Thinking
in
Java

Second Edition

Bruce Eckel
President, MindView, Inc.

ISBN 0-13-027363-5

9 780130 273635

Comments from readers:

Much better than any other Java book I've seen. Make that "by an order of magnitude"... very complete, with excellent right-to-the-point examples and intelligent, not dumbed-down, explanations ... In contrast to many other Java books I found it to be unusually mature, consistent, intellectually honest, well-written and precise. IMHO, an ideal book for studying Java. **Anatoly Vorobey, Technion University, Haifa, Israel**

One of the absolutely best programming tutorials I've seen for any language. **Joakim Ziegler, FIX sysop**

Thank you for your wonderful, wonderful book on Java. **Dr. Gavin Pillay, Registrar, King Edward VIII Hospital, South Africa**

Thank you again for your awesome book. I was really floundering (being a non-C programmer), but your book has brought me up to speed as fast as I could read it. It's really cool to be able to understand the underlying principles and concepts from the start, rather than having to try to build that conceptual model through trial and error. Hopefully I will be able to attend your seminar in the not-too-distant future. **Randall R. Hawley, Automation Technician, Eli Lilly & Co.**

The best computer book writing I have seen. **Tom Holland**

This is one of the best books I've read about a programming language... The best book ever written on Java. **Ravindra Pai, Oracle Corporation, SUNOS product line**

This is the best book on Java that I have ever found! You have done a great job. Your depth is amazing. I will be purchasing the book when it is published. I have been learning Java since October 96. I have read a few books, and consider yours a "MUST READ." These past few months we have been focused on a product written entirely in Java. Your book has helped solidify topics I was shaky on and has expanded my knowledge base. I have even used some of your explanations as information in interviewing contractors to help our team. I have found how much Java knowledge they have by asking them about things I have learned from reading your book (e.g., the difference between arrays and Vectors). Your book is great! **Steve Wilkinson, Senior Staff Specialist, MCI Telecommunications**

Great book. Best book on Java I have seen so far. **Jeff Sinclair, Software Engineer, Kestral Computing**

Thank you for *Thinking in Java*. It's time someone went beyond mere language description to a thoughtful, penetrating analytic tutorial that doesn't kowtow to The Manufacturers. I've read almost all the others—only yours and Patrick Winston's have found a place in my heart. I'm already recommending it to customers. Thanks again. **Richard Brooks, Java Consultant, Sun Professional Services, Dallas**

Other books cover the WHAT of Java (describing the syntax and the libraries) or the HOW of Java (practical programming examples). *Thinking in Java* is the only book I know that explains the WHY of Java; why it was designed the way it was, why it works the way it does, why it sometimes doesn't work, why it's better than C++, why it's not. Although it also does a good job of teaching the what and how of the language, *Thinking in Java* is definitely the thinking person's choice in a Java book. **Robert S. Stephenson**

Thanks for writing a great book. The more I read it the better I like it. My students like it, too. **Chuck Iverson**

I just want to commend you for your work on *Thinking in Java*. It is people like you that dignify the future of the Internet and I just want to thank you for your effort. It is very much appreciated. **Patrick Barrell, Network Officer Mamco, QAF Mfg. Inc.**

Most of the Java books out there are fine for a start, and most just have beginning stuff and a lot of the same examples. Yours is by far the best advanced thinking book I've seen. Please publish it soon! ... I also bought *Thinking in C++* just because I was so impressed with *Thinking in Java*. **George Laframboise, LightWorx Technology Consulting, Inc.**

I wrote to you earlier about my favorable impressions regarding your *Thinking in C++* (a book that stands prominently on my shelf here at work). And today I've been able to delve into Java with your e-book in my virtual hand, and I must say (in my best Chevy Chase from *Modern Problems*) "I like it!" Very informative and explanatory, without reading like a dry textbook. You cover the most important yet the least covered concepts of Java development: the whys. **Sean Brady**

Your examples are clear and easy to understand. You took care of many important details of Java that can't be found easily in the weak Java documentation. And you don't waste the reader's time with the basic facts a programmer already knows. **Kai Engert, Innovative Software, Germany**

I'm a great fan of your *Thinking in C++* and have recommended it to associates. As I go through the electronic version of your Java book, I'm finding that you've retained the same high level of writing. Thank you! **Peter R. Neuwald**

VERY well-written Java book...I think you've done a GREAT job on it. As the leader of a Chicago-area Java special interest group, I've favorably mentioned your book and Web site several times at our recent meetings. I would like to use *Thinking in Java* as the basis for a part of each monthly SIG meeting, in which we review and discuss each chapter in succession. **Mark Ertes**

I really appreciate your work and your book is good. I recommend it here to our users and Ph.D. students. **Hugues Leroy // Irisa-Inria Rennes France, Head of Scientific Computing and Industrial Tranfert**

OK, I've only read about 40 pages of *Thinking in Java*, but I've already found it to be the most clearly written and presented programming book I've come across...and I'm a writer, myself, so I am probably a little critical. I have *Thinking in C++* on order and can't wait to crack it—I'm fairly new to programming and am hitting learning curves head-on everywhere. So this is just a quick note to say thanks for your excellent work. I had begun to burn a little low on enthusiasm from slogging through the mucky, murky prose of most computer books—even ones that came with glowing recommendations. I feel a whole lot better now. **Glenn Becker, Educational Theatre Association**

Thank you for making your wonderful book available. I have found it immensely useful in finally understanding what I experienced as confusing in Java and C++. Reading your book has been very satisfying. **Felix Bizaoui, Twin Oaks Industries, Louisa, Va.**

I must congratulate you on an excellent book. I decided to have a look at *Thinking in Java* based on my experience with *Thinking in C++*, and I was not disappointed. **Jaco van der Merwe, Software Specialist, DataFusion Systems Ltd, Stellenbosch, South Africa**

This has to be one of the best Java books I've seen. **E.F. Pritchard, Senior Software Engineer, Cambridge Animation Systems Ltd., United Kingdom**

Your book makes all the other Java books I've read or flipped through seem doubly useless and insulting. **Brett g Porter, Senior Programmer, Art & Logic**

I have been reading your book for a week or two and compared to the books I have read earlier on Java, your book seems to have given me a great start. I have recommended this book to a lot of my friends and they have rated it excellent. Please accept my congratulations for coming out with an excellent book. **Rama Krishna Bhupathi, Software Engineer, TCSI Corporation, San Jose**

Just wanted to say what a "brilliant" piece of work your book is. I've been using it as a major reference for in-house Java work. I find that the table of contents is just right for quickly locating the section that is required. It's also nice to see a book that is not just a rehash of the API nor treats the programmer like a dummy. **Grant Sayer, Java Components Group Leader, Ceedata Systems Pty Ltd, Australia**

Wow! A readable, in-depth Java book. There are a lot of poor (and admittedly a couple of good) Java books out there, but from what I've seen yours is definitely one of the best. **John Root, Web Developer, Department of Social Security, London**

I've *just* started *Thinking in Java*. I expect it to be very good because I really liked *Thinking in C++* (which I read as an experienced C++ programmer, trying to stay ahead of the curve). I'm somewhat less experienced in Java, but expect to be very satisfied. You are a wonderful author. **Kevin K. Lewis, Technologist, ObjectSpace, Inc.**

I think it's a great book. I learned all I know about Java from this book. Thank you for making it available for free over the Internet. If you wouldn't have I'd know nothing about Java at all. But the best thing is that your book isn't a commercial brochure for Java. It also shows the bad sides of Java. YOU have done a great job here. **Frederik Fix, Belgium**

I have been hooked to your books all the time. A couple of years ago, when I wanted to start with C++, it was *C++ Inside & Out* which took me around the fascinating world of C++. It helped me in getting better opportunities in life. Now, in pursuit of more knowledge and when I wanted to learn Java, I bumped into *Thinking in Java*—no doubts in my mind as to whether I need some other book. Just fantastic. It is more like rediscovering myself as I get along with the book. It is just a month since I started with Java, and heartfelt thanks to you, I am understanding it better now. **Anand Kumar S., Software Engineer, Computervision, India**

Your book stands out as an excellent general introduction. **Peter Robinson, University of Cambridge Computer Laboratory**

It's by far the best material I have come across to help me learn Java and I just want you to know how lucky I feel to have found it. THANKS! **Chuck Peterson, Product Leader, Internet Product Line, IVIS International**

The book is great. It's the third book on Java I've started and I'm about two-thirds of the way through it now. I plan to finish this one. I found out about it because it is used in some internal classes at Lucent Technologies and a friend told me the book was on the Net. Good work. **Jerry Nowlin, MTS, Lucent Technologies**

Of the six or so Java books I've accumulated to date, your *Thinking in Java* is by far the best and clearest. **Michael Van Waas, Ph.D., President, TMR Associates**

I just want to say thanks for *Thinking in Java*. What a wonderful book you've made here! Not to mention downloadable for free! As a student I find your books invaluable (I have a copy of *C++ Inside Out*, another great book about C++), because they not only teach me the how-to, but also the whys, which are of course very important in building a strong foundation in languages such as C++ or Java. I have quite a lot of friends here who love programming just as I do, and I've told them about your books. They think it's great! Thanks again! By the way, I'm Indonesian and I live in

Java. **Ray Frederick Djajadinata, Student at Trisakti University, Jakarta**

The mere fact that you have made this work free over the Net puts me into shock. I thought I'd let you know how much I appreciate and respect what you're doing. **Shane LeBouthillier, Computer Engineering student, University of Alberta, Canada**

I have to tell you how much I look forward to reading your monthly column. As a newbie to the world of object oriented programming, I appreciate the time and thoughtfulness that you give to even the most elementary topic. I have downloaded your book, but you can bet that I will purchase the hard copy when it is published. Thanks for all of your help. **Dan Cashmer, B. C. Ziegler & Co.**

Just want to congratulate you on a job well done. First I stumbled upon the PDF version of *Thinking in Java*. Even before I finished reading it, I ran to the store and found *Thinking in C++*. Now, I have been in the computer business for over eight years, as a consultant, software engineer, teacher/trainer, and recently as self-employed, so I'd like to think that I have seen enough (not "have seen it all," mind you, but enough). However, these books cause my girlfriend to call me a "geek." Not that I have anything against the concept—it is just that I thought this phase was well beyond me. But I find myself truly enjoying both books, like no other computer book I have touched or bought so far. Excellent writing style, very nice introduction of every new topic, and lots of wisdom in the books. Well done. **Simon Goland, simonsez@smartt.com, Simon Says Consulting, Inc.**

I must say that your *Thinking in Java* is great! That is exactly the kind of documentation I was looking for. Especially the sections about good and poor software design using Java. **Dirk Duehr, Lexikon Verlag, Bertelsmann AG, Germany**

Thank you for writing two great books (*Thinking in C++, Thinking in Java*). You have helped me immensely in my progression to object oriented programming. **Donald Lawson, DCL Enterprises**

Thank you for taking the time to write a really helpful book on Java. If teaching makes you understand something, by now you must be pretty pleased with yourself. **Dominic Turner, GEAC Support**

It's the best Java book I have ever read—and I read some. **Jean-Yves MENGANT, Chief Software Architect NAT-SYSTEM, Paris, France**

Thinking in Java gives the best coverage and explanation. Very easy to read, and I mean the code fragments as well. **Ron Chan, Ph.D., Expert Choice, Inc., Pittsburgh PA**

Your book is great. I have read lots of programming books and your book still adds insights to programming in my mind. **Ningjian Wang, Information System Engineer, The Vanguard Group**

Thinking in Java is an excellent and readable book. I recommend it to all my students. **Dr. Paul Gorman, Department of Computer Science, University of Otago, Dunedin, New Zealand**

You make it possible for the proverbial free lunch to exist, not just a soup kitchen type of lunch but a gourmet delight for those who appreciate good software and books about it. **Jose Suriol, Scylax Corporation**

Thanks for the opportunity of watching this book grow into a masterpiece! IT IS THE BEST book on the subject that I've read or browsed. **Jeff Lapchinsky, Programmer, Net Results Technologies**

Your book is concise, accessible and a joy to read. **Keith Ritchie, Java Research & Development Team, KL Group Inc.**

It truly is the best book I've read on Java! **Daniel Eng**

The best book I have seen on Java! **Rich Hoffarth, Senior Architect, West Group**

Thank you for a wonderful book. I'm having a lot of fun going through the chapters. **Fred Trimble, Actium Corporation**

You have mastered the art of slowly and successfully making us grasp the details. You make learning VERY easy and satisfying. Thank you for a truly wonderful tutorial. **Rajesh Rau, Software Consultant**

Thinking in Java rocks the free world! **Miko O'Sullivan, President, Idocs Inc.**

About *Thinking in C++*:

**Best Book! Winner of the
1995 Software Development Magazine Jolt Award!**

"This book is a tremendous achievement. You owe it to yourself to have a copy on your shelf. The chapter on iostreams is the most comprehensive and understandable treatment of that subject I've seen to date."

Al Stevens
Contributing Editor, *Doctor Dobbs Journal*

"Eckel's book is the only one to so clearly explain how to rethink program construction for object orientation. That the book is also an excellent tutorial on the ins and outs of C++ is an added bonus."

Andrew Binstock
Editor, *Unix Review*

"Bruce continues to amaze me with his insight into C++, and *Thinking in C++* is his best collection of ideas yet. If you want clear answers to difficult questions about C++, buy this outstanding book."

Gary Entsminger
Author, *The Tao of Objects*

"*Thinking in C++* patiently and methodically explores the issues of when and how to use inlines, references, operator overloading, inheritance, and dynamic objects, as well as advanced topics such as the proper use of templates, exceptions and multiple inheritance. The entire effort is woven in a fabric that includes Eckel's own philosophy of object and program design. A must for every C++ developer's bookshelf, *Thinking in C++* is the one C++ book you must have if you're doing serious development with C++."

Richard Hale Shaw
Contributing Editor, PC Magazine

Thinking
in
Java

Second Edition

Bruce Eckel
President, MindView, Inc.

 Prentice Hall
Upper Saddle River, New Jersey 07458
www.phptr.com

Library of Congress Cataloging-in-Publication Data
Eckel, Bruce.
    Thinking in Java / Bruce Eckel.--2nd ed.
        p.   cm.
    ISBN 0-13-027363-5
    1. Java (Computer program language) I. Title.
QA76.73.J38E25 2000
005.13'3--dc21   00-037522
                                                           CIP

Editorial/Production Supervision: Nicholas Radhuber
Acquisitions Editor: Paul Petralia
Manufacturing Manager: Maura Goldstaub
Marketing Manager: Bryan Gambrel
Cover Design: Daniel Will-Harris
Interior Design: Daniel Will-Harris, www.will-harris.com

The information in this book is distributed on an "as is" basis, without warranty. While every precaution has been taken in the preparation of this book, neither the author nor the publisher shall have any liability to any person or entitle with respect to any liability, loss or damage caused or alleged to be caused directly or indirectly by instructions contained in this book or by the computer software or hardware products described herein.

Prentice-Hall books are widely used by corporations and government agencies for training, marketing, and resale. The publisher offers discounts on this book when ordered in bulk quantities. For more information, contact the Corporate Sales Department at 800-382-3419, fax: 201-236-7141, email: *corpsales@prenhall.com* or write: Corporate Sales Department, Prentice Hall PTR, One Lake Street, Upper Saddle River, New Jersey 07458.

Java is a registered trademark of Sun Microsystems, Inc. Windows 95 and Windows NT are trademarks of Microsoft Corporation. All other product names and company names mentioned herein are the property of their respective owners.

Printed in the United States of America
10 9 8 7 6 5

ISBN 0-13-027363-5

Prentice-Hall International (UK) Limited, *London*
Prentice-Hall of Australia Pty. Limited, *Sydney*
Prentice-Hall Canada, Inc., *Toronto*
Prentice-Hall Hispanoamericana, S.A., *Mexico*
Prentice-Hall of India Private Limited, *New Delhi*
Prentice-Hall of Japan, Inc., *Tokyo*
Pearson Education Asia Ltd., *Singapore*
Editora Prentice-Hall do Brasil, Ltda., *Rio de Janeiro*

Bruce Eckel's Hands-On Java Seminar
Multimedia CD
It's like coming to the seminar!
Available at *www.BruceEckel.com*

➢ The *Hands-On Java Seminar* captured on a Multimedia CD!

➢ Overhead slides and synchronized audio voice narration for all the lectures. Just play it to see and hear the lectures!

➢ Created and narrated by Bruce Eckel.

➢ Based on the material in this book.

➢ Demo lecture available at *www.BruceEckel.com*

Dedication

To the person who, even now,
is creating the next great computer language

Overview

What's Inside

Preface

I suggested to my brother Todd, who is making the leap from hardware into programming, that the next big revolution will be in genetic engineering.

We'll have microbes designed to make food, fuel, and plastic; they'll clean up pollution and in general allow us to master the manipulation of the physical world for a fraction of what it costs now. I claimed that it would make the computer revolution look small in comparison.

Then I realized I was making a mistake common to science fiction writers: getting lost in the technology (which is of course easy to do in science fiction). An experienced writer knows that the story is never about the things; it's about the people. Genetics will have a very large impact on our lives, but I'm not so sure it will dwarf the computer revolution (which enables the genetic revolution)—or at least the information revolution. Information is about talking to each other: yes, cars and shoes and especially genetic cures are important, but in the end those are just trappings. What truly matters is how we relate to the world. And so much of that is about communication.

This book is a case in point. A majority of folks thought I was very bold or a little crazy to put the entire thing up on the Web. "Why would anyone buy it?" they asked. If I had been of a more conservative nature I wouldn't have done it, but I really didn't want to write another computer book in the same old way. I didn't know what would happen but it turned out to be the smartest thing I've ever done with a book.

For one thing, people started sending in corrections. This has been an amazing process, because folks have looked into every nook and cranny and caught both technical and grammatical errors, and I've been able to eliminate bugs of all sorts that I know would have otherwise slipped through. People have been simply terrific about this, very often saying "Now, I don't mean this in a critical way..." and then giving me a collection of errors I'm sure I never would have found. I feel like this has been a kind of group process and it has really made the book into something special.

But then I started hearing "OK, fine, it's nice you've put up an electronic version, but I want a printed and bound copy from a real publisher." I tried very hard to make it easy for everyone to print it out in a nice looking format but that didn't stem the demand for the published book. Most people don't want to read the entire book on screen, and hauling around a sheaf of papers, no matter how nicely printed, didn't appeal to them either. (Plus, I think it's not so cheap in terms of laser printer toner.) It seems that the computer revolution won't put publishers out of business, after all. However, one student suggested this may become a model for future publishing: books will be published on the Web first, and only if sufficient interest warrants it will the book be put on paper. Currently, the great majority of all books are financial failures, and perhaps this new approach could make the publishing industry more profitable.

This book became an enlightening experience for me in another way. I originally approached Java as "just another programming language," which in many senses it is. But as time passed and I studied it more deeply, I began to see that the fundamental intention of this language is different from all the other languages I have seen.

Programming is about managing complexity: the complexity of the problem you want to solve, laid upon the complexity of the machine in which it is solved. Because of this complexity, most of our programming projects fail. And yet, of all the programming languages of which I am aware, none of them have gone all-out and decided that their main design goal would be to conquer the complexity of developing and maintaining programs[1]. Of course, many language design decisions were made with complexity in mind, but at some point there were always some other issues that were considered essential to be added into the mix. Inevitably, those other issues are what cause programmers to eventually "hit the wall" with that language. For example, C++ had to be backwards-compatible with C (to allow easy migration for C programmers), as well as

---

[1] I take this back on the 2nd edition: I believe that the Python language comes closest to doing exactly that. See www.Python.org.

efficient. Those are both very useful goals and account for much of the success of C++, but they also expose extra complexity that prevents some projects from being finished (certainly, you can blame programmers and management, but if a language can help by catching your mistakes, why shouldn't it?). As another example, Visual Basic (VB) was tied to BASIC, which wasn't really designed to be an extensible language, so all the extensions piled upon VB have produced some truly horrible and unmaintainable syntax. Perl is backwards-compatible with Awk, Sed, Grep, and other Unix tools it was meant to replace, and as a result is often accused of producing "write-only code" (that is, after a few months you can't read it). On the other hand, C++, VB, Perl, and other languages like Smalltalk had some of their design efforts focused on the issue of complexity and as a result are remarkably successful in solving certain types of problems.

What has impressed me most as I have come to understand Java is what seems like an unflinching goal of reducing complexity *for the programmer*. As if to say "we don't care about anything except reducing the time and difficulty of producing robust code." In the early days, this goal has resulted in code that doesn't run very fast (although there have been many promises made about how quickly Java will someday run) but it has indeed produced amazing reductions in development time; half or less of the time that it takes to create an equivalent C++ program. This result alone can save incredible amounts of time and money, but Java doesn't stop there. It goes on to wrap all the complex tasks that have become important, such as multithreading and network programming, in language features or libraries that can at times make those tasks trivial. And finally, it tackles some really big complexity problems: cross-platform programs, dynamic code changes, and even security, each of which can fit on your complexity spectrum anywhere from "impediment" to "show-stopper." So despite the performance problems we've seen, the promise of Java is tremendous: it can make us significantly more productive programmers.

One of the places I see the greatest impact for this is on the Web. Network programming has always been hard, and Java makes it easy (and the Java language designers are working on making it even easier). Network programming is how we talk to each other more effectively and cheaper than we ever have with telephones (email alone has revolutionized many businesses). As we talk to each other more, amazing things begin to happen, possibly more amazing even than the promise of genetic engineering.

In all ways—creating the programs, working in teams to create the programs, building user interfaces so the programs can communicate with the user, running the programs on different types of machines, and easily writing programs that communicate across the Internet—Java increases the communication bandwidth *between people*. I think that perhaps the results of the communication revolution will not be seen from the effects of moving large quantities of bits around; we shall see the true revolution because we will all be able to talk to each other more easily: one-on-one, but also in groups and, as a planet. I've heard it suggested that the next revolution is the formation of a kind of global mind that results from enough people and enough interconnectedness. Java may or may not be the tool that foments that revolution, but at least the possibility has made me feel like I'm doing something meaningful by attempting to teach the language.

Preface to the 2nd edition

People have made many, many wonderful comments about the first edition of this book, which has naturally been very pleasant for me. However, every now and then someone will have complaints, and for some reason one complaint that comes up periodically is "the book is too big." In my mind it is faint damnation indeed if "too many pages" is your only complaint. (One is reminded of the Emperor of Austria's complaint about Mozart's work: "Too many notes!" Not that I am in any way trying to compare myself to Mozart.) In addition, I can only assume that such a complaint comes from someone who is yet to be acquainted with the vastness of the Java language itself, and has not seen the rest of the books on the subject—for example, my favorite reference is Cay Horstmann & Gary Cornell's *Core Java* (Prentice-Hall), which grew so big it had to be broken into two volumes. Despite this, one of the things I have attempted to do in this edition is trim out the portions that have become obsolete, or at least nonessential. I feel comfortable doing this because the original material remains on the Web site and the CD ROM that accompanies this book, in the form of the freely-downloadable first edition of the book (at *www.BruceEckel.com*). If you want the old stuff, it's still there, and this is a wonderful relief for an author. For example, you may notice that the original last chapter, "Projects," is no longer here; two of the projects have been integrated into other chapters, and the rest were no longer appropriate. Also, the "Design Pattens" chapter became too big and has been moved into a book of its own (also downloadable at the Web site). So, by all rights the book should be thinner.

But alas, it is not to be.

The biggest issue is the continuing development of the Java language itself, and in particular the expanding APIs that promise to provide standard interfaces for just about everything you'd like to do (and I won't be surprised to see the "JToaster" API eventually appear). Covering all these APIs is obviously beyond the scope of this book and is a task relegated to other authors, but some issues cannot be ignored. The biggest of these include server-side Java (primarily Servlets & Java Server pages, or *JSP*s), which is truly an excellent solution to the World Wide Web problem, wherein we've discovered that the various Web browser platforms are just not consistent enough to support client-side programming. In addition, there is the whole problem of easily creating applications to interact with databases, transactions, security, and the like, which is involved with Enterprise Java Beans (EJBs). These topics are wrapped into the chapter formerly called "Network Programming" and now called "Distributed Computing," a subject that is becoming essential to everyone. You'll also find this chapter has been expanded to include an overview of Jini (pronounced "genie," and it isn't an acronym, just a name), which is a cutting-edge technology that allows us to change the way we think about interconnected applications. And of course the book has been changed to use the Swing GUI library throughout. Again, if you want the old Java 1.0/1.1 stuff you can get it from the freely-downloadable book at *www.BruceEckel.com* (it is also included on this edition's new CD ROM, bound into the book; more on that a little later).

Aside from additional small language features added in Java 2 and corrections made throughout the book, the other major change is in the collections chapter (9), which now focuses on the Java 2 collections used throughout the book. I've also improved that chapter to more deeply go into some of the important issues of collections, in particular how a hash function works (so that you can know how to properly create one). There have been other movements and changes, including a rewrite of Chapter 1, and removal of some appendices and other material that I consider no longer necessary for the printed book, but those are the bulk of them. In general, I've tried to go over everything, remove from the 2nd edition what is no longer necessary (but which still exists in the electronic first edition), include changes, and improve everything I could. As the language continues to change—albeit not quite at the same breakneck pace as before—there will no doubt be further editions of this book.

For those of you who still can't stand the size of the book, I do apologize. Believe it or not, I have worked hard to keep it small. Despite the bulk, I feel like there may be enough alternatives to satisfy you. For one thing, the book is available electronically (from the Web site, and also on the CD ROM that accompanies this book), so if you carry your laptop you can carry the book on that with no extra weight. If you're really into slimming down, there are actually Palm Pilot versions of the book floating around. (One person told me he would read the book in bed on his Palm with the backlighting on to keep from annoying his wife. I can only hope that it helps send him to slumberland.) If you need it on paper, I know of people who print a chapter at a time and carry it in their briefcase to read on the train.

Java 2

At this writing, the release of Sun's *Java Development Kit* (JDK) 1.3 is imminent, and the proposed changes for JDK 1.4 have been publicized. Although these version numbers are still in the "ones," the standard way to refer to any version of the language that is JDK 1.2 or greater is to call it "Java 2." This indicates the very significant changes between "old Java"—which had many warts that I complained about in the first edition of this book—and this more modern and improved version of the language, which has far fewer warts and many additions and nice designs.

This book is written for Java 2. I have the great luxury of getting rid of all the old stuff and writing to only the new, improved language because the old information still exists in the electronic 1st edition on the Web and on the CD ROM (which is where you can go if you're stuck using a pre-Java-2 version of the language). Also, because anyone can freely download the

JDK from java.sun.com, it means that by writing to Java 2 I'm not imposing a financial hardship on someone by forcing them to upgrade.

There is a bit of a catch, however. JDK 1.3 has some improvements that I'd really like to use, but the version of Java that is currently being released for Linux is JDK 1.2.2. Linux (see www.Linux.org) is a very important development in conjunction with Java, because it is fast becoming the most important server platform out there—fast, reliable, robust, secure, well-maintained, and free, a true revolution in the history of computing (I don't think we've ever seen all of those features in any tool before). And Java has found a very important niche in server-side programming in the form of *Servlets*, a technology that is a huge improvement over the traditional CGI programming (this is covered in the "Distributed Programming" chapter).

So although I would like to only use the very newest features, it's critical that everything compiles under Linux, and so when you unpack the source code and compile it under that OS (with the latest JDK) you'll discover that everything will compile. However, you will find that I've put notes about features in JDK 1.3 here and there.

The CD ROM

Another bonus with this edition is the CD ROM that is packaged in the back of the book. I've resisted putting CD ROMs in the back of my books in the past because I felt the extra charge for a few Kbytes of source code on this enormous CD was not justified, preferring instead to allow people to download such things from my Web site. However, you'll soon see that this CD ROM is different.

The CD does contain the source code from the book, but it also contains the book in its entirety, in several electronic formats. My favorite of these is the HTML format, because it is fast and fully indexed—you just click on an entry in the index or table of contents and you're immediately at that portion of the book.

The bulk of the 300+ Megabytes of the CD, however, is a full multimedia course called *Thinking in C: Foundations for C++ & Java*. I originally commissioned Chuck Allison to create this seminar-on-CD ROM as a stand-alone product, but decided to include it with the second editions of both *Thinking in C++* and *Thinking in Java* because of the consistent experience of having people come to seminars without an adequate background in C. The thinking apparently goes "I'm a smart programmer and I don't *want* to learn C, but rather C++ or Java, so I'll just skip C and go directly to C++/Java." After arriving at the seminar, it slowly dawns on folks that the prerequisite of understanding C syntax is there for a very good reason. By including the CD ROM with the book, we can ensure that everyone attends a seminar with adequate preparation.

The CD also allows the book to appeal to a wider audience. Even though Chapter 3 (Controlling program flow) does cover the fundamentals of the parts of Java that come from C, the CD is a gentler introduction, and assumes even less about the student's programming background than does the book. It is my hope that by including the CD more people will be able to be brought into the fold of Java programming.

Introduction

Like any human language, Java provides a way to express concepts. If successful, this medium of expression will be significantly easier and more flexible than the alternatives as problems grow larger and more complex.

You can't look at Java as just a collection of features—some of the features make no sense in isolation. You can use the sum of the parts only if you are thinking about *design*, not simply coding. And to understand Java in this way, you must understand the problems with it and with programming in general. This book discusses programming problems, why they are problems, and the approach Java has taken to solve them. Thus, the set of features I explain in each chapter are based on the way I see a particular type of problem being solved with the language. In this way I hope to move you, a little at a time, to the point where the Java mindset becomes your native tongue.

Throughout, I'll be taking the attitude that you want to build a model in your head that allows you to develop a deep understanding of the language; if you encounter a puzzle you'll be able to feed it to your model and deduce the answer.

Prerequisites

This book assumes that you have some programming familiarity: you understand that a program is a collection of statements, the idea of a subroutine/function/macro, control statements such as "if" and looping constructs such as "while," etc. However, you might have learned this in many places, such as programming with a macro language or working with a tool like Perl. As long as you've programmed to the point where you feel comfortable with the basic ideas of programming, you'll be able to work through this book. Of course, the book will be *easier* for the C programmers and more so for the C++ programmers, but don't count yourself out if you're not experienced with those languages (but come willing to work hard; also, the multimedia CD that accompanies this book will bring you up to speed on the basic C syntax necessary to learn Java). I'll be introducing the concepts of object-oriented programming (OOP) and Java's basic control mechanisms, so you'll be exposed to those, and the first exercises will involve the basic control-flow statements.

Although references will often be made to C and C++ language features, these are not intended to be insider comments, but instead to help all programmers put Java in perspective with those languages, from which, after all, Java is descended. I will attempt to make these references simple and to explain anything that I think a non- C/C++ programmer would not be familiar with.

Learning Java

At about the same time that my first book *Using C++* (Osborne/McGraw-Hill, 1989) came out, I began teaching that language. Teaching programming languages has become my profession; I've seen nodding heads, blank faces, and puzzled expressions in audiences all over the world since 1989. As I began giving in-house training with smaller groups of people, I discovered something during the exercises. Even those people who were smiling and nodding were confused about many issues. I found out, by chairing the C++ track at the Software Development Conference for a number of years (and later the Java track), that I and other speakers tended to give the typical audience too many topics too fast. So eventually, through both variety in the audience level and the way that I presented the material, I would end up losing some portion of the audience. Maybe it's asking too much, but because I am one of those people resistant to traditional lecturing (and for most people, I believe, such resistance results from boredom), I wanted to try to keep everyone up to speed.

For a time, I was creating a number of different presentations in fairly short order. Thus, I ended up learning by experiment and iteration (a technique that also works well in Java program design). Eventually I developed a course using everything I had learned from my teaching experience—one that I would be happy giving for a long time. It tackles the learning problem in discrete, easy-to-digest steps, and in a hands-on seminar (the ideal learning situation) there are exercises following each of the short lessons. I now give this course in public Java seminars, which you can find out about at *www.BruceEckel.com*. (The introductory seminar is also available as a CD ROM. Information is available at the same Web site.)

The feedback that I get from each seminar helps me change and refocus the material until I think it works well as a teaching medium. But this book isn't just seminar notes—I tried to pack as much information as I could within these pages, and structured it to draw you through onto the next subject. More than anything, the book is designed to serve the solitary reader who is struggling with a new programming language.

Goals

Like my previous book *Thinking in C++*, this book has come to be structured around the process of teaching the language. In particular, my motivation is to create something that provides me with a way to teach the language in my own seminars. When I think of a chapter in the book, I think in terms of what makes a good lesson during a seminar. My goal is to get bite-sized pieces that can be taught in a reasonable amount of time, followed by exercises that are feasible to accomplish in a classroom situation.

My goals in this book are to:

1.   Present the material one simple step at a time so that you can easily digest each concept before moving on.

2.   Use examples that are as simple and short as possible. This sometimes prevents me from tackling "real world" problems, but I've found that beginners are usually happier when they can understand every detail of an example rather than being impressed by the scope of the problem it solves. Also, there's a severe limit to the amount of code that can be absorbed in a classroom situation. For this I will no doubt receive criticism for using "toy examples," but I'm willing to accept that in favor of producing something pedagogically useful.

3. Carefully sequence the presentation of features so that you aren't seeing something that you haven't been exposed to. Of course, this isn't always possible; in those situations, a brief introductory description is given.

4. Give you what I think is important for you to understand about the language, rather than everything I know. I believe there is an information importance hierarchy, and that there are some facts that 95 percent of programmers will never need to know and that just confuse people and adds to their perception of the complexity of the language. To take an example from C, if you memorize the operator precedence table (I never did), you can write clever code. But if you need to think about it, it will also confuse the reader/maintainer of that code. So forget about precedence, and use parentheses when things aren't clear.

5. Keep each section focused enough so that the lecture time—and the time between exercise periods—is small. Not only does this keep the audience's minds more active and involved during a hands-on seminar, but it gives the reader a greater sense of accomplishment.

6. Provide you with a solid foundation so that you can understand the issues well enough to move on to more difficult coursework and books.

Online documentation

The Java language and libraries from Sun Microsystems (a free download) come with documentation in electronic form, readable using a Web browser, and virtually every third party implementation of Java has this or an equivalent documentation system. Almost all the books published on Java have duplicated this documentation. So you either already have it or you can download it, and unless necessary, this book will not repeat that documentation because it's usually much faster if you find the class descriptions with your Web browser than if you look them up in a book (and the on-line documentation is probably more up-to-date). This book will provide extra descriptions of the classes only when it's necessary to supplement the documentation so you can understand a particular example.

Chapters

This book was designed with one thing in mind: the way people learn the Java language. Seminar audience feedback helped me understand the difficult parts that needed illumination. In the areas where I got ambitious and included too many features all at once, I came to know—through the process of presenting the material—that if you include a lot of new features, you need to explain them all, and this easily compounds the student's confusion. As a result, I've taken a great deal of trouble to introduce the features as few at a time as possible.

The goal, then, is for each chapter to teach a single feature, or a small group of associated features, without relying on additional features. That way you can digest each piece in the context of your current knowledge before moving on.

Here is a brief description of the chapters contained in the book, which correspond to lectures and exercise periods in my hands-on seminars.

Chapter 1:   ***Introduction to Objects***

This chapter is an overview of what object-oriented programming is all about, including the answer to the basic question "What's an object?", interface vs. implementation, abstraction and encapsulation, messages and functions, inheritance and composition, and the all-important polymorphism. You'll also get an overview of issues of object creation such as constructors, where the objects live, where to put them once they're created, and the magical garbage collector that cleans up the objects that are no longer needed. Other issues will be introduced, including error handling with exceptions, multithreading for responsive user interfaces, and networking and the Internet. You'll learn what makes Java special, why it's been so successful, and about object-oriented analysis and design.

Chapter 2:   ***Everything is an Object***

This chapter moves you to the point where you can write your first Java program, so it must give an overview of the essentials, including the concept of a *reference* to an object;

how to create an object; an introduction to primitive types and arrays; scoping and the way objects are destroyed by the garbage collector; how everything in Java is a new data type (class) and how to create your own classes; functions, arguments, and return values; name visibility and using components from other libraries; the **static** keyword; and comments and embedded documentation.

Chapter 3:   ***Controlling Program Flow***
This chapter begins with all of the operators that come to Java from C and C++. In addition, you'll discover common operator pitfalls, casting, promotion, and precedence. This is followed by the basic control-flow and selection operations that you get with virtually any programming language: choice with if-else; looping with for and while; quitting a loop with break and continue as well as Java's labeled break and labeled continue (which account for the "missing goto" in Java); and selection using switch. Although much of this material has common threads with C and C++ code, there are some differences. In addition, all the examples will be full Java examples so you'll get more comfortable with what Java looks like.

Chapter 4:   ***Initialization & Cleanup***
This chapter begins by introducing the constructor, which guarantees proper initialization. The definition of the constructor leads into the concept of function overloading (since you might want several constructors). This is followed by a discussion of the process of cleanup, which is not always as simple as it seems. Normally, you just drop an object when you're done with it and the garbage collector eventually comes along and releases the memory. This portion explores the garbage collector and some of its idiosyncrasies. The chapter concludes with a closer look at how things are initialized: automatic member initialization, specifying member initialization, the order of initialization, **static** initialization and array initialization.

Chapter 5: **_Hiding the Implementation_**

This chapter covers the way that code is packaged together, and why some parts of a library are exposed while other parts are hidden. It begins by looking at the **package** and **import** keywords, which perform file-level packaging and allow you to build libraries of classes. It then examines subject of directory paths and file names. The remainder of the chapter looks at the **public**, **private,** and **protected** keywords, the concept of "friendly" access, and what the different levels of access control mean when used in various contexts.

Chapter 6: **_Reusing Classes_**

The concept of inheritance is standard in virtually all OOP languages. It's a way to take an existing class and add to its functionality (as well as change it, the subject of Chapter 7). Inheritance is often a way to reuse code by leaving the "base class" the same, and just patching things here and there to produce what you want. However, inheritance isn't the only way to make new classes from existing ones. You can also embed an object inside your new class with _composition_. In this chapter you'll learn about these two ways to reuse code in Java, and how to apply them.

Chapter 7: **_Polymorphism_**

On your own, you might take nine months to discover and understand polymorphism, a cornerstone of OOP. Through small, simple examples you'll see how to create a family of types with inheritance and manipulate objects in that family through their common base class. Java's polymorphism allows you to treat all objects in this family generically, which means the bulk of your code doesn't rely on specific type information. This makes your programs extensible, so building programs and code maintenance is easier and cheaper.

Chapter 8: **_Interfaces & Inner Classes_**

Java provides a third way to set up a reuse relationship, through the _interface_, which is a pure abstraction of the interface of an object. The **interface** is more than just an

---

abstract class taken to the extreme, since it allows you to perform a variation on C++'s "multiple inheritance," by creating a class that can be upcast to more than one base type.

At first, inner classes look like a simple code hiding mechanism: you place classes inside other classes. You'll learn, however, that the inner class does more than that—it knows about and can communicate with the surrounding class—and that the kind of code you can write with inner classes is more elegant and clear, although it is a new concept to most and takes some time to become comfortable with design using inner classes.

Chapter 9:   ***Holding your Objects***

It's a fairly simple program that has only a fixed quantity of objects with known lifetimes. In general, your programs will always be creating new objects at a variety of times that will be known only while the program is running. In addition, you won't know until run-time the quantity or even the exact type of the objects you need. To solve the general programming problem, you need to create any number of objects, anytime, anywhere. This chapter explores in depth the container library that Java 2 supplies to hold objects while you're working with them: the simple arrays and more sophisticated containers (data structures) such as **ArrayList** and **HashMap**.

Chapter 10:   ***Error Handling with Exceptions***

The basic philosophy of Java is that badly-formed code will not be run. As much as possible, the compiler catches problems, but sometimes the problems—either programmer error or a natural error condition that occurs as part of the normal execution of the program—can be detected and dealt with only at run-time. Java has *exception handling* to deal with any problems that arise while the program is running. This chapter examines how the keywords **try**, **catch**, **throw**, **throws**, and **finally** work in Java; when you should throw exceptions and what to do when you catch them. In addition, you'll see Java's standard exceptions, how to create your own, what happens with exceptions in constructors, and how exception handlers are located.

Chapter 11: **The Java I/O System**

Theoretically, you can divide any program into three parts: input, process, and output. This implies that I/O (input/output) is an important part of the equation. In this chapter you'll learn about the different classes that Java provides for reading and writing files, blocks of memory, and the console. The distinction between "old" I/O and "new" Java I/O will be shown. In addition, this chapter examines the process of taking an object, "streaming" it (so that it can be placed on disk or sent across a network) and reconstructing it, which is handled for you with Java's *object serialization*. Also, Java's compression libraries, which are used in the Java ARchive file format (JAR), are examined.

Chapter 12: **Run-Time Type Identification**

Java run-time type identification (RTTI) lets you find the exact type of an object when you have a reference to only the base type. Normally, you'll want to intentionally ignore the exact type of an object and let Java's dynamic binding mechanism (polymorphism) implement the correct behavior for that type. But occasionally it is very helpful to know the exact type of an object for which you have only a base reference. Often this information allows you to perform a special-case operation more efficiently. This chapter explains what RTTI is for, how to use it, and how to get rid of it when it doesn't belong there. In addition, this chapter introduces the Java *reflection* mechanism.

Chapter 13: **Creating Windows and Applets**

Java comes with the "Swing" GUI library, which is a set of classes that handle windowing in a portable fashion. These windowed programs can either be applets or stand-alone applications. This chapter is an introduction to Swing and the creation of World Wide Web applets. The important "JavaBeans" technology is introduced. This is fundamental for the creation of Rapid-Application Development (RAD) program-building tools.

Chapter 14: *Multiple Threads*

Java provides a built-in facility to support multiple concurrent subtasks, called *threads*, running within a single program. (Unless you have multiple processors on your machine, this is only the *appearance* of multiple subtasks.) Although these can be used anywhere, threads are most apparent when trying to create a responsive user interface so, for example, a user isn't prevented from pressing a button or entering data while some processing is going on. This chapter looks at the syntax and semantics of multithreading in Java.

Chapter 15: *Distributed Computing*

All the Java features and libraries seem to really come together when you start writing programs to work across networks. This chapter explores communication across networks and the Internet, and the classes that Java provides to make this easier. It introduces the very important concepts of *Servlets* and *JSPs* (for server-side programming), along *with Java DataBase Connectivity* (JDBC), and *Remote Method Invocation* (RMI). Finally, there's an introduction to the new technologies of *JINI, JavaSpaces*, and *Enterprise JavaBeans* (EJBs).

Appendix A: *Passing & Returning Objects*

Since the only way you talk to objects in Java is through references, the concepts of passing an object into a function and returning an object from a function have some interesting consequences. This appendix explains what you need to know to manage objects when you're moving in and out of functions, and also shows the **String** class, which uses a different approach to the problem.

Appendix B: *The Java Native Interface (JNI)*

A totally portable Java program has serious drawbacks: speed and the inability to access platform-specific services. When you know the platform that you're running on, it's possible to dramatically speed up certain operations by making them *native methods*, which are functions that are written in another programming language (currently, only C/C++ is supported). This appendix gives you enough of an introduction to this feature that you should be able to create simple examples that interface with non-Java code.

Appendix C: *Java Programming Guidelines*
This appendix contains suggestions to help guide you while performing low-level program design and writing code.

Appendix D: *Recommended Reading*
A list of some of the Java books I've found particularly useful.

Exercises

I've discovered that simple exercises are exceptionally useful to complete a student's understanding during a seminar, so you'll find a set at the end of each chapter.

Most exercises are designed to be easy enough that they can be finished in a reasonable amount of time in a classroom situation while the instructor observes, making sure that all the students are absorbing the material. Some exercises are more advanced to prevent boredom for experienced students. The majority are designed to be solved in a short time and test and polish your knowledge. Some are more challenging, but none present major challenges. (Presumably, you'll find those on your own—or more likely they'll find you).

Solutions to selected exercises can be found in the electronic document *The Thinking in Java Annotated Solution Guide*, available for a small fee from www.BruceEckel.com.

Multimedia CD ROM

There are two multimedia CDs associated with this book. The first is bound into the book itself: *Thinking in C*, described at the end of the preface, which prepares you for the book by bringing you up to speed on the necessary C syntax you need to be able to understand Java.

A second Multimedia CD ROM is available, which is based on the contents of the book. This CD ROM is a separate product and contains the **entire** contents of the week-long "Hands-On Java" training seminar. This is more than 15 hours of lectures that I have recorded, synchronized with hundreds of slides of information. Because the seminar is based on this book, it is an ideal accompaniment.

The CD ROM contains all the lectures (with the important exception of personalized attention!) from the five-day full-immersion training seminars. We believe that it sets a new standard for quality.

The Hands-On Java CD ROM is available only by ordering directly from the Web site *www.BruceEckel.com.*

Source code

All the source code for this book is available as copyrighted freeware, distributed as a single package, by visiting the Web site *www.BruceEckel.com.* To make sure that you get the most current version, this is the official site for distribution of the code and the electronic version of the book. You can find mirrored versions of the electronic book and the code on other sites (some of these sites are found at *www.BruceEckel.com*), but you should check the official site to ensure that the mirrored version is actually the most recent edition. You may distribute the code in classroom and other educational situations.

The primary goal of the copyright is to ensure that the source of the code is properly cited, and to prevent you from republishing the code in print media without permission. (As long as the source is cited, using examples from the book in most media is generally not a problem.)

In each source code file you will find a reference to the following copyright notice:

```
//:! :CopyRight.txt
Copyright ©2000 Bruce Eckel
Source code file from the 2nd edition of the book
"Thinking in Java." All rights reserved EXCEPT as
allowed by the following statements:
You can freely use this file
```

for your own work (personal or commercial), including modifications and distribution in executable form only. Permission is granted to use this file in classroom situations, including its use in presentation materials, as long as the book "Thinking in Java" is cited as the source. Except in classroom situations, you cannot copy and distribute this code; instead, the sole distribution point is http://www.BruceEckel.com (and official mirror sites) where it is freely available. You cannot remove this copyright and notice. You cannot distribute modified versions of the source code in this package. You cannot use this file in printed media without the express permission of the author. Bruce Eckel makes no representation about the suitability of this software for any purpose. It is provided "as is" without express or implied warranty of any kind, including any implied warranty of merchantability, fitness for a particular purpose or non-infringement. The entire risk as to the quality and performance of the software is with you. Bruce Eckel and the publisher shall not be liable for any damages suffered by you or any third party as a result of using or distributing software. In no event will Bruce Eckel or the publisher be liable for any lost revenue, profit, or data, or for direct, indirect, special, consequential, incidental, or punitive damages, however caused and regardless of the theory of liability, arising out of the use of or inability to use software, even if Bruce Eckel and the publisher have been advised of the possibility of such damages. Should the software prove defective, you assume the cost of all necessary servicing, repair, or correction. If you think you've found an error, please submit the correction using the form you will find at www.BruceEckel.com. (Please use the same form for non-code errors found in the book.)
///:~

You may use the code in your projects and in the classroom (including your presentation materials) as long as the copyright notice that appears in each source file is retained.

Coding standards

In the text of this book, identifiers (function, variable, and class names) are set in **bold**. Most keywords are also set in bold, except for those keywords that are used so much that the bolding can become tedious, such as "class."

I use a particular coding style for the examples in this book. This style follows the style that Sun itself uses in virtually all of the code you will find at its site (see *java.sun.com/docs/codeconv/index.html*), and seems to be supported by most Java development environments. If you've read my other works, you'll also notice that Sun's coding style coincides with mine—this pleases me, although I had nothing to do with it. The subject of formatting style is good for hours of hot debate, so I'll just say I'm not trying to dictate correct style via my examples; I have my own motivation for using the style that I do. Because Java is a free-form programming language, you can continue to use whatever style you're comfortable with.

The programs in this book are files that are included by the word processor in the text, directly from compiled files. Thus, the code files printed in the book should all work without compiler errors. The errors that *should* cause compile-time error messages are commented out with the comment **//!** so they can be easily discovered and tested using automatic means. Errors discovered and reported to the author will appear first in the distributed source code and later in updates of the book (which will also appear on the Web site *www.BruceEckel.com*).

Java versions

I generally rely on the Sun implementation of Java as a reference when determining whether behavior is correct.

Over time, Sun has released three major versions of Java: 1.0, 1.1 and 2 (which is called version 2 even though the releases of the JDK from Sun continue to use the numbering scheme of 1.2, 1.3, 1.4, etc.). Version 2 seems to finally bring Java into the prime time, in particular where user interface tools are concerned. This book focuses on and is tested with Java 2, although I do sometimes make concessions to earlier features of Java 2 so that the code will compile under Linux (via the Linux JDK that was available at this writing).

If you need to learn about earlier releases of the language that are not covered in this edition, the first edition of the book is freely downloadable at *www.BruceEckel.com* and is also contained on the CD that is bound in with this book.

One thing you'll notice is that, when I do need to mention earlier versions of the language, I don't use the sub-revision numbers. In this book I will refer to Java 1.0, Java 1.1, and Java 2 only, to guard against typographical errors produced by further sub-revisioning of these products.

Seminars and mentoring

My company provides five-day, hands-on, public and in-house training seminars based on the material in this book. Selected material from each chapter represents a lesson, which is followed by a monitored exercise period so each student receives personal attention. The audio lectures and slides for the introductory seminar are also captured on CD ROM to provide at least some of the experience of the seminar without the travel and expense. For more information, go to *www.BruceEckel.com*.

My company also provides consulting, mentoring and walkthrough services to help guide your project through its development cycle— espccially your company's first Java project.

Errors

No matter how many tricks a writer uses to detect errors, some always creep in and these often leap off the page for a fresh reader.

There is an error submission form linked from the beginning of each chapter in the HTML version of this book (and on the CD ROM bound into the back of this book, and downloadable from *www.BruceEckel.com*) and also on the Web site itself, on the page for this book. If you discover anything you believe to be an error, please use this form to submit the error along with your suggested correction. If necessary, include the original source file and note any suggested modifications. Your help is appreciated.

Note on the cover design

The cover of *Thinking in Java* is inspired by the American Arts & Crafts Movement, which began near the turn of the century and reached its zenith between 1900 and 1920. It began in England as a reaction to both the machine production of the Industrial Revolution and the highly ornamental style of the Victorian era. Arts & Crafts emphasized spare design, the forms of nature as seen in the art nouveau movement, hand-crafting, and the importance of the individual craftsperson, and yet it did not eschew the use of modern tools. There are many echoes with the situation we have today: the turn of the century, the evolution from the raw beginnings of the computer revolution to something more refined and meaningful to individual persons, and the emphasis on software craftsmanship rather than just manufacturing code.

I see Java in this same way: as an attempt to elevate the programmer away from an operating-system mechanic and toward being a "software craftsman."

Both the author and the book/cover designer (who have been friends since childhood) find inspiration in this movement, and both own furniture, lamps, and other pieces that are either original or inspired by this period.

The other theme in this cover suggests a collection box that a naturalist might use to display the insect specimens that he or she has preserved. These insects are objects, which are placed within the box objects. The box objects are themselves placed within the "cover object," which illustrates the fundamental concept of aggregation in object-oriented programming. Of course, a programmer cannot help but make the association with "bugs," and here the bugs have been captured and presumably killed in a specimen jar, and finally confined within a small display box, as if to imply Java's ability to find, display, and subdue bugs (which is truly one of its most powerful attributes).

Acknowledgements

First, thanks to associates who have worked with me to give seminars, provide consulting, and develop teaching projects: Andrea Provaglio, Dave Bartlett (who also contributed significantly to Chapter 15), Bill Venners, and Larry O'Brien. I appreciate your patience as I continue to try to develop the best model for independent folks like us to work together. Thanks to Rolf André Klaedtke (Switzerland); Martin Vlcek, Martin Byer, Vlada & Pavel Lahoda, Martin the Bear, and Hanka (Prague); and Marco Cantu (Italy) for hosting me on my first self-organized European seminar tour.

Thanks to the Doyle Street Cohousing Community for putting up with me for the two years that it took me to write the first edition of this book (and for putting up with me at all). Thanks very much to Kevin and Sonda Donovan for subletting their great place in gorgeous Crested Butte, Colorado for the summer while I worked on the first edition of the book. Also thanks to the friendly residents of Crested Butte and the Rocky Mountain Biological Laboratory who make me feel so welcome.

Thanks to Claudette Moore at Moore Literary Agency for her tremendous patience and perseverance in getting me exactly what I wanted.

My first two books were published with Jeff Pepper as editor at Osborne/McGraw-Hill. Jeff appeared at the right place and the right time at Prentice-Hall and has cleared the path and made all the right things happen to make this a very pleasant publishing experience. Thanks, Jeff—it means a lot to me.

I'm especially indebted to Gen Kiyooka and his company Digigami, who graciously provided my Web server for the first several years of my presence on the Web. This was an invaluable learning aid.

Thanks to Cay Horstmann (co-author of *Core Java*, Prentice-Hall, 2000*)*, D'Arcy Smith (Symantec), and Paul Tyma (co-author of *Java Primer Plus*, The Waite Group, 1996), for helping me clarify concepts in the language.

Thanks to people who have spoken in my Java track at the Software Development Conference, and students in my seminars, who ask the questions I need to hear in order to make the material more clear.

Special thanks to Larry and Tina O'Brien, who helped turn my seminar into the original *Hands-On Java* CD ROM. (You can find out more at *www.BruceEckel.com*.)

Lots of people sent in corrections and I am indebted to them all, but particular thanks go to (for the first edition): Kevin Raulerson (found tons of great bugs), Bob Resendes (simply incredible), John Pinto, Joe Dante, Joe Sharp (all three were fabulous), David Combs (many grammar and clarification corrections), Dr. Robert Stephenson, John Cook, Franklin Chen, Zev Griner, David Karr, Leander A. Stroschein, Steve Clark, Charles A. Lee, Austin Maher, Dennis P. Roth, Roque Oliveira, Douglas Dunn, Dejan Ristic, Neil Galarneau, David B. Malkovsky, Steve Wilkinson, and a host of others. Prof. Ir. Marc Meurrens put in a great deal of effort to publicize and make the electronic version of the first edition of the book available in Europe.

There have been a spate of smart technical people in my life who have become friends and have also been both influential and unusual in that they do yoga and practice other forms of spiritual enhancement, which I find quite inspirational and instructional. They are Kraig Brockschmidt, Gen Kiyooka, and Andrea Provaglio, (who helps in the understanding of Java and programming in general in Italy, and now in the United States as an associate of the MindView team).

It's not that much of a surprise to me that understanding Delphi helped me understand Java, since there are many concepts and language design decisions in common. My Delphi friends provided assistance by helping me gain insight into that marvelous programming environment. They are Marco Cantu (another Italian—perhaps being steeped in Latin gives one aptitude for programming languages?), Neil Rubenking (who used to do the yoga/vegetarian/Zen thing until he discovered computers), and of course Zack Urlocker, a long-time pal whom I've traveled the world with.

My friend Richard Hale Shaw's insights and support have been very helpful (and Kim's, too). Richard and I spent many months giving seminars together and trying to work out the perfect learning experience for the attendees. Thanks also to KoAnn Vikoren, Eric Faurot, Marco Pardi, and the rest of the cast and crew at MFI. Thanks especially to Tara Arrowood, who re-inspired me about the possibilities of conferences.

The book design, cover design, and cover photo were created by my friend Daniel Will-Harris, noted author and designer (*www.Will-Harris.com*), who used to play with rub-on letters in junior high school while he awaited the invention of computers and desktop publishing, and complained of me mumbling over my algebra problems. However, I produced the camera-ready pages myself, so the typesetting errors are mine. Microsoft® Word 97 for Windows was used to write the book and to create camera-ready pages in Adobe Acrobat; the book was created directly from the Acrobat PDF files. (As a tribute to the electronic age, I happened to be overseas both times the final version of the book was produced—the first edition was sent from Capetown, South Africa and the second edition was posted from Prague). The body typeface is *Georgia* and the headlines are in *Verdana*. The cover typeface is *ITC Rennie Mackintosh*.

Thanks to the vendors who created the compilers: Borland, the Blackdown group (for Linux), and of course, Sun.

A special thanks to all my teachers and all my students (who are my teachers as well). The most fun writing teacher was Gabrielle Rico (author of *Writing the Natural Way*, Putnam, 1983). I'll always treasure the terrific week at Esalen.

The supporting cast of friends includes, but is not limited to: Andrew Binstock, Steve Sinofsky, JD Hildebrandt, Tom Keffer, Brian McElhinney, Brinkley Barr, Bill Gates at *Midnight Engineering Magazine*, Larry Constantine and Lucy Lockwood, Greg Perry, Dan Putterman, Christi Westphal, Gene Wang, Dave Mayer, David Intersimone, Andrea Rosenfield, Claire Sawyers, more Italians (Laura Fallai, Corrado, Ilsa, and Cristina Giustozzi), Chris and Laura Strand, the Almquists, Brad Jerbic, Marilyn Cvitanic, the Mabrys, the Haflingers, the Pollocks, Peter Vinci, the Robbins Families, the Moelter Families (and the McMillans), Michael Wilk, Dave Stoner, Laurie Adams, the Cranstons, Larry Fogg, Mike and Karen Sequeira, Gary Entsminger and Allison Brody, Kevin Donovan and Sonda Eastlack, Chester and Shannon Andersen, Joe Lordi, Dave and

Brenda Bartlett, David Lee, the Rentschlers, the Sudeks, Dick, Patty, and Lee Eckel, Lynn and Todd, and their families. And of course, Mom and Dad.

Internet contributors

Thanks to those who helped me rewrite the examples to use the Swing library, and for other assistance: Jon Shvarts, Thomas Kirsch, Rahim Adatia, Rajesh Jain, Ravi Manthena, Banu Rajamani, Jens Brandt, Nitin Shivaram, Malcolm Davis, and everyone who expressed support. This really helped me jump-start the project.

1: Introduction to Objects

The genesis of the computer revolution was in a machine. The genesis of our programming languages thus tends to look like that machine.

But computers are not so much machines as they are mind amplification tools ("bicycles for the mind," as Steve Jobs is fond of saying) and a different kind of expressive medium. As a result, the tools are beginning to look less like machines and more like parts of our minds, and also like other forms of expression such as writing, painting, sculpture, animation, and filmmaking. Object-oriented programming (OOP) is part of this movement toward using the computer as an expressive medium.

This chapter will introduce you to the basic concepts of OOP, including an overview of development methods. This chapter, and this book, assume that you have had experience in a procedural programming language, although not necessarily C. If you think you need more preparation in programming and the syntax of C before tackling this book, you should work through the *Thinking in C: Foundations for C++ and Java* training CD ROM, bound in with this book and also available at *www.BruceEckel.com*.

This chapter is background and supplementary material. Many people do not feel comfortable wading into object-oriented programming without understanding the big picture first. Thus, there are many concepts that are introduced here to give you a solid overview of OOP. However, many other people don't get the big picture concepts until they've seen some of the mechanics first; these people may become bogged down and lost without some code to get their hands on. If you're part of this latter group and are eager to get to the specifics of the language, feel free to jump past this chapter—skipping it at this point will not prevent you from writing programs or learning the language. However, you will want to come back here eventually to fill in your knowledge so you can understand why objects are important and how to design with them.

The progress of abstraction

All programming languages provide abstractions. It can be argued that the complexity of the problems you're able to solve is directly related to the kind and quality of abstraction. By "kind" I mean, "What is it that you are abstracting?" Assembly language is a small abstraction of the underlying machine. Many so-called "imperative" languages that followed (such as Fortran, BASIC, and C) were abstractions of assembly language. These languages are big improvements over assembly language, but their primary abstraction still requires you to think in terms of the structure of the computer rather than the structure of the problem you are trying to solve. The programmer must establish the association between the machine model (in the "solution space," which is the place where you're modeling that problem, such as a computer) and the model of the problem that is actually being solved (in the "problem space," which is the place where the problem exists). The effort required to perform this mapping, and the fact that it is extrinsic to the programming language, produces programs that are difficult to write and expensive to maintain, and as a side effect created the entire "programming methods" industry.

The alternative to modeling the machine is to model the problem you're trying to solve. Early languages such as LISP and APL chose particular views of the world ("All problems are ultimately lists" or "All problems are algorithmic," respectively). PROLOG casts all problems into chains of decisions. Languages have been created for constraint-based programming and for programming exclusively by manipulating graphical symbols. (The latter proved to be too restrictive.) Each of these approaches is a good solution to the particular class of problem they're designed to solve, but when you step outside of that domain they become awkward.

The object-oriented approach goes a step further by providing tools for the programmer to represent elements in the problem space. This representation is general enough that the programmer is not constrained to any particular type of problem. We refer to the elements in the problem space and their representations in the solution space as "objects." (Of course, you will also need other objects that don't have problem-space analogs.) The idea is that the program is allowed to adapt itself to the lingo of the problem by adding new types of objects, so when you read the code describing the solution, you're reading words that also express the problem. This is a more flexible and powerful language abstraction than what we've had before. Thus, OOP allows you to describe the problem in terms of the problem, rather than in terms of the computer where the solution will run. There's still a connection back to the computer, though. Each object looks quite a bit like a little computer; it has a state, and it has operations that you can ask it to perform. However, this doesn't seem like such a bad analogy to objects in the real world—they all have characteristics and behaviors.

Some language designers have decided that object-oriented programming by itself is not adequate to easily solve all programming problems, and advocate the combination of various approaches into *multiparadigm* programming languages.[1]

Alan Kay summarized five basic characteristics of Smalltalk, the first successful object-oriented language and one of the languages upon which Java is based. These characteristics represent a pure approach to object-oriented programming:

1. **Everything is an object.** Think of an object as a fancy variable; it stores data, but you can "make requests" to that object, asking it to perform operations on itself. In theory, you can take any conceptual component in the problem you're trying to solve (dogs, buildings, services, etc.) and represent it as an object in your program.

2. **A program is a bunch of objects telling each other what to do by sending messages**. To make a request of an object, you "send a message" to that object. More concretely, you

---

[1] See *Multiparadigm Programming in Leda* by Timothy Budd (Addison-Wesley 1995).

can think of a message as a request to call a function that belongs to a particular object.

3. **Each object has its own memory made up of other objects**. Put another way, you create a new kind of object by making a package containing existing objects. Thus, you can build complexity in a program while hiding it behind the simplicity of objects.

4. **Every object has a type**. Using the parlance, each object is an *instance* of a *class*, in which "class" is synonymous with "type." The most important distinguishing characteristic of a class is "What messages can you send to it?"

5. **All objects of a particular type can receive the same messages**. This is actually a loaded statement, as you will see later. Because an object of type "circle" is also an object of type "shape," a circle is guaranteed to accept shape messages. This means you can write code that talks to shapes and automatically handle anything that fits the description of a shape. This *substitutability* is one of the most powerful concepts in OOP.

An object has an interface

Aristotle was probably the first to begin a careful study of the concept of *type;* he spoke of "the class of fishes and the class of birds." The idea that all objects, while being unique, are also part of a class of objects that have characteristics and behaviors in common was used directly in the first object-oriented language, Simula-67, with its fundamental keyword **class** that introduces a new type into a program.

Simula, as its name implies, was created for developing simulations such as the classic "bank teller problem." In this, you have a bunch of tellers, customers, accounts, transactions, and units of money—a lot of "objects." Objects that are identical except for their state during a program's execution are grouped together into "classes of objects" and that's where the keyword **class** came from. Creating abstract data types (classes) is a fundamental concept in object-oriented programming. Abstract data types work almost exactly like built-in types: You can create variables of a type (called *objects* or *instances* in object-oriented parlance) and manipulate those variables (called *sending messages* or *requests;* you send a message and the object figures out what to do with it). The members (elements) of each class share some commonality: every account has a balance, every teller can accept a deposit, etc. At the same time, each member has its own state, each account has a different balance, each teller has a name. Thus, the tellers, customers, accounts, transactions, etc., can each be represented with a unique entity in the computer program. This entity is the object, and each object belongs to a particular class that defines its characteristics and behaviors.

So, although what we really do in object-oriented programming is create new data types, virtually all object-oriented programming languages use the "class" keyword. When you see the word "type" think "class" and vice versa[2].

Since a class describes a set of objects that have identical characteristics (data elements) and behaviors (functionality), a class is really a data type because a floating point number, for example, also has a set of characteristics and behaviors. The difference is that a programmer defines a class to fit a problem rather than being forced to use an existing data type that was designed to represent a unit of storage in a machine. You extend the programming language by adding new data types specific to your needs. The programming system welcomes the new classes and gives them all the care and type-checking that it gives to built-in types.

The object-oriented approach is not limited to building simulations. Whether or not you agree that any program is a simulation of the system you're designing, the use of OOP techniques can easily reduce a large set of problems to a simple solution.

Once a class is established, you can make as many objects of that class as you like, and then manipulate those objects as if they are the elements that exist in the problem you are trying to solve. Indeed, one of the challenges of object-oriented programming is to create a one-to-one

---

[2] Some people make a distinction, stating that type determines the interface while class is a particular implementation of that interface.

mapping between the elements in the problem space and objects in the solution space.

But how do you get an object to do useful work for you? There must be a way to make a request of the object so that it will do something, such as complete a transaction, draw something on the screen, or turn on a switch. And each object can satisfy only certain requests. The requests you can make of an object are defined by its *interface,* and the type is what determines the interface. A simple example might be a representation of a light bulb:

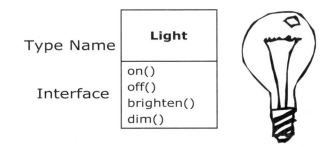

```
Light lt = new Light();
lt.on();
```

The interface establishes *what* requests you can make for a particular object. However, there must be code somewhere to satisfy that request. This, along with the hidden data, comprises the *implementation.* From a procedural programming standpoint, it's not that complicated. A type has a function associated with each possible request, and when you make a particular request to an object, that function is called. This process is usually summarized by saying that you "send a message" (make a request) to an object, and the object figures out what to do with that message (it executes code).

Here, the name of the type/class is **Light**, the name of this particular **Light** object is **lt**, and the requests that you can make of a **Light** object are to turn it on, turn it off, make it brighter, or make it dimmer. You create a **Light** object by defining a "reference" (**lt**) for that object and calling **new** to request a new object of that type. To send a message to the object, you state the name of the object and connect it to the message request with a period (dot). From the standpoint of the user of a predefined class, that's pretty much all there is to programming with objects.

The diagram shown above follows the format of the *Unified Modeling Language* (UML). Each class is represented by a box, with the type name in the top portion of the box, any data members that you care to describe in the middle portion of the box, and the *member functions* (the functions that belong to this object, which receive any messages you send to that object) in the bottom portion of the box. Often, only the name of the class and the public member functions are shown in UML design diagrams, and so the middle portion is not shown. If you're interested only in the class name, then the bottom portion doesn't need to be shown, either.

The hidden implementation

It is helpful to break up the playing field into *class creators* (those who create new data types) and *client programmers*[3] (the class consumers who use the data types in their applications). The goal of the client programmer is to collect a toolbox full of classes to use for rapid application development. The goal of the class creator is to build a class that exposes only what's necessary to the client programmer and keeps everything else hidden. Why? Because if it's hidden, the client programmer can't use it, which means that the class creator can change the hidden portion at will without worrying about the impact to anyone else. The hidden portion usually represents the tender insides of an object that could easily be corrupted by a careless or uninformed client programmer, so hiding the implementation reduces program bugs. The concept of implementation hiding cannot be overemphasized.

In any relationship it's important to have boundaries that are respected by all parties involved. When you create a library, you establish a relationship with the client programmer, who is also a programmer, but

---

[3] I'm indebted to my friend Scott Meyers for this term.

one who is putting together an application by using your library, possibly to build a bigger library.

If all the members of a class are available to everyone, then the client programmer can do anything with that class and there's no way to enforce rules. Even though you might really prefer that the client programmer not directly manipulate some of the members of your class, without access control there's no way to prevent it. Everything's naked to the world.

So the first reason for access control is to keep client programmers' hands off portions they shouldn't touch—parts that are necessary for the internal machinations of the data type but not part of the interface that users need in order to solve their particular problems. This is actually a service to users because they can easily see what's important to them and what they can ignore.

The second reason for access control is to allow the library designer to change the internal workings of the class without worrying about how it will affect the client programmer. For example, you might implement a particular class in a simple fashion to ease development, and then later discover that you need to rewrite it in order to make it run faster. If the interface and implementation are clearly separated and protected, you can accomplish this easily.

Java uses three explicit keywords to set the boundaries in a class: **public**, **private**, and **protected**. Their use and meaning are quite straightforward. These *access specifiers* determine who can use the definitions that follow. **public** means the following definitions are available to everyone. The **private** keyword, on the other hand, means that no one can access those definitions except you, the creator of the type, inside member functions of that type. **private** is a brick wall between you and the client programmer. If someone tries to access a **private** member, they'll get a compile-time error. **protected** acts like **private**, with the exception that an inheriting class has access to **protected** members, but not **private** members. Inheritance will be introduced shortly.

Java also has a "default" access, which comes into play if you don't use one of the aforementioned specifiers. This is sometimes called "friendly" access because classes can access the friendly members of other classes in the same package, but outside of the package those same friendly members appear to be **private**.

Reusing the implementation

Once a class has been created and tested, it should (ideally) represent a useful unit of code. It turns out that this reusability is not nearly so easy to achieve as many would hope; it takes experience and insight to produce a good design. But once you have such a design, it begs to be reused. Code reuse is one of the greatest advantages that object-oriented programming languages provide.

The simplest way to reuse a class is to just use an object of that class directly, but you can also place an object of that class inside a new class. We call this "creating a member object." Your new class can be made up of any number and type of other objects, in any combination that you need to achieve the functionality desired in your new class. Because you are composing a new class from existing classes, this concept is called *composition* (or more generally, *aggregation*). Composition is often referred to as a "has-a" relationship, as in "a car has an engine."

(The above UML diagram indicates composition with the filled diamond, which states there is one car. I will typically use a simpler form: just a line, without the diamond, to indicate an association.[4])

Composition comes with a great deal of flexibility. The member objects of your new class are usually private, making them inaccessible to the client programmers who are using the class. This allows you to change those

---

[4] This is usually enough detail for most diagrams, and you don't need to get specific about whether you're using aggregation or composition.

members without disturbing existing client code. You can also change the member objects at run-time, to dynamically change the behavior of your program. Inheritance, which is described next, does not have this flexibility since the compiler must place compile-time restrictions on classes created with inheritance.

Because inheritance is so important in object-oriented programming it is often highly emphasized, and the new programmer can get the idea that inheritance should be used everywhere. This can result in awkward and overly complicated designs. Instead, you should first look to composition when creating new classes, since it is simpler and more flexible. If you take this approach, your designs will be cleaner. Once you've had some experience, it will be reasonably obvious when you need inheritance.

Inheritance: reusing the interface

By itself, the idea of an object is a convenient tool. It allows you to package data and functionality together by *concept*, so you can represent an appropriate problem-space idea rather than being forced to use the idioms of the underlying machine. These concepts are expressed as fundamental units in the programming language by using the **class** keyword.

It seems a pity, however, to go to all the trouble to create a class and then be forced to create a brand new one that might have similar functionality. It's nicer if we can take the existing class, clone it, and then make additions and modifications to the clone. This is effectively what you get with *inheritance*, with the exception that if the original class (called the *base* or *super* or *parent* class) is changed, the modified "clone" (called the *derived* or *inherited* or *sub* or *child* class) also reflects those changes.

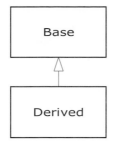

(The arrow in the above UML diagram points from the derived class to the base class. As you will see, there can be more than one derived class.)

A type does more than describe the constraints on a set of objects; it also has a relationship with other types. Two types can have characteristics and behaviors in common, but one type may contain more characteristics than another and may also handle more messages (or handle them differently). Inheritance expresses this similarity between types using the concept of base types and derived types. A base type contains all of the characteristics and behaviors that are shared among the types derived from it. You create a base type to represent the core of your ideas about some objects in your system. From the base type, you derive other types to express the different ways that this core can be realized.

For example, a trash-recycling machine sorts pieces of trash. The base type is "trash," and each piece of trash has a weight, a value, and so on, and can be shredded, melted, or decomposed. From this, more specific types of trash are derived that may have additional characteristics (a bottle has a color) or behaviors (an aluminum can may be crushed, a steel can is magnetic). In addition, some behaviors may be different (the value of paper depends on its type and condition). Using inheritance, you can build a type hierarchy that expresses the problem you're trying to solve in terms of its types.

A second example is the classic "shape" example, perhaps used in a computer-aided design system or game simulation. The base type is "shape," and each shape has a size, a color, a position, and so on. Each shape can be drawn, erased, moved, colored, etc. From this, specific types of shapes are derived (inherited): circle, square, triangle, and so on, each of which may have additional characteristics and behaviors. Certain shapes can be flipped, for example. Some behaviors may be different, such as when you want to calculate the area of a shape. The type hierarchy embodies both the similarities and differences between the shapes.

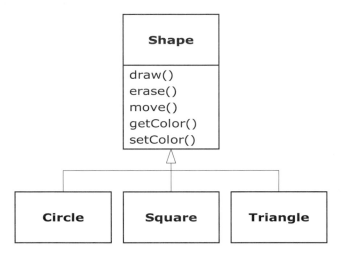

Casting the solution in the same terms as the problem is tremendously beneficial because you don't need a lot of intermediate models to get from a description of the problem to a description of the solution. With objects, the type hierarchy is the primary model, so you go directly from the description of the system in the real world to the description of the system in code. Indeed, one of the difficulties people have with object-oriented design is that it's too simple to get from the beginning to the end. A mind trained to look for complex solutions is often stumped by this simplicity at first.

When you inherit from an existing type, you create a new type. This new type contains not only all the members of the existing type (although the **private** ones are hidden away and inaccessible), but more important, it duplicates the interface of the base class. That is, all the messages you can send to objects of the base class you can also send to objects of the derived class. Since we know the type of a class by the messages we can send to it, this means that the derived class *is the same type as the base class*. In the previous example, "a circle is a shape." This type equivalence via inheritance is one of the fundamental gateways in understanding the meaning of object-oriented programming.

Since both the base class and derived class have the same interface, there must be some implementation to go along with that interface. That is, there must be some code to execute when an object receives a particular message. If you simply inherit a class and don't do anything else, the methods from the base-class interface come right along into the derived class. That means objects of the derived class have not only the same type, they also have the same behavior, which isn't particularly interesting.

You have two ways to differentiate your new derived class from the original base class. The first is quite straightforward: You simply add brand new functions to the derived class. These new functions are not part of the base class interface. This means that the base class simply didn't do as much as you wanted it to, so you added more functions. This simple and primitive use for inheritance is, at times, the perfect solution to your problem. However, you should look closely for the possibility that your base class might also need these additional functions. This process of discovery and iteration of your design happens regularly in object-oriented programming.

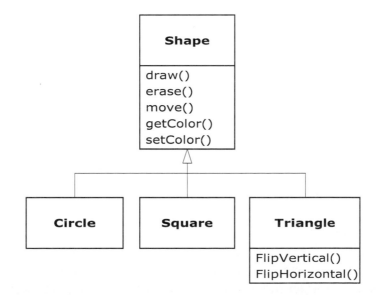

Although inheritance may sometimes imply (especially in Java, where the keyword that indicates inheritance is **extends**) that you are going to add new functions to the interface, that's not necessarily true. The second and more important way to differentiate your new class is to *change* the behavior of an existing base-class function. This is referred to as *overriding* that function.

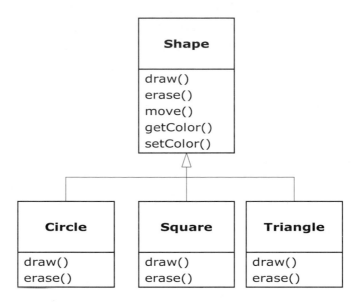

To override a function, you simply create a new definition for the function in the derived class. You're saying, "I'm using the same interface function here, but I want it to do something different for my new type."

Is-a vs. is-like-a relationships

There's a certain debate that can occur about inheritance: Should inheritance override *only* base-class functions (and not add new member functions that aren't in the base class)? This would mean that the derived type is *exactly* the same type as the base class since it has exactly the same interface. As a result, you can exactly substitute an object of the derived class for an object of the base class. This can be thought of as *pure substitution*, and it's often referred to as the *substitution principle*. In a sense, this is the ideal way to treat inheritance. We often refer to the relationship between the base class and derived classes in this case as an *is-a* relationship, because you can say "a circle *is a* shape." A test for inheritance is to determine whether you can state the is-a relationship about the classes and have it make sense.

There are times when you must add new interface elements to a derived type, thus extending the interface and creating a new type. The new type can still be substituted for the base type, but the substitution isn't perfect because your new functions are not accessible from the base type. This can be described as an *is-like-a*[5] relationship; the new type has the interface of the old type but it also contains other functions, so you can't really say it's exactly the same. For example, consider an air conditioner. Suppose your house is wired with all the controls for cooling; that is, it has an interface that allows you to control cooling. Imagine that the air conditioner breaks down and you replace it with a heat pump, which can both heat and cool. The heat pump *is-like-an* air conditioner, but it can do more. Because the control system of your house is designed only to control cooling, it is restricted to communication with the cooling part of the new object. The interface of the new object has been extended, and the existing system doesn't know about anything except the original interface.

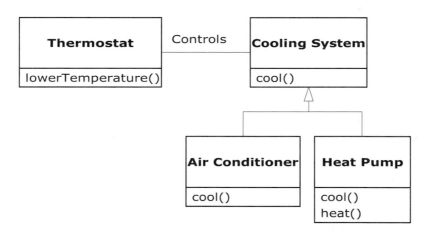

Of course, once you see this design it becomes clear that the base class "cooling system" is not general enough, and should be renamed to "temperature control system" so that it can also include heating—at which point the substitution principle will work. However, the diagram above is an example of what can happen in design and in the real world.

----

[5] My term.

When you see the substitution principle it's easy to feel like this approach (pure substitution) is the only way to do things, and in fact it *is* nice if your design works out that way. But you'll find that there are times when it's equally clear that you must add new functions to the interface of a derived class. With inspection both cases should be reasonably obvious.

Interchangeable objects with polymorphism

When dealing with type hierarchies, you often want to treat an object not as the specific type that it is, but instead as its base type. This allows you to write code that doesn't depend on specific types. In the shape example, functions manipulate generic shapes without respect to whether they're circles, squares, triangles, or some shape that hasn't even been defined yet. All shapes can be drawn, erased, and moved, so these functions simply send a message to a shape object; they don't worry about how the object copes with the message.

Such code is unaffected by the addition of new types, and adding new types is the most common way to extend an object-oriented program to handle new situations. For example, you can derive a new subtype of shape called pentagon without modifying the functions that deal only with generic shapes. This ability to extend a program easily by deriving new subtypes is important because it greatly improves designs while reducing the cost of software maintenance.

There's a problem, however, with attempting to treat derived-type objects as their generic base types (circles as shapes, bicycles as vehicles, cormorants as birds, etc.). If a function is going to tell a generic shape to draw itself, or a generic vehicle to steer, or a generic bird to move, the compiler cannot know at compile-time precisely what piece of code will be executed. That's the whole point—when the message is sent, the programmer doesn't *want* to know what piece of code will be executed; the draw function can be applied equally to a circle, a square, or a triangle, and the object will execute the proper code depending on its specific type. If you don't have to know what piece of code will be executed, then when you add a new subtype, the code it executes can be different without requiring changes to the function call. Therefore, the compiler cannot know precisely what piece of code is executed, so what does it do? For example, in the following diagram the **BirdController** object just works with generic **Bird** objects, and does not know what exact type they are. This is convenient from **BirdController**'s perspective because it doesn't have to write special code to determine the exact type of **Bird** it's working with, or that **Bird**'s behavior. So how does it happen that, when **move( )** is called while ignoring the specific type of **Bird**, the right behavior will occur (a **Goose** runs, flies, or swims, and a **Penguin** runs or swims)?

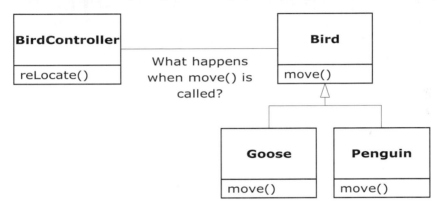

The answer is the primary twist in object-oriented programming: the compiler cannot make a function call in the traditional sense. The function call generated by a non-OOP compiler causes what is called *early binding*, a term you may not have heard before because you've never thought about it any other way. It means the compiler generates a call to a specific function name, and the linker resolves this call to the absolute address of the code to be executed. In OOP, the program cannot determine the address of the code until run-time, so some other scheme is necessary when a message is sent to a generic object.

To solve the problem, object-oriented languages use the concept of *late binding*. When you send a message to an object, the code being called isn't determined until run-time. The compiler does ensure that the function exists and performs type checking on the arguments and return value (a language in which this isn't true is called *weakly typed*), but it doesn't know the exact code to execute.

To perform late binding, Java uses a special bit of code in lieu of the absolute call. This code calculates the address of the function body, using information stored in the object (this process is covered in great detail in Chapter 7). Thus, each object can behave differently according to the contents of that special bit of code. When you send a message to an object, the object actually does figure out what to do with that message.

In some languages (C++, in particular) you must explicitly state that you want a function to have the flexibility of late-binding properties. In these languages, by default, member functions are *not* dynamically bound. This caused problems, so in Java dynamic binding is the default and you don't need to remember to add any extra keywords in order to get polymorphism.

Consider the shape example. The family of classes (all based on the same uniform interface) was diagrammed earlier in this chapter. To demonstrate polymorphism, we want to write a single piece of code that ignores the specific details of type and talks only to the base class. That code is *decoupled* from type-specific information, and thus is simpler to write and easier to understand. And, if a new type—a **Hexagon**, for example—is added through inheritance, the code you write will work just as well for the new type of **Shape** as it did on the existing types. Thus, the program is *extensible*.

If you write a method in Java (as you will soon learn how to do):

```
void doStuff(Shape s) {
  s.erase();
  // ...
  s.draw();
}
```

This function speaks to any **Shape**, so it is independent of the specific type of object that it's drawing and erasing. If in some other part of the program we use the **doStuff( )** function:

```
Circle c = new Circle();
Triangle t = new Triangle();
Line l = new Line();
doStuff(c);
doStuff(t);
```

```
doStuff(l);
```

The calls to **doStuff( )** automatically work correctly, regardless of the exact type of the object.

This is actually a pretty amazing trick. Consider the line:

```
doStuff(c);
```

What's happening here is that a **Circle** is being passed into a function that's expecting a **Shape**. Since a **Circle** *is* a **Shape** it can be treated as one by **doStuff( )**. That is, any message that **doStuff( )** can send to a **Shape**, a **Circle** can accept. So it is a completely safe and logical thing to do.

We call this process of treating a derived type as though it were its base type *upcasting*. The name *cast* is used in the sense of casting into a mold and the *up* comes from the way the inheritance diagram is typically arranged, with the base type at the top and the derived classes fanning out downward. Thus, casting to a base type is moving up the inheritance diagram: "upcasting."

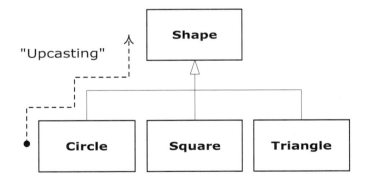

An object-oriented program contains some upcasting somewhere, because that's how you decouple yourself from knowing about the exact type you're working with. Look at the code in **doStuff( )**:

```
s.erase();
// ...
s.draw();
```

Notice that it doesn't say "If you're a **Circle**, do this, if you're a **Square**, do that, etc." If you write that kind of code, which checks for all the possible types that a **Shape** can actually be, it's messy and you need to change it every time you add a new kind of **Shape**. Here, you just say "You're a shape, I know you can **erase( )** and **draw( )** yourself, do it, and take care of the details correctly."

What's impressive about the code in **doStuff( )** is that, somehow, the right thing happens. Calling **draw( )** for **Circle** causes different code to be executed than when calling **draw( )** for a **Square** or a **Line**, but when the **draw( )** message is sent to an anonymous **Shape**, the correct behavior occurs based on the actual type of the **Shape**. This is amazing because, as mentioned earlier, when the Java compiler is compiling the code for **doStuff( )**, it cannot know exactly what types it is dealing with. So ordinarily, you'd expect it to end up calling the version of **erase( )** and **draw( )** for the base class **Shape**, and not for the specific **Circle**, **Square**, or **Line**. And yet the right thing happens because of polymorphism. The compiler and run-time system handle the details; all you need to know is that it happens, and more important how to design with it. When you send a message to an object, the object will do the right thing, even when upcasting is involved.

Abstract base classes and interfaces

Often in a design, you want the base class to present *only* an interface for its derived classes. That is, you don't want anyone to actually create an object of the base class, only to upcast to it so that its interface can be used. This is accomplished by making that class *abstract* using the **abstract** keyword. If anyone tries to make an object of an **abstract** class, the compiler prevents them. This is a tool to enforce a particular design.

You can also use the **abstract** keyword to describe a method that hasn't been implemented yet—as a stub indicating "here is an interface function for all types inherited from this class, but at this point I don't have any implementation for it." An **abstract** method may be created only inside an **abstract** class. When the class is inherited, that method must be implemented, or the inheriting class becomes **abstract** as well. Creating an **abstract** method allows you to put a method in an interface without being forced to provide a possibly meaningless body of code for that method.

The **interface** keyword takes the concept of an **abstract** class one step further by preventing any function definitions at all. The **interface** is a very handy and commonly used tool, as it provides the perfect separation of interface and implementation. In addition, you can combine many interfaces together, if you wish, whereas inheriting from multiple regular classes or abstract classes is not possible.

Object landscapes and lifetimes

Technically, OOP is just about abstract data typing, inheritance, and polymorphism, but other issues can be at least as important. The remainder of this section will cover these issues.

One of the most important factors is the way objects are created and destroyed. Where is the data for an object and how is the lifetime of the object controlled? There are different philosophies at work here. C++ takes the approach that control of efficiency is the most important issue, so it gives the programmer a choice. For maximum run-time speed, the storage and lifetime can be determined while the program is being written, by placing the objects on the stack (these are sometimes called *automatic* or *scoped* variables) or in the static storage area. This places a priority on the speed of storage allocation and release, and control of these can be very valuable in some situations. However, you sacrifice flexibility because you must know the exact quantity, lifetime, and type of objects while you're writing the program. If you are trying to solve a more general problem such as computer-aided design, warehouse management, or air-traffic control, this is too restrictive.

The second approach is to create objects dynamically in a pool of memory called the heap. In this approach, you don't know until run-time how many objects you need, what their lifetime is, or what their exact type is. Those are determined at the spur of the moment while the program is running. If you need a new object, you simply make it on the heap at the

---

point that you need it. Because the storage is managed dynamically, at run-time, the amount of time required to allocate storage on the heap is significantly longer than the time to create storage on the stack. (Creating storage on the stack is often a single assembly instruction to move the stack pointer down, and another to move it back up.) The dynamic approach makes the generally logical assumption that objects tend to be complicated, so the extra overhead of finding storage and releasing that storage will not have an important impact on the creation of an object. In addition, the greater flexibility is essential to solve the general programming problem.

Java uses the second approach, exclusively[6]. Every time you want to create an object, you use the **new** keyword to build a dynamic instance of that object.

There's another issue, however, and that's the lifetime of an object. With languages that allow objects to be created on the stack, the compiler determines how long the object lasts and can automatically destroy it. However, if you create it on the heap the compiler has no knowledge of its lifetime. In a language like C++, you must determine programmatically when to destroy the object, which can lead to memory leaks if you don't do it correctly (and this is a common problem in C++ programs). Java provides a feature called a garbage collector that automatically discovers when an object is no longer in use and destroys it. A garbage collector is much more convenient because it reduces the number of issues that you must track and the code you must write. More important, the garbage collector provides a much higher level of insurance against the insidious problem of memory leaks (which has brought many a C++ project to its knees).

The rest of this section looks at additional factors concerning object lifetimes and landscapes.

---

[6] Primitive types, which you'll learn about later, are a special case.

Collections and iterators

If you don't know how many objects you're going to need to solve a particular problem, or how long they will last, you also don't know how to store those objects. How can you know how much space to create for those objects? You can't, since that information isn't known until run-time.

The solution to most problems in object-oriented design seems flippant: you create another type of object. The new type of object that solves this particular problem holds references to other objects. Of course, you can do the same thing with an array, which is available in most languages. But there's more. This new object, generally called a *container* (also called a *collection*, but the Java library uses that term in a different sense so this book will use "container"), will expand itself whenever necessary to accommodate everything you place inside it. So you don't need to know how many objects you're going to hold in a container. Just create a container object and let it take care of the details.

Fortunately, a good OOP language comes with a set of containers as part of the package. In C++, it's part of the Standard C++ Library and is sometimes called the Standard Template Library (STL). Object Pascal has containers in its Visual Component Library (VCL). Smalltalk has a very complete set of containers. Java also has containers in its standard library. In some libraries, a generic container is considered good enough for all needs, and in others (Java, for example) the library has different types of containers for different needs: a vector (called an **ArrayList** in Java) for consistent access to all elements, and a linked list for consistent insertion at all elements, for example, so you can choose the particular type that fits your needs. Container libraries may also include sets, queues, hash tables, trees, stacks, etc.

All containers have some way to put things in and get things out; there are usually functions to add elements to a container, and others to fetch those elements back out. But fetching elements can be more problematic, because a single-selection function is restrictive. What if you want to manipulate or compare a set of elements in the container instead of just one?

The solution is an iterator, which is an object whose job is to select the elements within a container and present them to the user of the iterator. As a class, it also provides a level of abstraction. This abstraction can be used to separate the details of the container from the code that's accessing that container. The container, via the iterator, is abstracted to be simply a sequence. The iterator allows you to traverse that sequence without worrying about the underlying structure—that is, whether it's an **ArrayList**, a **LinkedList**, a **Stack**, or something else. This gives you the flexibility to easily change the underlying data structure without disturbing the code in your program. Java began (in version 1.0 and 1.1) with a standard iterator, called **Enumeration**, for all of its container classes. Java 2 has added a much more complete container library that contains an iterator called **Iterator** that does more than the older **Enumeration**.

From a design standpoint, all you really want is a sequence that can be manipulated to solve your problem. If a single type of sequence satisfied all of your needs, there'd be no reason to have different kinds. There are two reasons that you need a choice of containers. First, containers provide different types of interfaces and external behavior. A stack has a different interface and behavior than that of a queue, which is different from that of a set or a list. One of these might provide a more flexible solution to your problem than the other. Second, different containers have different efficiencies for certain operations. The best example is an **ArrayList** and a **LinkedList**. Both are simple sequences that can have identical interfaces and external behaviors. But certain operations can have radically different costs. Randomly accessing elements in an **ArrayList** is a constant-time operation; it takes the same amount of time regardless of the element you select. However, in a **LinkedList** it is expensive to move through the list to randomly select an element, and it takes longer to find an element that is further down the list. On the other hand, if you want to insert an element in the middle of a sequence, it's much cheaper in a **LinkedList** than in an **ArrayList**. These and other operations have different efficiencies depending on the underlying structure of the sequence. In the design phase, you might start with a **LinkedList** and, when tuning for performance, change to an **ArrayList**. Because of the abstraction via iterators, you can change from one to the other with minimal impact on your code.

In the end, remember that a container is only a storage cabinet to put objects in. If that cabinet solves all of your needs, it doesn't really matter how it is implemented (a basic concept with most types of objects). If you're working in a programming environment that has built-in overhead due to other factors, then the cost difference between an **ArrayList** and a **LinkedList** might not matter. You might need only one type of sequence. You can even imagine the "perfect" container abstraction, which can automatically change its underlying implementation according to the way it is used.

The singly rooted hierarchy

One of the issues in OOP that has become especially prominent since the introduction of C++ is whether all classes should ultimately be inherited from a single base class. In Java (as with virtually all other OOP languages) the answer is "yes" and the name of this ultimate base class is simply **Object**. It turns out that the benefits of the singly rooted hierarchy are many.

All objects in a singly rooted hierarchy have an interface in common, so they are all ultimately the same type. The alternative (provided by C++) is that you don't know that everything is the same fundamental type. From a backward-compatibility standpoint this fits the model of C better and can be thought of as less restrictive, but when you want to do full-on object-oriented programming you must then build your own hierarchy to provide the same convenience that's built into other OOP languages. And in any new class library you acquire, some other incompatible interface will be used. It requires effort (and possibly multiple inheritance) to work the new interface into your design. Is the extra "flexibility" of C++ worth it? If you need it—if you have a large investment in C—it's quite valuable. If you're starting from scratch, other alternatives such as Java can often be more productive.

All objects in a singly rooted hierarchy (such as Java provides) can be guaranteed to have certain functionality. You know you can perform certain basic operations on every object in your system. A singly rooted hierarchy, along with creating all objects on the heap, greatly simplifies argument passing (one of the more complex topics in C++).

A singly rooted hierarchy makes it much easier to implement a garbage collector (which is conveniently built into Java). The necessary support can be installed in the base class, and the garbage collector can thus send the appropriate messages to every object in the system. Without a singly rooted hierarchy and a system to manipulate an object via a reference, it is difficult to implement a garbage collector.

Since run-time type information is guaranteed to be in all objects, you'll never end up with an object whose type you cannot determine. This is especially important with system level operations, such as exception handling, and to allow greater flexibility in programming.

Collection libraries and support for easy collection use

Because a container is a tool that you'll use frequently, it makes sense to have a library of containers that are built in a reusable fashion, so you can take one off the shelf and plug it into your program. Java provides such a library, which should satisfy most needs.

Downcasting vs. templates/generics

To make these containers reusable, they hold the one universal type in Java that was previously mentioned: **Object**. The singly rooted hierarchy means that everything is an **Object**, so a container that holds **Object**s can hold anything. This makes containers easy to reuse.

To use such a container, you simply add object references to it, and later ask for them back. But, since the container holds only **Object**s, when you add your object reference into the container it is upcast to **Object**, thus losing its identity. When you fetch it back, you get an **Object** reference, and not a reference to the type that you put in. So how do you turn it back into something that has the useful interface of the object that you put into the container?

Here, the cast is used again, but this time you're not casting up the inheritance hierarchy to a more general type, you cast down the hierarchy to a more specific type. This manner of casting is called downcasting. With upcasting, you know, for example, that a **Circle** is a type of **Shape** so it's safe to upcast, but you don't know that an **Object** is necessarily a **Circle** or a **Shape** so it's hardly safe to downcast unless you know that's what you're dealing with.

It's not completely dangerous, however, because if you downcast to the wrong thing you'll get a run-time error called an *exception,* which will be described shortly. When you fetch object references from a container, though, you must have some way to remember exactly what they are so you can perform a proper downcast.

Downcasting and the run-time checks require extra time for the running program, and extra effort from the programmer. Wouldn't it make sense to somehow create the container so that it knows the types that it holds, eliminating the need for the downcast and a possible mistake? The solution is parameterized types, which are classes that the compiler can automatically customize to work with particular types. For example, with a parameterized container, the compiler could customize that container so that it would accept only Shapes and fetch only Shapes.

Parameterized types are an important part of C++, partly because C++ has no singly rooted hierarchy. In C++, the keyword that implements parameterized types is "template." Java currently has no parameterized types since it is possible for it to get by—however awkwardly—using the singly rooted hierarchy. However, a current proposal for parameterized types uses a syntax that is strikingly similar to C++ templates.

The housekeeping dilemma: who should clean up?

Each object requires resources in order to exist, most notably memory. When an object is no longer needed it must be cleaned up so that these resources are released for reuse. In simple programming situations the question of how an object is cleaned up doesn't seem too challenging: you create the object, use it for as long as it's needed, and then it should be destroyed. It's not hard, however, to encounter situations in which the situation is more complex.

Suppose, for example, you are designing a system to manage air traffic for an airport. (The same model might also work for managing crates in a warehouse, or a video rental system, or a kennel for boarding pets.) At first it seems simple: make a container to hold airplanes, then create a new airplane and place it in the container for each airplane that enters the air-traffic-control zone. For cleanup, simply delete the appropriate airplane object when a plane leaves the zone.

But perhaps you have some other system to record data about the planes; perhaps data that doesn't require such immediate attention as the main controller function. Maybe it's a record of the flight plans of all the small planes that leave the airport. So you have a second container of small planes, and whenever you create a plane object you also put it in this second container if it's a small plane. Then some background process performs operations on the objects in this container during idle moments.

Now the problem is more difficult: how can you possibly know when to destroy the objects? When you're done with the object, some other part of the system might not be. This same problem can arise in a number of other situations, and in programming systems (such as C++) in which you must explicitly delete an object when you're done with it this can become quite complex.

With Java, the garbage collector is designed to take care of the problem of releasing the memory (although this doesn't include other aspects of cleaning up an object). The garbage collector "knows" when an object is no longer in use, and it then automatically releases the memory for that object. This (combined with the fact that all objects are inherited from the single root class **Object** and that you can create objects only one way, on the heap) makes the process of programming in Java much simpler than programming in C++. You have far fewer decisions to make and hurdles to overcome.

Garbage collectors vs. efficiency and flexibility

If all this is such a good idea, why didn't they do the same thing in C++? Well of course there's a price you pay for all this programming convenience, and that price is run-time overhead. As mentioned before, in C++ you can create objects on the stack, and in this case they're automatically cleaned up (but you don't have the flexibility of creating as many as you want at run-time). Creating objects on the stack is the most efficient way to allocate storage for objects and to free that storage. Creating objects on the heap can be much more expensive. Always inheriting from a base class and making all function calls polymorphic also exacts a small toll. But the garbage collector is a particular problem because you never quite know when it's going to start up or how long it will take. This means that there's an inconsistency in the rate of execution of a Java program, so you can't use it in certain situations, such as when the rate of execution of a program is uniformly critical. (These are generally called real time programs, although not all real time programming problems are this stringent.)

The designers of the C++ language, trying to woo C programmers (and most successfully, at that), did not want to add any features to the language that would impact the speed or the use of C++ in any situation where programmers might otherwise choose C. This goal was realized, but at the price of greater complexity when programming in C++. Java is simpler than C++, but the trade-off is in efficiency and sometimes applicability. For a significant portion of programming problems, however, Java is the superior choice.

Exception handling: dealing with errors

Ever since the beginning of programming languages, error handling has been one of the most difficult issues. Because it's so hard to design a good error handling scheme, many languages simply ignore the issue, passing the problem on to library designers who come up with halfway measures that can work in many situations but can easily be circumvented, generally by just ignoring them. A major problem with most error handling schemes is that they rely on programmer vigilance in following an agreed-upon convention that is not enforced by the language. If the programmer is not vigilant—often the case if they are in a hurry—these schemes can easily be forgotten.

Exception handling wires error handling directly into the programming language and sometimes even the operating system. An exception is an object that is "thrown" from the site of the error and can be "caught" by an appropriate exception handler designed to handle that particular type of error. It's as if exception handling is a different, parallel path of execution that can be taken when things go wrong. And because it uses a separate execution path, it doesn't need to interfere with your normally executing code. This makes that code simpler to write since you aren't constantly forced to check for errors. In addition, a thrown exception is unlike an error value that's returned from a function or a flag that's set by a function in order to indicate an error condition—these can be ignored. An exception cannot be ignored, so it's guaranteed to be dealt with at some point. Finally, exceptions provide a way to reliably recover from a bad situation. Instead of just exiting you are often able to set things right and restore the execution of a program, which produces much more robust programs.

Java's exception handling stands out among programming languages, because in Java, exception handling was wired in from the beginning and you're forced to use it. If you don't write your code to properly handle exceptions, you'll get a compile-time error message. This guaranteed consistency makes error handling much easier.

It's worth noting that exception handling isn't an object-oriented feature, although in object-oriented languages the exception is normally represented with an object. Exception handling existed before object-oriented languages.

Multithreading

A fundamental concept in computer programming is the idea of handling more than one task at a time. Many programming problems require that the program be able to stop what it's doing, deal with some other problem, and then return to the main process. The solution has been approached in many ways. Initially, programmers with low-level knowledge of the machine wrote interrupt service routines and the suspension of the main process was initiated through a hardware interrupt. Although this worked well, it was difficult and nonportable, so it made moving a program to a new type of machine slow and expensive.

Sometimes interrupts are necessary for handling time-critical tasks, but there's a large class of problems in which you're simply trying to partition the problem into separately running pieces so that the whole program can be more responsive. Within a program, these separately running pieces are called threads, and the general concept is called *multithreading*. A common example of multithreading is the user interface. By using threads, a user can press a button and get a quick response rather than being forced to wait until the program finishes its current task.

Ordinarily, threads are just a way to allocate the time of a single processor. But if the operating system supports multiple processors, each thread can be assigned to a different processor and they can truly run in parallel. One of the convenient features of multithreading at the language level is that the programmer doesn't need to worry about whether there are many processors or just one. The program is logically divided into threads and if the machine has more than one processor then the program runs faster, without any special adjustments.

All this makes threading sound pretty simple. There is a catch: shared resources. If you have more than one thread running that's expecting to access the same resource you have a problem. For example, two processes can't simultaneously send information to a printer. To solve the problem, resources that can be shared, such as the printer, must be locked while they are being used. So a thread locks a resource, completes its task, and then releases the lock so that someone else can use the resource.

Java's threading is built into the language, which makes a complicated subject much simpler. The threading is supported on an object level, so one thread of execution is represented by one object. Java also provides limited resource locking. It can lock the memory of any object (which is, after all, one kind of shared resource) so that only one thread can use it at a time. This is accomplished with the **synchronized** keyword. Other types of resources must be locked explicitly by the programmer, typically by creating an object to represent the lock that all threads must check before accessing that resource.

Persistence

When you create an object, it exists for as long as you need it, but under no circumstances does it exist when the program terminates. While this makes sense at first, there are situations in which it would be incredibly useful if an object could exist and hold its information even while the program wasn't running. Then the next time you started the program, the object would be there and it would have the same information it had the previous time the program was running. Of course, you can get a similar effect by writing the information to a file or to a database, but in the spirit of making everything an object it would be quite convenient to be able to declare an object persistent and have all the details taken care of for you.

Java provides support for "lightweight persistence," which means that you can easily store objects on disk and later retrieve them. The reason it's "lightweight" is that you're still forced to make explicit calls to do the storage and retrieval. In addition, JavaSpaces (described in Chapter 15) provide for a kind of persistent storage of objects. In some future release more complete support for persistence might appear.

Java and the Internet

If Java is, in fact, yet another computer programming language, you may question why it is so important and why it is being promoted as a revolutionary step in computer programming. The answer isn't immediately obvious if you're coming from a traditional programming perspective. Although Java is very useful for solving traditional stand-alone programming problems, it is also important because it will solve programming problems on the World Wide Web.

What is the Web?

The Web can seem a bit of a mystery at first, with all this talk of "surfing," "presence," and "home pages." There has even been a growing reaction against "Internet-mania," questioning the economic value and outcome of such a sweeping movement. It's helpful to step back and see what it really is, but to do this you must understand client/server systems, another aspect of computing that's full of confusing issues.

Client/Server computing

The primary idea of a client/server system is that you have a central repository of information—some kind of data, often in a database—that you want to distribute on demand to some set of people or machines. A key to the client/server concept is that the repository of information is centrally located so that it can be changed and so that those changes will propagate out to the information consumers. Taken together, the information repository, the software that distributes the information, and the machine(s) where the information and software reside is called the server. The software that resides on the remote machine, communicates with the server, fetches the information, processes it, and then displays it on the remote machine is called the *client*.

The basic concept of client/server computing, then, is not so complicated. The problems arise because you have a single server trying to serve many clients at once. Generally, a database management system is involved so the designer "balances" the layout of data into tables for optimal use. In addition, systems often allow a client to insert new information into a server. This means you must ensure that one client's new data doesn't walk over another client's new data, or that data isn't lost in the process of adding it to the database. (This is called transaction processing.) As client software changes, it must be built, debugged, and installed on the client machines, which turns out to be more complicated and expensive than you might think. It's especially problematic to support multiple types of computers and operating systems. Finally, there's the all-important performance issue: you might have hundreds of clients making requests of your server at any one time, and so any small delay is crucial. To minimize latency, programmers work hard to offload processing tasks, often to the client machine, but sometimes to other machines at the server site, using so-called *middleware*. (Middleware is also used to improve maintainability.)

The simple idea of distributing information to people has so many layers of complexity in implementing it that the whole problem can seem hopelessly enigmatic. And yet it's crucial: client/server computing accounts for roughly half of all programming activities. It's responsible for everything from taking orders and credit-card transactions to the distribution of any kind of data—stock market, scientific, government, you name it. What we've come up with in the past is individual solutions to individual problems, inventing a new solution each time. These were hard to create and hard to use, and the user had to learn a new interface for each one. The entire client/server problem needs to be solved in a big way.

The Web as a giant server

The Web is actually one giant client/server system. It's a bit worse than that, since you have all the servers and clients coexisting on a single network at once. You don't need to know that, since all you care about is connecting to and interacting with one server at a time (even though you might be hopping around the world in your search for the correct server).

Initially it was a simple one-way process. You made a request of a server and it handed you a file, which your machine's browser software (i.e., the client) would interpret by formatting onto your local machine. But in short order people began wanting to do more than just deliver pages from a server. They wanted full client/server capability so that the client could feed information back to the server, for example, to do database lookups on the server, to add new information to the server, or to place an order (which required more security than the original systems offered). These are the changes we've been seeing in the development of the Web.

The Web browser was a big step forward: the concept that one piece of information could be displayed on any type of computer without change. However, browsers were still rather primitive and rapidly bogged down by the demands placed on them. They weren't particularly interactive, and tended to clog up both the server and the Internet because any time you needed to do something that required programming you had to send information back to the server to be processed. It could take many seconds or minutes to find out you had misspelled something in your request. Since the browser was just a viewer it couldn't perform even the simplest computing tasks. (On the other hand, it was safe, since it couldn't execute any programs on your local machine that might contain bugs or viruses.)

To solve this problem, different approaches have been taken. To begin with, graphics standards have been enhanced to allow better animation and video within browsers. The remainder of the problem can be solved only by incorporating the ability to run programs on the client end, under the browser. This is called client-side programming.

Client-side programming

The Web's initial server-browser design provided for interactive content, but the interactivity was completely provided by the server. The server produced static pages for the client browser, which would simply interpret and display them. Basic HTML contains simple mechanisms for data gathering: text-entry boxes, check boxes, radio boxes, lists and drop-down lists, as well as a button that can only be programmed to reset the data on the form or "submit" the data on the form back to the server. This submission passes through the Common Gateway Interface (CGI) provided on all Web servers. The text within the submission tells CGI what to do with it. The most common action is to run a program located on the server in a directory that's typically called "cgi-bin." (If you watch the address window at the top of your browser when you push a button on a Web page, you can sometimes see "cgi-bin" within all the gobbledygook there.) These programs can be written in most languages. Perl is a common choice because it is designed for text manipulation and is interpreted, so it can be installed on any server regardless of processor or operating system.

Many powerful Web sites today are built strictly on CGI, and you can in fact do nearly anything with it. However, Web sites built on CGI programs can rapidly become overly complicated to maintain, and there is also the problem of response time. The response of a CGI program depends on how much data must be sent, as well as the load on both the server and the Internet. (On top of this, starting a CGI program tends to be slow.) The initial designers of the Web did not foresee how rapidly this bandwidth would be exhausted for the kinds of applications people developed. For example, any sort of dynamic graphing is nearly impossible to perform with consistency because a GIF file must be created and moved from the server to the client for each version of the graph. And you've no doubt had direct experience with something as simple as validating the data on an input form. You press the submit button on a page; the data is shipped back to the server; the server starts a CGI program that discovers an error, formats an HTML page informing you of the error, and then sends the page back to you; you must then back up a page and try again. Not only is this slow, it's inelegant.

The solution is client-side programming. Most machines that run Web browsers are powerful engines capable of doing vast work, and with the original static HTML approach they are sitting there, just idly waiting for the server to dish up the next page. Client-side programming means that the Web browser is harnessed to do whatever work it can, and the result for the user is a much speedier and more interactive experience at your Web site.

The problem with discussions of client-side programming is that they aren't very different from discussions of programming in general. The parameters are almost the same, but the platform is different: a Web browser is like a limited operating system. In the end, you must still program, and this accounts for the dizzying array of problems and solutions produced by client-side programming. The rest of this section provides an overview of the issues and approaches in client-side programming.

Plug-ins

One of the most significant steps forward in client-side programming is the development of the plug-in. This is a way for a programmer to add new functionality to the browser by downloading a piece of code that plugs itself into the appropriate spot in the browser. It tells the browser "from now on you can perform this new activity." (You need to download the plug-in only once.) Some fast and powerful behavior is added to browsers via plug-ins, but writing a plug-in is not a trivial task, and isn't something you'd want to do as part of the process of building a particular site. The value of the plug-in for client-side programming is that it allows an expert programmer to develop a new language and add that language to a browser without the permission of the browser manufacturer. Thus, plug-ins provide a "back door" that allows the creation of new client-side programming languages (although not all languages are implemented as plug-ins).

Scripting languages

Plug-ins resulted in an explosion of scripting languages. With a scripting language you embed the source code for your client-side program directly into the HTML page, and the plug-in that interprets that language is automatically activated while the HTML page is being displayed. Scripting languages tend to be reasonably easy to understand and, because they are simply text that is part of an HTML page, they load very quickly as part of the single server hit required to procure that page. The trade-off is that your code is exposed for everyone to see (and steal). Generally, however, you aren't doing amazingly sophisticated things with scripting languages so this is not too much of a hardship.

This points out that the scripting languages used inside Web browsers are really intended to solve specific types of problems, primarily the creation of richer and more interactive graphical user interfaces (GUIs). However, a scripting language might solve 80 percent of the problems encountered in client-side programming. Your problems might very well fit completely within that 80 percent, and since scripting languages can allow easier and faster development, you should probably consider a scripting language before looking at a more involved solution such as Java or ActiveX programming.

The most commonly discussed browser scripting languages are JavaScript (which has nothing to do with Java; it's named that way just to grab some of Java's marketing momentum), VBScript (which looks like Visual Basic), and Tcl/Tk, which comes from the popular cross-platform GUI-building language. There are others out there, and no doubt more in development.

JavaScript is probably the most commonly supported. It comes built into both Netscape Navigator and the Microsoft Internet Explorer (IE). In addition, there are probably more JavaScript books available than there are for the other browser languages, and some tools automatically create pages using JavaScript. However, if you're already fluent in Visual Basic or Tcl/Tk, you'll be more productive using those scripting languages rather than learning a new one. (You'll have your hands full dealing with the Web issues already.)

Java

If a scripting language can solve 80 percent of the client-side programming problems, what about the other 20 percent—the "really hard stuff?" The most popular solution today is Java. Not only is it a powerful programming language built to be secure, cross-platform, and international, but Java is being continually extended to provide language features and libraries that elegantly handle problems that are difficult in traditional programming languages, such as multithreading, database access, network programming, and distributed computing. Java allows client-side programming via the *applet*.

An applet is a mini-program that will run only under a Web browser. The applet is downloaded automatically as part of a Web page (just as, for example, a graphic is automatically downloaded). When the applet is activated it executes a program. This is part of its beauty—it provides you with a way to automatically distribute the client software from the server at the time the user needs the client software, and no sooner. The user gets the latest version of the client software without fail and without difficult reinstallation. Because of the way Java is designed, the programmer needs to create only a single program, and that program automatically works with all computers that have browsers with built-in Java interpreters. (This safely includes the vast majority of machines.) Since Java is a full-fledged programming language, you can do as much work as possible on the client before and after making requests of the server. For example, you won't need to send a request form across the Internet to discover that you've gotten a date or some other parameter wrong, and your client computer can quickly do the work of plotting data instead of waiting for the server to make a plot and ship a graphic image back to you. Not only do you get the immediate win of speed and responsiveness, but the general network traffic and load on servers can be reduced, preventing the entire Internet from slowing down.

One advantage a Java applet has over a scripted program is that it's in compiled form, so the source code isn't available to the client. On the other hand, a Java applet can be decompiled without too much trouble, but hiding your code is often not an important issue. Two other factors can be important. As you will see later in this book, a compiled Java applet can comprise many modules and take multiple server "hits" (accesses) to download. (In Java 1.1 and higher this is minimized by Java archives, called JAR files, that allow all the required modules to be packaged together and compressed for a single download.) A scripted program will just be integrated into the Web page as part of its text (and will generally be smaller and reduce server hits). This could be important to the responsiveness of your Web site. Another factor is the all-important learning curve. Regardless of what you've heard, Java is not a trivial language to learn. If you're a Visual Basic programmer, moving to VBScript will be your fastest solution, and since it will probably solve most typical client/server problems you might be hard pressed to justify learning Java. If you're experienced with a scripting language you will certainly benefit from looking at JavaScript or VBScript before committing to Java, since they might fit your needs handily and you'll be more productive sooner.

ActiveX

To some degree, the competitor to Java is Microsoft's ActiveX, although it takes a completely different approach. ActiveX was originally a Windows-only solution, although it is now being developed via an independent consortium to become cross-platform. Effectively, ActiveX says "if your program connects to its environment just so, it can be dropped into a Web page and run under a browser that supports ActiveX." (IE directly supports ActiveX and Netscape does so using a plug-in.) Thus, ActiveX does not constrain you to a particular language. If, for example, you're already an experienced Windows programmer using a language such as C++, Visual Basic, or Borland's Delphi, you can create ActiveX components with almost no changes to your programming knowledge. ActiveX also provides a path for the use of legacy code in your Web pages.

Security

Automatically downloading and running programs across the Internet can sound like a virus-builder's dream. ActiveX especially brings up the thorny issue of security in client-side programming. If you click on a Web site, you might automatically download any number of things along with the HTML page: GIF files, script code, compiled Java code, and ActiveX components. Some of these are benign; GIF files can't do any harm, and scripting languages are generally limited in what they can do. Java was

---

also designed to run its applets within a "sandbox" of safety, which prevents it from writing to disk or accessing memory outside the sandbox.

ActiveX is at the opposite end of the spectrum. Programming with ActiveX is like programming Windows—you can do anything you want. So if you click on a page that downloads an ActiveX component, that component might cause damage to the files on your disk. Of course, programs that you load onto your computer that are not restricted to running inside a Web browser can do the same thing. Viruses downloaded from Bulletin-Board Systems (BBSs) have long been a problem, but the speed of the Internet amplifies the difficulty.

The solution seems to be "digital signatures," whereby code is verified to show who the author is. This is based on the idea that a virus works because its creator can be anonymous, so if you remove the anonymity individuals will be forced to be responsible for their actions. This seems like a good plan because it allows programs to be much more functional, and I suspect it will eliminate malicious mischief. If, however, a program has an unintentional destructive bug it will still cause problems.

The Java approach is to prevent these problems from occurring, via the sandbox. The Java interpreter that lives on your local Web browser examines the applet for any untoward instructions as the applet is being loaded. In particular, the applet cannot write files to disk or erase files (one of the mainstays of viruses). Applets are generally considered to be safe, and since this is essential for reliable client/server systems, any bugs in the Java language that allow viruses are rapidly repaired. (It's worth noting that the browser software actually enforces these security restrictions, and some browsers allow you to select different security levels to provide varying degrees of access to your system.)

You might be skeptical of this rather draconian restriction against writing files to your local disk. For example, you may want to build a local database or save data for later use offline. The initial vision seemed to be that eventually everyone would get online to do anything important, but that was soon seen to be impractical (although low-cost "Internet appliances" might someday satisfy the needs of a significant segment of users). The solution is the "signed applet" that uses public-key encryption to verify that an applet does indeed come from where it claims it does. A signed applet can still trash your disk, but the theory is that since you can now hold the applet creator accountable they won't do vicious things. Java provides a framework for digital signatures so that you will eventually be able to allow an applet to step outside the sandbox if necessary.

Digital signatures have missed an important issue, which is the speed that people move around on the Internet. If you download a buggy program and it does something untoward, how long will it be before you discover the damage? It could be days or even weeks. By then, how will you track down the program that's done it? And what good will it do you at that point?

Internet vs. intranet

The Web is the most general solution to the client/server problem, so it makes sense that you can use the same technology to solve a subset of the problem, in particular the classic client/server problem *within* a company. With traditional client/server approaches you have the problem of multiple types of client computers, as well as the difficulty of installing new client software, both of which are handily solved with Web browsers and client-side programming. When Web technology is used for an information network that is restricted to a particular company, it is referred to as an intranet. Intranets provide much greater security than the Internet, since you can physically control access to the servers within your company. In terms of training, it seems that once people understand the general concept of a browser it's much easier for them to deal with differences in the way pages and applets look, so the learning curve for new kinds of systems seems to be reduced.

The security problem brings us to one of the divisions that seems to be automatically forming in the world of client-side programming. If your program is running on the Internet, you don't know what platform it will be working under, and you want to be extra careful that you don't disseminate buggy code. You need something cross-platform and secure, like a scripting language or Java.

If you're running on an intranet, you might have a different set of constraints. It's not uncommon that your machines could all be Intel/Windows platforms. On an intranet, you're responsible for the quality of your own code and can repair bugs when they're discovered. In addition, you might already have a body of legacy code that you've been using in a more traditional client/server approach, whereby you must physically install client programs every time you do an upgrade. The time wasted in installing upgrades is the most compelling reason to move to browsers, because upgrades are invisible and automatic. If you are involved in such an intranet, the most sensible approach to take is the shortest path that allows you to use your existing code base, rather than trying to recode your programs in a new language.

When faced with this bewildering array of solutions to the client-side programming problem, the best plan of attack is a cost-benefit analysis. Consider the constraints of your problem and what would be the shortest path to your solution. Since client-side programming is still programming, it's always a good idea to take the fastest development approach for your particular situation. This is an aggressive stance to prepare for inevitable encounters with the problems of program development.

Server-side programming

This whole discussion has ignored the issue of server-side programming. What happens when you make a request of a server? Most of the time the request is simply "send me this file." Your browser then interprets the file in some appropriate fashion: as an HTML page, a graphic image, a Java applet, a script program, etc. A more complicated request to a server generally involves a database transaction. A common scenario involves a request for a complex database search, which the server then formats into an HTML page and sends to you as the result. (Of course, if the client has more intelligence via Java or a scripting language, the raw data can be sent and formatted at the client end, which will be faster and less load on the server.) Or you might want to register your name in a database when you join a group or place an order, which will involve changes to that database. These database requests must be processed via some code on the server side, which is generally referred to as server-side programming. Traditionally, server-side programming has been performed using Perl and CGI scripts, but more sophisticated systems have been appearing. These include Java-based Web servers that allow you to perform all your server-side programming in Java by writing what are called servlets. Servlets and their offspring, JSPs, are two of the most compelling reasons that companies who develop Web sites are moving to Java, especially because they eliminate the problems of dealing with differently abled browsers.

A separate arena: applications

Much of the brouhaha over Java has been over applets. Java is actually a general-purpose programming language that can solve any type of problem—at least in theory. And as pointed out previously, there might be more effective ways to solve most client/server problems. When you move out of the applet arena (and simultaneously release the restrictions, such as the one against writing to disk) you enter the world of general-purpose applications that run standalone, without a Web browser, just like any ordinary program does. Here, Java's strength is not only in its portability, but also its programmability. As you'll see throughout this book, Java has many features that allow you to create robust programs in a shorter period than with previous programming languages.

Be aware that this is a mixed blessing. You pay for the improvements through slower execution speed (although there is significant work going on in this area—JDK 1.3, in particular, introduces the so-called "hotspot" performance improvements). Like any language, Java has built-in limitations that might make it inappropriate to solve certain types of programming problems. Java is a rapidly evolving language, however, and as each new release comes out it becomes more and more attractive for solving larger sets of problems.

Analysis and design

The object-oriented paradigm is a new and different way of thinking about programming. Many folks have trouble at first knowing how to approach an OOP project. Once you know that everything is supposed to be an object, and as you learn to think more in an object-oriented style, you can begin to create "good" designs that take advantage of all the benefits that OOP has to offer.

A *method* (often called a *methodology*) is a set of processes and heuristics used to break down the complexity of a programming problem. Many OOP methods have been formulated since the dawn of object-oriented programming. This section will give you a feel for what you're trying to accomplish when using a method.

Especially in OOP, methodology is a field of many experiments, so it is important to understand what problem the method is trying to solve before you consider adopting one. This is particularly true with Java, in which the programming language is intended to reduce the complexity (compared to C) involved in expressing a program. This may in fact alleviate the need for ever-more-complex methodologies. Instead, simple methodologies may suffice in Java for a much larger class of problems than you could handle using simple methodologies with procedural languages.

It's also important to realize that the term "methodology" is often too grand and promises too much. Whatever you do now when you design and write a program is a method. It may be your own method, and you may not be conscious of doing it, but it is a process you go through as you create. If it is an effective process, it may need only a small tune-up to work with Java. If you are not satisfied with your productivity and the way your programs turn out, you may want to consider adopting a formal method, or choosing pieces from among the many formal methods.

While you're going through the development process, the most important issue is this: Don't get lost. It's easy to do. Most of the analysis and design methods are intended to solve the largest of problems. Remember that most projects don't fit into that category, so you can usually have successful analysis and design with a relatively small subset of what a method recommends[7]. But some sort of process, no matter how limited, will generally get you on your way in a much better fashion than simply beginning to code.

It's also easy to get stuck, to fall into "analysis paralysis," where you feel like you can't move forward because you haven't nailed down every little detail at the current stage. Remember, no matter how much analysis you do, there are some things about a system that won't reveal themselves

---

[7] An excellent example of this is *UML Distilled*, 2nd edition, by Martin Fowler (Addison-Wesley 2000), which reduces the sometimes-overwhelming UML process to a manageable subset.

until design time, and more things that won't reveal themselves until you're coding, or not even until a program is up and running. Because of this, it's crucial to move fairly quickly through analysis and design, and to implement a test of the proposed system.

This point is worth emphasizing. Because of the history we've had with procedural languages, it is commendable that a team will want to proceed carefully and understand every minute detail before moving to design and implementation. Certainly, when creating a DBMS, it pays to understand a customer's needs thoroughly. But a DBMS is in a class of problems that is very well-posed and well-understood; in many such programs, the database structure *is* the problem to be tackled. The class of programming problem discussed in this chapter is of the "wild-card" (my term) variety, in which the solution isn't simply re-forming a well-known solution, but instead involves one or more "wild-card factors"—elements for which there is no well-understood previous solution, and for which research is necessary[8]. Attempting to thoroughly analyze a wild-card problem before moving into design and implementation results in analysis paralysis because you don't have enough information to solve this kind of problem during the analysis phase. Solving such a problem requires iteration through the whole cycle, and that requires risk-taking behavior (which makes sense, because you're trying to do something new and the potential rewards are higher). It may seem like the risk is compounded by "rushing" into a preliminary implementation, but it can instead reduce the risk in a wild-card project because you're finding out early whether a particular approach to the problem is viable. Product development is risk management.

It's often proposed that you "build one to throw away." With OOP, you may still throw *part* of it away, but because code is encapsulated into classes, during the first pass you will inevitably produce some useful class designs and develop some worthwhile ideas about the system design that do not need to be thrown away. Thus, the first rapid pass at a problem not

---

[8] My rule of thumb for estimating such projects: If there's more than one wild card, don't even try to plan how long it's going to take or how much it will cost until you've created a working prototype. There are too many degrees of freedom.

---

only produces critical information for the next analysis, design, and implementation pass, it also creates a code foundation.

That said, if you're looking at a methodology that contains tremendous detail and suggests many steps and documents, it's still difficult to know when to stop. Keep in mind what you're trying to discover:

1.   What are the objects? (How do you partition your project into its component parts?)

2.   What are their interfaces? (What messages do you need to send to each object?)

If you come up with nothing more than the objects and their interfaces, then you can write a program. For various reasons you might need more descriptions and documents than this, but you can't get away with any less.

The process can be undertaken in five phases, and a Phase 0 that is just the initial commitment to using some kind of structure.

Phase 0: Make a plan

You must first decide what steps you're going to have in your process. It sounds simple (in fact, *all* of this sounds simple), and yet people often don't make this decision before they start coding. If your plan is "let's jump in and start coding," fine. (Sometimes that's appropriate when you have a well-understood problem.) At least agree that this is the plan.

You might also decide at this phase that some additional process structure is necessary, but not the whole nine yards. Understandably, some programmers like to work in "vacation mode," in which no structure is imposed on the process of developing their work; "It will be done when it's done." This can be appealing for a while, but I've found that having a few milestones along the way helps to focus and galvanize your efforts around those milestones instead of being stuck with the single goal of "finish the project." In addition, it divides the project into more bite-sized pieces and makes it seem less threatening (plus the milestones offer more opportunities for celebration).

When I began to study story structure (so that I will someday write a novel) I was initially resistant to the idea of structure, feeling that I wrote best when I simply let it flow onto the page. But I later realized that when I write about computers the structure is clear enough to me that I don't have to think about it very much. But I still structure my work, albeit only semi-consciously in my head. Even if you think that your plan is to just start coding, you still somehow go through the subsequent phases while asking and answering certain questions.

The mission statement

Any system you build, no matter how complicated, has a fundamental purpose; the business that it's in, the basic need that it satisfies. If you can look past the user interface, the hardware- or system-specific details, the coding algorithms and the efficiency problems, you will eventually find the core of its being—simple and straightforward. Like the so-called *high concept* from a Hollywood movie, you can describe it in one or two sentences. This pure description is the starting point.

The high concept is quite important because it sets the tone for your project; it's a mission statement. You won't necessarily get it right the first time (you may be in a later phase of the project before it becomes completely clear), but keep trying until it feels right. For example, in an air-traffic control system you may start out with a high concept focused on the system that you're building: "The tower program keeps track of the aircraft." But consider what happens when you shrink the system to a very small airfield; perhaps there's only a human controller, or none at all. A more useful model won't concern the solution you're creating as much as it describes the problem: "Aircraft arrive, unload, service and reload, then depart."

Phase 1: What are we making?

In the previous generation of program design (called *procedural design*), this is called "creating the *requirements analysis* and *system specification*." These, of course, were places to get lost; intimidatingly named documents that could become big projects in their own right. Their intention was good, however. The requirements analysis says "Make a list of the guidelines we will use to know when the job is done and the customer is satisfied." The system specification says "Here's a description of *what* the program will do (not *how*) to satisfy the requirements." The requirements analysis is really a contract between you and the customer (even if the customer works within your company, or is some other object or system). The system specification is a top-level exploration into the problem and in some sense a discovery of whether it can be done and how long it will take. Since both of these will require consensus among people (and because they will usually change over time), I think it's best to keep them as bare as possible—ideally, to lists and basic diagrams—to save time. You might have other constraints that require you to expand them into bigger documents, but by keeping the initial document small and concise, it can be created in a few sessions of group brainstorming with a leader who dynamically creates the description. This not only solicits input from everyone, it also fosters initial buy-in and agreement by everyone on the team. Perhaps most importantly, it can kick off a project with a lot of enthusiasm.

It's necessary to stay focused on the heart of what you're trying to accomplish in this phase: determine what the system is supposed to do. The most valuable tool for this is a collection of what are called "use cases." Use cases identify key features in the system that will reveal some of the fundamental classes you'll be using. These are essentially descriptive answers to questions like[9]:

- "Who will use this system?"
- "What can those actors do with the system?"
- "How does *this* actor do *that* with this system?"
- "How else might this work if someone else were doing this, or if the same actor had a different objective?" (to reveal variations)
- "What problems might happen while doing this with the system?" (to reveal exceptions)

If you are designing an auto-teller, for example, the use case for a particular aspect of the functionality of the system is able to describe what the auto-teller does in every possible situation. Each of these "situations"

---

[9] Thanks for help from James H Jarrett.

is referred to as a *scenario,* and a use case can be considered a collection of scenarios. You can think of a scenario as a question that starts with: "What does the system do if...?" For example, "What does the auto-teller do if a customer has just deposited a check within the last 24 hours, and there's not enough in the account without the check having cleared to provide a desired withdrawal?"

Use case diagrams are intentionally simple to prevent you from getting bogged down in system implementation details prematurely:

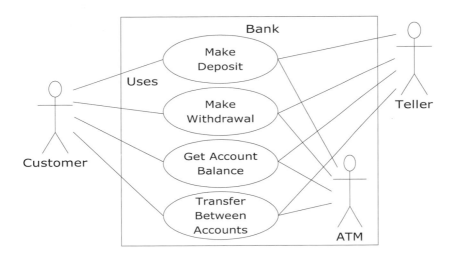

Each stick person represents an "actor," which is typically a human or some other kind of free agent. (These can even be other computer systems, as is the case with "ATM.") The box represents the boundary of your system. The ellipses represent the use cases, which are descriptions of valuable work that can be performed with the system. The lines between the actors and the use cases represent the interactions.

It doesn't matter how the system is actually implemented, as long as it looks like this to the user.

A use case does not need to be terribly complex, even if the underlying system is complex. It is only intended to show the system as it appears to the user. For example:

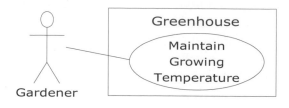

The use cases produce the requirements specifications by determining all the interactions that the user may have with the system. You try to discover a full set of use cases for your system, and once you've done that you have the core of what the system is supposed to do. The nice thing about focusing on use cases is that they always bring you back to the essentials and keep you from drifting off into issues that aren't critical for getting the job done. That is, if you have a full set of use cases, you can describe your system and move onto the next phase. You probably won't get it all figured out perfectly on the first try, but that's OK. Everything will reveal itself in time, and if you demand a perfect system specification at this point you'll get stuck.

If you do get stuck, you can kick-start this phase by using a rough approximation tool: describe the system in a few paragraphs and then look for nouns and verbs. The nouns can suggest actors, context of the use case (e.g., "lobby"), or artifacts manipulated in the use case. Verbs can suggest interactions between actors and use cases, and specify steps within the use case. You'll also discover that nouns and verbs produce objects and messages during the design phase (and note that use cases describe interactions between subsystems, so the "noun and verb" technique can be used only as a brainstorming tool as it does not generate use cases) [10].

The boundary between a use case and an actor can point out the existence of a user interface, but it does not define such a user interface. For a process of defining and creating user interfaces, see *Software for Use* by

---

[10] More information on use cases can be found in *Applying Use Cases* by Schneider & Winters (Addison-Wesley 1998) and *Use Case Driven Object Modeling with UML* by Rosenberg (Addison-Wesley 1999).

Larry Constantine and Lucy Lockwood, (Addison-Wesley Longman, 1999) or go to *www.ForUse.com*.

Although it's a black art, at this point some kind of basic scheduling is important. You now have an overview of what you're building, so you'll probably be able to get some idea of how long it will take. A lot of factors come into play here. If you estimate a long schedule then the company might decide not to build it (and thus use their resources on something more reasonable—that's a *good* thing). Or a manager might have already decided how long the project should take and will try to influence your estimate. But it's best to have an honest schedule from the beginning and deal with the tough decisions early. There have been a lot of attempts to come up with accurate scheduling techniques (much like techniques to predict the stock market), but probably the best approach is to rely on your experience and intuition. Get a gut feeling for how long it will really take, then double that and add 10 percent. Your gut feeling is probably correct; you *can* get something working in that time. The "doubling" will turn that into something decent, and the 10 percent will deal with the final polishing and details[11]. However you want to explain it, and regardless of the moans and manipulations that happen when you reveal such a schedule, it just seems to work out that way.

Phase 2: How will we build it?

In this phase you must come up with a design that describes what the classes look like and how they will interact. An excellent technique in determining classes and interactions is the *Class-Responsibility-Collaboration* (CRC) card. Part of the value of this tool is that it's so low-tech: you start out with a set of blank 3 x 5 cards, and you write on them. Each card represents a single class, and on the card you write:

1.   The name of the class. It's important that this name capture the essence of what the class does, so that it makes sense at a glance.

---

[11] My personal take on this has changed lately. Doubling and adding 10 percent will give you a reasonably accurate estimate (assuming there are not too many wild-card factors), but you still have to work quite diligently to finish in that time. If you want time to really make it elegant and to enjoy yourself in the process, the correct multiplier is more like three or four times, I believe.

---

2.   The "responsibilities" of the class: what it should do. This can typically be summarized by just stating the names of the member functions (since those names should be descriptive in a good design), but it does not preclude other notes. If you need to seed the process, look at the problem from a lazy programmer's standpoint: What objects would you like to magically appear to solve your problem?

3.   The "collaborations" of the class: what other classes does it interact with? "Interact" is an intentionally broad term; it could mean aggregation or simply that some other object exists that will perform services for an object of the class. Collaborations should also consider the audience for this class. For example, if you create a class **Firecracker**, who is going to observe it, a **Chemist** or a **Spectator**? The former will want to know what chemicals go into the construction, and the latter will respond to the colors and shapes released when it explodes.

You may feel like the cards should be bigger because of all the information you'd like to get on them, but they are intentionally small, not only to keep your classes small but also to keep you from getting into too much detail too early. If you can't fit all you need to know about a class on a small card, the class is too complex (either you're getting too detailed, or you should create more than one class). The ideal class should be understood at a glance. The idea of CRC cards is to assist you in coming up with a first cut of the design so that you can get the big picture and then refine your design.

One of the great benefits of CRC cards is in communication. It's best done real time, in a group, without computers. Each person takes responsibility for several classes (which at first have no names or other information). You run a live simulation by solving one scenario at a time, deciding which messages are sent to the various objects to satisfy each scenario. As you go through this process, you discover the classes that you need along with their responsibilities and collaborations, and you fill out the cards as you do this. When you've moved through all the use cases, you should have a fairly complete first cut of your design.

Before I began using CRC cards, the most successful consulting experiences I had when coming up with an initial design involved standing in front of a team—who hadn't built an OOP project before—and drawing objects on a whiteboard. We talked about how the objects should communicate with each other, and erased some of them and replaced them with other objects. Effectively, I was managing all the "CRC cards" on the whiteboard. The team (who knew what the project was supposed to do) actually created the design; they "owned" the design rather than having it given to them. All I was doing was guiding the process by asking the right questions, trying out the assumptions, and taking the feedback from the team to modify those assumptions. The true beauty of the process was that the team learned how to do object-oriented design not by reviewing abstract examples, but by working on the one design that was most interesting to them at that moment: theirs.

Once you've come up with a set of CRC cards, you may want to create a more formal description of your design using UML[12]. You don't need to use UML, but it can be helpful, especially if you want to put up a diagram on the wall for everyone to ponder, which is a good idea. An alternative to UML is a textual description of the objects and their interfaces, or, depending on your programming language, the code itself[13].

UML also provides an additional diagramming notation for describing the dynamic model of your system. This is helpful in situations in which the state transitions of a system or subsystem are dominant enough that they need their own diagrams (such as in a control system). You may also need to describe the data structures, for systems or subsystems in which data is a dominant factor (such as a database).

You'll know you're done with Phase 2 when you have described the objects and their interfaces. Well, most of them—there are usually a few that slip through the cracks and don't make themselves known until Phase 3. But that's OK. All you are concerned with is that you eventually discover all of your objects. It's nice to discover them early in the process, but OOP

---

[12] For starters, I recommend the aforementioned *UML Distilled*, 2nd edition.

[13] Python (www.Python.org) is often used as "executable pseudocode."

provides enough structure so that it's not so bad if you discover them later. In fact, the design of an object tends to happen in five stages, throughout the process of program development.

Five stages of object design

The design life of an object is not limited to the time when you're writing the program. Instead, the design of an object appears over a sequence of stages. It's helpful to have this perspective because you stop expecting perfection right away; instead, you realize that the understanding of what an object does and what it should look like happens over time. This view also applies to the design of various types of programs; the pattern for a particular type of program emerges through struggling again and again with that problem (This is chronicled in the book *Thinking in Patterns with Java*, downloadable at *www.BruceEckel.com*). Objects, too, have their patterns that emerge through understanding, use, and reuse.

1. Object discovery. This stage occurs during the initial analysis of a program. Objects may be discovered by looking for external factors and boundaries, duplication of elements in the system, and the smallest conceptual units. Some objects are obvious if you already have a set of class libraries. Commonality between classes suggesting base classes and inheritance may appear right away, or later in the design process.

2. Object assembly. As you're building an object you'll discover the need for new members that didn't appear during discovery. The internal needs of the object may require other classes to support it.

3. System construction. Once again, more requirements for an object may appear at this later stage. As you learn, you evolve your objects. The need for communication and interconnection with other objects in the system may change the needs of your classes or require new classes. For example, you may discover the need for facilitator or helper classes, such as a linked list, that contain little or no state information and simply help other classes function.

4. System extension. As you add new features to a system you may discover that your previous design doesn't support easy system extension. With this new information, you can restructure parts of the system, possibly adding new classes or class hierarchies.

5. Object reuse. This is the real stress test for a class. If someone tries to reuse it in an entirely new situation, they'll probably discover some shortcomings. As you change a class to adapt to more new programs, the general principles of the class will become clearer, until you have a truly reusable type. However, don't expect most objects from a system design to be reusable—it is perfectly acceptable for the bulk of your objects to be system-specific. Reusable types tend to be less common, and they must solve more general problems in order to be reusable.

Guidelines for object development

These stages suggest some guidelines when thinking about developing your classes:

1. Let a specific problem generate a class, then let the class grow and mature during the solution of other problems.

2. Remember, discovering the classes you need (and their interfaces) is the majority of the system design. If you already had those classes, this would be an easy project.

3. Don't force yourself to know everything at the beginning; learn as you go. This will happen anyway.

4. Start programming; get something working so you can prove or disprove your design. Don't fear that you'll end up with procedural-style spaghetti code—classes partition the problem and help control anarchy and entropy. Bad classes do not break good classes.

5. Always keep it simple. Little clean objects with obvious utility are better than big complicated interfaces. When decision points come up, use an Occam's Razor approach: Consider the choices and select the one that is simplest, because simple classes are almost always best. Start small and simple, and you can expand the class interface when you understand it better. As time goes on, it's difficult to remove elements from a class.

Phase 3: Build the core

This is the initial conversion from the rough design into a compiling and executing body of code that can be tested, and especially that will prove or disprove your architecture. This is not a one-pass process, but rather the beginning of a series of steps that will iteratively build the system, as you'll see in Phase 4.

Your goal is to find the core of your system architecture that needs to be implemented in order to generate a running system, no matter how incomplete that system is in this initial pass. You're creating a framework that you can build on with further iterations. You're also performing the first of many system integrations and tests, and giving the stakeholders feedback about what their system will look like and how it is progressing. Ideally, you are also exposing some of the critical risks. You'll probably also discover changes and improvements that can be made to your original architecture—things you would not have learned without implementing the system.

Part of building the system is the reality check that you get from testing against your requirements analysis and system specification (in whatever form they exist). Make sure that your tests verify the requirements and use cases. When the core of the system is stable, you're ready to move on and add more functionality.

Phase 4: Iterate the use cases

Once the core framework is running, each feature set you add is a small project in itself. You add a feature set during an *iteration*, a reasonably short period of development.

How big is an iteration? Ideally, each iteration lasts one to three weeks (this can vary based on the implementation language). At the end of that period, you have an integrated, tested system with more functionality than it had before. But what's particularly interesting is the basis for the iteration: a single use case. Each use case is a package of related functionality that you build into the system all at once, during one iteration. Not only does this give you a better idea of what the scope of a use case should be, but it also gives more validation to the idea of a use case, since the concept isn't discarded after analysis and design, but instead it is a fundamental unit of development throughout the software-building process.

You stop iterating when you achieve target functionality or an external deadline arrives and the customer can be satisfied with the current version. (Remember, software is a subscription business.) Because the process is iterative, you have many opportunities to ship a product rather than a single endpoint; open-source projects work exclusively in an iterative, high-feedback environment, which is precisely what makes them successful.

An iterative development process is valuable for many reasons. You can reveal and resolve critical risks early, the customers have ample opportunity to change their minds, programmer satisfaction is higher, and the project can be steered with more precision. But an additional important benefit is the feedback to the stakeholders, who can see by the current state of the product exactly where everything lies. This may reduce or eliminate the need for mind-numbing status meetings and increase the confidence and support from the stakeholders.

Phase 5: Evolution

This is the point in the development cycle that has traditionally been called "maintenance," a catch-all term that can mean everything from "getting it to work the way it was really supposed to in the first place" to "adding features that the customer forgot to mention" to the more traditional "fixing the bugs that show up" and "adding new features as the need arises." So many misconceptions have been applied to the term "maintenance" that it has taken on a slightly deceiving quality, partly because it suggests that you've actually built a pristine program and all you need to do is change parts, oil it, and keep it from rusting. Perhaps there's a better term to describe what's going on.

I'll use the term *evolution*[14]. That is, "You won't get it right the first time, so give yourself the latitude to learn and to go back and make changes." You might need to make a lot of changes as you learn and understand the problem more deeply. The elegance you'll produce if you evolve until you get it right will pay off, both in the short and the long term. Evolution is

---

[14] At least one aspect of evolution is covered in Martin Fowler's book *Refactoring: improving the design of existing code* (Addison-Wesley 1999), which uses Java examples exclusively.

where your program goes from good to great, and where those issues that you didn't really understand in the first pass become clear. It's also where your classes can evolve from single-project usage to reusable resources.

What it means to "get it right" isn't just that the program works according to the requirements and the use cases. It also means that the internal structure of the code makes sense to you, and feels like it fits together well, with no awkward syntax, oversized objects, or ungainly exposed bits of code. In addition, you must have some sense that the program structure will survive the changes that it will inevitably go through during its lifetime, and that those changes can be made easily and cleanly. This is no small feat. You must not only understand what you're building, but also how the program will evolve (what I call the *vector of change*). Fortunately, object-oriented programming languages are particularly adept at supporting this kind of continuing modification—the boundaries created by the objects are what tend to keep the structure from breaking down. They also allow you to make changes—ones that would seem drastic in a procedural program—without causing earthquakes throughout your code. In fact, support for evolution might be the most important benefit of OOP.

With evolution, you create something that at least approximates what you think you're building, and then you kick the tires, compare it to your requirements, and see where it falls short. Then you can go back and fix it by redesigning and reimplementing the portions of the program that didn't work right[15]. You might actually need to solve the problem, or an aspect of the problem, several times before you hit on the right solution. (A study of *Design Patterns* is usually helpful here. You can find information in *Thinking in Patterns with Java*, downloadable at *www.BruceEckel.com*.)

---

[15] This is something like "rapid prototyping," where you were supposed to build a quick-and-dirty version so that you could learn about the system, and then throw away your prototype and build it right. The trouble with rapid prototyping is that people didn't throw away the prototype, but instead built upon it. Combined with the lack of structure in procedural programming, this often leads to messy systems that are expensive to maintain.

Evolution also occurs when you build a system, see that it matches your requirements, and then discover it wasn't actually what you wanted. When you see the system in operation, you find that you really wanted to solve a different problem. If you think this kind of evolution is going to happen, then you owe it to yourself to build your first version as quickly as possible so you can find out if it is indeed what you want.

Perhaps the most important thing to remember is that by default—by definition, really—if you modify a class, its super- and subclasses will still function. You need not fear modification (especially if you have a built-in set of unit tests to verify the correctness of your modifications). Modification won't necessarily break the program, and any change in the outcome will be limited to subclasses and/or specific collaborators of the class you change.

Plans pay off

Of course you wouldn't build a house without a lot of carefully drawn plans. If you build a deck or a dog house your plans won't be so elaborate, but you'll probably still start with some kind of sketches to guide you on your way. Software development has gone to extremes. For a long time, people didn't have much structure in their development, but then big projects began failing. In reaction, we ended up with methodologies that had an intimidating amount of structure and detail, primarily intended for those big projects. These methodologies were too scary to use—it looked like you'd spend all your time writing documents and no time programming. (This was often the case.) I hope that what I've shown you here suggests a middle path—a sliding scale. Use an approach that fits your needs (and your personality). No matter how minimal you choose to make it, *some* kind of plan will make a big improvement in your project as opposed to no plan at all. Remember that, by most estimates, over 50 percent of projects fail (some estimates go up to 70 percent!).

By following a plan—preferably one that is simple and brief—and coming up with design structure before coding, you'll discover that things fall together far more easily than if you dive in and start hacking. You'll also realize a great deal of satisfaction. It's my experience that coming up with an elegant solution is deeply satisfying at an entirely different level; it feels closer to art than technology. And elegance always pays off; it's not a frivolous pursuit. Not only does it give you a program that's easier to build and debug, but it's also easier to understand and maintain, and that's where the financial value lies.

Extreme programming

I have studied analysis and design techniques, on and off, since I was in graduate school. The concept of *Extreme Programming* (XP) is the most radical, and delightful, that I've seen. You can find it chronicled in *Extreme Programming Explained* by Kent Beck (Addison-Wesley, 2000) and on the Web at *www.xprogramming.com*.

XP is both a philosophy about programming work and a set of guidelines to do it. Some of these guidelines are reflected in other recent methodologies, but the two most important and distinct contributions, in my opinion, are "write tests first" and "pair programming." Although he argues strongly for the whole process, Beck points out that if you adopt only these two practices you'll greatly improve your productivity and reliability.

Write tests first

Testing has traditionally been relegated to the last part of a project, after you've "gotten everything working, but just to be sure." It's implicitly had a low priority, and people who specialize in it have not been given a lot of status and have often even been cordoned off in a basement, away from the "real programmers." Test teams have responded in kind, going so far as to wear black clothing and cackling with glee whenever they break something (to be honest, I've had this feeling myself when breaking compilers).

XP completely revolutionizes the concept of testing by giving it equal (or even greater) priority than the code. In fact, you write the tests *before* you write the code that will be tested, and the tests stay with the code forever. The tests must be executed successfully every time you do an integration of the project (which is often, sometimes more than once a day).

Writing tests first has two extremely important effects.

First, it forces a clear definition of the interface of a class. I've often suggested that people "imagine the perfect class to solve a particular problem" as a tool when trying to design the system. The XP testing strategy goes further than that—it specifies exactly what the class must look like, to the consumer of that class, and exactly how the class must behave. In no uncertain terms. You can write all the prose, or create all the diagrams you want, describing how a class should behave and what it looks like, but nothing is as real as a set of tests. The former is a wish list, but the tests are a contract that is enforced by the compiler and the running program. It's hard to imagine a more concrete description of a class than the tests.

While creating the tests, you are forced to completely think out the class and will often discover needed functionality that might be missed during the thought experiments of UML diagrams, CRC cards, use cases, etc.

The second important effect of writing the tests first comes from running the tests every time you do a build of your software. This activity gives you the other half of the testing that's performed by the compiler. If you look at the evolution of programming languages from this perspective, you'll see that the real improvements in the technology have actually revolved around testing. Assembly language checked only for syntax, but C imposed some semantic restrictions, and these prevented you from making certain types of mistakes. OOP languages impose even more semantic restrictions, which if you think about it are actually forms of testing. "Is this data type being used properly?" and "Is this function being called properly?" are the kinds of tests that are being performed by the compiler or run-time system. We've seen the results of having these tests built into the language: people have been able to write more complex systems, and get them to work, with much less time and effort. I've puzzled over why this is, but now I realize it's the tests: you do something wrong, and the safety net of the built-in tests tells you there's a problem and points you to where it is.

But the built-in testing afforded by the design of the language can only go so far. At some point, *you* must step in and add the rest of the tests that produce a full suite (in cooperation with the compiler and run-time system) that verifies all of your program. And, just like having a compiler watching over your shoulder, wouldn't you want these tests helping you right from the beginning? That's why you write them first, and run them automatically with every build of your system. Your tests become an extension of the safety net provided by the language.

One of the things that I've discovered about the use of more and more powerful programming languages is that I am emboldened to try more brazen experiments, because I know that the language will keep me from wasting my time chasing bugs. The XP test scheme does the same thing for your entire project. Because you know your tests will always catch any problems that you introduce (and you regularly add any new tests as you think of them), you can make big changes when you need to without worrying that you'll throw the whole project into complete disarray. This is incredibly powerful.

Pair programming

Pair programming goes against the rugged individualism that we've been indoctrinated into from the beginning, through school (where we succeed or fail on our own, and working with our neighbors is considered "cheating"), and media, especially Hollywood movies in which the hero is usually fighting against mindless conformity[16]. Programmers, too, are considered paragons of individuality—"cowboy coders" as Larry Constantine likes to say. And yet XP, which is itself battling against conventional thinking, says that code should be written with two people per workstation. And that this should be done in an area with a group of workstations, without the barriers that the facilities-design people are so fond of. In fact, Beck says that the first task of converting to XP is to arrive with screwdrivers and Allen wrenches and take apart everything that gets in the way.[17] (This will require a manager who can deflect the ire of the facilities department.)

---

[16] Although this may be a more American perspective, the stories of Hollywood reach everywhere.

[17] Including (especially) the PA system. I once worked in a company that insisted on broadcasting every phone call that arrived for every executive, and it constantly interrupted our productivity (but the managers couldn't begin to conceive of stifling such an important service as the PA). Finally, when no one was looking I started snipping speaker wires.

The value of pair programming is that one person is actually doing the coding while the other is thinking about it. The thinker keeps the big picture in mind—not only the picture of the problem at hand, but the guidelines of XP. If two people are working, it's less likely that one of them will get away with saying, "I don't want to write the tests first," for example. And if the coder gets stuck, they can swap places. If both of them get stuck, their musings may be overheard by someone else in the work area who can contribute. Working in pairs keeps things flowing and on track. Probably more important, it makes programming a lot more social and fun.

I've begun using pair programming during the exercise periods in some of my seminars and it seems to significantly improve everyone's experience.

Why Java succeeds

The reason Java has been so successful is that the goal was to solve many of the problems facing developers today. The goal of Java is improved productivity. This productivity comes in many ways, but the language is designed to aid you as much as possible, while hindering you as little as possible with arbitrary rules or any requirement that you use a particular set of features. Java is designed to be practical; Java language design decisions were based on providing the maximum benefits to the programmer.

Systems are easier to express and understand

Classes designed to fit the problem tend to express it better. This means that when you write the code, you're describing your solution in the terms of the problem space ("Put the grommet in the bin") rather than the terms of the computer, which is the solution space ("Set the bit in the chip that means that the relay will close"). You deal with higher-level concepts and can do much more with a single line of code.

The other benefit of this ease of expression is maintenance, which (if reports can be believed) takes a huge portion of the cost over a program's lifetime. If a program is easier to understand, then it's easier to maintain.

This can also reduce the cost of creating and maintaining the documentation.

Maximal leverage with libraries

The fastest way to create a program is to use code that's already written: a library. A major goal in Java is to make library use easier. This is accomplished by casting libraries into new data types (classes), so that bringing in a library means adding new types to the language. Because the Java compiler takes care of how the library is used—guaranteeing proper initialization and cleanup, and ensuring that functions are called properly—you can focus on what you want the library to do, not how you have to do it.

Error handling

Error handling in C is a notorious problem, and one that is often ignored—finger-crossing is usually involved. If you're building a large, complex program, there's nothing worse than having an error buried somewhere with no clue as to where it came from. Java *exception handling* is a way to guarantee that an error is noticed, and that something happens as a result.

Programming in the large

Many traditional languages have built-in limitations to program size and complexity. BASIC, for example, can be great for pulling together quick solutions for certain classes of problems, but if the program gets more than a few pages long, or ventures out of the normal problem domain of that language, it's like trying to swim through an ever-more viscous fluid. There's no clear line that tells you when your language is failing you, and even if there were, you'd ignore it. You don't say, "My BASIC program just got too big; I'll have to rewrite it in C!" Instead, you try to shoehorn a few more lines in to add that one new feature. So the extra costs come creeping up on you.

Java is designed to aid *programming in the large*—that is, to erase those creeping-complexity boundaries between a small program and a large one. You certainly don't need to use OOP when you're writing a "hello world" style utility program, but the features are there when you need them. And the compiler is aggressive about ferreting out bug-producing errors for small and large programs alike.

Strategies for transition

If you buy into OOP, your next question is probably, "How can I get my manager/colleagues/department/peers to start using objects?" Think about how you—one independent programmer—would go about learning to use a new language and a new programming paradigm. You've done it before. First comes education and examples; then comes a trial project to give you a feel for the basics without doing anything too confusing. Then comes a "real world" project that actually does something useful. Throughout your first projects you continue your education by reading, asking questions of experts, and trading hints with friends. This is the approach many experienced programmers suggest for the switch to Java. Switching an entire company will of course introduce certain group dynamics, but it will help at each step to remember how one person would do it.

Guidelines

Here are some guidelines to consider when making the transition to OOP and Java:

1. Training

The first step is some form of education. Remember the company's investment in code, and try not to throw everything into disarray for six to nine months while everyone puzzles over how interfaces work. Pick a small group for indoctrination, preferably one composed of people who are curious, work well together, and can function as their own support network while they're learning Java.

An alternative approach that is sometimes suggested is the education of all company levels at once, including overview courses for strategic managers as well as design and programming courses for project builders. This is especially good for smaller companies making fundamental shifts in the way they do things, or at the division level of larger companies. Because the cost is higher, however, some may choose to start with project-level training, do a pilot project (possibly with an outside mentor), and let the project team become the teachers for the rest of the company.

2. Low-risk project

Try a low-risk project first and allow for mistakes. Once you've gained some experience, you can either seed other projects from members of this first team or use the team members as an OOP technical support staff. This first project may not work right the first time, so it should not be mission-critical for the company. It should be simple, self-contained, and instructive; this means that it should involve creating classes that will be meaningful to the other programmers in the company when they get their turn to learn Java.

3. Model from success

Seek out examples of good object-oriented design before starting from scratch. There's a good probability that someone has solved your problem already, and if they haven't solved it exactly you can probably apply what you've learned about abstraction to modify an existing design to fit your needs. This is the general concept of *design patterns,* covered in *Thinking in Patterns with Java*, downloadable at *www.BruceEckel.com.*

4. Use existing class libraries

The primary economic motivation for switching to OOP is the easy use of existing code in the form of class libraries (in particular, the Standard Java libraries, which are covered throughout this book). The shortest application development cycle will result when you can create and use objects from off-the-shelf libraries. However, some new programmers don't understand this, are unaware of existing class libraries, or, through fascination with the language, desire to write classes that may already exist. Your success with OOP and Java will be optimized if you make an effort to seek out and reuse other people's code early in the transition process.

5. Don't rewrite existing code in Java

It is not usually the best use of your time to take existing, functional code and rewrite it in Java. (If you must turn it into objects, you can interface to the C or C++ code using the Java Native Interface, described in

Appendix B.) There are incremental benefits, especially if the code is slated for reuse. But chances are you aren't going to see the dramatic increases in productivity that you hope for in your first few projects unless that project is a new one. Java and OOP shine best when taking a project from concept to reality.

Management obstacles

If you're a manager, your job is to acquire resources for your team, to overcome barriers to your team's success, and in general to try to provide the most productive and enjoyable environment so your team is most likely to perform those miracles that are always being asked of you. Moving to Java falls in all three of these categories, and it would be wonderful if it didn't cost you anything as well. Although moving to Java may be cheaper—depending on your constraints—than the OOP alternatives for a team of C programmers (and probably for programmers in other procedural languages), it isn't free, and there are obstacles you should be aware of before trying to sell the move to Java within your company and embarking on the move itself.

Startup costs

The cost of moving to Java is more than just the acquisition of Java compilers (the Sun Java compiler is free, so this is hardly an obstacle). Your medium- and long-term costs will be minimized if you invest in training (and possibly mentoring for your first project) and also if you identify and purchase class libraries that solve your problem rather than trying to build those libraries yourself. These are hard-money costs that must be factored into a realistic proposal. In addition, there are the hidden costs in loss of productivity while learning a new language and possibly a new programming environment. Training and mentoring can certainly minimize these, but team members must overcome their own struggles to understand the new technology. During this process they will make more mistakes (this is a feature, because acknowledged mistakes are the fastest path to learning) and be less productive. Even then, with some types of programming problems, the right classes, and the right development environment, it's possible to be more productive while you're learning Java (even considering that you're making more mistakes and writing fewer lines of code per day) than if you'd stayed with C.

Performance issues

A common question is, "Doesn't OOP automatically make my programs a lot bigger and slower?" The answer is, "It depends." The extra safety features in Java have traditionally extracted a performance penalty over a language like C++. Technologies such as "hotspot" and compilation technologies have improved the speed significantly in most cases, and efforts continue toward higher performance.

When your focus is on rapid prototyping, you can throw together components as fast as possible while ignoring efficiency issues. If you're using any third-party libraries, these are usually already optimized by their vendors; in any case it's not an issue while you're in rapid-development mode. When you have a system that you like, if it's small and fast enough, then you're done. If not, you begin tuning with a profiling tool, looking first for speedups that can be done by rewriting small portions of code. If that doesn't help, you look for modifications that can be made in the underlying implementation so no code that uses a particular class needs to be changed. Only if nothing else solves the problem do you need to change the design. The fact that performance is so critical in that portion of the design is an indicator that it must be part of the primary design criteria. You have the benefit of finding this out early using rapid development.

If you find a function that is a particular bottleneck, you can rewrite it in C/C++ using Java's *native methods*, the subject of Appendix B.

Common design errors

When starting your team into OOP and Java, programmers will typically go through a series of common design errors. This often happens due to insufficient feedback from experts during the design and implementation of early projects, because no experts have been developed within the company, and because there may be resistance to retaining consultants. It's easy to feel that you understand OOP too early in the cycle and go off on a bad tangent. Something that's obvious to someone experienced with the language may be a subject of great internal debate for a novice. Much of this trauma can be skipped by using an experienced outside expert for training and mentoring.

Java vs. C++?

Java looks a lot like C++, and so naturally it would seem that C++ will be replaced by Java. But I'm starting to question this logic. For one thing, C++ still has some features that Java doesn't, and although there have been a lot of promises about Java someday being as fast or faster than C++, we've seen steady improvements but no dramatic breakthroughs. Also, there seems to be a continuing interest in C++, so I don't think that language is going away any time soon. (Languages seem to hang around. Speaking at one of my "Intermediate/Advanced Java Seminars," Allen Holub asserted that the two most commonly used languages are Rexx and COBOL, in that order.)

I'm beginning to think that the strength of Java lies in a slightly different arena than that of C++. C++ is a language that doesn't try to fit a mold. Certainly it has been adapted in a number of ways to solve particular problems. Some C++ tools combine libraries, component models, and code-generation tools to solve the problem of developing windowed end-user applications (for Microsoft Windows). And yet, what do the vast majority of Windows developers use? Microsoft's Visual Basic (VB). This despite the fact that VB produces the kind of code that becomes unmanageable when the program is only a few pages long (and syntax that can be positively mystifying). As successful and popular as VB is, it's not a very good example of language design. It would be nice to have the ease and power of VB without the resulting unmanageable code. And that's where I think Java will shine: as the "next VB." You may or may not shudder to hear this, but think about it: so much of Java is intended to make it easy for the programmer to solve application-level problems like networking and cross-platform UI, and yet it has a language design that allows the creation of very large and flexible bodies of code. Add to this the fact that Java has the most robust type checking and error handling systems I've ever seen in a language and you have the makings of a significant leap forward in programming productivity.

Should you use Java instead of C++ for your project? Other than Web applets, there are two issues to consider. First, if you want to use a lot of existing C++ libraries (and you'll certainly get a lot of productivity gains there), or if you have an existing C or C++ code base, Java might slow your development down rather than speeding it up.

If you're developing all your code primarily from scratch, then the simplicity of Java over C++ will significantly shorten your development time—the anecdotal evidence (stories from C++ teams that I've talked to who have switched to Java) suggests a doubling of development speed over C++. If Java performance doesn't matter or you can somehow compensate for it, sheer time-to-market issues make it difficult to choose C++ over Java.

The biggest issue is performance. Interpreted Java has been slow, even 20 to 50 times slower than C in the original Java interpreters. This has improved greatly over time, but it will still remain an important number. Computers are about speed; if it wasn't significantly faster to do something on a computer then you'd do it by hand. (I've even heard it suggested that you start with Java, to gain the short development time, then use a tool and support libraries to translate your code to C++, if you need faster execution speed.)

The key to making Java feasible for most development projects is the appearance of speed improvements like so-called "just-in time" (JIT) compilers, Sun's own "hotspot" technology, and even native code compilers. Of course, native code compilers will eliminate the touted cross-platform execution of the compiled programs, but they will also bring the speed of the executable closer to that of C and C++. And cross-compiling a program in Java should be a lot easier than doing so in C or C++. (In theory, you just recompile, but that promise has been made before for other languages.)

You can find comparisons of Java and C++ and observations about Java realities in the appendices of the first edition of this book (Available on this book's accompanying CD ROM, as well as at *www.BruceEckel.com).*

Summary

This chapter attempts to give you a feel for the broad issues of object-oriented programming and Java, including why OOP is different, and why Java in particular is different, concepts of OOP methodologies, and finally

---

the kinds of issues you will encounter when moving your own company to OOP and Java.

OOP and Java may not be for everyone. It's important to evaluate your own needs and decide whether Java will optimally satisfy those needs, or if you might be better off with another programming system (including the one you're currently using). If you know that your needs will be very specialized for the foreseeable future and if you have specific constraints that may not be satisfied by Java, then you owe it to yourself to investigate the alternatives[18]. Even if you eventually choose Java as your language, you'll at least understand what the options were and have a clear vision of why you took that direction.

You know what a procedural program looks like: data definitions and function calls. To find the meaning of such a program you have to work a little, looking through the function calls and low-level concepts to create a model in your mind. This is the reason we need intermediate representations when designing procedural programs—by themselves, these programs tend to be confusing because the terms of expression are oriented more toward the computer than to the problem you're solving.

Because Java adds many new concepts on top of what you find in a procedural language, your natural assumption may be that the **main( )** in a Java program will be far more complicated than for the equivalent C program. Here, you'll be pleasantly surprised: A well-written Java program is generally far simpler and much easier to understand than the equivalent C program. What you'll see are the definitions of the objects that represent concepts in your problem space (rather than the issues of the computer representation) and messages sent to those objects to represent the activities in that space. One of the delights of object-oriented programming is that, with a well-designed program, it's easy to understand the code by reading it. Usually there's a lot less code as well, because many of your problems will be solved by reusing existing library code.

_____

[18] In particular, I recommend looking at Python (http://www.Python.org).

2: Everything is an Object

Although it is based on C++, Java is more of a "pure" object-oriented language.

Both C++ and Java are hybrid languages, but in Java the designers felt that the hybridization was not as important as it was in C++. A hybrid language allows multiple programming styles; the reason C++ is hybrid is to support backward compatibility with the C language. Because C++ is a superset of the C language, it includes many of that language's undesirable features, which can make some aspects of C++ overly complicated.

The Java language assumes that you want to do only object-oriented programming. This means that before you can begin you must shift your mindset into an object-oriented world (unless it's already there). The benefit of this initial effort is the ability to program in a language that is simpler to learn and to use than many other OOP languages. In this chapter we'll see the basic components of a Java program and we'll learn that everything in Java is an object, even a Java program.

You manipulate objects with references

Each programming language has its own means of manipulating data. Sometimes the programmer must be constantly aware of what type of manipulation is going on. Are you manipulating the object directly, or are you dealing with some kind of indirect representation (a pointer in C or C++) that must be treated with a special syntax?

All this is simplified in Java. You treat everything as an object, so there is a single consistent syntax that you use everywhere. Although you *treat* everything as an object, the identifier you manipulate is actually a "reference" to an object[1]. You might imagine this scene as a television (the object) with your remote control (the reference). As long as you're holding this reference, you have a connection to the television, but when someone says "change the channel" or "lower the volume," what you're manipulating is the reference, which in turn modifies the object. If you want to move around the room and still control the television, you take the remote/reference with you, not the television.

Also, the remote control can stand on its own, with no television. That is, just because you have a reference doesn't mean there's necessarily an object connected to it. So if you want to hold a word or sentence, you create a **String** reference:

```
String s;
```

But here you've created *only* the reference, not an object. If you decided to send a message to **s** at this point, you'll get an error (at run-time) because **s** isn't actually attached to anything (there's no television). A safer practice, then, is always to initialize a reference when you create it:

```
String s = "asdf";
```

---

[1] This can be a flashpoint. There are those who say "clearly, it's a pointer," but this presumes an underlying implementation. Also, Java references are much more akin to C++ references than pointers in their syntax. In the first edition of this book, I chose to invent a new term, "handle," because C++ references and Java references have some important differences. I was coming out of C++ and did not want to confuse the C++ programmers whom I assumed would be the largest audience for Java. In the 2nd edition, I decided that "reference" was the more commonly used term, and that anyone changing from C++ would have a lot more to cope with than the terminology of references, so they might as well jump in with both feet. However, there are people who disagree even with the term "reference." I read in one book where it was "completely wrong to say that Java supports pass by reference," because Java object identifiers (according to that author) are *actually* "object references." And (he goes on) everything is *actually* pass by value. So you're not passing by reference, you're "passing an object reference by value." One could argue for the precision of such convoluted explanations, but I think my approach simplifies the understanding of the concept without hurting anything (well, the language lawyers may claim that I'm lying to you, but I'll say that I'm providing an appropriate abstraction.)

However, this uses a special Java feature: strings can be initialized with quoted text. Normally, you must use a more general type of initialization for objects.

You must create all the objects

When you create a reference, you want to connect it with a new object. You do so, in general, with the **new** keyword. **new** says, "Make me a new one of these objects." So in the above example, you can say:

```
String s = new String("asdf");
```

Not only does this mean "Make me a new **String**," but it also gives information about *how* to make the **String** by supplying an initial character string.

Of course, **String** is not the only type that exists. Java comes with a plethora of ready-made types. What's more important is that you can create your own types. In fact, that's the fundamental activity in Java programming, and it's what you'll be learning about in the rest of this book.

Where storage lives

It's useful to visualize some aspects of how things are laid out while the program is running, in particular how memory is arranged. There are six different places to store data:

1. **Registers**. This is the fastest storage because it exists in a place different from that of other storage: inside the processor. However, the number of registers is severely limited, so registers are allocated by the compiler according to its needs. You don't have direct control, nor do you see any evidence in your programs that registers even exist.

2. **The stack**. This lives in the general RAM (random-access memory) area, but has direct support from the processor via its *stack pointer*. The stack pointer is moved down to create new

memory and moved up to release that memory. This is an extremely fast and efficient way to allocate storage, second only to registers. The Java compiler must know, while it is creating the program, the exact size and lifetime of all the data that is stored on the stack, because it must generate the code to move the stack pointer up and down. This constraint places limits on the flexibility of your programs, so while some Java storage exists on the stack— in particular, object references—Java objects themselves are not placed on the stack.

3. **The heap**. This is a general-purpose pool of memory (also in the RAM area) where all Java objects live. The nice thing about the heap is that, unlike the stack, the compiler doesn't need to know how much storage it needs to allocate from the heap or how long that storage must stay on the heap. Thus, there's a great deal of flexibility in using storage on the heap. Whenever you need to create an object, you simply write the code to create it using **new**, and the storage is allocated on the heap when that code is executed. Of course there's a price you pay for this flexibility: it takes more time to allocate heap storage than it does to allocate stack storage (that is, if you even *could* create objects on the stack in Java, as you can in C++).

4. **Static storage**. "Static" is used here in the sense of "in a fixed location" (although it's also in RAM). Static storage contains data that is available for the entire time a program is running. You can use the **static** keyword to specify that a particular element of an object is static, but Java objects themselves are never placed in static storage.

5. **Constant storage**. Constant values are often placed directly in the program code, which is safe since they can never change. Sometimes constants are cordoned off by themselves so that they can be optionally placed in read-only memory (ROM).

6. **Non-RAM storage**. If data lives completely outside a program it can exist while the program is not running, outside the control of the program. The two primary examples of this are *streamed objects,* in which objects are turned into streams of bytes, generally

to be sent to another machine, and *persistent objects,* in which the objects are placed on disk so they will hold their state even when the program is terminated. The trick with these types of storage is turning the objects into something that can exist on the other medium, and yet can be resurrected into a regular RAM-based object when necessary. Java provides support for *lightweight persistence*, and future versions of Java might provide more complete solutions for persistence.

Special case: primitive types

There is a group of types that gets special treatment; you can think of these as "primitive" types that you use quite often in your programming. The reason for the special treatment is that to create an object with **new**—especially a small, simple variable—isn't very efficient because **new** places objects on the heap. For these types Java falls back on the approach taken by C and C++. That is, instead of creating the variable using **new**, an "automatic" variable is created that *is not a reference*. The variable holds the value, and it's placed on the stack so it's much more efficient.

Java determines the size of each primitive type. These sizes don't change from one machine architecture to another as they do in most languages. This size invariance is one reason Java programs are so portable.

Primitive type	Size	Minimum	Maximum	Wrapper type
boolean	—	—	—	**Boolean**
char	16-bit	Unicode 0	Unicode $2^{16}- 1$	**Character**
byte	8-bit	-128	+127	**Byte**
short	16-bit	-2^{15}	$+2^{15}-1$	**Short**
int	32-bit	-2^{31}	$+2^{31}-1$	**Integer**
long	64-bit	-2^{63}	$+2^{63}-1$	**Long**
float	32-bit	IEEE754	IEEE754	**Float**
double	64-bit	IEEE754	IEEE754	**Double**
void	—	—	—	**Void**

All numeric types are signed, so don't go looking for unsigned types.

The size of the **boolean** type is not explicitly defined; it is only specified to be able to take the literal values **true** or **false**.

The primitive data types also have "wrapper" classes for them. That means that if you want to make a nonprimitive object on the heap to represent that primitive type, you use the associated wrapper. For example:

```
char c = 'x';
Character C = new Character(c);
```

Or you could also use:

```
Character C = new Character('x');
```

The reasons for doing this will be shown in a later chapter.

High-precision numbers

Java includes two classes for performing high-precision arithmetic: **BigInteger** and **BigDecimal**. Although these approximately fit into the same category as the "wrapper" classes, neither one has a primitive analogue.

Both classes have methods that provide analogues for the operations that you perform on primitive types. That is, you can do anything with a **BigInteger** or **BigDecimal** that you can with an **int** or **float**, it's just that you must use method calls instead of operators. Also, since there's more involved, the operations will be slower. You're exchanging speed for accuracy.

BigInteger supports arbitrary-precision integers. This means that you can accurately represent integral values of any size without losing any information during operations.

BigDecimal is for arbitrary-precision fixed-point numbers; you can use these for accurate monetary calculations, for example.

Consult your online documentation for details about the constructors and methods you can call for these two classes.

Arrays in Java

Virtually all programming languages support arrays. Using arrays in C and C++ is perilous because those arrays are only blocks of memory. If a program accesses the array outside of its memory block or uses the memory before initialization (common programming errors) there will be unpredictable results.

One of the primary goals of Java is safety, so many of the problems that plague programmers in C and C++ are not repeated in Java. A Java array is guaranteed to be initialized and cannot be accessed outside of its range. The range checking comes at the price of having a small amount of memory overhead on each array as well as verifying the index at run-time, but the assumption is that the safety and increased productivity is worth the expense.

When you create an array of objects, you are really creating an array of references, and each of those references is automatically initialized to a special value with its own keyword: **null**. When Java sees **null**, it recognizes that the reference in question isn't pointing to an object. You must assign an object to each reference before you use it, and if you try to use a reference that's still **null,** the problem will be reported at run-time. Thus, typical array errors are prevented in Java.

You can also create an array of primitives. Again, the compiler guarantees initialization because it zeroes the memory for that array.

Arrays will be covered in detail in later chapters.

You never need to destroy an object

In most programming languages, the concept of the lifetime of a variable occupies a significant portion of the programming effort. How long does the variable last? If you are supposed to destroy it, when should you? Confusion over variable lifetimes can lead to a lot of bugs, and this section shows how Java greatly simplifies the issue by doing all the cleanup work for you.

Scoping

Most procedural languages have the concept of *scope*. This determines both the visibility and lifetime of the names defined within that scope. In C, C++, and Java, scope is determined by the placement of curly braces **{}**. So for example:

```
{
  int x = 12;
  /* only x available */
  {
    int q = 96;
    /* both x & q available */
  }
  /* only x available */
  /* q "out of scope" */
}
```

A variable defined within a scope is available only to the end of that scope.

Indentation makes Java code easier to read. Since Java is a free-form language, the extra spaces, tabs, and carriage returns do not affect the resulting program.

Note that you *cannot* do the following, even though it is legal in C and C++:

```
{
  int x = 12;
  {
    int x = 96; /* illegal */
  }
}
```

The compiler will announce that the variable **x** has already been defined. Thus the C and C++ ability to "hide" a variable in a larger scope is not allowed because the Java designers thought that it led to confusing programs.

Scope of objects

Java objects do not have the same lifetimes as primitives. When you create a Java object using **new**, it hangs around past the end of the scope. Thus if you use:

```
{
  String s = new String("a string");
} /* end of scope */
```

the reference **s** vanishes at the end of the scope. However, the **String** object that **s** was pointing to is still occupying memory. In this bit of code, there is no way to access the object because the only reference to it is out of scope. In later chapters you'll see how the reference to the object can be passed around and duplicated during the course of a program.

It turns out that because objects created with **new** stay around for as long as you want them, a whole slew of C++ programming problems simply vanish in Java. The hardest problems seem to occur in C++ because you don't get any help from the language in making sure that the objects are available when they're needed. And more important, in C++ you must make sure that you destroy the objects when you're done with them.

That brings up an interesting question. If Java leaves the objects lying around, what keeps them from filling up memory and halting your program? This is exactly the kind of problem that would occur in C++. This is where a bit of magic happens. Java has a *garbage collector*, which looks at all the objects that were created with **new** and figures out which ones are not being referenced anymore. Then it releases the memory for those objects, so the memory can be used for new objects. This means that you never need to worry about reclaiming memory yourself. You simply create objects, and when you no longer need them they will go away by themselves. This eliminates a certain class of programming problem: the so-called "memory leak," in which a programmer forgets to release memory.

Creating new data types: class

If everything is an object, what determines how a particular class of object looks and behaves? Put another way, what establishes the *type* of an object? You might expect there to be a keyword called "type," and that certainly would have made sense. Historically, however, most object-oriented languages have used the keyword **class** to mean "I'm about to tell you what a new type of object looks like." The **class** keyword (which is so common that it will not be emboldened throughout this book) is followed by the name of the new type. For example:

```
class ATypeName { /* class body goes here */ }
```

This introduces a new type, so you can now create an object of this type using **new**:

```
ATypeName a = new ATypeName();
```

In **ATypeName**, the class body consists only of a comment (the stars and slashes and what is inside, which will be discussed later in this chapter), so there is not too much that you can do with it. In fact, you cannot tell it to do much of anything (that is, you cannot send it any interesting messages) until you define some methods for it.

Fields and methods

When you define a class (and all you do in Java is define classes, make objects of those classes, and send messages to those objects), you can put two types of elements in your class: data members (sometimes called *fields*), and member functions (typically called *methods*). A data member is an object of any type that you can communicate with via its reference. It can also be one of the primitive types (which isn't a reference). If it is a reference to an object, you must initialize that reference to connect it to an actual object (using **new**, as seen earlier) in a special function called a *constructor* (described fully in Chapter 4). If it is a primitive type you can initialize it directly at the point of definition in the class. (As you'll see later, references can also be initialized at the point of definition.)

Each object keeps its own storage for its data members; the data members are not shared among objects. Here is an example of a class with some data members:

```
class DataOnly {
    int i;
    float f;
    boolean b;
}
```

This class doesn't *do* anything, but you can create an object:

```
DataOnly d = new DataOnly();
```

You can assign values to the data members, but you must first know how to refer to a member of an object. This is accomplished by stating the name of the object reference, followed by a period (dot), followed by the name of the member inside the object:

```
objectReference.member
```

For example:

```
d.i = 47;
d.f = 1.1f;
d.b = false;
```

It is also possible that your object might contain other objects that contain data you'd like to modify. For this, you just keep "connecting the dots." For example:

```
myPlane.leftTank.capacity = 100;
```

The **DataOnly** class cannot do much of anything except hold data, because it has no member functions (methods). To understand how those work, you must first understand *arguments* and *return values*, which will be described shortly.

Default values for primitive members

When a primitive data type is a member of a class, it is guaranteed to get a default value if you do not initialize it:

Primitive type	Default
boolean	false
char	'\u0000' (null)
byte	(byte)0
short	(short)0
int	0
long	0L
float	0.0f
double	0.0d

Note carefully that the default values are what Java guarantees when the variable is used *as a member of a class*. This ensures that member variables of primitive types will always be initialized (something C++ doesn't do), reducing a source of bugs. However, this initial value may not be correct or even legal for the program you are writing. It's best to always explicitly initialize your variables.

This guarantee doesn't apply to "local" variables—those that are not fields of a class. Thus, if within a function definition you have:

```
int x;
```

Then **x** will get some arbitrary value (as in C and C++); it will not automatically be initialized to zero. You are responsible for assigning an appropriate value before you use **x**. If you forget, Java definitely improves on C++: you get a compile-time error telling you the variable might not have been initialized. (Many C++ compilers will warn you about uninitialized variables, but in Java these are errors.)

Methods, arguments, and return values

Up until now, the term *function* has been used to describe a named subroutine. The term that is more commonly used in Java is *method,* as in "a way to do something." If you want, you can continue thinking in terms of functions. It's really only a syntactic difference, but from now on "method" will be used in this book rather than "function."

Methods in Java determine the messages an object can receive. In this section you will learn how simple it is to define a method.

The fundamental parts of a method are the name, the arguments, the return type, and the body. Here is the basic form:

```
returnType methodName( /* argument list */ ) {
  /* Method body */
}
```

The return type is the type of the value that pops out of the method after you call it. The argument list gives the types and names for the information you want to pass into the method. The method name and argument list together uniquely identify the method.

Methods in Java can be created only as part of a class. A method can be called only for an object,[2] and that object must be able to perform that method call. If you try to call the wrong method for an object, you'll get an error message at compile-time. You call a method for an object by naming the object followed by a period (dot), followed by the name of the method and its argument list, like this: **objectName.methodName(arg1, arg2, arg3)**. For example, suppose you have a method **f( )** that takes no arguments and returns a value of type **int**. Then, if you have an object called **a** for which **f( )** can be called, you can say this:

```
int x = a.f();
```

The type of the return value must be compatible with the type of **x**.

This act of calling a method is commonly referred to as *sending a message to an object*. In the above example, the message is **f( )** and the object is **a**. Object-oriented programming is often summarized as simply "sending messages to objects."

---

[2] **static** methods, which you'll learn about soon, can be called *for the class*, without an object.

The argument list

The method argument list specifies what information you pass into the method. As you might guess, this information—like everything else in Java—takes the form of objects. So, what you must specify in the argument list are the types of the objects to pass in and the name to use for each one. As in any situation in Java where you seem to be handing objects around, you are actually passing references[3]. The type of the reference must be correct, however. If the argument is supposed to be a **String**, what you pass in must be a string.

Consider a method that takes a **String** as its argument. Here is the definition, which must be placed within a class definition for it to be compiled:

```
int storage(String s) {
  return s.length() * 2;
}
```

This method tells you how many bytes are required to hold the information in a particular **String.** (Each **char** in a **String** is 16 bits, or two bytes, long, to support Unicode characters.) The argument is of type **String** and is called **s**. Once **s** is passed into the method, you can treat it just like any other object. (You can send messages to it.) Here, the **length( )** method is called, which is one of the methods for **String**s; it returns the number of characters in a string.

You can also see the use of the **return** keyword, which does two things. First, it means "leave the method, I'm done." Second, if the method produces a value, that value is placed right after the **return** statement. In this case, the return value is produced by evaluating the expression **s.length( ) * 2**.

You can return any type you want, but if you don't want to return anything at all, you do so by indicating that the method returns **void**. Here are some examples:

---

[3] With the usual exception of the aforementioned "special" data types **boolean, char, byte**, **short**, **int**, **long, float,** and **double**. In general, though, you pass objects, which really means you pass references to objects.

```
boolean flag() { return true; }
float naturalLogBase() { return 2.718f; }
void nothing() { return; }
void nothing2() {}
```

When the return type is **void**, then the **return** keyword is used only to exit the method, and is therefore unnecessary when you reach the end of the method. You can return from a method at any point, but if you've given a non-**void** return type then the compiler will force you (with error messages) to return the appropriate type of value regardless of where you return.

At this point, it can look like a program is just a bunch of objects with methods that take other objects as arguments and send messages to those other objects. That is indeed much of what goes on, but in the following chapter you'll learn how to do the detailed low-level work by making decisions within a method. For this chapter, sending messages will suffice.

Building a Java program

There are several other issues you must understand before seeing your first Java program.

Name visibility

A problem in any programming language is the control of names. If you use a name in one module of the program, and another programmer uses the same name in another module, how do you distinguish one name from another and prevent the two names from "clashing?" In C this is a particular problem because a program is often an unmanageable sea of names. C++ classes (on which Java classes are based) nest functions within classes so they cannot clash with function names nested within other classes. However, C++ still allowed global data and global functions, so clashing was still possible. To solve this problem, C++ introduced *namespaces* using additional keywords.

Java was able to avoid all of this by taking a fresh approach. To produce an unambiguous name for a library, the specifier used is not unlike an Internet domain name. In fact, the Java creators want you to use your

---

Internet domain name in reverse since those are guaranteed to be unique. Since my domain name is **BruceEckel.com**, my utility library of foibles would be named **com.bruceeckel.utility.foibles**. After your reversed domain name, the dots are intended to represent subdirectories.

In Java 1.0 and Java 1.1 the domain extensions **com**, **edu**, **org**, **net**, etc., were capitalized by convention, so the library would appear: **COM.bruceeckel.utility.foibles**. Partway through the development of Java 2, however, it was discovered that this caused problems, and so now the entire package name is lowercase.

This mechanism means that all of your files automatically live in their own namespaces, and each class within a file must have a unique identifier. So you do not need to learn special language features to solve this problem—the language takes care of it for you.

Using other components

Whenever you want to use a predefined class in your program, the compiler must know how to locate it. Of course, the class might already exist in the same source code file that it's being called from. In that case, you simply use the class—even if the class doesn't get defined until later in the file. Java eliminates the "forward referencing" problem so you don't need to think about it.

What about a class that exists in some other file? You might think that the compiler should be smart enough to simply go and find it, but there is a problem. Imagine that you want to use a class of a particular name, but more than one definition for that class exists (presumably these are different definitions). Or worse, imagine that you're writing a program, and as you're building it you add a new class to your library that conflicts with the name of an existing class.

To solve this problem, you must eliminate all potential ambiguities. This is accomplished by telling the Java compiler exactly what classes you want using the **import** keyword. **import** tells the compiler to bring in a *package*, which is a library of classes. (In other languages, a library could consist of functions and data as well as classes, but remember that all code in Java must be written inside a class.)

Most of the time you'll be using components from the standard Java libraries that come with your compiler. With these, you don't need to worry about long, reversed domain names; you just say, for example:

```
import java.util.ArrayList;
```

to tell the compiler that you want to use Java's **ArrayList** class. However, **util** contains a number of classes and you might want to use several of them without declaring them all explicitly. This is easily accomplished by using '*' to indicate a wild card:

```
import java.util.*;
```

It is more common to import a collection of classes in this manner than to import classes individually.

The **static** keyword

Ordinarily, when you create a class you are describing how objects of that class look and how they will behave. You don't actually get anything until you create an object of that class with **new**, and at that point data storage is created and methods become available.

But there are two situations in which this approach is not sufficient. One is if you want to have only one piece of storage for a particular piece of data, regardless of how many objects are created, or even if no objects are created. The other is if you need a method that isn't associated with any particular object of this class. That is, you need a method that you can call even if no objects are created. You can achieve both of these effects with the **static** keyword. When you say something is **static**, it means that data or method is not tied to any particular object instance of that class. So even if you've never created an object of that class you can call a **static** method or access a piece of **static** data. With ordinary, non-**static** data and methods you must create an object and use that object to access the data or method, since non-**static** data and methods must know the particular object they are working with. Of course, since **static** methods don't need any objects to be created before they are used, they cannot *directly* access non-**static** members or methods by simply calling those other members without referring to a named object (since non-**static** members and methods must be tied to a particular object).

Some object-oriented languages use the terms *class data* and *class methods*, meaning that the data and methods exist only for the class as a whole, and not for any particular objects of the class. Sometimes the Java literature uses these terms too.

To make a data member or method **static**, you simply place the keyword before the definition. For example, the following produces a **static** data member and initializes it:

```
class StaticTest {
    static int i = 47;
}
```

Now even if you make two **StaticTest** objects, there will still be only one piece of storage for **StaticTest.i.** Both objects will share the same **i.** Consider:

```
StaticTest st1 = new StaticTest();
StaticTest st2 = new StaticTest();
```

At this point, both **st1.i** and **st2.i** have the same value of 47 since they refer to the same piece of memory.

There are two ways to refer to a **static** variable. As indicated above, you can name it via an object, by saying, for example, **st2.i.** You can also refer to it directly through its class name, something you cannot do with a non-static member. (This is the preferred way to refer to a **static** variable since it emphasizes that variable's **static** nature.)

```
StaticTest.i++;
```

The **++** operator increments the variable. At this point, both **st1.i** and **st2.i** will have the value 48.

Similar logic applies to static methods. You can refer to a static method either through an object as you can with any method, or with the special additional syntax **ClassName.method( )**. You define a static method in a similar way:

```
class StaticFun {
  static void incr() { StaticTest.i++; }
}
```

You can see that the **StaticFun** method **incr( )** increments the **static** data **i**. You can call **incr( )** in the typical way, through an object:

```
StaticFun sf = new StaticFun();
sf.incr();
```

Or, because **incr( )** is a static method, you can call it directly through its class:

```
StaticFun.incr();
```

While **static**, when applied to a data member, definitely changes the way the data is created (one for each class vs. the non-**static** one for each object), when applied to a method it's not so dramatic. An important use of **static** for methods is to allow you to call that method without creating an object. This is essential, as we will see, in defining the **main( )** method that is the entry point for running an application.

Like any method, a **static** method can create or use named objects of its type, so a **static** method is often used as a "shepherd" for a flock of instances of its own type.

Your first Java program

Finally, here's the program.[4] It starts by printing a string, and then the date, using the **Date** class from the Java standard library. Note that an additional style of comment is introduced here: the '//', which is a comment until the end of the line:

```
// HelloDate.java
```

---

[4] Some programming environments will flash programs up on the screen and close them before you've had a chance to see the results. You can put in the following bit of code at the end of **main( )** to pause the output:

```
try {
  System.in.read();
} catch(Exception e) {}
```

This will pause the output until you press "Enter" (or any other key). This code involves concepts that will not be introduced until much later in the book, so you won't understand it until then, but it will do the trick.

```
import java.util.*;

public class HelloDate {
  public static void main(String[] args) {
    System.out.println("Hello, it's: ");
    System.out.println(new Date());
  }
}
```

At the beginning of each program file, you must place the **import** statement to bring in any extra classes you'll need for the code in that file. Note that I say "extra;" that's because there's a certain library of classes that are automatically brought into every Java file: **java.lang**. Start up your Web browser and look at the documentation from Sun. (If you haven't downloaded it from *java.sun.com* or otherwise installed the Java documentation, do so now). If you look at the list of the packages, you'll see all the different class libraries that come with Java. Select **java.lang**. This will bring up a list of all the classes that are part of that library. Since **java.lang** is implicitly included in every Java code file, these classes are automatically available. There's no **Date** class listed in **java.lang**, which means you must import another library to use that. If you don't know the library where a particular class is, or if you want to see all of the classes, you can select "Tree" in the Java documentation. Now you can find every single class that comes with Java. Then you can use the browser's "find" function to find **Date**. When you do you'll see it listed as **java.util.Date**, which lets you know that it's in the **util** library and that you must **import java.util.*** in order to use **Date**.

If you go back to the beginning, select **java.lang** and then **System**, you'll see that the **System** class has several fields, and if you select **out** you'll discover that it's a **static PrintStream** object. Since it's **static** you don't need to create anything. The **out** object is always there and you can just use it. What you can do with this **out** object is determined by the type it is: a **PrintStream**. Conveniently, **PrintStream** is shown in the description as a hyperlink, so if you click on that you'll see a list of all the methods you can call for **PrintStream**. There are quite a few and these will be covered later in this book. For now all we're interested in is **println( )**, which in effect means "print what I'm giving you out to the console and end with a new line." Thus, in any Java program you write you can say **System.out.println("things")** whenever you want to print something to the console.

The name of the class is the same as the name of the file. When you're creating a stand-alone program such as this one, one of the classes in the file must have the same name as the file. (The compiler complains if you don't do this.) That class must contain a method called **main( )** with the signature shown:

```
public static void main(String[] args) {
```

The **public** keyword means that the method is available to the outside world (described in detail in Chapter 5). The argument to **main( )** is an array of **String** objects. The **args** won't be used in this program, but the Java compiler insists that they be there because they hold the arguments invoked on the command line.

The line that prints the date is quite interesting:

```
System.out.println(new Date());
```

Consider the argument: a **Date** object is being created just to send its value to **println( )**. As soon as this statement is finished, that **Date** is unnecessary, and the garbage collector can come along and get it anytime. We don't need to worry about cleaning it up.

Compiling and running

To compile and run this program, and all the other programs in this book, you must first have a Java programming environment. There are a number of third-party development environments, but in this book we will assume that you are using the JDK from Sun, which is free. If you are using another development system, you will need to look in the documentation for that system to determine how to compile and run programs.

Get on the Internet and go to *java.sun.com*. There you will find information and links that will lead you through the process of downloading and installing the JDK for your particular platform.

Once the JDK is installed, and you've set up your computer's path information so that it will find **javac** and **java**, download and unpack the

---

source code for this book (you can find it on the CD ROM that's bound in with this book, or at *www.BruceEckel.com*). This will create a subdirectory for each chapter in this book. Move to subdirectory **c02** and type:

```
javac HelloDate.java
```

This command should produce no response. If you get any kind of an error message it means you haven't installed the JDK properly and you need to investigate those problems.

On the other hand, if you just get your command prompt back, you can type:

```
java HelloDate
```

and you'll get the message and the date as output.

This is the process you can use to compile and run each of the programs in this book. However, you will see that the source code for this book also has a file called **makefile** in each chapter, and this contains "make" commands for automatically building the files for that chapter. See this book's Web page at *www.BruceEckel.com* for details on how to use the makefiles.

Comments and embedded documentation

There are two types of comments in Java. The first is the traditional C-style comment that was inherited by C++. These comments begin with a /* and continue, possibly across many lines, until a */. Note that many programmers will begin each line of a continued comment with a *, so you'll often see:

```
/* This is a comment
 *  that continues
 *  across lines
 */
```

Remember, however, that everything inside the /* and */ is ignored, so there's no difference in saying:

```
/* This is a comment that
continues across lines */
```

The second form of comment comes from C++. It is the single-line comment, which starts at a // and continues until the end of the line. This type of comment is convenient and commonly used because it's easy. You don't need to hunt on the keyboard to find / and then * (instead, you just press the same key twice), and you don't need to close the comment. So you will often see:

```
// this is a one-line comment
```

Comment documentation

One of the thoughtful parts of the Java language is that the designers didn't consider writing code to be the only important activity—they also thought about documenting it. Possibly the biggest problem with documenting code has been maintaining that documentation. If the documentation and the code are separate, it becomes a hassle to change the documentation every time you change the code. The solution seems simple: link the code to the documentation. The easiest way to do this is to put everything in the same file. To complete the picture, however, you need a special comment syntax to mark special documentation, and a tool to extract those comments and put them in a useful form. This is what Java has done.

The tool to extract the comments is called *javadoc.* It uses some of the technology from the Java compiler to look for special comment tags you put in your programs. It not only extracts the information marked by these tags, but it also pulls out the class name or method name that adjoins the comment. This way you can get away with the minimal amount of work to generate decent program documentation.

The output of javadoc is an HTML file that you can view with your Web browser. This tool allows you to create and maintain a single source file and automatically generate useful documentation. Because of javadoc we have a standard for creating documentation, and it's easy enough that we can expect or even demand documentation with all Java libraries.

Syntax

All of the javadoc commands occur only within /** comments. The comments end with */ as usual. There are two primary ways to use javadoc: embed HTML, or use "doc tags." Doc tags are commands that start with a '@' and are placed at the beginning of a comment line. (A leading '*', however, is ignored.)

There are three "types" of comment documentation, which correspond to the element the comment precedes: class, variable, or method. That is, a class comment appears right before the definition of a class; a variable comment appears right in front of the definition of a variable, and a method comment appears right in front of the definition of a method. As a simple example:

```
/** A class comment */
public class docTest {
  /** A variable comment */
  public int i;
  /** A method comment */
  public void f() {}
}
```

Note that javadoc will process comment documentation for only **public** and **protected** members. Comments for **private** and "friendly" members (see Chapter 5) are ignored and you'll see no output. (However, you can use the **-private** flag to include **private** members as well.) This makes sense, since only **public** and **protected** members are available outside the file, which is the client programmer's perspective. However, all **class** comments are included in the output.

The output for the above code is an HTML file that has the same standard format as all the rest of the Java documentation, so users will be comfortable with the format and can easily navigate your classes. It's worth entering the above code, sending it through javadoc and viewing the resulting HTML file to see the results.

Embedded HTML

Javadoc passes HTML commands through to the generated HTML document. This allows you full use of HTML; however, the primary motive is to let you format code, such as:

```
/**
* <pre>
* System.out.println(new Date());
* </pre>
*/
```

You can also use HTML just as you would in any other Web document to format the regular text in your descriptions:

```
/**
* You can <em>even</em> insert a list:
* <ol>
* <li> Item one
* <li> Item two
* <li> Item three
* </ol>
*/
```

Note that within the documentation comment, asterisks at the beginning of a line are thrown away by javadoc, along with leading spaces. Javadoc reformats everything so that it conforms to the standard documentation appearance. Don't use headings such as **<h1>** or **<hr>** as embedded HTML because javadoc inserts its own headings and yours will interfere with them.

All types of comment documentation—class, variable, and method—can support embedded HTML.

@see: referring to other classes

All three types of comment documentation (class, variable, and method) can contain **@see** tags, which allow you to refer to the documentation in other classes. Javadoc will generate HTML with the **@see** tags hyperlinked to the other documentation. The forms are:

```
@see classname
```

```
@see fully-qualified-classname
@see fully-qualified-classname#method-name
```

Each one adds a hyperlinked "See Also" entry to the generated documentation. Javadoc will not check the hyperlinks you give it to make sure they are valid.

Class documentation tags

Along with embedded HTML and **@see** references, class documentation can include tags for version information and the author's name. Class documentation can also be used for *interfaces* (see Chapter 8).

@version

This is of the form:

```
@version version-information
```

in which **version-information** is any significant information you see fit to include. When the **-version** flag is placed on the javadoc command line, the version information will be called out specially in the generated HTML documentation.

@author

This is of the form:

```
@author author-information
```

in which **author-information** is, presumably, your name, but it could also include your email address or any other appropriate information. When the **-author** flag is placed on the javadoc command line, the author information will be called out specially in the generated HTML documentation.

You can have multiple author tags for a list of authors, but they must be placed consecutively. All the author information will be lumped together into a single paragraph in the generated HTML.

@since

This tag allows you to indicate the version of this code that began using a particular feature. You'll see it appearing in the HTML Java documentation to indicate what version of the JDK is used.

Variable documentation tags

Variable documentation can include only embedded HTML and **@see** references.

Method documentation tags

As well as embedded documentation and **@see** references, methods allow documentation tags for parameters, return values, and exceptions.

@param

This is of the form:

```
@param parameter-name description
```

in which **parameter-name** is the identifier in the parameter list, and **description** is text that can continue on subsequent lines. The description is considered finished when a new documentation tag is encountered. You can have any number of these, presumably one for each parameter.

@return

This is of the form:

```
@return description
```

in which **description** gives you the meaning of the return value. It can continue on subsequent lines.

@throws

Exceptions will be demonstrated in Chapter 10, but briefly they are objects that can be "thrown" out of a method if that method fails. Although only one exception object can emerge when you call a method, a particular method might produce any number of different types of

---

exceptions, all of which need descriptions. So the form for the exception tag is:

```
@throws fully-qualified-class-name description
```

in which **fully-qualified-class-name** gives an unambiguous name of an exception class that's defined somewhere, and **description** (which can continue on subsequent lines) tells you why this particular type of exception can emerge from the method call.

@deprecated

This is used to tag features that were superseded by an improved feature. The deprecated tag is a suggestion that you no longer use this particular feature, since sometime in the future it is likely to be removed. A method that is marked **@deprecated** causes the compiler to issue a warning if it is used.

Documentation example

Here is the first Java program again, this time with documentation comments added:

```java
//: c02:HelloDate.java
import java.util.*;

/** The first Thinking in Java example program.
 * Displays a string and today's date.
 * @author Bruce Eckel
 * @author www.BruceEckel.com
 * @version 2.0
 */
public class HelloDate {
  /** Sole entry point to class & application
   * @param args array of string arguments
   * @return No return value
   * @exception exceptions No exceptions thrown
   */
  public static void main(String[] args) {
    System.out.println("Hello, it's: ");
    System.out.println(new Date());
  }
```

```
} ///:~
```

The first line of the file uses my own technique of putting a ':' as a special marker for the comment line containing the source file name. That line contains the path information to the file (in this case, **c02** indicates Chapter 2) followed by the file name[5]. The last line also finishes with a comment, and this one indicates the end of the source code listing, which allows it to be automatically extracted from the text of this book and checked with a compiler.

Coding style

The unofficial standard in Java is to capitalize the first letter of a class name. If the class name consists of several words, they are run together (that is, you don't use underscores to separate the names), and the first letter of each embedded word is capitalized, such as:

```
class AllTheColorsOfTheRainbow { // ...
```

For almost everything else: methods, fields (member variables), and object reference names, the accepted style is just as it is for classes *except* that the first letter of the identifier is lowercase. For example:

```
class AllTheColorsOfTheRainbow {
  int anIntegerRepresentingColors;
  void changeTheHueOfTheColor(int newHue) {
    // ...
  }
  // ...
}
```

Of course, you should remember that the user must also type all these long names, and so be merciful.

The Java code you will see in the Sun libraries also follows the placement of open-and-close curly braces that you see used in this book.

---

[5] A tool that I created using Python (see www.Python.org) uses this information to extract the code files, put them in appropriate subdirectories, and create makefiles.

Summary

In this chapter you have seen enough of Java programming to understand how to write a simple program, and you have gotten an overview of the language and some of its basic ideas. However, the examples so far have all been of the form "do this, then do that, then do something else." What if you want the program to make choices, such as "if the result of doing this is red, do that; if not, then do something else"? The support in Java for this fundamental programming activity will be covered in the next chapter.

Exercises

Solutions to selected exercises can be found in the electronic document *The Thinking in Java Annotated Solution Guide*, available for a small fee from *www.BruceEckel.com*.

1. Following the **HelloDate.java** example in this chapter, create a "hello, world" program that simply prints out that statement. You need only a single method in your class (the "main" one that gets executed when the program starts). Remember to make it **static** and to include the argument list, even though you don't use the argument list. Compile the program with **javac** and run it using **java**. If you are using a different development environment than the JDK, learn how to compile and run programs in that environment.

2. Find the code fragments involving **ATypeName** and turn them into a program that compiles and runs.

3. Turn the **DataOnly** code fragments into a program that compiles and runs.

4. Modify Exercise 3 so that the values of the data in **DataOnly** are assigned to and printed in **main( )**.

5. Write a program that includes and calls the **storage( )** method defined as a code fragment in this chapter.

6. Turn the **StaticFun** code fragments into a working program.

---

7.   Write a program that prints three arguments taken from the command line. To do this, you'll need to index into the command-line array of **String**s.

8.   Turn the **AllTheColorsOfTheRainbow** example into a program that compiles and runs.

9.   Find the code for the second version of **HelloDate.java**, which is the simple comment documentation example. Execute **javadoc** on the file and view the results with your Web browser.

10.   Turn **docTest** into a file that compiles and then run it through **javadoc**. Verify the resulting documentation with your Web browser.

11.   Add an HTML list of items to the documentation in Exercise 10.

12.   Take the program in Exercise 1 and add comment documentation to it. Extract this comment documentation into an HTML file using **javadoc** and view it with your Web browser.

3: Controlling Program Flow

Like a sentient creature, a program must manipulate its world and make choices during execution.

In Java you manipulate objects and data using operators, and you make choices with execution control statements. Java was inherited from C++, so most of these statements and operators will be familiar to C and C++ programmers. Java has also added some improvements and simplifications.

If you find yourself floundering a bit in this chapter, make sure you go through the multimedia CD ROM bound into this book: *Thinking in C: Foundations for Java and C++*. It contains audio lectures, slides, exercises, and solutions specifically designed to bring you up to speed with the C syntax necessary to learn Java.

Using Java operators

An operator takes one or more arguments and produces a new value. The arguments are in a different form than ordinary method calls, but the effect is the same. You should be reasonably comfortable with the general concept of operators from your previous programming experience. Addition (+), subtraction and unary minus (-), multiplication (*), division (/), and assignment (=) all work much the same in any programming language.

All operators produce a value from their operands. In addition, an operator can change the value of an operand. This is called a *side effect*. The most common use for operators that modify their operands is to generate the side effect, but you should keep in mind that the value produced is available for your use just as in operators without side effects.

Almost all operators work only with primitives. The exceptions are '=', '==' and '!=', which work with all objects (and are a point of confusion for objects). In addition, the **String** class supports '+' and '+='.

Precedence

Operator precedence defines how an expression evaluates when several operators are present. Java has specific rules that determine the order of evaluation. The easiest one to remember is that multiplication and division happen before addition and subtraction. Programmers often forget the other precedence rules, so you should use parentheses to make the order of evaluation explicit. For example:

```
A = X + Y - 2/2 + Z;
```

has a very different meaning from the same statement with a particular grouping of parentheses:

```
A = X + (Y - 2)/(2 + Z);
```

Assignment

Assignment is performed with the operator =. It means "take the value of the right-hand side (often called the *rvalue*) and copy it into the left-hand side (often called the *lvalue*). An rvalue is any constant, variable or expression that can produce a value, but an lvalue must be a distinct, named variable. (That is, there must be a physical space to store a value.) For instance, you can assign a constant value to a variable (**A = 4;**), but you cannot assign anything to constant value—it cannot be an lvalue. (You can't say **4 = A;**.)

Assignment of primitives is quite straightforward. Since the primitive holds the actual value and not a reference to an object, when you assign primitives you copy the contents from one place to another. For example, if you say **A = B** for primitives, then the contents of **B** are copied into **A**. If you then go on to modify **A**, **B** is naturally unaffected by this modification. As a programmer, this is what you've come to expect for most situations.

When you assign objects, however, things change. Whenever you manipulate an object, what you're manipulating is the reference, so when you assign "from one object to another" you're actually copying a reference from one place to another. This means that if you say **C = D** for objects, you end up with both **C** and **D** pointing to the object that, originally, only **D** pointed to. The following example will demonstrate this.

Here's the example:

```
//: c03:Assignment.java
// Assignment with objects is a bit tricky.

class Number {
  int i;
}

public class Assignment {
  public static void main(String[] args) {
    Number n1 = new Number();
    Number n2 = new Number();
    n1.i = 9;
    n2.i = 47;
    System.out.println("1: n1.i: " + n1.i +
      ", n2.i: " + n2.i);
    n1 = n2;
    System.out.println("2: n1.i: " + n1.i +
      ", n2.i: " + n2.i);
    n1.i = 27;
    System.out.println("3: n1.i: " + n1.i +
      ", n2.i: " + n2.i);
  }
} ///:~
```

The **Number** class is simple, and two instances of it (**n1** and **n2**) are created within **main( )**. The **i** value within each **Number** is given a different value, and then **n2** is assigned to **n1**, and **n1** is changed. In many programming languages you would expect **n1** and **n2** to be independent at all times, but because you've assigned a reference here's the output you'll see:

```
1: n1.i: 9, n2.i: 47
2: n1.i: 47, n2.i: 47
3: n1.i: 27, n2.i: 27
```

Changing the **n1** object appears to change the **n2** object as well! This is because both **n1** and **n2** contain the same reference, which is pointing to the same object. (The original reference that was in **n1** that pointed to the object holding a value of 9 was overwritten during the assignment and effectively lost; its object will be cleaned up by the garbage collector.)

This phenomenon is often called *aliasing* and it's a fundamental way that Java works with objects. But what if you don't want aliasing to occur in this case? You could forego the assignment and say:

```
n1.i = n2.i;
```

This retains the two separate objects instead of tossing one and tying **n1** and **n2** to the same object, but you'll soon realize that manipulating the fields within objects is messy and goes against good object-oriented design principles. This is a nontrivial topic, so it is left for Appendix A, which is devoted to aliasing. In the meantime, you should keep in mind that assignment for objects can add surprises.

Aliasing during method calls

Aliasing will also occur when you pass an object into a method:

```
//: c03:PassObject.java
// Passing objects to methods may not be what
// you're used to.

class Letter {
  char c;
}

public class PassObject {
  static void f(Letter y) {
    y.c = 'z';
  }
  public static void main(String[] args) {
    Letter x = new Letter();
    x.c = 'a';
    System.out.println("1: x.c: " + x.c);
    f(x);
    System.out.println("2: x.c: " + x.c);
  }
```

```
} ///:~
```

In many programming languages, the method **f( )** would appear to be making a copy of its argument **Letter y** inside the scope of the method. But once again a reference is being passed so the line

```
y.c = 'z';
```

is actually changing the object outside of **f( )**. The output shows this:

```
1: x.c: a
2: x.c: z
```

Aliasing and its solution is a complex issue and, although you must wait until Appendix A for all the answers, you should be aware of it at this point so you can watch for pitfalls.

Mathematical operators

The basic mathematical operators are the same as the ones available in most programming languages: addition (+), subtraction (-), division (/), multiplication (*) and modulus (%, which produces the remainder from integer division). Integer division truncates, rather than rounds, the result.

Java also uses a shorthand notation to perform an operation and an assignment at the same time. This is denoted by an operator followed by an equal sign, and is consistent with all the operators in the language (whenever it makes sense). For example, to add 4 to the variable **x** and assign the result to **x**, use: **x += 4**.

This example shows the use of the mathematical operators:

```
//: c03:MathOps.java
// Demonstrates the mathematical operators.
import java.util.*;

public class MathOps {
  // Create a shorthand to save typing:
  static void prt(String s) {
    System.out.println(s);
  }
  // shorthand to print a string and an int:
```

```
  static void pInt(String s, int i) {
    prt(s + " = " + i);
  }
  // shorthand to print a string and a float:
  static void pFlt(String s, float f) {
    prt(s + " = " + f);
  }
  public static void main(String[] args) {
    // Create a random number generator,
    // seeds with current time by default:
    Random rand = new Random();
    int i, j, k;
    // '%' limits maximum value to 99:
    j = rand.nextInt() % 100;
    k = rand.nextInt() % 100;
    pInt("j",j);  pInt("k",k);
    i = j + k; pInt("j + k", i);
    i = j - k; pInt("j - k", i);
    i = k / j; pInt("k / j", i);
    i = k * j; pInt("k * j", i);
    i = k % j; pInt("k % j", i);
    j %= k; pInt("j %= k", j);
    // Floating-point number tests:
    float u,v,w;  // applies to doubles, too
    v = rand.nextFloat();
    w = rand.nextFloat();
    pFlt("v", v); pFlt("w", w);
    u = v + w; pFlt("v + w", u);
    u = v - w; pFlt("v - w", u);
    u = v * w; pFlt("v * w", u);
    u = v / w; pFlt("v / w", u);
    // the following also works for
    // char, byte, short, int, long,
    // and double:
    u += v; pFlt("u += v", u);
    u -= v; pFlt("u -= v", u);
    u *= v; pFlt("u *= v", u);
    u /= v; pFlt("u /= v", u);
  }
} ///:~
```

The first thing you will see are some shorthand methods for printing: the **prt( )** method prints a **String**, the **pInt( )** prints a **String** followed by an **int** and the **pFlt( )** prints a **String** followed by a **float**. Of course, they all ultimately end up using **System.out.println( )**.

To generate numbers, the program first creates a **Random** object. Because no arguments are passed during creation, Java uses the current time as a seed for the random number generator. The program generates a number of different types of random numbers with the **Random** object simply by calling different methods: **nextInt( )**, **nextLong( )**, **nextFloat( )** or **nextDouble( )**.

The modulus operator, when used with the result of the random number generator, limits the result to an upper bound of the operand minus one (99 in this case).

Unary minus and plus operators

The unary minus (-) and unary plus (+) are the same operators as binary minus and plus. The compiler figures out which use is intended by the way you write the expression. For instance, the statement

```
x = -a;
```

has an obvious meaning. The compiler is able to figure out:

```
x = a * -b;
```

but the reader might get confused, so it is clearer to say:

```
x = a * (-b);
```

The unary minus produces the negative of the value. Unary plus provides symmetry with unary minus, although it doesn't have any effect.

Auto increment and decrement

Java, like C, is full of shortcuts. Shortcuts can make code much easier to type, and either easier or harder to read.

Two of the nicer shortcuts are the increment and decrement operators (often referred to as the auto-increment and auto-decrement operators). The decrement operator is -- and means "decrease by one unit." The

---

increment operator is ++ and means "increase by one unit." If **a** is an **int**, for example, the expression **++a** is equivalent to (**a = a + 1**). Increment and decrement operators produce the value of the variable as a result.

There are two versions of each type of operator, often called the prefix and postfix versions. Pre-increment means the **++** operator appears before the variable or expression, and post-increment means the **++** operator appears after the variable or expression. Similarly, pre-decrement means the **--** operator appears before the variable or expression, and post-decrement means the **--** operator appears after the variable or expression. For pre-increment and pre-decrement, (i.e., **++a** or **--a**), the operation is performed and the value is produced. For post-increment and post-decrement (i.e. **a++** or **a--**), the value is produced, then the operation is performed. As an example:

```
//: c03:AutoInc.java
// Demonstrates the ++ and -- operators.

public class AutoInc {
  public static void main(String[] args) {
    int i = 1;
    prt("i : " + i);
    prt("++i : " + ++i); // Pre-increment
    prt("i++ : " + i++); // Post-increment
    prt("i : " + i);
    prt("--i : " + --i); // Pre-decrement
    prt("i-- : " + i--); // Post-decrement
    prt("i : " + i);
  }
  static void prt(String s) {
    System.out.println(s);
  }
} ///:~
```

The output for this program is:

```
i : 1
++i : 2
i++ : 2
i : 3
--i : 2
```

```
i-- : 2
i : 1
```

You can see that for the prefix form you get the value after the operation has been performed, but with the postfix form you get the value before the operation is performed. These are the only operators (other than those involving assignment) that have side effects. (That is, they change the operand rather than using just its value.)

The increment operator is one explanation for the name C++, implying "one step beyond C." In an early Java speech, Bill Joy (one of the creators), said that "Java=C++--" (C plus plus minus minus), suggesting that Java is C++ with the unnecessary hard parts removed and therefore a much simpler language. As you progress in this book you'll see that many parts are simpler, and yet Java isn't *that* much easier than C++.

Relational operators

Relational operators generate a **boolean** result. They evaluate the relationship between the values of the operands. A relational expression produces **true** if the relationship is true, and **false** if the relationship is untrue. The relational operators are less than (<), greater than (>), less than or equal to (<=), greater than or equal to (>=), equivalent (==) and not equivalent (!=). Equivalence and nonequivalence works with all built-in data types, but the other comparisons won't work with type **boolean**.

Testing object equivalence

The relational operators == and != also work with all objects, but their meaning often confuses the first-time Java programmer. Here's an example:

```
//: c03:Equivalence.java

public class Equivalence {
  public static void main(String[] args) {
    Integer n1 = new Integer(47);
    Integer n2 = new Integer(47);
    System.out.println(n1 == n2);
    System.out.println(n1 != n2);
  }
```

```
} ///:~
```

The expression **System.out.println(n1 == n2)** will print the result of the **boolean** comparison within it. Surely the output should be **true** and then **false**, since both **Integer** objects are the same. But while the *contents* of the objects are the same, the references are not the same and the operators == and != compare object references. So the output is actually **false** and then **true**. Naturally, this surprises people at first.

What if you want to compare the actual contents of an object for equivalence? You must use the special method **equals( )** that exists for all objects (not primitives, which work fine with == and !=). Here's how it's used:

```
//: c03:EqualsMethod.java

public class EqualsMethod {
  public static void main(String[] args) {
    Integer n1 = new Integer(47);
    Integer n2 = new Integer(47);
    System.out.println(n1.equals(n2));
  }
} ///:~
```

The result will be **true**, as you would expect. Ah, but it's not as simple as that. If you create your own class, like this:

```
//: c03:EqualsMethod2.java

class Value {
  int i;
}

public class EqualsMethod2 {
  public static void main(String[] args) {
    Value v1 = new Value();
    Value v2 = new Value();
    v1.i = v2.i = 100;
    System.out.println(v1.equals(v2));
  }
} ///:~
```

you're back to square one: the result is **false**. This is because the default behavior of **equals( )** is to compare references. So unless you *override* **equals( )** in your new class you won't get the desired behavior. Unfortunately, you won't learn about overriding until Chapter 7, but being aware of the way **equals( )** behaves might save you some grief in the meantime.

Most of the Java library classes implement **equals( )** so that it compares the contents of objects instead of their references.

Logical operators

The logical operators AND (&&), OR (||) and NOT (!) produce a **boolean** value of **true** or **false** based on the logical relationship of its arguments. This example uses the relational and logical operators:

```
//: c03:Bool.java
// Relational and logical operators.
import java.util.*;

public class Bool {
  public static void main(String[] args) {
    Random rand = new Random();
    int i = rand.nextInt() % 100;
    int j = rand.nextInt() % 100;
    prt("i = " + i);
    prt("j = " + j);
    prt("i > j is " + (i > j));
    prt("i < j is " + (i < j));
    prt("i >= j is " + (i >= j));
    prt("i <= j is " + (i <= j));
    prt("i == j is " + (i == j));
    prt("i != j is " + (i != j));

    // Treating an int as a boolean is
    // not legal Java
//! prt("i && j is " + (i && j));
//! prt("i || j is " + (i || j));
//! prt("!i is " + !i);

    prt("(i < 10) && (j < 10) is "
```

```
          + ((i < 10) && (j < 10)) );
    prt("(i < 10) || (j < 10) is "
          + ((i < 10) || (j < 10)) );
  }
  static void prt(String s) {
    System.out.println(s);
  }
} ///:~
```

You can apply AND, OR, or NOT to **boolean** values only. You can't use a non-**boolean** as if it were a **boolean** in a logical expression as you can in C and C++. You can see the failed attempts at doing this commented out with a //! comment marker. The subsequent expressions, however, produce **boolean** values using relational comparisons, then use logical operations on the results.

One output listing looked like this:

```
i = 85
j = 4
i > j is true
i < j is false
i >= j is true
i <= j is false
i == j is false
i != j is true
(i < 10) && (j < 10) is false
(i < 10) || (j < 10) is true
```

Note that a **boolean** value is automatically converted to an appropriate text form if it's used where a **String** is expected.

You can replace the definition for **int** in the above program with any other primitive data type except **boolean**. Be aware, however, that the comparison of floating-point numbers is very strict. A number that is the tiniest fraction different from another number is still "not equal." A number that is the tiniest bit above zero is still nonzero.

Short-circuiting

When dealing with logical operators you run into a phenomenon called "short circuiting." This means that the expression will be evaluated only

---

Thinking in Java

until the truth or falsehood of the entire expression can be unambiguously determined. As a result, all the parts of a logical expression might not be evaluated. Here's an example that demonstrates short-circuiting:

```
//: c03:ShortCircuit.java
// Demonstrates short-circuiting behavior.
// with logical operators.

public class ShortCircuit {
  static boolean test1(int val) {
    System.out.println("test1(" + val + ")");
    System.out.println("result: " + (val < 1));
    return val < 1;
  }
  static boolean test2(int val) {
    System.out.println("test2(" + val + ")");
    System.out.println("result: " + (val < 2));
    return val < 2;
  }
  static boolean test3(int val) {
    System.out.println("test3(" + val + ")");
    System.out.println("result: " + (val < 3));
    return val < 3;
  }
  public static void main(String[] args) {
    if(test1(0) && test2(2) && test3(2))
      System.out.println("expression is true");
    else
      System.out.println("expression is false");
  }
} ///:~
```

Each test performs a comparison against the argument and returns true or false. It also prints information to show you that it's being called. The tests are used in the expression:

```
if(test1(0) && test2(2) && test3(2))
```

You might naturally think that all three tests would be executed, but the output shows otherwise:

```
test1(0)
```

```
result: true
test2(2)
result: false
expression is false
```

The first test produced a **true** result, so the expression evaluation continues. However, the second test produced a **false** result. Since this means that the whole expression must be **false**, why continue evaluating the rest of the expression? It could be expensive. The reason for short-circuiting, in fact, is precisely that; you can get a potential performance increase if all the parts of a logical expression do not need to be evaluated.

Bitwise operators

The bitwise operators allow you to manipulate individual bits in an integral primitive data type. Bitwise operators perform boolean algebra on the corresponding bits in the two arguments to produce the result.

The bitwise operators come from C's low-level orientation; you were often manipulating hardware directly and had to set the bits in hardware registers. Java was originally designed to be embedded in TV set-top boxes, so this low-level orientation still made sense. However, you probably won't use the bitwise operators much.

The bitwise AND operator (**&**) produces a one in the output bit if both input bits are one; otherwise it produces a zero. The bitwise OR operator (|) produces a one in the output bit if either input bit is a one and produces a zero only if both input bits are zero. The bitwise EXCLUSIVE OR, or XOR (^), produces a one in the output bit if one or the other input bit is a one, but not both. The bitwise NOT (~, also called the *ones complement* operator) is a unary operator; it takes only one argument. (All other bitwise operators are binary operators.) Bitwise NOT produces the opposite of the input bit—a one if the input bit is zero, a zero if the input bit is one.

The bitwise operators and logical operators use the same characters, so it is helpful to have a mnemonic device to help you remember the meanings: since bits are "small," there is only one character in the bitwise operators.

Bitwise operators can be combined with the = sign to unite the operation and assignment: **&=**, |= and ^= are all legitimate. (Since ~ is a unary operator it cannot be combined with the = sign.)

The **boolean** type is treated as a one-bit value so it is somewhat different. You can perform a bitwise AND, OR and XOR, but you can't perform a bitwise NOT (presumably to prevent confusion with the logical NOT). For **boolean**s the bitwise operators have the same effect as the logical operators except that they do not short circuit. Also, bitwise operations on **boolean**s include an XOR logical operator that is not included under the list of "logical" operators. You're prevented from using **boolean**s in shift expressions, which is described next.

Shift operators

The shift operators also manipulate bits. They can be used solely with primitive, integral types. The left-shift operator (<<) produces the operand to the left of the operator shifted to the left by the number of bits specified after the operator (inserting zeroes at the lower-order bits). The signed right-shift operator (>>) produces the operand to the left of the operator shifted to the right by the number of bits specified after the operator. The signed right shift >> uses *sign extension*: if the value is positive, zeroes are inserted at the higher-order bits; if the value is negative, ones are inserted at the higher-order bits. Java has also added the unsigned right shift >>>, which uses *zero extension*: regardless of the sign, zeroes are inserted at the higher-order bits. This operator does not exist in C or C++.

If you shift a **char**, **byte,** or **short**, it will be promoted to **int** before the shift takes place, and the result will be an **int**. Only the five low-order bits of the right-hand side will be used. This prevents you from shifting more than the number of bits in an **int**. If you're operating on a **long**, you'll get a **long** result. Only the six low-order bits of the right-hand side will be used so you can't shift more than the number of bits in a **long**.

Shifts can be combined with the equal sign (<<= or >>= or >>>=). The lvalue is replaced by the lvalue shifted by the rvalue. There is a problem, however, with the unsigned right shift combined with assignment. If you use it with **byte** or **short** you don't get the correct results. Instead, these are promoted to **int** and right shifted, but then truncated as they are assigned back into their variables, so you get **-1** in those cases. The following example demonstrates this:

```
//: c03:URShift.java
// Test of unsigned right shift.

public class URShift {
  public static void main(String[] args) {
    int i = -1;
    i >>>= 10;
    System.out.println(i);
    long l = -1;
    l >>>= 10;
    System.out.println(l);
    short s = -1;
    s >>>= 10;
    System.out.println(s);
    byte b = -1;
    b >>>= 10;
    System.out.println(b);
    b = -1;
    System.out.println(b>>>10);
  }
} ///:~
```

In the last line, the resulting value is not assigned back into **b**, but is printed directly and so the correct behavior occurs.

Here's an example that demonstrates the use of all the operators involving bits:

```
//: c03:BitManipulation.java
// Using the bitwise operators.
import java.util.*;

public class BitManipulation {
  public static void main(String[] args) {
    Random rand = new Random();
    int i = rand.nextInt();
    int j = rand.nextInt();
    pBinInt("-1", -1);
    pBinInt("+1", +1);
```

```
    int maxpos = 2147483647;
    pBinInt("maxpos", maxpos);
    int maxneg = -2147483648;
    pBinInt("maxneg", maxneg);
    pBinInt("i", i);
    pBinInt("~i", ~i);
    pBinInt("-i", -i);
    pBinInt("j", j);
    pBinInt("i & j", i & j);
    pBinInt("i | j", i | j);
    pBinInt("i ^ j", i ^ j);
    pBinInt("i << 5", i << 5);
    pBinInt("i >> 5", i >> 5);
    pBinInt("(~i) >> 5", (~i) >> 5);
    pBinInt("i >>> 5", i >>> 5);
    pBinInt("(~i) >>> 5", (~i) >>> 5);

    long l = rand.nextLong();
    long m = rand.nextLong();
    pBinLong("-1L", -1L);
    pBinLong("+1L", +1L);
    long ll = 9223372036854775807L;
    pBinLong("maxpos", ll);
    long lln = -9223372036854775808L;
    pBinLong("maxneg", lln);
    pBinLong("l", l);
    pBinLong("~l", ~l);
    pBinLong("-l", -l);
    pBinLong("m", m);
    pBinLong("l & m", l & m);
    pBinLong("l | m", l | m);
    pBinLong("l ^ m", l ^ m);
    pBinLong("l << 5", l << 5);
    pBinLong("l >> 5", l >> 5);
    pBinLong("(~l) >> 5", (~l) >> 5);
    pBinLong("l >>> 5", l >>> 5);
    pBinLong("(~l) >>> 5", (~l) >>> 5);
  }
  static void pBinInt(String s, int i) {
    System.out.println(
      s + ", int: " + i + ", binary: ");
```

```
        System.out.print("   ");
        for(int j = 31; j >=0; j--)
          if(((1 << j) &  i) != 0)
            System.out.print("1");
          else
            System.out.print("0");
        System.out.println();
    }
    static void pBinLong(String s, long l) {
      System.out.println(
        s + ", long: " + l + ", binary: ");
      System.out.print("   ");
      for(int i = 63; i >=0; i--)
        if(((1L << i) & l) != 0)
          System.out.print("1");
        else
          System.out.print("0");
      System.out.println();
    }
} ///:~
```

The two methods at the end, **pBinInt( )** and **pBinLong( )** take an **int** or a **long**, respectively, and print it out in binary format along with a descriptive string. You can ignore the implementation of these for now.

You'll note the use of **System.out.print( )** instead of **System.out.println( )**. The **print( )** method does not emit a new line, so it allows you to output a line in pieces.

As well as demonstrating the effect of all the bitwise operators for **int** and **long**, this example also shows the minimum, maximum, +1 and -1 values for **int** and **long** so you can see what they look like. Note that the high bit represents the sign: 0 means positive and 1 means negative. The output for the **int** portion looks like this:

```
-1, int: -1, binary:
    11111111111111111111111111111111
+1, int: 1, binary:
    00000000000000000000000000000001
maxpos, int: 2147483647, binary:
    01111111111111111111111111111111
```

```
maxneg, int: -2147483648, binary:
    10000000000000000000000000000000
i, int: 59081716, binary:
    00000011100001011000001111110100
~i, int: -59081717, binary:
    11111100011110100111110000001011
-i, int: -59081716, binary:
    11111100011110100111110000001100
j, int: 198850956, binary:
    00001011110110100011100110001100
i & j, int: 58720644, binary:
    00000011100000000000000110000100
i | j, int: 199212028, binary:
    00001011110111111011101111111100
i ^ j, int: 140491384, binary:
    00001000010111111011101001111000
i << 5, int: 1890614912, binary:
    01110000101100000111111010000000
i >> 5, int: 1846303, binary:
    00000000000111000010110000011111
(~i) >> 5, int: -1846304, binary:
    11111111111000111101001111100000
i >>> 5, int: 1846303, binary:
    00000000000111000010110000011111
(~i) >>> 5, int: 132371424, binary:
    00000111111000111101001111100000
```

The binary representation of the numbers is referred to as *signed two's complement*.

Ternary if-else operator

This operator is unusual because it has three operands. It is truly an operator because it produces a value, unlike the ordinary if-else statement that you'll see in the next section of this chapter. The expression is of the form:

```
boolean-exp ? value0 : value1
```

If *boolean-exp* evaluates to **true**, *value0* is evaluated and its result becomes the value produced by the operator. If *boolean-exp* is **false**,

---

value1 is evaluated and its result becomes the value produced by the operator.

Of course, you could use an ordinary **if-else** statement (described later), but the ternary operator is much terser. Although C (where this operator originated) prides itself on being a terse language, and the ternary operator might have been introduced partly for efficiency, you should be somewhat wary of using it on an everyday basis—it's easy to produce unreadable code.

The conditional operator can be used for its side effects or for the value it produces, but in general you want the value since that's what makes the operator distinct from the **if-else**. Here's an example:

```
static int ternary(int i) {
   return i < 10 ? i * 100 : i * 10;
}
```

You can see that this code is more compact than what you'd need to write without the ternary operator:

```
static int alternative(int i) {
   if (i < 10)
      return i * 100;
   else
      return i * 10;
}
```

The second form is easier to understand, and doesn't require a lot more typing. So be sure to ponder your reasons when choosing the ternary operator.

The comma operator

The comma is used in C and C++ not only as a separator in function argument lists, but also as an operator for sequential evaluation. The sole place that the comma *operator* is used in Java is in **for** loops, which will be described later in this chapter.

String operator +

There's one special usage of an operator in Java: the + operator can be used to concatenate strings, as you've already seen. It seems a natural use of the + even though it doesn't fit with the traditional way that + is used. This capability seemed like a good idea in C++, so *operator overloading* was added to C++ to allow the C++ programmer to add meanings to almost any operator. Unfortunately, operator overloading combined with some of the other restrictions in C++ turns out to be a fairly complicated feature for programmers to design into their classes. Although operator overloading would have been much simpler to implement in Java than it was in C++, this feature was still considered too complex, so Java programmers cannot implement their own overloaded operators as C++ programmers can.

The use of the **String** + has some interesting behavior. If an expression begins with a **String**, then all operands that follow must be **String**s (remember that the compiler will turn a quoted sequence of characters into a **String**):

```java
int x = 0, y = 1, z = 2;
String sString = "x, y, z ";
System.out.println(sString + x + y + z);
```

Here, the Java compiler will convert **x**, **y**, and **z** into their **String** representations instead of adding them together first. And if you say:

```java
System.out.println(x + sString);
```

Java will turn **x** into a **String**.

Common pitfalls when using operators

One of the pitfalls when using operators is trying to get away without parentheses when you are even the least bit uncertain about how an expression will evaluate. This is still true in Java.

An extremely common error in C and C++ looks like this:

```java
while(x = y) {
```

```
        // ....
}
```

The programmer was trying to test for equivalence (==) rather than do an assignment. In C and C++ the result of this assignment will always be **true** if **y** is nonzero, and you'll probably get an infinite loop. In Java, the result of this expression is not a **boolean,** and the compiler expects a **boolean** and won't convert from an **int**, so it will conveniently give you a compile-time error and catch the problem before you ever try to run the program. So the pitfall never happens in Java. (The only time you won't get a compile-time error is when **x** and **y** are **boolean**, in which case **x = y** is a legal expression, and in the above case, probably an error.)

A similar problem in C and C++ is using bitwise AND and OR instead of the logical versions. Bitwise AND and OR use one of the characters (**&** or **|**) while logical AND and OR use two (**&&** and **||**). Just as with = and ==, it's easy to type just one character instead of two. In Java, the compiler again prevents this because it won't let you cavalierly use one type where it doesn't belong.

Casting operators

The word *cast* is used in the sense of "casting into a mold." Java will automatically change one type of data into another when appropriate. For instance, if you assign an integral value to a floating-point variable, the compiler will automatically convert the **int** to a **float**. Casting allows you to make this type conversion explicit, or to force it when it wouldn't normally happen.

To perform a cast, put the desired data type (including all modifiers) inside parentheses to the left of any value. Here's an example:

```
void casts() {
  int i = 200;
  long l = (long)i;
  long l2 = (long)200;
}
```

As you can see, it's possible to perform a cast on a numeric value as well as on a variable. In both casts shown here, however, the cast is superfluous, since the compiler will automatically promote an **int** value to a **long** when necessary. However, you are allowed to use superfluous casts in to make a point or to make your code more clear. In other situations, a cast may be essential just to get the code to compile.

In C and C++, casting can cause some headaches. In Java, casting is safe, with the exception that when you perform a so-called *narrowing conversion* (that is, when you go from a data type that can hold more information to one that doesn't hold as much) you run the risk of losing information. Here the compiler forces you to do a cast, in effect saying "this can be a dangerous thing to do—if you want me to do it anyway you must make the cast explicit." With a *widening conversion* an explicit cast is not needed because the new type will more than hold the information from the old type so that no information is ever lost.

Java allows you to cast any primitive type to any other primitive type, except for **boolean,** which doesn't allow any casting at all. Class types do not allow casting. To convert one to the other there must be special methods. (**String** is a special case, and you'll find out later in this book that objects can be cast within a *family* of types; an **Oak** can be cast to a **Tree** and vice-versa, but not to a foreign type such as a **Rock**.)

Literals

Ordinarily when you insert a literal value into a program the compiler knows exactly what type to make it. Sometimes, however, the type is ambiguous. When this happens you must guide the compiler by adding some extra information in the form of characters associated with the literal value. The following code shows these characters:

```
//: c03:Literals.java

class Literals {
  char c = 0xffff; // max char hex value
  byte b = 0x7f; // max byte hex value
  short s = 0x7fff; // max short hex value
  int i1 = 0x2f; // Hexadecimal (lowercase)
  int i2 = 0X2F; // Hexadecimal (uppercase)
  int i3 = 0177; // Octal (leading zero)
  // Hex and Oct also work with long.
  long n1 = 200L; // long suffix
  long n2 = 200l; // long suffix
```

```
  long n3 = 200;
//! long 16(200); // not allowed
  float f1 = 1;
  float f2 = 1F; // float suffix
  float f3 = 1f; // float suffix
  float f4 = 1e-45f; // 10 to the power
  float f5 = 1e+9f; // float suffix
  double d1 = 1d; // double suffix
  double d2 = 1D; // double suffix
  double d3 = 47e47d; // 10 to the power
} ///:~
```

Hexadecimal (base 16), which works with all the integral data types, is denoted by a leading **0x** or **0X** followed by 0—9 and a—f either in upper or lowercase. If you try to initialize a variable with a value bigger than it can hold (regardless of the numerical form of the value), the compiler will give you an error message. Notice in the above code the maximum possible hexadecimal values for **char**, **byte,** and **short**. If you exceed these, the compiler will automatically make the value an **int** and tell you that you need a narrowing cast for the assignment. You'll know you've stepped over the line.

Octal (base 8) is denoted by a leading zero in the number and digits from 0-7. There is no literal representation for binary numbers in C, C++ or Java.

A trailing character after a literal value establishes its type. Upper or lowercase **L** means **long**, upper or lowercase **F** means **float** and upper or lowercase **D** means **double**.

Exponents use a notation that I've always found rather dismaying: **1.39 e-47f**. In science and engineering, 'e' refers to the base of natural logarithms, approximately 2.718. (A more precise **double** value is available in Java as **Math.E**.) This is used in exponentiation expressions such as $1.39 \times e^{-47}$, which means 1.39×2.718^{-47}. However, when FORTRAN was invented they decided that **e** would naturally mean "ten to the power," which is an odd decision because FORTRAN was designed for science and engineering and one would think its designers would be sensitive about introducing such an ambiguity.[1] At any rate, this custom was followed in C, C++ and now Java. So if you're used to thinking in terms of **e** as the base of natural logarithms, you must do a mental translation when you see an expression such as **1.39 e-47f** in Java; it means 1.39×10^{-47}.

Note that you don't need to use the trailing character when the compiler can figure out the appropriate type. With

```
long n3 = 200;
```

there's no ambiguity, so an **L** after the 200 would be superfluous. However, with

```
float f4 = 1e-47f; // 10 to the power
```

the compiler normally takes exponential numbers as doubles, so without the trailing **f** it will give you an error telling you that you must use a cast to convert **double** to **float**.

Promotion

You'll discover that if you perform any mathematical or bitwise operations on primitive data types that are smaller than an **int** (that is, **char**, **byte**, or **short**), those values will be promoted to **int** before performing the operations, and the resulting value will be of type **int**. So if you want to assign back into the smaller type, you must use a cast. (And, since you're assigning back into a smaller type, you might be losing information.) In general, the largest data type in an expression is the one that determines

---

[1] John Kirkham writes, "I started computing in 1962 using FORTRAN II on an IBM 1620. At that time, and throughout the 1960s and into the 1970s, FORTRAN was an all uppercase language. This probably started because many of the early input devices were old teletype units that used 5 bit Baudot code, which had no lowercase capability. The 'E' in the exponential notation was also always upper case and was never confused with the natural logarithm base 'e', which is always lowercase. The 'E' simply stood for exponential, which was for the base of the number system used—usually 10. At the time octal was also widely used by programmers. Although I never saw it used, if I had seen an octal number in exponential notation I would have considered it to be base 8. The first time I remember seeing an exponential using a lowercase 'e' was in the late 1970s and I also found it confusing. The problem arose as lowercase crept into FORTRAN, not at its beginning. We actually had functions to use if you really wanted to use the natural logarithm base, but they were all uppercase."

the size of the result of that expression; if you multiply a **float** and a **double**, the result will be **double**; if you add an **int** and a **long**, the result will be **long**.

Java has no "sizeof"

In C and C++, the **sizeof( )** operator satisfies a specific need: it tells you the number of bytes allocated for data items. The most compelling need for **sizeof( )** in C and C++ is portability. Different data types might be different sizes on different machines, so the programmer must find out how big those types are when performing operations that are sensitive to size. For example, one computer might store integers in 32 bits, whereas another might store integers as 16 bits. Programs could store larger values in integers on the first machine. As you might imagine, portability is a huge headache for C and C++ programmers.

Java does not need a **sizeof( )** operator for this purpose because all the data types are the same size on all machines. You do not need to think about portability on this level—it is designed into the language.

Precedence revisited

Upon hearing me complain about the complexity of remembering operator precedence during one of my seminars, a student suggested a mnemonic that is simultaneously a commentary: "Ulcer Addicts Really Like C A lot."

Mnemonic	Operator type	Operators
Ulcer	Unary	+ - ++ --
Addicts	Arithmetic (and shift)	* / % + - << >>
Really	Relational	> < >= <= == !=
Like	Logical (and bitwise)	&& || & | ^
C	Conditional (ternary)	A > B ? X : Y
A Lot	Assignment	= (and compound assignment like *=)

Of course, with the shift and bitwise operators distributed around the table it is not a perfect mnemonic, but for non-bit operations it works.

A compendium of operators

The following example shows which primitive data types can be used with particular operators. Basically, it is the same example repeated over and over, but using different primitive data types. The file will compile without error because the lines that would cause errors are commented out with a //!.

```
//: c03:AllOps.java
// Tests all the operators on all the
// primitive data types to show which
// ones are accepted by the Java compiler.

class AllOps {
  // To accept the results of a boolean test:
  void f(boolean b) {}
  void boolTest(boolean x, boolean y) {
    // Arithmetic operators:
    //! x = x * y;
    //! x = x / y;
    //! x = x % y;
    //! x = x + y;
    //! x = x - y;
    //! x++;
    //! x--;
    //! x = +y;
    //! x = -y;
    // Relational and logical:
    //! f(x > y);
    //! f(x >= y);
    //! f(x < y);
    //! f(x <= y);
    f(x == y);
    f(x != y);
    f(!y);
    x = x && y;
    x = x || y;
    // Bitwise operators:
    //! x = ~y;
    x = x & y;
    x = x | y;
```

```
      x = x ^ y;
      //! x = x << 1;
      //! x = x >> 1;
      //! x = x >>> 1;
      // Compound assignment:
      //! x += y;
      //! x -= y;
      //! x *= y;
      //! x /= y;
      //! x %= y;
      //! x <<= 1;
      //! x >>= 1;
      //! x >>>= 1;
      x &= y;
      x ^= y;
      x |= y;
      // Casting:
      //! char c = (char)x;
      //! byte B = (byte)x;
      //! short s = (short)x;
      //! int i = (int)x;
      //! long l = (long)x;
      //! float f = (float)x;
      //! double d = (double)x;
    }
    void charTest(char x, char y) {
      // Arithmetic operators:
      x = (char)(x * y);
      x = (char)(x / y);
      x = (char)(x % y);
      x = (char)(x + y);
      x = (char)(x - y);
      x++;
      x--;
      x = (char)+y;
      x = (char)-y;
      // Relational and logical:
      f(x > y);
      f(x >= y);
      f(x < y);
      f(x <= y);
```

```java
    f(x == y);
    f(x != y);
    //! f(!x);
    //! f(x && y);
    //! f(x || y);
    // Bitwise operators:
    x= (char)~y;
    x = (char)(x & y);
    x  = (char)(x | y);
    x = (char)(x ^ y);
    x = (char)(x << 1);
    x = (char)(x >> 1);
    x = (char)(x >>> 1);
    // Compound assignment:
    x += y;
    x -= y;
    x *= y;
    x /= y;
    x %= y;
    x <<= 1;
    x >>= 1;
    x >>>= 1;
    x &= y;
    x ^= y;
    x |= y;
    // Casting:
    //! boolean b = (boolean)x;
    byte B = (byte)x;
    short s = (short)x;
    int i = (int)x;
    long l = (long)x;
    float f = (float)x;
    double d = (double)x;
  }
  void byteTest(byte x, byte y) {
    // Arithmetic operators:
    x = (byte)(x* y);
    x = (byte)(x / y);
    x = (byte)(x % y);
    x = (byte)(x + y);
    x = (byte)(x - y);
```

```
x++;
x--;
x = (byte)+ y;
x = (byte)- y;
// Relational and logical:
f(x > y);
f(x >= y);
f(x < y);
f(x <= y);
f(x == y);
f(x != y);
//! f(!x);
//! f(x && y);
//! f(x || y);
// Bitwise operators:
x = (byte)~y;
x = (byte)(x & y);
x = (byte)(x | y);
x = (byte)(x ^ y);
x = (byte)(x << 1);
x = (byte)(x >> 1);
x = (byte)(x >>> 1);
// Compound assignment:
x += y;
x -= y;
x *= y;
x /= y;
x %= y;
x <<= 1;
x >>= 1;
x >>>= 1;
x &= y;
x ^= y;
x |= y;
// Casting:
//! boolean b = (boolean)x;
char c = (char)x;
short s = (short)x;
int i = (int)x;
long l = (long)x;
float f = (float)x;
```

```
    double d = (double)x;
  }
  void shortTest(short x, short y) {
    // Arithmetic operators:
    x = (short)(x * y);
    x = (short)(x / y);
    x = (short)(x % y);
    x = (short)(x + y);
    x = (short)(x - y);
    x++;
    x--;
    x = (short)+y;
    x = (short)-y;
    // Relational and logical:
    f(x > y);
    f(x >= y);
    f(x < y);
    f(x <= y);
    f(x == y);
    f(x != y);
    //! f(!x);
    //! f(x && y);
    //! f(x || y);
    // Bitwise operators:
    x = (short)~y;
    x = (short)(x & y);
    x = (short)(x | y);
    x = (short)(x ^ y);
    x = (short)(x << 1);
    x = (short)(x >> 1);
    x = (short)(x >>> 1);
    // Compound assignment:
    x += y;
    x -= y;
    x *= y;
    x /= y;
    x %= y;
    x <<= 1;
    x >>= 1;
    x >>>= 1;
    x &= y;
```

```
    x ^= y;
    x |= y;
    // Casting:
    //! boolean b = (boolean)x;
    char c = (char)x;
    byte B = (byte)x;
    int i = (int)x;
    long l = (long)x;
    float f = (float)x;
    double d = (double)x;
  }
  void intTest(int x, int y) {
    // Arithmetic operators:
    x = x * y;
    x = x / y;
    x = x % y;
    x = x + y;
    x = x - y;
    x++;
    x--;
    x = +y;
    x = -y;
    // Relational and logical:
    f(x > y);
    f(x >= y);
    f(x < y);
    f(x <= y);
    f(x == y);
    f(x != y);
    //! f(!x);
    //! f(x && y);
    //! f(x || y);
    // Bitwise operators:
    x = ~y;
    x = x & y;
    x = x | y;
    x = x ^ y;
    x = x << 1;
    x = x >> 1;
    x = x >>> 1;
    // Compound assignment:
```

```
        x += y;
        x -= y;
        x *= y;
        x /= y;
        x %= y;
        x <<= 1;
        x >>= 1;
        x >>>= 1;
        x &= y;
        x ^= y;
        x |= y;
        // Casting:
        //! boolean b = (boolean)x;
        char c = (char)x;
        byte B = (byte)x;
        short s = (short)x;
        long l = (long)x;
        float f = (float)x;
        double d = (double)x;
    }
    void longTest(long x, long y) {
        // Arithmetic operators:
        x = x * y;
        x = x / y;
        x = x % y;
        x = x + y;
        x = x - y;
        x++;
        x--;
        x = +y;
        x = -y;
        // Relational and logical:
        f(x > y);
        f(x >= y);
        f(x < y);
        f(x <= y);
        f(x == y);
        f(x != y);
        //! f(!x);
        //! f(x && y);
        //! f(x || y);
```

```java
    // Bitwise operators:
    x = ~y;
    x = x & y;
    x = x | y;
    x = x ^ y;
    x = x << 1;
    x = x >> 1;
    x = x >>> 1;
    // Compound assignment:
    x += y;
    x -= y;
    x *= y;
    x /= y;
    x %= y;
    x <<= 1;
    x >>= 1;
    x >>>= 1;
    x &= y;
    x ^= y;
    x |= y;
    // Casting:
    //! boolean b = (boolean)x;
    char c = (char)x;
    byte B = (byte)x;
    short s = (short)x;
    int i = (int)x;
    float f = (float)x;
    double d = (double)x;
  }
  void floatTest(float x, float y) {
    // Arithmetic operators:
    x = x * y;
    x = x / y;
    x = x % y;
    x = x + y;
    x = x - y;
    x++;
    x--;
    x = +y;
    x = -y;
    // Relational and logical:
```

```
      f(x > y);
      f(x >= y);
      f(x < y);
      f(x <= y);
      f(x == y);
      f(x != y);
      //! f(!x);
      //! f(x && y);
      //! f(x || y);
      // Bitwise operators:
      //! x = ~y;
      //! x = x & y;
      //! x = x | y;
      //! x = x ^ y;
      //! x = x << 1;
      //! x = x >> 1;
      //! x = x >>> 1;
      // Compound assignment:
      x += y;
      x -= y;
      x *= y;
      x /= y;
      x %= y;
      //! x <<= 1;
      //! x >>= 1;
      //! x >>>= 1;
      //! x &= y;
      //! x ^= y;
      //! x |= y;
      // Casting:
      //! boolean b = (boolean)x;
      char c = (char)x;
      byte B = (byte)x;
      short s = (short)x;
      int i = (int)x;
      long l = (long)x;
      double d = (double)x;
    }
    void doubleTest(double x, double y) {
      // Arithmetic operators:
      x = x * y;
```

```
x = x / y;
x = x % y;
x = x + y;
x = x - y;
x++;
x--;
x = +y;
x = -y;
// Relational and logical:
f(x > y);
f(x >= y);
f(x < y);
f(x <= y);
f(x == y);
f(x != y);
//! f(!x);
//! f(x && y);
//! f(x || y);
// Bitwise operators:
//! x = ~y;
//! x = x & y;
//! x = x | y;
//! x = x ^ y;
//! x = x << 1;
//! x = x >> 1;
//! x = x >>> 1;
// Compound assignment:
x += y;
x -= y;
x *= y;
x /= y;
x %= y;
//! x <<= 1;
//! x >>= 1;
//! x >>>= 1;
//! x &= y;
//! x ^= y;
//! x |= y;
// Casting:
//! boolean b = (boolean)x;
char c = (char)x;
```

```
    byte B = (byte)x;
    short s = (short)x;
    int i = (int)x;
    long l = (long)x;
    float f = (float)x;
  }
} ///:~
```

Note that **boolean** is quite limited. You can assign to it the values **true** and **false**, and you can test it for truth or falsehood, but you cannot add booleans or perform any other type of operation on them.

In **char**, **byte**, and **short** you can see the effect of promotion with the arithmetic operators. Each arithmetic operation on any of those types results in an **int** result, which must be explicitly cast back to the original type (a narrowing conversion that might lose information) to assign back to that type. With **int** values, however, you do not need to cast, because everything is already an **int**. Don't be lulled into thinking everything is safe, though. If you multiply two **int**s that are big enough, you'll overflow the result. The following example demonstrates this:

```
//: c03:Overflow.java
// Surprise! Java lets you overflow.

public class Overflow {
  public static void main(String[] args) {
    int big = 0x7fffffff; // max int value
    prt("big = " + big);
    int bigger = big * 4;
    prt("bigger = " + bigger);
  }
  static void prt(String s) {
    System.out.println(s);
  }
} ///:~
```

The output of this is:

```
big = 2147483647
bigger = -4
```

and you get no errors or warnings from the compiler, and no exceptions at run-time. Java is good, but it's not *that* good.

Compound assignments do *not* require casts for **char**, **byte,** or **short**, even though they are performing promotions that have the same results as the direct arithmetic operations. On the other hand, the lack of the cast certainly simplifies the code.

You can see that, with the exception of **boolean**, any primitive type can be cast to any other primitive type. Again, you must be aware of the effect of a narrowing conversion when casting to a smaller type, otherwise you might unknowingly lose information during the cast.

Execution control

Java uses all of C's execution control statements, so if you've programmed with C or C++ then most of what you see will be familiar. Most procedural programming languages have some kind of control statements, and there is often overlap among languages. In Java, the keywords include **if-else**, **while**, **do-while**, **for**, and a selection statement called **switch**. Java does not, however, support the much-maligned **goto** (which can still be the most expedient way to solve certain types of problems). You can still do a goto-like jump, but it is much more constrained than a typical **goto**.

true and false

All conditional statements use the truth or falsehood of a conditional expression to determine the execution path. An example of a conditional expression is **A == B**. This uses the conditional operator == to see if the value of **A** is equivalent to the value of **B**. The expression returns **true** or **false**. Any of the relational operators you've seen earlier in this chapter can be used to produce a conditional statement. Note that Java doesn't allow you to use a number as a **boolean**, even though it's allowed in C and C++ (where truth is nonzero and falsehood is zero). If you want to use a non-**boolean** in a **boolean** test, such as **if(a)**, you must first convert it to a **boolean** value using a conditional expression, such as **if(a != 0)**.

if-else

The **if-else** statement is probably the most basic way to control program flow. The **else** is optional, so you can use **if** in two forms:

```
if(Boolean-expression)
  statement
```

or

```
if(Boolean-expression)
  statement
else
  statement
```

The conditional must produce a **boolean** result. The *statement* means either a simple statement terminated by a semicolon or a compound statement, which is a group of simple statements enclosed in braces. Any time the word "*statement*" is used, it always implies that the statement can be simple or compound.

As an example of **if-else**, here is a **test( )** method that will tell you whether a guess is above, below, or equivalent to a target number:

```
//: c03:IfElse.java
public class IfElse {
  static int test(int testval, int target) {
    int result = 0;
    if(testval > target)
      result = +1;
    else if(testval < target)
      result = -1;
    else
      result = 0; // Match
    return result;
  }
  public static void main(String[] args) {
    System.out.println(test(10, 5));
    System.out.println(test(5, 10));
    System.out.println(test(5, 5));
  }
} ///:~
```

It is conventional to indent the body of a control flow statement so the reader might easily determine where it begins and ends.

return

The **return** keyword has two purposes: it specifies what value a method will return (if it doesn't have a **void** return value) and it causes that value to be returned immediately. The **test( )** method above can be rewritten to take advantage of this:

```
//: c03:IfElse2.java
public class IfElse2 {
  static int test(int testval, int target) {
    int result = 0;
    if(testval > target)
      return +1;
    else if(testval < target)
      return -1;
    else
      return 0; // Match
  }
  public static void main(String[] args) {
    System.out.println(test(10, 5));
    System.out.println(test(5, 10));
    System.out.println(test(5, 5));
  }
} ///:~
```

There's no need for **else** because the method will not continue after executing a **return**.

Iteration

while, **do-while** and **for** control looping and are sometimes classified as *iteration statements*. A *statement* repeats until the controlling *Boolean-expression* evaluates to false. The form for a **while** loop is

```
while(Boolean-expression)
  statement
```

The *Boolean-expression* is evaluated once at the beginning of the loop and again before each further iteration of the *statement*.

Here's a simple example that generates random numbers until a particular condition is met:

```
//: c03:WhileTest.java
// Demonstrates the while loop.

public class WhileTest {
  public static void main(String[] args) {
    double r = 0;
    while(r < 0.99d) {
      r = Math.random();
      System.out.println(r);
    }
  }
} ///:~
```

This uses the **static** method **random( )** in the **Math** library, which generates a **double** value between 0 and 1. (It includes 0, but not 1.) The conditional expression for the **while** says "keep doing this loop until the number is 0.99 or greater." Each time you run this program you'll get a different-sized list of numbers.

do-while

The form for **do-while** is

```
do
   statement
while(Boolean-expression);
```

The sole difference between **while** and **do-while** is that the statement of the **do-while** always executes at least once, even if the expression evaluates to false the first time. In a **while**, if the conditional is false the first time the statement never executes. In practice, **do-while** is less common than **while**.

for

A **for** loop performs initialization before the first iteration. Then it performs conditional testing and, at the end of each iteration, some form of "stepping." The form of the **for** loop is:

```
for(initialization; Boolean-expression; step)
    statement
```

Any of the expressions *initialization, Boolean-expression* or *step* can be empty. The expression is tested before each iteration, and as soon as it evaluates to **false** execution will continue at the line following the **for** statement. At the end of each loop, the *step* executes.

for loops are usually used for "counting" tasks:

```
//: c03:ListCharacters.java
// Demonstrates "for" loop by listing
// all the ASCII characters.

public class ListCharacters {
  public static void main(String[] args) {
  for( char c = 0; c < 128; c++)
    if (c != 26 )   // ANSI Clear screen
      System.out.println(
        "value: " + (int)c +
        " character: " + c);

  }
} ///:~
```

Note that the variable **c** is defined at the point where it is used, inside the control expression of the **for** loop, rather than at the beginning of the block denoted by the open curly brace. The scope of **c** is the expression controlled by the **for**.

Traditional procedural languages like C require that all variables be defined at the beginning of a block so when the compiler creates a block it can allocate space for those variables. In Java and C++ you can spread your variable declarations throughout the block, defining them at the point that you need them. This allows a more natural coding style and makes code easier to understand.

You can define multiple variables within a **for** statement, but they must be of the same type:

```
for(int i = 0, j = 1;
    i < 10 && j != 11;
    i++, j++)
```

```
  /* body of for loop */;
```

The **int** definition in the **for** statement covers both **i** and **j**. The ability to define variables in the control expression is limited to the **for** loop. You cannot use this approach with any of the other selection or iteration statements.

The comma operator

Earlier in this chapter I stated that the comma *operator* (not the comma *separator*, which is used to separate definitions and function arguments) has only one use in Java: in the control expression of a **for** loop. In both the initialization and step portions of the control expression you can have a number of statements separated by commas, and those statements will be evaluated sequentially. The previous bit of code uses this ability. Here's another example:

```
//: c03:CommaOperator.java
public class CommaOperator {
  public static void main(String[] args) {
    for(int i = 1, j = i + 10; i < 5;
        i++, j = i * 2) {
      System.out.println("i= " + i + " j= " + j);
    }
  }
} ///:~
```

Here's the output:

```
i= 1 j= 11
i= 2 j= 4
i= 3 j= 6
i= 4 j= 8
```

You can see that in both the initialization and step portions the statements are evaluated in sequential order. Also, the initialization portion can have any number of definitions *of one type*.

break and continue

Inside the body of any of the iteration statements you can also control the flow of the loop by using **break** and **continue**. **break** quits the loop without executing the rest of the statements in the loop. **continue** stops the execution of the current iteration and goes back to the beginning of the loop to begin the next iteration.

This program shows examples of **break** and **continue** within **for** and **while** loops:

```
//: c03:BreakAndContinue.java
// Demonstrates break and continue keywords.

public class BreakAndContinue {
  public static void main(String[] args) {
    for(int i = 0; i < 100; i++) {
      if(i == 74) break; // Out of for loop
      if(i % 9 != 0) continue; // Next iteration
      System.out.println(i);
    }
    int i = 0;
    // An "infinite loop":
    while(true) {
      i++;
      int j = i * 27;
      if(j == 1269) break; // Out of loop
      if(i % 10 != 0) continue; // Top of loop
      System.out.println(i);
    }
  }
} ///:~
```

In the **for** loop the value of **i** never gets to 100 because the **break** statement breaks out of the loop when **i** is 74. Normally, you'd use a **break** like this only if you didn't know when the terminating condition was going to occur. The **continue** statement causes execution to go back to the top of the iteration loop (thus incrementing **i**) whenever **i** is not evenly divisible by 9. When it is, the value is printed.

The second portion shows an "infinite loop" that would, in theory, continue forever. However, inside the loop there is a **break** statement that will break out of the loop. In addition, you'll see that the **continue** moves back to the top of the loop without completing the remainder.

(Thus printing happens in the second loop only when the value of **i** is divisible by 10.) The output is:

```
0
9
18
27
36
45
54
63
72
10
20
30
40
```

The value 0 is printed because 0 % 9 produces 0.

A second form of the infinite loop is **for(;;)**. The compiler treats both **while(true)** and **for(;;)** in the same way so whichever one you use is a matter of programming taste.

The infamous "goto"

The **goto** keyword has been present in programming languages from the beginning. Indeed, **goto** was the genesis of program control in assembly language: "if condition A, then jump here, otherwise jump there." If you read the assembly code that is ultimately generated by virtually any compiler, you'll see that program control contains many jumps. However, a **goto** is a jump at the source-code level, and that's what brought it into disrepute. If a program will always jump from one point to another, isn't there some way to reorganize the code so the flow of control is not so jumpy? **goto** fell into true disfavor with the publication of the famous "Goto considered harmful" paper by Edsger Dijkstra, and since then goto-bashing has been a popular sport, with advocates of the cast-out keyword scurrying for cover.

As is typical in situations like this, the middle ground is the most fruitful. The problem is not the use of **goto**, but the overuse of **goto**—in rare situations **goto** is actually the best way to structure control flow.

Although **goto** is a reserved word in Java, it is not used in the language; Java has no **goto**. However, it does have something that looks a bit like a jump tied in with the **break** and **continue** keywords. It's not a jump but rather a way to break out of an iteration statement. The reason it's often thrown in with discussions of **goto** is because it uses the same mechanism: a label.

A label is an identifier followed by a colon, like this:

```
label1:
```

The *only* place a label is useful in Java is right before an iteration statement. And that means *right* before—it does no good to put any other statement between the label and the iteration. And the sole reason to put a label before an iteration is if you're going to nest another iteration or a switch inside it. That's because the **break** and **continue** keywords will normally interrupt only the current loop, but when used with a label they'll interrupt the loops up to where the label exists:

```
label1:
outer-iteration {
  inner-iteration {
    //...
    break; // 1
    //...
    continue;   // 2
    //...
    continue label1; // 3
    //...
    break label1;   // 4
  }
}
```

In case 1, the **break** breaks out of the inner iteration and you end up in the outer iteration. In case 2, the **continue** moves back to the beginning of the inner iteration. But in case 3, the **continue label1** breaks out of the inner iteration *and* the outer iteration, all the way back to **label1**. Then it does in fact continue the iteration, but starting at the outer iteration. In case 4, the **break label1** also breaks all the way out to **label1**, but it does not re-enter the iteration. It actually does break out of both iterations.

Here is an example using **for** loops:

```
//: c03:LabeledFor.java
// Java's "labeled for" loop.

public class LabeledFor {
  public static void main(String[] args) {
    int i = 0;
    outer: // Can't have statements here
    for(; true ;) { // infinite loop
      inner: // Can't have statements here
      for(; i < 10; i++) {
        prt("i = " + i);
        if(i == 2) {
          prt("continue");
          continue;
        }
        if(i == 3) {
          prt("break");
          i++; // Otherwise i never
               // gets incremented.
          break;
        }
        if(i == 7) {
          prt("continue outer");
          i++; // Otherwise i never
               // gets incremented.
          continue outer;
        }
        if(i == 8) {
          prt("break outer");
          break outer;
        }
        for(int k = 0; k < 5; k++) {
          if(k == 3) {
            prt("continue inner");
            continue inner;
          }
        }
      }
    }
  }
```

```
    // Can't break or continue
    // to labels here
  }
  static void prt(String s) {
    System.out.println(s);
  }
} ///:~
```

This uses the **prt( )** method that has been defined in the other examples.

Note that **break** breaks out of the **for** loop, and that the increment-expression doesn't occur until the end of the pass through the **for** loop. Since **break** skips the increment expression, the increment is performed directly in the case of **i == 3**. The **continue outer** statement in the case of **i == 7** also goes to the top of the loop and also skips the increment, so it too is incremented directly.

Here is the output:

```
i = 0
continue inner
i = 1
continue inner
i = 2
continue
i = 3
break
i = 4
continue inner
i = 5
continue inner
i = 6
continue inner
i = 7
continue outer
i = 8
break outer
```

If not for the **break outer** statement, there would be no way to get out of the outer loop from within an inner loop, since **break** by itself can break out of only the innermost loop. (The same is true for **continue**.)

Of course, in the cases where breaking out of a loop will also exit the method, you can simply use a **return**.

Here is a demonstration of labeled **break** and **continue** statements with **while** loops:

```java
//: c03:LabeledWhile.java
// Java's "labeled while" loop.

public class LabeledWhile {
  public static void main(String[] args) {
    int i = 0;
    outer:
    while(true) {
      prt("Outer while loop");
      while(true) {
        i++;
        prt("i = " + i);
        if(i == 1) {
          prt("continue");
          continue;
        }
        if(i == 3) {
          prt("continue outer");
          continue outer;
        }
        if(i == 5) {
          prt("break");
          break;
        }
        if(i == 7) {
          prt("break outer");
          break outer;
        }
      }
    }
  }
  static void prt(String s) {
    System.out.println(s);
  }
} ///:~
```

The same rules hold true for **while**:

1. A plain **continue** goes to the top of the innermost loop and continues.

2. A labeled **continue** goes to the label and re-enters the loop right after that label.

3. A **break** "drops out of the bottom" of the loop.

4. A labeled **break** drops out of the bottom of the end of the loop denoted by the label.

The output of this method makes it clear:

```
Outer while loop
i = 1
continue
i = 2
i = 3
continue outer
Outer while loop
i = 4
i = 5
break
Outer while loop
i = 6
i = 7
break outer
```

It's important to remember that the *only* reason to use labels in Java is when you have nested loops and you want to **break** or **continue** through more than one nested level.

In Dijkstra's "goto considered harmful" paper, what he specifically objected to was the labels, not the goto. He observed that the number of bugs seems to increase with the number of labels in a program. Labels and gotos make programs difficult to analyze statically, since it introduces cycles in the program execution graph. Note that Java labels don't suffer from this problem, since they are constrained in their placement and can't be used to transfer control in an ad hoc manner. It's also interesting to note that this is a case where a language feature is made more useful by restricting the power of the statement.

switch

The **switch** is sometimes classified as a *selection statement*. The **switch** statement selects from among pieces of code based on the value of an integral expression. Its form is:

```
switch(integral-selector) {
  case integral-value1 : statement; break;
  case integral-value2 : statement; break;
  case integral-value3 : statement; break;
  case integral-value4 : statement; break;
  case integral-value5 : statement; break;
        // ...
  default: statement;
}
```

Integral-selector is an expression that produces an integral value. The **switch** compares the result of *integral-selector* to each *integral-value*. If it finds a match, the corresponding *statement* (simple or compound) executes. If no match occurs, the **default** *statement* executes.

You will notice in the above definition that each **case** ends with a **break**, which causes execution to jump to the end of the **switch** body. This is the conventional way to build a **switch** statement, but the **break** is optional. If it is missing, the code for the following case statements execute until a **break** is encountered. Although you don't usually want this kind of behavior, it can be useful to an experienced programmer. Note the last statement, following the **default**, doesn't have a **break** because the execution just falls through to where the **break** would have taken it anyway. You could put a **break** at the end of the **default** statement with no harm if you considered it important for style's sake.

The **switch** statement is a clean way to implement multi-way selection (i.e., selecting from among a number of different execution paths), but it requires a selector that evaluates to an integral value such as **int** or **char**. If you want to use, for example, a string or a floating-point number as a selector, it won't work in a **switch** statement. For non-integral types, you must use a series of **if** statements.

Here's an example that creates letters randomly and determines whether they're vowels or consonants:

```
//: c03:VowelsAndConsonants.java
// Demonstrates the switch statement.

public class VowelsAndConsonants {
  public static void main(String[] args) {
    for(int i = 0; i < 100; i++) {
      char c = (char)(Math.random() * 26 + 'a');
      System.out.print(c + ": ");
      switch(c) {
      case 'a':
      case 'e':
      case 'i':
      case 'o':
      case 'u':
                System.out.println("vowel");
                break;
      case 'y':
      case 'w':
                System.out.println(
                  "Sometimes a vowel");
                break;
      default:
                System.out.println("consonant");
      }
    }
  }
} ///:~
```

Since **Math.random( )** generates a value between 0 and 1, you need only multiply it by the upper bound of the range of numbers you want to produce (26 for the letters in the alphabet) and add an offset to establish the lower bound.

Although it appears you're switching on a character here, the **switch** statement is actually using the integral value of the character. The singly-quoted characters in the **case** statements also produce integral values that are used for comparison.

Notice how the **case**s can be "stacked" on top of each other to provide multiple matches for a particular piece of code. You should also be aware that it's essential to put the **break** statement at the end of a particular case, otherwise control will simply drop through and continue processing on the next case.

Calculation details

The statement:

```
char c = (char)(Math.random() * 26 + 'a');
```

deserves a closer look. **Math.random( )** produces a **double**, so the value 26 is converted to a **double** to perform the multiplication, which also produces a **double**. This means that **'a'** must be converted to a **double** to perform the addition. The **double** result is turned back into a **char** with a cast.

What does the cast to **char** do? That is, if you have the value 29.7 and you cast it to a **char**, is the resulting value 30 or 29? The answer to this can be seen in this example:

```
//: c03:CastingNumbers.java
// What happens when you cast a float
// or double to an integral value?

public class CastingNumbers {
  public static void main(String[] args) {
    double
      above = 0.7,
      below = 0.4;
    System.out.println("above: " + above);
    System.out.println("below: " + below);
    System.out.println(
      "(int)above: " + (int)above);
    System.out.println(
      "(int)below: " + (int)below);
    System.out.println(
      "(char)('a' + above): " +
      (char)('a' + above));
    System.out.println(
      "(char)('a' + below): " +
```

```
          (char)('a' + below));
    }
} ///:~
```

The output is:

```
above: 0.7
below: 0.4
(int)above: 0
(int)below: 0
(char)('a' + above): a
(char)('a' + below): a
```

So the answer is that casting from a **float** or **double** to an integral value always truncates.

A second question concerns **Math.random( )**. Does it produce a value from zero to one, inclusive or exclusive of the value '1'? In math lingo, is it (0,1), or [0,1], or (0,1] or [0,1)? (The square bracket means "includes" whereas the parenthesis means "doesn't include.") Again, a test program might provide the answer:

```
//: c03:RandomBounds.java
// Does Math.random() produce 0.0 and 1.0?

public class RandomBounds {
  static void usage() {
    System.out.println("Usage: \n\t" +
      "RandomBounds lower\n\t" +
      "RandomBounds upper");
    System.exit(1);
  }
  public static void main(String[] args) {
    if(args.length != 1) usage();
    if(args[0].equals("lower")) {
      while(Math.random() != 0.0)
        ; // Keep trying
      System.out.println("Produced 0.0!");
    }
    else if(args[0].equals("upper")) {
      while(Math.random() != 1.0)
        ; // Keep trying
```

```
        System.out.println("Produced 1.0!");
      }
    else
      usage();
  }
} ///:~
```

To run the program, you type a command line of either:

```
java RandomBounds lower
```

or

```
java RandomBounds upper
```

In both cases you are forced to break out of the program manually, so it would *appear* that **Math.random( )** never produces either 0.0 or 1.0. But this is where such an experiment can be deceiving. If you consider[2] that there are about 2^{62} different double fractions between 0 and 1, the likelihood of reaching any one value experimentally might exceed the lifetime of one computer, or even one experimenter. It turns out that 0.0 *is* included in the output of **Math.random( )**. Or, in math lingo, it is [0,1).

Summary

This chapter concludes the study of fundamental features that appear in most programming languages: calculation, operator precedence, type

---

[2] Chuck Allison writes: The total number of numbers in a floating-point number system is
2(M-m+1)b^(p-1) + 1
where **b** is the base (usually 2), **p** is the precision (digits in the mantissa), **M** is the largest exponent, and **m** is the smallest exponent. IEEE 754 uses:
M = 1023, m = -1022, p = 53, b = 2
so the total number of numbers is
2(1023+1022+1)2^52
= 2((2^10-1) + (2^10-1))2^52
= (2^10-1)2^54
= 2^64 - 2^54
Half of these numbers (corresponding to exponents in the range [-1022, 0]) are less than 1 in magnitude (both positive and negative), so 1/4 of that expression, or 2^62 - 2^52 + 1 (approximately 2^62) is in the range [0,1). See my paper at http://www.freshsources.com/1995006a.htm (last of text).

casting, and selection and iteration. Now you're ready to begin taking steps that move you closer to the world of object-oriented programming. The next chapter will cover the important issues of initialization and cleanup of objects, followed in the subsequent chapter by the essential concept of implementation hiding.

Exercises

Solutions to selected exercises can be found in the electronic document *The Thinking in Java Annotated Solution Guide*, available for a small fee from *www.BruceEckel.com*.

1.   There are two expressions in the section labeled "precedence" early in this chapter. Put these expressions into a program and demonstrate that they produce different results.

2.   Put the methods ternary( ) and alternative( ) into a working program.

3.   From the sections labeled "if-else" and "return", put the methods test( ) and test2( ) into a working program.

4.   Write a program that prints values from one to 100.

5.   Modify Exercise 4 so that the program exits by using the break keyword at value 47. Try using return instead.

6.   Write a function that takes two String arguments, and uses all the Boolean comparisons to compare the two Strings and print the results. For the == and !=, also perform the equals( ) test. In main( ), call your function with some different String objects.

7.   Write a program that generates 25 random int values. For each value, use an if-then-else statement to classify it as greater than, less than or equal to a second randomly-generated value.

8.   Modify Exercise 7 so that your code is surrounded by an "infinite" while loop. It will then run until you interrupt it from the keyboard (typically by pressing Control-C).

9.   Write a program that uses two nested for loops and the modulus operator (%) to detect and print prime numbers (integral numbers

that are not evenly divisible by any other numbers except for themselves and 1).

10. Create a switch statement that prints a message for each case, and put the switch inside a for loop that tries each case. Put a break after each case and test it, then remove the breaks and see what happens.

4: Initialization & Cleanup

As the computer revolution progresses, "unsafe" programming has become one of the major culprits that makes programming expensive.

Two of these safety issues are *initialization* and *cleanup*. Many C bugs occur when the programmer forgets to initialize a variable. This is especially true with libraries when users don't know how to initialize a library component, or even that they must. Cleanup is a special problem because it's easy to forget about an element when you're done with it, since it no longer concerns you. Thus, the resources used by that element are retained and you can easily end up running out of resources (most notably, memory).

C++ introduced the concept of a *constructor*, a special method automatically called when an object is created. Java also adopted the constructor, and in addition has a garbage collector that automatically releases memory resources when they're no longer being used. This chapter examines the issues of initialization and cleanup, and their support in Java.

Guaranteed initialization with the constructor

You can imagine creating a method called **initialize( )** for every class you write. The name is a hint that it should be called before using the object. Unfortunately, this means the user must remember to call the method. In Java, the class designer can guarantee initialization of every object by providing a special method called a *constructor*. If a class has a constructor, Java automatically calls that constructor when an object is created, before users can even get their hands on it. So initialization is guaranteed.

The next challenge is what to name this method. There are two issues. The first is that any name you use could clash with a name you might like to use as a member in the class. The second is that because the compiler is responsible for calling the constructor, it must always know which method to call. The C++ solution seems the easiest and most logical, so it's also used in Java: the name of the constructor is the same as the name of the class. It makes sense that such a method will be called automatically on initialization.

Here's a simple class with a constructor:

```
//: c04:SimpleConstructor.java
// Demonstration of a simple constructor.

class Rock {
  Rock() { // This is the constructor
    System.out.println("Creating Rock");
  }
}

public class SimpleConstructor {
  public static void main(String[] args) {
    for(int i = 0; i < 10; i++)
      new Rock();
  }
} ///:~
```

Now, when an object is created:

```
new Rock();
```

storage is allocated and the constructor is called. It is guaranteed that the object will be properly initialized before you can get your hands on it.

Note that the coding style of making the first letter of all methods lowercase does not apply to constructors, since the name of the constructor must match the name of the class *exactly*.

Like any method, the constructor can have arguments to allow you to specify *how* an object is created. The above example can easily be changed so the constructor takes an argument:

```
//: c04:SimpleConstructor2.java
// Constructors can have arguments.

class Rock2 {
  Rock2(int i) {
    System.out.println(
      "Creating Rock number " + i);
  }
}

public class SimpleConstructor2 {
  public static void main(String[] args) {
    for(int i = 0; i < 10; i++)
      new Rock2(i);
  }
} ///:~
```

Constructor arguments provide you with a way to provide parameters for the initialization of an object. For example, if the class **Tree** has a constructor that takes a single integer argument denoting the height of the tree, you would create a **Tree** object like this:

```
Tree t = new Tree(12);   // 12-foot tree
```

If **Tree(int)** is your only constructor, then the compiler won't let you create a **Tree** object any other way.

Constructors eliminate a large class of problems and make the code easier to read. In the preceding code fragment, for example, you don't see an explicit call to some **initialize( )** method that is conceptually separate from definition. In Java, definition and initialization are unified concepts—you can't have one without the other.

The constructor is an unusual type of method because it has no return value. This is distinctly different from a **void** return value, in which the method returns nothing but you still have the option to make it return something else. Constructors return nothing and you don't have an option. If there was a return value, and if you could select your own, the compiler would somehow need to know what to do with that return value.

Method overloading

One of the important features in any programming language is the use of names. When you create an object, you give a name to a region of storage. A method is a name for an action. By using names to describe your system, you create a program that is easier for people to understand and change. It's a lot like writing prose—the goal is to communicate with your readers.

You refer to all objects and methods by using names. Well-chosen names make it easier for you and others to understand your code.

A problem arises when mapping the concept of nuance in human language onto a programming language. Often, the same word expresses a number of different meanings—it's *overloaded*. This is useful, especially when it comes to trivial differences. You say "wash the shirt," "wash the car," and "wash the dog." It would be silly to be forced to say, "shirtWash the shirt," "carWash the car," and "dogWash the dog" just so the listener doesn't need to make any distinction about the action performed. Most human languages are redundant, so even if you miss a few words, you can still determine the meaning. We don't need unique identifiers—we can deduce meaning from context.

Most programming languages (C in particular) require you to have a unique identifier for each function. So you could not have one function called **print( )** for printing integers and another called **print( )** for printing floats—each function requires a unique name.

In Java (and C++), another factor forces the overloading of method names: the constructor. Because the constructor's name is predetermined by the name of the class, there can be only one constructor name. But what if you want to create an object in more than one way? For example, suppose you build a class that can initialize itself in a standard way or by reading information from a file. You need two constructors, one that takes no arguments (the *default* constructor, also called the *no-arg* constructor), and one that takes a **String** as an argument, which is the name of the file from which to initialize the object. Both are constructors, so they must have the same name—the name of the class. Thus, *method overloading* is essential to allow the same method name to be used with different argument types. And although method overloading is a must for constructors, it's a general convenience and can be used with any method.

Here's an example that shows both overloaded constructors and overloaded ordinary methods:

```
//: c04:Overloading.java
// Demonstration of both constructor
// and ordinary method overloading.
import java.util.*;

class Tree {
  int height;
  Tree() {
    prt("Planting a seedling");
    height = 0;
  }
  Tree(int i) {
    prt("Creating new Tree that is "
        + i + " feet tall");
    height = i;
  }
  void info() {
    prt("Tree is " + height
        + " feet tall");
  }
  void info(String s) {
    prt(s + ": Tree is "
        + height + " feet tall");
  }
  static void prt(String s) {
    System.out.println(s);
  }
}

public class Overloading {
  public static void main(String[] args) {
    for(int i = 0; i < 5; i++) {
```

```
      Tree t = new Tree(i);
      t.info();
      t.info("overloaded method");
    }
    // Overloaded constructor:
    new Tree();
  }
} ///:~
```

A **Tree** object can be created either as a seedling, with no argument, or as a plant grown in a nursery, with an existing height. To support this, there are two constructors, one that takes no arguments (we call constructors that take no arguments *default constructors*[1]) and one that takes the existing height.

You might also want to call the **info( )** method in more than one way. For example, with a **String** argument if you have an extra message you want printed, and without if you have nothing more to say. It would seem strange to give two separate names to what is obviously the same concept. Fortunately, method overloading allows you to use the same name for both.

Distinguishing overloaded methods

If the methods have the same name, how can Java know which method you mean? There's a simple rule: each overloaded method must take a unique list of argument types.

If you think about this for a second, it makes sense: how else could a programmer tell the difference between two methods that have the same name, other than by the types of their arguments?

Even differences in the ordering of arguments are sufficient to distinguish two methods: (Although you don't normally want to take this approach, as it produces difficult-to-maintain code.)

---

[1] In some of the Java literature from Sun they instead refer to these with the clumsy but descriptive name "no-arg constructors." The term "default constructor" has been in use for many years and so I will use that.

```
//: c04:OverloadingOrder.java
// Overloading based on the order of
// the arguments.

public class OverloadingOrder {
  static void print(String s, int i) {
    System.out.println(
      "String: " + s +
      ", int: " + i);
  }
  static void print(int i, String s) {
    System.out.println(
      "int: " + i +
      ", String: " + s);
  }
  public static void main(String[] args) {
    print("String first", 11);
    print(99, "Int first");
  }
} ///:~
```

The two **print( )** methods have identical arguments, but the order is different, and that's what makes them distinct.

Overloading with primitives

A primitive can be automatically promoted from a smaller type to a larger one and this can be slightly confusing in combination with overloading. The following example demonstrates what happens when a primitive is handed to an overloaded method:

```
//: c04:PrimitiveOverloading.java
// Promotion of primitives and overloading.

public class PrimitiveOverloading {
  // boolean can't be automatically converted
  static void prt(String s) {
    System.out.println(s);
  }

  void f1(char x) { prt("f1(char)"); }
```

```java
void f1(byte x) { prt("f1(byte)"); }
void f1(short x) { prt("f1(short)"); }
void f1(int x) { prt("f1(int)"); }
void f1(long x) { prt("f1(long)"); }
void f1(float x) { prt("f1(float)"); }
void f1(double x) { prt("f1(double)"); }

void f2(byte x) { prt("f2(byte)"); }
void f2(short x) { prt("f2(short)"); }
void f2(int x) { prt("f2(int)"); }
void f2(long x) { prt("f2(long)"); }
void f2(float x) { prt("f2(float)"); }
void f2(double x) { prt("f2(double)"); }

void f3(short x) { prt("f3(short)"); }
void f3(int x) { prt("f3(int)"); }
void f3(long x) { prt("f3(long)"); }
void f3(float x) { prt("f3(float)"); }
void f3(double x) { prt("f3(double)"); }

void f4(int x) { prt("f4(int)"); }
void f4(long x) { prt("f4(long)"); }
void f4(float x) { prt("f4(float)"); }
void f4(double x) { prt("f4(double)"); }

void f5(long x) { prt("f5(long)"); }
void f5(float x) { prt("f5(float)"); }
void f5(double x) { prt("f5(double)"); }

void f6(float x) { prt("f6(float)"); }
void f6(double x) { prt("f6(double)"); }

void f7(double x) { prt("f7(double)"); }

void testConstVal() {
  prt("Testing with 5");
  f1(5);f2(5);f3(5);f4(5);f5(5);f6(5);f7(5);
}
void testChar() {
  char x = 'x';
  prt("char argument:");
```

```
    f1(x);f2(x);f3(x);f4(x);f5(x);f6(x);f7(x);
  }
  void testByte() {
    byte x = 0;
    prt("byte argument:");
    f1(x);f2(x);f3(x);f4(x);f5(x);f6(x);f7(x);
  }
  void testShort() {
    short x = 0;
    prt("short argument:");
    f1(x);f2(x);f3(x);f4(x);f5(x);f6(x);f7(x);
  }
  void testInt() {
    int x = 0;
    prt("int argument:");
    f1(x);f2(x);f3(x);f4(x);f5(x);f6(x);f7(x);
  }
  void testLong() {
    long x = 0;
    prt("long argument:");
    f1(x);f2(x);f3(x);f4(x);f5(x);f6(x);f7(x);
  }
  void testFloat() {
    float x = 0;
    prt("float argument:");
    f1(x);f2(x);f3(x);f4(x);f5(x);f6(x);f7(x);
  }
  void testDouble() {
    double x = 0;
    prt("double argument:");
    f1(x);f2(x);f3(x);f4(x);f5(x);f6(x);f7(x);
  }
  public static void main(String[] args) {
    PrimitiveOverloading p =
      new PrimitiveOverloading();
    p.testConstVal();
    p.testChar();
    p.testByte();
    p.testShort();
    p.testInt();
    p.testLong();
```

```
    p.testFloat();
    p.testDouble();
  }
} ///:~
```

If you view the output of this program, you'll see that the constant value 5 is treated as an **int**, so if an overloaded method is available that takes an **int** it is used. In all other cases, if you have a data type that is smaller than the argument in the method, that data type is promoted. **char** produces a slightly different effect, since if it doesn't find an exact **char** match, it is promoted to **int**.

What happens if your argument is *bigger* than the argument expected by the overloaded method? A modification of the above program gives the answer:

```
//: c04:Demotion.java
// Demotion of primitives and overloading.

public class Demotion {
  static void prt(String s) {
    System.out.println(s);
  }

  void f1(char x) { prt("f1(char)"); }
  void f1(byte x) { prt("f1(byte)"); }
  void f1(short x) { prt("f1(short)"); }
  void f1(int x) { prt("f1(int)"); }
  void f1(long x) { prt("f1(long)"); }
  void f1(float x) { prt("f1(float)"); }
  void f1(double x) { prt("f1(double)"); }

  void f2(char x) { prt("f2(char)"); }
  void f2(byte x) { prt("f2(byte)"); }
  void f2(short x) { prt("f2(short)"); }
  void f2(int x) { prt("f2(int)"); }
  void f2(long x) { prt("f2(long)"); }
  void f2(float x) { prt("f2(float)"); }

  void f3(char x) { prt("f3(char)"); }
  void f3(byte x) { prt("f3(byte)"); }
```

```
    void f3(short x) { prt("f3(short)"); }
    void f3(int x) { prt("f3(int)"); }
    void f3(long x) { prt("f3(long)"); }

    void f4(char x) { prt("f4(char)"); }
    void f4(byte x) { prt("f4(byte)"); }
    void f4(short x) { prt("f4(short)"); }
    void f4(int x) { prt("f4(int)"); }

    void f5(char x) { prt("f5(char)"); }
    void f5(byte x) { prt("f5(byte)"); }
    void f5(short x) { prt("f5(short)"); }

    void f6(char x) { prt("f6(char)"); }
    void f6(byte x) { prt("f6(byte)"); }

    void f7(char x) { prt("f7(char)"); }

    void testDouble() {
      double x = 0;
      prt("double argument:");
      f1(x);f2((float)x);f3((long)x);f4((int)x);
      f5((short)x);f6((byte)x);f7((char)x);
    }
    public static void main(String[] args) {
      Demotion p = new Demotion();
      p.testDouble();
    }
} ///:~
```

Here, the methods take narrower primitive values. If your argument is wider then you must *cast* to the necessary type using the type name in parentheses. If you don't do this, the compiler will issue an error message.

You should be aware that this is a *narrowing conversion,* which means you might lose information during the cast. This is why the compiler forces you to do it—to flag the narrowing conversion.

Overloading on return values

It is common to wonder "Why only class names and method argument lists? Why not distinguish between methods based on their return values?" For example, these two methods, which have the same name and arguments, are easily distinguished from each other:

```
void f() {}
int f() {}
```

This works fine when the compiler can unequivocally determine the meaning from the context, as in **int x = f( )**. However, you can call a method and ignore the return value; this is often referred to as *calling a method for its side effect* since you don't care about the return value but instead want the other effects of the method call. So if you call the method this way:

```
f();
```

how can Java determine which **f( )** should be called? And how could someone reading the code see it? Because of this sort of problem, you cannot use return value types to distinguish overloaded methods.

Default constructors

As mentioned previously, a default constructor (a.k.a. a "no-arg" constructor) is one without arguments, used to create a "vanilla object." If you create a class that has no constructors, the compiler will automatically create a default constructor for you. For example:

```
//: c04:DefaultConstructor.java

class Bird {
  int i;
}

public class DefaultConstructor {
  public static void main(String[] args) {
    Bird nc = new Bird(); // default!
  }
} ///:~
```

The line

```
new Bird();
```

creates a new object and calls the default constructor, even though one was not explicitly defined. Without it we would have no method to call to build our object. However, if you define any constructors (with or without arguments), the compiler will *not* synthesize one for you:

```
class Bush {
  Bush(int i) {}
  Bush(double d) {}
}
```

Now if you say:

```
new Bush();
```

the compiler will complain that it cannot find a constructor that matches. It's as if when you don't put in any constructors, the compiler says "You are bound to need *some* constructor, so let me make one for you." But if you write a constructor, the compiler says "You've written a constructor so you know what you're doing; if you didn't put in a default it's because you meant to leave it out."

The **this** keyword

If you have two objects of the same type called **a** and **b**, you might wonder how it is that you can call a method **f( )** for both those objects:

```
class Banana { void f(int i) { /* ... */ } }
Banana a = new Banana(), b = new Banana();
a.f(1);
b.f(2);
```

If there's only one method called **f( )**, how can that method know whether it's being called for the object **a** or **b**?

To allow you to write the code in a convenient object-oriented syntax in which you "send a message to an object," the compiler does some undercover work for you. There's a secret first argument passed to the method **f( )**, and that argument is the reference to the object that's being manipulated. So the two method calls above become something like:

```
Banana.f(a,1);
Banana.f(b,2);
```

This is internal and you can't write these expressions and get the compiler to accept them, but it gives you an idea of what's happening.

Suppose you're inside a method and you'd like to get the reference to the current object. Since that reference is passed *secretly* by the compiler, there's no identifier for it. However, for this purpose there's a keyword: **this**. The **this** keyword—which can be used only inside a method— produces the reference to the object the method has been called for. You can treat this reference just like any other object reference. Keep in mind that if you're calling a method of your class from within another method of your class, you don't need to use **this**; you simply call the method. The current **this** reference is automatically used for the other method. Thus you can say:

```
class Apricot {
  void pick() { /* ... */ }
  void pit() { pick(); /* ... */ }
}
```

Inside **pit( )**, you *could* say **this.pick( )** but there's no need to. The compiler does it for you automatically. The **this** keyword is used only for those special cases in which you need to explicitly use the reference to the current object. For example, it's often used in **return** statements when you want to return the reference to the current object:

```
//: c04:Leaf.java
// Simple use of the "this" keyword.

public class Leaf {
  int i = 0;
  Leaf increment() {
    i++;
    return this;
  }
  void print() {
    System.out.println("i = " + i);
  }
  public static void main(String[] args) {
```

```
      Leaf x = new Leaf();
      x.increment().increment().increment().print();
  }
} ///:~
```

Because **increment( )** returns the reference to the current object via the **this** keyword, multiple operations can easily be performed on the same object.

Calling constructors from constructors

When you write several constructors for a class, there are times when you'd like to call one constructor from another to avoid duplicating code. You can do this using the **this** keyword.

Normally, when you say **this**, it is in the sense of "this object" or "the current object," and by itself it produces the reference to the current object. In a constructor, the **this** keyword takes on a different meaning when you give it an argument list: it makes an explicit call to the constructor that matches that argument list. Thus you have a straightforward way to call other constructors:

```
//: c04:Flower.java
// Calling constructors with "this."

public class Flower {
  int petalCount = 0;
  String s = new String("null");
  Flower(int petals) {
    petalCount = petals;
    System.out.println(
      "Constructor w/ int arg only, petalCount= "
      + petalCount);
  }
  Flower(String ss) {
    System.out.println(
      "Constructor w/ String arg only, s=" + ss);
    s = ss;
  }
  Flower(String s, int petals) {
    this(petals);
//!    this(s); // Can't call two!
```

```
    this.s = s; // Another use of "this"
    System.out.println("String & int args");
  }
  Flower() {
    this("hi", 47);
    System.out.println(
      "default constructor (no args)");
  }
  void print() {
//!    this(11); // Not inside non-constructor!
    System.out.println(
      "petalCount = " + petalCount + " s = "+ s);
  }
  public static void main(String[] args) {
    Flower x = new Flower();
    x.print();
  }
} ///:~
```

The constructor **Flower(String s, int petals)** shows that, while you can call one constructor using **this**, you cannot call two. In addition, the constructor call must be the first thing you do or you'll get a compiler error message.

This example also shows another way you'll see **this** used. Since the name of the argument **s** and the name of the member data **s** are the same, there's an ambiguity. You can resolve it by saying **this.s** to refer to the member data. You'll often see this form used in Java code, and it's used in numerous places in this book.

In **print( )** you can see that the compiler won't let you call a constructor from inside any method other than a constructor.

The meaning of **static**

With the **this** keyword in mind, you can more fully understand what it means to make a method **static**. It means that there is no **this** for that particular method. You cannot call non-**static** methods from inside

static methods[2] (although the reverse is possible), and you can call a **static** method for the class itself, without any object. In fact, that's primarily what a **static** method is for. It's as if you're creating the equivalent of a global function (from C). Except global functions are not permitted in Java, and putting the **static** method inside a class allows it access to other **static** methods and to **static** fields.

Some people argue that **static** methods are not object-oriented since they do have the semantics of a global function; with a **static** method you don't send a message to an object, since there's no **this**. This is probably a fair argument, and if you find yourself using a *lot* of static methods you should probably rethink your strategy. However, **static**s are pragmatic and there are times when you genuinely need them, so whether or not they are "proper OOP" should be left to the theoreticians. Indeed, even Smalltalk has the equivalent in its "class methods."

Cleanup: finalization and garbage collection

Programmers know about the importance of initialization, but often forget the importance of cleanup. After all, who needs to clean up an **int**? But with libraries, simply "letting go" of an object once you're done with it is not always safe. Of course, Java has the garbage collector to reclaim the memory of objects that are no longer used. Now consider a very unusual case. Suppose your object allocates "special" memory without using **new**. The garbage collector knows only how to release memory allocated *with* **new**, so it won't know how to release the object's "special" memory. To handle this case, Java provides a method called **finalize( )** that you can define for your class. Here's how it's *supposed* to work. When the garbage collector is ready to release the storage used for your object, it will first call **finalize( )**, and only on the next garbage-collection pass will it

---

[2] The one case in which this is possible occurs if you pass a reference to an object into the **static** method. Then, via the reference (which is now effectively **this**), you can call non-**static** methods and access non-**static** fields. But typically if you want to do something like this you'll just make an ordinary, non-**static** method.

---

reclaim the object's memory. So if you choose to use **finalize( )**, it gives you the ability to perform some important cleanup *at the time of garbage collection*.

This is a potential programming pitfall because some programmers, especially C++ programmers, might initially mistake **finalize( )** for the *destructor* in C++, which is a function that is always called when an object is destroyed. But it is important to distinguish between C++ and Java here, because in C++ *objects always get destroyed* (in a bug-free program), whereas in Java objects do not always get garbage-collected. Or, put another way:

Garbage collection is not destruction.

If you remember this, you will stay out of trouble. What it means is that if there is some activity that must be performed before you no longer need an object, you must perform that activity yourself. Java has no destructor or similar concept, so you must create an ordinary method to perform this cleanup. For example, suppose in the process of creating your object it draws itself on the screen. If you don't explicitly erase its image from the screen, it might never get cleaned up. If you put some kind of erasing functionality inside **finalize( )**, then if an object is garbage-collected, the image will first be removed from the screen, but if it isn't, the image will remain. So a second point to remember is:

Your objects might not get garbage-collected.

You might find that the storage for an object never gets released because your program never nears the point of running out of storage. If your program completes and the garbage collector never gets around to releasing the storage for any of your objects, that storage will be returned to the operating system *en masse* as the program exits. This is a good thing, because garbage collection has some overhead, and if you never do it you never incur that expense.

What is **finalize( )** for?

You might believe at this point that you should not use **finalize( )** as a general-purpose cleanup method. What good is it?

A third point to remember is:

Garbage collection is only about memory.

That is, the sole reason for the existence of the garbage collector is to recover memory that your program is no longer using. So any activity that is associated with garbage collection, most notably your **finalize( )** method, must also be only about memory and its deallocation.

Does this mean that if your object contains other objects **finalize( )** should explicitly release those objects? Well, no—the garbage collector takes care of the release of all object memory regardless of how the object is created. It turns out that the need for **finalize( )** is limited to special cases, in which your object can allocate some storage in some way other than creating an object. But, you might observe, everything in Java is an object so how can this be?

It would seem that **finalize( )** is in place because of the possibility that you'll do something C-like by allocating memory using a mechanism other than the normal one in Java. This can happen primarily through *native methods*, which are a way to call non-Java code from Java. (Native methods are discussed in Appendix B.) C and C++ are the only languages currently supported by native methods, but since they can call subprograms in other languages, you can effectively call anything. Inside the non-Java code, C's **malloc( )** family of functions might be called to allocate storage, and unless you call **free( )** that storage will not be released, causing a memory leak. Of course, **free( )** is a C and C++ function, so you'd need to call it in a native method inside your **finalize( )**.

After reading this, you probably get the idea that you won't use **finalize( )** much. You're correct; it is not the appropriate place for normal cleanup to occur. So where should normal cleanup be performed?

You must perform cleanup

To clean up an object, the user of that object must call a cleanup method at the point the cleanup is desired. This sounds pretty straightforward, but it collides a bit with the C++ concept of the destructor. In C++, all objects are destroyed. Or rather, all objects *should be* destroyed. If the

C++ object is created as a local (i.e., on the stack—not possible in Java), then the destruction happens at the closing curly brace of the scope in which the object was created. If the object was created using **new** (like in Java) the destructor is called when the programmer calls the C++ operator **delete** (which doesn't exist in Java). If the C++ programmer forgets to call **delete**, the destructor is never called and you have a memory leak, plus the other parts of the object never get cleaned up. This kind of bug can be very difficult to track down.

In contrast, Java doesn't allow you to create local objects—you must always use **new**. But in Java, there's no "delete" to call to release the object since the garbage collector releases the storage for you. So from a simplistic standpoint you could say that because of garbage collection, Java has no destructor. You'll see as this book progresses, however, that the presence of a garbage collector does not remove the need for or utility of destructors. (And you should never call **finalize( )** directly, so that's not an appropriate avenue for a solution.) If you want some kind of cleanup performed other than storage release you must *still* explicitly call an appropriate method in Java, which is the equivalent of a C++ destructor without the convenience.

One of the things **finalize( )** can be useful for is observing the process of garbage collection. The following example shows you what's going on and summarizes the previous descriptions of garbage collection:

```
//: c04:Garbage.java
// Demonstration of the garbage
// collector and finalization

class Chair {
  static boolean gcrun = false;
  static boolean f = false;
  static int created = 0;
  static int finalized = 0;
  int i;
  Chair() {
    i = ++created;
    if(created == 47)
      System.out.println("Created 47");
  }
```

```java
  public void finalize() {
    if(!gcrun) {
      // The first time finalize() is called:
      gcrun = true;
      System.out.println(
        "Beginning to finalize after " +
        created + " Chairs have been created");
    }
    if(i == 47) {
      System.out.println(
        "Finalizing Chair #47, " +
        "Setting flag to stop Chair creation");
      f = true;
    }
    finalized++;
    if(finalized >= created)
      System.out.println(
        "All " + finalized + " finalized");
  }
}

public class Garbage {
  public static void main(String[] args) {
    // As long as the flag hasn't been set,
    // make Chairs and Strings:
    while(!Chair.f) {
      new Chair();
      new String("To take up space");
    }
    System.out.println(
      "After all Chairs have been created:\n" +
      "total created = " + Chair.created +
      ", total finalized = " + Chair.finalized);
    // Optional arguments force garbage
    // collection & finalization:
    if(args.length > 0) {
      if(args[0].equals("gc") ||
         args[0].equals("all")) {
        System.out.println("gc():");
        System.gc();
      }
```

```
      if(args[0].equals("finalize") ||
         args[0].equals("all")) {
        System.out.println("runFinalization():");
        System.runFinalization();
      }
    }
    System.out.println("bye!");
  }
} ///:~
```

The above program creates many **Chair** objects, and at some point after the garbage collector begins running, the program stops creating **Chair**s. Since the garbage collector can run at any time, you don't know exactly when it will start up, so there's a flag called **gcrun** to indicate whether the garbage collector has started running yet. A second flag **f** is a way for **Chair** to tell the **main( )** loop that it should stop making objects. Both of these flags are set within **finalize( )**, which is called during garbage collection.

Two other **static** variables, **created** and **finalized**, keep track of the number of **Chair**s created versus the number that get finalized by the garbage collector. Finally, each **Chair** has its own (non-**static**) **int i** so it can keep track of what number it is. When **Chair** number 47 is finalized, the flag is set to **true** to bring the process of **Chair** creation to a stop.

All this happens in **main( )**, in the loop

```
    while(!Chair.f) {
      new Chair();
      new String("To take up space");
    }
```

You might wonder how this loop could ever finish, since there's nothing inside the loop that changes the value of **Chair.f**. However, the **finalize( )** process will, eventually, when it finalizes number 47.

The creation of a **String** object during each iteration is simply extra storage being allocated to encourage the garbage collector to kick in, which it will do when it starts to get nervous about the amount of memory available.

When you run the program, you provide a command-line argument of "gc," "finalize," or "all." The "gc" argument will call the **System.gc( )** method (to force execution of the garbage collector). Using the "finalize" argument calls **System.runFinalization( )** which—in theory—will cause any unfinalized objects to be finalized. And "all" causes both methods to be called.

The behavior of this program and the version in the first edition of this book shows that the whole issue of garbage collection and finalization has been evolving, with much of the evolution happening behind closed doors. In fact, by the time you read this, the behavior of the program may have changed once again.

If **System.gc( )** is called, then finalization happens to all the objects. This was not necessarily the case with previous implementations of the JDK, although the documentation claimed otherwise. In addition, you'll see that it doesn't seem to make any difference whether **System.runFinalization( )** is called.

However, you will see that only if **System.gc( )** is called after all the objects are created and discarded will all the finalizers be called. If you do not call **System.gc( )**, then only some of the objects will be finalized. In Java 1.1, a method **System.runFinalizersOnExit( )** was introduced that caused programs to run all the finalizers as they exited, but the design turned out to be buggy and the method was deprecated. This is yet another clue that the Java designers were thrashing about trying to solve the garbage collection and finalization problem. We can only hope that things have been worked out in Java 2.

The preceding program shows that the promise that finalizers will always be run holds true, but only if you explicitly force it to happen yourself. If you don't cause **System.gc( )** to be called, you'll get an output like this:

```
Created 47
Beginning to finalize after 3486 Chairs have been
created
Finalizing Chair #47, Setting flag to stop Chair
creation
After all Chairs have been created:
total created = 3881, total finalized = 2684
```

```
bye!
```

Thus, not all finalizers get called by the time the program completes. If **System.gc( )** is called, it will finalize and destroy all the objects that are no longer in use up to that point.

Remember that neither garbage collection nor finalization is guaranteed. If the Java Virtual Machine (JVM) isn't close to running out of memory, then it will (wisely) not waste time recovering memory through garbage collection.

The death condition

 In general, you can't rely on **finalize( )** being called, and you must create separate "cleanup" functions and call them explicitly. So it appears that **finalize( )** is only useful for obscure memory cleanup that most programmers will never use. However, there is a very interesting use of **finalize( )** which does not rely on it being called every time. This is the verification of the *death condition*[3] of an object.

At the point that you're no longer interested in an object—when it's ready to be cleaned up—that object should be in a state whereby its memory can be safely released. For example, if the object represents an open file, that file should be closed by the programmer before the object is garbage-collected. If any portions of the object are not properly cleaned up, then you have a bug in your program that could be very difficult to find. The value of **finalize( )** is that it can be used to discover this condition, even if it isn't always called. If one of the finalizations happens to reveal the bug, then you discover the problem, which is all you really care about.

Here's a simple example of how you might use it:

```
//: c04:DeathCondition.java
// Using finalize() to detect an object that
// hasn't been properly cleaned up.

class Book {
```

---

[3] A term coined by Bill Venners (www.artima.com) during a seminar that he and I were giving together.

```
  boolean checkedOut = false;
  Book(boolean checkOut) {
    checkedOut = checkOut;
  }
  void checkIn() {
    checkedOut = false;
  }
  public void finalize() {
    if(checkedOut)
      System.out.println("Error: checked out");
  }
}

public class DeathCondition {
  public static void main(String[] args) {
    Book novel = new Book(true);
    // Proper cleanup:
    novel.checkIn();
    // Drop the reference, forget to clean up:
    new Book(true);
    // Force garbage collection & finalization:
    System.gc();
  }
} ///:~
```

The death condition is that all **Book** objects are supposed to be checked in before they are garbage-collected, but in **main( )** a programmer error doesn't check in one of the books. Without **finalize( )** to verify the death condition, this could be a difficult bug to find.

Note that **System.gc( )** is used to force finalization (and you should do this during program development to speed debugging). But even if it isn't, it's highly probable that the errant **Book** will eventually be discovered through repeated executions of the program (assuming the program allocates enough storage to cause the garbage collector to execute).

How a garbage collector works

If you come from a programming language where allocating objects on the heap is expensive, you may naturally assume that Java's scheme of allocating everything (except primitives) on the heap is expensive.

However, it turns out that the garbage collector can have a significant impact on *increasing* the speed of object creation. This might sound a bit odd at first—that storage release affects storage allocation—but it's the way some JVMs work and it means that allocating storage for heap objects in Java can be nearly as fast as creating storage on the stack in other languages.

For example, you can think of the C++ heap as a yard where each object stakes out its own piece of turf. This real estate can become abandoned sometime later and must be reused. In some JVMs, the Java heap is quite different; it's more like a conveyor belt that moves forward every time you allocate a new object. This means that object storage allocation is remarkably rapid. The "heap pointer" is simply moved forward into virgin territory, so it's effectively the same as C++'s stack allocation. (Of course, there's a little extra overhead for bookkeeping but it's nothing like searching for storage.)

Now you might observe that the heap isn't in fact a conveyor belt, and if you treat it that way you'll eventually start paging memory a lot (which is a big performance hit) and later run out. The trick is that the garbage collector steps in and while it collects the garbage it compacts all the objects in the heap so that you've effectively moved the "heap pointer" closer to the beginning of the conveyor belt and further away from a page fault. The garbage collector rearranges things and makes it possible for the high-speed, infinite-free-heap model to be used while allocating storage.

To understand how this works, you need to get a little better idea of the way the different garbage collector (GC) schemes work. A simple but slow GC technique is reference counting. This means that each object contains a reference counter, and every time a reference is attached to an object the reference count is increased. Every time a reference goes out of scope or is set to **null**, the reference count is decreased. Thus, managing reference counts is a small but constant overhead that happens throughout the lifetime of your program. The garbage collector moves through the entire list of objects and when it finds one with a reference count of zero it releases that storage. The one drawback is that if objects circularly refer to each other they can have nonzero reference counts while still being garbage. Locating such self-referential groups requires significant extra work for the garbage collector. Reference counting is commonly used to explain one kind of garbage collection but it doesn't seem to be used in any JVM implementations.

In faster schemes, garbage collection is not based on reference counting. Instead, it is based on the idea that any nondead object must ultimately be traceable back to a reference that lives either on the stack or in static storage. The chain might go through several layers of objects. Thus, if you start in the stack and the static storage area and walk through all the references you'll find all the live objects. For each reference that you find, you must trace into the object that it points to and then follow all the references in *that* object, tracing into the objects they point to, etc., until you've moved through the entire web that originated with the reference on the stack or in static storage. Each object that you move through must still be alive. Note that there is no problem with detached self-referential groups—these are simply not found, and are therefore automatically garbage.

In the approach described here, the JVM uses an *adaptive* garbage-collection scheme, and what it does with the live objects that it locates depends on the variant currently being used. One of these variants is *stop-and-copy*. This means that—for reasons that will become apparent—the program is first stopped (this is not a background collection scheme). Then, each live object that is found is copied from one heap to another, leaving behind all the garbage. In addition, as the objects are copied into the new heap they are packed end-to-end, thus compacting the new heap (and allowing new storage to simply be reeled off the end as previously described).

Of course, when an object is moved from one place to another, all references that point at (i.e., that *reference*) the object must be changed. The reference that goes from the heap or the static storage area to the object can be changed right away, but there can be other references pointing to this object that will be encountered later during the "walk." These are fixed up as they are found (you could imagine a table that maps old addresses to new ones).

There are two issues that make these so-called "copy collectors" inefficient. The first is the idea that you have two heaps and you slosh all the memory back and forth between these two separate heaps, maintaining twice as much memory as you actually need. Some JVMs deal with this by allocating the heap in chunks as needed and simply copying from one chunk to another.

The second issue is the copying. Once your program becomes stable it might be generating little or no garbage. Despite that, a copy collector will still copy all the memory from one place to another, which is wasteful. To prevent this, some JVMs detect that no new garbage is being generated and switch to a different scheme (this is the "adaptive" part). This other scheme is called *mark and sweep*, and it's what earlier versions of Sun's JVM used all the time. For general use, mark and sweep is fairly slow, but when you know you're generating little or no garbage it's fast.

Mark and sweep follows the same logic of starting from the stack and static storage and tracing through all the references to find live objects. However, each time it finds a live object that object is marked by setting a flag in it, but the object isn't collected yet. Only when the marking process is finished does the sweep occur. During the sweep, the dead objects are released. However, no copying happens, so if the collector chooses to compact a fragmented heap it does so by shuffling objects around.

The "stop-and-copy" refers to the idea that this type of garbage collection is *not* done in the background; instead, the program is stopped while the GC occurs. In the Sun literature you'll find many references to garbage collection as a low-priority background process, but it turns out that the GC was not implemented that way, at least in earlier versions of the Sun JVM. Instead, the Sun garbage collector ran when memory got low. In addition, mark-and-sweep requires that the program be stopped.

As previously mentioned, in the JVM described here memory is allocated in big blocks. If you allocate a large object, it gets its own block. Strict stop-and-copy requires copying every live object from the source heap to a new heap before you could free the old one, which translates to lots of memory. With blocks, the GC can typically use dead blocks to copy objects to as it collects. Each block has a *generation count* to keep track of whether it's alive. In the normal case, only the blocks created since the last GC are compacted; all other blocks get their generation count bumped if they have been referenced from somewhere. This handles the normal case of lots of short-lived temporary objects. Periodically, a full sweep is made—large objects are still not copied (just get their generation count bumped) and blocks containing small objects are copied and compacted. The JVM monitors the efficiency of GC and if it becomes a waste of time because all objects are long-lived then it switches to mark-and-sweep. Similarly, the JVM keeps track of how successful mark-and-sweep is, and if the heap starts to become fragmented it switches back to stop-and-copy. This is where the "adaptive" part comes in, so you end up with a mouthful: "adaptive generational stop-and-copy mark-and-sweep."

There are a number of additional speedups possible in a JVM. An especially important one involves the operation of the loader and Just-In-Time (JIT) compiler. When a class must be loaded (typically, the first time you want to create an object of that class), the **.class** file is located and the byte codes for that class are brought into memory. At this point, one approach is to simply JIT all the code, but this has two drawbacks: it takes a little more time, which, compounded throughout the life of the program, can add up; and it increases the size of the executable (byte codes are significantly more compact than expanded JIT code) and this might cause paging, which definitely slows down a program. An alternative approach is *lazy evaluation,* which means that the code is not JIT compiled until necessary. Thus, code that never gets executed might never get JIT compiled.

Member initialization

Java goes out of its way to guarantee that variables are properly initialized before they are used. In the case of variables that are defined locally to a method, this guarantee comes in the form of a compile-time error. So if you say:

```
void f() {
  int i;
  i++;
}
```

you'll get an error message that says that **i** might not have been initialized. Of course, the compiler could have given **i** a default value, but it's more likely that this is a programmer error and a default value would have covered that up. Forcing the programmer to provide an initialization value is more likely to catch a bug.

If a primitive is a data member of a class, however, things are a bit different. Since any method can initialize or use that data, it might not be practical to force the user to initialize it to its appropriate value before the data is used. However, it's unsafe to leave it with a garbage value, so each primitive data member of a class is guaranteed to get an initial value. Those values can be seen here:

```java
//: c04:InitialValues.java
// Shows default initial values.

class Measurement {
  boolean t;
  char c;
  byte b;
  short s;
  int i;
  long l;
  float f;
  double d;
  void print() {
    System.out.println(
      "Data type      Initial value\n" +
      "boolean        " + t + "\n" +
      "char           [" + c + "] "+ (int)c +"\n"+
      "byte           " + b + "\n" +
      "short          " + s + "\n" +
      "int            " + i + "\n" +
      "long           " + l + "\n" +
      "float          " + f + "\n" +
      "double         " + d);
  }
}

public class InitialValues {
  public static void main(String[] args) {
    Measurement d = new Measurement();
    d.print();
    /* In this case you could also say:
```

```
      new Measurement().print();
      */
  }
} ///:~
```

The output of this program is:

```
Data type          Initial value
boolean            false
char               [ ] 0
byte               0
short              0
int                0
long               0
float              0.0
double             0.0
```

The **char** value is a zero, which prints as a space.

You'll see later that when you define an object reference inside a class without initializing it to a new object, that reference is given a special value of **null** (which is a Java keyword).

You can see that even though the values are not specified, they automatically get initialized. So at least there's no threat of working with uninitialized variables.

Specifying initialization

What happens if you want to give a variable an initial value? One direct way to do this is simply to assign the value at the point you define the variable in the class. (Notice you cannot do this in C++, although C++ novices always try.) Here the field definitions in class **Measurement** are changed to provide initial values:

```
class Measurement {
  boolean b = true;
  char c = 'x';
  byte B = 47;
  short s = 0xff;
  int i = 999;
  long l = 1;
  float f = 3.14f;
```

```
double d = 3.14159;
//. . .
```

You can also initialize nonprimitive objects in this same way. If **Depth** is a class, you can insert a variable and initialize it like so:

```
class Measurement {
  Depth o = new Depth();
  boolean b = true;
  // . . .
```

If you haven't given **o** an initial value and you try to use it anyway, you'll get a run-time error called an *exception* (covered in Chapter 10).

You can even call a method to provide an initialization value:

```
class CInit {
  int i = f();
  //...
}
```

This method can have arguments, of course, but those arguments cannot be other class members that haven't been initialized yet. Thus, you can do this:

```
class CInit {
  int i = f();
  int j = g(i);
  //...
}
```

But you cannot do this:

```
class CInit {
  int j = g(i);
  int i = f();
  //...
}
```

This is one place in which the compiler, appropriately, *does* complain about forward referencing, since this has to do with the order of initialization and not the way the program is compiled.

This approach to initialization is simple and straightforward. It has the limitation that *every* object of type **Measurement** will get these same initialization values. Sometimes this is exactly what you need, but at other times you need more flexibility.

Constructor initialization

The constructor can be used to perform initialization, and this gives you greater flexibility in your programming since you can call methods and perform actions at run-time to determine the initial values. There's one thing to keep in mind, however: you aren't precluding the automatic initialization, which happens before the constructor is entered. So, for example, if you say:

```
class Counter {
  int i;
  Counter() { i = 7; }
  // . . .
```

then **i** will first be initialized to 0, then to 7. This is true with all the primitive types and with object references, including those that are given explicit initialization at the point of definition. For this reason, the compiler doesn't try to force you to initialize elements in the constructor at any particular place, or before they are used—initialization is already guaranteed[4].

Order of initialization

Within a class, the order of initialization is determined by the order that the variables are defined within the class. The variable definitions may be scattered throughout and in between method definitions, but the variables are initialized before any methods can be called—even the constructor. For example:

```
//: c04:OrderOfInitialization.java
// Demonstrates initialization order.
```

---

[4] In contrast, C++ has the *constructor initializer list* that causes initialization to occur before entering the constructor body, and is enforced for objects. See *Thinking in C++, 2nd edition* (available on this book's CD ROM and at *www.BruceEckel.com*).

```java
// When the constructor is called to create a
// Tag object, you'll see a message:
class Tag {
  Tag(int marker) {
    System.out.println("Tag(" + marker + ")");
  }
}

class Card {
  Tag t1 = new Tag(1); // Before constructor
  Card() {
    // Indicate we're in the constructor:
    System.out.println("Card()");
    t3 = new Tag(33); // Reinitialize t3
  }
  Tag t2 = new Tag(2); // After constructor
  void f() {
    System.out.println("f()");
  }
  Tag t3 = new Tag(3); // At end
}

public class OrderOfInitialization {
  public static void main(String[] args) {
    Card t = new Card();
    t.f(); // Shows that construction is done
  }
} ///:~
```

In **Card**, the definitions of the **Tag** objects are intentionally scattered about to prove that they'll all get initialized before the constructor is entered or anything else can happen. In addition, **t3** is reinitialized inside the constructor. The output is:

```
Tag(1)
Tag(2)
Tag(3)
Card()
Tag(33)
f()
```

Thus, the **t3** reference gets initialized twice, once before and once during the constructor call. (The first object is dropped, so it can be garbage-collected later.) This might not seem efficient at first, but it guarantees proper initialization—what would happen if an overloaded constructor were defined that did *not* initialize **t3** and there wasn't a "default" initialization for **t3** in its definition?

Static data initialization

When the data is **static** the same thing happens; if it's a primitive and you don't initialize it, it gets the standard primitive initial values. If it's a reference to an object, it's **null** unless you create a new object and attach your reference to it.

If you want to place initialization at the point of definition, it looks the same as for non-**static**s. There's only a single piece of storage for a **static**, regardless of how many objects are created. But the question arises of when the **static** storage gets initialized. An example makes this question clear:

```
//: c04:StaticInitialization.java
// Specifying initial values in a
// class definition.

class Bowl {
  Bowl(int marker) {
    System.out.println("Bowl(" + marker + ")");
  }
  void f(int marker) {
    System.out.println("f(" + marker + ")");
  }
}

class Table {
  static Bowl b1 = new Bowl(1);
  Table() {
    System.out.println("Table()");
    b2.f(1);
  }
  void f2(int marker) {
    System.out.println("f2(" + marker + ")");
```

```
    }
    static Bowl b2 = new Bowl(2);
}

class Cupboard {
    Bowl b3 = new Bowl(3);
    static Bowl b4 = new Bowl(4);
    Cupboard() {
        System.out.println("Cupboard()");
        b4.f(2);
    }
    void f3(int marker) {
        System.out.println("f3(" + marker + ")");
    }
    static Bowl b5 = new Bowl(5);
}

public class StaticInitialization {
    public static void main(String[] args) {
        System.out.println(
            "Creating new Cupboard() in main");
        new Cupboard();
        System.out.println(
            "Creating new Cupboard() in main");
        new Cupboard();
        t2.f2(1);
        t3.f3(1);
    }
    static Table t2 = new Table();
    static Cupboard t3 = new Cupboard();
} ///:~
```

Bowl allows you to view the creation of a class, and **Table** and **Cupboard** create **static** members of **Bowl** scattered through their class definitions. Note that **Cupboard** creates a non-**static Bowl b3** prior to the **static** definitions. The output shows what happens:

```
Bowl(1)
Bowl(2)
Table()
f(1)
```

```
Bowl(4)
Bowl(5)
Bowl(3)
Cupboard()
f(2)
Creating new Cupboard() in main
Bowl(3)
Cupboard()
f(2)
Creating new Cupboard() in main
Bowl(3)
Cupboard()
f(2)
f2(1)
f3(1)
```

The **static** initialization occurs only if it's necessary. If you don't create a **Table** object and you never refer to **Table.b1** or **Table.b2**, the **static** **Bowl b1** and **b2** will never be created. However, they are initialized only when the *first* **Table** object is created (or the first **static** access occurs). After that, the **static** objects are not reinitialized.

The order of initialization is **static**s first, if they haven't already been initialized by a previous object creation, and then the non-**static** objects. You can see the evidence of this in the output.

It's helpful to summarize the process of creating an object. Consider a class called **Dog**:

1.   The first time an object of type **Dog** is created, *or* the first time a **static** method or **static** field of class **Dog** is accessed, the Java interpreter must locate **Dog.class**, which it does by searching through the classpath.

2.   As **Dog.class** is loaded (creating a **Class** object, which you'll learn about later), all of its **static** initializers are run. Thus, **static** initialization takes place only once, as the **Class** object is loaded for the first time.

3.   When you create a **new Dog( )**, the construction process for a **Dog** object first allocates enough storage for a **Dog** object on the heap.

4.   This storage is wiped to zero, automatically setting all the primitives in that **Dog** object to their default values (zero for numbers and the equivalent for **boolean** and **char**) and the references to **null**.

5.   Any initializations that occur at the point of field definition are executed.

6.   Constructors are executed. As you shall see in Chapter 6, this might actually involve a fair amount of activity, especially when inheritance is involved.

Explicit static initialization

Java allows you to group other **static** initializations inside a special "**static** construction clause" (sometimes called a *static block*) in a class. It looks like this:

```
class Spoon {
  static int i;
  static {
    i = 47;
  }
  // . . .
```

It appears to be a method, but it's just the **static** keyword followed by a method body. This code, like other **static** initializations, is executed only once, the first time you make an object of that class *or* the first time you access a **static** member of that class (even if you never make an object of that class). For example:

```
//: c04:ExplicitStatic.java
// Explicit static initialization
// with the "static" clause.

class Cup {
  Cup(int marker) {
    System.out.println("Cup(" + marker + ")");
```

```
    }
    void f(int marker) {
      System.out.println("f(" + marker + ")");
    }
}

class Cups {
  static Cup c1;
  static Cup c2;
  static {
    c1 = new Cup(1);
    c2 = new Cup(2);
  }
  Cups() {
    System.out.println("Cups()");
  }
}

public class ExplicitStatic {
  public static void main(String[] args) {
    System.out.println("Inside main()");
    Cups.c1.f(99);  // (1)
  }
  // static Cups x = new Cups();  // (2)
  // static Cups y = new Cups();  // (2)
} ///:~
```

The **static** initializers for **Cups** run when either the access of the **static** object **c1** occurs on the line marked (1), or if line (1) is commented out and the lines marked (2) are uncommented. If both (1) and (2) are commented out, the **static** initialization for **Cups** never occurs. Also, it doesn't matter if one or both of the lines marked (2) are uncommented; the static initialization only occurs once.

Non-static instance initialization

Java provides a similar syntax for initializing non-**static** variables for each object. Here's an example:

```
//: c04:Mugs.java
// Java "Instance Initialization."
```

```
class Mug {
  Mug(int marker) {
    System.out.println("Mug(" + marker + ")");
  }
  void f(int marker) {
    System.out.println("f(" + marker + ")");
  }
}

public class Mugs {
  Mug c1;
  Mug c2;
  {
    c1 = new Mug(1);
    c2 = new Mug(2);
    System.out.println("c1 & c2 initialized");
  }
  Mugs() {
    System.out.println("Mugs()");
  }
  public static void main(String[] args) {
    System.out.println("Inside main()");
    Mugs x = new Mugs();
  }
} ///:~
```

You can see that the instance initialization clause:

```
  {
    c1 = new Mug(1);
    c2 = new Mug(2);
    System.out.println("c1 & c2 initialized");
  }
```

looks exactly like the static initialization clause except for the missing **static** keyword. This syntax is necessary to support the initialization of *anonymous inner classes* (see Chapter 8).

Array initialization

Initializing arrays in C is error-prone and tedious. C++ uses *aggregate initialization* to make it much safer[5]. Java has no "aggregates" like C++, since everything is an object in Java. It does have arrays, and these are supported with array initialization.

An array is simply a sequence of either objects or primitives, all the same type and packaged together under one identifier name. Arrays are defined and used with the square-brackets *indexing operator* **[ ]**. To define an array you simply follow your type name with empty square brackets:

```
int[] a1;
```

You can also put the square brackets after the identifier to produce exactly the same meaning:

```
int a1[];
```

This conforms to expectations from C and C++ programmers. The former style, however, is probably a more sensible syntax, since it says that the type is "an **int** array." That style will be used in this book.

The compiler doesn't allow you to tell it how big the array is. This brings us back to that issue of "references." All that you have at this point is a reference to an array, and there's been no space allocated for the array. To create storage for the array you must write an initialization expression. For arrays, initialization can appear anywhere in your code, but you can also use a special kind of initialization expression that must occur at the point where the array is created. This special initialization is a set of values surrounded by curly braces. The storage allocation (the equivalent of using **new**) is taken care of by the compiler in this case. For example:

```
int[] a1 = { 1, 2, 3, 4, 5 };
```

So why would you ever define an array reference without an array?

---

[5] See *Thinking in C++, 2nd edition* for a complete description of C++ aggregate initialization.

```
int[] a2;
```

Well, it's possible to assign one array to another in Java, so you can say:

```
a2 = a1;
```

What you're really doing is copying a reference, as demonstrated here:

```
//: c04:Arrays.java
// Arrays of primitives.

public class Arrays {
  public static void main(String[] args) {
    int[] a1 = { 1, 2, 3, 4, 5 };
    int[] a2;
    a2 = a1;
    for(int i = 0; i < a2.length; i++)
      a2[i]++;
    for(int i = 0; i < a1.length; i++)
      System.out.println(
        "a1[" + i + "] = " + a1[i]);
  }
} ///:~
```

You can see that **a1** is given an initialization value while **a2** is not; **a2** is assigned later—in this case, to another array.

There's something new here: all arrays have an intrinsic member (whether they're arrays of objects or arrays of primitives) that you can query—but not change—to tell you how many elements there are in the array. This member is **length**. Since arrays in Java, like C and C++, start counting from element zero, the largest element you can index is **length - 1**. If you go out of bounds, C and C++ quietly accept this and allow you to stomp all over your memory, which is the source of many infamous bugs. However, Java protects you against such problems by causing a run-time error (an *exception*, the subject of Chapter 10) if you step out of bounds. Of course, checking every array access costs time and code and there's no way to turn it off, which means that array accesses might be a source of inefficiency in your program if they occur at a critical juncture. For Internet security and programmer productivity, the Java designers thought that this was a worthwhile trade-off.

What if you don't know how many elements you're going to need in your array while you're writing the program? You simply use **new** to create the elements in the array. Here, **new** works even though it's creating an array of primitives (**new** won't create a nonarray primitive):

```
//: c04:ArrayNew.java
// Creating arrays with new.
import java.util.*;

public class ArrayNew {
  static Random rand = new Random();
  static int pRand(int mod) {
    return Math.abs(rand.nextInt()) % mod + 1;
  }
  public static void main(String[] args) {
    int[] a;
    a = new int[pRand(20)];
    System.out.println(
      "length of a = " + a.length);
    for(int i = 0; i < a.length; i++)
      System.out.println(
        "a[" + i + "] = " + a[i]);
  }
} ///:~
```

Since the size of the array is chosen at random (using the **pRand( )** method), it's clear that array creation is actually happening at run-time. In addition, you'll see from the output of this program that array elements of primitive types are automatically initialized to "empty" values. (For numerics and **char**, this is zero, and for **boolean**, it's **false**.)

Of course, the array could also have been defined and initialized in the same statement:

```
int[] a = new int[pRand(20)];
```

If you're dealing with an array of nonprimitive objects, you must always use **new**. Here, the reference issue comes up again because what you create is an array of references. Consider the wrapper type **Integer,** which is a class and not a primitive:

```
//: c04:ArrayClassObj.java
```

```
// Creating an array of nonprimitive objects.
import java.util.*;

public class ArrayClassObj {
  static Random rand = new Random();
  static int pRand(int mod) {
    return Math.abs(rand.nextInt()) % mod + 1;
  }
  public static void main(String[] args) {
    Integer[] a = new Integer[pRand(20)];
    System.out.println(
      "length of a = " + a.length);
    for(int i = 0; i < a.length; i++) {
      a[i] = new Integer(pRand(500));
      System.out.println(
        "a[" + i + "] = " + a[i]);
    }
  }
} ///:~
```

Here, even after **new** is called to create the array:

```
Integer[] a = new Integer[pRand(20)];
```

it's only an array of references, and not until the reference itself is initialized by creating a new **Integer** object is the initialization complete:

```
a[i] = new Integer(pRand(500));
```

If you forget to create the object, however, you'll get an exception at run-time when you try to read the empty array location.

Take a look at the formation of the **String** object inside the print statements. You can see that the reference to the **Integer** object is automatically converted to produce a **String** representing the value inside the object.

It's also possible to initialize arrays of objects using the curly-brace-enclosed list. There are two forms:

```
//: c04:ArrayInit.java
// Array initialization.
```

```
public class ArrayInit {
  public static void main(String[] args) {
    Integer[] a = {
      new Integer(1),
      new Integer(2),
      new Integer(3),
    };

    Integer[] b = new Integer[] {
      new Integer(1),
      new Integer(2),
      new Integer(3),
    };
  }
} ///:~
```

This is useful at times, but it's more limited since the size of the array is determined at compile-time. The final comma in the list of initializers is optional. (This feature makes for easier maintenance of long lists.)

The second form of array initialization provides a convenient syntax to create and call methods that can produce the same effect as C's *variable argument lists* (known as "varargs" in C). These can include unknown quantity of arguments as well as unknown types. Since all classes are ultimately inherited from the common root class **Object** (a subject you will learn more about as this book progresses), you can create a method that takes an array of **Object** and call it like this:

```
//: c04:VarArgs.java
// Using the array syntax to create
// variable argument lists.

class A { int i; }

public class VarArgs {
  static void f(Object[] x) {
    for(int i = 0; i < x.length; i++)
      System.out.println(x[i]);
  }
  public static void main(String[] args) {
    f(new Object[] {
```

```
        new Integer(47), new VarArgs(),
        new Float(3.14), new Double(11.11) });
    f(new Object[] {"one", "two", "three" });
    f(new Object[] {new A(), new A(), new A()});
  }
} ///:~
```

At this point, there's not much you can do with these unknown objects, and this program uses the automatic **String** conversion to do something useful with each **Object**. In Chapter 12, which covers *run-time type identification* (RTTI), you'll learn how to discover the exact type of such objects so that you can do something more interesting with them.

Multidimensional arrays

Java allows you to easily create multidimensional arrays:

```
//: c04:MultiDimArray.java
// Creating multidimensional arrays.
import java.util.*;

public class MultiDimArray {
  static Random rand = new Random();
  static int pRand(int mod) {
    return Math.abs(rand.nextInt()) % mod + 1;
  }
  static void prt(String s) {
    System.out.println(s);
  }
  public static void main(String[] args) {
    int[][] a1 = {
      { 1, 2, 3, },
      { 4, 5, 6, },
    };
    for(int i = 0; i < a1.length; i++)
      for(int j = 0; j < a1[i].length; j++)
        prt("a1[" + i + "][" + j +
          "] = " + a1[i][j]);
    // 3-D array with fixed length:
    int[][][] a2 = new int[2][2][4];
    for(int i = 0; i < a2.length; i++)
```

```java
        for(int j = 0; j < a2[i].length; j++)
          for(int k = 0; k < a2[i][j].length;
              k++)
            prt("a2[" + i + "][" +
                j + "][" + k +
                "] = " + a2[i][j][k]);
    // 3-D array with varied-length vectors:
    int[][][] a3 = new int[pRand(7)][][];
    for(int i = 0; i < a3.length; i++) {
      a3[i] = new int[pRand(5)][];
      for(int j = 0; j < a3[i].length; j++)
        a3[i][j] = new int[pRand(5)];
    }
    for(int i = 0; i < a3.length; i++)
      for(int j = 0; j < a3[i].length; j++)
        for(int k = 0; k < a3[i][j].length;
            k++)
          prt("a3[" + i + "][" +
              j + "][" + k +
              "] = " + a3[i][j][k]);
    // Array of nonprimitive objects:
    Integer[][] a4 = {
      { new Integer(1), new Integer(2) },
      { new Integer(3), new Integer(4) },
      { new Integer(5), new Integer(6) },
    };
    for(int i = 0; i < a4.length; i++)
      for(int j = 0; j < a4[i].length; j++)
        prt("a4[" + i + "][" + j +
            "] = " + a4[i][j]);
    Integer[][] a5;
    a5 = new Integer[3][];
    for(int i = 0; i < a5.length; i++) {
      a5[i] = new Integer[3];
      for(int j = 0; j < a5[i].length; j++)
        a5[i][j] = new Integer(i*j);
    }
    for(int i = 0; i < a5.length; i++)
      for(int j = 0; j < a5[i].length; j++)
        prt("a5[" + i + "][" + j +
            "] = " + a5[i][j]);
```

```
  }
} ///:~
```

The code used for printing uses **length** so that it doesn't depend on fixed array sizes.

The first example shows a multidimensional array of primitives. You delimit each vector in the array with curly braces:

```
int[][] a1 = {
  { 1, 2, 3, },
  { 4, 5, 6, },
};
```

Each set of square brackets moves you into the next level of the array.

The second example shows a three-dimensional array allocated with **new**. Here, the whole array is allocated at once:

```
int[][][] a2 = new int[2][2][4];
```

But the third example shows that each vector in the arrays that make up the matrix can be of any length:

```
int[][][] a3 = new int[pRand(7)][][];
for(int i = 0; i < a3.length; i++) {
  a3[i] = new int[pRand(5)][];
  for(int j = 0; j < a3[i].length; j++)
    a3[i][j] = new int[pRand(5)];
}
```

The first **new** creates an array with a random-length first element and the rest undetermined. The second **new** inside the **for** loop fills out the elements but leaves the third index undetermined until you hit the third **new**.

You will see from the output that array values are automatically initialized to zero if you don't give them an explicit initialization value.

You can deal with arrays of nonprimitive objects in a similar fashion, which is shown in the fourth example, demonstrating the ability to collect many **new** expressions with curly braces:

```
Integer[][] a4 = {
```

```
      { new Integer(1), new Integer(2) },
      { new Integer(3), new Integer(4) },
      { new Integer(5), new Integer(6) },
   };
```

The fifth example shows how an array of nonprimitive objects can be built up piece by piece:

```
   Integer[][] a5;
   a5 = new Integer[3][];
   for(int i = 0; i < a5.length; i++) {
     a5[i] = new Integer[3];
     for(int j = 0; j < a5[i].length; j++)
       a5[i][j] = new Integer(i*j);
   }
```

The **i*j** is just to put an interesting value into the **Integer**.

Summary

This seemingly elaborate mechanism for initialization, the constructor, should give you a strong hint about the critical importance placed on initialization in the language. As Stroustrup was designing C++, one of the first observations he made about productivity in C was that improper initialization of variables causes a significant portion of programming problems. These kinds of bugs are hard to find, and similar issues apply to improper cleanup. Because constructors allow you to *guarantee* proper initialization and cleanup (the compiler will not allow an object to be created without the proper constructor calls), you get complete control and safety.

In C++, destruction is quite important because objects created with **new** must be explicitly destroyed. In Java, the garbage collector automatically releases the memory for all objects, so the equivalent cleanup method in Java isn't necessary much of the time. In cases where you don't need destructor-like behavior, Java's garbage collector greatly simplifies programming, and adds much-needed safety in managing memory. Some garbage collectors can even clean up other resources like graphics and file handles. However, the garbage collector does add a run-time cost, the expense of which is difficult to put into perspective because of the overall slowness of Java interpreters at this writing. As this changes, we'll be able to discover if the overhead of the garbage collector will preclude the use of Java for certain types of programs. (One of the issues is the unpredictability of the garbage collector.)

Because of the guarantee that all objects will be constructed, there's actually more to the constructor than what is shown here. In particular, when you create new classes using either *composition* or *inheritance* the guarantee of construction also holds, and some additional syntax is necessary to support this. You'll learn about composition, inheritance, and how they affect constructors in future chapters.

Exercises

Solutions to selected exercises can be found in the electronic document *The Thinking in Java Annotated Solution Guide*, available for a small fee from *www.BruceEckel.com*.

1. Create a class with a default constructor (one that takes no arguments) that prints a message. Create an object of this class.

2. Add an overloaded constructor to Exercise 1 that takes a **String** argument and prints it along with your message.

3. Create an array of object references of the class you created in Exercise 2, but don't actually create objects to assign into the array. When you run the program, notice whether the initialization messages from the constructor calls are printed.

4. Complete Exercise 3 by creating objects to attach to the array of references.

5. Create an array of **String** objects and assign a string to each element. Print the array using a **for** loop.

6. Create a class called **Dog** with an overloaded **bark( )** method. This method should be overloaded based on various primitive data types, and print different types of barking, howling, etc., depending on which overloaded version is called. Write a **main( )** that calls all the different versions.

7.   Modify Exercise 6 so that two of the overloaded methods have two arguments (of two different types), but in reversed order relative to each other. Verify that this works.

8.   Create a class without a constructor, and then create an object of that class in **main( )** to verify that the default constructor is automatically synthesized.

9.   Create a class with two methods. Within the first method, call the second method twice: the first time without using **this**, and the second time using **this**.

10.   Create a class with two (overloaded) constructors. Using **this**, call the second constructor inside the first one.

11.   Create a class with a **finalize( )** method that prints a message. In **main( )**, create an object of your class. Explain the behavior of your program.

12.   Modify Exercise 11 so that your **finalize( )** will always be called.

13.   Create a class called **Tank** that can be filled and emptied, and has a *death condition* that it must be empty when the object is cleaned up. Write a **finalize( )** that verifies this death condition. In **main( )**, test the possible scenarios that can occur when your **Tank** is used.

14.   Create a class containing an **int** and a **char** that are not initialized, and print their values to verify that Java performs default initialization.

15.   Create a class containing an uninitialized **String** reference. Demonstrate that this reference is initialized by Java to **null**.

16.   Create a class with a **String** field that is initialized at the point of definition, and another one that is initialized by the constructor. What is the difference between the two approaches?

17.   Create a class with a **static String** field that is initialized at the point of definition, and another one that is initialized by the **static**

block. Add a **static** method that prints both fields and demonstrates that they are both initialized before they are used.

18.   Create a class with a **String** that is initialized using "instance initialization." Describe a use for this feature (other than the one specified in this book).

19.   Write a method that creates and initializes a two-dimensional array of **double**. The size of the array is determined by the arguments of the method, and the initialization values are a range determined by beginning and ending values that are also arguments of the method. Create a second method that will print the array generated by the first method. In **main( )** test the methods by creating and printing several different sizes of arrays.

20.   Repeat Exercise 19 for a three-dimensional array.

21.   Comment the line marked (1) in **ExplicitStatic.java** and verify that the static initialization clause is not called. Now uncomment one of the lines marked (2) and verify that the static initialization clause *is* called. Now uncomment the other line marked (2) and verify that static initialization only occurs once.

22.   Experiment with **Garbage.java** by running the program using the arguments "gc," "finalize," or "all." Repeat the process and see if you detect any patterns in the output. Change the code so that **System.runFinalization( )** is called *before* **System.gc( )** and observe the results.

5: Hiding the Implementation

A primary consideration in object-oriented design is "separating the things that change from the things that stay the same."

This is particularly important for libraries. The user (*client programmer*) of that library must be able to rely on the part they use, and know that they won't need to rewrite code if a new version of the library comes out. On the flip side, the library creator must have the freedom to make modifications and improvements with the certainty that the client programmer's code won't be affected by those changes.

This can be achieved through convention. For example, the library programmer must agree to not remove existing methods when modifying a class in the library, since that would break the client programmer's code. The reverse situation is thornier, however. In the case of a data member, how can the library creator know which data members have been accessed by client programmers? This is also true with methods that are only part of the implementation of a class, and not meant to be used directly by the client programmer. But what if the library creator wants to rip out an old implementation and put in a new one? Changing any of those members might break a client programmer's code. Thus the library creator is in a strait jacket and can't change anything.

To solve this problem, Java provides *access specifiers* to allow the library creator to say what is available to the client programmer and what is not. The levels of access control from "most access" to "least access" are **public**, **protected**, "friendly" (which has no keyword), and **private**. From the previous paragraph you might think that, as a library designer, you'll want to keep everything as "private" as possible, and expose only the methods that you want the client programmer to use. This is exactly right, even though it's often counterintuitive for people who program in other languages (especially C) and are used to accessing everything without restriction. By the end of this chapter you should be convinced of the value of access control in Java.

The concept of a library of components and the control over who can access the components of that library is not complete, however. There's still the question of how the components are bundled together into a cohesive library unit. This is controlled with the **package** keyword in Java, and the access specifiers are affected by whether a class is in the same package or in a separate package. So to begin this chapter, you'll learn how library components are placed into packages. Then you'll be able to understand the complete meaning of the access specifiers.

package: the library unit

A package is what you get when you use the **import** keyword to bring in an entire library, such as

```
import java.util.*;
```

This brings in the entire utility library that's part of the standard Java distribution. Since, for example, the class **ArrayList** is in **java.util**, you can now either specify the full name **java.util.ArrayList** (which you can do without the **import** statement), or you can simply say **ArrayList** (because of the **import**).

If you want to bring in a single class, you can name that class in the **import** statement

```
import java.util.ArrayList;
```

Now you can use **ArrayList** with no qualification. However, none of the other classes in **java.util** are available.

The reason for all this importing is to provide a mechanism to manage "name spaces." The names of all your class members are insulated from each other. A method **f( )** inside a class **A** will not clash with an **f( )** that has the same signature (argument list) in class **B**. But what about the class names? Suppose you create a **stack** class that is installed on a machine that already has a **stack** class that's written by someone else? With Java on the Internet, this can happen without the user knowing it, since classes can get downloaded automatically in the process of running a Java program.

This potential clashing of names is why it's important to have complete control over the name spaces in Java, and to be able to create a completely unique name regardless of the constraints of the Internet.

So far, most of the examples in this book have existed in a single file and have been designed for local use, and haven't bothered with package names. (In this case the class name is placed in the "default package.") This is certainly an option, and for simplicity's sake this approach will be used whenever possible throughout the rest of this book. However, if you're planning to create libraries or programs that are friendly to other Java programs on the same machine, you must think about preventing class name clashes.

When you create a source-code file for Java, it's commonly called a *compilation unit* (sometimes a *translation unit*). Each compilation unit must have a name ending in **.java**, and inside the compilation unit there can be a **public** class that must have the same name as the file (including capitalization, but excluding the **.java** filename extension). There can be only *one* **public** class in each compilation unit, otherwise the compiler will complain. The rest of the classes in that compilation unit, if there are any, are hidden from the world outside that package because they're *not* **public**, and they comprise "support" classes for the main **public** class.

When you compile a **.java** file you get an output file with exactly the same name but an extension of **.class** *for each class in the* **.java** file. Thus you can cnd up with quite a few **.class** files from a small number of **.java** files. If you've programmed with a compiled language, you might be used to the compiler spitting out an intermediate form (usually an "obj" file) that is then packaged together with others of its kind using a linker (to create an executable file) or a librarian (to create a library). That's not how Java works. A working program is a bunch of **.class** files, which can be packaged and compressed into a JAR file (using Java's **jar** archiver).

The Java interpreter is responsible for finding, loading, and interpreting these files[1].

A library is also a bunch of these class files. Each file has one class that is **public** (you're not forced to have a **public** class, but it's typical), so there's one component for each file. If you want to say that all these components (that are in their own separate **.java** and **.class** files) belong together, that's where the **package** keyword comes in.

When you say:

```
package mypackage;
```

at the beginning of a file (if you use a **package** statement, it *must* appear as the first noncomment in the file), you're stating that this compilation unit is part of a library named **mypackage**. Or, put another way, you're saying that the **public** class name within this compilation unit is under the umbrella of the name **mypackage**, and if anyone wants to use the name they must either fully specify the name or use the **import** keyword in combination with **mypackage** (using the choices given previously). Note that the convention for Java package names is to use all lowercase letters, even for intermediate words.

For example, suppose the name of the file is **MyClass.java**. This means there can be one and only one **public** class in that file, and the name of that class must be **MyClass** (including the capitalization):

```
package mypackage;
public class MyClass {
  // . . .
```

Now, if someone wants to use **MyClass** or, for that matter, any of the other **public** classes in **mypackage**, they must use the **import** keyword to make the name or names in **mypackage** available. The alternative is to give the fully qualified name:

```
mypackage.MyClass m = new mypackage.MyClass();
```

---

[1] There's nothing in Java that forces the use of an interpreter. There exist native-code Java compilers that generate a single executable file.

The **import** keyword can make this much cleaner:

```
import mypackage.*;
// . . .
MyClass m = new MyClass();
```

It's worth keeping in mind that what the **package** and **import** keywords allow you to do, as a library designer, is to divide up the single global name space so you won't have clashing names, no matter how many people get on the Internet and start writing classes in Java.

Creating unique package names

You might observe that, since a package never really gets "packaged" into a single file, a package could be made up of many **.class** files, and things could get a bit cluttered. To prevent this, a logical thing to do is to place all the **.class** files for a particular package into a single directory; that is, use the hierarchical file structure of the operating system to your advantage. This is one way that Java references the problem of clutter; you'll see the other way later when the **jar** utility is introduced.

Collecting the package files into a single subdirectory solves two other problems: creating unique package names, and finding those classes that might be buried in a directory structure someplace. This is accomplished, as was introduced in Chapter 2, by encoding the path of the location of the **.class** file into the name of the **package**. The compiler enforces this, but by convention, the first part of the **package** name is the Internet domain name of the creator of the class, reversed. Since Internet domain names are guaranteed to be unique, *if* you follow this convention it's guaranteed that your **package** name will be unique and thus you'll never have a name clash. (That is, until you lose the domain name to someone else who starts writing Java code with the same path names as you did.) Of course, if you don't have your own domain name then you must fabricate an unlikely combination (such as your first and last name) to create unique package names. If you've decided to start publishing Java code it's worth the relatively small effort to get a domain name.

The second part of this trick is resolving the **package** name into a directory on your machine, so when the Java program runs and it needs to load the **.class** file (which it does dynamically, at the point in the program where it needs to create an object of that particular class, or the first time you access a **static** member of the class), it can locate the directory where the **.class** file resides.

The Java interpreter proceeds as follows. First, it finds the environment variable CLASSPATH (set via the operating system, sometimes by the installation program that installs Java or a Java-based tool on your machine). CLASSPATH contains one or more directories that are used as roots for a search for **.class** files. Starting at that root, the interpreter will take the package name and replace each dot with a slash to generate a path name from the CLASSPATH root (so **package foo.bar.baz** becomes **foo\bar\baz** or **foo/bar/baz** or possibly something else, depending on your operating system). This is then concatenated to the various entries in the CLASSPATH. That's where it looks for the **.class** file with the name corresponding to the class you're trying to create. (It also searches some standard directories relative to where the Java interpreter resides).

To understand this, consider my domain name, which is **bruceeckel.com**. By reversing this, **com.bruceeckel** establishes my unique global name for my classes. (The com, cdu, org, etc., extension was formerly capitalized in Java packages, but this was changed in Java 2 so the entire package name is lowercase.) I can further subdivide this by deciding that I want to create a library named **simple**, so I'll end up with a package name:

```
package com.bruceeckel.simple;
```

Now this package name can be used as an umbrella name space for the following two files:

```
//: com:bruceeckel:simple:Vector.java
// Creating a package.
package com.bruceeckel.simple;

public class Vector {
  public Vector() {
    System.out.println(
      "com.bruceeckel.util.Vector");
  }
} ///:~
```

When you create your own packages, you'll discover that the **package** statement must be the first noncomment code in the file. The second file looks much the same:

```
//: com:bruceeckel:simple:List.java
// Creating a package.
package com.bruceeckel.simple;

public class List {
  public List() {
    System.out.println(
      "com.bruceeckel.util.List");
  }
} ///:~
```

Both of these files are placed in the subdirectory on my system:

```
C:\DOC\JavaT\com\bruceeckel\simple
```

If you walk back through this, you can see the package name **com.bruceeckel.simple**, but what about the first portion of the path? That's taken care of in the CLASSPATH environment variable, which is, on my machine:

```
CLASSPATH=.;D:\JAVA\LIB;C:\DOC\JavaT
```

You can see that the CLASSPATH can contain a number of alternative search paths.

There's a variation when using JAR files, however. You must put the name of the JAR file in the classpath, not just the path where it's located. So for a JAR named **grape.jar** your classpath would include:

```
CLASSPATH=.;D:\JAVA\LIB;C:\flavors\grape.jar
```

Once the classpath is set up properly, the following file can be placed in any directory:

```
//: c05:LibTest.java
// Uses the library.
import com.bruceeckel.simple.*;

public class LibTest {
```

```
  public static void main(String[] args) {
    Vector v = new Vector();
    List l = new List();
  }
} ///:~
```

When the compiler encounters the **import** statement, it begins searching at the directories specified by CLASSPATH, looking for subdirectory com\bruceeckel\simple, then seeking the compiled files of the appropriate names (**Vector.class** for **Vector** and **List.class** for **List**). Note that both the classes and the desired methods in **Vector** and **List** must be **public**.

Setting the CLASSPATH has been such a trial for beginning Java users (it was for me, when I started) that Sun made the JDK in Java 2 a bit smarter. You'll find that, when you install it, even if you don't set a CLASSPATH you'll be able to compile and run basic Java programs. To compile and run the source-code package for this book (available on the CD ROM packaged with this book, or at *www.BruceEckel.com*), however, you will need to make some modifications to your CLASSPATH (these are explained in the source-code package).

Collisions

What happens if two libraries are imported via * and they include the same names? For example, suppose a program does this:

```
import com.bruceeckel.simple.*;
import java.util.*;
```

Since **java.util.*** also contains a **Vector** class, this causes a potential collision. However, as long as you don't write the code that actually causes the collision, everything is OK—this is good because otherwise you might end up doing a lot of typing to prevent collisions that would never happen.

The collision *does* occur if you now try to make a **Vector**:

```
Vector v = new Vector();
```

Which **Vector** class does this refer to? The compiler can't know, and the reader can't know either. So the compiler complains and forces you to be explicit. If I want the standard Java **Vector**, for example, I must say:

```
java.util.Vector v = new java.util.Vector();
```

Since this (along with the CLASSPATH) completely specifies the location of that **Vector**, there's no need for the **import java.util.*** statement unless I'm using something else from **java.util**.

A custom tool library

With this knowledge, you can now create your own libraries of tools to reduce or eliminate duplicate code. Consider, for example, creating an alias for **System.out.println( )** to reduce typing. This can be part of a package called **tools**:

```
//: com:bruceeckel:tools:P.java
// The P.rint & P.rintln shorthand.
package com.bruceeckel.tools;

public class P {
  public static void rint(String s) {
    System.out.print(s);
  }
  public static void rintln(String s) {
    System.out.println(s);
  }
} ///:~
```

You can use this shorthand to print a **String** either with a newline (**P.rintln( )**) or without a newline (**P.rint( )**).

You can guess that the location of this file must be in a directory that starts at one of the CLASSPATH locations, then continues **com/bruceeckel/tools**. After compiling, the **P.class** file can be used anywhere on your system with an **import** statement:

```
//: c05:ToolTest.java
// Uses the tools library.
import com.bruceeckel.tools.*;

public class ToolTest {
  public static void main(String[] args) {
    P.rintln("Available from now on!");
    P.rintln("" + 100); // Force it to be a String
```

```
    P.rintln("" + 100L);
    P.rintln("" + 3.14159);
  }
} ///:~
```

Notice that all objects can easily be forced into **String** representations by putting them in a **String** expression; in the above case, starting the expression with an empty **String** does the trick. But this brings up an interesting observation. If you call **System.out.println(100)**, it works without casting it to a **String**. With some extra overloading, you can get the **P** class to do this as well (this is an exercise at the end of this chapter).

So from now on, whenever you come up with a useful new utility, you can add it to the **tools** directory. (Or to your own personal **util** or **tools** directory.)

Using imports to change behavior

A feature that is missing from Java is C's *conditional compilation*, which allows you to change a switch and get different behavior without changing any other code. The reason such a feature was left out of Java is probably because it is most often used in C to solve cross-platform issues: different portions of the code are compiled depending on the platform that the code is being compiled for. Since Java is intended to be automatically cross-platform, such a feature should not be necessary.

However, there are other valuable uses for conditional compilation. A very common use is for debugging code. The debugging features are enabled during development, and disabled in the shipping product. Allen Holub (*www.holub.com*) came up with the idea of using packages to mimic conditional compilation. He used this to create a Java version of C's very useful *assertion mechanism*, whereby you can say "this should be true" or "this should be false" and if the statement doesn't agree with your assertion you'll find out about it. Such a tool is quite helpful during debugging.

Here is the class that you'll use for debugging:

```
//: com:bruceeckel:tools:debug:Assert.java
// Assertion tool for debugging.
package com.bruceeckel.tools.debug;
```

```
public class Assert {
  private static void perr(String msg) {
    System.err.println(msg);
  }
  public final static void is_true(boolean exp) {
    if(!exp) perr("Assertion failed");
  }
  public final static void is_false(boolean exp){
    if(exp) perr("Assertion failed");
  }
  public final static void
  is_true(boolean exp, String msg) {
    if(!exp) perr("Assertion failed: " + msg);
  }
  public final static void
  is_false(boolean exp, String msg) {
    if(exp) perr("Assertion failed: " + msg);
  }
} ///:~
```

This class simply encapsulates Boolean tests, which print error messages if they fail. In Chapter 10, you'll learn about a more sophisticated tool for dealing with errors called *exception handling*, but the **perr( )** method will work fine in the meantime.

The output is printed to the console *standard error* stream by writing to **System.err**.

When you want to use this class, you add a line in your program:

```
import com.bruceeckel.tools.debug.*;
```

To remove the assertions so you can ship the code, a second **Assert** class is created, but in a different package:

```
//: com:bruceeckel:tools:Assert.java
// Turning off the assertion output
// so you can ship the program.
package com.bruceeckel.tools;

public class Assert {
```

```
    public final static void is_true(boolean exp){}
    public final static void is_false(boolean exp){}
    public final static void
    is_true(boolean exp, String msg) {}
    public final static void
    is_false(boolean exp, String msg) {}
} ///:~
```

Now if you change the previous **import** statement to:

```
import com.bruceeckel.tools.*;
```

The program will no longer print assertions. Here's an example:

```
//: c05:TestAssert.java
// Demonstrating the assertion tool.
// Comment the following, and uncomment the
// subsequent line to change assertion behavior:
import com.bruceeckel.tools.debug.*;
// import com.bruceeckel.tools.*;

public class TestAssert {
  public static void main(String[] args) {
    Assert.is_true((2 + 2) == 5);
    Assert.is_false((1 + 1) == 2);
    Assert.is_true((2 + 2) == 5, "2 + 2 == 5");
    Assert.is_false((1 + 1) == 2, "1 +1 != 2");
  }
} ///:~
```

By changing the **package** that's imported, you change your code from the
debug version to the production version. This technique can be used for
any kind of conditional code.

Package caveat

It's worth remembering that anytime you create a package, you implicitly
specify a directory structure when you give the package a name. The
package *must* live in the directory indicated by its name, which must be a
directory that is searchable starting from the CLASSPATH.
Experimenting with the **package** keyword can be a bit frustrating at first,
because unless you adhere to the package-name to directory-path rule,

you'll get a lot of mysterious run-time messages about not being able to find a particular class, even if that class is sitting there in the same directory. If you get a message like this, try commenting out the **package** statement, and if it runs you'll know where the problem lies.

Java access specifiers

When used, the Java access specifiers **public**, **protected**, and **private** are placed in front of each definition for each member in your class, whether it's a field or a method. Each access specifier controls the access for only that particular definition. This is a distinct contrast to C++, in which the access specifier controls all the definitions following it until another access specifier comes along.

One way or another, everything has some kind of access specified for it. In the following sections, you'll learn all about the various types of access, starting with the default access.

"Friendly"

What if you give no access specifier at all, as in all the examples before this chapter? The default access has no keyword, but it is commonly referred to as "friendly." It means that all the other classes in the current package have access to the friendly member, but to all the classes outside of this package the member appears to be **private**. Since a compilation unit—a file—can belong only to a single package, all the classes within a single compilation unit are automatically friendly with each other. Thus, friendly elements are also said to have *package access*.

Friendly access allows you to group related classes together in a package so that they can easily interact with each other. When you put classes together in a package (thus granting mutual access to their friendly members; e.g., making them "friends") you "own" the code in that package. It makes sense that only code you own should have friendly access to other code you own. You could say that friendly access gives a meaning or a reason for grouping classes together in a package. In many languages the way you organize your definitions in files can be willy-nilly, but in Java you're compelled to organize them in a sensible fashion. In

---

addition, you'll probably want to exclude classes that shouldn't have access to the classes being defined in the current package.

The class controls which code has access to its members. There's no magic way to "break in." Code from another package can't show up and say, "Hi, I'm a friend of **Bob**'s!" and expect to see the **protected**, friendly, and **private** members of **Bob**. The only way to grant access to a member is to:

1. Make the member **public**. Then everybody, everywhere, can access it.

2. Make the member friendly by leaving off any access specifier, and put the other classes in the same package. Then the other classes can access the member.

3. As you'll see in Chapter 6, when inheritance is introduced, an inherited class can access a **protected** member as well as a **public** member (but not **private** members). It can access friendly members only if the two classes are in the same package. But don't worry about that now.

4. Provide "accessor/mutator" methods (also known as "get/set" methods) that read and change the value. This is the most civilized approach in terms of OOP, and it is fundamental to JavaBeans, as you'll see in Chapter 13.

public: interface access

When you use the **public** keyword, it means that the member declaration that immediately follows **public** is available to everyone, in particular to the client programmer who uses the library. Suppose you define a package **dessert** containing the following compilation unit:

```
//: c05:dessert:Cookie.java
// Creates a library.
package c05.dessert;

public class Cookie {
  public Cookie() {
    System.out.println("Cookie constructor");
  }
```

```
  void bite() { System.out.println("bite"); }
} ///:~
```

Remember, **Cookie.java** must reside in a subdirectory called **dessert**, in a directory under **c05** (indicating Chapter 5 of this book) that must be under one of the CLASSPATH directories. Don't make the mistake of thinking that Java will always look at the current directory as one of the starting points for searching. If you don't have a '.' as one of the paths in your CLASSPATH, Java won't look there.

Now if you create a program that uses **Cookie**:

```
//: c05:Dinner.java
// Uses the library.
import c05.dessert.*;

public class Dinner {
  public Dinner() {
    System.out.println("Dinner constructor");
  }
  public static void main(String[] args) {
    Cookie x = new Cookie();
    //! x.bite(); // Can't access
  }
} ///:~
```

you can create a **Cookie** object, since its constructor is **public** and the class is **public**. (We'll look more at the concept of a **public** class later.) However, the **bite( )** member is inaccessible inside **Dinner.java** since **bite( )** is friendly only within package **dessert**.

The default package

You might be surprised to discover that the following code compiles, even though it would appear that it breaks the rules:

```
//: c05:Cake.java
// Accesses a class in a
// separate compilation unit.

class Cake {
  public static void main(String[] args) {
```

```
    Pie x = new Pie();
    x.f();
  }
} ///:~
```

In a second file, in the same directory:

```
//: c05:Pie.java
// The other class.

class Pie {
  void f() { System.out.println("Pie.f()"); }
} ///:~
```

You might initially view these as completely foreign files, and yet **Cake** is able to create a **Pie** object and call its **f( )** method! (Note that you must have '.' in your CLASSPATH in order for the files to compile.) You'd typically think that **Pie** and **f( )** are friendly and therefore not available to **Cake**. They *are* friendly—that part is correct. The reason that they are available in **Cake.java** is because they are in the same directory and have no explicit package name. Java treats files like this as implicitly part of the "default package" for that directory, and therefore friendly to all the other files in that directory.

private: you can't touch that!

The **private** keyword means that no one can access that member except that particular class, inside methods of that class. Other classes in the same package cannot access **private** members, so it's as if you're even insulating the class against yourself. On the other hand, it's not unlikely that a package might be created by several people collaborating together, so **private** allows you to freely change that member without concern that it will affect another class in the same package.

The default "friendly" package access often provides an adequate amount of hiding; remember, a "friendly" member is inaccessible to the user of the package. This is nice, since the default access is the one that you normally use (and the one that you'll get if you forget to add any access control). Thus, you'll typically think about access for the members that you explicitly want to make **public** for the client programmer, and as a result, you might not initially think you'll use the **private** keyword often since it's tolerable to get away without it. (This is a distinct contrast with C++.) However, it turns out that the consistent use of **private** is very important, especially where multithreading is concerned. (As you'll see in Chapter 14.)

Here's an example of the use of **private**:

```
//: c05:IceCream.java
// Demonstrates "private" keyword.

class Sundae {
  private Sundae() {}
  static Sundae makeASundae() {
    return new Sundae();
  }
}

public class IceCream {
  public static void main(String[] args) {
    //! Sundae x = new Sundae();
    Sundae x = Sundae.makeASundae();
  }
} ///:~
```

This shows an example in which **private** comes in handy: you might want to control how an object is created and prevent someone from directly accessing a particular constructor (or all of them). In the example above, you cannot create a **Sundae** object via its constructor; instead you must call the **makeASundae( )** method to do it for you[2].

Any method that you're certain is only a "helper" method for that class can be made **private,** to ensure that you don't accidentally use it elsewhere in the package and thus prohibit yourself from changing or removing the method. Making a method **private** guarantees that you retain this option.

---

[2] There's another effect in this case: Since the default constructor is the only one defined, and it's **private**, it will prevent inheritance of this class. (A subject that will be introduced in Chapter 6.)

The same is true for a **private** field inside a class. Unless you must expose the underlying implementation (which is a much rarer situation than you might think), you should make all fields **private**. However, just because a reference to an object is **private** inside a class doesn't mean that some other object can't have a **public** reference to the same object. (See Appendix A for issues about aliasing.)

protected: "sort of friendly"

The **protected** access specifier requires a jump ahead to understand. First, you should be aware that you don't need to understand this section to continue through this book up through inheritance (Chapter 6). But for completeness, here is a brief description and example using **protected**.

The **protected** keyword deals with a concept called *inheritance*, which takes an existing class and adds new members to that class without touching the existing class, which we refer to as the *base class*. You can also change the behavior of existing members of the class. To inherit from an existing class, you say that your new class **extends** an existing class, like this:

```
class Foo extends Bar {
```

The rest of the class definition looks the same.

If you create a new package and you inherit from a class in another package, the only members you have access to are the **public** members of the original package. (Of course, if you perform the inheritance in the *same* package, you have the normal package access to all the "friendly" members.) Sometimes the creator of the base class would like to take a particular member and grant access to derived classes but not the world in general. That's what **protected** does. If you refer back to the file **Cookie.java**, the following class *cannot* access the "friendly" member:

```
//: c05:ChocolateChip.java
// Can't access friendly member
// in another class.
import c05.dessert.*;

public class ChocolateChip extends Cookie {
  public ChocolateChip() {
```

```
    System.out.println(
      "ChocolateChip constructor");
  }
  public static void main(String[] args) {
    ChocolateChip x = new ChocolateChip();
    //! x.bite(); // Can't access bite
  }
} ///:~
```

One of the interesting things about inheritance is that if a method **bite( )** exists in class **Cookie**, then it also exists in any class inherited from **Cookie**. But since **bite( )** is "friendly" in a foreign package, it's unavailable to us in this one. Of course, you could make it **public**, but then everyone would have access and maybe that's not what you want. If we change the class **Cookie** as follows:

```
public class Cookie {
  public Cookie() {
    System.out.println("Cookie constructor");
  }
  protected void bite() {
    System.out.println("bite");
  }
}
```

then **bite( )** still has "friendly" access within package **dessert**, but it is also accessible to anyone inheriting from **Cookie**. However, it is *not* **public**.

Interface and implementation

Access control is often referred to as *implementation hiding*. Wrapping data and methods within classes in combination with implementation hiding is often called *encapsulation*[3]. The result is a data type with characteristics and behaviors.

---

[3] However, people often refer to implementation hiding alone as encapsulation.

Access control puts boundaries within a data type for two important reasons. The first is to establish what the client programmers can and can't use. You can build your internal mechanisms into the structure without worrying that the client programmers will accidentally treat the internals as part of the interface that they should be using.

This feeds directly into the second reason, which is to separate the interface from the implementation. If the structure is used in a set of programs, but client programmers can't do anything but send messages to the **public** interface, then you can change anything that's *not* **public** (e.g., "friendly," **protected**, or **private**) without requiring modifications to client code.

We're now in the world of object-oriented programming, where a **class** is actually describing "a class of objects," as you would describe a class of fishes or a class of birds. Any object belonging to this class will share these characteristics and behaviors. The class is a description of the way all objects of this type will look and act.

In the original OOP language, Simula-67, the keyword **class** was used to describe a new data type. The same keyword has been used for most object-oriented languages. This is the focal point of the whole language: the creation of new data types that are more than just boxes containing data and methods.

The class is the fundamental OOP concept in Java. It is one of the keywords that will *not* be set in bold in this book—it becomes annoying with a word repeated as often as "class."

For clarity, you might prefer a style of creating classes that puts the **public** members at the beginning, followed by the **protected**, friendly, and **private** members. The advantage is that the user of the class can then read down from the top and see first what's important to them (the **public** members, because they can be accessed outside the file), and stop reading when they encounter the non-**public** members, which are part of the internal implementation:

```
public class X {
  public void pub1( ) { /* . . . */ }
  public void pub2( ) { /* . . . */ }
```

```
    public void pub3( ) { /* . . . */ }
    private void priv1( ) { /* . . . */ }
    private void priv2( ) { /* . . . */ }
    private void priv3( ) { /* . . . */ }
    private int i;
    // . . .
}
```

This will make it only partially easier to read because the interface and implementation are still mixed together. That is, you still see the source code—the implementation—because it's right there in the class. In addition, the comment documentation supported by javadoc (described in Chapter 2) lessens the importance of code readability by the client programmer. Displaying the interface to the consumer of a class is really the job of the *class browser*, a tool whose job is to look at all the available classes and show you what you can do with them (i.e., what members are available) in a useful fashion. By the time you read this, browsers should be an expected part of any good Java development tool.

Class access

In Java, the access specifiers can also be used to determine which classes *within* a library will be available to the users of that library. If you want a class to be available to a client programmer, you place the **public** keyword somewhere before the opening brace of the class body. This controls whether the client programmer can even create an object of the class.

To control the access of a class, the specifier must appear before the keyword **class**. Thus you can say:

```
public class Widget {
```

Now if the name of your library is **mylib** any client programmer can access **Widget** by saying

```
import mylib.Widget;
```

or

```
import mylib.*;
```

However, there's an extra set of constraints:

1. There can be only one **public** class per compilation unit (file). The idea is that each compilation unit has a single public interface represented by that **public** class. It can have as many supporting "friendly" classes as you want. If you have more than one **public** class inside a compilation unit, the compiler will give you an error message.

2. The name of the **public** class must exactly match the name of the file containing the compilation unit, including capitalization. So for **Widget**, the name of the file must be **Widget.java**, not **widget.java** or **WIDGET.java**. Again, you'll get a compile-time error if they don't agree.

3. It is possible, though not typical, to have a compilation unit with no **public** class at all. In this case, you can name the file whatever you like.

What if you've got a class inside **mylib** that you're just using to accomplish the tasks performed by **Widget** or some other **public** class in **mylib**? You don't want to go to the bother of creating documentation for the client programmer, and you think that sometime later you might want to completely change things and rip out your class altogether, substituting a different one. To give you this flexibility, you need to ensure that no client programmers become dependent on your particular implementation details hidden inside **mylib**. To accomplish this, you just leave the **public** keyword off the class, in which case it becomes friendly. (That class can be used only within that package.)

Note that a class cannot be **private** (that would make it accessible to no one but the class), or **protected**[4]. So you have only two choices for class access: "friendly" or **public**. If you don't want anyone else to have access to that class, you can make all the constructors **private**, thereby

---

[4] Actually, an *inner class* can be private or protected, but that's a special case. These will be introduced in Chapter 7.

preventing anyone but you, inside a **static** member of the class, from creating an object of that class[5]. Here's an example:

```
//: c05:Lunch.java
// Demonstrates class access specifiers.
// Make a class effectively private
// with private constructors:

class Soup {
  private Soup() {}
  // (1) Allow creation via static method:
  public static Soup makeSoup() {
    return new Soup();
  }
  // (2) Create a static object and
  // return a reference upon request.
  // (The "Singleton" pattern):
  private static Soup ps1 = new Soup();
  public static Soup access() {
    return ps1;
  }
  public void f() {}
}

class Sandwich { // Uses Lunch
  void f() { new Lunch(); }
}

// Only one public class allowed per file:
public class Lunch {
  void test() {
    // Can't do this! Private constructor:
    //! Soup priv1 = new Soup();
    Soup priv2 = Soup.makeSoup();
    Sandwich f1 = new Sandwich();
    Soup.access().f();
  }
} ///:~
```

---

[5] You can also do it by inheriting (Chapter 6) from that class.

Up to now, most of the methods have been returning either **void** or a primitive type, so the definition:

```
public static Soup access() {
   return ps1;
}
```

might look a little confusing at first. The word before the method name (**access**) tells what the method returns. So far this has most often been **void,** which means it returns nothing. But you can also return a reference to an object, which is what happens here. This method returns a reference to an object of class **Soup**.

The **class Soup** shows how to prevent direct creation of a class by making all the constructors **private**. Remember that if you don't explicitly create at least one constructor, the default constructor (a constructor with no arguments) will be created for you. By writing the default constructor, it won't be created automatically. By making it **private**, no one can create an object of that class. But now how does anyone use this class? The above example shows two options. First, a **static** method is created that creates a new **Soup** and returns a reference to it. This could be useful if you want to do some extra operations on the **Soup** before returning it, or if you want to keep count of how many **Soup** objects to create (perhaps to restrict their population).

The second option uses what's called a *design pattern*, which is covered in *Thinking in Patterns with Java*, downloadable at *www.BruceEckel.com*. This particular pattern is called a "singleton" because it allows only a single object to ever be created. The object of class **Soup** is created as a **static private** member of **Soup**, so there's one and only one, and you can't get at it except through the **public** method **access( )**.

As previously mentioned, if you don't put an access specifier for class access it defaults to "friendly." This means that an object of that class can be created by any other class in the package, but not outside the package. (Remember, all the files within the same directory that don't have explicit **package** declarations are implicitly part of the default package for that directory.) However, if a **static** member of that class is **public**, the client programmer can still access that **static** member even though they cannot create an object of that class.

Summary

In any relationship it's important to have boundaries that are respected by all parties involved. When you create a library, you establish a relationship with the user of that library—the client programmer—who is another programmer, but one putting together an application or using your library to build a bigger library.

Without rules, client programmers can do anything they want with all the members of a class, even if you might prefer they don't directly manipulate some of the members. Everything's naked to the world.

This chapter looked at how classes are built to form libraries; first, the way a group of classes is packaged within a library, and second, the way the class controls access to its members.

It is estimated that a C programming project begins to break down somewhere between 50K and 100K lines of code because C has a single "name space" so names begin to collide, causing an extra management overhead. In Java, the **package** keyword, the package naming scheme, and the **import** keyword give you complete control over names, so the issue of name collision is easily avoided.

There are two reasons for controlling access to members. The first is to keep users' hands off tools that they shouldn't touch; tools that are necessary for the internal machinations of the data type, but not part of the interface that users need to solve their particular problems. So making methods and fields **private** is a service to users because they can easily see what's important to them and what they can ignore. It simplifies their understanding of the class.

The second and most important reason for access control is to allow the library designer to change the internal workings of the class without worrying about how it will affect the client programmer. You might build a class one way at first, and then discover that restructuring your code will provide much greater speed. If the interface and implementation are clearly separated and protected, you can accomplish this without forcing the user to rewrite their code.

Access specifiers in Java give valuable control to the creator of a class. The users of the class can clearly see exactly what they can use and what to ignore. More important, though, is the ability to ensure that no user becomes dependent on any part of the underlying implementation of a class. If you know this as the creator of the class, you can change the underlying implementation with the knowledge that no client programmer will be affected by the changes because they can't access that part of the class.

When you have the ability to change the underlying implementation, you can not only improve your design later, but you also have the freedom to make mistakes. No matter how carefully you plan and design you'll make mistakes. Knowing that it's relatively safe to make these mistakes means you'll be more experimental, you'll learn faster, and you'll finish your project sooner.

The public interface to a class is what the user *does* see, so that is the most important part of the class to get "right" during analysis and design. Even that allows you some leeway for change. If you don't get the interface right the first time, you can *add* more methods, as long as you don't remove any that client programmers have already used in their code.

Exercises

Solutions to selected exercises can be found in the electronic document *The Thinking in Java Annotated Solution Guide*, available for a small fee from *www.BruceEckel.com*.

1. Write a program that creates an **ArrayList** object without explicitly importing **java.util.***.

2. In the section labeled "package: the library unit," turn the code fragments concerning **mypackage** into a compiling and running set of Java files.

3. In the section labeled "Collisions," take the code fragments and turn them into a program, and verify that collisions do in fact occur.

4. Generalize the class **P** defined in this chapter by adding all the overloaded versions of **rint( )** and **rintln( )** necessary to handle all the different basic Java types.

5.   Change the import statement in **TestAssert.java** to enable and disable the assertion mechanism.

6.   Create a class with **public**, **private**, **protected**, and "friendly" data members and method members. Create an object of this class and see what kind of compiler messages you get when you try to access all the class members. Be aware that classes in the same directory are part of the "default" package.

7.   Create a class with **protected** data. Create a second class in the same file with a method that manipulates the **protected** data in the first class.

8.   Change the class **Cookie** as specified in the section labeled "**protected**: 'sort of friendly.'" Verify that **bite( )** is not **public**.

9.   In the section titled "Class access" you'll find code fragments describing **mylib** and **Widget**. Create this library, then create a **Widget** in a class that is not part of the **mylib** package.

10.   Create a new directory and edit your CLASSPATH to include that new directory. Copy the **P.class** file (produced by compiling **com.bruceeckel.tools.P.java**) to your new directory and then change the names of the file, the **P** class inside and the method names. (You might also want to add additional output to watch how it works.) Create another program in a different directory that uses your new class.

11.   Following the form of the example **Lunch.java**, create a class called **ConnectionManager** that manages a fixed array of **Connection** objects. The client programmer must not be able to explicitly create **Connection** objects, but can only get them via a **static** method in **ConnectionManager**. When the **ConnectionManager** runs out of objects, it returns a **null** reference. Test the classes in **main( )**.

12.   Create the following file in the c05/local directory (presumably in your CLASSPATH):

```
///: c05:local:PackagedClass.java
package c05.local;
```

```
class PackagedClass {
  public PackagedClass() {
    System.out.println(
      "Creating a packaged class");
  }
} ///:~
```

Then create the following file in a directory other than c05:

```
///: c05:foreign:Foreign.java
package c05.foreign;
import c05.local.*;
public class Foreign {
    public static void main (String[] args) {
        PackagedClass pc = new PackagedClass();
    }
} ///:~
```

Explain why the compiler generates an error. Would making the **Foreign** class part of the **c05.local** package change anything?

6: Reusing Classes

One of the most compelling features about Java is code reuse. But to be revolutionary, you've got to be able to do a lot more than copy code and change it.

That's the approach used in procedural languages like C, and it hasn't worked very well. Like everything in Java, the solution revolves around the class. You reuse code by creating new classes, but instead of creating them from scratch, you use existing classes that someone has already built and debugged.

The trick is to use the classes without soiling the existing code. In this chapter you'll see two ways to accomplish this. The first is quite straightforward: You simply create objects of your existing class inside the new class. This is called *composition,* because the new class is composed of objects of existing classes. You're simply reusing the functionality of the code, not its form.

The second approach is more subtle. It creates a new class as a *type of* an existing class. You literally take the form of the existing class and add code to it without modifying the existing class. This magical act is called *inheritance*, and the compiler does most of the work. Inheritance is one of the cornerstones of object-oriented programming, and has additional implications that will be explored in Chapter 7.

It turns out that much of the syntax and behavior are similar for both composition and inheritance (which makes sense because they are both ways of making new types from existing types). In this chapter, you'll learn about these code reuse mechanisms.

Composition syntax

Until now, composition has been used quite frequently. You simply place object references inside new classes. For example, suppose you'd like an object that holds several **String** objects, a couple of primitives, and an object of another class. For the nonprimitive objects, you put references inside your new class, but you define the primitives directly:

```
//: c06:SprinklerSystem.java
// Composition for code reuse.

class WaterSource {
  private String s;
  WaterSource() {
    System.out.println("WaterSource()");
    s = new String("Constructed");
  }
  public String toString() { return s; }
}

public class SprinklerSystem {
  private String valve1, valve2, valve3, valve4;
  WaterSource source;
  int i;
  float f;
  void print() {
    System.out.println("valve1 = " + valve1);
    System.out.println("valve2 = " + valve2);
    System.out.println("valve3 = " + valve3);
    System.out.println("valve4 = " + valve4);
    System.out.println("i = " + i);
    System.out.println("f = " + f);
    System.out.println("source = " + source);
  }
  public static void main(String[] args) {
    SprinklerSystem x = new SprinklerSystem();
    x.print();
  }
} ///:~
```

One of the methods defined in **WaterSource** is special: **toString( )**. You will learn later that every nonprimitive object has a **toString( )** method, and it's called in special situations when the compiler wants a **String** but it's got one of these objects. So in the expression:

```
System.out.println("source = " + source);
```

the compiler sees you trying to add a **String** object ("**source = **") to a **WaterSource**. This doesn't make sense to it, because you can only "add" a **String** to another **String**, so it says "I'll turn **source** into a **String** by calling **toString( )**!" After doing this it can combine the two **Strings** and pass the resulting **String** to **System.out.println( )**. Any time you want to allow this behavior with a class you create you need only write a **toString( )** method.

At first glance, you might assume—Java being as safe and careful as it is—that the compiler would automatically construct objects for each of the references in the above code; for example, calling the default constructor for **WaterSource** to initialize **source**. The output of the print statement is in fact:

```
valve1 = null
valve2 = null
valve3 = null
valve4 = null
i = 0
f = 0.0
source = null
```

Primitives that are fields in a class are automatically initialized to zero, as noted in Chapter 2. But the object references are initialized to **null**, and if you try to call methods for any of them you'll get an exception. It's actually pretty good (and useful) that you can still print them out without throwing an exception.

It makes sense that the compiler doesn't just create a default object for every reference because that would incur unnecessary overhead in many cases. If you want the references initialized, you can do it:

1. At the point the objects are defined. This means that they'll always be initialized before the constructor is called.

2. In the constructor for that class.

3. Right before you actually need to use the object. This is often called *lazy initialization*. It can reduce overhead in situations where the object doesn't need to be created every time.

All three approaches are shown here:

```
//: c06:Bath.java
// Constructor initialization with composition.

class Soap {
  private String s;
  Soap() {
    System.out.println("Soap()");
    s = new String("Constructed");
  }
  public String toString() { return s; }
}

public class Bath {
  private String
    // Initializing at point of definition:
    s1 = new String("Happy"),
    s2 = "Happy",
    s3, s4;
  Soap castille;
  int i;
  float toy;
  Bath() {
    System.out.println("Inside Bath()");
    s3 = new String("Joy");
    i = 47;
    toy = 3.14f;
    castille = new Soap();
  }
  void print() {
    // Delayed initialization:
    if(s4 == null)
      s4 = new String("Joy");
    System.out.println("s1 = " + s1);
    System.out.println("s2 = " + s2);
    System.out.println("s3 = " + s3);
    System.out.println("s4 = " + s4);
    System.out.println("i = " + i);
    System.out.println("toy = " + toy);
    System.out.println("castille = " + castille);
```

```
  }
  public static void main(String[] args) {
    Bath b = new Bath();
    b.print();
  }
} ///:~
```

Note that in the **Bath** constructor a statement is executed before any of the initializations take place. When you don't initialize at the point of definition, there's still no guarantee that you'll perform any initialization before you send a message to an object reference—except for the inevitable run-time exception.

Here's the output for the program:

```
Inside Bath()
Soap()
s1 = Happy
s2 = Happy
s3 = Joy
s4 = Joy
i = 47
toy = 3.14
castille = Constructed
```

When **print( )** is called it fills in **s4** so that all the fields are properly initialized by the time they are used.

Inheritance syntax

Inheritance is an integral part of Java (and OOP languages in general). It turns out that you're always doing inheritance when you create a class, because unless you explicitly inherit from some other class, you implicitly inherit from Java's standard root class **Object**.

The syntax for composition is obvious, but to perform inheritance there's a distinctly different form. When you inherit, you say "This new class is like that old class." You state this in code by giving the name of the class as usual, but before the opening brace of the class body, put the keyword **extends** followed by the name of the *base class*. When you do this, you automatically get all the data members and methods in the base class. Here's an example:

```
//: c06:Detergent.java
// Inheritance syntax & properties.

class Cleanser {
  private String s = new String("Cleanser");
  public void append(String a) { s += a; }
  public void dilute() { append(" dilute()"); }
  public void apply() { append(" apply()"); }
  public void scrub() { append(" scrub()"); }
  public void print() { System.out.println(s); }
  public static void main(String[] args) {
    Cleanser x = new Cleanser();
    x.dilute(); x.apply(); x.scrub();
    x.print();
  }
}

public class Detergent extends Cleanser {
  // Change a method:
  public void scrub() {
    append(" Detergent.scrub()");
    super.scrub(); // Call base-class version
  }
  // Add methods to the interface:
  public void foam() { append(" foam()"); }
  // Test the new class:
  public static void main(String[] args) {
    Detergent x = new Detergent();
    x.dilute();
    x.apply();
    x.scrub();
    x.foam();
    x.print();
    System.out.println("Testing base class:");
    Cleanser.main(args);
  }
} ///:~
```

This demonstrates a number of features. First, in the **Cleanser** **append( )** method, **String**s are concatenated to **s** using the += operator, which is one of the operators (along with '+') that the Java designers "overloaded" to work with **String**s.

Second, both **Cleanser** and **Detergent** contain a **main( )** method. You can create a **main( )** for each one of your classes, and it's often recommended to code this way so that your test code is wrapped in with the class. Even if you have a lot of classes in a program, only the **main( )** for the class invoked on the command line will be called. (As long as **main( )** is **public**, it doesn't matter whether the class that it's part of is **public**.) So in this case, when you say **java Detergent**, **Detergent.main( )** will be called. But you can also say **java Cleanser** to invoke **Cleanser.main( )**, even though **Cleanser** is not a **public** class. This technique of putting a **main( )** in each class allows easy unit testing for each class. And you don't need to remove the **main( )** when you're finished testing; you can leave it in for later testing.

Here, you can see that **Detergent.main( )** calls **Cleanser.main( )** explicitly, passing it the same arguments from the command line (however, you could pass it any **String** array).

It's important that all of the methods in **Cleanser** are **public**. Remember that if you leave off any access specifier the member defaults to "friendly," which allows access only to package members. Thus, *within this package*, anyone could use those methods if there were no access specifier. **Detergent** would have no trouble, for example. However, if a class from some other package were to inherit from **Cleanser** it could access only **public** members. So to plan for inheritance, as a general rule make all fields **private** and all methods **public**. (**protected** members also allow access by derived classes; you'll learn about this later.) Of course, in particular cases you must make adjustments, but this is a useful guideline.

Note that **Cleanser** has a set of methods in its interface: **append( )**, **dilute( )**, **apply( )**, **scrub( )**, and **print( )**. Because **Detergent** is *derived from* **Cleanser** (via the **extends** keyword) it automatically gets all these methods in its interface, even though you don't see them all explicitly defined in **Detergent**. You can think of inheritance, then, as *reusing the interface.* (The implementation also comes with it, but that part isn't the primary point.)

As seen in **scrub( )**, it's possible to take a method that's been defined in the base class and modify it. In this case, you might want to call the method from the base class inside the new version. But inside **scrub( )** you cannot simply call **scrub( )**, since that would produce a recursive call, which isn't what you want. To solve this problem Java has the keyword **super** that refers to the "superclass" that the current class has been inherited from. Thus the expression **super.scrub( )** calls the base-class version of the method **scrub( )**.

When inheriting you're not restricted to using the methods of the base class. You can also add new methods to the derived class exactly the way you put any method in a class: just define it. The method **foam( )** is an example of this.

In **Detergent.main( )** you can see that for a **Detergent** object you can call all the methods that are available in **Cleanser** as well as in **Detergent** (i.e., **foam( )**).

Initializing the base class

Since there are now two classes involved—the base class and the derived class—instead of just one, it can be a bit confusing to try to imagine the resulting object produced by a derived class. From the outside, it looks like the new class has the same interface as the base class and maybe some additional methods and fields. But inheritance doesn't just copy the interface of the base class. When you create an object of the derived class, it contains within it a *subobject* of the base class. This subobject is the same as if you had created an object of the base class by itself. It's just that, from the outside, the subobject of the base class is wrapped within the derived-class object.

Of course, it's essential that the base-class subobject be initialized correctly and there's only one way to guarantee that: perform the initialization in the constructor, by calling the base-class constructor, which has all the appropriate knowledge and privileges to perform the base-class initialization. Java automatically inserts calls to the base-class constructor in the derived-class constructor. The following example shows this working with three levels of inheritance:

```
//: c06:Cartoon.java
// Constructor calls during inheritance.

class Art {
  Art() {
    System.out.println("Art constructor");
  }
}

class Drawing extends Art {
  Drawing() {
    System.out.println("Drawing constructor");
  }
}

public class Cartoon extends Drawing {
  Cartoon() {
    System.out.println("Cartoon constructor");
  }
  public static void main(String[] args) {
    Cartoon x = new Cartoon();
  }
} ///:~
```

The output for this program shows the automatic calls:

```
Art constructor
Drawing constructor
Cartoon constructor
```

You can see that the construction happens from the base "outward," so the base class is initialized before the derived-class constructors can access it.

Even if you don't create a constructor for **Cartoon( )**, the compiler will synthesize a default constructor for you that calls the base class constructor.

Constructors with arguments

The above example has default constructors; that is, they don't have any arguments. It's easy for the compiler to call these because there's no question about what arguments to pass. If your class doesn't have default arguments, or if you want to call a base-class constructor that has an argument, you must explicitly write the calls to the base-class constructor using the **super** keyword and the appropriate argument list:

```
//: c06:Chess.java
// Inheritance, constructors and arguments.

class Game {
  Game(int i) {
    System.out.println("Game constructor");
  }
}

class BoardGame extends Game {
  BoardGame(int i) {
    super(i);
    System.out.println("BoardGame constructor");
  }
}

public class Chess extends BoardGame {
  Chess() {
    super(11);
    System.out.println("Chess constructor");
  }
  public static void main(String[] args) {
    Chess x = new Chess();
  }
} ///:~
```

If you don't call the base-class constructor in **BoardGame( )**, the compiler will complain that it can't find a constructor of the form **Game( )**. In addition, the call to the base-class constructor *must* be the first thing you do in the derived-class constructor. (The compiler will remind you if you get it wrong.)

Catching base constructor exceptions

As just noted, the compiler forces you to place the base-class constructor call first in the body of the derived-class constructor. This means nothing else can appear before it. As you'll see in Chapter 10, this also prevents a derived-class constructor from catching any exceptions that come from a base class. This can be inconvenient at times.

Combining composition and inheritance

It is very common to use composition and inheritance together. The following example shows the creation of a more complex class, using both inheritance and composition, along with the necessary constructor initialization:

```
//: c06:PlaceSetting.java
// Combining composition & inheritance.

class Plate {
  Plate(int i) {
    System.out.println("Plate constructor");
  }
}

class DinnerPlate extends Plate {
  DinnerPlate(int i) {
    super(i);
    System.out.println(
      "DinnerPlate constructor");
  }
}

class Utensil {
  Utensil(int i) {
    System.out.println("Utensil constructor");
  }
}
```

```java
class Spoon extends Utensil {
  Spoon(int i) {
    super(i);
    System.out.println("Spoon constructor");
  }
}

class Fork extends Utensil {
  Fork(int i) {
    super(i);
    System.out.println("Fork constructor");
  }
}

class Knife extends Utensil {
  Knife(int i) {
    super(i);
    System.out.println("Knife constructor");
  }
}

// A cultural way of doing something:
class Custom {
  Custom(int i) {
    System.out.println("Custom constructor");
  }
}

public class PlaceSetting extends Custom {
  Spoon sp;
  Fork frk;
  Knife kn;
  DinnerPlate pl;
  PlaceSetting(int i) {
    super(i + 1);
    sp = new Spoon(i + 2);
    frk = new Fork(i + 3);
    kn = new Knife(i + 4);
    pl = new DinnerPlate(i + 5);
    System.out.println(
      "PlaceSetting constructor");
```

```
    }
  public static void main(String[] args) {
    PlaceSetting x = new PlaceSetting(9);
  }
} ///:~
```

While the compiler forces you to initialize the base classes, and requires that you do it right at the beginning of the constructor, it doesn't watch over you to make sure that you initialize the member objects, so you must remember to pay attention to that.

Guaranteeing proper cleanup

Java doesn't have the C++ concept of a *destructor*, a method that is automatically called when an object is destroyed. The reason is probably that in Java the practice is simply to forget about objects rather than to destroy them, allowing the garbage collector to reclaim the memory as necessary.

Often this is fine, but there are times when your class might perform some activities during its lifetime that require cleanup. As mentioned in Chapter 4, you can't know when the garbage collector will be called, or if it will be called. So if you want something cleaned up for a class, you must explicitly write a special method to do it, and make sure that the client programmer knows that they must call this method. On top of this—as described in Chapter 10 ("Error Handling with Exceptions")—you must guard against an exception by putting such cleanup in a **finally** clause.

Consider an example of a computer-aided design system that draws pictures on the screen:

```
//: c06:CADSystem.java
// Ensuring proper cleanup.
import java.util.*;

class Shape {
  Shape(int i) {
    System.out.println("Shape constructor");
  }
  void cleanup() {
    System.out.println("Shape cleanup");
```

```java
    }
  }

class Circle extends Shape {
  Circle(int i) {
    super(i);
    System.out.println("Drawing a Circle");
  }
  void cleanup() {
    System.out.println("Erasing a Circle");
    super.cleanup();
  }
}

class Triangle extends Shape {
  Triangle(int i) {
    super(i);
    System.out.println("Drawing a Triangle");
  }
  void cleanup() {
    System.out.println("Erasing a Triangle");
    super.cleanup();
  }
}

class Line extends Shape {
  private int start, end;
  Line(int start, int end) {
    super(start);
    this.start = start;
    this.end = end;
    System.out.println("Drawing a Line: " +
            start + ", " + end);
  }
  void cleanup() {
    System.out.println("Erasing a Line: " +
            start + ", " + end);
    super.cleanup();
  }
}
```

```java
public class CADSystem extends Shape {
  private Circle c;
  private Triangle t;
  private Line[] lines = new Line[10];
  CADSystem(int i) {
    super(i + 1);
    for(int j = 0; j < 10; j++)
      lines[j] = new Line(j, j*j);
    c = new Circle(1);
    t = new Triangle(1);
    System.out.println("Combined constructor");
  }
  void cleanup() {
    System.out.println("CADSystem.cleanup()");
    // The order of cleanup is the reverse
    // of the order of initialization
    t.cleanup();
    c.cleanup();
    for(int i = lines.length - 1; i >= 0; i--)
      lines[i].cleanup();
    super.cleanup();
  }
  public static void main(String[] args) {
    CADSystem x = new CADSystem(47);
    try {
      // Code and exception handling...
    } finally {
      x.cleanup();
    }
  }
} ///:~
```

Everything in this system is some kind of **Shape** (which is itself a kind of **Object** since it's implicitly inherited from the root class). Each class redefines **Shape**'s **cleanup( )** method in addition to calling the base-class version of that method using **super**. The specific **Shape** classes—**Circle**, **Triangle** and **Line**—all have constructors that "draw," although any method called during the lifetime of the object could be responsible for doing something that needs cleanup. Each class has its own **cleanup( )** method to restore nonmemory things back to the way they were before the object existed.

In **main( )**, you can see two keywords that are new, and won't officially be introduced until Chapter 10: **try** and **finally**. The **try** keyword indicates that the block that follows (delimited by curly braces) is a *guarded region*, which means that it is given special treatment. One of these special treatments is that the code in the **finally** clause following this guarded region is *always* executed, no matter how the **try** block exits. (With exception handling, it's possible to leave a **try** block in a number of nonordinary ways.) Here, the **finally** clause is saying "always call **cleanup( )** for **x**, no matter what happens." These keywords will be explained thoroughly in Chapter 10.

Note that in your cleanup method you must also pay attention to the calling order for the base-class and member-object cleanup methods in case one subobject depends on another. In general, you should follow the same form that is imposed by a C++ compiler on its destructors: First perform all of the cleanup work specific to your class, in the reverse order of creation. (In general, this requires that base-class elements still be viable.) Then call the base-class cleanup method, as demonstrated here.

There can be many cases in which the cleanup issue is not a problem; you just let the garbage collector do the work. But when you must do it explicitly, diligence and attention is required.

Order of garbage collection

There's not much you can rely on when it comes to garbage collection. The garbage collector might never be called. If it is, it can reclaim objects in any order it wants. It's best to not rely on garbage collection for anything but memory reclamation. If you want cleanup to take place, make your own cleanup methods and don't rely on **finalize( )**. (As mentioned in Chapter 4, Java can be forced to call all the finalizers.)

Name hiding

Only C++ programmers might be surprised by name hiding, since it works differently in that language. If a Java base class has a method name that's overloaded several times, redefining that method name in the derived class will *not* hide any of the base-class versions. Thus overloading works regardless of whether the method was defined at this level or in a base class:

```
//: c06:Hide.java
// Overloading a base-class method name
// in a derived class does not hide the
// base-class versions.

class Homer {
  char doh(char c) {
    System.out.println("doh(char)");
    return 'd';
  }
  float doh(float f) {
    System.out.println("doh(float)");
    return 1.0f;
  }
}

class Milhouse {}

class Bart extends Homer {
  void doh(Milhouse m) {}
}

class Hide {
  public static void main(String[] args) {
    Bart b = new Bart();
    b.doh(1); // doh(float) used
    b.doh('x');
    b.doh(1.0f);
    b.doh(new Milhouse());
  }
} ///:~
```

As you'll see in the next chapter, it's far more common to override methods of the same name using exactly the same signature and return type as in the base class. It can be confusing otherwise (which is why C++ disallows it, to prevent you from making what is probably a mistake).

Choosing composition vs. inheritance

Both composition and inheritance allow you to place subobjects inside your new class. You might wonder about the difference between the two, and when to choose one over the other.

Composition is generally used when you want the features of an existing class inside your new class, but not its interface. That is, you embed an object so that you can use it to implement functionality in your new class, but the user of your new class sees the interface you've defined for the new class rather than the interface from the embedded object. For this effect, you embed **private** objects of existing classes inside your new class.

Sometimes it makes sense to allow the class user to directly access the composition of your new class; that is, to make the member objects **public**. The member objects use implementation hiding themselves, so this is a safe thing to do. When the user knows you're assembling a bunch of parts, it makes the interface easier to understand. A **car** object is a good example:

```
//: c06:Car.java
// Composition with public objects.

class Engine {
  public void start() {}
  public void rev() {}
  public void stop() {}
}

class Wheel {
  public void inflate(int psi) {}
}

class Window {
  public void rollup() {}
  public void rolldown() {}
```

```
  }

class Door {
  public Window window = new Window();
  public void open() {}
  public void close() {}
}

public class Car {
  public Engine engine = new Engine();
  public Wheel[] wheel = new Wheel[4];
  public Door left = new Door(),
      right = new Door(); // 2-door
  public Car() {
    for(int i = 0; i < 4; i++)
      wheel[i] = new Wheel();
  }
  public static void main(String[] args) {
    Car car = new Car();
    car.left.window.rollup();
    car.wheel[0].inflate(72);
  }
} ///:~
```

Because the composition of a car is part of the analysis of the problem
(and not simply part of the underlying design), making the members
public assists the client programmer's understanding of how to use the
class and requires less code complexity for the creator of the class.
However, keep in mind that this is a special case and that in general you
should make fields **private**.

When you inherit, you take an existing class and make a special version of
it. In general, this means that you're taking a general-purpose class and
specializing it for a particular need. With a little thought, you'll see that it
would make no sense to compose a car using a vehicle object—a car
doesn't contain a vehicle, it *is* a vehicle. The *is-a* relationship is expressed
with inheritance, and the *has-a* relationship is expressed with
composition.

---

protected

Now that you've been introduced to inheritance, the keyword **protected** finally has meaning. In an ideal world, **private** members would always be hard-and-fast **private**, but in real projects there are times when you want to make something hidden from the world at large and yet allow access for members of derived classes. The **protected** keyword is a nod to pragmatism. It says "This is **private** as far as the class user is concerned, but available to anyone who inherits from this class or anyone else in the same **package**." That is, **protected** in Java is automatically "friendly."

The best tack to take is to leave the data members **private**—you should always preserve your right to change the underlying implementation. You can then allow controlled access to inheritors of your class through **protected** methods:

```
//: c06:Orc.java
// The protected keyword.
import java.util.*;

class Villain {
  private int i;
  protected int read() { return i; }
  protected void set(int ii) { i = ii; }
  public Villain(int ii) { i = ii; }
  public int value(int m) { return m*i; }
}

public class Orc extends Villain {
  private int j;
  public Orc(int jj) { super(jj); j = jj; }
  public void change(int x) { set(x); }
} ///:~
```

You can see that **change( )** has access to **set( )** because it's **protected**.

Incremental development

One of the advantages of inheritance is that it supports *incremental development* by allowing you to introduce new code without causing bugs in existing code. This also isolates new bugs inside the new code. By inheriting from an existing, functional class and adding data members and methods (and redefining existing methods), you leave the existing code—that someone else might still be using—untouched and unbugged. If a bug happens, you know that it's in your new code, which is much shorter and easier to read than if you had modified the body of existing code.

It's rather amazing how cleanly the classes are separated. You don't even need the source code for the methods in order to reuse the code. At most, you just import a package. (This is true for both inheritance and composition.)

It's important to realize that program development is an incremental process, just like human learning. You can do as much analysis as you want, but you still won't know all the answers when you set out on a project. You'll have much more success—and more immediate feedback—if you start out to "grow" your project as an organic, evolutionary creature, rather than constructing it all at once like a glass-box skyscraper.

Although inheritance for experimentation can be a useful technique, at some point after things stabilize you need to take a new look at your class hierarchy with an eye to collapsing it into a sensible structure. Remember that underneath it all, inheritance is meant to express a relationship that says "This new class is a *type of* that old class." Your program should not be concerned with pushing bits around, but instead with creating and manipulating objects of various types to express a model in the terms that come from the problem space.

Upcasting

The most important aspect of inheritance is not that it provides methods for the new class. It's the relationship expressed between the new class and the base class. This relationship can be summarized by saying "The new class *is a type of* the existing class."

This description is not just a fanciful way of explaining inheritance—it's supported directly by the language. As an example, consider a base class called **Instrument** that represents musical instruments, and a derived class called **Wind**. Because inheritance means that all of the methods in the base class are also available in the derived class, any message you can send to the base class can also be sent to the derived class. If the **Instrument** class has a **play( )** method, so will **Wind** instruments. This means we can accurately say that a **Wind** object is also a type of **Instrument**. The following example shows how the compiler supports this notion:

```
//: c06:Wind.java
// Inheritance & upcasting.
import java.util.*;

class Instrument {
  public void play() {}
  static void tune(Instrument i) {
    // ...
    i.play();
  }
}

// Wind objects are instruments
// because they have the same interface:
class Wind extends Instrument {
  public static void main(String[] args) {
    Wind flute = new Wind();
    Instrument.tune(flute); // Upcasting
  }
} ///:~
```

What's interesting in this example is the **tune( )** method, which accepts an **Instrument** reference. However, in **Wind.main( )** the **tune( )** method is called by giving it a **Wind** reference. Given that Java is particular about type checking, it seems strange that a method that accepts one type will readily accept another type, until you realize that a **Wind** object is also an **Instrument** object, and there's no method that

tune( ) could call for an **Instrument** that isn't also in **Wind**. Inside **tune( )**, the code works for **Instrument** and anything derived from **Instrument**, and the act of converting a **Wind** reference into an **Instrument** reference is called *upcasting*.

Why "upcasting"?

The reason for the term is historical, and based on the way class inheritance diagrams have traditionally been drawn: with the root at the top of the page, growing downward. (Of course, you can draw your diagrams any way you find helpful.) The inheritance diagram for **Wind.java** is then:

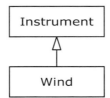

Casting from derived to base moves *up* on the inheritance diagram, so it's commonly referred to as *upcasting*. Upcasting is always safe because you're going from a more specific type to a more general type. That is, the derived class is a superset of the base class. It might contain more methods than the base class, but it must contain *at least* the methods in the base class. The only thing that can occur to the class interface during the upcast is that it can lose methods, not gain them. This is why the compiler allows upcasting without any explicit casts or other special notation.

You can also perform the reverse of upcasting, called *downcasting*, but this involves a dilemma that is the subject of Chapter 12.

Composition vs. inheritance revisited

In object-oriented programming, the most likely way that you'll create and use code is by simply packaging data and methods together into a class, and using objects of that class. You'll also use existing classes to build new classes with composition. Less frequently, you'll use inheritance. So although inheritance gets a lot of emphasis while learning

OOP, it doesn't mean that you should use it everywhere you possibly can. On the contrary, you should use it sparingly, only when it's clear that inheritance is useful. One of the clearest ways to determine whether you should use composition or inheritance is to ask whether you'll ever need to upcast from your new class to the base class. If you must upcast, then inheritance is necessary, but if you don't need to upcast, then you should look closely at whether you need inheritance. The next chapter (polymorphism) provides one of the most compelling reasons for upcasting, but if you remember to ask "Do I need to upcast?" you'll have a good tool for deciding between composition and inheritance.

The **final** keyword

Java's **final** keyword has slightly different meanings depending on the context, but in general it says "This cannot be changed." You might want to prevent changes for two reasons: design or efficiency. Because these two reasons are quite different, it's possible to misuse the **final** keyword.

The following sections discuss the three places where **final** can be used: for data, methods, and classes.

Final data

Many programming languages have a way to tell the compiler that a piece of data is "constant." A constant is useful for two reasons:

1.   It can be a *compile-time constant* that won't ever change.

2.   It can be a value initialized at run-time that you don't want changed.

In the case of a compile-time constant, the compiler is allowed to "fold" the constant value into any calculations in which it's used; that is, the calculation can be performed at compile-time, eliminating some run-time overhead. In Java, these sorts of constants must be primitives and are expressed using the **final** keyword. A value must be given at the time of definition of such a constant.

A field that is both **static** and **final** has only one piece of storage that cannot be changed.

When using **final** with object references rather than primitives the meaning gets a bit confusing. With a primitive, **final** makes the *value* a constant, but with an object reference, **final** makes the *reference* a constant. Once the reference is initialized to an object, it can never be changed to point to another object. However, the object itself can be modified; Java does not provide a way to make any arbitrary object a constant. (You can, however, write your class so that objects have the effect of being constant.) This restriction includes arrays, which are also objects.

Here's an example that demonstrates **final** fields:

```
//: c06:FinalData.java
// The effect of final on fields.

class Value {
  int i = 1;
}

public class FinalData {
  // Can be compile-time constants
  final int i1 = 9;
  static final int VAL_TWO = 99;
  // Typical public constant:
  public static final int VAL_THREE = 39;
  // Cannot be compile-time constants:
  final int i4 = (int)(Math.random()*20);
  static final int i5 = (int)(Math.random()*20);

  Value v1 = new Value();
  final Value v2 = new Value();
  static final Value v3 = new Value();
  // Arrays:
  final int[] a = { 1, 2, 3, 4, 5, 6 };

  public void print(String id) {
    System.out.println(
      id + ": " + "i4 = " + i4 +
      ", i5 = " + i5);
  }
  public static void main(String[] args) {
```

```
    FinalData fd1 = new FinalData();
    //! fd1.i1++; // Error: can't change value
    fd1.v2.i++; // Object isn't constant!
    fd1.v1 = new Value(); // OK -- not final
    for(int i = 0; i < fd1.a.length; i++)
      fd1.a[i]++; // Object isn't constant!
    //! fd1.v2 = new Value(); // Error: Can't
    //! fd1.v3 = new Value(); // change reference
    //! fd1.a = new int[3];

    fd1.print("fd1");
    System.out.println("Creating new FinalData");
    FinalData fd2 = new FinalData();
    fd1.print("fd1");
    fd2.print("fd2");
  }
} ///:~
```

Since **i1** and **VAL_TWO** are **final** primitives with compile-time values, they can both be used as compile-time constants and are not different in any important way. **VAL_THREE** is the more typical way you'll see such constants defined: **public** so they're usable outside the package, **static** to emphasize that there's only one, and **final** to say that it's a constant. Note that **final static** primitives with constant initial values (that is, compile-time constants) are named with all capitals by convention, with words separated by underscores (This is just like C constants, which is where the convention originated.) Also note that **i5** cannot be known at compile-time, so it is not capitalized.

Just because something is **final** doesn't mean that its value is known at compile-time. This is demonstrated by initializing **i4** and **i5** at run-time using randomly generated numbers. This portion of the example also shows the difference between making a **final** value **static** or non-**static**. This difference shows up only when the values are initialized at run-time, since the compile-time values are treated the same by the compiler. (And presumably optimized out of existence.) The difference is shown in the output from one run:

```
fd1: i4 = 15, i5 = 9
Creating new FinalData
fd1: i4 = 15, i5 = 9
```

```
fd2: i4 = 10, i5 = 9
```

Note that the values of **i4** for **fd1** and **fd2** are unique, but the value for **i5** is not changed by creating the second **FinalData** object. That's because it's **static** and is initialized once upon loading and not each time a new object is created.

The variables **v1** through **v4** demonstrate the meaning of a **final** reference. As you can see in **main( )**, just because **v2** is **final** doesn't mean that you can't change its value. However, you cannot rebind **v2** to a new object, precisely because it's **final**. That's what **final** means for a reference. You can also see the same meaning holds true for an array, which is just another kind of reference. (There is no way that I know of to make the array references themselves **final**.) Making references **final** seems less useful than making primitives **final**.

Blank finals

Java allows the creation of *blank finals*, which are fields that are declared as **final** but are not given an initialization value. In all cases, the blank final *must* be initialized before it is used, and the compiler ensures this. However, blank finals provide much more flexibility in the use of the **final** keyword since, for example, a **final** field inside a class can now be different for each object and yet it retains its immutable quality. Here's an example:

```
//: c06:BlankFinal.java
// "Blank" final data members.

class Poppet { }

class BlankFinal {
  final int i = 0; // Initialized final
  final int j; // Blank final
  final Poppet p; // Blank final reference
  // Blank finals MUST be initialized
  // in the constructor:
  BlankFinal() {
    j = 1; // Initialize blank final
    p = new Poppet();
  }
```

```
  BlankFinal(int x) {
    j = x; // Initialize blank final
    p = new Poppet();
  }
  public static void main(String[] args) {
    BlankFinal bf = new BlankFinal();
  }
} ///:~
```

You're forced to perform assignments to **final**s either with an expression at the point of definition of the field or in every constructor. This way it's guaranteed that the **final** field is always initialized before use.

Final arguments

Java allows you to make arguments **final** by declaring them as such in the argument list. This means that inside the method you cannot change what the argument reference points to:

```
//: c06:FinalArguments.java
// Using "final" with method arguments.

class Gizmo {
  public void spin() {}
}

public class FinalArguments {
  void with(final Gizmo g) {
    //! g = new Gizmo(); // Illegal -- g is final
  }
  void without(Gizmo g) {
    g = new Gizmo(); // OK -- g not final
    g.spin();
  }
  // void f(final int i) { i++; } // Can't change
  // You can only read from a final primitive:
  int g(final int i) { return i + 1; }
  public static void main(String[] args) {
    FinalArguments bf = new FinalArguments();
    bf.without(null);
    bf.with(null);
  }
```

```
} ///:~
```

Note that you can still assign a **null** reference to an argument that's final without the compiler catching it, just like you can with a non-**final** argument.

The methods **f( )** and **g( )** show what happens when primitive arguments are **final**: you can read the argument, but you can't change it.

Final methods

There are two reasons for **final** methods. The first is to put a "lock" on the method to prevent any inheriting class from changing its meaning. This is done for design reasons when you want to make sure that a method's behavior is retained during inheritance and cannot be overridden.

The second reason for **final** methods is efficiency. If you make a method **final**, you are allowing the compiler to turn any calls to that method into *inline* calls. When the compiler sees a **final** method call it can (at its discretion) skip the normal approach of inserting code to perform the method call mechanism (push arguments on the stack, hop over to the method code and execute it, hop back and clean off the stack arguments, and deal with the return value) and instead replace the method call with a copy of the actual code in the method body. This eliminates the overhead of the method call. Of course, if a method is big, then your code begins to bloat and you probably won't see any performance gains from inlining, since any improvements will be dwarfed by the amount of time spent inside the method. It is implied that the Java compiler is able to detect these situations and choose wisely whether to inline a **final** method. However, it's better to not trust that the compiler is able to do this and make a method **final** only if it's quite small or if you want to explicitly prevent overriding.

final and private

Any **private** methods in a class are implicitly **final**. Because you can't access a **private** method, you can't override it (even though the compiler doesn't give an error message if you try to override it, you haven't overridden the method, you've just created a new method). You can add the **final** specifier to a **private** method but it doesn't give that method any extra meaning.

This issue can cause confusion, because if you try to override a **private** method (which is implicitly **final**) it seems to work:

```
//: c06:FinalOverridingIllusion.java
// It only looks like you can override
// a private or private final method.

class WithFinals {
  // Identical to "private" alone:
  private final void f() {
    System.out.println("WithFinals.f()");
  }
  // Also automatically "final":
  private void g() {
    System.out.println("WithFinals.g()");
  }
}

class OverridingPrivate extends WithFinals {
  private final void f() {
    System.out.println("OverridingPrivate.f()");
  }
  private void g() {
    System.out.println("OverridingPrivate.g()");
  }
}

class OverridingPrivate2
  extends OverridingPrivate {
  public final void f() {
    System.out.println("OverridingPrivate2.f()");
  }
  public void g() {
    System.out.println("OverridingPrivate2.g()");
  }
}

public class FinalOverridingIllusion {
```

```
public static void main(String[] args) {
  OverridingPrivate2 op2 =
    new OverridingPrivate2();
  op2.f();
  op2.g();
  // You can upcast:
  OverridingPrivate op = op2;
  // But you can't call the methods:
  //! op.f();
  //! op.g();
  // Same here:
  WithFinals wf = op2;
  //! wf.f();
  //! wf.g();
  }
} ///:~
```

"Overriding" can only occur if something is part of the base-class interface. That is, you must be able to upcast an object to its base type and call the same method (the point of this will become clear in the next chapter). If a method is **private**, it isn't part of the base-class interface. It is just some code that's hidden away inside the class, and it just happens to have that name, but if you create a **public**, **protected** or "friendly" method in the derived class, there's no connection to the method that might happen to have that name in the base class. Since a **private** method is unreachable and effectively invisible, it doesn't factor into anything except for the code organization of the class for which it was defined.

Final classes

When you say that an entire class is **final** (by preceding its definition with the **final** keyword), you state that you don't want to inherit from this class or allow anyone else to do so. In other words, for some reason the design of your class is such that there is never a need to make any changes, or for safety or security reasons you don't want subclassing. Alternatively, you might be dealing with an efficiency issue, and you want to make sure that any activity involved with objects of this class are as efficient as possible.

```
//: c06:Jurassic.java
// Making an entire class final.
```

```
class SmallBrain {}

final class Dinosaur {
  int i = 7;
  int j = 1;
  SmallBrain x = new SmallBrain();
  void f() {}
}

//! class Further extends Dinosaur {}
// error: Cannot extend final class 'Dinosaur'

public class Jurassic {
  public static void main(String[] args) {
    Dinosaur n = new Dinosaur();
    n.f();
    n.i = 40;
    n.j++;
  }
} ///:~
```

Note that the data members can be **final** or not, as you choose. The same rules apply to **final** for data members regardless of whether the class is defined as **final**. Defining the class as **final** simply prevents inheritance—nothing more. However, because it prevents inheritance all methods in a **final** class are implicitly **final**, since there's no way to override them. So the compiler has the same efficiency options as it does if you explicitly declare a method **final**.

You can add the **final** specifier to a method in a **final** class, but it doesn't add any meaning.

Final caution

It can seem to be sensible to make a method **final** while you're designing a class. You might feel that efficiency is very important when using your class and that no one could possibly want to override your methods anyway. Sometimes this is true.

But be careful with your assumptions. In general, it's difficult to anticipate how a class can be reused, especially a general-purpose class. If you define a method as **final** you might prevent the possibility of reusing your class through inheritance in some other programmer's project simply because you couldn't imagine it being used that way.

The standard Java library is a good example of this. In particular, the Java 1.0/1.1 **Vector** class was commonly used and might have been even more useful if, in the name of efficiency, all the methods hadn't been made **final**. It's easily conceivable that you might want to inherit and override with such a fundamentally useful class, but the designers somehow decided this wasn't appropriate. This is ironic for two reasons. First, **Stack** is inherited from **Vector**, which says that a **Stack** *is* a **Vector**, which isn't really true from a logical standpoint. Second, many of the most important methods of **Vector**, such as **addElement( )** and **elementAt( )** are **synchronized**. As you will see in Chapter 14, this incurs a significant performance overhead that probably wipes out any gains provided by **final**. This lends credence to the theory that programmers are consistently bad at guessing where optimizations should occur. It's just too bad that such a clumsy design made it into the standard library where we must all cope with it. (Fortunately, the Java 2 container library replaces **Vector** with **ArrayList**, which behaves much more civilly. Unfortunately, there's still plenty of new code being written that uses the old container library.)

It's also interesting to note that **Hashtable**, another important standard library class, does *not* have any **final** methods. As mentioned elsewhere in this book, it's quite obvious that some classes were designed by completely different people than others. (You'll see that the method names in **Hashtable** are much briefer compared to those in **Vector**, another piece of evidence.) This is precisely the sort of thing that should *not* be obvious to consumers of a class library. When things are inconsistent it just makes more work for the user. Yet another paean to the value of design and code walkthroughs. (Note that the Java 2 container library replaces **Hashtable** with **HashMap**.)

Initialization and class loading

In more traditional languages, programs are loaded all at once as part of the startup process. This is followed by initialization, and then the program begins. The process of initialization in these languages must be carefully controlled so that the order of initialization of **static**s doesn't cause trouble. C++, for example, has problems if one **static** expects another **static** to be valid before the second one has been initialized.

Java doesn't have this problem because it takes a different approach to loading. Because everything in Java is an object, many activities become easier, and this is one of them. As you will learn more fully in the next chapter, the compiled code for each class exists in its own separate file. That file isn't loaded until the code is needed. In general, you can say that "Class code is loaded at the point of first use." This is often not until the first object of that class is constructed, but loading also occurs when a **static** field or **static** method is accessed.

The point of first use is also where the **static** initialization takes place. All the **static** objects and the **static** code block will be initialized in textual order (that is, the order that you write them down in the class definition) at the point of loading. The **static**s, of course, are initialized only once.

Initialization with inheritance

It's helpful to look at the whole initialization process, including inheritance, to get a full picture of what happens. Consider the following code:

```
//: c06:Beetle.java
// The full process of initialization.

class Insect {
  int i = 9;
  int j;
  Insect() {
    prt("i = " + i + ", j = " + j);
```

```
      j = 39;
   }
   static int x1 =
      prt("static Insect.x1 initialized");
   static int prt(String s) {
      System.out.println(s);
      return 47;
   }
}

public class Beetle extends Insect {
   int k = prt("Beetle.k initialized");
   Beetle() {
      prt("k = " + k);
      prt("j = " + j);
   }
   static int x2 =
      prt("static Beetle.x2 initialized");
   public static void main(String[] args) {
      prt("Beetle constructor");
      Beetle b = new Beetle();
   }
} ///:~
```

The output for this program is:

```
static Insect.x1 initialized
static Beetle.x2 initialized
Beetle constructor
i = 9, j = 0
Beetle.k initialized
k = 47
j = 39
```

The first thing that happens when you run Java on **Beetle** is that you try to access **Beetle.main( )** (a **static** method), so the loader goes out and finds the compiled code for the **Beetle** class (this happens to be in a file called **Beetle.class**). In the process of loading it, the loader notices that it has a base class (that's what the **extends** keyword says), which it then loads. This will happen whether or not you're going to make an object of that base class. (Try commenting out the object creation to prove it to yourself.)

If the base class has a base class, that second base class would then be loaded, and so on. Next, the **static** initialization in the root base class (in this case, **Insect**) is performed, and then the next derived class, and so on. This is important because the derived-class static initialization might depend on the base class member being initialized properly.

At this point, the necessary classes have all been loaded so the object can be created. First, all the primitives in this object are set to their default values and the object references are set to **null**—this happens in one fell swoop by setting the memory in the object to binary zero. Then the base-class constructor will be called. In this case the call is automatic, but you can also specify the base-class constructor call (as the first operation in the **Beetle( )** constructor) using **super**. The base class construction goes through the same process in the same order as the derived-class constructor. After the base-class constructor completes, the instance variables are initialized in textual order. Finally, the rest of the body of the constructor is executed.

Summary

Both inheritance and composition allow you to create a new type from existing types. Typically, however, you use composition to reuse existing types as part of the underlying implementation of the new type, and inheritance when you want to reuse the interface. Since the derived class has the base-class interface, it can be *upcast* to the base, which is critical for polymorphism, as you'll see in the next chapter.

Despite the strong emphasis on inheritance in object-oriented programming, when you start a design you should generally prefer composition during the first cut and use inheritance only when it is clearly necessary. Composition tends to be more flexible. In addition, by using the added artifice of inheritance with your member type, you can change the exact type, and thus the behavior, of those member objects at run-time. Therefore, you can change the behavior of the composed object at run-time.

Although code reuse through composition and inheritance is helpful for rapid project development, you'll generally want to redesign your class hierarchy before allowing other programmers to become dependent on it. Your goal is a hierarchy in which each class has a specific use and is neither too big (encompassing so much functionality that it's unwieldy to reuse) nor annoyingly small (you can't use it by itself or without adding functionality).

Exercises

Solutions to selected exercises can be found in the electronic document *The Thinking in Java Annotated Solution Guide*, available for a small fee from *www.BruceEckel.com*.

1. Create two classes, **A** and **B**, with default constructors (empty argument lists) that announce themselves. Inherit a new class called **C** from **A**, and create a member of class **B** inside **C**. Do not create a constructor for **C**. Create an object of class **C** and observe the results.

2. Modify Exercise 1 so that **A** and **B** have constructors with arguments instead of default constructors. Write a constructor for **C** and perform all initialization within **C**'s constructor.

3. Create a simple class. Inside a second class, define a field for an object of the first class. Use lazy initialization to instantiate this object.

4. Inherit a new class from class **Detergent**. Override **scrub( )** and add a new method called **sterilize( )**.

5. Take the file **Cartoon.java** and comment out the constructor for the **Cartoon** class. Explain what happens.

6. Take the file **Chess.java** and comment out the constructor for the **Chess** class. Explain what happens.

7. Prove that default constructors are created for you by the compiler.

8. Prove that the base-class constructors are (a) always called, and (b) called before derived-class constructors.

---

9. Create a base class with only a nondefault constructor, and a derived class with both a default and nondefault constructor. In the derived-class constructors, call the base-class constructor.

10. Create a class called **Root** that contains an instance of each of classes (that you also create) named **Component1**, **Component2**, and **Component3**. Derive a class **Stem** from **Root** that also contains an instance of each "component." All classes should have default constructors that print a message about that class.

11. Modify Exercise 10 so that each class only has nondefault constructors.

12. Add a proper hierarchy of **cleanup( )** methods to all the classes in Exercise 11.

13. Create a class with a method that is overloaded three times. Inherit a new class, add a new overloading of the method, and show that all four methods are available in the derived class.

14. In **Car.java** add a **service( )** method to **Engine** and call this method in **main( )**.

15. Create a class inside a package. Your class should contain a **protected** method. Outside of the package, try to call the **protected** method and explain the results. Now inherit from your class and call the **protected** method from inside a method of your derived class.

16. Create a class called **Amphibian**. From this, inherit a class called **Frog**. Put appropriate methods in the base class. In **main( )**, create a **Frog** and upcast it to **Amphibian**, and demonstrate that all the methods still work.

17. Modify Exercise 16 so that **Frog** overrides the method definitions from the base class (provides new definitions using the same method signatures). Note what happens in **main( )**.

18. Create a class with a **static final** field and a **final** field and demonstrate the difference between the two.

19.   Create a class with a blank **final** reference to an object. Perform
        the initialization of the blank **final** inside a method (not the
        constructor) right before you use it. Demonstrate the guarantee
        that the **final** must be initialized before use, and that it cannot be
        changed once initialized.

20.   Create a class with a **final** method. Inherit from that class and
        attempt to override that method.

21.   Create a **final** class and attempt to inherit from it.

22.   Prove that class loading takes place only once. Prove that loading
        may be caused by either the creation of the first instance of that
        class, or the access of a **static** member.

23.   In **Beetle.java**, inherit a specific type of beetle from class
        Beetle, following the same format as the existing classes. Trace
        and explain the output.

7: Polymorphism

Polymorphism is the third essential feature of an object-oriented programming language, after data abstraction and inheritance.

It provides another dimension of separation of interface from implementation, to decouple *what* from *how*. Polymorphism allows improved code organization and readability as well as the creation of *extensible* programs that can be "grown" not only during the original creation of the project but also when new features are desired.

Encapsulation creates new data types by combining characteristics and behaviors. Implementation hiding separates the interface from the implementation by making the details **private**. This sort of mechanical organization makes ready sense to someone with a procedural programming background. But polymorphism deals with decoupling in terms of *types*. In the last chapter, you saw how inheritance allows the treatment of an object as its own type *or* its base type. This ability is critical because it allows many types (derived from the same base type) to be treated as if they were one type, and a single piece of code to work on all those different types equally. The polymorphic method call allows one type to express its distinction from another, similar type, as long as they're both derived from the same base type. This distinction is expressed through differences in behavior of the methods that you can call through the base class.

In this chapter, you'll learn about polymorphism (also called *dynamic binding* or *late binding* or *run-time binding*) starting from the basics, with simple examples that strip away everything but the polymorphic behavior of the program.

Upcasting revisited

In Chapter 6 you saw how an object can be used as its own type or as an object of its base type. Taking an object reference and treating it as a reference to its base type is called *upcasting,* because of the way inheritance trees are drawn with the base class at the top.

You also saw a problem arise, which is embodied in the following:

```java
//: c07:music:Music.java
// Inheritance & upcasting.

class Note {
  private int value;
  private Note(int val) { value = val; }
  public static final Note
    MIDDLE_C = new Note(0),
    C_SHARP  = new Note(1),
    B_FLAT   = new Note(2);
} // Etc.

class Instrument {
  public void play(Note n) {
    System.out.println("Instrument.play()");
  }
}

// Wind objects are instruments
// because they have the same interface:
class Wind extends Instrument {
  // Redefine interface method:
  public void play(Note n) {
    System.out.println("Wind.play()");
  }
}

public class Music {
  public static void tune(Instrument i) {
    // ...
    i.play(Note.MIDDLE_C);
  }
  public static void main(String[] args) {
    Wind flute = new Wind();
    tune(flute); // Upcasting
  }
```

```
} ///:~
```

The method **Music.tune( )** accepts an **Instrument** reference, but also anything derived from **Instrument**. In **main( )**, you can see this happening as a **Wind** reference is passed to **tune( )**, with no cast necessary. This is acceptable; the interface in **Instrument** must exist in **Wind**, because **Wind** is inherited from **Instrument**. Upcasting from **Wind** to **Instrument** may "narrow" that interface, but it cannot make it anything less than the full interface to **Instrument**.

Forgetting the object type

This program might seem strange to you. Why should anyone intentionally *forget* the type of an object? This is what happens when you upcast, and it seems like it could be much more straightforward if **tune( )** simply takes a **Wind** reference as its argument. This brings up an essential point: If you did that, you'd need to write a new **tune( )** for every type of **Instrument** in your system. Suppose we follow this reasoning and add **Stringed** and **Brass** instruments:

```java
//: c07:music2:Music2.java
// Overloading instead of upcasting.

class Note {
  private int value;
  private Note(int val) { value = val; }
  public static final Note
    MIDDLE_C = new Note(0),
    C_SHARP = new Note(1),
    B_FLAT = new Note(2);
} // Etc.

class Instrument {
  public void play(Note n) {
    System.out.println("Instrument.play()");
  }
}

class Wind extends Instrument {
  public void play(Note n) {
    System.out.println("Wind.play()");
```

```
    }
  }

class Stringed extends Instrument {
  public void play(Note n) {
    System.out.println("Stringed.play()");
  }
}

class Brass extends Instrument {
  public void play(Note n) {
    System.out.println("Brass.play()");
  }
}

public class Music2 {
  public static void tune(Wind i) {
    i.play(Note.MIDDLE_C);
  }
  public static void tune(Stringed i) {
    i.play(Note.MIDDLE_C);
  }
  public static void tune(Brass i) {
    i.play(Note.MIDDLE_C);
  }
  public static void main(String[] args) {
    Wind flute = new Wind();
    Stringed violin = new Stringed();
    Brass frenchHorn = new Brass();
    tune(flute); // No upcasting
    tune(violin);
    tune(frenchHorn);
  }
} ///:~
```

This works, but there's a major drawback: You must write type-specific methods for each new **Instrument** class you add. This means more programming in the first place, but it also means that if you want to add a new method like **tune( )** or a new type of **Instrument**, you've got a lot of work to do. Add the fact that the compiler won't give you any error messages if you forget to overload one of your methods and the whole process of working with types becomes unmanageable.

Wouldn't it be much nicer if you could just write a single method that takes the base class as its argument, and not any of the specific derived classes? That is, wouldn't it be nice if you could forget that there are derived classes, and write your code to talk only to the base class?

That's exactly what polymorphism allows you to do. However, most programmers who come from a procedural programming background have a bit of trouble with the way polymorphism works.

The twist

The difficulty with **Music.java** can be seen by running the program. The output is **Wind.play( )**. This is clearly the desired output, but it doesn't seem to make sense that it would work that way. Look at the **tune( )** method:

```
public static void tune(Instrument i) {
  // ...
  i.play(Note.MIDDLE_C);
}
```

It receives an **Instrument** reference. So how can the compiler possibly know that this **Instrument** reference points to a **Wind** in this case and not a **Brass** or **Stringed**? The compiler can't. To get a deeper understanding of the issue, it's helpful to examine the subject of *binding*.

Method-call binding

Connecting a method call to a method body is called *binding*. When binding is performed before the program is run (by the compiler and linker, if there is one), it's called *early binding*. You might not have heard the term before because it has never been an option with procedural languages. C compilers have only one kind of method call, and that's early binding.

The confusing part of the above program revolves around early binding because the compiler cannot know the correct method to call when it has only an **Instrument** reference.

The solution is called *late binding*, which means that the binding occurs at run-time based on the type of object. Late binding is also called *dynamic binding* or *run-time binding*. When a language implements late binding, there must be some mechanism to determine the type of the object at run-time and to call the appropriate method. That is, the compiler still doesn't know the object type, but the method-call mechanism finds out and calls the correct method body. The late-binding mechanism varies from language to language, but you can imagine that some sort of type information must be installed in the objects.

All method binding in Java uses late binding unless a method has been declared **final**. This means that ordinarily you don't need to make any decisions about whether late binding will occur—it happens automatically.

Why would you declare a method **final**? As noted in the last chapter, it prevents anyone from overriding that method. Perhaps more important, it effectively "turns off" dynamic binding, or rather it tells the compiler that dynamic binding isn't necessary. This allows the compiler to generate slightly more efficient code for **final** method calls. However, in most cases it won't make any overall performance difference in your program, so it's best to only use **final** as a design decision, and not as an attempt to improve performance.

Producing the right behavior

Once you know that all method binding in Java happens polymorphically via late binding, you can write your code to talk to the base class and know that all the derived-class cases will work correctly using the same code. Or to put it another way, you "send a message to an object and let the object figure out the right thing to do."

The classic example in OOP is the "shape" example. This is commonly used because it is easy to visualize, but unfortunately it can confuse novice programmers into thinking that OOP is just for graphics programming, which is of course not the case.

The shape example has a base class called **Shape** and various derived types: **Circle**, **Square**, **Triangle**, etc. The reason the example works so well is that it's easy to say "a circle is a type of shape" and be understood. The inheritance diagram shows the relationships:

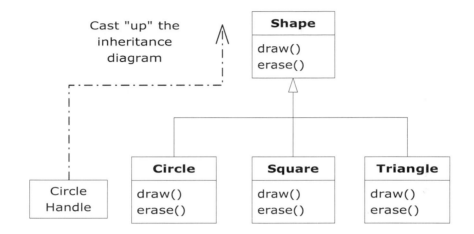

The upcast could occur in a statement as simple as:

```
Shape s = new Circle();
```

Here, a **Circle** object is created and the resulting reference is immediately assigned to a **Shape**, which would seem to be an error (assigning one type to another); and yet it's fine because a **Circle** *is* a **Shape** by inheritance. So the compiler agrees with the statement and doesn't issue an error message.

Suppose you call one of the base-class methods (that have been overridden in the derived classes):

```
s.draw();
```

Again, you might expect that **Shape**'s **draw( )** is called because this is, after all, a **Shape** reference—so how could the compiler know to do anything else? And yet the proper **Circle.draw( )** is called because of late binding (polymorphism).

The following example puts it a slightly different way:

```
//: c07:Shapes.java
```

```java
// Polymorphism in Java.

class Shape {
  void draw() {}
  void erase() {}
}

class Circle extends Shape {
  void draw() {
    System.out.println("Circle.draw()");
  }
  void erase() {
    System.out.println("Circle.erase()");
  }
}

class Square extends Shape {
  void draw() {
    System.out.println("Square.draw()");
  }
  void erase() {
    System.out.println("Square.erase()");
  }
}

class Triangle extends Shape {
  void draw() {
    System.out.println("Triangle.draw()");
  }
  void erase() {
    System.out.println("Triangle.erase()");
  }
}

public class Shapes {
  public static Shape randShape() {
    switch((int)(Math.random() * 3)) {
      default:
      case 0: return new Circle();
      case 1: return new Square();
      case 2: return new Triangle();
```

```
      }
    }
    public static void main(String[] args) {
      Shape[] s = new Shape[9];
      // Fill up the array with shapes:
      for(int i = 0; i < s.length; i++)
        s[i] = randShape();
      // Make polymorphic method calls:
      for(int i = 0; i < s.length; i++)
        s[i].draw();
    }
} ///:~
```

The base class **Shape** establishes the common interface to anything inherited from **Shape**—that is, all shapes can be drawn and erased. The derived classes override these definitions to provide unique behavior for each specific type of shape.

The main class **Shapes** contains a **static** method **randShape( )** that produces a reference to a randomly-selected **Shape** object each time you call it. Note that the upcasting happens in each of the **return** statements, which take a reference to a **Circle**, **Square**, or **Triangle** and sends it out of the method as the return type, **Shape**. So whenever you call this method you never get a chance to see what specific type it is, since you always get back a plain **Shape** reference.

main( ) contains an array of **Shape** references filled through calls to **randShape( )**. At this point you know you have **Shape**s, but you don't know anything more specific than that (and neither does the compiler). However, when you step through this array and call **draw( )** for each one, the correct type-specific behavior magically occurs, as you can see from one output example:

```
Circle.draw()
Triangle.draw()
Circle.draw()
Circle.draw()
Circle.draw()
Square.draw()
Triangle.draw()
Square.draw()
```

```
Square.draw()
```

Of course, since the shapes are all chosen randomly each time, your runs will have different results. The point of choosing the shapes randomly is to drive home the understanding that the compiler can have no special knowledge that allows it to make the correct calls at compile-time. All the calls to **draw( )** are made through dynamic binding.

Extensibility

Now let's return to the musical instrument example. Because of polymorphism, you can add as many new types as you want to the system without changing the **tune( )** method. In a well-designed OOP program, most or all of your methods will follow the model of **tune( )** and communicate only with the base-class interface. Such a program is *extensible* because you can add new functionality by inheriting new data types from the common base class. The methods that manipulate the base-class interface will not need to be changed at all to accommodate the new classes.

Consider what happens if you take the instrument example and add more methods in the base class and a number of new classes. Here's the diagram:

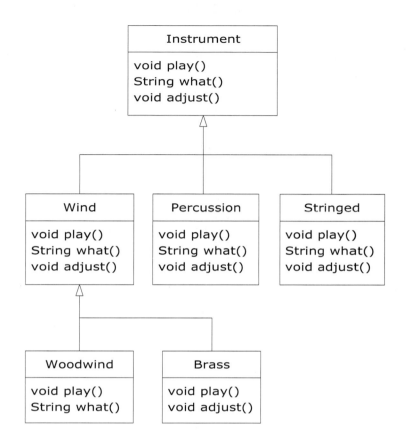

All these new classes work correctly with the old, unchanged **tune( )** method. Even if **tune( )** is in a separate file and new methods are added to the interface of **Instrument**, **tune( )** works correctly without recompilation. Here is the implementation of the above diagram:

```
//: c07:music3:Music3.java
// An extensible program.
import java.util.*;

class Instrument {
  public void play() {
    System.out.println("Instrument.play()");
  }
  public String what() {
    return "Instrument";
  }
  public void adjust() {}
```

```java
}

class Wind extends Instrument {
  public void play() {
    System.out.println("Wind.play()");
  }
  public String what() { return "Wind"; }
  public void adjust() {}
}

class Percussion extends Instrument {
  public void play() {
    System.out.println("Percussion.play()");
  }
  public String what() { return "Percussion"; }
  public void adjust() {}
}

class Stringed extends Instrument {
  public void play() {
    System.out.println("Stringed.play()");
  }
  public String what() { return "Stringed"; }
  public void adjust() {}
}

class Brass extends Wind {
  public void play() {
    System.out.println("Brass.play()");
  }
  public void adjust() {
    System.out.println("Brass.adjust()");
  }
}

class Woodwind extends Wind {
  public void play() {
    System.out.println("Woodwind.play()");
  }
  public String what() { return "Woodwind"; }
}
```

```
public class Music3 {
  // Doesn't care about type, so new types
  // added to the system still work right:
  static void tune(Instrument i) {
    // ...
    i.play();
  }
  static void tuneAll(Instrument[] e) {
    for(int i = 0; i < e.length; i++)
      tune(e[i]);
  }
  public static void main(String[] args) {
    Instrument[] orchestra = new Instrument[5];
    int i = 0;
    // Upcasting during addition to the array:
    orchestra[i++] = new Wind();
    orchestra[i++] = new Percussion();
    orchestra[i++] = new Stringed();
    orchestra[i++] = new Brass();
    orchestra[i++] = new Woodwind();
    tuneAll(orchestra);
  }
} ///:~
```

The new methods are **what( )**, which returns a **String** reference with a description of the class, and **adjust( )**, which provides some way to adjust each instrument.

In **main( )**, when you place something inside the **Instrument** array you automatically upcast to **Instrument**.

You can see that the **tune( )** method is blissfully ignorant of all the code changes that have happened around it, and yet it works correctly. This is exactly what polymorphism is supposed to provide. Your code changes don't cause damage to parts of the program that should not be affected. Put another way, polymorphism is one of the most important techniques that allow the programmer to "separate the things that change from the things that stay the same."

Overriding vs. overloading

Let's take a different look at the first example in this chapter. In the following program, the interface of the method **play( )** is changed in the process of overriding it, which means that you haven't *overridden* the method, but instead *overloaded* it. The compiler allows you to overload methods so it gives no complaint. But the behavior is probably not what you want. Here's the example:

```
//: c07:WindError.java
// Accidentally changing the interface.

class NoteX {
  public static final int
    MIDDLE_C = 0, C_SHARP = 1, C_FLAT = 2;
}

class InstrumentX {
  public void play(int NoteX) {
    System.out.println("InstrumentX.play()");
  }
}

class WindX extends InstrumentX {
  // OOPS! Changes the method interface:
  public void play(NoteX n) {
    System.out.println("WindX.play(NoteX n)");
  }
}

public class WindError {
  public static void tune(InstrumentX i) {
    // ...
    i.play(NoteX.MIDDLE_C);
  }
  public static void main(String[] args) {
    WindX flute = new WindX();
    tune(flute); // Not the desired behavior!
  }
} ///:~
```

There's another confusing aspect thrown in here. In **InstrumentX**, the **play( )** method takes an **int** that has the identifier **NoteX**. That is, even though **NoteX** is a class name, it can also be used as an identifier without complaint. But in **WindX**, **play( )** takes a **NoteX** reference that has an identifier **n**. (Although you could even say **play(NoteX NoteX)** without an error.) Thus it appears that the programmer intended to override **play( )** but mistyped the method a bit. The compiler, however, assumed that an overload and not an override was intended. Note that if you follow the standard Java naming convention, the argument identifier would be **noteX** (lowercase 'n'), which would distinguish it from the class name.

In **tune**, the **InstrumentX i** is sent the **play( )** message, with one of **NoteX**'s members (**MIDDLE_C**) as an argument. Since **NoteX** contains **int** definitions, this means that the **int** version of the now-overloaded **play( )** method is called, and since that has *not* been overridden the base-class version is used.

The output is:

```
InstrumentX.play()
```

This certainly doesn't appear to be a polymorphic method call. Once you understand what's happening, you can fix the problem fairly easily, but imagine how difficult it might be to find the bug if it's buried in a program of significant size.

Abstract classes and methods

In all the instrument examples, the methods in the base class **Instrument** were always "dummy" methods. If these methods are ever called, you've done something wrong. That's because the intent of **Instrument** is to create a *common interface* for all the classes derived from it.

The only reason to establish this common interface is so it can be expressed differently for each different subtype. It establishes a basic form, so you can say what's in common with all the derived classes.

Another way of saying this is to call **Instrument** an *abstract base class* (or simply an *abstract class*). You create an abstract class when you want to manipulate a set of classes through this common interface. All derived-class methods that match the signature of the base-class declaration will be called using the dynamic binding mechanism. (However, as seen in the last section, if the method's name is the same as the base class but the arguments are different, you've got overloading, which probably isn't what you want.)

If you have an abstract class like **Instrument**, objects of that class almost always have no meaning. That is, **Instrument** is meant to express only the interface, and not a particular implementation, so creating an **Instrument** object makes no sense, and you'll probably want to prevent the user from doing it. This can be accomplished by making all the methods in **Instrument** print error messages, but that delays the information until run-time and requires reliable exhaustive testing on the user's part. It's always better to catch problems at compile-time.

Java provides a mechanism for doing this called the *abstract method*[1]. This is a method that is incomplete; it has only a declaration and no method body. Here is the syntax for an abstract method declaration:

```
abstract void f();
```

A class containing abstract methods is called an *abstract class*. If a class contains one or more abstract methods, the class must be qualified as **abstract**. (Otherwise, the compiler gives you an error message.)

If an abstract class is incomplete, what is the compiler supposed to do when someone tries to make an object of that class? It cannot safely create an object of an abstract class, so you get an error message from the compiler. This way the compiler ensures the purity of the abstract class, and you don't need to worry about misusing it.

If you inherit from an abstract class and you want to make objects of the new type, you must provide method definitions for all the abstract methods in the base class. If you don't (and you may choose not to), then

---

[1] For C++ programmers, this is the analogue of C++'s *pure virtual function*.

the derived class is also abstract and the compiler will force you to qualify *that* class with the **abstract** keyword.

It's possible to create a class as **abstract** without including any **abstract** methods. This is useful when you've got a class in which it doesn't make sense to have any **abstract** methods, and yet you want to prevent any instances of that class.

The **Instrument** class can easily be turned into an **abstract** class. Only some of the methods will be **abstract**, since making a class abstract doesn't force you to make all the methods **abstract**. Here's what it looks like:

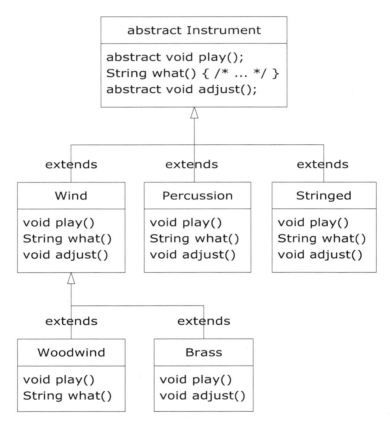

Here's the orchestra example modified to use **abstract** classes and methods:

```
//: c07:music4:Music4.java
```

```java
// Abstract classes and methods.
import java.util.*;

abstract class Instrument {
  int i; // storage allocated for each
  public abstract void play();
  public String what() {
    return "Instrument";
  }
  public abstract void adjust();
}

class Wind extends Instrument {
  public void play() {
    System.out.println("Wind.play()");
  }
  public String what() { return "Wind"; }
  public void adjust() {}
}

class Percussion extends Instrument {
  public void play() {
    System.out.println("Percussion.play()");
  }
  public String what() { return "Percussion"; }
  public void adjust() {}
}

class Stringed extends Instrument {
  public void play() {
    System.out.println("Stringed.play()");
  }
  public String what() { return "Stringed"; }
  public void adjust() {}
}

class Brass extends Wind {
  public void play() {
    System.out.println("Brass.play()");
  }
  public void adjust() {
```

```
      System.out.println("Brass.adjust()");
    }
}

class Woodwind extends Wind {
  public void play() {
    System.out.println("Woodwind.play()");
  }
  public String what() { return "Woodwind"; }
}

public class Music4 {
  // Doesn't care about type, so new types
  // added to the system still work right:
  static void tune(Instrument i) {
    // ...
    i.play();
  }
  static void tuneAll(Instrument[] e) {
    for(int i = 0; i < e.length; i++)
      tune(e[i]);
  }
  public static void main(String[] args) {
    Instrument[] orchestra = new Instrument[5];
    int i = 0;
    // Upcasting during addition to the array:
    orchestra[i++] = new Wind();
    orchestra[i++] = new Percussion();
    orchestra[i++] = new Stringed();
    orchestra[i++] = new Brass();
    orchestra[i++] = new Woodwind();
    tuneAll(orchestra);
  }
} ///:~
```

You can see that there's really no change except in the base class.

It's helpful to create **abstract** classes and methods because they make the abstractness of a class explicit, and tell both the user and the compiler how it was intended to be used.

Constructors and polymorphism

As usual, constructors are different from other kinds of methods. This is also true when polymorphism is involved. Even though constructors are not polymorphic (although you can have a kind of "virtual constructor," as you will see in Chapter 12), it's important to understand the way constructors work in complex hierarchies and with polymorphism. This understanding will help you avoid unpleasant entanglements.

Order of constructor calls

The order of constructor calls was briefly discussed in Chapter 4 and again in Chapter 6, but that was before polymorphism was introduced.

A constructor for the base class is always called in the constructor for a derived class, chaining up the inheritance hierarchy so that a constructor for every base class is called. This makes sense because the constructor has a special job: to see that the object is built properly. A derived class has access to its own members only, and not to those of the base class (whose members are typically **private**). Only the base-class constructor has the proper knowledge and access to initialize its own elements. Therefore, it's essential that all constructors get called, otherwise the entire object wouldn't be constructed. That's why the compiler enforces a constructor call for every portion of a derived class. It will silently call the default constructor if you don't explicitly call a base-class constructor in the derived-class constructor body. If there is no default constructor, the compiler will complain. (In the case where a class has no constructors, the compiler will automatically synthesize a default constructor.)

Let's take a look at an example that shows the effects of composition, inheritance, and polymorphism on the order of construction:

```
//: c07:Sandwich.java
// Order of constructor calls.

class Meal {
  Meal() { System.out.println("Meal()"); }
```

```
  }

class Bread {
  Bread() { System.out.println("Bread()"); }
}

class Cheese {
  Cheese() { System.out.println("Cheese()"); }
}

class Lettuce {
  Lettuce() { System.out.println("Lettuce()"); }
}

class Lunch extends Meal {
  Lunch() { System.out.println("Lunch()"); }
}

class PortableLunch extends Lunch {
  PortableLunch() {
    System.out.println("PortableLunch()");
  }
}

class Sandwich extends PortableLunch {
  Bread b = new Bread();
  Cheese c = new Cheese();
  Lettuce l = new Lettuce();
  Sandwich() {
    System.out.println("Sandwich()");
  }
  public static void main(String[] args) {
    new Sandwich();
  }
} ///:~
```

This example creates a complex class out of other classes, and each class has a constructor that announces itself. The important class is **Sandwich**, which reflects three levels of inheritance (four, if you count the implicit inheritance from **Object**) and three member objects. When a **Sandwich** object is created in **main( )**, the output is:

```
Meal()
Lunch()
PortableLunch()
Bread()
Cheese()
Lettuce()
Sandwich()
```

This means that the order of constructor calls for a complex object is as follows:

1. The base-class constructor is called. This step is repeated recursively such that the root of the hierarchy is constructed first, followed by the next-derived class, etc., until the most-derived class is reached.

2. Member initializers are called in the order of declaration.

3. The body of the derived-class constructor is called.

The order of the constructor calls is important. When you inherit, you know all about the base class and can access any **public** and **protected** members of the base class. This means that you must be able to assume that all the members of the base class are valid when you're in the derived class. In a normal method, construction has already taken place, so all the members of all parts of the object have been built. Inside the constructor, however, you must be able to assume that all members that you use have been built. The only way to guarantee this is for the base-class constructor to be called first. Then when you're in the derived-class constructor, all the members you can access in the base class have been initialized. "Knowing that all members are valid" inside the constructor is also the reason that, whenever possible, you should initialize all member objects (that is, objects placed in the class using composition) at their point of definition in the class (e.g., **b**, **c**, and **l** in the example above). If you follow this practice, you will help ensure that all base class members *and* member objects of the current object have been initialized. Unfortunately, this doesn't handle every case, as you will see in the next section.

Inheritance and **finalize( )**

When you use composition to create a new class, you never worry about finalizing the member objects of that class. Each member is an independent object, and thus is garbage collected and finalized regardless of whether it happens to be a member of your class. With inheritance, however, you must override **finalize( )** in the derived class if you have any special cleanup that must happen as part of garbage collection. When you override **finalize( )** in an inherited class, it's important to remember to call the base-class version of **finalize( )**, since otherwise the base-class finalization will not happen. The following example proves this:

```
//: c07:Frog.java
// Testing finalize with inheritance.

class DoBaseFinalization {
  public static boolean flag = false;
}

class Characteristic {
  String s;
  Characteristic(String c) {
    s = c;
    System.out.println(
      "Creating Characteristic " + s);
  }
  protected void finalize() {
    System.out.println(
      "finalizing Characteristic " + s);
  }
}

class LivingCreature {
  Characteristic p =
    new Characteristic("is alive");
  LivingCreature() {
    System.out.println("LivingCreature()");
  }
  protected void finalize() throws Throwable {
    System.out.println(
      "LivingCreature finalize");
```

```
    // Call base-class version LAST!
    if(DoBaseFinalization.flag)
      super.finalize();
  }
}

class Animal extends LivingCreature {
  Characteristic p =
    new Characteristic("has heart");
  Animal() {
    System.out.println("Animal()");
  }
  protected void finalize() throws Throwable {
    System.out.println("Animal finalize");
    if(DoBaseFinalization.flag)
      super.finalize();
  }
}

class Amphibian extends Animal {
  Characteristic p =
    new Characteristic("can live in water");
  Amphibian() {
    System.out.println("Amphibian()");
  }
  protected void finalize() throws Throwable {
    System.out.println("Amphibian finalize");
    if(DoBaseFinalization.flag)
      super.finalize();
  }
}

public class Frog extends Amphibian {
  Frog() {
    System.out.println("Frog()");
  }
  protected void finalize() throws Throwable {
    System.out.println("Frog finalize");
    if(DoBaseFinalization.flag)
      super.finalize();
  }
```

```
  public static void main(String[] args) {
    if(args.length != 0 &&
       args[0].equals("finalize"))
       DoBaseFinalization.flag = true;
    else
      System.out.println("Not finalizing bases");
    new Frog(); // Instantly becomes garbage
    System.out.println("Bye!");
    // Force finalizers to be called:
    System.gc();
  }
} ///:~
```

The class **DoBaseFinalization** simply holds a flag that indicates to each class in the hierarchy whether to call **super.finalize( )**. This flag is set based on a command-line argument, so you can view the behavior with and without base-class finalization.

Each class in the hierarchy also contains a member object of class **Characteristic**. You will see that regardless of whether the base class finalizers are called, the **Characteristic** member objects are always finalized.

Each overridden **finalize( )** must have access to at least **protected** members since the **finalize( )** method in class **Object** is **protected** and the compiler will not allow you to reduce the access during inheritance. ("Friendly" is less accessible than **protected**.)

In **Frog.main( )**, the **DoBaseFinalization** flag is configured and a single **Frog** object is created. Remember that garbage collection—and in particular finalization—might not happen for any particular object, so to enforce this, the call to **System.gc( )** triggers garbage collection, and thus finalization. Without base-class finalization, the output is:

```
Not finalizing bases
Creating Characteristic is alive
LivingCreature()
Creating Characteristic has heart
Animal()
Creating Characteristic can live in water
Amphibian()
```

```
Frog()
Bye!
Frog finalize
finalizing Characteristic is alive
finalizing Characteristic has heart
finalizing Characteristic can live in water
```

You can see that, indeed, no finalizers are called for the base classes of **Frog** (the member objects *are* finalized, as you would expect). But if you add the "finalize" argument on the command line, you get:

```
Creating Characteristic is alive
LivingCreature()
Creating Characteristic has heart
Animal()
Creating Characteristic can live in water
Amphibian()
Frog()
bye!
Frog finalize
Amphibian finalize
Animal finalize
LivingCreature finalize
finalizing Characteristic is alive
finalizing Characteristic has heart
finalizing Characteristic can live in water
```

Although the order the member objects are finalized is the same order that they are created, technically the order of finalization of objects is unspecified. With base classes, however, you have control over the order of finalization. The best order to use is the one that's shown here, which is the reverse of the order of initialization. Following the form that's used in C++ for destructors, you should perform the derived-class finalization first, then the base-class finalization. That's because the derived-class finalization could call some methods in the base class that require that the base-class components are still alive, so you must not destroy them prematurely.

Behavior of polymorphic methods inside constructors

The hierarchy of constructor calls brings up an interesting dilemma. What happens if you're inside a constructor and you call a dynamically bound method of the object being constructed? Inside an ordinary method you can imagine what will happen—the dynamically bound call is resolved at run-time because the object cannot know whether it belongs to the class that the method is in or some class derived from it. For consistency, you might think this is what should happen inside constructors.

This is not exactly the case. If you call a dynamically bound method inside a constructor, the overridden definition for that method is used. However, the *effect* can be rather unexpected, and can conceal some difficult-to-find bugs.

Conceptually, the constructor's job is to bring the object into existence (which is hardly an ordinary feat). Inside any constructor, the entire object might be only partially formed—you can know only that the base-class objects have been initialized, but you cannot know which classes are inherited from you. A dynamically bound method call, however, reaches "outward" into the inheritance hierarchy. It calls a method in a derived class. If you do this inside a constructor, you call a method that might manipulate members that haven't been initialized yet—a sure recipe for disaster.

You can see the problem in the following example:

```
//: c07:PolyConstructors.java
// Constructors and polymorphism
// don't produce what you might expect.

abstract class Glyph {
  abstract void draw();
  Glyph() {
    System.out.println("Glyph() before draw()");
    draw();
    System.out.println("Glyph() after draw()");
  }
}
```

```
class RoundGlyph extends Glyph {
  int radius = 1;
  RoundGlyph(int r) {
    radius = r;
    System.out.println(
      "RoundGlyph.RoundGlyph(), radius = "
      + radius);
  }
  void draw() {
    System.out.println(
      "RoundGlyph.draw(), radius = " + radius);
  }
}

public class PolyConstructors {
  public static void main(String[] args) {
    new RoundGlyph(5);
  }
} ///:~
```

In **Glyph**, the **draw( )** method is **abstract**, so it is designed to be overridden. Indeed, you are forced to override it in **RoundGlyph**. But the **Glyph** constructor calls this method, and the call ends up in **RoundGlyph.draw( )**, which would seem to be the intent. But look at the output:

```
Glyph() before draw()
RoundGlyph.draw(), radius = 0
Glyph() after draw()
RoundGlyph.RoundGlyph(), radius = 5
```

When **Glyph**'s constructor calls **draw( )**, the value of **radius** isn't even the default initial value 1. It's 0. This would probably result in either a dot or nothing at all being drawn on the screen, and you'd be left staring, trying to figure out why the program won't work.

The order of initialization described in the previous section isn't quite complete, and that's the key to solving the mystery. The actual process of initialization is:

1.   The storage allocated for the object is initialized to binary zero before anything else happens.

2.   The base-class constructors are called as described previously. At this point, the overridden **draw( )** method is called (yes, *before* the **RoundGlyph** constructor is called), which discovers a **radius** value of zero, due to step 1.

3.   Member initializers are called in the order of declaration.

4.   The body of the derived-class constructor is called.

There's an upside to this, which is that everything is at least initialized to zero (or whatever zero means for that particular data type) and not just left as garbage. This includes object references that are embedded inside a class via composition, which become **null**. So if you forget to initialize that reference you'll get an exception at run-time. Everything else gets zero, which is usually a telltale value when looking at output.

On the other hand, you should be pretty horrified at the outcome of this program. You've done a perfectly logical thing, and yet the behavior is mysteriously wrong, with no complaints from the compiler. (C++ produces more rational behavior in this situation.) Bugs like this could easily be buried and take a long time to discover.

As a result, a good guideline for constructors is, "Do as little as possible to set the object into a good state, and if you can possibly avoid it, don't call any methods." The only safe methods to call inside a constructor are those that are **final** in the base class. (This also applies to **private** methods, which are automatically **final**.) These cannot be overridden and thus cannot produce this kind of surprise.

Designing with inheritance

Once you learn about polymorphism, it can seem that everything ought to be inherited because polymorphism is such a clever tool. This can burden your designs; in fact if you choose inheritance first when you're using an existing class to make a new class, things can become needlessly complicated.

A better approach is to choose composition first, when it's not obvious which one you should use. Composition does not force a design into an inheritance hierarchy. But composition is also more flexible since it's possible to dynamically choose a type (and thus behavior) when using composition, whereas inheritance requires an exact type to be known at compile-time. The following example illustrates this:

```java
//: c07:Transmogrify.java
// Dynamically changing the behavior of
// an object via composition.

abstract class Actor {
  abstract void act();
}

class HappyActor extends Actor {
  public void act() {
    System.out.println("HappyActor");
  }
}

class SadActor extends Actor {
  public void act() {
    System.out.println("SadActor");
  }
}

class Stage {
  Actor a = new HappyActor();
  void change() { a = new SadActor(); }
  void go() { a.act(); }
}

public class Transmogrify {
  public static void main(String[] args) {
    Stage s = new Stage();
    s.go(); // Prints "HappyActor"
    s.change();
    s.go(); // Prints "SadActor"
  }
} ///:~
```

A **Stage** object contains a reference to an **Actor**, which is initialized to a **HappyActor** object. This means **go( )** produces a particular behavior. But since a reference can be rebound to a different object at run-time, a reference for a **SadActor** object can be substituted in **a** and then the behavior produced by **go( )** changes. Thus you gain dynamic flexibility at run-time. (This is also called the *State Pattern*. See *Thinking in Patterns with Java*, downloadable at *www.BruceEckel.com*.) In contrast, you can't decide to inherit differently at run-time; that must be completely determined at compile-time.

A general guideline is "Use inheritance to express differences in behavior, and fields to express variations in state." In the above example, both are used: two different classes are inherited to express the difference in the **act( )** method, and **Stage** uses composition to allow its state to be changed. In this case, that change in state happens to produce a change in behavior.

Pure inheritance vs. extension

When studying inheritance, it would seem that the cleanest way to create an inheritance hierarchy is to take the "pure" approach. That is, only methods that have been established in the base class or **interface** are to be overridden in the derived class, as seen in this diagram:

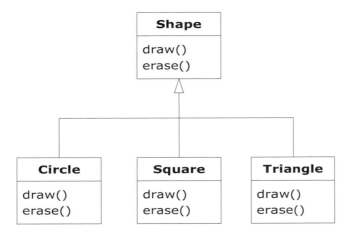

This can be termed a pure "is-a" relationship because the interface of a class establishes what it is. Inheritance guarantees that any derived class will have the interface of the base class and nothing less. If you follow the above diagram, derived classes will also have *no more* than the base class interface.

This can be thought of as *pure substitution*, because derived class objects can be perfectly substituted for the base class, and you never need to know any extra information about the subclasses when you're using them:

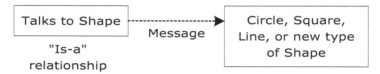

That is, the base class can receive any message you can send to the derived class because the two have exactly the same interface. All you need to do is upcast from the derived class and never look back to see what exact type of object you're dealing with. Everything is handled through polymorphism.

When you see it this way, it seems like a pure "is-a" relationship is the only sensible way to do things, and any other design indicates muddled thinking and is by definition broken. This too is a trap. As soon as you start thinking this way, you'll turn around and discover that extending the interface (which, unfortunately, the keyword **extends** seems to encourage) is the perfect solution to a particular problem. This could be termed an "is-like-a" relationship because the derived class is *like* the base class—it has the same fundamental interface—but it has other features that require additional methods to implement:

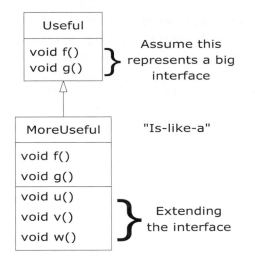

While this is also a useful and sensible approach (depending on the situation) it has a drawback. The extended part of the interface in the derived class is not available from the base class, so once you upcast you can't call the new methods:

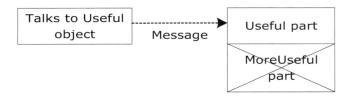

If you're not upcasting in this case, it won't bother you, but often you'll get into a situation in which you need to rediscover the exact type of the object so you can access the extended methods of that type. The following section shows how this is done.

Downcasting and run-time type identification

Since you lose the specific type information via an *upcast* (moving up the inheritance hierarchy), it makes sense that to retrieve the type information—that is, to move back down the inheritance hierarchy—you use a *downcast*. However, you know an upcast is always safe; the base

---

class cannot have a bigger interface than the derived class, therefore every message you send through the base class interface is guaranteed to be accepted. But with a downcast, you don't really know that a shape (for example) is actually a circle. It could instead be a triangle or square or some other type.

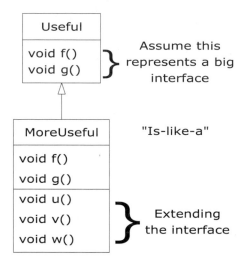

To solve this problem there must be some way to guarantee that a downcast is correct, so you won't accidentally cast to the wrong type and then send a message that the object can't accept. This would be quite unsafe.

In some languages (like C++) you must perform a special operation in order to get a type-safe downcast, but in Java *every cast* is checked! So even though it looks like you're just performing an ordinary parenthesized cast, at run-time this cast is checked to ensure that it is in fact the type you think it is. If it isn't, you get a **ClassCastException**. This act of checking types at run-time is called *run-time type identification* (RTTI). The following example demonstrates the behavior of RTTI:

```
//: c07:RTTI.java
// Downcasting & Run-time Type
// Identification (RTTI).
import java.util.*;

class Useful {
  public void f() {}
```

```
      public void g() {}
}

class MoreUseful extends Useful {
  public void f() {}
  public void g() {}
  public void u() {}
  public void v() {}
  public void w() {}
}

public class RTTI {
  public static void main(String[] args) {
    Useful[] x = {
      new Useful(),
      new MoreUseful()
    };
    x[0].f();
    x[1].g();
    // Compile-time: method not found in Useful:
    //! x[1].u();
    ((MoreUseful)x[1]).u(); // Downcast/RTTI
    ((MoreUseful)x[0]).u(); // Exception thrown
  }
} ///:~
```

As in the diagram, **MoreUseful** extends the interface of **Useful**. But since it's inherited, it can also be upcast to a **Useful**. You can see this happening in the initialization of the array **x** in **main( )**. Since both objects in the array are of class **Useful**, you can send the **f( )** and **g( )** methods to both, and if you try to call **u( )** (which exists only in **MoreUseful**) you'll get a compile-time error message.

If you want to access the extended interface of a **MoreUseful** object, you can try to downcast. If it's the correct type, it will be successful. Otherwise, you'll get a **ClassCastException**. You don't need to write any special code for this exception, since it indicates a programmer error that could happen anywhere in a program.

There's more to RTTI than a simple cast. For example, there's a way to see what type you're dealing with *before* you try to downcast it. All of Chapter

12 is devoted to the study of different aspects of Java run-time type identification.

Summary

Polymorphism means "different forms." In object-oriented programming, you have the same face (the common interface in the base class) and different forms using that face: the different versions of the dynamically bound methods.

You've seen in this chapter that it's impossible to understand, or even create, an example of polymorphism without using data abstraction and inheritance. Polymorphism is a feature that cannot be viewed in isolation (like a **switch** statement can, for example), but instead works only in concert, as part of a "big picture" of class relationships. People are often confused by other, non-object-oriented features of Java, like method overloading, which are sometimes presented as object-oriented. Don't be fooled: If it isn't late binding, it isn't polymorphism.

To use polymorphism—and thus object-oriented techniques—effectively in your programs you must expand your view of programming to include not just members and messages of an individual class, but also the commonality among classes and their relationships with each other. Although this requires significant effort, it's a worthy struggle, because the results are faster program development, better code organization, extensible programs, and easier code maintenance.

Exercises

Solutions to selected exercises can be found in the electronic document *The Thinking in Java Annotated Solution Guide*, available for a small fee from *www.BruceEckel.com*.

1.   Add a new method in the base class of **Shapes.java** that prints a message, but don't override it in the derived classes. Explain what happens. Now override it in one of the derived classes but not the others, and see what happens. Finally, override it in all the derived classes.

2.   Add a new type of **Shape** to **Shapes.java** and verify in **main( )** that polymorphism works for your new type as it does in the old types.

3.   Change **Music3.java** so that **what( )** becomes the root **Object** method **toString( )**. Try printing the **Instrument** objects using **System.out.println( )** (without any casting).

4.   Add a new type of **Instrument** to **Music3.java** and verify that polymorphism works for your new type.

5.   Modify **Music3.java** so that it randomly creates **Instrument** objects the way **Shapes.java** does.

6.   Create an inheritance hierarchy of **Rodent: Mouse, Gerbil, Hamster**, etc. In the base class, provide methods that are common to all **Rodent**s, and override these in the derived classes to perform different behaviors depending on the specific type of **Rodent**. Create an array of **Rodent**, fill it with different specific types of **Rodent**s, and call your base-class methods to see what happens.

7.   Modify Exercise 6 so that **Rodent** is an **abstract** class. Make the methods of **Rodent** abstract whenever possible.

8.   Create a class as **abstract** without including any **abstract** methods, and verify that you cannot create any instances of that class.

9.   Add class **Pickle** to **Sandwich.java**.

10.   Modify Exercise 6 so that it demonstrates the order of initialization of the base classes and derived classes. Now add member objects to both the base and derived classes, and show the order in which their initialization occurs during construction.

11.   Create a 3-level inheritance hierarchy. Each class in the hierarchy should have a **finalize( )** method, and it should properly call the base-class version of **finalize( )**. Demonstrate that your hierarchy works properly.

12.   Create a base class with two methods. In the first method, call the second method. Inherit a class and override the second method. Create an object of the derived class, upcast it to the base type, and call the first method. Explain what happens.

13.   Create a base class with an **abstract print( )** method that is overridden in a derived class. The overridden version of the method prints the value of an **int** variable defined in the derived class. At the point of definition of this variable, give it a nonzero value. In the base-class constructor, call this method. In **main( )**, create an object of the derived type, and then call its **print( )** method. Explain the results.

14.   Following the example in **Transmogrify.java**, create a **Starship** class containing an **AlertStatus** reference that can indicate three different states. Include methods to change the states.

15.   Create an **abstract** class with no methods. Derive a class and add a method. Create a **static** method that takes a reference to the base class, downcasts it to the derived class, and calls the method. In **main( )**, demonstrate that it works. Now put the **abstract** declaration for the method in the base class, thus eliminating the need for the downcast.

8: Interfaces & Inner Classes

Interfaces and inner classes provide more sophisticated ways to organize and control the objects in your system.

C++, for example, does not contain such mechanisms, although the clever programmer may simulate them. The fact that they exist in Java indicates that they were considered important enough to provide direct support through language keywords.

In Chapter 7, you learned about the **abstract** keyword, which allows you to create one or more methods in a class that have no definitions—you provide part of the interface without providing a corresponding implementation, which is created by inheritors. The **interface** keyword produces a completely abstract class, one that provides no implementation at all. You'll learn that the **interface** is more than just an abstract class taken to the extreme, since it allows you to perform a variation on C++'s "multiple inheritance," by creating a class that can be upcast to more than one base type.

At first, inner classes look like a simple code-hiding mechanism: you place classes inside other classes. You'll learn, however, that the inner class does more than that—it knows about and can communicate with the surrounding class—and that the kind of code you can write with inner classes is more elegant and clear, although it is a new concept to most. It takes some time to become comfortable with design using inner classes.

Interfaces

The **interface** keyword takes the **abstract** concept one step further. You could think of it as a "pure" **abstract** class. It allows the creator to establish the form for a class: method names, argument lists, and return types, but no method bodies. An **interface** can also contain fields, but these are implicitly **static** and **final**. An **interface** provides only a form, but no implementation.

An **interface** says: "This is what all classes that *implement* this particular interface will look like." Thus, any code that uses a particular **interface** knows what methods might be called for that **interface**, and that's all. So the **interface** is used to establish a "protocol" between classes. (Some object-oriented programming languages have a keyword called *protocol* to do the same thing.)

To create an **interface**, use the **interface** keyword instead of the **class** keyword. Like a class, you can add the **public** keyword before the **interface** keyword (but only if that **interface** is defined in a file of the same name) or leave it off to give "friendly" status so that it is only usable within the same package.

To make a class that conforms to a particular **interface** (or group of **interface**s) use the **implements** keyword. You're saying "The **interface** is what it looks like but now I'm going to say how it *works*." Other than that, it looks like inheritance. The diagram for the instrument example shows this:

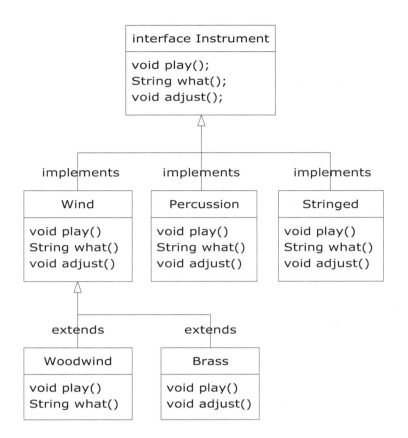

Once you've implemented an **interface**, that implementation becomes an ordinary class that can be extended in the regular way.

You can choose to explicitly declare the method declarations in an **interface** as **public**. But they are **public** even if you don't say it. So when you **implement** an **interface**, the methods from the **interface** must be defined as **public**. Otherwise they would default to "friendly," and you'd be reducing the accessibility of a method during inheritance, which is not allowed by the Java compiler.

You can see this in the modified version of the **Instrument** example. Note that every method in the **interface** is strictly a declaration, which is the only thing the compiler allows. In addition, none of the methods in **Instrument** are declared as **public**, but they're automatically **public** anyway:

```
//: c08:music5:Music5.java
```

```
// Interfaces.
import java.util.*;

interface Instrument {
  // Compile-time constant:
  int i = 5; // static & final
  // Cannot have method definitions:
  void play(); // Automatically public
  String what();
  void adjust();
}

class Wind implements Instrument {
  public void play() {
    System.out.println("Wind.play()");
  }
  public String what() { return "Wind"; }
  public void adjust() {}
}

class Percussion implements Instrument {
  public void play() {
    System.out.println("Percussion.play()");
  }
  public String what() { return "Percussion"; }
  public void adjust() {}
}

class Stringed implements Instrument {
  public void play() {
    System.out.println("Stringed.play()");
  }
  public String what() { return "Stringed"; }
  public void adjust() {}
}

class Brass extends Wind {
  public void play() {
    System.out.println("Brass.play()");
  }
  public void adjust() {
```

```
      System.out.println("Brass.adjust()");
    }
  }

class Woodwind extends Wind {
  public void play() {
    System.out.println("Woodwind.play()");
  }
  public String what() { return "Woodwind"; }
}

public class Music5 {
  // Doesn't care about type, so new types
  // added to the system still work right:
  static void tune(Instrument i) {
    // ...
    i.play();
  }
  static void tuneAll(Instrument[] e) {
    for(int i = 0; i < e.length; i++)
      tune(e[i]);
  }
  public static void main(String[] args) {
    Instrument[] orchestra = new Instrument[5];
    int i = 0;
    // Upcasting during addition to the array:
    orchestra[i++] = new Wind();
    orchestra[i++] = new Percussion();
    orchestra[i++] = new Stringed();
    orchestra[i++] = new Brass();
    orchestra[i++] = new Woodwind();
    tuneAll(orchestra);
  }
} ///:~
```

The rest of the code works the same. It doesn't matter if you are upcasting to a "regular" class called **Instrument**, an **abstract** class called **Instrument**, or to an **interface** called **Instrument**. The behavior is the same. In fact, you can see in the **tune( )** method that there isn't any evidence about whether **Instrument** is a "regular" class, an **abstract** class, or an **interface**. This is the intent: Each approach gives the programmer different control over the way objects are created and used.

"Multiple inheritance" in Java

The **interface** isn't simply a "more pure" form of **abstract** class. It has a higher purpose than that. Because an **interface** has no implementation at all—that is, there is no storage associated with an **interface**—there's nothing to prevent many **interface**s from being combined. This is valuable because there are times when you need to say "An **x** is an **a** *and* a **b** *and* a **c**." In C++, this act of combining multiple class interfaces is called *multiple inheritance*, and it carries some rather sticky baggage because each class can have an implementation. In Java, you can perform the same act, but only one of the classes can have an implementation, so the problems seen in C++ do not occur with Java when combining multiple interfaces:

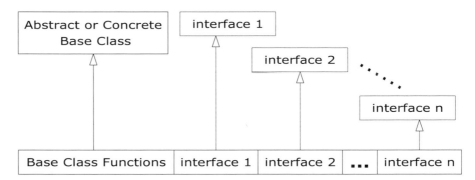

In a derived class, you aren't forced to have a base class that is either an **abstract** or "concrete" (one with no **abstract** methods). If you *do* inherit from a non-**interface**, you can inherit from only one. All the rest of the base elements must be **interface**s. You place all the interface names after the **implements** keyword and separate them with commas. You can have as many **interface**s as you want—each one becomes an independent type that you can upcast to. The following example shows a concrete class combined with several **interface**s to produce a new class:

```
//: c08:Adventure.java
// Multiple interfaces.
import java.util.*;
```

```
interface CanFight {
  void fight();
}

interface CanSwim {
  void swim();
}

interface CanFly {
  void fly();
}

class ActionCharacter {
  public void fight() {}
}

class Hero extends ActionCharacter
    implements CanFight, CanSwim, CanFly {
  public void swim() {}
  public void fly() {}
}

public class Adventure {
  static void t(CanFight x) { x.fight(); }
  static void u(CanSwim x) { x.swim(); }
  static void v(CanFly x) { x.fly(); }
  static void w(ActionCharacter x) { x.fight(); }
  public static void main(String[] args) {
    Hero h = new Hero();
    t(h); // Treat it as a CanFight
    u(h); // Treat it as a CanSwim
    v(h); // Treat it as a CanFly
    w(h); // Treat it as an ActionCharacter
  }
} ///:~
```

You can see that **Hero** combines the concrete class **ActionCharacter**
with the interfaces **CanFight**, **CanSwim**, and **CanFly**. When you
combine a concrete class with interfaces this way, the concrete class must
come first, then the interfaces. (The compiler gives an error otherwise.)

Note that the signature for **fight( )** is the same in the **interface CanFight** and the class **ActionCharacter**, and that **fight( )** is *not* provided with a definition in **Hero**. The rule for an **interface** is that you can inherit from it (as you will see shortly), but then you've got another **interface**. If you want to create an object of the new type, it must be a class with all definitions provided. Even though **Hero** does not explicitly provide a definition for **fight( )**, the definition comes along with **ActionCharacter** so it is automatically provided and it's possible to create objects of **Hero**.

In class **Adventure**, you can see that there are four methods that take as arguments the various interfaces and the concrete class. When a **Hero** object is created, it can be passed to any of these methods, which means it is being upcast to each **interface** in turn. Because of the way interfaces are designed in Java, this works without a hitch and without any particular effort on the part of the programmer.

Keep in mind that the core reason for interfaces is shown in the above example: to be able to upcast to more than one base type. However, a second reason for using interfaces is the same as using an **abstract** base class: to prevent the client programmer from making an object of this class and to establish that it is only an interface. This brings up a question: Should you use an **interface** or an **abstract** class? An **interface** gives you the benefits of an **abstract** class *and* the benefits of an **interface**, so if it's possible to create your base class without any method definitions or member variables you should always prefer **interface**s to **abstract** classes. In fact, if you know something is going to be a base class, your first choice should be to make it an **interface**, and only if you're forced to have method definitions or member variables should you change to an **abstract** class, or if necessary a concrete class.

Name collisions when combining interfaces

You can encounter a small pitfall when implementing multiple interfaces. In the above example, both **CanFight** and **ActionCharacter** have an identical **void fight( )** method. This is no problem because the method is identical in both cases, but what if it's not? Here's an example:

```
//: c08:InterfaceCollision.java
```

```
interface I1 { void f(); }
interface I2 { int f(int i); }
interface I3 { int f(); }
class C { public int f() { return 1; } }

class C2 implements I1, I2 {
  public void f() {}
  public int f(int i) { return 1; } // overloaded
}

class C3 extends C implements I2 {
  public int f(int i) { return 1; } // overloaded
}

class C4 extends C implements I3 {
  // Identical, no problem:
  public int f() { return 1; }
}

// Methods differ only by return type:
//! class C5 extends C implements I1 {}
//! interface I4 extends I1, I3 {} ///:~
```

The difficulty occurs because overriding, implementation, and overloading get unpleasantly mixed together, and overloaded functions cannot differ only by return type. When the last two lines are uncommented, the error messages say it all:

```
InterfaceCollision.java:23: f() in C cannot
implement f() in I1; attempting to use
incompatible return type
found   : int
required: void
InterfaceCollision.java:24: interfaces I3 and I1 are
incompatible; both define f
(), but with different return type
```

Using the same method names in different interfaces that are intended to be combined generally causes confusion in the readability of the code, as well. Strive to avoid it.

Extending an interface with inheritance

You can easily add new method declarations to an **interface** using inheritance, and you can also combine several **interface**s into a new **interface** with inheritance. In both cases you get a new **interface**, as seen in this example:

```
//: c08:HorrorShow.java
// Extending an interface with inheritance.

interface Monster {
  void menace();
}

interface DangerousMonster extends Monster {
  void destroy();
}

interface Lethal {
  void kill();
}

class DragonZilla implements DangerousMonster {
  public void menace() {}
  public void destroy() {}
}

interface Vampire
    extends DangerousMonster, Lethal {
  void drinkBlood();
}

class HorrorShow {
  static void u(Monster b) { b.menace(); }
  static void v(DangerousMonster d) {
    d.menace();
    d.destroy();
  }
  public static void main(String[] args) {
```

```
      DragonZilla if2 = new DragonZilla();
      u(if2);
      v(if2);
  }
} ///:~
```

DangerousMonster is a simple extension to **Monster** that produces a new **interface**. This is implemented in **DragonZilla**.

The syntax used in **Vampire** works *only* when inheriting interfaces. Normally, you can use **extends** with only a single class, but since an **interface** can be made from multiple other interfaces, **extends** can refer to multiple base interfaces when building a new **interface**. As you can see, the **interface** names are simply separated with commas.

Grouping constants

Because any fields you put into an **interface** are automatically **static** and **final**, the **interface** is a convenient tool for creating groups of constant values, much as you would with an **enum** in C or C++. For example:

```
//: c08:Months.java
// Using interfaces to create groups of constants.
package c08;

public interface Months {
  int
    JANUARY = 1, FEBRUARY = 2, MARCH = 3,
    APRIL = 4, MAY = 5, JUNE = 6, JULY = 7,
    AUGUST = 8, SEPTEMBER = 9, OCTOBER = 10,
    NOVEMBER = 11, DECEMBER = 12;
} ///:~
```

Notice the Java style of using all uppercase letters (with underscores to separate multiple words in a single identifier) for **static final**s that have constant initializers.

The fields in an **interface** are automatically **public**, so it's unnecessary to specify that.

Now you can use the constants from outside the package by importing **c08.*** or **c08.Months** just as you would with any other package, and

---

referencing the values with expressions like **Months.JANUARY**. Of course, what you get is just an **int**, so there isn't the extra type safety that C++'s **enum** has, but this (commonly used) technique is certainly an improvement over hard-coding numbers into your programs. (That approach is often referred to as using "magic numbers" and it produces very difficult-to-maintain code.)

If you do want extra type safety, you can build a class like this[1]:

```
//: c08:Month2.java
// A more robust enumeration system.
package c08;

public final class Month2 {
  private String name;
  private Month2(String nm) { name = nm; }
  public String toString() { return name; }
  public final static Month2
    JAN = new Month2("January"),
    FEB = new Month2("February"),
    MAR = new Month2("March"),
    APR = new Month2("April"),
    MAY = new Month2("May"),
    JUN = new Month2("June"),
    JUL = new Month2("July"),
    AUG = new Month2("August"),
    SEP = new Month2("September"),
    OCT = new Month2("October"),
    NOV = new Month2("November"),
    DEC = new Month2("December");
  public final static Month2[] month =  {
    JAN, JAN, FEB, MAR, APR, MAY, JUN,
    JUL, AUG, SEP, OCT, NOV, DEC
  };
  public static void main(String[] args) {
    Month2 m = Month2.JAN;
    System.out.println(m);
    m = Month2.month[12];
```

---

[1] This approach was inspired by an e-mail from Rich Hoffarth.

```
      System.out.println(m);
      System.out.println(m == Month2.DEC);
      System.out.println(m.equals(Month2.DEC));
    }
} ///:~
```

The class is called **Month2**, since there's already a **Month** in the standard Java library. It's a **final** class with a **private** constructor so no one can inherit from it or make any instances of it. The only instances are the **final static** ones created in the class itself: **JAN, FEB, MAR,** etc. These objects are also used in the array **month**, which lets you choose months by number instead of by name. (Notice the extra **JAN** in the array to provide an offset by one, so that December is month 12.) In **main( )** you can see the type safety: **m** is a **Month2** object so it can be assigned only to a **Month2**. The previous example **Months.java** provided only **int** values, so an **int** variable intended to represent a month could actually be given any integer value, which wasn't very safe.

This approach also allows you to use **==** or **equals( )** interchangeably, as shown at the end of **main( )**.

Initializing fields in interfaces

Fields defined in interfaces are automatically **static** and **final**. These cannot be "blank finals," but they can be initialized with nonconstant expressions. For example:

```
//: c08:RandVals.java
// Initializing interface fields with
// non-constant initializers.
import java.util.*;

public interface RandVals {
  int rint = (int)(Math.random() * 10);
  long rlong = (long)(Math.random() * 10);
  float rfloat = (float)(Math.random() * 10);
  double rdouble = Math.random() * 10;
} ///:~
```

Since the fields are **static**, they are initialized when the class is first loaded, which happens when any of the fields are accessed for the first time. Here's a simple test:

```
//: c08:TestRandVals.java

public class TestRandVals {
  public static void main(String[] args) {
    System.out.println(RandVals.rint);
    System.out.println(RandVals.rlong);
    System.out.println(RandVals.rfloat);
    System.out.println(RandVals.rdouble);
  }
} ///:~
```

The fields, of course, are not part of the interface but instead are stored in the **static** storage area for that interface.

Nesting interfaces

[2]Interfaces may be nested within classes and within other interfaces. This reveals a number of very interesting features:

```
//: c08:NestingInterfaces.java

class A {
  interface B {
    void f();
  }
  public class BImp implements B {
    public void f() {}
  }
  private class BImp2 implements B {
    public void f() {}
  }
  public interface C {
    void f();
  }
```

---

[2] Thanks to Martin Danner for asking this question during a seminar.

```
    class CImp implements C {
      public void f() {}
    }
    private class CImp2 implements C {
      public void f() {}
    }
    private interface D {
      void f();
    }
    private class DImp implements D {
      public void f() {}
    }
    public class DImp2 implements D {
      public void f() {}
    }
    public D getD() { return new DImp2(); }
    private D dRef;
    public void receiveD(D d) {
      dRef = d;
      dRef.f();
    }
}

interface E {
  interface G {
    void f();
  }
  // Redundant "public":
  public interface H {
    void f();
  }
  void g();
  // Cannot be private within an interface:
  //! private interface I {}
}

public class NestingInterfaces {
  public class BImp implements A.B {
    public void f() {}
  }
  class CImp implements A.C {
```

```
      public void f() {}
  }
  // Cannot implement a private interface except
  // within that interface's defining class:
  //! class DImp implements A.D {
  //!  public void f() {}
  //! }
  class EImp implements E {
    public void g() {}
  }
  class EGImp implements E.G {
    public void f() {}
  }
  class EImp2 implements E {
    public void g() {}
    class EG implements E.G {
      public void f() {}
    }
  }
  public static void main(String[] args) {
    A a = new A();
    // Can't access A.D:
    //! A.D ad = a.getD();
    // Doesn't return anything but A.D:
    //! A.DImp2 di2 = a.getD();
    // Cannot access a member of the interface:
    //! a.getD().f();
    // Only another A can do anything with getD():
    A a2 = new A();
    a2.receiveD(a.getD());
  }
} ///:~
```

The syntax for nesting an interface within a class is reasonably obvious, and just like non-nested interfaces these can have **public** or "friendly" visibility. You can also see that both **public** and "friendly" nested interfaces can be implemented as a **public**, "friendly," and **private** nested classes.

As a new twist, interfaces can also be **private** as seen in **A.D** (the same qualification syntax is used for nested interfaces as for nested classes).

What good is a **private** nested interface? You might guess that it can only be implemented as a **private** nested class as in **DImp**, but **A.DImp2** shows that it can also be implemented as a **public** class. However, **A.DImp2** can only be used as itself. You are not allowed to mention the fact that it implements the **private** interface, so implementing a **private** interface is a way to force the definition of the methods in that interface without adding any type information (that is, without allowing any upcasting).

The method **getD( )** produces a further quandary concerning the **private** interface: it's a **public** method that returns a reference to a **private** interface. What can you do with the return value of this method? In **main( )**, you can see several attempts to use the return value, all of which fail. The only thing that works is if the return value is handed to an object that has permission to use it—in this case, another **A**, via the **received( )** method.

Interface **E** shows that interfaces can be nested within each other. However, the rules about interfaces—in particular, that all interface elements must be **public**—are strictly enforced here, so an interface nested within another interface is automatically **public** and cannot be made **private**.

NestingInterfaces shows the various ways that nested interfaces can be implemented. In particular, notice that when you implement an interface, you are not required to implement any interfaces nested within. Also, **private** interfaces cannot be implemented outside of their defining classes.

Initially, these features may seem like they are added strictly for syntactic consistency, but I generally find that once you know about a feature, you often discover places where it is useful.

Inner classes

It's possible to place a class definition within another class definition. This is called an *inner class*. The inner class is a valuable feature because it allows you to group classes that logically belong together and to control the visibility of one within the other. However, it's important to understand that inner classes are distinctly different from composition.

Often, while you're learning about them, the need for inner classes isn't immediately obvious. At the end of this section, after all of the syntax and semantics of inner classes have been described, you'll find examples that should make clear the benefits of inner classes.

You create an inner class just as you'd expect—by placing the class definition inside a surrounding class:

```java
//: c08:Parcel1.java
// Creating inner classes.

public class Parcel1 {
  class Contents {
    private int i = 11;
    public int value() { return i; }
  }
  class Destination {
    private String label;
    Destination(String whereTo) {
      label = whereTo;
    }
    String readLabel() { return label; }
  }
  // Using inner classes looks just like
  // using any other class, within Parcel1:
  public void ship(String dest) {
    Contents c = new Contents();
    Destination d = new Destination(dest);
    System.out.println(d.readLabel());
  }
  public static void main(String[] args) {
    Parcel1 p = new Parcel1();
    p.ship("Tanzania");
  }
} ///:~
```

The inner classes, when used inside **ship( )**, look just like the use of any other classes. Here, the only practical difference is that the names are nested within **Parcel1**. You'll see in a while that this isn't the only difference.

More typically, an outer class will have a method that returns a reference to an inner class, like this:

```
//: c08:Parcel2.java
// Returning a reference to an inner class.

public class Parcel2 {
  class Contents {
    private int i = 11;
    public int value() { return i; }
  }
  class Destination {
    private String label;
    Destination(String whereTo) {
      label = whereTo;
    }
    String readLabel() { return label; }
  }
  public Destination to(String s) {
    return new Destination(s);
  }
  public Contents cont() {
    return new Contents();
  }
  public void ship(String dest) {
    Contents c = cont();
    Destination d = to(dest);
    System.out.println(d.readLabel());
  }
  public static void main(String[] args) {
    Parcel2 p = new Parcel2();
    p.ship("Tanzania");
    Parcel2 q = new Parcel2();
    // Defining references to inner classes:
    Parcel2.Contents c = q.cont();
    Parcel2.Destination d = q.to("Borneo");
  }
} ///:~
```

If you want to make an object of the inner class anywhere except from within a non-**static** method of the outer class, you must specify the type of that object as *OuterClassName.InnerClassName*, as seen in **main( )**.

Inner classes and upcasting

So far, inner classes don't seem that dramatic. After all, if it's hiding you're after, Java already has a perfectly good hiding mechanism—just allow the class to be "friendly" (visible only within a package) rather than creating it as an inner class.

However, inner classes really come into their own when you start upcasting to a base class, and in particular to an **interface**. (The effect of producing an interface reference from an object that implements it is essentially the same as upcasting to a base class.) That's because the inner class—the implementation of the **interface**—can then be completely unseen and unavailable to anyone, which is convenient for hiding the implementation. All you get back is a reference to the base class or the **interface**.

First, the common interfaces will be defined in their own files so they can be used in all the examples:

```
//: c08:Destination.java
public interface Destination {
  String readLabel();
} ///:~
```

```
//: c08:Contents.java
public interface Contents {
  int value();
} ///:~
```

Now **Contents** and **Destination** represent interfaces available to the client programmer. (The **interface**, remember, automatically makes all of its members **public**.)

When you get back a reference to the base class or the **interface**, it's possible that you can't even find out the exact type, as shown here:

```
//: c08:Parcel3.java
// Returning a reference to an inner class.
```

```
public class Parcel3 {
  private class PContents implements Contents {
    private int i = 11;
    public int value() { return i; }
  }
  protected class PDestination
      implements Destination {
    private String label;
    private PDestination(String whereTo) {
      label = whereTo;
    }
    public String readLabel() { return label; }
  }
  public Destination dest(String s) {
    return new PDestination(s);
  }
  public Contents cont() {
    return new PContents();
  }
}

class Test {
  public static void main(String[] args) {
    Parcel3 p = new Parcel3();
    Contents c = p.cont();
    Destination d = p.dest("Tanzania");
    // Illegal -- can't access private class:
    //! Parcel3.PContents pc = p.new PContents();
  }
} ///:~
```

Note that since **main( )** is in **Test**, when you want to run this program you don't execute **Parcel3**, but instead:

```
java Test
```

In the example, **main( )** must be in a separate class in order to demonstrate the privateness of the inner class **PContents**.

In **Parcel3**, something new has been added: the inner class **PContents** is **private** so no one but **Parcel3** can access it. **PDestination** is

---

protected, so no one but **Parcel3**, classes in the **Parcel3** package (since **protected** also gives package access—that is, **protected** is also "friendly"), and the inheritors of **Parcel3** can access **PDestination**. This means that the client programmer has restricted knowledge and access to these members. In fact, you can't even downcast to a **private** inner class (or a **protected** inner class unless you're an inheritor), because you can't access the name, as you can see in **class Test**. Thus, the **private** inner class provides a way for the class designer to completely prevent any type-coding dependencies and to completely hide details about implementation. In addition, extension of an **interface** is useless from the client programmer's perspective since the client programmer cannot access any additional methods that aren't part of the **public interface** class. This also provides an opportunity for the Java compiler to generate more efficient code.

Normal (non-inner) classes cannot be made **private** or **protected**—only **public** or "friendly."

Inner classes
in methods and scopes

What you've seen so far encompasses the typical use for inner classes. In general, the code that you'll write and read involving inner classes will be "plain" inner classes that are simple and easy to understand. However, the design for inner classes is quite complete and there are a number of other, more obscure, ways that you can use them if you choose: inner classes can be created within a method or even an arbitrary scope. There are two reasons for doing this:

1. As shown previously, you're implementing an interface of some kind so that you can create and return a reference.

2. You're solving a complicated problem and you want to create a class to aid in your solution, but you don't want it publicly available.

In the following examples, the previous code will be modified to use:

1. A class defined within a method

---

2. A class defined within a scope inside a method

3. An anonymous class implementing an interface

4. An anonymous class extending a class that has a nondefault constructor

5. An anonymous class that performs field initialization

6. An anonymous class that performs construction using instance initialization (anonymous inner classes cannot have constructors)

Although it's an ordinary class with an implementation, **Wrapping** is also being used as a common "interface" to its derived classes:

```
//: c08:Wrapping.java
public class Wrapping {
  private int i;
  public Wrapping(int x) { i = x; }
  public int value() { return i; }
} ///:~
```

You'll notice above that **Wrapping** has a constructor that requires an argument, to make things a bit more interesting.

The first example shows the creation of an entire class within the scope of a method (instead of the scope of another class):

```
//: c08:Parcel4.java
// Nesting a class within a method.

public class Parcel4 {
  public Destination dest(String s) {
    class PDestination
        implements Destination {
      private String label;
      private PDestination(String whereTo) {
        label = whereTo;
      }
      public String readLabel() { return label; }
    }
    return new PDestination(s);
  }
```

```
    public static void main(String[] args) {
      Parcel4 p = new Parcel4();
      Destination d = p.dest("Tanzania");
    }
} ///:~
```

The class **PDestination** is part of **dest( )** rather than being part of **Parcel4**. (Also notice that you could use the class identifier **PDestination** for an inner class inside each class in the same subdirectory without a name clash.) Therefore, **PDestination** cannot be accessed outside of **dest( )**. Notice the upcasting that occurs in the return statement—nothing comes out of **dest( )** except a reference to **Destination**, the base class. Of course, the fact that the name of the class **PDestination** is placed inside **dest( )** doesn't mean that **PDestination** is not a valid object once **dest( )** returns.

The next example shows how you can nest an inner class within any arbitrary scope:

```
//: c08:Parcel5.java
// Nesting a class within a scope.

public class Parcel5 {
  private void internalTracking(boolean b) {
    if(b) {
      class TrackingSlip {
        private String id;
        TrackingSlip(String s) {
          id = s;
        }
        String getSlip() { return id; }
      }
      TrackingSlip ts = new TrackingSlip("slip");
      String s = ts.getSlip();
    }
    // Can't use it here! Out of scope:
    //! TrackingSlip ts = new TrackingSlip("x");
  }
  public void track() { internalTracking(true); }
  public static void main(String[] args) {
    Parcel5 p = new Parcel5();
```

```
      p.track();
    }
} ///:~
```

The class **TrackingSlip** is nested inside the scope of an **if** statement. This does not mean that the class is conditionally created—it gets compiled along with everything else. However, it's not available outside the scope in which it is defined. Other than that, it looks just like an ordinary class.

Anonymous inner classes

The next example looks a little strange:

```
//: c08:Parcel6.java
// A method that returns an anonymous inner class.

public class Parcel6 {
  public Contents cont() {
    return new Contents() {
      private int i = 11;
      public int value() { return i; }
    }; // Semicolon required in this case
  }
  public static void main(String[] args) {
    Parcel6 p = new Parcel6();
    Contents c = p.cont();
  }
} ///:~
```

The **cont( )** method combines the creation of the return value with the definition of the class that represents that return value! In addition, the class is anonymous—it has no name. To make matters a bit worse, it looks like you're starting out to create a **Contents** object:

```
return new Contents()
```

But then, before you get to the semicolon, you say, "But wait, I think I'll slip in a class definition":

```
return new Contents() {
  private int i = 11;
  public int value() { return i; }
```

```
};
```

What this strange syntax means is: "Create an object of an anonymous class that's inherited from **Contents**." The reference returned by the **new** expression is automatically upcast to a **Contents** reference. The anonymous inner-class syntax is a shorthand for:

```
class MyContents implements Contents {
  private int i = 11;
  public int value() { return i; }
}
return new MyContents();
```

In the anonymous inner class, **Contents** is created using a default constructor. The following code shows what to do if your base class needs a constructor with an argument:

```
//: c08:Parcel7.java
// An anonymous inner class that calls
// the base-class constructor.

public class Parcel7 {
  public Wrapping wrap(int x) {
    // Base constructor call:
    return new Wrapping(x) {
      public int value() {
        return super.value() * 47;
      }
    }; // Semicolon required
  }
  public static void main(String[] args) {
    Parcel7 p = new Parcel7();
    Wrapping w = p.wrap(10);
  }
} ///:~
```

That is, you simply pass the appropriate argument to the base-class constructor, seen here as the **x** passed in **new Wrapping(x)**. An anonymous class cannot have a constructor where you would normally call **super( )**.

In both of the previous examples, the semicolon doesn't mark the end of the class body (as it does in C++). Instead, it marks the end of the expression that happens to contain the anonymous class. Thus, it's identical to the use of the semicolon everywhere else.

What happens if you need to perform some kind of initialization for an object of an anonymous inner class? Since it's anonymous, there's no name to give the constructor—so you can't have a constructor. You can, however, perform initialization at the point of definition of your fields:

```
//: c08:Parcel8.java
// An anonymous inner class that performs
// initialization. A briefer version
// of Parcel5.java.

public class Parcel8 {
  // Argument must be final to use inside
  // anonymous inner class:
  public Destination dest(final String dest) {
    return new Destination() {
      private String label = dest;
      public String readLabel() { return label; }
    };
  }
  public static void main(String[] args) {
    Parcel8 p = new Parcel8();
    Destination d = p.dest("Tanzania");
  }
} ///:~
```

If you're defining an anonymous inner class and want to use an object that's defined outside the anonymous inner class, the compiler requires that the outside object be **final**. This is why the argument to **dest( )** is **final**. If you forget, you'll get a compile-time error message.

As long as you're simply assigning a field, the above approach is fine. But what if you need to perform some constructor-like activity? With *instance initialization*, you can, in effect, create a constructor for an anonymous inner class:

```
//: c08:Parcel9.java
```

```
// Using "instance initialization" to perform
// construction on an anonymous inner class.

public class Parcel9 {
  public Destination
  dest(final String dest, final float price) {
    return new Destination() {
      private int cost;
      // Instance initialization for each object:
      {
        cost = Math.round(price);
        if(cost > 100)
          System.out.println("Over budget!");
      }
      private String label = dest;
      public String readLabel() { return label; }
    };
  }
  public static void main(String[] args) {
    Parcel9 p = new Parcel9();
    Destination d = p.dest("Tanzania", 101.395F);
  }
} ///:~
```

Inside the instance initializer you can see code that couldn't be executed as part of a field initializer (that is, the **if** statement). So in effect, an instance initializer is the constructor for an anonymous inner class. Of course, it's limited; you can't overload instance initializers so you can have only one of these constructors.

The link to the outer class

So far, it appears that inner classes are just a name-hiding and code-organization scheme, which is helpful but not totally compelling. However, there's another twist. When you create an inner class, an object of that inner class has a link to the enclosing object that made it, and so it can access the members of that enclosing object—*without* any special qualifications. In addition, inner classes have access rights to all the elements in the enclosing class[3]. The following example demonstrates this:

```
//: c08:Sequence.java
// Holds a sequence of Objects.

interface Selector {
  boolean end();
  Object current();
  void next();
}

public class Sequence {
  private Object[] obs;
  private int next = 0;
  public Sequence(int size) {
    obs = new Object[size];
  }
  public void add(Object x) {
    if(next < obs.length) {
      obs[next] = x;
      next++;
    }
  }
  private class SSelector implements Selector {
    int i = 0;
    public boolean end() {
      return i == obs.length;
    }
    public Object current() {
      return obs[i];
    }
    public void next() {
      if(i < obs.length) i++;
    }
  }
```

---

[3] This is very different from the design of *nested classes* in C++, which is simply a name-hiding mechanism. There is no link to an enclosing object and no implied permissions in C++.

```
  public Selector getSelector() {
    return new SSelector();
  }
  public static void main(String[] args) {
    Sequence s = new Sequence(10);
    for(int i = 0; i < 10; i++)
      s.add(Integer.toString(i));
    Selector sl = s.getSelector();
    while(!sl.end()) {
      System.out.println(sl.current());
      sl.next();
    }
  }
} ///:~
```

The **Sequence** is simply a fixed-sized array of **Object** with a class wrapped around it. You call **add( )** to add a new **Object** to the end of the sequence (if there's room left). To fetch each of the objects in a **Sequence**, there's an interface called **Selector**, which allows you to see if you're at the **end( )**, to look at the **current( ) Object**, and to move to the **next( ) Object** in the **Sequence**. Because **Selector** is an **interface**, many other classes can implement the **interface** in their own ways, and many methods can take the **interface** as an argument, in order to create generic code.

Here, the **SSelector** is a **private** class that provides **Selector** functionality. In **main( )**, you can see the creation of a **Sequence**, followed by the addition of a number of **String** objects. Then, a **Selector** is produced with a call to **getSelector( )** and this is used to move through the **Sequence** and select each item.

At first, the creation of **SSelector** looks like just another inner class. But examine it closely. Note that each of the methods **end( )**, **current( ),** and **next( )** refer to **obs**, which is a reference that isn't part of **SSelector**, but is instead a **private** field in the enclosing class. However, the inner class can access methods and fields from the enclosing class as if they owned them. This turns out to be very convenient, as you can see in the above example.

So an inner class has automatic access to the members of the enclosing class. How can this happen? The inner class must keep a reference to the particular object of the enclosing class that was responsible for creating it. Then when you refer to a member of the enclosing class, that (hidden) reference is used to select that member. Fortunately, the compiler takes care of all these details for you, but you can also understand now that an object of an inner class can be created only in association with an object of the enclosing class. Construction of the inner class object requires the reference to the object of the enclosing class, and the compiler will complain if it cannot access that reference. Most of the time this occurs without any intervention on the part of the programmer.

static inner classes

If you don't need a connection between the inner class object and the outer class object, then you can make the inner class **static**. To understand the meaning of **static** when applied to inner classes, you must remember that the object of an ordinary inner class implicitly keeps a reference to the object of the enclosing class that created it. This is not true, however, when you say an inner class is **static**. A **static** inner class means:

1. You don't need an outer-class object in order to create an object of a **static** inner class.

2. You can't access an outer-class object from an object of a **static** inner class.

static inner classes are different than non-**static** inner classes in another way, as well. Fields and methods in non-**static** inner classes can only be at the outer level of a class, so non-**static** inner classes cannot have **static** data, **static** fields, or **static** inner classes. However, **static** inner classes can have all of these:

```
//: c08:Parcel10.java
// Static inner classes.

public class Parcel10 {
  private static class PContents
  implements Contents {
    private int i = 11;
    public int value() { return i; }
  }
```

```
  protected static class PDestination
      implements Destination {
    private String label;
    private PDestination(String whereTo) {
      label = whereTo;
    }
    public String readLabel() { return label; }
    // Static inner classes can contain
    // other static elements:
    public static void f() {}
    static int x = 10;
    static class AnotherLevel {
      public static void f() {}
      static int x = 10;
    }
  }
  public static Destination dest(String s) {
    return new PDestination(s);
  }
  public static Contents cont() {
    return new PContents();
  }
  public static void main(String[] args) {
    Contents c = cont();
    Destination d = dest("Tanzania");
  }
} ///:~
```

In **main( )**, no object of **Parcel10** is necessary; instead you use the normal syntax for selecting a **static** member to call the methods that return references to **Contents** and **Destination**.

As you will see shortly, in an ordinary (non-**static**) inner class, the link to the outer class object is achieved with a special **this** reference. A **static** inner class does not have this special **this** reference, which makes it analogous to a **static** method.

Normally you can't put any code inside an **interface**, but a **static** inner class can be part of an **interface**. Since the class is **static** it doesn't violate the rules for interfaces—the **static** inner class is only placed inside the namespace of the interface:

```
//: c08:IInterface.java
// Static inner classes inside interfaces.

interface IInterface {
  static class Inner {
    int i, j, k;
    public Inner() {}
    void f() {}
  }
} ///:~
```

Earlier in this book I suggested putting a **main( )** in every class to act as a test bed for that class. One drawback to this is the amount of extra compiled code you must carry around. If this is a problem, you can use a **static** inner class to hold your test code:

```
//: c08:TestBed.java
// Putting test code in a static inner class.

class TestBed {
  TestBed() {}
  void f() { System.out.println("f()"); }
  public static class Tester {
    public static void main(String[] args) {
      TestBed t = new TestBed();
      t.f();
    }
  }
} ///:~
```

This generates a separate class called **TestBed$Tester** (to run the program, you say **java TestBed$Tester**). You can use this class for testing, but you don't need to include it in your shipping product.

Referring to the outer class object

If you need to produce the reference to the outer class object, you name the outer class followed by a dot and **this**. For example, in the class **Sequence.SSelector**, any of its methods can produce the stored reference to the outer class **Sequence** by saying **Sequence.this**. The resulting reference is automatically the correct type. (This is known and checked at compile-time, so there is no run-time overhead.)

Sometimes you want to tell some other object to create an object of one of its inner classes. To do this you must provide a reference to the other outer class object in the **new** expression, like this:

```
//: c08:Parcel11.java
// Creating instances of inner classes.

public class Parcel11 {
  class Contents {
    private int i = 11;
    public int value() { return i; }
  }
  class Destination {
    private String label;
    Destination(String whereTo) {
      label = whereTo;
    }
    String readLabel() { return label; }
  }
  public static void main(String[] args) {
    Parcel11 p = new Parcel11();
    // Must use instance of outer class
    // to create an instances of the inner class:
    Parcel11.Contents c = p.new Contents();
    Parcel11.Destination d =
      p.new Destination("Tanzania");
  }
} ///:~
```

To create an object of the inner class directly, you don't follow the same form and refer to the outer class name **Parcel11** as you might expect, but instead you must use an *object* of the outer class to make an object of the inner class:

```
Parcel11.Contents c = p.new Contents();
```

Thus, it's not possible to create an object of the inner class unless you already have an object of the outer class. This is because the object of the inner class is quietly connected to the object of the outer class that it was made from. However, if you make a **static** inner class, then it doesn't need a reference to the outer class object.

Reaching outward from a multiply-nested class

[4]It doesn't matter how deeply an inner class may be nested—it can transparently access all of the members of all the classes it is nested within, as seen here:

```
//: c08:MultiNestingAccess.java
// Nested classes can access all members of all
// levels of the classes they are nested within.

class MNA {
  private void f() {}
  class A {
    private void g() {}
    public class B {
      void h() {
        g();
        f();
      }
    }
  }
}

public class MultiNestingAccess {
  public static void main(String[] args) {
    MNA mna = new MNA();
    MNA.A mnaa = mna.new A();
    MNA.A.B mnaab = mnaa.new B();
    mnaab.h();
  }
} ///:~
```

------

[4] Thanks again to Martin Danner.

You can see that in **MNA.A.B**, the methods **g( )** and **f( )** are callable without any qualification (despite the fact that they are **private**). This example also demonstrates the syntax necessary to create objects of multiply-nested inner classes when you create the objects in a different class. The ".**new**" syntax produces the correct scope so you do not have to qualify the class name in the constructor call.

Inheriting from inner classes

Because the inner class constructor must attach to a reference of the enclosing class object, things are slightly complicated when you inherit from an inner class. The problem is that the "secret" reference to the enclosing class object *must* be initialized, and yet in the derived class there's no longer a default object to attach to. The answer is to use a syntax provided to make the association explicit:

```
//: c08:InheritInner.java
// Inheriting an inner class.

class WithInner {
  class Inner {}
}

public class InheritInner
    extends WithInner.Inner {
  //! InheritInner() {} // Won't compile
  InheritInner(WithInner wi) {
    wi.super();
  }
  public static void main(String[] args) {
    WithInner wi = new WithInner();
    InheritInner ii = new InheritInner(wi);
  }
} ///:~
```

You can see that **InheritInner** is extending only the inner class, not the outer one. But when it comes time to create a constructor, the default one is no good and you can't just pass a reference to an enclosing object. In addition, you must use the syntax

```
enclosingClassReference.super();
```

inside the constructor. This provides the necessary reference and the program will then compile.

Can inner classes be overridden?

What happens when you create an inner class, then inherit from the enclosing class and redefine the inner class? That is, is it possible to override an inner class? This seems like it would be a powerful concept, but "overriding" an inner class as if it were another method of the outer class doesn't really do anything:

```
//: c08:BigEgg.java
// An inner class cannot be overriden
// like a method.

class Egg {
  protected class Yolk {
    public Yolk() {
      System.out.println("Egg.Yolk()");
    }
  }
  private Yolk y;
  public Egg() {
    System.out.println("New Egg()");
    y = new Yolk();
  }
}

public class BigEgg extends Egg {
  public class Yolk {
    public Yolk() {
      System.out.println("BigEgg.Yolk()");
    }
  }
  public static void main(String[] args) {
    new BigEgg();
  }
} ///:~
```

The default constructor is synthesized automatically by the compiler, and this calls the base-class default constructor. You might think that since a

BigEgg is being created, the "overridden" version of **Yolk** would be used, but this is not the case. The output is:

```
New Egg()
Egg.Yolk()
```

This example simply shows that there isn't any extra inner class magic going on when you inherit from the outer class. The two inner classes are completely separate entities, each in their own namespace. However, it's still possible to explicitly inherit from the inner class:

```
//: c08:BigEgg2.java
// Proper inheritance of an inner class.

class Egg2 {
  protected class Yolk {
    public Yolk() {
      System.out.println("Egg2.Yolk()");
    }
    public void f() {
      System.out.println("Egg2.Yolk.f()");
    }
  }
  private Yolk y = new Yolk();
  public Egg2() {
    System.out.println("New Egg2()");
  }
  public void insertYolk(Yolk yy) { y = yy; }
  public void g() { y.f(); }
}

public class BigEgg2 extends Egg2 {
  public class Yolk extends Egg2.Yolk {
    public Yolk() {
      System.out.println("BigEgg2.Yolk()");
    }
    public void f() {
      System.out.println("BigEgg2.Yolk.f()");
    }
  }
  public BigEgg2() { insertYolk(new Yolk()); }
  public static void main(String[] args) {
```

```
      Egg2 e2 = new BigEgg2();
      e2.g();
  }
} ///:~
```

Now **BigEgg2.Yolk** explicitly **extends Egg2.Yolk** and overrides its
methods. The method **insertYolk( )** allows **BigEgg2** to upcast one of its
own **Yolk** objects into the **y** reference in **Egg2**, so when **g( )** calls **y.f( )**
the overridden version of **f( )** is used. The output is:

```
Egg2.Yolk()
New Egg2()
Egg2.Yolk()
BigEgg2.Yolk()
BigEgg2.Yolk.f()
```

The second call to **Egg2.Yolk( )** is the base-class constructor call of the
BigEgg2.Yolk constructor. You can see that the overridden version of
f( ) is used when **g( )** is called.

Inner class identifiers

Since every class produces a **.class** file that holds all the information
about how to create objects of this type (this information produces a
"meta-class" called the **Class** object), you might guess that inner classes
must also produce **.class** files to contain the information for *their* **Class**
objects. The names of these files/classes have a strict formula: the name
of the enclosing class, followed by a '**$**', followed by the name of the inner
class. For example, the **.class** files created by **InheritInner.java**
include:

```
InheritInner.class
WithInner$Inner.class
WithInner.class
```

If inner classes are anonymous, the compiler simply starts generating
numbers as inner class identifiers. If inner classes are nested within inner
classes, their names are simply appended after a '**$**' and the outer class
identifier(s).

Although this scheme of generating internal names is simple and straightforward, it's also robust and handles most situations[5]. Since it is the standard naming scheme for Java, the generated files are automatically platform-independent. (Note that the Java compiler is changing your inner classes in all sorts of other ways in order to make them work.)

Why inner classes?

At this point you've seen a lot of syntax and semantics describing the way inner classes work, but this doesn't answer the question of why they exist. Why did Sun go to so much trouble to add this fundamental language feature?

Typically, the inner class inherits from a class or implements an **interface**, and the code in the inner class manipulates the outer class object that it was created within. So you could say that an inner class provides a kind of window into the outer class.

A question that cuts to the heart of inner classes is this: if I just need a reference to an **interface**, why don't I just make the outer class implement that **interface**? The answer is "If that's all you need, then that's how you should do it." So what is it that distinguishes an inner class implementing an **interface** from an outer class implementing the same **interface**? The answer is that you can't always have the convenience of **interface**s—sometimes you're working with implementations. So the most compelling reason for inner classes is:

> *Each inner class can independently inherit from an implementation. Thus, the inner class is not limited by whether the outer class is already inheriting from an implementation.*

Without the ability that inner classes provide to inherit—in effect—from more than one concrete or **abstract** class, some design and programming problems would be intractable. So one way to look at the inner class is as

---

[5] On the other hand, '$' is a meta-character to the Unix shell and so you'll sometimes have trouble when listing the **.class** files. This is a bit strange coming from Sun, a Unix-based company. My guess is that they weren't considering this issue, but instead thought you'd naturally focus on the source-code files.

the completion of the solution of the multiple-inheritance problem. Interfaces solve part of the problem, but inner classes effectively allow "multiple implementation inheritance." That is, inner classes effectively allow you to inherit from more than one non-**interface**.

To see this in more detail, consider a situation where you have two interfaces that must somehow be implemented within a class. Because of the flexibility of interfaces, you have two choices: a single class or an inner class:

```
//: c08:MultiInterfaces.java
// Two ways that a class can
// implement multiple interfaces.

interface A {}
interface B {}

class X implements A, B {}

class Y implements A {
  B makeB() {
    // Anonymous inner class:
    return new B() {};
  }
}

public class MultiInterfaces {
  static void takesA(A a) {}
  static void takesB(B b) {}
  public static void main(String[] args) {
    X x = new X();
    Y y = new Y();
    takesA(x);
    takesA(y);
    takesB(x);
    takesB(y.makeB());
  }
} ///:~
```

Of course, this assumes that the structure of your code makes logical sense either way. However, you'll ordinarily have some kind of guidance

---

from the nature of the problem about whether to use a single class or an inner class. But without any other constraints, in the above example the approach you take doesn't really make much difference from an implementation standpoint. Both of them work.

However, if you have **abstract** or concrete classes instead of **interface**s, you are suddenly limited to using inner classes if your class must somehow implement both of the others:

```
//: c08:MultiImplementation.java
// With concrete or abstract classes, inner
// classes are the only way to produce the effect
// of "multiple implementation inheritance."

class C {}
abstract class D {}

class Z extends C {
  D makeD() { return new D() {}; }
}

public class MultiImplementation {
  static void takesC(C c) {}
  static void takesD(D d) {}
  public static void main(String[] args) {
    Z z = new Z();
    takesC(z);
    takesD(z.makeD());
  }
} ///:~
```

If you didn't need to solve the "multiple implementation inheritance" problem, you could conceivably code around everything else without the need for inner classes. But with inner classes you have these additional features:

1.   The inner class can have multiple instances, each with its own state information that is independent of the information in the outer class object.

2. In a single outer class you can have several inner classes, each of which implement the same **interface** or inherit from the same class in a different way. An example of this will be shown shortly.

3. The point of creation of the inner class object is not tied to the creation of the outer class object.

4. There is no potentially confusing "is-a" relationship with the inner class; it's a separate entity.

As an example, if **Sequence.java** did not use inner classes, you'd have to say "a **Sequence** is a **Selector**," and you'd only be able to have one **Selector** in existence for a particular **Sequence**. Also, you can have a second method, **getRSelector( )**, that produces a **Selector** that moves backward through the sequence. This kind of flexibility is only available with inner classes.

Closures & Callbacks

A *closure* is a callable object that retains information from the scope in which it was created. From this definition, you can see that an inner class is an object-oriented closure, because it doesn't just contain each piece of information from the outer class object ("the scope in which it was created"), but it automatically holds a reference back to the whole outer class object, where it has permission to manipulate all the members, even **private** ones.

One of the most compelling arguments made to include some kind of pointer mechanism in Java was to allow *callbacks*. With a callback, some other object is given a piece of information that allows it to call back into the originating object at some later point. This is a very powerful concept, as you will see in Chapters 13 and 16. If a callback is implemented using a pointer, however, you must rely on the programmer to behave and not misuse the pointer. As you've seen by now, Java tends to be more careful than that, so pointers were not included in the language.

The closure provided by the inner class is a perfect solution; more flexible and far safer than a pointer. Here's a simple example:

```
//: c08:Callbacks.java
// Using inner classes for callbacks
```

```java
interface Incrementable {
  void increment();
}

// Very simple to just implement the interface:
class Callee1 implements Incrementable {
  private int i = 0;
  public void increment() {
    i++;
    System.out.println(i);
  }
}

class MyIncrement {
  public void increment() {
    System.out.println("Other operation");
  }
  public static void f(MyIncrement mi) {
    mi.increment();
  }
}

// If your class must implement increment() in
// some other way, you must use an inner class:
class Callee2 extends MyIncrement {
  private int i = 0;
  private void incr() {
    i++;
    System.out.println(i);
  }
  private class Closure implements Incrementable {
    public void increment() { incr(); }
  }
  Incrementable getCallbackReference() {
    return new Closure();
  }
}

class Caller {
  private Incrementable callbackReference;
```

```
    Caller(Incrementable cbh) {
      callbackReference = cbh;
    }
    void go() {
      callbackReference.increment();
    }
  }

public class Callbacks {
  public static void main(String[] args) {
    Callee1 c1 = new Callee1();
    Callee2 c2 = new Callee2();
    MyIncrement.f(c2);
    Caller caller1 = new Caller(c1);
    Caller caller2 =
      new Caller(c2.getCallbackReference());
    caller1.go();
    caller1.go();
    caller2.go();
    caller2.go();
  }
} ///:~
```

This example also provides a further distinction between implementing an interface in an outer class vs. doing so in an inner class. **Callee1** is clearly the simpler solution in terms of the code. **Callee2** inherits from **MyIncrement** which already has a different **increment( )** method which does something unrelated to that which is expected by the **Incrementable** interface. When **MyIncrement** is inherited into **Callee2**, **increment( )** can't be overridden for use by **Incrementable**, so you're forced to provide a separate implementation using an inner class. Also note that when you create an inner class you do not add to or modify the interface of the outer class.

Notice that everything except **getCallbackReference( )** in **Callee2** is **private**. To allow *any* connection to the outside world, the **interface Incrementable** is essential. Here you can see how **interface**s allow for a complete separation of interface from implementation.

The inner class **Closure** simply implements **Incrementable** to provide a hook back into **Callee2**—but a safe hook. Whoever gets the

Incrementable reference can, of course, only call **increment( )** and has no other abilities (unlike a pointer, which would allow you to run wild).

Caller takes an **Incrementable** reference in its constructor (although the capturing of the callback reference could happen at any time) and then, sometime latter, uses the reference to "call back" into the **Callee** class.

The value of the callback is in its flexibility—you can dynamically decide what functions will be called at run-time. The benefit of this will become more evident in Chapter 13, where callbacks are used everywhere to implement graphical user interface (GUI) functionality.

Inner classes & control frameworks

A more concrete example of the use of inner classes can be found in something that I will refer to here as a *control framework*.

An *application framework* is a class or a set of classes that's designed to solve a particular type of problem. To apply an application framework, you inherit from one or more classes and override some of the methods. The code you write in the overridden methods customizes the general solution provided by that application framework, in order to solve your specific problem. The control framework is a particular type of application framework dominated by the need to respond to events; a system that primarily responds to events is called an *event-driven system*. One of the most important problems in application programming is the graphical user interface (GUI), which is almost entirely event-driven. As you will see in Chapter 13, the Java Swing library is a control framework that elegantly solves the GUI problem and that heavily uses inner classes.

To see how inner classes allow the simple creation and use of control frameworks, consider a control framework whose job is to execute events whenever those events are "ready." Although "ready" could mean anything, in this case the default will be based on clock time. What follows is a control framework that contains no specific information about what it's controlling. First, here is the interface that describes any control event. It's an **abstract** class instead of an actual **interface** because the default

---

behavior is to perform the control based on time, so some of the
implementation can be included here:

```
//: c08:controller:Event.java
// The common methods for any control event.
package c08.controller;

abstract public class Event {
  private long evtTime;
  public Event(long eventTime) {
    evtTime = eventTime;
  }
  public boolean ready() {
    return System.currentTimeMillis() >= evtTime;
  }
  abstract public void action();
  abstract public String description();
} ///:~
```

The constructor simply captures the time when you want the **Event** to
run, while **ready( )** tells you when it's time to run it. Of course, **ready( )**
could be overridden in a derived class to base the **Event** on something
other than time.

action( ) is the method that's called when the **Event** is **ready( )**, and
description( ) gives textual information about the **Event**.

The following file contains the actual control framework that manages
and fires events. The first class is really just a "helper" class whose job is
to hold **Event** objects. You can replace it with any appropriate container,
and in Chapter 9 you'll discover other containers that will do the trick
without requiring you to write this extra code:

```
//: c08:controller:Controller.java
// Along with Event, the generic
// framework for all control systems:
package c08.controller;

// This is just a way to hold Event objects.
class EventSet {
  private Event[] events = new Event[100];
  private int index = 0;
```

```java
    private int next = 0;
    public void add(Event e) {
      if(index >= events.length)
        return; // (In real life, throw exception)
      events[index++] = e;
    }
    public Event getNext() {
      boolean looped = false;
      int start = next;
      do {
        next = (next + 1) % events.length;
        // See if it has looped to the beginning:
        if(start == next) looped = true;
        // If it loops past start, the list
        // is empty:
        if((next == (start + 1) % events.length)
            && looped)
          return null;
      } while(events[next] == null);
      return events[next];
    }
    public void removeCurrent() {
      events[next] = null;
    }
  }

public class Controller {
  private EventSet es = new EventSet();
  public void addEvent(Event c) { es.add(c); }
  public void run() {
    Event e;
    while((e = es.getNext()) != null) {
      if(e.ready()) {
        e.action();
        System.out.println(e.description());
        es.removeCurrent();
      }
    }
  }
} ///:~
```

EventSet arbitrarily holds 100 **Event**s. (If a "real" container from Chapter 9 is used here you don't need to worry about its maximum size, since it will resize itself). The **index** is used to keep track of the next available space, and **next** is used when you're looking for the next **Event** in the list, to see whether you've looped around. This is important during a call to **getNext( )**, because **Event** objects are removed from the list (using **removeCurrent( )**) once they're run, so **getNext( )** will encounter holes in the list as it moves through it.

Note that **removeCurrent( )** doesn't just set some flag indicating that the object is no longer in use. Instead, it sets the reference to **null**. This is important because if the garbage collector sees a reference that's still in use then it can't clean up the object. If you think your references might hang around (as they would here), then it's a good idea to set them to **null** to give the garbage collector permission to clean them up.

Controller is where the actual work goes on. It uses an **EventSet** to hold its **Event** objects, and **addEvent( )** allows you to add new events to this list. But the important method is **run( )**. This method loops through the **EventSet**, hunting for an **Event** object that's **ready( )** to run. For each one it finds **ready( )**, it calls the **action( )** method, prints out the **description( ),** and then removes the **Event** from the list.

Note that so far in this design you know nothing about exactly *what* an **Event** does. And this is the crux of the design; how it "separates the things that change from the things that stay the same." Or, to use my term, the "vector of change" is the different actions of the various kinds of **Event** objects, and you express different actions by creating different **Event** subclasses.

This is where inner classes come into play. They allow two things:

1. To create the entire implementation of a control-framework application in a single class, thereby encapsulating everything that's unique about that implementation. Inner classes are used to express the many different kinds of **action( )** necessary to solve the problem. In addition, the following example uses **private** inner classes so the implementation is completely hidden and can be changed with impunity.

2.   Inner classes keep this implementation from becoming awkward, since you're able to easily access any of the members in the outer class. Without this ability the code might become unpleasant enough that you'd end up seeking an alternative.

Consider a particular implementation of the control framework designed to control greenhouse functions[6]. Each action is entirely different: turning lights, water, and thermostats on and off, ringing bells, and restarting the system. But the control framework is designed to easily isolate this different code. Inner classes allow you to have multiple derived versions of the same base class, **Event**, within a single class. For each type of action you inherit a new **Event** inner class, and write the control code inside of **action( )**.

As is typical with an application framework, the class **GreenhouseControls** is inherited from **Controller**:

```
//: c08:GreenhouseControls.java
// This produces a specific application of the
// control system, all in a single class. Inner
// classes allow you to encapsulate different
// functionality for each type of event.
import c08.controller.*;

public class GreenhouseControls
    extends Controller {
  private boolean light = false;
  private boolean water = false;
  private String thermostat = "Day";
  private class LightOn extends Event {
    public LightOn(long eventTime) {
      super(eventTime);
    }
    public void action() {
      // Put hardware control code here to
      // physically turn on the light.
      light = true;
```

---

[6] For some reason this has always been a pleasing problem for me to solve; it came from my earlier book *C++ Inside & Out*, but Java allows a much more elegant solution.

```
      }
    public String description() {
      return "Light is on";
    }
  }
  private class LightOff extends Event {
    public LightOff(long eventTime) {
      super(eventTime);
    }
    public void action() {
      // Put hardware control code here to
      // physically turn off the light.
      light = false;
    }
    public String description() {
      return "Light is off";
    }
  }
  private class WaterOn extends Event {
    public WaterOn(long eventTime) {
      super(eventTime);
    }
    public void action() {
      // Put hardware control code here
      water = true;
    }
    public String description() {
      return "Greenhouse water is on";
    }
  }
  private class WaterOff extends Event {
    public WaterOff(long eventTime) {
      super(eventTime);
    }
    public void action() {
      // Put hardware control code here
      water = false;
    }
    public String description() {
      return "Greenhouse water is off";
    }
```

```
  }
  private class ThermostatNight extends Event {
    public ThermostatNight(long eventTime) {
      super(eventTime);
    }
    public void action() {
      // Put hardware control code here
      thermostat = "Night";
    }
    public String description() {
      return "Thermostat on night setting";
    }
  }
  private class ThermostatDay extends Event {
    public ThermostatDay(long eventTime) {
      super(eventTime);
    }
    public void action() {
      // Put hardware control code here
      thermostat = "Day";
    }
    public String description() {
      return "Thermostat on day setting";
    }
  }
  // An example of an action() that inserts a
  // new one of itself into the event list:
  private int rings;
  private class Bell extends Event {
    public Bell(long eventTime) {
      super(eventTime);
    }
    public void action() {
      // Ring every 2 seconds, 'rings' times:
      System.out.println("Bing!");
      if(--rings > 0)
        addEvent(new Bell(
          System.currentTimeMillis() + 2000));
    }
    public String description() {
      return "Ring bell";
```

```
      }
    }
    private class Restart extends Event {
      public Restart(long eventTime) {
        super(eventTime);
      }
      public void action() {
        long tm = System.currentTimeMillis();
        // Instead of hard-wiring, you could parse
        // configuration information from a text
        // file here:
        rings = 5;
        addEvent(new ThermostatNight(tm));
        addEvent(new LightOn(tm + 1000));
        addEvent(new LightOff(tm + 2000));
        addEvent(new WaterOn(tm + 3000));
        addEvent(new WaterOff(tm + 8000));
        addEvent(new Bell(tm + 9000));
        addEvent(new ThermostatDay(tm + 10000));
        // Can even add a Restart object!
        addEvent(new Restart(tm + 20000));
      }
      public String description() {
        return "Restarting system";
      }
    }
    public static void main(String[] args) {
      GreenhouseControls gc =
        new GreenhouseControls();
      long tm = System.currentTimeMillis();
      gc.addEvent(gc.new Restart(tm));
      gc.run();
    }
} ///:~
```

Note that **light, water, thermostat,** and **rings** all belong to the outer
class **GreenhouseControls**, and yet the inner classes can access those
fields without qualification or special permission. Also, most of the
action( ) methods involve some sort of hardware control, which would
most likely involve calls to non-Java code.

Most of the **Event** classes look similar, but **Bell** and **Restart** are special. **Bell** rings, and if it hasn't yet rung enough times it adds a new **Bell** object to the event list, so it will ring again later. Notice how inner classes *almost* look like multiple inheritance: **Bell** has all the methods of **Event** and it also appears to have all the methods of the outer class **GreenhouseControls**.

Restart is responsible for initializing the system, so it adds all the appropriate events. Of course, a more flexible way to accomplish this is to avoid hard-coding the events and instead read them from a file. (An exercise in Chapter 11 asks you to modify this example to do just that.) Since **Restart( )** is just another **Event** object, you can also add a **Restart** object within **Restart.action( )** so that the system regularly restarts itself. And all you need to do in **main( )** is create a **GreenhouseControls** object and add a **Restart** object to get it going.

This example should move you a long way toward appreciating the value of inner classes, especially when used within a control framework. However, in Chapter 13 you'll see how elegantly inner classes are used to describe the actions of a graphical user interface. By the time you finish that chapter you should be fully convinced.

Summary

Interfaces and inner classes are more sophisticated concepts than what you'll find in many OOP languages. For example, there's nothing like them in C++. Together, they solve the same problem that C++ attempts to solve with its multiple inheritance (MI) feature. However, MI in C++ turns out to be rather difficult to use, while Java interfaces and inner classes are, by comparison, much more accessible.

Although the features themselves are reasonably straightforward, the use of these features is a design issue, much the same as polymorphism. Over time, you'll become better at recognizing situations where you should use an interface, or an inner class, or both. But at this point in this book you should at least be comfortable with the syntax and semantics. As you see these language features in use you'll eventually internalize them.

Exercises

Solutions to selected exercises can be found in the electronic document *The Thinking in Java Annotated Solution Guide*, available for a small fee from *www.BruceEckel.com*.

1. Prove that the fields in an **interface** are implicitly **static** and **final**.

2. Create an **interface** containing three methods, in its own **package**. Implement the interface in a different **package**.

3. Prove that all the methods in an **interface** are automatically **public**.

4. In **c07:Sandwich.java**, create an interface called **FastFood** (with appropriate methods) and change **Sandwich** so that it also implements **FastFood**.

5. Create three **interface**s, each with two methods. Inherit a new **interface** from the three, adding a new method. Create a class by implementing the new **interface** and also inheriting from a concrete class. Now write four methods, each of which takes one of the four **interface**s as an argument. In **main( )**, create an object of your class and pass it to each of the methods.

6. Modify Exercise 5 by creating an **abstract** class and inheriting that into the derived class.

7. Modify **Music5.java** by adding a **Playable interface**. Remove the **play( )** declaration from **Instrument**. Add **Playable** to the derived classes by including it in the **implements** list. Change **tune( )** so that it takes a **Playable** instead of an **Instrument**.

8. Change Exercise 6 in Chapter 7 so that **Rodent** is an **interface**.

9. In **Adventure.java**, add an **interface** called **CanClimb**, following the form of the other interfaces.

10. Write a program that imports and uses **Month2.java**.

11. Following the example given in **Month2.java**, create an enumeration of days of the week.

---

12.   Create an **interface** with at least one method, in its own package. Create a class in a separate package. Add a **protected** inner class that implements the **interface**. In a third package, inherit from your class and, inside a method, return an object of the **protected** inner class, upcasting to the **interface** during the return.

13.   Create an **interface** with at least one method, and implement that **interface** by defining an inner class within a method, which returns a reference to your **interface**.

14.   Repeat Exercise 13 but define the inner class within a scope within a method.

15.   Repeat Exercise 13 using an anonymous inner class.

16.   Create a **private** inner class that implements a **public interface**. Write a method that returns a reference to an instance of the **private** inner class, upcast to the **interface**. Show that the inner class is completely hidden by trying to downcast to it.

17.   Create a class with a nondefault constructor and no default constructor. Create a second class that has a method which returns a reference to the first class. Create the object to return by making an anonymous inner class that inherits from the first class.

18.   Create a class with a **private** field and a **private** method. Create an inner class with a method that modifies the outer class field and calls the outer class method. In a second outer class method, create an object of the inner class and call it's method, then show the effect on the outer class object.

19.   Repeat Exercise 18 using an anonymous inner class.

20.   Create a class containing a **static** inner class. In **main( )**, create an instance of the inner class.

21.   Create an **interface** containing a **static** inner class. Implement this **interface** and create an instance of the inner class.

22.   Create a class containing an inner class that itself contains an inner class. Repeat this using **static** inner classes. Note the names of the **.class** files produced by the compiler.

23.   Create a class with an inner class. In a separate class, make an instance of the inner class.

24.   Create a class with an inner class that has a nondefault constructor. Create a second class with an inner class that inherits from the first inner class.

25.   Repair the problem in **WindError.java**.

26.   Modify **Sequence.java** by adding a method **getRSelector( )** that produces a different implementation of the **Selector interface** that moves backward through the sequence from the end to the beginning.

27.   Create an **interface U** with three methods. Create a class **A** with a method that produces a reference to a **U** by building an anonymous inner class. Create a second class **B** that contains an array of **U**. **B** should have one method that accepts and stores a reference to a **U** in the array, a second method that sets a reference in the array (specified by the method argument) to **null** and a third method that moves through the array and calls the methods in **U**. In **main( )**, create a group of **A** objects and a single **B**. Fill the **B** with **U** references produced by the **A** objects. Use the **B** to call back into all the **A** objects. Remove some of the **U** references from the **B**.

28.   In **GreenhouseControls.java**, add **Event** inner classes that turn fans on and off.

29.   Show that an inner class has access to the **private** elements of its outer class. Determine whether the reverse is true.

9: Holding Your Objects

It's a fairly simple program that has only a fixed quantity of objects with known lifetimes.

In general, your programs will always be creating new objects based on some criteria that will be known only at the time the program is running. You won't know until run-time the quantity or even the exact type of the objects you need. To solve the general programming problem, you need to be able to create any number of objects, anytime, anywhere. So you can't rely on creating a named reference to hold each one of your objects:

```
MyObject myReference;
```

since you'll never know how many of these you'll actually need.

To solve this rather essential problem, Java has several ways to hold objects (or rather, references to objects). The built-in type is the array, which has been discussed before. Also, the Java utilities library has a reasonably complete set of *container classes* (also known as *collection classes*, but because the Java 2 libraries use the name **Collection** to refer to a particular subset of the library, I shall use the more inclusive term "container"). Containers provide sophisticated ways to hold and even manipulate your objects.

Arrays

Most of the necessary introduction to arrays is in the last section of Chapter 4, which showed how you define and initialize an array. Holding objects is the focus of this chapter, and an array is just one way to hold objects. But there are a number of other ways to hold objects, so what makes an array special?

There are two issues that distinguish arrays from other types of containers: efficiency and type. The array is the most efficient way that Java provides to store and randomly access a sequence of objects (actually, object references). The array is a simple linear sequence, which makes element access fast, but you pay for this speed: when you create an array object, its size is fixed and cannot be changed for the lifetime of that array object. You might suggest creating an array of a particular size and then, if you run out of space, creating a new one and moving all the references from the old one to the new one. This is the behavior of the **ArrayList** class, which will be studied later in this chapter. However, because of the overhead of this size flexibility, an **ArrayList** is measurably less efficient than an array.

The **vector** container class in C++ *does* know the type of objects it holds, but it has a different drawback when compared with arrays in Java: the C++ **vector**'s **operator[]** doesn't do bounds checking, so you can run past the end[1]. In Java, you get bounds checking regardless of whether you're using an array or a container—you'll get a **RuntimeException** if you exceed the bounds. As you'll learn in Chapter 10, this type of exception indicates a programmer error, and thus you don't need to check for it in your code. As an aside, the reason the C++ **vector** doesn't check bounds with every access is speed—in Java you have the constant performance overhead of bounds checking all the time for both arrays and containers.

The other generic container classes that will be studied in this chapter, **List**, **Set**, and **Map**, all deal with objects as if they had no specific type. That is, they treat them as type **Object**, the root class of all classes in Java. This works fine from one standpoint: you need to build only one container, and any Java object will go into that container. (Except for primitives—these can be placed in containers as constants using the Java primitive wrapper classes, or as changeable values by wrapping in your own class.) This is the second place where an array is superior to the generic containers: when you create an array, you create it to hold a specific type. This means that you get compile-time type checking to

_____

[1] It's possible, however, to ask how big the **vector** is, and the **at( )** method *does* perform bounds checking.

prevent you from putting the wrong type in, or mistaking the type that you're extracting. Of course, Java will prevent you from sending an inappropriate message to an object, either at compile-time or at run-time. So it's not much riskier one way or the other, it's just nicer if the compiler points it out to you, faster at run-time, and there's less likelihood that the end user will get surprised by an exception.

For efficiency and type checking it's always worth trying to use an array if you can. However, when you're trying to solve a more general problem arrays can be too restrictive. After looking at arrays, the rest of this chapter will be devoted to the container classes provided by Java.

Arrays are first-class objects

Regardless of what type of array you're working with, the array identifier is actually a reference to a true object that's created on the heap. This is the object that holds the references to the other objects, and it can be created either implicitly, as part of the array initialization syntax, or explicitly with a **new** expression. Part of the array object (in fact, the only field or method you can access) is the read-only **length** member that tells you how many elements can be stored in that array object. The '**[]**' syntax is the only other access that you have to the array object.

The following example shows the various ways that an array can be initialized, and how the array references can be assigned to different array objects. It also shows that arrays of objects and arrays of primitives are almost identical in their use. The only difference is that arrays of objects hold references, while arrays of primitives hold the primitive values directly.

```
//: c09:ArraySize.java
// Initialization & re-assignment of arrays.

class Weeble {} // A small mythical creature

public class ArraySize {
  public static void main(String[] args) {
    // Arrays of objects:
    Weeble[] a; // Null reference
    Weeble[] b = new Weeble[5]; // Null references
```

```java
Weeble[] c = new Weeble[4];
for(int i = 0; i < c.length; i++)
  c[i] = new Weeble();
// Aggregate initialization:
Weeble[] d = {
  new Weeble(), new Weeble(), new Weeble()
};
// Dynamic aggregate initialization:
a = new Weeble[] {
  new Weeble(), new Weeble()
};
System.out.println("a.length=" + a.length);
System.out.println("b.length = " + b.length);
// The references inside the array are
// automatically initialized to null:
for(int i = 0; i < b.length; i++)
  System.out.println("b[" + i + "]=" + b[i]);
System.out.println("c.length = " + c.length);
System.out.println("d.length = " + d.length);
a = d;
System.out.println("a.length = " + a.length);

// Arrays of primitives:
int[] e; // Null reference
int[] f = new int[5];
int[] g = new int[4];
for(int i = 0; i < g.length; i++)
  g[i] = i*i;
int[] h = { 11, 47, 93 };
// Compile error: variable e not initialized:
//!System.out.println("e.length=" + e.length);
System.out.println("f.length = " + f.length);
// The primitives inside the array are
// automatically initialized to zero:
for(int i = 0; i < f.length; i++)
  System.out.println("f[" + i + "]=" + f[i]);
System.out.println("g.length = " + g.length);
System.out.println("h.length = " + h.length);
e = h;
System.out.println("e.length = " + e.length);
e = new int[] { 1, 2 };
```

```
      System.out.println("e.length = " + e.length);
    }
} ///:~
```

Here's the output from the program:

```
b.length = 5
b[0]=null
b[1]=null
b[2]=null
b[3]=null
b[4]=null
c.length = 4
d.length = 3
a.length = 3
a.length = 2
f.length = 5
f[0]=0
f[1]=0
f[2]=0
f[3]=0
f[4]=0
g.length = 4
h.length = 3
e.length = 3
e.length = 2
```

The array **a** is initially just a **null** reference, and the compiler prevents you from doing anything with this reference until you've properly initialized it. The array **b** is initialized to point to an array of **Weeble** references, but no actual **Weeble** objects are ever placed in that array. However, you can still ask what the size of the array is, since **b** is pointing to a legitimate object. This brings up a slight drawback: you can't find out how many elements are actually *in* the array, since **length** tells you only how many elements *can* be placed in the array; that is, the size of the array object, not the number of elements it actually holds. However, when an array object is created its references are automatically initialized to **null**, so you can see whether a particular array slot has an object in it by checking to see whether it's **null**. Similarly, an array of primitives is automatically initialized to zero for numeric types, **(char)0** for **char**, and **false** for **boolean**.

Array **c** shows the creation of the array object followed by the assignment of **Weeble** objects to all the slots in the array. Array **d** shows the "aggregate initialization" syntax that causes the array object to be created (implicitly with **new** on the heap, just like for array **c**) *and* initialized with **Weeble** objects, all in one statement.

The next array initialization could be thought of as a "dynamic aggregate initialization." The aggregate initialization used by **d** must be used at the point of **d**'s definition, but with the second syntax you can create and initialize an array object anywhere. For example, suppose **hide( )** is a method that takes an array of **Weeble** objects. You could call it by saying:

```
hide(d);
```

but you can also dynamically create the array you want to pass as the argument:

```
hide(new Weeble[] { new Weeble(), new Weeble() });
```

In some situations this new syntax provides a more convenient way to write code.

The expression

```
a = d;
```

shows how you can take a reference that's attached to one array object and assign it to another array object, just as you can do with any other type of object reference. Now both **a** and **d** are pointing to the same array object on the heap.

The second part of **ArraySize.java** shows that primitive arrays work just like object arrays *except* that primitive arrays hold the primitive values directly.

Containers of primitives

Container classes can hold only references to objects. An array, however, can be created to hold primitives directly, as well as references to objects. It *is* possible to use the "wrapper" classes such as **Integer**, **Double,** etc. to place primitive values inside a container, but the wrapper classes for primitives can be awkward to use. In addition, it's much more efficient to

---

create and access an array of primitives than a container of wrapped primitives.

Of course, if you're using a primitive type and you need the flexibility of a container that automatically expands when more space is needed, the array won't work and you're forced to use a container of wrapped primitives. You might think that there should be a specialized type of **ArrayList** for each of the primitive data types, but Java doesn't provide this for you. Some sort of templatizing mechanism might someday provide a better way for Java to handle this problem.[2]

Returning an array

Suppose you're writing a method and you don't just want to return just one thing, but a whole bunch of things. Languages like C and C++ make this difficult because you can't just return an array, only a pointer to an array. This introduces problems because it becomes messy to control the lifetime of the array, which easily leads to memory leaks.

Java takes a similar approach, but you just "return an array." Actually, of course, you're returning a reference to an array, but with Java you never worry about responsibility for that array—it will be around as long as you need it, and the garbage collector will clean it up when you're done.

As an example, consider returning an array of **String**:

```
//: c09:IceCream.java
// Returning arrays from methods.

public class IceCream {
  static String[] flav = {
    "Chocolate", "Strawberry",
    "Vanilla Fudge Swirl", "Mint Chip",
    "Mocha Almond Fudge", "Rum Raisin",
    "Praline Cream", "Mud Pie"
  };
  static String[] flavorSet(int n) {
```

---

[2] This is one of the places where C++ is distinctly superior to Java, since C++ supports *parameterized types* with the **template** keyword.

```
   // Force it to be positive & within bounds:
   n = Math.abs(n) % (flav.length + 1);
   String[] results = new String[n];
   boolean[] picked =
     new boolean[flav.length];
   for (int i = 0; i < n; i++) {
     int t;
     do
       t = (int)(Math.random() * flav.length);
     while (picked[t]);
     results[i] = flav[t];
     picked[t] = true;
   }
   return results;
  }
  public static void main(String[] args) {
    for(int i = 0; i < 20; i++) {
      System.out.println(
        "flavorSet(" + i + ") = ");
      String[] fl = flavorSet(flav.length);
      for(int j = 0; j < fl.length; j++)
        System.out.println("\t" + fl[j]);
    }
  }
} ///:~
```

The method **flavorSet( )** creates an array of **String** called **results**. The size of this array is **n**, determined by the argument you pass into the method. Then it proceeds to choose flavors randomly from the array **flav** and place them into **results**, which it finally returns. Returning an array is just like returning any other object—it's a reference. It's not important that the array was created within **flavorSet( )**, or that the array was created anyplace else, for that matter. The garbage collector takes care of cleaning up the array when you're done with it, and the array will persist for as long as you need it.

As an aside, notice that when **flavorSet( )** chooses flavors randomly, it ensures that a random choice hasn't been picked before. This is performed in a **do** loop that keeps making random choices until it finds one that's not already in the **picked** array. (Of course, a **String** comparison could also have been performed to see if the random choice

was already in the **results** array, but **String** comparisons are inefficient.)
If it's successful, it adds the entry and finds the next one (**i** gets
incremented).

main( ) prints out 20 full sets of flavors, so you can see that **flavorSet( )**
chooses the flavors in a random order each time. It's easiest to see this if
you redirect the output into a file. And while you're looking at the file,
remember, you just *want* the ice cream, you don't *need* it.

The **Arrays** class

In **java.util**, you'll find the **Arrays** class, which holds a set of **static**
methods that perform utility functions for arrays. There are four basic
functions: **equals( )**, to compare two arrays for equality; **fill( )**, to fill an
array with a value; **sort( )**, to sort the array; and **binarySearch( )**, to
find an element in a sorted array. All of these methods are overloaded for
all the primitive types and **Object**s. In addition, there's a single **asList( )**
method that takes any array and turns it into a **List** container—which
you'll learn about later in this chapter.

While useful, the **Arrays** class stops short of being fully functional. For
example, it would be nice to be able to easily print the elements of an
array without having to code a **for** loop by hand every time. And as you'll
see, the **fill( )** method only takes a single value and places it in the array,
so if you wanted—for example—to fill an array with randomly generated
numbers, **fill( )** is no help.

Thus it makes sense to supplement the **Arrays** class with some additional
utilities, which will be placed in the **package com.bruceeckel.util** for
convenience. These will print an array of any type, and fill an array with
values or objects that are created by an object called a *generator* that you
can define.

Because code needs to be created for each primitive type as well as
Object, there's a lot of nearly duplicated code[3]. For example, a

---

[3] The C++ programmer will note how much the code could be collapsed with the use of
default arguments and templates. The Python programmer will note that this entire library
would be largely unnecessary in that language.

"generator" interface is required for each type because the return type of **next( )** must be different in each case:

```
//: com:bruceeckel:util:Generator.java
package com.bruceeckel.util;
public interface Generator {
  Object next();
} ///:~
```

```
//: com:bruceeckel:util:BooleanGenerator.java
package com.bruceeckel.util;
public interface BooleanGenerator {
  boolean next();
} ///:~
```

```
//: com:bruceeckel:util:ByteGenerator.java
package com.bruceeckel.util;
public interface ByteGenerator {
  byte next();
} ///:~
```

```
//: com:bruceeckel:util:CharGenerator.java
package com.bruceeckel.util;
public interface CharGenerator {
  char next();
} ///:~
```

```
//: com:bruceeckel:util:ShortGenerator.java
package com.bruceeckel.util;
public interface ShortGenerator {
  short next();
} ///:~
```

```
//: com:bruceeckel:util:IntGenerator.java
package com.bruceeckel.util;
public interface IntGenerator {
  int next();
} ///:~
```

```
//: com:bruceeckel:util:LongGenerator.java
package com.bruceeckel.util;
```

```
public interface LongGenerator {
  long next();
} ///:~

//: com:bruceeckel:util:FloatGenerator.java
package com.bruceeckel.util;
public interface FloatGenerator {
  float next();
} ///:~

//: com:bruceeckel:util:DoubleGenerator.java
package com.bruceeckel.util;
public interface DoubleGenerator {
  double next();
} ///:~
```

Arrays2 contains a variety of **print( )** functions, overloaded for each type. You can simply print an array, you can add a message before the array is printed, or you can print a range of elements within an array. The **print( )** code is self-explanatory:

```
//: com:bruceeckel:util:Arrays2.java
// A supplement to java.util.Arrays, to provide
// additional useful functionality when working
// with arrays. Allows any array to be printed,
// and to be filled via a user-defined
// "generator" object.
package com.bruceeckel.util;
import java.util.*;

public class Arrays2 {
  private static void
  start(int from, int to, int length) {
    if(from != 0 || to != length)
      System.out.print("["+ from +":"+ to +"] ");
    System.out.print("(");
  }
  private static void end() {
    System.out.println(")");
  }
  public static void print(Object[] a) {
```

```java
    print(a, 0, a.length);
  }
  public static void
  print(String msg, Object[] a) {
    System.out.print(msg + " ");
    print(a, 0, a.length);
  }
  public static void
  print(Object[] a, int from, int to){
    start(from, to, a.length);
    for(int i = from; i < to; i++) {
      System.out.print(a[i]);
      if(i < to -1)
        System.out.print(", ");
    }
    end();
  }
  public static void print(boolean[] a) {
      print(a, 0, a.length);
  }
  public static void
  print(String msg, boolean[] a) {
    System.out.print(msg + " ");
    print(a, 0, a.length);
  }
  public static void
  print(boolean[] a, int from, int to) {
    start(from, to, a.length);
    for(int i = from; i < to; i++) {
      System.out.print(a[i]);
      if(i < to -1)
        System.out.print(", ");
    }
    end();
  }
  public static void print(byte[] a) {
      print(a, 0, a.length);
  }
  public static void
  print(String msg, byte[] a) {
    System.out.print(msg + " ");
```

```
      print(a, 0, a.length);
  }
  public static void
  print(byte[] a, int from, int to) {
    start(from, to, a.length);
    for(int i = from; i < to; i++) {
      System.out.print(a[i]);
      if(i < to -1)
        System.out.print(", ");
    }
    end();
  }
  public static void print(char[] a) {
      print(a, 0, a.length);
  }
  public static void
  print(String msg, char[] a) {
    System.out.print(msg + " ");
    print(a, 0, a.length);
  }
  public static void
  print(char[] a, int from, int to) {
    start(from, to, a.length);
    for(int i = from; i < to; i++) {
      System.out.print(a[i]);
      if(i < to -1)
        System.out.print(", ");
    }
    end();
  }
  public static void print(short[] a) {
      print(a, 0, a.length);
  }
  public static void
  print(String msg, short[] a) {
    System.out.print(msg + " ");
    print(a, 0, a.length);
  }
  public static void
  print(short[] a, int from, int to) {
    start(from, to, a.length);
```

```java
    for(int i = from; i < to; i++) {
      System.out.print(a[i]);
      if(i < to - 1)
        System.out.print(", ");
    }
    end();
  }
  public static void print(int[] a) {
      print(a, 0, a.length);
  }
  public static void
  print(String msg, int[] a) {
    System.out.print(msg + " ");
    print(a, 0, a.length);
  }
  public static void
  print(int[] a, int from, int to) {
    start(from, to, a.length);
    for(int i = from; i < to; i++) {
      System.out.print(a[i]);
      if(i < to - 1)
        System.out.print(", ");
    }
    end();
  }
  public static void print(long[] a) {
    print(a, 0, a.length);
  }
  public static void
  print(String msg, long[] a) {
    System.out.print(msg + " ");
    print(a, 0, a.length);
  }
  public static void
  print(long[] a, int from, int to) {
    start(from, to, a.length);
    for(int i = from; i < to; i++) {
      System.out.print(a[i]);
      if(i < to - 1)
        System.out.print(", ");
    }
```

```
      end();
    }
    public static void print(float[] a) {
        print(a, 0, a.length);
    }
    public static void
    print(String msg, float[] a) {
      System.out.print(msg + " ");
      print(a, 0, a.length);
    }
    public static void
    print(float[] a, int from, int to) {
      start(from, to, a.length);
      for(int i = from; i < to; i++) {
        System.out.print(a[i]);
        if(i < to - 1)
          System.out.print(", ");
      }
      end();
    }
    public static void print(double[] a) {
        print(a, 0, a.length);
    }
    public static void
    print(String msg, double[] a) {
      System.out.print(msg + " ");
      print(a, 0, a.length);
    }
    public static void
    print(double[] a, int from, int to){
      start(from, to, a.length);
      for(int i = from; i < to; i++) {
        System.out.print(a[i]);
        if(i < to - 1)
          System.out.print(", ");
      }
      end();
    }
    // Fill an array using a generator:
    public static void
    fill(Object[] a, Generator gen) {
```

```java
    fill(a, 0, a.length, gen);
  }
  public static void
  fill(Object[] a, int from, int to,
      Generator gen){
    for(int i = from; i < to; i++)
      a[i] = gen.next();
  }
  public static void
  fill(boolean[] a, BooleanGenerator gen) {
      fill(a, 0, a.length, gen);
  }
  public static void
  fill(boolean[] a, int from, int to,
      BooleanGenerator gen) {
    for(int i = from; i < to; i++)
      a[i] = gen.next();
  }
  public static void
  fill(byte[] a, ByteGenerator gen) {
      fill(a, 0, a.length, gen);
  }
  public static void
  fill(byte[] a, int from, int to,
      ByteGenerator gen) {
    for(int i = from; i < to; i++)
      a[i] = gen.next();
  }
  public static void
  fill(char[] a, CharGenerator gen) {
      fill(a, 0, a.length, gen);
  }
  public static void
  fill(char[] a, int from, int to,
      CharGenerator gen) {
    for(int i = from; i < to; i++)
      a[i] = gen.next();
  }
  public static void
  fill(short[] a, ShortGenerator gen) {
      fill(a, 0, a.length, gen);
```

```
  }
  public static void
  fill(short[] a, int from, int to,
        ShortGenerator gen) {
    for(int i = from; i < to; i++)
      a[i] = gen.next();
  }
  public static void
  fill(int[] a, IntGenerator gen) {
      fill(a, 0, a.length, gen);
  }
  public static void
  fill(int[] a, int from, int to,
        IntGenerator gen) {
    for(int i = from; i < to; i++)
      a[i] = gen.next();
  }
  public static void
  fill(long[] a, LongGenerator gen) {
      fill(a, 0, a.length, gen);
  }
  public static void
  fill(long[] a, int from, int to,
        LongGenerator gen) {
    for(int i = from; i < to; i++)
      a[i] = gen.next();
  }
  public static void
  fill(float[] a, FloatGenerator gen) {
      fill(a, 0, a.length, gen);
  }
  public static void
  fill(float[] a, int from, int to,
        FloatGenerator gen) {
    for(int i = from; i < to; i++)
      a[i] = gen.next();
  }
  public static void
  fill(double[] a, DoubleGenerator gen) {
      fill(a, 0, a.length, gen);
  }
```

```java
public static void
fill(double[] a, int from, int to,
     DoubleGenerator gen){
  for(int i = from; i < to; i++)
    a[i] = gen.next();
}
private static Random r = new Random();
public static class RandBooleanGenerator
implements BooleanGenerator {
  public boolean next() {
    return r.nextBoolean();
  }
}
public static class RandByteGenerator
implements ByteGenerator {
  public byte next() {
    return (byte)r.nextInt();
  }
}
static String ssource =
  "ABCDEFGHIJKLMNOPQRSTUVWXYZ" +
  "abcdefghijklmnopqrstuvwxyz";
static char[] src = ssource.toCharArray();
public static class RandCharGenerator
implements CharGenerator {
  public char next() {
    int pos = Math.abs(r.nextInt());
    return src[pos % src.length];
  }
}
public static class RandStringGenerator
implements Generator {
  private int len;
  private RandCharGenerator cg =
    new RandCharGenerator();
  public RandStringGenerator(int length) {
    len = length;
  }
  public Object next() {
    char[] buf = new char[len];
    for(int i = 0; i < len; i++)
```

```
      buf[i] = cg.next();
      return new String(buf);
    }
  }
  public static class RandShortGenerator
  implements ShortGenerator {
    public short next() {
      return (short)r.nextInt();
    }
  }
  public static class RandIntGenerator
  implements IntGenerator {
    private int mod = 10000;
    public RandIntGenerator() {}
    public RandIntGenerator(int modulo) {
      mod = modulo;
    }
    public int next() {
      return r.nextInt() % mod;
    }
  }
  public static class RandLongGenerator
  implements LongGenerator {
    public long next() { return r.nextLong(); }
  }
  public static class RandFloatGenerator
  implements FloatGenerator {
    public float next() { return r.nextFloat(); }
  }
  public static class RandDoubleGenerator
  implements DoubleGenerator {
    public double next() {return r.nextDouble();}
  }
} ///:~
```

To fill an array of elements using a generator, the **fill( )** method takes a
reference to an appropriate generator **interface**, which has a **next( )**
method that will somehow produce an object of the right type (depending
on how the interface is implemented). The **fill( )** method simply calls
next( ) until the desired range has been filled. Now you can create any

---

generator by implementing the appropriate **interface**, and use your
generator with **fill( )**.

Random data generators are useful for testing, so a set of inner classes is
created to implement all the primitive generator interfaces, as well as a
String generator to represent **Object**. You can see that
RandStringGenerator uses **RandCharGenerator** to fill an array of
characters, which is then turned into a **String**. The size of the array is
determined by the constructor argument.

To generate numbers that aren't too large, **RandIntGenerator** defaults
to a modulus of 10,000, but the overloaded constructor allows you to
choose a smaller value.

Here's a program to test the library, and to demonstrate how it is used:

```
//: c09:TestArrays2.java
// Test and demonstrate Arrays2 utilities
import com.bruceeckel.util.*;

public class TestArrays2 {
  public static void main(String[] args) {
    int size = 6;
    // Or get the size from the command line:
    if(args.length != 0)
      size = Integer.parseInt(args[0]);
    boolean[] a1 = new boolean[size];
    byte[] a2 = new byte[size];
    char[] a3 = new char[size];
    short[] a4 = new short[size];
    int[] a5 = new int[size];
    long[] a6 = new long[size];
    float[] a7 = new float[size];
    double[] a8 = new double[size];
    String[] a9 = new String[size];
    Arrays2.fill(a1,
      new Arrays2.RandBooleanGenerator());
    Arrays2.print(a1);
    Arrays2.print("a1 = ", a1);
    Arrays2.print(a1, size/3, size/3 + size/3);
    Arrays2.fill(a2,
```

```
          new Arrays2.RandByteGenerator());
      Arrays2.print(a2);
      Arrays2.print("a2 = ", a2);
      Arrays2.print(a2, size/3, size/3 + size/3);
      Arrays2.fill(a3,
          new Arrays2.RandCharGenerator());
      Arrays2.print(a3);
      Arrays2.print("a3 = ", a3);
      Arrays2.print(a3, size/3, size/3 + size/3);
      Arrays2.fill(a4,
          new Arrays2.RandShortGenerator());
      Arrays2.print(a4);
      Arrays2.print("a4 = ", a4);
      Arrays2.print(a4, size/3, size/3 + size/3);
      Arrays2.fill(a5,
          new Arrays2.RandIntGenerator());
      Arrays2.print(a5);
      Arrays2.print("a5 = ", a5);
      Arrays2.print(a5, size/3, size/3 + size/3);
      Arrays2.fill(a6,
          new Arrays2.RandLongGenerator());
      Arrays2.print(a6);
      Arrays2.print("a6 = ", a6);
      Arrays2.print(a6, size/3, size/3 + size/3);
      Arrays2.fill(a7,
          new Arrays2.RandFloatGenerator());
      Arrays2.print(a7);
      Arrays2.print("a7 = ", a7);
      Arrays2.print(a7, size/3, size/3 + size/3);
      Arrays2.fill(a8,
          new Arrays2.RandDoubleGenerator());
      Arrays2.print(a8);
      Arrays2.print("a8 = ", a8);
      Arrays2.print(a8, size/3, size/3 + size/3);
      Arrays2.fill(a9,
          new Arrays2.RandStringGenerator(7));
      Arrays2.print(a9);
      Arrays2.print("a9 = ", a9);
      Arrays2.print(a9, size/3, size/3 + size/3);
  }
} ///:~
```

The **size** parameter has a default value, but you can also set it from the command line.

Filling an array

The Java standard library **Arrays** also has a **fill( )** method, but that is rather trivial—it only duplicates a single value into each location, or in the case of objects, copies the same reference into each location. Using **Arrays2.print( )**, the **Arrays.fill( )** methods can be easily demonstrated:

```
//: c09:FillingArrays.java
// Using Arrays.fill()
import com.bruceeckel.util.*;
import java.util.*;

public class FillingArrays {
  public static void main(String[] args) {
    int size = 6;
    // Or get the size from the command line:
    if(args.length != 0)
      size = Integer.parseInt(args[0]);
    boolean[] a1 = new boolean[size];
    byte[] a2 = new byte[size];
    char[] a3 = new char[size];
    short[] a4 = new short[size];
    int[] a5 = new int[size];
    long[] a6 = new long[size];
    float[] a7 = new float[size];
    double[] a8 = new double[size];
    String[] a9 = new String[size];
    Arrays.fill(a1, true);
    Arrays2.print("a1 = ", a1);
    Arrays.fill(a2, (byte)11);
    Arrays2.print("a2 = ", a2);
    Arrays.fill(a3, 'x');
    Arrays2.print("a3 = ", a3);
    Arrays.fill(a4, (short)17);
    Arrays2.print("a4 = ", a4);
    Arrays.fill(a5, 19);
    Arrays2.print("a5 = ", a5);
```

```
      Arrays.fill(a6, 23);
      Arrays2.print("a6 = ", a6);
      Arrays.fill(a7, 29);
      Arrays2.print("a7 = ", a7);
      Arrays.fill(a8, 47);
      Arrays2.print("a8 = ", a8);
      Arrays.fill(a9, "Hello");
      Arrays2.print("a9 = ", a9);
      // Manipulating ranges:
      Arrays.fill(a9, 3, 5, "World");
      Arrays2.print("a9 = ", a9);
    }
} ///:~
```

You can either fill the entire array, or—as the last two statements show—a range of elements. But since you can only provide a single value to use for filling using **Arrays.fill( )**, the **Arrays2.fill( )** methods produce much more interesting results.

Copying an array

The Java standard library provides a **static** method, **System.arraycopy( )**, which can make much faster copies of an array than if you use a **for** loop to perform the copy by hand. **System.arraycopy( )** is overloaded to handle all types. Here's an example that manipulates arrays of **int**:

```
//: c09:CopyingArrays.java
// Using System.arraycopy()
import com.bruceeckel.util.*;
import java.util.*;

public class CopyingArrays {
  public static void main(String[] args) {
    int[] i = new int[25];
    int[] j = new int[25];
    Arrays.fill(i, 47);
    Arrays.fill(j, 99);
    Arrays2.print("i = ", i);
    Arrays2.print("j = ", j);
    System.arraycopy(i, 0, j, 0, i.length);
```

```
    Arrays2.print("j = ", j);
    int[] k = new int[10];
    Arrays.fill(k, 103);
    System.arraycopy(i, 0, k, 0, k.length);
    Arrays2.print("k = ", k);
    Arrays.fill(k, 103);
    System.arraycopy(k, 0, i, 0, k.length);
    Arrays2.print("i = ", i);
    // Objects:
    Integer[] u = new Integer[10];
    Integer[] v = new Integer[5];
    Arrays.fill(u, new Integer(47));
    Arrays.fill(v, new Integer(99));
    Arrays2.print("u = ", u);
    Arrays2.print("v = ", v);
    System.arraycopy(v, 0,
      u, u.length/2, v.length);
    Arrays2.print("u = ", u);
  }
} ///:~
```

The arguments to **arraycopy( )** are the source array, the offset into the
source array from whence to start copying, the destination array, the
offset into the destination array where the copying begins, and the
number of elements to copy. Naturally, any violation of the array
boundaries will cause an exception.

The example shows that both primitive arrays and object arrays can be
copied. However, if you copy arrays of objects then only the references get
copied—there's no duplication of the objects themselves. This is called a
shallow copy (see Appendix A).

Comparing arrays

Arrays provides the overloaded method **equals( )** to compare entire
arrays for equality. Again, these are overloaded for all the primitives, and
for **Object**. To be equal, the arrays must have the same number of
elements and each element must be equivalent to each corresponding
element in the other array, using the **equals( )** for each element. (For
primitives, that primitive's wrapper class **equals( )** is used; for example,
Integer.equals( ) for **int**.) Here's an example:

```
//: c09:ComparingArrays.java
// Using Arrays.equals()
import java.util.*;

public class ComparingArrays {
  public static void main(String[] args) {
    int[] a1 = new int[10];
    int[] a2 = new int[10];
    Arrays.fill(a1, 47);
    Arrays.fill(a2, 47);
    System.out.println(Arrays.equals(a1, a2));
    a2[3] = 11;
    System.out.println(Arrays.equals(a1, a2));
    String[] s1 = new String[5];
    Arrays.fill(s1, "Hi");
    String[] s2 = {"Hi", "Hi", "Hi", "Hi", "Hi"};
    System.out.println(Arrays.equals(s1, s2));
  }
} ///:~
```

Originally, **a1** and **a2** are exactly equal, so the output is "true," but then one of the elements is changed so the second line of output is "false." In the last case, all the elements of **s1** point to the same object, but **s2** has five unique objects. However, array equality is based on contents (via **Object.equals( )**) and so the result is "true."

Array element comparisons

One of the missing features in the Java 1.0 and 1.1 libraries is algorithmic operations—even simple sorting. This was a rather confusing situation to someone expecting an adequate standard library. Fortunately, Java 2 remedies the situation, at least for the sorting problem.

A problem with writing generic sorting code is that sorting must perform comparisons based on the actual type of the object. Of course, one approach is to write a different sorting method for every different type, but you should be able to recognize that this does not produce code that is easily reused for new types.

A primary goal of programming design is to "separate things that change from things that stay the same," and here, the code that stays the same is

---

the general sort algorithm, but the thing that changes from one use to the next is the way objects are compared. So instead of hard-wiring the comparison code into many different sort routines, the technique of the *callback* is used. With a callback, the part of the code that varies from case to case is encapsulated inside its own class, and the part of the code that's always the same will call back to the code that changes. That way you can make different objects to express different ways of comparison and feed them to the same sorting code.

In Java 2, there are two ways to provide comparison functionality. The first is with the *natural comparison method* that is imparted to a class by implementing the **java.lang.Comparable** interface. This is a very simple interface with a single method, **compareTo( )**. This method takes another **Object** as an argument, and produces a negative value if the argument is less than the current object, zero if the argument is equal, and a positive value if the argument is greater than the current object.

Here's a class that implements **Comparable** and demonstrates the comparability by using the Java standard library method **Arrays.sort( )**:

```
//: c09:CompType.java
// Implementing Comparable in a class.
import com.bruceeckel.util.*;
import java.util.*;

public class CompType implements Comparable {
  int i;
  int j;
  public CompType(int n1, int n2) {
    i = n1;
    j = n2;
  }
  public String toString() {
    return "[i = " + i + ", j = " + j + "]";
  }
  public int compareTo(Object rv) {
    int rvi = ((CompType)rv).i;
    return (i < rvi ? -1 : (i == rvi ? 0 : 1));
  }
  private static Random r = new Random();
  private static int randInt() {
```

```
      return Math.abs(r.nextInt()) % 100;
    }
  public static Generator generator() {
    return new Generator() {
      public Object next() {
        return new CompType(randInt(),randInt());
      }
    };
  }
  public static void main(String[] args) {
    CompType[] a = new CompType[10];
    Arrays2.fill(a, generator());
    Arrays2.print("before sorting, a = ", a);
    Arrays.sort(a);
    Arrays2.print("after sorting, a = ", a);
  }
} ///:~
```

When you define the comparison function, you are responsible for deciding what it means to compare one of your objects to another. Here, only the **i** values are used in the comparison, and the **j** values are ignored.

The **static randInt( )** method produces positive values between zero and 100, and the **generator( )** method produces an object that implements the **Generator** interface, by creating an anonymous inner class (see Chapter 8). This builds **CompType** objects by initializing them with random values. In **main( )**, the generator is used to fill an array of **CompType**, which is then sorted. If **Comparable** hadn't been implemented, then you'd get a compile-time error message when you tried to call **sort( )**.

Now suppose someone hands you a class that doesn't implement **Comparable**, or they hand you this class that *does* implement **Comparable**, but you decide you don't like the way it works and would rather have a different comparison function for the type. To do this, you use the second approach for comparing objects, by creating a separate class that implements an interface called **Comparator**. This has two methods, **compare( )** and **equals( )**. However, you don't have to implement **equals( )** except for special performance needs, because anytime you create a class it is implicitly inherited from **Object**, which has an **equals( )**. So you can just use the default **Object equals( )** and satisfy the contract imposed by the interface.

The **Collections** class (which we'll look at more later) contains a single **Comparator** that reverses the natural sorting order. This can easily be applied to the **CompType**:

```
//: c09:Reverse.java
// The Collecions.reverseOrder() Comparator.
import com.bruceeckel.util.*;
import java.util.*;

public class Reverse {
  public static void main(String[] args) {
    CompType[] a = new CompType[10];
    Arrays2.fill(a, CompType.generator());
    Arrays2.print("before sorting, a = ", a);
    Arrays.sort(a, Collections.reverseOrder());
    Arrays2.print("after sorting, a = ", a);
  }
} ///:~
```

The call to **Collections.reverseOrder( )** produces the reference to the **Comparator**.

As a second example, the following **Comparator** compares **CompType** objects based on their **j** values rather than their **i** values:

```
//: c09:ComparatorTest.java
// Implementing a Comparator for a class.
import com.bruceeckel.util.*;
import java.util.*;

class CompTypeComparator implements Comparator {
  public int compare(Object o1, Object o2) {
    int j1 = ((CompType)o1).j;
    int j2 = ((CompType)o2).j;
    return (j1 < j2 ? -1 : (j1 == j2 ? 0 : 1));
  }
}

public class ComparatorTest {
```

```
  public static void main(String[] args) {
    CompType[] a = new CompType[10];
    Arrays2.fill(a, CompType.generator());
    Arrays2.print("before sorting, a = ", a);
    Arrays.sort(a, new CompTypeComparator());
    Arrays2.print("after sorting, a = ", a);
  }
} ///:~
```

The **compare( )** method must return a negative integer, zero, or a
positive integer if the first argument is less than, equal to, or greater than
the second, respectively.

Sorting an array

With the built-in sorting methods, you can sort any array of primitives,
and any array of objects that either implements **Comparable** or has an
associated **Comparator**. This fills a big hole in the Java libraries—
believe it or not, there was no support in Java 1.0 or 1.1 for sorting
Strings! Here's an example that generates random **String** objects and
sorts them:

```
//: c09:StringSorting.java
// Sorting an array of Strings.
import com.bruceeckel.util.*;
import java.util.*;

public class StringSorting {
  public static void main(String[] args) {
    String[] sa = new String[30];
    Arrays2.fill(sa,
      new Arrays2.RandStringGenerator(5));
    Arrays2.print("Before sorting: ", sa);
    Arrays.sort(sa);
    Arrays2.print("After sorting: ", sa);
  }
} ///:~
```

One thing you'll notice about the output in the **String** sorting algorithm is
that it's *lexicographic*, so it puts all the words starting with uppercase
letters first, followed by all the words starting with lowercase letters.

(Telephone books are typically sorted this way.) You may also want to group the words together regardless of case, and you can do this by defining a **Comparator** class, thereby overriding the default **String Comparable** behavior. For reuse, this will be added to the "util" package:

```
//: com:bruceeckel:util:AlphabeticComparator.java
// Keeping upper and lowercase letters together.
package com.bruceeckel.util;
import java.util.*;

public class AlphabeticComparator
implements Comparator{
  public int compare(Object o1, Object o2) {
    String s1 = (String)o1;
    String s2 = (String)o2;
    return s1.toLowerCase().compareTo(
      s2.toLowerCase());
  }
} ///:~
```

Each **String** is converted to lowercase before the comparison. **String**'s built-in **compareTo( )** method provides the desired functionality.

Here's a test using **AlphabeticComparator**:

```
//: c09:AlphabeticSorting.java
// Keeping upper and lowercase letters together.
import com.bruceeckel.util.*;
import java.util.*;

public class AlphabeticSorting {
  public static void main(String[] args) {
    String[] sa = new String[30];
    Arrays2.fill(sa,
      new Arrays2.RandStringGenerator(5));
    Arrays2.print("Before sorting: ", sa);
    Arrays.sort(sa, new AlphabeticComparator());
    Arrays2.print("After sorting: ", sa);
  }
} ///:~
```

The sorting algorithm that's used in the Java standard library is designed to be optimal for the particular type you're sorting—a Quicksort for primitives, and a stable merge sort for objects. So you shouldn't need to spend any time worrying about performance unless your profiling tool points you to the sorting process as a bottleneck.

Searching a sorted array

Once an array is sorted, you can perform a fast search for a particular item using **Arrays.binarySearch( )**. However, it's very important that you do not try to use **binarySearch( )** on an unsorted array; the results will be unpredictable. The following example uses a **RandIntGenerator** to fill an array, then to produces values to search for:

```
//: c09:ArraySearching.java
// Using Arrays.binarySearch().
import com.bruceeckel.util.*;
import java.util.*;

public class ArraySearching {
  public static void main(String[] args) {
    int[] a = new int[100];
    Arrays2.RandIntGenerator gen =
      new Arrays2.RandIntGenerator(1000);
    Arrays2.fill(a, gen);
    Arrays.sort(a);
    Arrays2.print("Sorted array: ", a);
    while(true) {
      int r = gen.next();
      int location = Arrays.binarySearch(a, r);
      if(location >= 0) {
        System.out.println("Location of " + r +
          " is " + location + ", a[" +
          location + "] = " + a[location]);
        break; // Out of while loop
      }
    }
  }
} ///:~
```

In the **while** loop, random values are generated as search items, until one of them is found.

Arrays.binarySearch( ) produces a value greater than or equal to zero if the search item is found. Otherwise, it produces a negative value representing the place that the element should be inserted if you are maintaining the sorted array by hand. The value produced is

```
-(insertion point) - 1
```

The insertion point is the index of the first element greater than the key, or **a.size( )**, if all elements in the array are less than the specified key.

If the array contains duplicate elements, there is no guarantee which one will be found. The algorithm is thus not really designed to support duplicate elements, as much as tolerate them. If you need a sorted list of nonduplicated elements, however, use a **TreeSet**, which will be introduced later in this chapter. This takes care of all the details for you automatically. Only in cases of performance bottlenecks should you replace the **TreeSet** with a hand-maintained array.

If you have sorted an object array using a **Comparator** (primitive arrays do not allow sorting with a **Comparator**), you must include that same **Comparator** when you perform a **binarySearch( )** (using the overloaded version of the function that's provided). For example, the **AlphabeticSorting.java** program can be modified to perform a search:

```
//: c09:AlphabeticSearch.java
// Searching with a Comparator.
import com.bruceeckel.util.*;
import java.util.*;

public class AlphabeticSearch {
  public static void main(String[] args) {
    String[] sa = new String[30];
    Arrays2.fill(sa,
      new Arrays2.RandStringGenerator(5));
    AlphabeticComparator comp =
      new AlphabeticComparator();
    Arrays.sort(sa, comp);
    int index =
```

```
            Arrays.binarySearch(sa, sa[10], comp);
        System.out.println("Index = " + index);
    }
} ///:~
```

The **Comparator** must be passed to the overloaded **binarySearch( )** as the third argument. In the above example, success is guaranteed because the search item is plucked out of the array itself.

Array summary

To summarize what you've seen so far, your first and most efficient choice to hold a group of objects should be an array, and you're forced into this choice if you want to hold a group of primitives. In the remainder of this chapter we'll look at the more general case, when you don't know at the time you're writing the program how many objects you're going to need, or if you need a more sophisticated way to store your objects. Java provides a library of *container classes* to solve this problem, the basic types of which are **List**, **Set**, and **Map**. You can solve a surprising number of problems using these tools.

Among their other characteristics—**Set**, for example, holds only one object of each value, and **Map** is an *associative array* that lets you associate any object with any other object—the Java container classes will automatically resize themselves. So, unlike arrays, you can put in any number of objects and you don't need to worry about how big to make the container while you're writing the program.

Introduction to containers

To me, container classes are one of the most powerful tools for raw development because they significantly increase your programming muscle. The Java 2 containers represent a thorough redesign[4] of the rather poor showings in Java 1.0 and 1.1. Some of the redesign makes things tighter and more sensible. It also fills out the functionality of the

---

[4] By Joshua Bloch at Sun.

containers library, providing the behavior of linked lists, queues, and deques (double-ended queues, pronounced "decks").

The design of a containers library is difficult (true of most library design problems). In C++, the container classes covered the bases with many different classes. This was better than what was available prior to the C++ container classes (nothing), but it didn't translate well into Java. On the other extreme, I've seen a containers library that consists of a single class, "container," which acts like both a linear sequence and an associative array at the same time. The Java 2 container library strikes a balance: the full functionality that you expect from a mature container library, but easier to learn and use than the C++ container classes and other similar container libraries. The result can seem a bit odd in places. Unlike some of the decisions made in the early Java libraries, these oddities were not accidents, but carefully considered decisions based on trade-offs in complexity. It might take you a little while to get comfortable with some aspects of the library, but I think you'll find yourself rapidly acquiring and using these new tools.

The Java 2 container library takes the issue of "holding your objects" and divides it into two distinct concepts:

1. **Collection**: a group of individual elements, often with some rule applied to them. A **List** must hold the elements in a particular sequence, and a **Set** cannot have any duplicate elements. (A *bag*, which is not implemented in the Java container library—since **List**s provide you with enough of that functionality—has no such rules.)

2. **Map**: a group of key-value object pairs. At first glance, this might seem like it ought to be a **Collection** of pairs, but when you try to implement it that way the design gets awkward, so it's clearer to make it a separate concept. On the other hand, it's convenient to look at portions of a **Map** by creating a **Collection** to represent that portion. Thus, a **Map** can return a **Set** of its keys, a **Collection** of its values, or a **Set** of its pairs. **Map**s, like arrays, can easily be expanded to multiple dimensions without adding new concepts: you simply make a **Map** whose values are **Map**s (and the values of *those* **Map**s can be **Map**s, etc.).

We will first look at the general features of containers, then go into details, and finally learn why there are different versions of some containers, and how to choose between them.

Printing containers

Unlike arrays, the containers print nicely without any help. Here's an example that also introduces you to the basic types of containers:

```
//: c09:PrintingContainers.java
// Containers print themselves automatically.
import java.util.*;

public class PrintingContainers {
  static Collection fill(Collection c) {
    c.add("dog");
    c.add("dog");
    c.add("cat");
    return c;
  }
  static Map fill(Map m) {
    m.put("dog", "Bosco");
    m.put("dog", "Spot");
    m.put("cat", "Rags");
    return m;
  }
  public static void main(String[] args) {
    System.out.println(fill(new ArrayList()));
    System.out.println(fill(new HashSet()));
    System.out.println(fill(new HashMap()));
  }
} ///:~
```

As mentioned before, there are two basic categories in the Java container library. The distinction is based on the number of items that are held in each location of the container. The **Collection** category only holds one item in each location (the name is a bit misleading since entire container libraries are often called "collections"). It includes the **List**, which holds a group of items in a specified sequence, and the **Set**, which only allows the addition of one item of each type. The **ArrayList** is a type of **List**, and

HashSet is a type of **Set**. To add items to any **Collection**, there's an **add( )** method.

The **Map** holds key-value pairs, rather like a mini database. The above program uses one flavor of **Map**, the **HashMap**. If you have a **Map** that associates states with their capitals and you want to know the capital of Ohio, you look it up—almost as if you were indexing into an array. (Maps are also called *associative arrays*.) To add elements to a **Map** there's a **put( )** method that takes a key and a value as arguments. The above example only shows adding elements and does not look the elements up after they're added. That will be shown later.

The overloaded **fill( )** methods fill **Collection**s and **Map**s, respectively. If you look at the output, you can see that the default printing behavior (provided via the container's various **toString( )** methods) produces quite readable results, so no additional printing support is necessary as it was with arrays:

```
[dog, dog, cat]
[cat, dog]
{cat=Rags, dog=Spot}
```

A **Collection** is printed surrounded by square braces, with each element separated by a comma. A **Map** is surrounded by curly braces, with each key and value associated with an equal sign (keys on the left, values on the right).

You can also immediately see the basic behavior of the different containers. The **List** holds the objects exactly as they are entered, without any reordering or editing. The **Set**, however, only accepts one of each object and it uses its own internal ordering method (in general, you are only concerned with whether or not something is a member of the **Set**, not the order in which it appears—for that you'd use a **List**). And the **Map** also only accepts one of each type of item, based on the key, and it also has its own internal ordering and does not care about the order in which you enter the items.

Filling containers

Although the problem of printing the containers is taken care of, filling containers suffers from the same deficiency as **java.util.Arrays**. Just like **Arrays**, there is a companion class called **Collections** containing **static** utility methods including one called **fill( )**. This **fill( )** also just duplicates a single object reference throughout the container, and also only works for **List** objects and not **Set**s or **Map**s:

```
//: c09:FillingLists.java
// The Collections.fill() method.
import java.util.*;

public class FillingLists {
  public static void main(String[] args) {
    List list = new ArrayList();
    for(int i = 0; i < 10; i++)
      list.add("");
    Collections.fill(list, "Hello");
    System.out.println(list);
  }
} ///:~
```

This method is made even less useful by the fact that it can only replace elements that are already in the **List**, and will not add new elements.

To be able to create interesting examples, here is a complementary **Collections2** library (part of **com.bruceeckel.util** for convenience) with a **fill( )** method that uses a generator to add elements, and allows you to specify the number of elements you want to **add( )**. The **Generator interface** defined previously will work for **Collection**s, but the **Map** requires its own generator **interface** since a pair of objects (one key and one value) must be produced by each call to **next( )**. Here is the **Pair** class:

```
//: com:bruceeckel:util:Pair.java
package com.bruceeckel.util;
public class Pair {
  public Object key, value;
  Pair(Object k, Object v) {
    key = k;
    value = v;
  }
} ///:~
```

Next, the generator **interface** that produces the **Pair**:

```
//: com:bruceeckel:util:MapGenerator.java
package com.bruceeckel.util;
public interface MapGenerator {
  Pair next();
} ///:~
```

With these, a set of utilities for working with the container classes can be developed:

```
//: com:bruceeckel:util:Collections2.java
// To fill any type of container
// using a generator object.
package com.bruceeckel.util;
import java.util.*;

public class Collections2 {
  // Fill an array using a generator:
  public static void
  fill(Collection c, Generator gen, int count) {
    for(int i = 0; i < count; i++)
      c.add(gen.next());
  }
  public static void
  fill(Map m, MapGenerator gen, int count) {
    for(int i = 0; i < count; i++) {
      Pair p = gen.next();
      m.put(p.key, p.value);
    }
  }
  public static class RandStringPairGenerator
  implements MapGenerator {
    private Arrays2.RandStringGenerator gen;
    public RandStringPairGenerator(int len) {
      gen = new Arrays2.RandStringGenerator(len);
    }
    public Pair next() {
      return new Pair(gen.next(), gen.next());
    }
  }
  // Default object so you don't have
  // to create your own:
  public static RandStringPairGenerator rsp =
```

```
    new RandStringPairGenerator(10);
  public static class StringPairGenerator
  implements MapGenerator {
    private int index = -1;
    private String[][] d;
    public StringPairGenerator(String[][] data) {
      d = data;
    }
    public Pair next() {
      // Force the index to wrap:
      index = (index + 1) % d.length;
      return new Pair(d[index][0], d[index][1]);
    }
    public StringPairGenerator reset() {
      index = -1;
      return this;
    }
  }
  // Use a predefined dataset:
  public static StringPairGenerator geography =
    new StringPairGenerator(
      CountryCapitals.pairs);
  // Produce a sequence from a 2D array:
  public static class StringGenerator
  implements Generator {
    private String[][] d;
    private int position;
    private int index = -1;
    public
    StringGenerator(String[][] data, int pos) {
      d = data;
      position = pos;
    }
    public Object next() {
      // Force the index to wrap:
      index = (index + 1) % d.length;
      return d[index][position];
    }
    public StringGenerator reset() {
      index = -1;
      return this;
```

```
      }
    }
  // Use a predefined dataset:
  public static StringGenerator countries =
    new StringGenerator(CountryCapitals.pairs,0);
  public static StringGenerator capitals =
    new StringGenerator(CountryCapitals.pairs,1);
} ///:~
```

Both versions of **fill( )** take an argument that determines the number of items to add to the container. In addition, there are two generators for the map: **RandStringPairGenerator**, which creates any number of pairs of gibberish **String**s with length determined by the constructor argument; and **StringPairGenerator**, which produces pairs of **String**s given a two-dimensional array of **String**. The **StringGenerator** also takes a two-dimensional array of **String** but generates single items rather than **Pair**s. The **static rsp**, **geography**, **countries**, and **capitals** objects provide prebuilt generators, the last three using all the countries of the world and their capitals. Note that if you try to create more pairs than are available, the generators will loop around to the beginning, and if you are pulling the pairs into a **Map**, the duplicates will just be ignored.

Here is the predefined dataset, which consists of country names and their capitals. It is set in a small font to prevent taking up unnecessary space:

```
//: com:bruceeckel:util:CountryCapitals.java
package com.bruceeckel.util;
public class CountryCapitals {
  public static final String[][] pairs = {
    // Africa
    {"ALGERIA","Algiers"}, {"ANGOLA","Luanda"},
    {"BENIN","Porto-Novo"}, {"BOTSWANA","Gaberone"},
    {"BURKINA FASO","Ouagadougou"}, {"BURUNDI","Bujumbura"},
    {"CAMEROON","Yaounde"}, {"CAPE VERDE","Praia"},
    {"CENTRAL AFRICAN REPUBLIC","Bangui"},
    {"CHAD","N'djamena"},  {"COMOROS","Moroni"},
    {"CONGO","Brazzaville"}, {"DJIBOUTI","Dijibouti"},
    {"EGYPT","Cairo"}, {"EQUATORIAL GUINEA","Malabo"},
    {"ERITREA","Asmara"}, {"ETHIOPIA","Addis Ababa"},
    {"GABON","Libreville"}, {"THE GAMBIA","Banjul"},
    {"GHANA","Accra"}, {"GUINEA","Conakry"},
    {"GUINEA","-"}, {"BISSAU","Bissau"},
    {"CETE D'IVOIR (IVORY COAST)","Yamoussoukro"},
    {"KENYA","Nairobi"}, {"LESOTHO","Maseru"},
    {"LIBERIA","Monrovia"}, {"LIBYA","Tripoli"},
```

```
{"MADAGASCAR","Antananarivo"}, {"MALAWI","Lilongwe"},
{"MALI","Bamako"}, {"MAURITANIA","Nouakchott"},
{"MAURITIUS","Port Louis"}, {"MOROCCO","Rabat"},
{"MOZAMBIQUE","Maputo"}, {"NAMIBIA","Windhoek"},
{"NIGER","Niamey"}, {"NIGERIA","Abuja"},
{"RWANDA","Kigali"}, {"SAO TOME E PRINCIPE","Sao Tome"},
{"SENEGAL","Dakar"}, {"SEYCHELLES","Victoria"},
{"SIERRA LEONE","Freetown"}, {"SOMALIA","Mogadishu"},
{"SOUTH AFRICA","Pretoria/Cape Town"}, {"SUDAN","Khartoum"},
{"SWAZILAND","Mbabane"}, {"TANZANIA","Dodoma"},
{"TOGO","Lome"}, {"TUNISIA","Tunis"},
{"UGANDA","Kampala"},
{"DEMOCRATIC REPUBLIC OF THE CONGO (ZAIRE)","Kinshasa"},
{"ZAMBIA","Lusaka"}, {"ZIMBABWE","Harare"},
// Asia
{"AFGHANISTAN","Kabul"}, {"BAHRAIN","Manama"},
{"BANGLADESH","Dhaka"}, {"BHUTAN","Thimphu"},
{"BRUNEI","Bandar Seri Begawan"}, {"CAMBODIA","Phnom Penh"},
{"CHINA","Beijing"}, {"CYPRUS","Nicosia"},
{"INDIA","New Delhi"}, {"INDONESIA","Jakarta"},
{"IRAN","Tehran"}, {"IRAQ","Baghdad"},
{"ISRAEL","Jerusalem"}, {"JAPAN","Tokyo"},
{"JORDAN","Amman"}, {"KUWAIT","Kuwait City"},
{"LAOS","Vientiane"}, {"LEBANON","Beirut"},
{"MALAYSIA","Kuala Lumpur"}, {"THE MALDIVES","Male"},
{"MONGOLIA","Ulan Bator"}, {"MYANMAR (BURMA)","Rangoon"},
{"NEPAL","Katmandu"}, {"NORTH KOREA","P'yongyang"},
{"OMAN","Muscat"}, {"PAKISTAN","Islamabad"},
{"PHILIPPINES","Manila"}, {"QATAR","Doha"},
{"SAUDI ARABIA","Riyadh"}, {"SINGAPORE","Singapore"},
{"SOUTH KOREA","Seoul"}, {"SRI LANKA","Colombo"},
{"SYRIA","Damascus"}, {"TAIWAN (REPUBLIC OF CHINA)","Taipei"},
{"THAILAND","Bangkok"}, {"TURKEY","Ankara"},
{"UNITED ARAB EMIRATES","Abu Dhabi"}, {"VIETNAM","Hanoi"},
{"YEMEN","Sana'a"},
// Australia and Oceania
{"AUSTRALIA","Canberra"}, {"FIJI","Suva"},
{"KIRIBATI","Bairiki"},
{"MARSHALL ISLANDS","Dalap-Uliga-Darrit"},
{"MICRONESIA","Palikir"}, {"NAURU","Yaren"},
{"NEW ZEALAND","Wellington"}, {"PALAU","Koror"},
{"PAPUA NEW GUINEA","Port Moresby"},
{"SOLOMON ISLANDS","Honaira"}, {"TONGA","Nuku'alofa"},
{"TUVALU","Fongafale"}, {"VANUATU","< Port-Vila"},
{"WESTERN SAMOA","Apia"},
// Eastern Europe and former USSR
{"ARMENIA","Yerevan"}, {"AZERBAIJAN","Baku"},
{"BELARUS (BYELORUSSIA)","Minsk"}, {"GEORGIA","Tbilisi"},
{"KAZAKSTAN","Almaty"}, {"KYRGYZSTAN","Alma-Ata"},
{"MOLDOVA","Chisinau"}, {"RUSSIA","Moscow"},
{"TAJIKISTAN","Dushanbe"}, {"TURKMENISTAN","Ashkabad"},
{"UKRAINE","Kyiv"}, {"UZBEKISTAN","Tashkent"},
```

```java
    // Europe
    {"ALBANIA","Tirana"}, {"ANDORRA","Andorra la Vella"},
    {"AUSTRIA","Vienna"}, {"BELGIUM","Brussels"},
    {"BOSNIA","-"}, {"HERZEGOVINA","Sarajevo"},
    {"CROATIA","Zagreb"}, {"CZECH REPUBLIC","Prague"},
    {"DENMARK","Copenhagen"}, {"ESTONIA","Tallinn"},
    {"FINLAND","Helsinki"}, {"FRANCE","Paris"},
    {"GERMANY","Berlin"}, {"GREECE","Athens"},
    {"HUNGARY","Budapest"}, {"ICELAND","Reykjavik"},
    {"IRELAND","Dublin"}, {"ITALY","Rome"},
    {"LATVIA","Riga"}, {"LIECHTENSTEIN","Vaduz"},
    {"LITHUANIA","Vilnius"}, {"LUXEMBOURG","Luxembourg"},
    {"MACEDONIA","Skopje"}, {"MALTA","Valletta"},
    {"MONACO","Monaco"}, {"MONTENEGRO","Podgorica"},
    {"THE NETHERLANDS","Amsterdam"}, {"NORWAY","Oslo"},
    {"POLAND","Warsaw"}, {"PORTUGAL","Lisbon"},
    {"ROMANIA","Bucharest"}, {"SAN MARINO","San Marino"},
    {"SERBIA","Belgrade"}, {"SLOVAKIA","Bratislava"},
    {"SLOVENIA","Ljujiana"}, {"SPAIN","Madrid"},
    {"SWEDEN","Stockholm"}, {"SWITZERLAND","Berne"},
    {"UNITED KINGDOM","London"}, {"VATICAN CITY","---"},
    // North and Central America
    {"ANTIGUA AND BARBUDA","Saint John's"}, {"BAHAMAS","Nassau"},
    {"BARBADOS","Bridgetown"}, {"BELIZE","Belmopan"},
    {"CANADA","Ottawa"}, {"COSTA RICA","San Jose"},
    {"CUBA","Havana"}, {"DOMINICA","Roseau"},
    {"DOMINICAN REPUBLIC","Santo Domingo"},
    {"EL SALVADOR","San Salvador"}, {"GRENADA","Saint George's"},
    {"GUATEMALA","Guatemala City"}, {"HAITI","Port-au-Prince"},
    {"HONDURAS","Tegucigalpa"}, {"JAMAICA","Kingston"},
    {"MEXICO","Mexico City"}, {"NICARAGUA","Managua"},
    {"PANAMA","Panama City"}, {"ST. KITTS","-"},
    {"NEVIS","Basseterre"}, {"ST. LUCIA","Castries"},
    {"ST. VINCENT AND THE GRENADINES","Kingstown"},
    {"UNITED STATES OF AMERICA","Washington, D.C."},
    // South America
    {"ARGENTINA","Buenos Aires"},
    {"BOLIVIA","Sucre (legal)/La Paz(administrative)"},
    {"BRAZIL","Brasilia"}, {"CHILE","Santiago"},
    {"COLOMBIA","Bogota"}, {"ECUADOR","Quito"},
    {"GUYANA","Georgetown"}, {"PARAGUAY","Asuncion"},
    {"PERU","Lima"}, {"SURINAME","Paramaribo"},
    {"TRINIDAD AND TOBAGO","Port of Spain"},
    {"URUGUAY","Montevideo"}, {"VENEZUELA","Caracas"},
  };
} ///:~
```

This is simply a two-dimensional array of **String** data[5]. Here's a simple test using the **fill( )** methods and generators:

```
//: c09:FillTest.java
import com.bruceeckel.util.*;
import java.util.*;

public class FillTest {
  static Generator sg =
    new Arrays2.RandStringGenerator(7);
  public static void main(String[] args) {
    List list = new ArrayList();
    Collections2.fill(list, sg, 25);
    System.out.println(list + "\n");
    List list2 = new ArrayList();
    Collections2.fill(list2,
      Collections2.capitals, 25);
    System.out.println(list2 + "\n");
    Set set = new HashSet();
    Collections2.fill(set, sg, 25);
    System.out.println(set + "\n");
    Map m = new HashMap();
    Collections2.fill(m, Collections2.rsp, 25);
    System.out.println(m + "\n");
    Map m2 = new HashMap();
    Collections2.fill(m2,
      Collections2.geography, 25);
    System.out.println(m2);
  }
} ///:~
```

With these tools you can easily test the various containers by filling them with interesting data.

---

[5] This data was found on the Internet, then processed by creating a Python program (see *www.Python.org*).

Container disadvantage: unknown type

The "disadvantage" to using the Java containers is that you lose type information when you put an object into a container. This happens because the programmer of that container class had no idea what specific type you wanted to put in the container, and making the container hold only your type would prevent it from being a general-purpose tool. So instead, the container holds references to **Object**, which is the root of all the classes so it holds any type. (Of course, this doesn't include primitive types, since they aren't inherited from anything.) This is a great solution, except:

1. Since the type information is thrown away when you put an object reference into a container, there's no restriction on the type of object that can be put into your container, even if you mean it to hold only, say, cats. Someone could just as easily put a dog into the container.

2. Since the type information is lost, the only thing the container knows that it holds is a reference to an object. You must perform a cast to the correct type before you use it.

On the up side, Java won't let you *misuse* the objects that you put into a container. If you throw a dog into a container of cats and then try to treat everything in the container as a cat, you'll get a run-time exception when you pull the dog reference out of the cat container and try to cast it to a cat.

Here's an example using the basic workhorse container, **ArrayList**. For starters, you can think of **ArrayList** as "an array that automatically expands itself." Using an **ArrayList** is straightforward: create one, put objects in using **add( ),** and later get them out with **get( )** using an index—just like you would with an array but without the square brackets[6].

---

[6] This is a place where operator overloading would be nice.

ArrayList also has a method **size( )** to let you know how many elements have been added so you don't inadvertently run off the end and cause an exception.

First, **Cat** and **Dog** classes are created:

```
//: c09:Cat.java
public class Cat {
  private int catNumber;
  Cat(int i) { catNumber = i; }
  void print() {
    System.out.println("Cat #" + catNumber);
  }
} ///:~
```

```
//: c09:Dog.java
public class Dog {
  private int dogNumber;
  Dog(int i) { dogNumber = i; }
  void print() {
    System.out.println("Dog #" + dogNumber);
  }
} ///:~
```

Cats and **Dog**s are placed into the container, then pulled out:

```
//: c09:CatsAndDogs.java
// Simple container example.
import java.util.*;

public class CatsAndDogs {
  public static void main(String[] args) {
    ArrayList cats = new ArrayList();
    for(int i = 0; i < 7; i++)
      cats.add(new Cat(i));
    // Not a problem to add a dog to cats:
    cats.add(new Dog(7));
    for(int i = 0; i < cats.size(); i++)
      ((Cat)cats.get(i)).print();
    // Dog is detected only at run-time
  }
} ///:~
```

The classes **Cat** and **Dog** are distinct—they have nothing in common except that they are **Object**s. (If you don't explicitly say what class you're inheriting from, you automatically inherit from **Object**.) Since **ArrayList** holds **Object**s, you can not only put **Cat** objects into this container using the **ArrayList** method **add( )**, but you can also add **Dog** objects without complaint at either compile-time or run-time. When you go to fetch out what you think are **Cat** objects using the **ArrayList** method **get( )**, you get back a reference to an object that you must cast to a **Cat**. Then you need to surround the entire expression with parentheses to force the evaluation of the cast before calling the **print( )** method for **Cat**, otherwise you'll get a syntax error. Then, at run-time, when you try to cast the **Dog** object to a **Cat**, you'll get an exception.

This is more than just an annoyance. It's something that can create difficult-to-find bugs. If one part (or several parts) of a program inserts objects into a container, and you discover only in a separate part of the program through an exception that a bad object was placed in the container, then you must find out where the bad insert occurred. On the upside, it's convenient to start with some standardized container classes for programming, despite the scarcity and awkwardness.

Sometimes it works anyway

It turns out that in some cases things seem to work correctly without casting back to your original type. One case is quite special: the **String** class has some extra help from the compiler to make it work smoothly. Whenever the compiler expects a **String** object and it hasn't got one, it will automatically call the **toString( )** method that's defined in **Object** and can be overridden by any Java class. This method produces the desired **String** object, which is then used wherever it was wanted.

Thus, all you need to do to make objects of your class print is to override the **toString( )** method, as shown in the following example:

```
//: c09:Mouse.java
// Overriding toString().
public class Mouse {
  private int mouseNumber;
  Mouse(int i) { mouseNumber = i; }
  // Override Object.toString():
```

```java
  public String toString() {
    return "This is Mouse #" + mouseNumber;
  }
  public int getNumber() {
    return mouseNumber;
  }
} ///:~

//: c09:WorksAnyway.java
// In special cases, things just
// seem to work correctly.
import java.util.*;

class MouseTrap {
  static void caughtYa(Object m) {
    Mouse mouse = (Mouse)m; // Cast from Object
    System.out.println("Mouse: " +
      mouse.getNumber());
  }
}

public class WorksAnyway {
  public static void main(String[] args) {
    ArrayList mice = new ArrayList();
    for(int i = 0; i < 3; i++)
      mice.add(new Mouse(i));
    for(int i = 0; i < mice.size(); i++) {
      // No cast necessary, automatic
      // call to Object.toString():
      System.out.println(
        "Free mouse: " + mice.get(i));
      MouseTrap.caughtYa(mice.get(i));
    }
  }
} ///:~
```

You can see **toString( )** overridden in **Mouse**. In the second **for** loop in **main( )** you find the statement:

```java
System.out.println("Free mouse: " + mice.get(i));
```

After the '+' sign the compiler expects to see a **String** object. **get( )** produces an **Object**, so to get the desired **String** the compiler implicitly calls **toString( )**. Unfortunately, you can work this kind of magic only with **String**; it isn't available for any other type.

A second approach to hiding the cast has been placed inside **MouseTrap**. The **caughtYa( )** method accepts not a **Mouse**, but an **Object,** which it then casts to a **Mouse**. This is quite presumptuous, of course, since by accepting an **Object** anything could be passed to the method. However, if the cast is incorrect—if you passed the wrong type— you'll get an exception at run-time. This is not as good as compile-time checking but it's still robust. Note that in the use of this method:

```
MouseTrap.caughtYa(mice.get(i));
```

no cast is necessary.

Making a type-conscious **ArrayList**

You might not want to give up on this issue just yet. A more ironclad solution is to create a new class using the **ArrayList**, such that it will accept only your type and produce only your type:

```
//: c09:MouseList.java
// A type-conscious ArrayList.
import java.util.*;

public class MouseList {
  private ArrayList list = new ArrayList();
  public void add(Mouse m) {
    list.add(m);
  }
  public Mouse get(int index) {
    return (Mouse)list.get(index);
  }
  public int size() { return list.size(); }
} ///:~
```

Here's a test for the new container:

```
//: c09:MouseListTest.java
public class MouseListTest {
```

```
  public static void main(String[] args) {
    MouseList mice = new MouseList();
    for(int i = 0; i < 3; i++)
      mice.add(new Mouse(i));
    for(int i = 0; i < mice.size(); i++)
      MouseTrap.caughtYa(mice.get(i));
  }
} ///:~
```

This is similar to the previous example, except that the new **MouseList**
class has a **private** member of type **ArrayList**, and methods just like
ArrayList. However, it doesn't accept and produce generic **Object**s, only
Mouse objects.

Note that if **MouseList** had instead been *inherited* from **ArrayList**, the
add(Mouse) method would simply overload the existing **add(Object)**
and there would still be no restriction on what type of objects could be
added. Thus, the **MouseList** becomes a *surrogate* to the **ArrayList**,
performing some activities before passing on the responsibility (see
Thinking in Patterns with Java, downloadable at *www.BruceEckel.com*).

Because a **MouseList** will accept only a **Mouse**, if you say:

```
mice.add(new Pigeon());
```

you will get an error message *at compile-time*. This approach, while more
tedious from a coding standpoint, will tell you immediately if you're using
a type improperly.

Note that no cast is necessary when using **get( )**—it's always a **Mouse**.

Parameterized types

This kind of problem isn't isolated—there are numerous cases in which
you need to create new types based on other types, and in which it is
useful to have specific type information at compile-time. This is the
concept of a *parameterized type*. In C++, this is directly supported by the
language with *templates*. It is likely that a future version of Java will
support some variation of parameterized types; the current front-runner
automatically creates classes similar to **MouseList**.

Iterators

In any container class, you must have a way to put things in and a way to get things out. After all, that's the primary job of a container—to hold things. In the **ArrayList**, **add( )** is the way that you insert objects, and **get( )** is *one* way to get things out. **ArrayList** is quite flexible—you can select anything at any time, and select multiple elements at once using different indexes.

If you want to start thinking at a higher level, there's a drawback: you need to know the exact type of the container in order to use it. This might not seem bad at first, but what if you start out using an **ArrayList**, and later on in your program you discover that because of the way you are using the container it would be much more efficient to use a **LinkedList** instead? Or suppose you'd like to write a piece of generic code that doesn't know or care what type of container it's working with, so that it could be used on different types of containers without rewriting that code?

The concept of an *iterator* can be used to achieve this abstraction. An iterator is an object whose job is to move through a sequence of objects and select each object in that sequence without the client programmer knowing or caring about the underlying structure of that sequence. In addition, an iterator is usually what's called a "light-weight" object: one that's cheap to create. For that reason, you'll often find seemingly strange constraints for iterators; for example, some iterators can move in only one direction.

The Java **Iterator** is an example of an iterator with these kinds of constraints. There's not much you can do with one except:

1. Ask a container to hand you an **Iterator** using a method called **iterator( )**. This **Iterator** will be ready to return the first element in the sequence on your first call to its **next( )** method.

2. Get the next object in the sequence with **next( )**.

3. See if there *are* any more objects in the sequence with **hasNext( )**.

4. Remove the last element returned by the iterator with **remove( )**.

That's all. It's a simple implementation of an iterator, but still powerful (and there's a more sophisticated **ListIterator** for **List**s). To see how it works, let's revisit the **CatsAndDogs.java** program from earlier in this chapter. In the original version, the method **get( )** was used to select each element, but in the following modified version an Iterator is used:

```
//: c09:CatsAndDogs2.java
// Simple container with Iterator.
import java.util.*;

public class CatsAndDogs2 {
  public static void main(String[] args) {
    ArrayList cats = new ArrayList();
    for(int i = 0; i < 7; i++)
      cats.add(new Cat(i));
    Iterator e = cats.iterator();
    while(e.hasNext())
      ((Cat)e.next()).print();
  }
} ///:~
```

You can see that the last few lines now use an **Iterator** to step through the sequence instead of a **for** loop. With the **Iterator**, you don't need to worry about the number of elements in the container. That's taken care of for you by **hasNext( )** and **next( )**.

As another example, consider the creation of a general-purpose printing method:

```
//: c09:HamsterMaze.java
// Using an Iterator.
import java.util.*;

class Hamster {
  private int hamsterNumber;
  Hamster(int i) { hamsterNumber = i; }
  public String toString() {
    return "This is Hamster #" + hamsterNumber;
  }
}
```

```
class Printer {
  static void printAll(Iterator e) {
    while(e.hasNext())
      System.out.println(e.next());
  }
}

public class HamsterMaze {
  public static void main(String[] args) {
    ArrayList v = new ArrayList();
    for(int i = 0; i < 3; i++)
      v.add(new Hamster(i));
    Printer.printAll(v.iterator());
  }
} ///:~
```

Look closely at **printAll( )**. Note that there's no information about the type of sequence. All you have is an **Iterator**, and that's all you need to know about the sequence: that you can get the next object, and that you can know when you're at the end. This idea of taking a container of objects and passing through it to perform an operation on each one is powerful, and will be seen throughout this book.

The example is even more generic, since it implicitly uses the **Object.toString( )** method. The **println( )** method is overloaded for all the primitive types as well as **Object**; in each case a **String** is automatically produced by calling the appropriate **toString( )** method.

Although it's unnecessary, you can be more explicit using a cast, which has the effect of calling **toString( )**:

```
System.out.println((String)e.next());
```

In general, however, you'll want to do something more than call **Object** methods, so you'll run up against the type-casting issue again. You must assume you've gotten an **Iterator** to a sequence of the particular type you're interested in, and cast the resulting objects to that type (getting a run-time exception if you're wrong).

Unintended recursion

Because (like every other class), the Java standard containers are inherited from **Object**, they contain a **toString( )** method. This has been overridden so that they can produce a **String** representation of themselves, including the objects they hold. Inside **ArrayList**, for example, the **toString( )** steps through the elements of the **ArrayList** and calls **toString( )** for each one. Suppose you'd like to print the address of your class. It seems to make sense to simply refer to **this** (in particular, C++ programmers are prone to this approach):

```
//: c09:InfiniteRecursion.java
// Accidental recursion.
import java.util.*;

public class InfiniteRecursion {
  public String toString() {
    return " InfiniteRecursion address: "
      + this + "\n";
  }
  public static void main(String[] args) {
    ArrayList v = new ArrayList();
    for(int i = 0; i < 10; i++)
      v.add(new InfiniteRecursion());
    System.out.println(v);
  }
} ///:~
```

If you simply create an **InfiniteRecursion** object and then print it, you'll get an endless sequence of exceptions. This is also true if you place the **InfiniteRecursion** objects in an **ArrayList** and print that **ArrayList** as shown here. What's happening is automatic type conversion for **String**s. When you say:

```
"InfiniteRecursion address: " + this
```

The compiler sees a **String** followed by a '+' and something that's not a **String**, so it tries to convert **this** to a **String**. It does this conversion by calling **toString( )**, which produces a recursive call.

If you really do want to print the address of the object in this case, the solution is to call the **Object toString( )** method, which does just that.

So instead of saying **this**, you'd say **super.toString( )**. (This only works if you're directly inheriting from **Object**, or if none of your parent classes have overridden the **toString( )** method.)

Container taxonomy

Collections and **Map**s may be implemented in different ways, according to your programming needs. It's helpful to look at a diagram of the Java 2 containers:

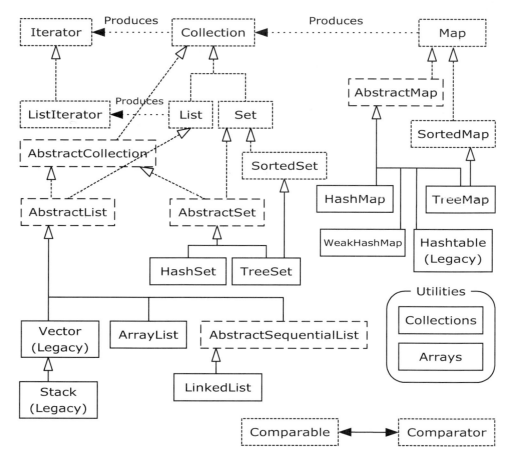

This diagram can be a bit overwhelming at first, but you'll see that there are really only three container components: **Map**, **List**, and **Set**, and only two or three implementations of each one (with, typically, a preferred version). When you see this, the containers are not so daunting.

The dotted boxes represent **interface**s, the dashed boxes represent **abstract** classes, and the solid boxes are regular (concrete) classes. The dotted-line arrows indicate that a particular class is implementing an **interface** (or in the case of an **abstract** class, partially implementing that **interface**). The solid arrows show that a class can produce objects of the class the arrow is pointing to. For example, any **Collection** can produce an **Iterator**, while a **List** can produce a **ListIterator** (as well as an ordinary **Iterator**, since **List** is inherited from **Collection**).

The interfaces that are concerned with holding objects are **Collection**, **List**, **Set**, and **Map**. Ideally, you'll write most of your code to talk to these interfaces, and the only place where you'll specify the precise type you're using is at the point of creation. So you can create a **List** like this:

```
List x = new LinkedList();
```

Of course, you can also decide to make **x** a **LinkedList** (instead of a generic **List**) and carry the precise type information around with **x**. The beauty (and the intent) of using the **interface** is that if you decide you want to change your implementation, all you need to do is change it at the point of creation, like this:

```
List x = new ArrayList();
```

The rest of your code can remain untouched (some of this genericity can also be achieved with iterators).

In the class hierarchy, you can see a number of classes whose names begin with "**Abstract**," and these can seem a bit confusing at first. They are simply tools that partially implement a particular interface. If you were making your own **Set**, for example, you wouldn't start with the **Set** interface and implement all the methods, instead you'd inherit from **AbstractSet** and do the minimal necessary work to make your new class. However, the containers library contains enough functionality to satisfy your needs virtually all the time. So for our purposes, you can ignore any class that begins with "**Abstract**."

Therefore, when you look at the diagram, you're really concerned with only those **interface**s at the top of the diagram and the concrete classes (those with solid boxes around them). You'll typically make an object of a concrete class, upcast it to the corresponding **interface**, and then use the

interface throughout the rest of your code. In addition, you do not need to consider the legacy elements when writing new code. Therefore, the diagram can be greatly simplified to look like this:

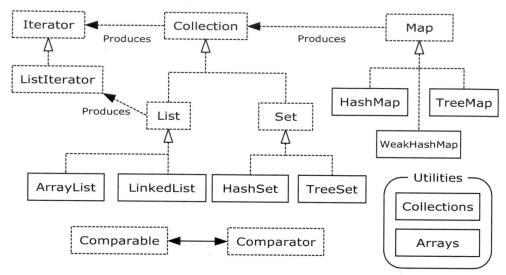

Now it only includes the interfaces and classes that you will encounter on a regular basis, and also the elements that we will focus on in this chapter.

Here's a simple example, which fills a **Collection** (represented here with an **ArrayList**) with **String** objects, and then prints each element in the **Collection**:

```
//: c09:SimpleCollection.java
// A simple example using Java 2 Collections.
import java.util.*;

public class SimpleCollection {
  public static void main(String[] args) {
    // Upcast because we just want to
    // work with Collection features
    Collection c = new ArrayList();
    for(int i = 0; i < 10; i++)
      c.add(Integer.toString(i));
    Iterator it = c.iterator();
    while(it.hasNext())
      System.out.println(it.next());
  }
```

```
} ///:~
```

The first line in **main( )** creates an **ArrayList** object and then upcasts it to a **Collection**. Since this example uses only the **Collection** methods, any object of a class inherited from **Collection** would work, but **ArrayList** is the typical workhorse **Collection**.

The **add( )** method, as its name suggests, puts a new element in the **Collection**. However, the documentation carefully states that **add( )** "ensures that this Container contains the specified element." This is to allow for the meaning of **Set**, which adds the element only if it isn't already there. With an **ArrayList**, or any sort of **List**, **add( )** always means "put it in," because **List**s don't care if there are duplicates.

All **Collection**s can produce an **Iterator** via their **iterator( )** method. Here, an **Iterator** is created and used to traverse the **Collection**, printing each element.

Collection functionality

The following table shows everything you can do with a **Collection** (not including the methods that automatically come through with **Object**), and thus, everything you can do with a **Set** or a **List**. (**List** also has additional functionality.) **Map**s are not inherited from **Collection**, and will be treated separately.

boolean add(Object)	Ensures that the container holds the argument. Returns false if it doesn't add the argument. (This is an "optional" method, described later in this chapter.)
boolean addAll(Collection)	Adds all the elements in the argument. Returns **true** if any elements were added. ("Optional.")
void clear( )	Removes all the elements in the container. ("Optional.")
boolean contains(Object)	**true** if the container holds the argument.
boolean containsAll(Collection)	**true** if the container holds all the elements in the argument.

boolean isEmpty( )	**true** if the container has no elements.
Iterator iterator( )	Returns an **Iterator** that you can use to move through the elements in the container.
boolean remove(Object)	If the argument is in the container, one instance of that element is removed. Returns **true** if a removal occurred. ("Optional.")
boolean removeAll(Collection)	Removes all the elements that are contained in the argument. Returns **true** if any removals occurred. ("Optional.")
boolean retainAll(Collection)	Retains only elements that are contained in the argument (an "intersection" from set theory). Returns **true** if any changes occurred. ("Optional.")
int size( )	Returns the number of elements in the container.
Object[] toArray( )	Returns an array containing all the elements in the container.
Object[] toArray(Object[] a)	Returns an array containing all the elements in the container, whose type is that of the array a rather than plain **Object** (you must cast the array to the right type).

Notice that there's no **get( )** function for random-access element selection. That's because **Collection** also includes **Set**, which maintains its own internal ordering (and thus makes random-access lookup meaningless). Thus, if you want to examine all the elements of a **Collection** you must use an iterator; that's the only way to fetch things back.

The following example demonstrates all of these methods. Again, these work with anything that inherits from **Collection**, but an **ArrayList** is used as a kind of "least-common denominator":

```
//: c09:Collection1.java
```

```java
// Things you can do with all Collections.
import java.util.*;
import com.bruceeckel.util.*;

public class Collection1 {
  public static void main(String[] args) {
    Collection c = new ArrayList();
    Collections2.fill(c,
      Collections2.countries, 10);
    c.add("ten");
    c.add("eleven");
    System.out.println(c);
    // Make an array from the List:
    Object[] array = c.toArray();
    // Make a String array from the List:
    String[] str =
      (String[])c.toArray(new String[1]);
    // Find max and min elements; this means
    // different things depending on the way
    // the Comparable interface is implemented:
    System.out.println("Collections.max(c) = " +
      Collections.max(c));
    System.out.println("Collections.min(c) = " +
      Collections.min(c));
    // Add a Collection to another Collection
    Collection c2 = new ArrayList();
    Collections2.fill(c2,
      Collections2.countries, 10);
    c.addAll(c2);
    System.out.println(c);
    c.remove(CountryCapitals.pairs[0][0]);
    System.out.println(c);
    c.remove(CountryCapitals.pairs[1][0]);
    System.out.println(c);
    // Remove all components that are in the
    // argument collection:
    c.removeAll(c2);
    System.out.println(c);
    c.addAll(c2);
    System.out.println(c);
    // Is an element in this Collection?
```

```
    String val = CountryCapitals.pairs[3][0];
    System.out.println(
      "c.contains(" + val  + ") = "
      + c.contains(val));
    // Is a Collection in this Collection?
    System.out.println(
      "c.containsAll(c2) = "+ c.containsAll(c2));
    Collection c3 = ((List)c).subList(3, 5);
    // Keep all the elements that are in both
    // c2 and c3 (an intersection of sets):
    c2.retainAll(c3);
    System.out.println(c);
    // Throw away all the elements
    // in c2 that also appear in c3:
    c2.removeAll(c3);
    System.out.println("c.isEmpty() = " +
      c.isEmpty());
    c = new ArrayList();
    Collections2.fill(c,
      Collections2.countries, 10);
    System.out.println(c);
    c.clear(); // Remove all elements
    System.out.println("after c.clear():");
    System.out.println(c);
  }
} ///:~
```

ArrayLists are created containing different sets of data and upcast to **Collection** objects, so it's clear that nothing other than the **Collection** interface is being used. **main( )** uses simple exercises to show all of the methods in **Collection**.

The following sections describe the various implementations of **List**, **Set**, and **Map** and indicate in each case (with an asterisk) which one should be your default choice. You'll notice that the legacy classes **Vector**, **Stack**, and **Hashtable** are *not* included because in all cases there are preferred classes within the Java 2 Containers.

List functionality

The basic **List** is quite simple to use, as you've seen so far with **ArrayList**. Although most of the time you'll just use **add( )** to insert objects, **get( )** to get them out one at a time, and **iterator( )** to get an **Iterator** to the sequence, there's also a set of other methods that can be useful.

In addition, there are actually two types of **List**: the basic **ArrayList**, which excels at randomly accessing elements, and the much more powerful **LinkedList** (which is not designed for fast random access, but has a much more general set of methods).

List (interface)	Order is the most important feature of a **List**; it promises to maintain elements in a particular sequence. **List** adds a number of methods to **Collection** that allow insertion and removal of elements in the middle of a **List**. (This is recommended only for a **LinkedList**.) A **List** will produce a **ListIterator**, and using this you can traverse the **List** in both directions, as well as insert and remove elements in the middle of the **List**.
ArrayList*	A **List** implemented with an array. Allows rapid random access to elements, but is slow when inserting and removing elements from the middle of a list. **ListIterator** should be used only for back-and-forth traversal of an **ArrayList**, but not for inserting and removing elements, which is expensive compared to **LinkedList**.
LinkedList	Provides optimal sequential access, with inexpensive insertions and deletions from the middle of the **List**. Relatively slow for random access. (Use **ArrayList** instead.) Also has **addFirst( )**, **addLast( )**, **getFirst( )**, **getLast( )**, **removeFirst( )**, and **removeLast( )** (which are not defined in any interfaces or base classes) to allow it to be used as a stack, a queue, and a deque.

The methods in the following example each cover a different group of activities: things that every list can do (**basicTest( )**), moving around

---

with an **Iterator** (**iterMotion( )**) versus changing things with an **Iterator** (**iterManipulation( )**), seeing the effects of **List** manipulation (**testVisual( )**), and operations available only to **LinkedList**s.

```java
//: c09:List1.java
// Things you can do with Lists.
import java.util.*;
import com.bruceeckel.util.*;

public class List1 {
  public static List fill(List a) {
    Collections2.countries.reset();
    Collections2.fill(a,
      Collections2.countries, 10);
    return a;
  }
  static boolean b;
  static Object o;
  static int i;
  static Iterator it;
  static ListIterator lit;
  public static void basicTest(List a) {
    a.add(1, "x"); // Add at location 1
    a.add("x"); // Add at end
    // Add a collection:
    a.addAll(fill(new ArrayList()));
    // Add a collection starting at location 3:
    a.addAll(3, fill(new ArrayList()));
    b = a.contains("1"); // Is it in there?
    // Is the entire collection in there?
    b = a.containsAll(fill(new ArrayList()));
    // Lists allow random access, which is cheap
    // for ArrayList, expensive for LinkedList:
    o = a.get(1); // Get object at location 1
    i = a.indexOf("1"); // Tell index of object
    b = a.isEmpty(); // Any elements inside?
    it = a.iterator(); // Ordinary Iterator
    lit = a.listIterator(); // ListIterator
    lit = a.listIterator(3); // Start at loc 3
    i = a.lastIndexOf("1"); // Last match
    a.remove(1); // Remove location 1
```

```java
    a.remove("3"); // Remove this object
    a.set(1, "y"); // Set location 1 to "y"
    // Keep everything that's in the argument
    // (the intersection of the two sets):
    a.retainAll(fill(new ArrayList()));
    // Remove everything that's in the argument:
    a.removeAll(fill(new ArrayList()));
    i = a.size(); // How big is it?
    a.clear(); // Remove all elements
  }
  public static void iterMotion(List a) {
    ListIterator it = a.listIterator();
    b = it.hasNext();
    b = it.hasPrevious();
    o = it.next();
    i = it.nextIndex();
    o = it.previous();
    i = it.previousIndex();
  }
  public static void iterManipulation(List a) {
    ListIterator it = a.listIterator();
    it.add("47");
    // Must move to an element after add():
    it.next();
    // Remove the element that was just produced:
    it.remove();
    // Must move to an element after remove():
    it.next();
    // Change the element that was just produced:
    it.set("47");
  }
  public static void testVisual(List a) {
    System.out.println(a);
    List b = new ArrayList();
    fill(b);
    System.out.print("b = ");
    System.out.println(b);
    a.addAll(b);
    a.addAll(fill(new ArrayList()));
    System.out.println(a);
    // Insert, remove, and replace elements
```

```
    // using a ListIterator:
    ListIterator x = a.listIterator(a.size()/2);
    x.add("one");
    System.out.println(a);
    System.out.println(x.next());
    x.remove();
    System.out.println(x.next());
    x.set("47");
    System.out.println(a);
    // Traverse the list backwards:
    x = a.listIterator(a.size());
    while(x.hasPrevious())
      System.out.print(x.previous() + " ");
    System.out.println();
    System.out.println("testVisual finished");
  }
  // There are some things that only
  // LinkedLists can do:
  public static void testLinkedList() {
    LinkedList ll = new LinkedList();
    fill(ll);
    System.out.println(ll);
    // Treat it like a stack, pushing:
    ll.addFirst("one");
    ll.addFirst("two");
    System.out.println(ll);
    // Like "peeking" at the top of a stack:
    System.out.println(ll.getFirst());
    // Like popping a stack:
    System.out.println(ll.removeFirst());
    System.out.println(ll.removeFirst());
    // Treat it like a queue, pulling elements
    // off the tail end:
    System.out.println(ll.removeLast());
    // With the above operations, it's a dequeue!
    System.out.println(ll);
  }
  public static void main(String[] args) {
    // Make and fill a new list each time:
    basicTest(fill(new LinkedList()));
    basicTest(fill(new ArrayList()));
```

```
    iterMotion(fill(new LinkedList()));
    iterMotion(fill(new ArrayList()));
    iterManipulation(fill(new LinkedList()));
    iterManipulation(fill(new ArrayList()));
    testVisual(fill(new LinkedList()));
    testLinkedList();
  }
} ///:~
```

In **basicTest( )** and **iterMotion( )** the calls are simply made to show
the proper syntax, and while the return value is captured, it is not used. In
some cases, the return value isn't captured since it isn't typically used.
You should look up the full usage of each of these methods in the online
documentation from *java.sun.com* before you use them.

Making a stack from a **LinkedList**

A stack is sometimes referred to as a "last-in, first-out" (LIFO) container.
That is, whatever you "push" on the stack last is the first item you can
"pop" out. Like all of the other containers in Java, what you push and pop
are **Object**s, so you must cast what you pop, unless you're just using
Object behavior.

The **LinkedList** has methods that directly implement stack functionality,
so you can also just use a **LinkedList** rather than making a stack class.
However, a stack class can sometimes tell the story better:

```
//: c09:StackL.java
// Making a stack from a LinkedList.
import java.util.*;
import com.bruceeckel.util.*;

public class StackL {
  private LinkedList list = new LinkedList();
  public void push(Object v) {
    list.addFirst(v);
  }
  public Object top() { return list.getFirst(); }
  public Object pop() {
    return list.removeFirst();
  }
```

```
    public static void main(String[] args) {
      StackL stack = new StackL();
      for(int i = 0; i < 10; i++)
        stack.push(Collections2.countries.next());
      System.out.println(stack.top());
      System.out.println(stack.top());
      System.out.println(stack.pop());
      System.out.println(stack.pop());
      System.out.println(stack.pop());
    }
} ///:~
```

If you want only stack behavior, inheritance is inappropriate here because it would produce a class with all the rest of the **LinkedList** methods (you'll see later that this very mistake was made by the Java 1.0 library designers with **Stack**).

Making a queue from a **LinkedList**

A *queue* is a *"first-in, first-out"* (FIFO) container. That is, you put things in at one end, and pull them out at the other. So the order in which you put them in will be the same order that they come out. **LinkedList** has methods to support queue behavior, so these can be used in a **Queue** class:

```
//: c09:Queue.java
// Making a queue from a LinkedList.
import java.util.*;

public class Queue {
  private LinkedList list = new LinkedList();
  public void put(Object v) { list.addFirst(v); }
  public Object get() {
    return list.removeLast();
  }
  public boolean isEmpty() {
    return list.isEmpty();
  }
  public static void main(String[] args) {
    Queue queue = new Queue();
    for(int i = 0; i < 10; i++)
```

```
      queue.put(Integer.toString(i));
    while(!queue.isEmpty())
      System.out.println(queue.get());
  }
} ///:~
```

You can also easily create a *deque* (double-ended queue) from a
LinkedList. This is like a queue, but you can add and remove elements
from either end.

Set functionality

Set has exactly the same interface as **Collection**, so there isn't any extra
functionality like there is with the two different **List**s. Instead, the **Set** is
exactly a **Collection**, it just has different behavior. (This is the ideal use
of inheritance and polymorphism: to express different behavior.) A **Set**
refuses to hold more than one instance of each object value (what
constitutes the "value" of an object is more complex, as you shall see).

Set (interface)	Each element that you add to the **Set** must be unique; otherwise the **Set** doesn't add the duplicate element. **Object**s added to a **Set** must define **equals( )** to establish object uniqueness. **Set** has exactly the same interface as **Collection**. The **Set** interface does not guarantee it will maintain its elements in any particular order.
HashSet*	For **Set**s where fast lookup time is important. **Object**s must also define **hashCode( )**.
TreeSet	An ordered **Set** backed by a tree. This way, you can extract an ordered sequence from a **Set**.

The following example does *not* show everything you can do with a **Set**,
since the interface is the same as **Collection**, and so was exercised in the
previous example. Instead, this demonstrates the behavior that makes a
Set unique:

```
//: c09:Set1.java
// Things you can do with Sets.
import java.util.*;
import com.bruceeckel.util.*;
```

```java
public class Set1 {
  static Collections2.StringGenerator gen =
    Collections2.countries;
  public static void testVisual(Set a) {
    Collections2.fill(a, gen.reset(), 10);
    Collections2.fill(a, gen.reset(), 10);
    Collections2.fill(a, gen.reset(), 10);
    System.out.println(a); // No duplicates!
    // Add another set to this one:
    a.addAll(a);
    a.add("one");
    a.add("one");
    a.add("one");
    System.out.println(a);
    // Look something up:
    System.out.println("a.contains(\"one\"): " +
      a.contains("one"));
  }
  public static void main(String[] args) {
    System.out.println("HashSet");
    testVisual(new HashSet());
    System.out.println("TreeSet");
    testVisual(new TreeSet());
  }
} ///:~
```

Duplicate values are added to the **Set**, but when it is printed you'll see the **Set** has accepted only one instance of each value.

When you run this program you'll notice that the order maintained by the **HashSet** is different from **TreeSet**, since each has a different way of storing elements so they can be located later. (**TreeSet** keeps them sorted, while **HashSet** uses a hashing function, which is designed specifically for rapid lookups.) When creating your own types, be aware that a **Set** needs a way to maintain a storage order, which means you must implement the **Comparable** interface and define the **compareTo( )** method. Here's an example:

```java
//: c09:Set2.java
// Putting your own type in a Set.
```

```
import java.util.*;

class MyType implements Comparable {
  private int i;
  public MyType(int n) { i = n; }
  public boolean equals(Object o) {
    return
      (o instanceof MyType)
      && (i == ((MyType)o).i);
  }
  public int hashCode() { return i; }
  public String toString() { return i + " "; }
  public int compareTo(Object o) {
    int i2 = ((MyType)o).i;
    return (i2 < i ? -1 : (i2 == i ? 0 : 1));
  }
}

public class Set2 {
  public static Set fill(Set a, int size) {
    for(int i = 0; i < size; i++)
      a.add(new MyType(i));
    return a;
  }
  public static void test(Set a) {
    fill(a, 10);
    fill(a, 10); // Try to add duplicates
    fill(a, 10);
    a.addAll(fill(new TreeSet(), 10));
    System.out.println(a);
  }
  public static void main(String[] args) {
    test(new HashSet());
    test(new TreeSet());
  }
} ///:~
```

The form for the definitions for **equals( )** and **hashCode( )** will be
described later in this chapter. You must define an **equals( )** in both
cases, but the **hashCode( )** is absolutely necessary only if the class will
be placed in a **HashSet** (which is likely, since that should generally be

---

your first choice as a **Set** implementation). However, as a programming style you should always override **hashCode( )** when you override **equals( )**. This process will be fully detailed later in this chapter.

In the **compareTo( )**, note that I did *not* use the "simple and obvious" form **return i-i2**. Although this is a common programming error, it would only work properly if **i** and **i2** were "unsigned" **int**s (if Java *had* an "unsigned" keyword, which it does not). It breaks for Java's signed **int**, which is not big enough to represent the difference of two signed **int**s. If **i** is a large positive integer and **j** is a large negative integer, **i-j** will overflow and return a negative value, which will not work.

SortedSet

If you have a **SortedSet** (of which **TreeSet** is the only one available), the elements are guaranteed to be in sorted order which allows additional functionality to be provided with these methods in the **SortedSet** interface:

Comparator comparator(): Produces the **Comparator** used for this **Set**, or **null** for natural ordering.

Object first(): Produces the lowest element.

Object last(): Produces the highest element.

SortedSet subSet(fromElement, toElement): Produces a view of this **Set** with elements from **fromElement**, inclusive, to **toElement**, exclusive.

SortedSet headSet(toElement): Produces a view of this **Set** with elements less than **toElement**.

SortedSet tailSet(fromElement): Produces a view of this **Set** with elements greater than or equal to **fromElement**.

Map functionality

An **ArrayList** allows you to select from a sequence of objects using a number, so in a sense it associates numbers to objects. But what if you'd like to select from a sequence of objects using some other criterion? A stack is an example: its selection criterion is "the last thing pushed on the stack." A powerful twist on this idea of "selecting from a sequence" is alternately termed a *map*, a *dictionary,* or an *associative array.* Conceptually, it seems like an **ArrayList**, but instead of looking up objects using a number, you look them up using *another object*! This is often a key process in a program.

The concept shows up in Java as the **Map** interface. The **put(Object key, Object value)** method adds a value (the thing you want), and associates it with a key (the thing you look it up with). **get(Object key)** produces the value given the corresponding key. You can also test a **Map** to see if it contains a key or a value with **containsKey( )** and **containsValue( )**.

The standard Java library contains two different types of **Map**s: **HashMap** and **TreeMap**. Both have the same interface (since they both implement **Map**), but they differ in one distinct way: efficiency. If you look at what must be done for a **get( )**, it seems pretty slow to search through (for example) an **ArrayList** for the key. This is where **HashMap** speeds things up. Instead of a slow search for the key, it uses a special value called a *hash code*. The hash code is a way to take some information in the object in question and turn it into a "relatively unique" **int** for that object. All Java objects can produce a hash code, and **hashCode( )** is a method in the root class **Object**. A **HashMap** takes the **hashCode( )** of the object and uses it to quickly hunt for the key. This results in a dramatic performance improvement[7].

Map (interface)	Maintains key-value associations (pairs), so you can look up a value using a key.
HashMap*	Implementation based on a hash table. (Use this instead of **Hashtable**.) Provides constant-time performance for inserting and locating pairs. Performance can be adjusted via constructors that allow you to set the *capacity* and *load factor* of the

---

[7] If these speedups still don't meet your performance needs, you can further accelerate table lookup by writing your own **Map** and customizing it to your particular types to avoid delays due to casting to and from **Object**s. To reach even higher levels of performance, speed enthusiasts can use Donald Knuth's *The Art of Computer Programming, Volume 3: Sorting and Searching, Second Edition* to replace overflow bucket lists with arrays that have two additional benefits: they can be optimized for disk storage characteristics and they can save most of the time of creating and garbage collecting individual records.

	hash table.
TreeMap	Implementation based on a red-black tree. When you view the keys or the pairs, they will be in sorted order (determined by **Comparable** or **Comparator**, discussed later). The point of a **TreeMap** is that you get the results in sorted order. **TreeMap** is the only **Map** with the **subMap( )** method, which allows you to return a portion of the tree.

Sometimes you'll also need to know the details of how hashing works, so we'll look at that a little later.

The following example uses the **Collections2.fill( )** method and the test data sets that were previously defined:

```
//: c09:Map1.java
// Things you can do with Maps.
import java.util.*;
import com.bruceeckel.util.*;

public class Map1 {
  static Collections2.StringPairGenerator geo =
    Collections2.geography;
  static Collections2.RandStringPairGenerator
    rsp = Collections2.rsp;
  // Producing a Set of the keys:
  public static void printKeys(Map m) {
    System.out.print("Size = " + m.size() +", ");
    System.out.print("Keys: ");
    System.out.println(m.keySet());
  }
  // Producing a Collection of the values:
  public static void printValues(Map m) {
    System.out.print("Values: ");
    System.out.println(m.values());
  }
  public static void test(Map m) {
    Collections2.fill(m, geo, 25);
    // Map has 'Set' behavior for keys:
    Collections2.fill(m, geo.reset(), 25);
```

```
      printKeys(m);
      printValues(m);
      System.out.println(m);
      String key = CountryCapitals.pairs[4][0];
      String value = CountryCapitals.pairs[4][1];
      System.out.println("m.containsKey(\"" + key +
        "\"): " + m.containsKey(key));
      System.out.println("m.get(\"" + key + "\"): "
        + m.get(key));
      System.out.println("m.containsValue(\""
        + value + "\"): " +
        m.containsValue(value));
      Map m2 = new TreeMap();
      Collections2.fill(m2, rsp, 25);
      m.putAll(m2);
      printKeys(m);
      key = m.keySet().iterator().next().toString();
      System.out.println("First key in map: "+key);
      m.remove(key);
      printKeys(m);
      m.clear();
      System.out.println("m.isEmpty(): "
        + m.isEmpty());
      Collections2.fill(m, geo.reset(), 25);
      // Operations on the Set change the Map:
      m.keySet().removeAll(m.keySet());
      System.out.println("m.isEmpty(): "
        + m.isEmpty());
    }
  public static void main(String[] args) {
    System.out.println("Testing HashMap");
    test(new HashMap());
    System.out.println("Testing TreeMap");
    test(new TreeMap());
  }
} ///:~
```

The **printKeys( )** and **printValues( )** methods are not only useful utilities, they also demonstrate how to produce **Collection** views of a **Map**. The **keySet( )** method produces a **Set** backed by the keys in the **Map**. Similar treatment is given to **values( )**, which produces a

---

Collection containing all the values in the **Map**. (Note that keys must be unique, while values may contain duplicates.) Since these **Collection**s are backed by the **Map**, any changes in a **Collection** will be reflected in the associated **Map**.

The rest of the program provides simple examples of each **Map** operation, and tests each type of **Map**.

As an example of the use of a **HashMap**, consider a program to check the randomness of Java's **Math.random( )** method. Ideally, it would produce a perfect distribution of random numbers, but to test this you need to generate a bunch of random numbers and count the ones that fall in the various ranges. A **HashMap** is perfect for this, since it associates objects with objects (in this case, the value object contains the number produced by **Math.random( )** along with the number of times that number appears):

```
//: c09:Statistics.java
// Simple demonstration of HashMap.
import java.util.*;

class Counter {
  int i = 1;
  public String toString() {
    return Integer.toString(i);
  }
}

class Statistics {
  public static void main(String[] args) {
    HashMap hm = new HashMap();
    for(int i = 0; i < 10000; i++) {
      // Produce a number between 0 and 20:
      Integer r =
        new Integer((int)(Math.random() * 20));
      if(hm.containsKey(r))
        ((Counter)hm.get(r)).i++;
      else
        hm.put(r, new Counter());
    }
    System.out.println(hm);
```

```
     }
} ///:~
```

In **main( )**, each time a random number is generated it is wrapped inside
an **Integer** object so that reference can be used with the **HashMap**. (You
can't use a primitive with a container, only an object reference.) The
containsKey( ) method checks to see if this key is already in the
container. (That is, has the number been found already?) If so, the **get( )**
method produces the associated value for the key, which in this case is a
Counter object. The value **i** inside the counter is incremented to indicate
that one more of this particular random number has been found.

If the key has not been found yet, the method **put( )** will place a new key-
value pair into the **HashMap**. Since **Counter** automatically initializes its
variable **i** to one when it's created, it indicates the first occurrence of this
particular random number.

To display the **HashMap**, it is simply printed. The **HashMap**
toString( ) method moves through all the key-value pairs and calls the
toString( ) for each one. The **Integer.toString( )** is predefined, and
you can see the **toString( )** for **Counter**. The output from one run (with
some line breaks added) is:

```
{19=526, 18=533, 17=460, 16=513, 15=521, 14=495,
 13=512, 12=483, 11=488, 10=487, 9=514, 8=523,
 7=497, 6=487, 5=480, 4=489, 3=509, 2=503, 1=475,
 0=505}
```

You might wonder at the necessity of the class **Counter,** which seems like
it doesn't even have the functionality of the wrapper class **Integer**. Why
not use **int** or **Integer**? Well, you can't use an **int** because all of the
containers can hold only **Object** references. After seeing containers the
wrapper classes might begin to make a little more sense to you, since you
can't put any of the primitive types in containers. However, the only thing
you *can* do with the Java wrappers is to initialize them to a particular
value and read that value. That is, there's no way to change a value once a
wrapper object has been created. This makes the **Integer** wrapper
immediately useless to solve our problem, so we're forced to create a new
class that does satisfy the need.

SortedMap

If you have a **SortedMap** (of which **TreeMap** is the only one available), the keys are guaranteed to be in sorted order which allows additional functionality to be provided with these methods in the **SortedMap** interface:

Comparator comparator(): Produces the comparator used for this **Map**, or **null** for natural ordering.

Object firstKey(): Produces the lowest key.

Object lastKey(): Produces the highest key.

SortedMap subMap(fromKey, toKey): Produces a view of this **Map** with keys from **fromKey**, inclusive, to **toKey**, exclusive.

SortedMap headMap(toKey): Produces a view of this **Map** with keys less than **toKey**.

SortedMap tailMap(fromKey): Produces a view of this **Map** with keys greater than or equal to **fromKey**.

Hashing and hash codes

In the previous example, a standard library class (**Integer**) was used as a key for the **HashMap**. It worked fine as a key, because it has all the necessary wiring to make it work correctly as a key. But a common pitfall occurs with **HashMap**s when you create your own classes to be used as keys. For example, consider a weather predicting system that matches **Groundhog** objects to **Prediction** objects. It seems fairly straightforward—you create the two classes, and use **Groundhog** as the key and **Prediction** as the value:

```
//: c09:SpringDetector.java
// Looks plausible, but doesn't work.
import java.util.*;

class Groundhog {
  int ghNumber;
  Groundhog(int n) { ghNumber = n; }
}

class Prediction {
```

```
    boolean shadow = Math.random() > 0.5;
    public String toString() {
      if(shadow)
        return "Six more weeks of Winter!";
      else
        return "Early Spring!";
    }
}

public class SpringDetector {
  public static void main(String[] args) {
    HashMap hm = new HashMap();
    for(int i = 0; i < 10; i++)
      hm.put(new Groundhog(i), new Prediction());
    System.out.println("hm = " + hm + "\n");
    System.out.println(
      "Looking up prediction for Groundhog #3:");
    Groundhog gh = new Groundhog(3);
    if(hm.containsKey(gh))
      System.out.println((Prediction)hm.get(gh));
    else
      System.out.println("Key not found: " + gh);
  }
} ///:~
```

Each **Groundhog** is given an identity number, so you can look up a **Prediction** in the **HashMap** by saying, "Give me the **Prediction** associated with **Groundhog** number 3." The **Prediction** class contains a **boolean** that is initialized using **Math.random( )**, and a **toString( )** that interprets the result for you. In **main( )**, a **HashMap** is filled with **Groundhog**s and their associated **Prediction**s. The **HashMap** is printed so you can see that it has been filled. Then a **Groundhog** with an identity number of 3 is used as a key to look up the prediction for **Groundhog** #3 (which you can see must be in the **Map**).

It seems simple enough, but it doesn't work. The problem is that **Groundhog** is inherited from the common root class **Object** (which is what happens if you don't specify a base class, thus all classes are ultimately inherited from **Object**). It is **Object**'s **hashCode( )** method that is used to generate the hash code for each object, and by default it just uses the address of its object. Thus, the first instance of

Groundhog(3) does *not* produce a hash code equal to the hash code for the second instance of **Groundhog(3)** that we tried to use as a lookup.

You might think that all you need to do is write an appropriate override for **hashCode( )**. But it still won't work until you've done one more thing: override the **equals( )** that is also part of **Object**. This method is used by the **HashMap** when trying to determine if your key is equal to any of the keys in the table. Again, the default **Object.equals( )** simply compares object addresses, so one **Groundhog(3)** is not equal to another **Groundhog(3)**.

Thus, to use your own classes as keys in a **HashMap**, you must override both **hashCode( )** and **equals( )**, as shown in the following solution to the problem above:

```
//: c09:SpringDetector2.java
// A class that's used as a key in a HashMap
// must override hashCode() and equals().
import java.util.*;

class Groundhog2 {
  int ghNumber;
  Groundhog2(int n) { ghNumber = n; }
  public int hashCode() { return ghNumber; }
  public boolean equals(Object o) {
    return (o instanceof Groundhog2)
      && (ghNumber == ((Groundhog2)o).ghNumber);
  }
}

public class SpringDetector2 {
  public static void main(String[] args) {
    HashMap hm = new HashMap();
    for(int i = 0; i < 10; i++)
      hm.put(new Groundhog2(i),new Prediction());
    System.out.println("hm = " + hm + "\n");
    System.out.println(
      "Looking up prediction for groundhog #3:");
    Groundhog2 gh = new Groundhog2(3);
    if(hm.containsKey(gh))
      System.out.println((Prediction)hm.get(gh));
```

```
    }
} ///:~
```

Note that this uses the **Prediction** class from the previous example, so **SpringDetector.java** must be compiled first or you'll get a compile-time error when you try to compile **SpringDetector2.java**.

Groundhog2.hashCode( ) returns the groundhog number as an identifier. In this example, the programmer is responsible for ensuring that no two groundhogs exist with the same ID number. The **hashCode( )** is not required to return a unique identifier (something you'll understand better later in this chapter), but the **equals( )** method must be able to strictly determine whether two objects are equivalent.

Even though it appears that the **equals( )** method is only checking to see whether the argument is an instance of **Groundhog2** (using the **instanceof** keyword, which is fully explained in Chapter 12), the **instanceof** actually quietly does a second sanity check, to see if the object is **null**, since **instanceof** produces **false** if the left-hand argument is **null**. Assuming it's the correct type and not **null**, the comparison is based on the actual **ghNumber**s. This time, when you run the program, you'll see it produces the correct output.

When creating your own class to use in a **HashSet**, you must pay attention to the same issues as when it is used as a key in a **HashMap**.

Understanding **hashCode( )**

The above example is only a start toward solving the problem correctly. It shows that if you do not override **hashCode( )** and **equals( )** for your key, the hashed data structure (**HashSet** or **HashMap**) will not be able to deal with your key properly. However, to get a good solution for the problem you need to understand what's going on inside the hashed data structure.

First, consider the motivation behind hashing: you want to look up an object using another object. But you can accomplish this with a **TreeSet** or **TreeMap**, too. It's also possible to implement your own **Map**. To do so, the **Map.entrySet( )** method must be supplied to produce a set of **Map.Entry** objects. **MPair** will be defined as the new type of

Map.Entry. In order for it to be placed in a **TreeSet** it must implement **equals( )** and be **Comparable**:

```
//: c09:MPair.java
// A Map implemented with ArrayLists.
import java.util.*;

public class MPair
implements Map.Entry, Comparable {
  Object key, value;
  MPair(Object k, Object v) {
    key = k;
    value = v;
  }
  public Object getKey() { return key; }
  public Object getValue() { return value; }
  public Object setValue(Object v){
    Object result = value;
    value = v;
    return result;
  }
  public boolean equals(Object o) {
    return key.equals(((MPair)o).key);
  }
  public int compareTo(Object rv) {
    return ((Comparable)key).compareTo(
      ((MPair)rv).key);
  }
} ///:~
```

Notice that the comparisons are only interested in the keys, so duplicate values are perfectly acceptable.

The following example implements a **Map** using a pair of **ArrayLists**:

```
//: c09:SlowMap.java
// A Map implemented with ArrayLists.
import java.util.*;
import com.bruceeckel.util.*;

public class SlowMap extends AbstractMap {
  private ArrayList
```

```java
      keys = new ArrayList(),
      values = new ArrayList();
    public Object put(Object key, Object value) {
      Object result = get(key);
      if(!keys.contains(key)) {
        keys.add(key);
        values.add(value);
      } else
        values.set(keys.indexOf(key), value);
      return result;
    }
    public Object get(Object key) {
      if(!keys.contains(key))
        return null;
      return values.get(keys.indexOf(key));
    }
    public Set entrySet() {
      Set entries = new HashSet();
      Iterator
        ki = keys.iterator(),
        vi = values.iterator();
      while(ki.hasNext())
        entries.add(new MPair(ki.next(), vi.next()));
      return entries;
    }
    public static void main(String[] args) {
      SlowMap m = new SlowMap();
      Collections2.fill(m,
        Collections2.geography, 25);
      System.out.println(m);
    }
} ///:~
```

The **put( )** method simply places the keys and values in corresponding **ArrayList**s. In **main( )**, a **SlowMap** is loaded and then printed to show that it works.

This shows that it's not that hard to produce a new type of **Map**. But as the name suggests, a **SlowMap** isn't very fast, so you probably wouldn't use it if you had an alternative available. The problem is in the lookup of the key: there is no order so a simple linear search is used, which is the slowest way to look something up.

The whole point of hashing is speed: hashing allows the lookup to happen quickly. Since the bottleneck is in the speed of the key lookup, one of the solutions to the problem could be by keeping the keys sorted and then using **Collections.binarySearch( )** to perform the lookup (an exercise at the end of this chapter will walk you through this process).

Hashing goes further by saying that all you want to do is to store the key *somewhere* so that it can be quickly found. As you've seen in this chapter, the fastest structure in which to store a group of elements is an array, so that will be used for representing the key information (note carefully that I said "key information," and not the key itself). Also seen in this chapter was the fact that an array, once allocated, cannot be resized, so we have a problem: we want to be able to store any number of values in the **Map**, but if the number of keys is fixed by the array size, how can this be?

The answer is that the array will not hold the keys. From the key object, a number will be derived that will index into the array. This number is the *hash code*, produced by the **hashCode( )** method (in computer science parlance, this is the *hash function*) defined in **Object** and presumably overridden by your class. To solve the problem of the fixed-size array, more than one key may produce the same index. That is, there may be *collisions*. Because of this, it doesn't matter how big the array is because each key object will land somewhere in that array.

So the process of looking up a value starts by computing the hash code and using it to index into the array. If you could guarantee that there were no collisions (which could be possible if you have a fixed number of values) then you'd have a *perfect hashing function*, but that's a special case. In all other cases, collisions are handled by *external chaining*: the array points not directly to a value, but instead to a list of values. These values are searched in a linear fashion using the **equals( )** method. Of course, this aspect of the search is much slower, but if the hash function is good there will only be a few values in each slot, at the most. So instead of searching through the entire list, you quickly jump to a slot where you have to compare a few entries to find the value. This is much faster, which is why the **HashMap** is so quick.

Knowing the basics of hashing, it's possible to implement a simple hashed **Map**:

```java
//: c09:SimpleHashMap.java
// A demonstration hashed Map.
import java.util.*;
import com.bruceeckel.util.*;

public class SimpleHashMap extends AbstractMap {
  // Choose a prime number for the hash table
  // size, to achieve a uniform distribution:
  private final static int SZ = 997;
  private LinkedList[] bucket= new LinkedList[SZ];
  public Object put(Object key, Object value) {
    Object result = null;
    int index = key.hashCode() % SZ;
    if(index < 0) index = -index;
    if(bucket[index] == null)
      bucket[index] = new LinkedList();
    LinkedList pairs = bucket[index];
    MPair pair = new MPair(key, value);
    ListIterator it = pairs.listIterator();
    boolean found = false;
    while(it.hasNext()) {
      Object iPair = it.next();
      if(iPair.equals(pair)) {
        result = ((MPair)iPair).getValue();
        it.set(pair); // Replace old with new
        found = true;
        break;
      }
    }
    if(!found)
      bucket[index].add(pair);
    return result;
  }
  public Object get(Object key) {
    int index = key.hashCode() % SZ;
    if(index < 0) index = -index;
    if(bucket[index] == null) return null;
    LinkedList pairs = bucket[index];
```

```
    MPair match = new MPair(key, null);
    ListIterator it = pairs.listIterator();
    while(it.hasNext()) {
      Object iPair = it.next();
      if(iPair.equals(match))
        return ((MPair)iPair).getValue();
    }
    return null;
  }
  public Set entrySet() {
    Set entries = new HashSet();
    for(int i = 0; i < bucket.length; i++) {
      if(bucket[i] == null) continue;
      Iterator it = bucket[i].iterator();
      while(it.hasNext())
        entries.add(it.next());
    }
    return entries;
  }
  public static void main(String[] args) {
    SimpleHashMap m = new SimpleHashMap();
    Collections2.fill(m,
      Collections2.geography, 25);
    System.out.println(m);
  }
} ///:~
```

Because the "slots" in a hash table are often referred to as *buckets,* the array that represents the actual table is called **bucket**. To promote even distribution, the number of buckets is typically a prime number. Notice that it is an array of **LinkedList**, which automatically provides for collisions—each new item is simply added to the end of the list.

The return value of **put( )** is **null** or, if the key was already in the list, the old value associated with that key. The return value is **result**, which is initialized to **null**, but if a key is discovered in the list then **result** is assigned to that key.

For both **put( )** and **get( )**, the first thing that happens is that the **hashCode( )** is called for the key, and the result is forced to a positive number. Then it is forced to fit into the **bucket** array using the modulus operator and the size of the array. If that location is **null**, it means there are no elements that hash to that location, so a new **LinkedList** is created to hold the object that just did. However, the normal process is to look through the list to see if there are duplicates, and if there are, the old value is put into **result** and the new value replaces the old. The **found** flag keeps track of whether an old key-value pair was found and, if not, the new pair is appended to the end of the list.

In **get( )**, you'll see very similar code as that contained in **put( )**, but simpler. The index is calculated into the **bucket** array, and if a **LinkedList** exists it is searched for a match.

entrySet( ) must find and traverse all the lists, adding them to the result **Set**. Once this method has been created, the **Map** can be tested by filling it with values and then printing them.

HashMap performance factors

To understand the issues, some terminology is necessary:

Capacity: The number of buckets in the table.

Initial capacity: The number of buckets when the table is created. **HashMap** and **HashSet**: have constructors that allow you to specify the initial capacity.

Size: The number of entries currently in the table.

Load factor: size/capacity. A load factor of 0 is an empty table, 0.5 is a half-full table, etc. A lightly-loaded table will have few collisions and so is optimal for insertions and lookups (but will slow down the process of traversing with an iterator). **HashMap** and **HashSet** have constructors that allow you to specify the load factor, which means that when this load factor is reached the container will automatically increase the capacity (the number of buckets) by roughly doubling it, and will redistribute the existing objects into the new set of buckets (this is called *rehashing*).

The default load factor used by **HashMap** is 0.75 (it doesn't rehash until the table is ¾ full). This seems to be a good trade-off between time and space costs. A higher load factor decreases the space required by the table but increases the lookup cost, which is important because lookup is what you do most of the time (including both **get( )** and **put( )**).

If you know that you'll be storing many entries in a **HashMap**, creating it with an appropriately large initial capacity will prevent the overhead of automatic rehashing.

Overriding **hashCode( )**

Now that you understand what's involved in the function of the **HashMap**, the issues involved in writing a **hashCode( )** will make more sense.

First of all, you don't have control of the creation of the actual value that's used to index into the array of buckets. That is dependent on the capacity of the particular **HashMap** object, and that capacity changes depending on how full the container is, and what the load factor is. The value produced by your **hashCode( )** will be further processed in order to create the bucket index (in **SimpleHashMap** the calculation is just a modulo by the size of the bucket array).

The most important factor in creating a **hashCode( )** is that, regardless of when **hashCode( )** is called, it produces the same value for a particular object every time it is called. If you end up with an object that produces one **hashCode( )** value when it is **put( )** into a **HashMap**, and another during a **get( )**, you won't be able to retrieve the objects. So if your **hashCode( )** depends on mutable data in the object the user must be made aware that changing the data will effectively produce a different key by generating a different **hashCode( )**.

In addition, you will probably *not* want to generate a **hashCode( )** that is based on unique object information—in particular, the value of **this** makes a bad **hashCode( )** because then you can't generate a new identical key to the one used to **put( )** the original key-value pair. This was the problem that occurred in **SpringDetector.java** because the default implementation of **hashCode( )** *does* use the object address. So you'll want to use information in the object that identifies the object in a meaningful way.

One example is found in the **String** class. **String**s have the special characteristic that if a program has several **String** objects that contain identical character sequences, then those **String** objects all map to the same memory (the mechanism for this is described in Appendix A). So it

makes sense that the **hashCode( )** produced by two separate instances of
new String("hello") should be identical. You can see it by running this
program:

```
//: c09:StringHashCode.java
public class StringHashCode {
  public static void main(String[] args) {
    System.out.println("Hello".hashCode());
    System.out.println("Hello".hashCode());
  }
} ///:~
```

For this to work, the **hashCode( )** for **String** must be based on the
contents of the **String**.

So for a **hashCode( )** to be effective, it must be fast and it must be
meaningful: that is, it must generate a value based on the contents of the
object. Remember that this value doesn't have to be unique—you should
lean toward speed rather than uniqueness—but between **hashCode( )**
and **equals( )** the identity of the object must be completely resolved.

Because the **hashCode( )** is further processed before the bucket index is
produced, the range of values is not important; it just needs to generate
an **int**.

There's one other factor: a good **hashCode( )** should result in an even
distribution of values. If the values tend to cluster, then the **HashMap** or
HashSet will be more heavily loaded in some areas and will not be as fast
as it could be with an evenly distributed hashing function.

Here's an example that follows these guidelines:

```
//: c09:CountedString.java
// Creating a good hashCode().
import java.util.*;

public class CountedString {
  private String s;
  private int id = 0;
  private static ArrayList created =
    new ArrayList();
  public CountedString(String str) {
```

```
      s = str;
      created.add(s);
      Iterator it = created.iterator();
      // Id is the total number of instances
      // of this string in use by CountedString:
      while(it.hasNext())
        if(it.next().equals(s))
          id++;
  }
  public String toString() {
    return "String: " + s + " id: " + id +
      " hashCode(): " + hashCode() + "\n";
  }
  public int hashCode() {
    return s.hashCode() * id;
  }
  public boolean equals(Object o) {
    return (o instanceof CountedString)
      && s.equals(((CountedString)o).s)
      && id == ((CountedString)o).id;
  }
  public static void main(String[] args) {
    HashMap m = new HashMap();
    CountedString[] cs = new CountedString[10];
    for(int i = 0; i < cs.length; i++) {
      cs[i] = new CountedString("hi");
      m.put(cs[i], new Integer(i));
    }
    System.out.println(m);
    for(int i = 0; i < cs.length; i++) {
      System.out.print("Looking up " + cs[i]);
      System.out.println(m.get(cs[i]));
    }
  }
} ///:~
```

CountedString includes a **String** and an **id** that represents the number
of **CountedString** objects that contain an identical **String**. The counting
is accomplished in the constructor by iterating through the **static**
ArrayList where all the **String**s are stored.

Both **hashCode( )** and **equals( )** produce results based on both fields; if they were just based on the **String** alone or the **id** alone there would be duplicate matches for distinct values.

Note how simple the **hashCode( )** is: **String**'s **hashCode( )** is multiplied by the **id**. Smaller is generally better (and faster) for **hashCode( )**.

In **main( )**, a bunch of **CountedString** objects are created, using the same **String** to show that the duplicates create unique values because of the count **id**. The **HashMap** is displayed so that you can see how it is stored internally (no discernible orders) and then each key is looked up individually to demonstrate that the lookup mechanism is working properly.

Holding references

The **java.lang.ref** library contains a set of classes that allow greater flexibility in garbage collection, which are especially useful when you have large objects that may cause memory exhaustion. There are three classes inherited from the abstract class **Reference**: **SoftReference**, **WeakReference**, and **PhantomReference**. Each of these provides a different level of indirection for the garbage collector, if the object in question is *only* reachable through one of these **Reference** objects.

If an object is *reachable* it means that somewhere in your program the object can be found. This could mean that you have an ordinary reference on the stack that goes right to the object, but you might also have a reference to an object that has a reference to the object in question; there could be many intermediate links. If an object is reachable, the garbage collector cannot release it because it's still in use by your program. If an object isn't reachable, there's no way for your program to use it so it's safe to garbage-collect that object.

You use **Reference** objects when you want to continue to hold onto a reference to that object—you want to be able to reach that object—but you also want to allow the garbage collector to release that object. Thus, you have a way to go on using the object, but if memory exhaustion is imminent you allow that object to be released.

You accomplish this by using a **Reference** object as an intermediary between you and the ordinary reference, *and* there must be no ordinary references to the object (ones that are not wrapped inside **Reference** objects). If the garbage collector discovers that an object is reachable through an ordinary reference, it will not release that object.

In the order **SoftReference**, **WeakReference**, and **PhantomReference**, each one is "weaker" than the last, and corresponds to a different level of reachability. Soft references are for implementing memory-sensitive caches. Weak references are for implementing "canonicalizing mappings"—where instances of objects can be simultaneously used in multiple places in a program, to save storage— that do not prevent their keys (or values) from being reclaimed. Phantom references are for scheduling pre-mortem cleanup actions in a more flexible way than is possible with the Java finalization mechanism.

With **SoftReference**s and **WeakReference**s, you have a choice about whether to place them on a **ReferenceQueue** (the device used for premortem cleanup actions), but a **PhantomReference** can only be built on a **ReferenceQueue**. Here's a simple demonstration:

```
//: c09:References.java
// Demonstrates Reference objects
import java.lang.ref.*;

class VeryBig {
  static final int SZ = 10000;
  double[] d = new double[SZ];
  String ident;
  public VeryBig(String id) { ident = id; }
  public String toString() { return ident; }
  public void finalize() {
    System.out.println("Finalizing " + ident);
  }
}

public class References {
  static ReferenceQueue rq= new ReferenceQueue();
  public static void checkQueue() {
    Object inq = rq.poll();
    if(inq != null)
```

```java
      System.out.println("In queue: " +
        (VeryBig)((Reference)inq).get());
  }
  public static void main(String[] args) {
    int size = 10;
    // Or, choose size via the command line:
    if(args.length > 0)
      size = Integer.parseInt(args[0]);
    SoftReference[] sa =
      new SoftReference[size];
    for(int i = 0; i < sa.length; i++) {
      sa[i] = new SoftReference(
        new VeryBig("Soft " + i), rq);
      System.out.println("Just created: " +
        (VeryBig)sa[i].get());
      checkQueue();
    }
    WeakReference[] wa =
      new WeakReference[size];
    for(int i = 0; i < wa.length; i++) {
      wa[i] = new WeakReference(
        new VeryBig("Weak " + i), rq);
      System.out.println("Just created: " +
        (VeryBig)wa[i].get());
      checkQueue();
    }
    SoftReference s = new SoftReference(
      new VeryBig("Soft"));
    WeakReference w = new WeakReference(
      new VeryBig("Weak"));
    System.gc();
    PhantomReference[] pa =
      new PhantomReference[size];
    for(int i = 0; i < pa.length; i++) {
      pa[i] = new PhantomReference(
        new VeryBig("Phantom " + i), rq);
      System.out.println("Just created: " +
        (VeryBig)pa[i].get());
      checkQueue();
    }
  }
}
```

```
} ///:~
```

When you run this program (you'll want to pipe the output through a "more" utility so that you can view the output in pages), you'll see that the objects are garbage-collected, even though you still have access to them through the **Reference** object (to get the actual object reference, you use **get( )**). You'll also see that the **ReferenceQueue** always produces a **Reference** containing a **null** object. To make use of this, you can inherit from the particular **Reference** class you're interested in and add more useful methods to the new type of **Reference**.

The **WeakHashMap**

The containers library has a special **Map** to hold weak references: the **WeakHashMap**. This class is designed to make the creation of canonicalized mappings easier. In such a mapping, you are saving storage by making only one instance of a particular value. When the program needs that value, it looks up the existing object in the mapping and uses that (rather than creating one from scratch). The mapping may make the values as part of its initialization, but it's more likely that the values are made on demand.

Since this is a storage-saving technique, it's very convenient that the **WeakHashMap** allows the garbage collector to automatically clean up the keys and values. You don't have to do anything special to the keys and values you want to place in the **WeakHashMap**; these are automatically wrapped in **WeakReference**s by the map. The trigger to allow cleanup is if the key is no longer in use, as demonstrated here:

```
//: c09:CanonicalMapping.java
// Demonstrates WeakHashMap.
import java.util.*;
import java.lang.ref.*;

class Key {
  String ident;
  public Key(String id) { ident = id; }
  public String toString() { return ident; }
  public int hashCode() {
    return ident.hashCode();
  }
```

```java
  public boolean equals(Object r) {
    return (r instanceof Key)
      && ident.equals(((Key)r).ident);
  }
  public void finalize() {
    System.out.println("Finalizing Key "+ ident);
  }
}

class Value {
  String ident;
  public Value(String id) { ident = id; }
  public String toString() { return ident; }
  public void finalize() {
    System.out.println("Finalizing Value "+ident);
  }
}

public class CanonicalMapping {
  public static void main(String[] args) {
    int size = 1000;
    // Or, choose size via the command line:
    if(args.length > 0)
      size = Integer.parseInt(args[0]);
    Key[] keys = new Key[size];
    WeakHashMap whm = new WeakHashMap();
    for(int i = 0; i < size; i++) {
      Key k = new Key(Integer.toString(i));
      Value v = new Value(Integer.toString(i));
      if(i % 3 == 0)
        keys[i] = k; // Save as "real" references
      whm.put(k, v);
    }
    System.gc();
  }
} ///:~
```

The **Key** class must have a **hashCode( )** and an **equals( )** since it is being used as a key in a hashed data structure, as described previously in this chapter.

When you run the program you'll see that the garbage collector will skip every third key, because an ordinary reference to that key has also been placed in the **keys** array and thus those objects cannot be garbage-collected.

Iterators revisited

We can now demonstrate the true power of the **Iterator**: the ability to separate the operation of traversing a sequence from the underlying structure of that sequence. In the following example, the class **PrintData** uses an **Iterator** to move through a sequence and call the **toString( )** method for every object. Two different types of containers are created—an **ArrayList** and a **HashMap**—and they are each filled with, respectively, **Mouse** and **Hamster** objects. (These classes are defined earlier in this chapter.) Because an **Iterator** hides the structure of the underlying container, **PrintData** doesn't know or care what kind of container the **Iterator** comes from:

```
//: c09:Iterators2.java
// Revisiting Iterators.
import java.util.*;

class PrintData {
  static void print(Iterator e) {
    while(e.hasNext())
      System.out.println(e.next());
  }
}

class Iterators2 {
  public static void main(String[] args) {
    ArrayList v = new ArrayList();
    for(int i = 0; i < 5; i++)
      v.add(new Mouse(i));
    HashMap m = new HashMap();
    for(int i = 0; i < 5; i++)
      m.put(new Integer(i), new Hamster(i));
    System.out.println("ArrayList");
    PrintData.print(v.iterator());
    System.out.println("HashMap");
```

```
        PrintData.print(m.entrySet().iterator());
    }
} ///:~
```

For the **HashMap**, the **entrySet( )** method produces a **Set** of **Map.entry** objects, which contain both the key and the value for each entry, so you see both of them printed.

Note that **PrintData.print( )** takes advantage of the fact that the objects in these containers are of class **Object** so the call **toString( )** by **System.out.println( )** is automatic. It's more likely that in your problem, you must make the assumption that your **Iterator** is walking through a container of some specific type. For example, you might assume that everything in the container is a **Shape** with a **draw( )** method. Then you must downcast from the **Object** that **Iterator.next( )** returns to produce a **Shape**.

Choosing an implementation

By now you should understand that there are really only three container components: **Map**, **List**, and **Set**, and only two or three implementations of each interface. If you need to use the functionality offered by a particular **interface**, how do you decide which particular implementation to use?

To understand the answer, you must be aware that each different implementation has its own features, strengths, and weaknesses. For example, you can see in the diagram that the "feature" of **Hashtable**, **Vector**, and **Stack** is that they are legacy classes, so that old code doesn't break. On the other hand, it's best if you don't use those for new (Java 2) code.

The distinction between the other containers often comes down to what they are "backed by"; that is, the data structures that physically implement your desired **interface**. This means that, for example, **ArrayList** and **LinkedList** implement the **List** interface so your program will produce the same results regardless of the one you use.

However, **ArrayList** is backed by an array, while the **LinkedList** is implemented in the usual way for a doubly linked list, as individual objects each containing data along with references to the previous and next elements in the list. Because of this, if you want to do many insertions and removals in the middle of a list, a **LinkedList** is the appropriate choice. (**LinkedList** also has additional functionality that is established in **AbstractSequentialList**.) If not, an **ArrayList** is typically faster.

As another example, a **Set** can be implemented as either a **TreeSet** or a **HashSet**. A **TreeSet** is backed by a **TreeMap** and is designed to produce a constantly sorted set. However, if you're going to have larger quantities in your **Set**, the performance of **TreeSet** insertions will get slow. When you're writing a program that needs a **Set**, you should choose **HashSet** by default, and change to **TreeSet** when it's more important to have a constantly sorted set.

Choosing between **List**s

The most convincing way to see the differences between the implementations of **List** is with a performance test. The following code establishes an inner base class to use as a test framework, then creates an array of anonymous inner classes, one for each different test. Each of these inner classes is called by the **test( )** method. This approach allows you to easily add and remove new kinds of tests.

```
//: c09:ListPerformance.java
// Demonstrates performance differences in Lists.
import java.util.*;
import com.bruceeckel.util.*;

public class ListPerformance {
  private abstract static class Tester {
    String name;
    int size; // Test quantity
    Tester(String name, int size) {
      this.name = name;
      this.size = size;
    }
    abstract void test(List a, int reps);
```

```
      }
    private static Tester[] tests = {
      new Tester("get", 300) {
        void test(List a, int reps) {
          for(int i = 0; i < reps; i++) {
            for(int j = 0; j < a.size(); j++)
              a.get(j);
          }
        }
      },
      new Tester("iteration", 300) {
        void test(List a, int reps) {
          for(int i = 0; i < reps; i++) {
            Iterator it = a.iterator();
            while(it.hasNext())
              it.next();
          }
        }
      },
      new Tester("insert", 5000) {
        void test(List a, int reps) {
          int half = a.size()/2;
          String s = "test";
          ListIterator it = a.listIterator(half);
          for(int i = 0; i < size * 10; i++)
            it.add(s);
        }
      },
      new Tester("remove", 5000) {
        void test(List a, int reps) {
          ListIterator it = a.listIterator(3);
          while(it.hasNext()) {
            it.next();
            it.remove();
          }
        }
      },
    };
    public static void test(List a, int reps) {
      // A trick to print out the class name:
      System.out.println("Testing " +
```

```
        a.getClass().getName());
    for(int i = 0; i < tests.length; i++) {
      Collections2.fill(a,
        Collections2.countries.reset(),
        tests[i].size);
      System.out.print(tests[i].name);
      long t1 = System.currentTimeMillis();
      tests[i].test(a, reps);
      long t2 = System.currentTimeMillis();
      System.out.println(": " + (t2 - t1));
    }
  }
  public static void testArray(int reps) {
    System.out.println("Testing array as List");
    // Can only do first two tests on an array:
    for(int i = 0; i < 2; i++) {
      String[] sa = new String[tests[i].size];
      Arrays2.fill(sa,
        Collections2.countries.reset());
      List a = Arrays.asList(sa);
      System.out.print(tests[i].name);
      long t1 = System.currentTimeMillis();
      tests[i].test(a, reps);
      long t2 = System.currentTimeMillis();
      System.out.println(": " + (t2 - t1));
    }
  }
  public static void main(String[] args) {
    int reps = 50000;
    // Or, choose the number of repetitions
    // via the command line:
    if(args.length > 0)
      reps = Integer.parseInt(args[0]);
    System.out.println(reps + " repetitions");
    testArray(reps);
    test(new ArrayList(), reps);
    test(new LinkedList(), reps);
    test(new Vector(), reps);
  }
} ///:~
```

The inner class **Tester** is **abstract**, to provide a base class for the specific tests. It contains a **String** to be printed when the test starts, a **size** parameter to be used by the test for quantity of elements or repetitions of tests, a constructor to initialize the fields, and an **abstract** method **test( )** that does the work. All the different types of tests are collected in one place, the array **tests**, which is initialized with different anonymous inner classes that inherit from **Tester**. To add or remove tests, simply add or remove an inner class definition from the array, and everything else happens automatically.

To compare array access to container access (primarily against **ArrayList**), a special test is created for arrays by wrapping one as a **List** using **Arrays.asList( )**. Note that only the first two tests can be performed in this case, because you cannot insert or remove elements from an array.

The **List** that's handed to **test( )** is first filled with elements, then each test in the **tests** array is timed. The results will vary from machine to machine; they are intended to give only an order of magnitude comparison between the performance of the different containers. Here is a summary of one run:

Type	Get	Iteration	Insert	Remove
array	1430	3850	na	na
ArrayList	3070	12200	500	46850
LinkedList	16320	9110	110	60
Vector	4890	16250	550	46850

As expected, arrays are faster than any container for random-access lookups and iteration. You can see that random accesses (**get( )**) are cheap for **ArrayList**s and expensive for **LinkedList**s. (Oddly, iteration is *faster* for a **LinkedList** than an **ArrayList**, which is a bit counterintuitive.) On the other hand, insertions and removals from the middle of a list are dramatically cheaper for a **LinkedList** than for an **ArrayList**—*especially* removals. **Vector** is generally not as fast as **ArrayList**, and it should be avoided; it's only in the library for legacy code support (the only reason it works in this program is because it was adapted to be a **List** in Java 2). The best approach is probably to choose

---

an **ArrayList** as your default, and to change to a **LinkedList** if you
discover performance problems due to many insertions and removals
from the middle of the list. And of course, if you are working with a fixed-
sized group of elements, use an array.

Choosing between **Set**s

You can choose between a **TreeSet** and a **HashSet**, depending on the
size of the **Set** (if you need to produce an ordered sequence from a **Set**,
use **TreeSet**). The following test program gives an indication of this
trade-off:

```
//: c09:SetPerformance.java
import java.util.*;
import com.bruceeckel.util.*;

public class SetPerformance {
  private abstract static class Tester {
    String name;
    Tester(String name) { this.name = name; }
    abstract void test(Set s, int size, int reps);
  }
  private static Tester[] tests = {
    new Tester("add") {
      void test(Set s, int size, int reps) {
        for(int i = 0; i < reps; i++) {
          s.clear();
          Collections2.fill(s,
            Collections2.countries.reset(),size);
        }
      }
    },
    new Tester("contains") {
      void test(Set s, int size, int reps) {
        for(int i = 0; i < reps; i++)
          for(int j = 0; j < size; j++)
            s.contains(Integer.toString(j));
      }
    },
    new Tester("iteration") {
      void test(Set s, int size, int reps) {
```

```java
      for(int i = 0; i < reps * 10; i++) {
        Iterator it = s.iterator();
        while(it.hasNext())
          it.next();
      }
    }
  },
};
public static void
test(Set s, int size, int reps) {
  System.out.println("Testing " +
    s.getClass().getName() + " size " + size);
  Collections2.fill(s,
    Collections2.countries.reset(), size);
  for(int i = 0; i < tests.length; i++) {
    System.out.print(tests[i].name);
    long t1 = System.currentTimeMillis();
    tests[i].test(s, size, reps);
    long t2 = System.currentTimeMillis();
    System.out.println(": " +
      ((double)(t2 - t1)/(double)size));
  }
}
public static void main(String[] args) {
  int reps = 50000;
  // Or, choose the number of repetitions
  // via the command line:
  if(args.length > 0)
    reps = Integer.parseInt(args[0]);
  // Small:
  test(new TreeSet(), 10, reps);
  test(new HashSet(), 10, reps);
  // Medium:
  test(new TreeSet(), 100, reps);
  test(new HashSet(), 100, reps);
  // Large:
  test(new TreeSet(), 1000, reps);
  test(new HashSet(), 1000, reps);
}
} ///:~
```

The following table shows the results of one run. (Of course, this will be different according to the computer and JVM you are using; you should run the test yourself as well):

Type	Test size	Add	Contains	Iteration
TreeSet	10	138.0	115.0	187.0
	100	189.5	151.1	206.5
	1000	150.6	177.4	40.04
HashSet	10	55.0	82.0	192.0
	100	45.6	90.0	202.2
	1000	36.14	106.5	39.39

The performance of **HashSet** is generally superior to **TreeSet** for all operations (but in particular addition and lookup, the two most important operations). The only reason **TreeSet** exists is because it maintains its elements in sorted order, so you only use it when you need a sorted **Set**.

Choosing between **Map**s

When choosing between implementations of **Map**, the size of the **Map** is what most strongly affects performance, and the following test program gives an indication of this trade-off:

```
//: c09:MapPerformance.java
// Demonstrates performance differences in Maps.
import java.util.*;
import com.bruceeckel.util.*;

public class MapPerformance {
  private abstract static class Tester {
    String name;
    Tester(String name) { this.name = name; }
    abstract void test(Map m, int size, int reps);
  }
  private static Tester[] tests = {
    new Tester("put") {
      void test(Map m, int size, int reps) {
        for(int i = 0; i < reps; i++) {
          m.clear();
```

```
              Collections2.fill(m,
                Collections2.geography.reset(), size);
            }
          }
        },
      new Tester("get") {
        void test(Map m, int size, int reps) {
          for(int i = 0; i < reps; i++)
            for(int j = 0; j < size; j++)
              m.get(Integer.toString(j));
        }
      },
      new Tester("iteration") {
        void test(Map m, int size, int reps) {
          for(int i = 0; i < reps * 10; i++) {
            Iterator it = m.entrySet().iterator();
            while(it.hasNext())
              it.next();
          }
        }
      },
    };
  public static void
  test(Map m, int size, int reps) {
    System.out.println("Testing " +
      m.getClass().getName() + " size " + size);
    Collections2.fill(m,
      Collections2.geography.reset(), size);
    for(int i = 0; i < tests.length; i++) {
      System.out.print(tests[i].name);
      long t1 = System.currentTimeMillis();
      tests[i].test(m, size, reps);
      long t2 = System.currentTimeMillis();
      System.out.println(": " +
        ((double)(t2 - t1)/(double)size));
    }
  }
  public static void main(String[] args) {
    int reps = 50000;
    // Or, choose the number of repetitions
    // via the command line:
```

```
  if(args.length > 0)
    reps = Integer.parseInt(args[0]);
  // Small:
  test(new TreeMap(), 10, reps);
  test(new HashMap(), 10, reps);
  test(new Hashtable(), 10, reps);
  // Medium:
  test(new TreeMap(), 100, reps);
  test(new HashMap(), 100, reps);
  test(new Hashtable(), 100, reps);
  // Large:
  test(new TreeMap(), 1000, reps);
  test(new HashMap(), 1000, reps);
  test(new Hashtable(), 1000, reps);
  }
} ///:~
```

Because the size of the map is the issue, you'll see that the timing tests divide the time by the size to normalize each measurement. Here is one set of results. (Yours will probably be different.)

Type	Test size	Put	Get	Iteration
TreeMap	10	143.0	110.0	186.0
	100	201.1	188.4	280.1
	1000	222.8	205.2	40.7
HashMap	10	66.0	83.0	197.0
	100	80.7	135.7	278.5
	1000	48.2	105.7	41.4
Hashtable	10	61.0	93.0	302.0
	100	90.6	143.3	329.0
	1000	54.1	110.95	47.3

As you might expect, **Hashtable** performance is roughly equivalent to **HashMap**. (You can also see that **HashMap** is generally a bit faster. **HashMap** is intended to replace **Hashtable**.) The **TreeMap** is generally slower than the **HashMap**, so why would you use it? So you could use it not as a **Map**, but as a way to create an ordered list. The behavior of a tree is such that it's always in order and doesn't have to be specially sorted. Once you fill a **TreeMap**, you can call **keySet( )** to get a **Set** view of the keys, then **toArray( )** to produce an array of those keys. You can then use the **static** method **Arrays.binarySearch( )** (discussed later) to rapidly find objects in your sorted array. Of course, you would probably only do this if, for some reason, the behavior of a **HashMap** was unacceptable, since **HashMap** is designed to rapidly find things. Also, you can easily create a **HashMap** from a **TreeMap** with a single object creation In the end, when you're using a **Map** your first choice should be **HashMap**, and only if you need a constantly sorted **Map** will you need **TreeMap**.

Sorting and searching
Lists

Utilities to perform sorting and searching for **List**s have the same names and signatures as those for sorting arrays of objects, but are **static** methods of **Collections** instead of **Arrays**. Here's an example, modified from **ArraySearching.java**:

```
//: c09:ListSortSearch.java
// Sorting and searching Lists with 'Collections.'
import com.bruceeckel.util.*;
import java.util.*;

public class ListSortSearch {
  public static void main(String[] args) {
    List list = new ArrayList();
    Collections2.fill(list,
      Collections2.capitals, 25);
    System.out.println(list + "\n");
    Collections.shuffle(list);
    System.out.println("After shuffling: "+list);
    Collections.sort(list);
    System.out.println(list + "\n");
    Object key = list.get(12);
    int index =
      Collections.binarySearch(list, key);
```

```
        System.out.println("Location of " + key +
            " is " + index + ", list.get(" +
            index + ") = " + list.get(index));
        AlphabeticComparator comp =
            new AlphabeticComparator();
        Collections.sort(list, comp);
        System.out.println(list + "\n");
        key = list.get(12);
        index =
            Collections.binarySearch(list, key, comp);
        System.out.println("Location of " + key +
            " is " + index + ", list.get(" +
            index + ") = " + list.get(index));
    }
} ///:~
```

The use of these methods is identical to the ones in **Arrays**, but you're using a **List** instead of an array. Just like searching and sorting with arrays, if you sort using a **Comparator** you must **binarySearch( )** using the same **Comparator**.

This program also demonstrates the **shufflc( )** method in **Collections**, which randomizes the order of a **List**.

Utilities

There are a number of other useful utilities in the **Collections** class:

enumeration(Collection)	Produces an old-style **Enumeration** for the argument.
max(Collection) min(Collection)	Produces the maximum or minimum element in the argument using the natural comparison method of the objects in the **Collection**.
max(Collection, Comparator) min(Collection, Comparator)	Produces the maximum or minimum element in the **Collection** using the **Comparator**.
reverse( )	Reverses all the elements in

	place.
copy(List dest, List src)	Copies elements from src to dest.
fill(List list, Object o)	Replaces all the elements of list with o.
nCopies(int n, Object o)	Returns an immutable **List** of size n whose references all point to o.

Note that **min( )** and **max( )** work with **Collection** objects, not with **List**s, so you don't need to worry about whether the **Collection** should be sorted or not. (As mentioned earlier, you *do* need to **sort( )** a **List** or an array before performing a **binarySearch( )**.)

Making a **Collection** or **Map** unmodifiable

Often it is convenient to create a read-only version of a **Collection** or **Map**. The **Collections** class allows you to do this by passing the original container into a method that hands back a read-only version. There are four variations on this method, one each for **Collection** (if you don't want to treat a **Collection** as a more specific type), **List**, **Set**, and **Map**. This example shows the proper way to build read-only versions of each:

```
//: c09:ReadOnly.java
// Using the Collections.unmodifiable methods.
import java.util.*;
import com.bruceeckel.util.*;

public class ReadOnly {
  static Collections2.StringGenerator gen =
    Collections2.countries;
  public static void main(String[] args) {
    Collection c = new ArrayList();
    Collections2.fill(c, gen, 25); // Insert data
    c = Collections.unmodifiableCollection(c);
    System.out.println(c); // Reading is OK
    c.add("one"); // Can't change it

    List a = new ArrayList();
```

```
   Collections2.fill(a, gen.reset(), 25);
   a = Collections.unmodifiableList(a);
   ListIterator lit = a.listIterator();
   System.out.println(lit.next()); // Reading OK
   lit.add("one"); // Can't change it

   Set s = new HashSet();
   Collections2.fill(s, gen.reset(), 25);
   s = Collections.unmodifiableSet(s);
   System.out.println(s); // Reading OK
   //! s.add("one"); // Can't change it

   Map m = new HashMap();
   Collections2.fill(m,
     Collections2.geography, 25);
   m = Collections.unmodifiableMap(m);
   System.out.println(m); // Reading OK
   //! m.put("Ralph", "Howdy!");
  }
} ///:~
```

In each case, you must fill the container with meaningful data *before* you make it read-only. Once it is loaded, the best approach is to replace the existing reference with the reference that is produced by the "unmodifiable" call. That way, you don't run the risk of accidentally changing the contents once you've made it unmodifiable. On the other hand, this tool also allows you to keep a modifiable container as **private** within a class and to return a read-only reference to that container from a method call. So you can change it from within the class, but everyone else can only read it.

Calling the "unmodifiable" method for a particular type does not cause compile-time checking, but once the transformation has occurred, any calls to methods that modify the contents of a particular container will produce an **UnsupportedOperationException**.

Synchronizing a **Collection** or **Map**

The **synchronized** keyword is an important part of the subject of *multithreading*, a more complicated topic that will not be introduced until Chapter 14. Here, I shall note only that the **Collections** class contains a way to automatically synchronize an entire container. The syntax is similar to the "unmodifiable" methods:

```
//: c09:Synchronization.java
// Using the Collections.synchronized methods.
import java.util.*;

public class Synchronization {
  public static void main(String[] args) {
    Collection c =
      Collections.synchronizedCollection(
        new ArrayList());
    List list = Collections.synchronizedList(
      new ArrayList());
    Set s = Collections.synchronizedSet(
      new HashSet());
    Map m = Collections.synchronizedMap(
      new HashMap());
  }
} ///:~
```

In this case, you immediately pass the new container through the appropriate "synchronized" method; that way there's no chance of accidentally exposing the unsynchronized version.

Fail fast

The Java containers also have a mechanism to prevent more than one process from modifying the contents of a container. The problem occurs if you're iterating through a container and some other process steps in and inserts, removes, or changes an object in that container. Maybe you've already passed that object, maybe it's ahead of you, maybe the size of the container shrinks after you call **size( )**—there are many scenarios for disaster. The Java containers library incorporates a *fail-fast* mechanism that looks for any changes to the container other than the ones your process is personally responsible for. If it detects that someone else is modifying the container, it immediately produces a **ConcurrentModificationException**. This is the "fail-fast" aspect—it doesn't try to detect a problem later on using a more complex algorithm.

It's quite easy to see the fail-fast mechanism in operation—all you have to do is create an iterator and then add something to the collection that the iterator is pointing to, like this:

```
//: c09:FailFast.java
// Demonstrates the "fail fast" behavior.
import java.util.*;

public class FailFast {
  public static void main(String[] args) {
    Collection c = new ArrayList();
    Iterator it = c.iterator();
    c.add("An object");
    // Causes an exception:
    String s = (String)it.next();
  }
} ///:~
```

The exception happens because something is placed in the container *after* the iterator is acquired from the container. The possibility that two parts of the program could be modifying the same container produces an uncertain state, so the exception notifies you that you should change your code—in this case, acquire the iterator *after* you have added all the elements to the container.

Note that you cannot benefit from this kind of monitoring when you're accessing the elements of a **List** using **get( )**.

Unsupported operations

It's possible to turn an array into a **List** with the **Arrays.asList( )** method:

```
//: c09:Unsupported.java
// Sometimes methods defined in the
// Collection interfaces don't work!
import java.util.*;

public class Unsupported {
  private static String[] s = {
    "one", "two", "three", "four", "five",
```

```
      "six", "seven", "eight", "nine", "ten",
  };
  static List a = Arrays.asList(s);
  static List a2 = a.subList(3, 6);
  public static void main(String[] args) {
    System.out.println(a);
    System.out.println(a2);
    System.out.println(
      "a.contains(" + s[0] + ") = " +
      a.contains(s[0]));
    System.out.println(
      "a.containsAll(a2) = " +
      a.containsAll(a2));
    System.out.println("a.isEmpty() = " +
      a.isEmpty());
    System.out.println(
      "a.indexOf(" + s[5] + ") = " +
      a.indexOf(s[5]));
    // Traverse backwards:
    ListIterator lit = a.listIterator(a.size());
    while(lit.hasPrevious())
      System.out.print(lit.previous() + " ");
    System.out.println();
    // Set the elements to different values:
    for(int i = 0; i < a.size(); i++)
      a.set(i, "47");
    System.out.println(a);
    // Compiles, but won't run:
    lit.add("X"); // Unsupported operation
    a.clear(); // Unsupported
    a.add("eleven"); // Unsupported
    a.addAll(a2); // Unsupported
    a.retainAll(a2); // Unsupported
    a.remove(s[0]); // Unsupported
    a.removeAll(a2); // Unsupported
  }
} ///:~
```

You'll discover that only a portion of the **Collection** and **List** interfaces
are actually implemented. The rest of the methods cause the unwelcome
appearance of something called an

UnsupportedOperationException. You'll learn all about exceptions in the next chapter, but the short story is that the **Collection interface**—as well as some of the other **interface**s in the Java containers library—contain "optional" methods, which might or might not be "supported" in the concrete class that **implements** that **interface**. Calling an unsupported method causes an **UnsupportedOperationException** to indicate a programming error.

"What?!?" you say, incredulous. "The whole point of **interface**s and base classes is that they promise these methods will do something meaningful! This breaks that promise—it says that not only will calling some methods *not* perform a meaningful behavior, they will stop the program! Type safety was just thrown out the window!"

It's not quite that bad. With a **Collection**, **List**, **Set**, or **Map**, the compiler still restricts you to calling only the methods in that **interface**, so it's not like Smalltalk (in which you can call any method for any object, and find out only when you run the program whether your call does anything). In addition, most methods that take a **Collection** as an argument only read from that **Collection**—all the "read" methods of **Collection** are *not* optional.

This approach prevents an explosion of interfaces in the design. Other designs for container libraries always seem to end up with a confusing plethora of interfaces to describe each of the variations on the main theme and are thus difficult to learn. It's not even possible to capture all of the special cases in **interface**s, because someone can always invent a new **interface**. The "unsupported operation" approach achieves an important goal of the Java containers library: the containers are simple to learn and use; unsupported operations are a special case that can be learned later. For this approach to work, however:

1. The **UnsupportedOperationException** must be a rare event. That is, for most classes all operations should work, and only in special cases should an operation be unsupported. This is true in the Java containers library, since the classes you'll use 99 percent of the time—**ArrayList**, **LinkedList**, **HashSet**, and **HashMap**, as well as the other concrete implementations—support all of the operations. The design does provide a "back door" if you want to

create a new **Collection** without providing meaningful definitions for all the methods in the **Collection interface**, and yet still fit it into the existing library.

2.   When an operation *is* unsupported, there should be reasonable likelihood that an **UnsupportedOperationException** will appear at implementation time, rather than after you've shipped the product to the customer. After all, it indicates a programming error: you've used an implementation incorrectly. This point is less certain, and is where the experimental nature of this design comes into play. Only over time will we find out how well it works.

In the example above, **Arrays.asList( )** produces a **List** that is backed by a fixed-size array. Therefore it makes sense that the only supported operations are the ones that don't change the size of the array. If, on the other hand, a new **interface** were required to express this different kind of behavior (called, perhaps, "**FixedSizeList**"), it would throw open the door to complexity and soon you wouldn't know where to start when trying to use the library.

The documentation for a method that takes a **Collection**, **List**, **Set**, or **Map** as an argument should specify which of the optional methods must be implemented. For example, sorting requires the **set( )** and **Iterator.set( )** methods, but not **add( )** and **remove( )**.

Java 1.0/1.1 containers

Unfortunately, a lot of code was written using the Java 1.0/1.1 containers, and even new code is sometimes written using these classes. So although you should never use the old containers when writing new code, you'll still need to be aware of them. However, the old containers were quite limited, so there's not that much to say about them. (Since they are in the past, I will try to refrain from overemphasizing some of the hideous design decisions.)

Vector & Enumeration

The only self-expanding sequence in Java 1.0/1.1 was the **Vector**, and so it saw a lot of use. Its flaws are too numerous to describe here (see the first edition of this book, available on this book's CD ROM and as a free download from *www.BruceEckel.com*). Basically, you can think of it as an **ArrayList** with long, awkward method names. In the Java 2 container library, **Vector** was adapted so that it could fit as a **Collection** and a **List**, so in the following example the **Collections2.fill( )** method is successfully used. This turns out to be a bit perverse, as it may confuse some people into thinking that **Vector** has gotten better, when it is actually included only to support pre-Java 2 code.

The Java 1.0/1.1 version of the iterator chose to invent a new name, "enumeration," instead of using a term that everyone was already familiar with. The **Enumeration** interface is smaller than **Iterator**, with only two methods, and it uses longer method names: **boolean hasMoreElements( )** produces **true** if this enumeration contains more elements, and **Object nextElement( )** returns the next element of this enumeration if there are any more (otherwise it throws an exception).

Enumeration is only an interface, not an implementation, and even new libraries sometimes still use the old **Enumeration**—which is unfortunate but generally harmless. Even though you should always use **Iterator** when you can in your own code, you must be prepared for libraries that want to hand you an **Enumeration**.

In addition, you can produce an **Enumeration** for any **Collection** by using the **Collections.enumeration( )** method, as seen in this example:

```
//: c09:Enumerations.java
// Java 1.0/1.1 Vector and Enumeration.
import java.util.*;
import com.bruceeckel.util.*;

class Enumerations {
  public static void main(String[] args) {
    Vector v = new Vector();
    Collections2.fill(
      v, Collections2.countries, 100);
    Enumeration e = v.elements();
    while(e.hasMoreElements())
      System.out.println(e.nextElement());
```

```
      // Produce an Enumeration from a Collection:
      e = Collections.enumeration(new ArrayList());
   }
} ///:~
```

The Java 1.0/1.1 **Vector** has only an **addElement( )** method, but **fill( )** uses the **add( )** method that was pasted on as **Vector** was turned into a **List**. To produce an **Enumeration**, you call **elements( )**, then you can use it to perform a forward iteration.

The last line creates an **ArrayList** and uses **enumeration( )** to adapt an **Enumeration** from the **ArrayList Iterator**. Thus, if you have old code that wants an **Enumeration**, you can still use the new containers.

Hashtable

As you've seen in the performance comparison in this chapter, the basic **Hashtable** is very similar to the **HashMap**, even down to the method names. There's no reason to use **Hashtable** instead of **HashMap** in new code.

Stack

The concept of the stack was introduced earlier, with the **LinkedList**. What's rather odd about the Java 1.0/1.1 **Stack** is that instead of using a **Vector** as a building block, **Stack** is *inherited* from **Vector**. So it has all of the characteristics and behaviors of a **Vector** plus some extra **Stack** behaviors. It's difficult to know whether the designers explicitly decided that this was an especially useful way of doing things, or whether it was just a naive design.

Here's a simple demonstration of **Stack** that pushes each line from a **String** array:

```
//: c09:Stacks.java
// Demonstration of Stack Class.
import java.util.*;

public class Stacks {
   static String[] months = {
      "January", "February", "March", "April",
```

```
      "May", "June", "July", "August", "September",
      "October", "November", "December" };
   public static void main(String[] args) {
     Stack stk = new Stack();
     for(int i = 0; i < months.length; i++)
       stk.push(months[i] + " ");
     System.out.println("stk = " + stk);
     // Treating a stack as a Vector:
     stk.addElement("The last line");
     System.out.println(
       "element 5 = " + stk.elementAt(5));
     System.out.println("popping elements:");
     while(!stk.empty())
       System.out.println(stk.pop());
   }
} ///:~
```

Each line in the **months** array is inserted into the **Stack** with **push( )**, and later fetched from the top of the stack with a **pop( )**. To make a point, **Vector** operations are also performed on the **Stack** object. This is possible because, by virtue of inheritance, a **Stack** *is* a **Vector**. Thus, all operations that can be performed on a **Vector** can also be performed on a **Stack**, such as **elementAt( )**.

As mentioned earlier, you should use a **LinkedList** when you want stack behavior.

BitSet

A **BitSet** is used if you want to efficiently store a lot of on-off information. It's efficient only from the standpoint of size; if you're looking for efficient access, it is slightly slower than using an array of some native type.

In addition, the minimum size of the **BitSet** is that of a **long**: 64 bits. This implies that if you're storing anything smaller, like 8 bits, a **BitSet** will be wasteful; you're better off creating your own class, or just an array, to hold your flags if size is an issue.

A normal container expands as you add more elements, and the **BitSet** does this as well. The following example shows how the **BitSet** works:

```
//: c09:Bits.java
```

```
// Demonstration of BitSet.
import java.util.*;

public class Bits {
  static void printBitSet(BitSet b) {
    System.out.println("bits: " + b);
    String bbits = new String();
    for(int j = 0; j < b.size() ; j++)
      bbits += (b.get(j) ? "1" : "0");
    System.out.println("bit pattern: " + bbits);
  }
  public static void main(String[] args) {
    Random rand = new Random();
    // Take the LSB of nextInt():
    byte bt = (byte)rand.nextInt();
    BitSet bb = new BitSet();
    for(int i = 7; i >=0; i--)
      if(((1 << i) &  bt) != 0)
        bb.set(i);
      else
        bb.clear(i);
    System.out.println("byte value: " + bt);
    printBitSet(bb);

    short st = (short)rand.nextInt();
    BitSet bs = new BitSet();
    for(int i = 15; i >=0; i--)
      if(((1 << i) &  st) != 0)
        bs.set(i);
      else
        bs.clear(i);
    System.out.println("short value: " + st);
    printBitSet(bs);

    int it = rand.nextInt();
    BitSet bi = new BitSet();
    for(int i = 31; i >=0; i--)
      if(((1 << i) &  it) != 0)
        bi.set(i);
      else
        bi.clear(i);
```

```
      System.out.println("int value: " + it);
      printBitSet(bi);

      // Test bitsets >= 64 bits:
      BitSet b127 = new BitSet();
      b127.set(127);
      System.out.println("set bit 127: " + b127);
      BitSet b255 = new BitSet(65);
      b255.set(255);
      System.out.println("set bit 255: " + b255);
      BitSet b1023 = new BitSet(512);
      b1023.set(1023);
      b1023.set(1024);
      System.out.println("set bit 1023: " + b1023);
  }
} ///:~
```

The random number generator is used to create a random **byte**, **short**, and **int**, and each one is transformed into a corresponding bit pattern in a **BitSet**. This works fine because a **BitSet** is 64 bits, so none of these cause it to increase in size. Then a **BitSet** of 512 bits is created. The constructor allocates storage for twice that number of bits. However, you can still set bit 1024 or greater.

Summary

To review the containers provided in the standard Java library:

1. An array associates numerical indices to objects. It holds objects of a known type so that you don't have to cast the result when you're looking up an object. It can be multidimensional, and it can hold primitives. However, its size cannot be changed once you create it.

2. A **Collection** holds single elements, while a **Map** holds associated pairs.

3. Like an array, a **List** also associates numerical indices to objects— you can think of arrays and **List**s as ordered containers. The **List** automatically resizes itself as you add more elements. But a **List** can hold only **Object reference**s, so it won't hold primitives and

you must always cast the result when you pull an **Object** reference out of a container.

4.   Use an **ArrayList** if you're doing a lot of random accesses, and a **LinkedList** if you will be doing a lot of insertions and removals in the middle of the list.

5.   The behavior of queues, deques, and stacks is provided via the **LinkedList**.

6.   A **Map** is a way to associate not numbers, but *objects* with other objects. The design of a **HashMap** is focused on rapid access, while a **TreeMap** keeps its keys in sorted order, and thus is not as fast as a **HashMap**.

7.   A **Set** only accepts one of each type of object. **HashSet**s provide maximally fast lookups, while **TreeSet**s keep the elements in sorted order.

8.   There's no need to use the legacy classes **Vector**, **Hashtable** and **Stack** in new code.

The containers are tools that you can use on a day-to-day basis to make your programs simpler, more powerful, and more effective.

Exercises

Solutions to selected exercises can be found in the electronic document *The Thinking in Java Annotated Solution Guide*, available for a small fee from *www.BruceEckel.com*.

1.   Create an array of **double** and **fill( )** it using **RandDoubleGenerator**. Print the results.

2.   Create a new class called **Gerbil** with an **int gerbilNumber** that's initialized in the constructor (similar to the **Mouse** example in this chapter). Give it a method called **hop( )** that prints out which gerbil number this is, and that it's hopping. Create an **ArrayList** and add a bunch of **Gerbil** objects to the **List**. Now use the **get( )** method to move through the **List** and call **hop( )** for each **Gerbil**.

---

3. Modify Exercise 2 so you use an **Iterator** to move through the **List** while calling **hop( )**.

4. Take the **Gerbil** class in Exercise 2 and put it into a **Map** instead, associating the name of the **Gerbil** as a **String** (the key) for each **Gerbil** (the value) you put in the table. Get an **Iterator** for the **keySet( )** and use it to move through the **Map**, looking up the **Gerbil** for each key and printing out the key and telling the **gerbil** to **hop( )**.

5. Create a **List** (try both **ArrayList** and **LinkedList**) and fill it using **Collections2.countries**. Sort the list and print it, then apply **Collections.shuffle( )** to the list repeatedly, printing it each time so that you can see how the **shuffle( )** method randomizes the list differently each time.

6. Demonstrate that you can't add anything but a **Mouse** to a **MouseList**.

7. Modify **MouseList.java** so that it inherits from **ArrayList** instead of using composition. Demonstrate the problem with this approach.

8. Repair **CatsAndDogs.java** by creating a **Cats** container (utilizing **ArrayList**) that will only accept and retrieve **Cat** objects.

9. Create a container that encapsulates an array of **String**, and that only adds **String**s and gets **String**s, so that there are no casting issues during use. If the internal array isn't big enough for the next add, your container should automatically resize it. In **main( )**, compare the performance of your container with an **ArrayList** holding **String**s.

10. Repeat Exercise 9 for a container of **int**, and compare the performance to an **ArrayList** holding **Integer** objects. In your performance comparison, include the process of incrementing each object in the container.

11. Using the utilities in **com.bruceeckel.util**, create an array of each primitive type and of **String**, then fill each array using an

appropriate generator, and print each array using the appropriate **print( )** method.

12. Create a generator that produces character names from your favorite movies (you can use *Snow White* or *Star Wars* as a fallback), and loops around to the beginning when it runs out of names. Use the utilities in **com.bruceeckel.util** to fill an array, an **ArrayList**, a **LinkedList** and both types of **Set**, then print each container.

13. Create a class containing two **String** objects, and make it **Comparable** so that the comparison only cares about the first **String**. Fill an array and an **ArrayList** with objects of your class, using the **geography** generator. Demonstrate that sorting works properly. Now make a **Comparator** that only cares about the second **String** and demonstrate that sorting works properly; also perform a binary search using your **Comparator**.

14. Modify Exercise 13 so that an alphabetic sort is used.

15. Use **Arrays2.RandStringGenerator** to fill a **TreeSet** but using alphabetic ordering. Print the **TreeSet** to verify the sort order.

16. Create both an **ArrayList** and a **LinkedList**, and fill each using the **Collections2.capitals** generator. Print each list using an ordinary **Iterator**, then insert one list into the other using a **ListIterator**, inserting at every other location. Now perform the insertion starting at the end of the first list and moving backward.

17. Write a method that uses an **Iterator** to step through a **Collection** and print the **hashCode( )** of each object in the container. Fill all the different types of **Collections** with objects and apply your method to each container.

18. Repair the problem in **InfiniteRecursion.java**.

19. Create a class, then make an initialized array of objects of your class. Fill a **List** from your array. Create a subset of your **List** using **subList( )**, and then remove this subset from your **List** using **removeAll( )**.

20. Change Exercise 6 in Chapter 7 to use an **ArrayList** to hold the **Rodent**s and an **Iterator** to move through the sequence of **Rodent**s. Remember that an **ArrayList** holds only **Object**s so you must use a cast when accessing individual **Rodent**s.

21. Following the **Queue.java** example, create a **Deque** class and test it.

22. Use a **TreeMap** in **Statistics.java**. Now add code that tests the performance difference between **HashMap** and **TreeMap** in that program.

23. Produce a **Map** and a **Set** containing all the countries that begin with 'A.'

24. Using **Collections2.countries**, fill a **Set** multiple times with the same data and verify that the **Set** ends up with only one of each instance. Try this with both kinds of **Set**.

25. Starting with **Statistics.java**, create a program that runs the test repeatedly and looks to see if any one number tends to appear more than the others in the results.

26. Rewrite **Statistics.java** using a **HashSet** of **Counter** objects (you'll have to modify **Counter** so that it will work in the **HashSet**). Which approach seems better?

27. Modify the class in Exercise 13 so that it will work with **HashSet**s and as a key in **HashMap**s.

28. Using **SlowMap.java** for inspiration, create a **SlowSet**.

29. Apply the tests in **Map1.java** to **SlowMap** to verify that it works. Fix anything in **SlowMap** that doesn't work correctly.

30. Implement the rest of the **Map** interface for **SlowMap**.

31. Modify **MapPerformance.java** to include tests of **SlowMap**.

32. Modify **SlowMap** so that instead of two **ArrayList**s, it holds a single **ArrayList** of **MPair** objects. Verify that the modified version works correctly. Using **MapPerformance.java**, test the

speed of your new **Map**. Now change the **put( )** method so that it performs a **sort( )** after each pair is entered, and modify **get( )** to use **Collections.binarySearch( )** to look up the key. Compare the performance of the new version with the old ones.

33.   Add a **char** field to **CountedString** that is also initialized in the constructor, and modify the **hashCode( )** and **equals( )** methods to include the value of this **char**.

34.   Modify **SimpleHashMap** so that it reports collisions, and test this by adding the same data set twice so that you see collisions.

35.   Modify **SimpleHashMap** so that it reports the number of "probes" necessary when collisions occur. That is, how many calls to **next( )** must be made on the **Iterator**s that walk the **LinkedList**s looking for matches?

36.   Implement the **clear( )** and **remove( )** methods for **SimpleHashMap**.

37.   Implement the rest of the **Map** interface for **SimpleHashMap**.

38.   Add a **private rehash( )** method to **SimpleHashMap** that is invoked when the load factor exceeds 0.75. During rehashing, double the number of buckets, then search for the first prime number greater than that to determine the new number of buckets.

39.   Following the example in **SimpleHashMap.java**, create and test a **SimpleHashSet**.

40.   Modify **SimpleHashMap** to use **ArrayList**s instead of **LinkedList**s. Modify **MapPerformance.java** to compare the performance of the two implementations.

41.   Using the HTML documentation for the JDK (downloadable from *java.sun.com*), look up the **HashMap** class. Create a **HashMap**, fill it with elements, and determine the load factor. Test the lookup speed with this map, then attempt to increase the speed by making a new **HashMap** with a larger initial capacity and copying the old

---

map into the new one, running your lookup speed test again on the new map.

42. In Chapter 8, locate the **GreenhouseControls.java** example, which consists of three files. In **Controller.java**, the class **EventSet** is just a container. Change the code to use a **LinkedList** instead of an **EventSet**. This will require more than just replacing **EventSet** with **LinkedList**; you'll also need to use an **Iterator** to cycle through the set of events.

43. (Challenging). Write your own hashed map class, customized for a particular key type: **String** for this example. Do not inherit it from **Map**. Instead, duplicate the methods so that the **put( )** and **get( )** methods specifically take **String** objects, not **Object**s, as keys. Everything that involves keys should not use generic types, but instead work with **String**s, to avoid the cost of upcasting and downcasting. Your goal is to make the fastest possible custom implementation. Modify **MapPerformance.java** to test your implementation vs. a **HashMap**.

44. (Challenging). Find the source code for **List** in the Java source code library that comes with all Java distributions. Copy this code and make a special version called **intList** that holds only **int**s. Consider what it would take to make a special version of **List** for all the primitive types. Now consider what happens if you want to make a linked list class that works with all the primitive types. If parameterized types are ever implemented in Java, they will provide a way to do this work for you automatically (as well as many other benefits).

10: Error Handling with Exceptions

The basic philosophy of Java is that "badly formed code will not be run."

The ideal time to catch an error is at compile-time, before you even try to run the program. However, not all errors can be detected at compile-time. The rest of the problems must be handled at run-time, through some formality that allows the originator of the error to pass appropriate information to a recipient who will know how to handle the difficulty properly.

In C and other earlier languages, there could be several of these formalities, and they were generally established by convention and not as part of the programming language. Typically, you returned a special value or set a flag, and the recipient was supposed to look at the value or the flag and determine that something was amiss. However, as the years passed, it was discovered that programmers who use a library tend to think of themselves as invincible—as in, "Yes, errors might happen to others, but not in *my* code." So, not too surprisingly, they wouldn't check for the error conditions (and sometimes the error conditions were too silly to check for[1]). If you *were* thorough enough to check for an error every time you called a method, your code could turn into an unreadable nightmare. Because programmers could still coax systems out of these languages they were resistant to admitting the truth: This approach to handling errors was a major limitation to creating large, robust, maintainable programs.

The solution is to take the casual nature out of error handling and to enforce formality. This actually has a long history, since implementations of *exception handling* go back to operating systems in the 1960s, and even

---

[1] The C programmer can look up the return value of **printf( )** for an example of this.

to BASIC's "**on error goto**." But C++ exception handling was based on Ada, and Java's is based primarily on C++ (although it looks even more like Object Pascal).

The word "exception" is meant in the sense of "I take exception to that." At the point where the problem occurs you might not know what to do with it, but you do know that you can't just continue on merrily; you must stop and somebody, somewhere, must figure out what to do. But you don't have enough information in the current context to fix the problem. So you hand the problem out to a higher context where someone is qualified to make the proper decision (much like a chain of command).

The other rather significant benefit of exceptions is that they clean up error handling code. Instead of checking for a particular error and dealing with it at multiple places in your program, you no longer need to check at the point of the method call (since the exception will guarantee that someone catches it). And, you need to handle the problem in only one place, the so-called *exception handler*. This saves you code, and it separates the code that describes what you want to do from the code that is executed when things go awry. In general, reading, writing, and debugging code becomes much clearer with exceptions than when using the old way of error handling.

Because exception handling is enforced by the Java compiler, there are only so many examples that can be written in this book without learning about exception handling. This chapter introduces you to the code you need to write to properly handle exceptions, and the way you can generate your own exceptions if one of your methods gets into trouble.

Basic exceptions

An *exceptional condition* is a problem that prevents the continuation of the method or scope that you're in. It's important to distinguish an exceptional condition from a normal problem, in which you have enough information in the current context to somehow cope with the difficulty. With an exceptional condition, you cannot continue processing because you don't have the information necessary to deal with the problem *in the current context*. All you can do is jump out of the current context and relegate that problem to a higher context. This is what happens when you throw an exception.

A simple example is a divide. If you're about to divide by zero, it's worth checking to make sure you don't go ahead and perform the divide. But what does it mean that the denominator is zero? Maybe you know, in the context of the problem you're trying to solve in that particular method, how to deal with a zero denominator. But if it's an unexpected value, you can't deal with it and so must throw an exception rather than continuing along that path.

When you throw an exception, several things happen. First, the exception object is created in the same way that any Java object is created: on the heap, with **new**. Then the current path of execution (the one you couldn't continue) is stopped and the reference for the exception object is ejected from the current context. At this point the exception handling mechanism takes over and begins to look for an appropriate place to continue executing the program. This appropriate place is the *exception handler,* whose job is to recover from the problem so the program can either try another tack or just continue.

As a simple example of throwing an exception, consider an object reference called **t**. It's possible that you might be passed a reference that hasn't been initialized, so you might want to check before trying to call a method using that object reference. You can send information about the error into a larger context by creating an object representing your information and "throwing" it out of your current context. This is called *throwing an exception.* Here's what it looks like:

```
if(t == null)
  throw new NullPointerException();
```

This throws the exception, which allows you—in the current context—to abdicate responsibility for thinking about the issue further. It's just magically handled somewhere else. Precisely *where* will be shown shortly.

Exception arguments

Like any object in Java, you always create exceptions on the heap using **new**, which allocates storage and calls a constructor. There are two constructors in all standard exceptions: the first is the default constructor, and the second takes a string argument so you can place pertinent information in the exception:

```
if(t == null)
  throw new NullPointerException("t = null");
```

This string can later be extracted using various methods, as will be shown shortly.

The keyword **throw** causes a number of relatively magical things to happen. Typically, you'll first use **new** to create an object that represents the error condition. You give the resulting reference to **throw**. The object is, in effect, "returned" from the method, even though that object type isn't normally what the method is designed to return. A simplistic way to think about exception handling is as an alternate return mechanism, although you get into trouble if you take that analogy too far. You can also exit from ordinary scopes by throwing an exception. But a value is returned, and the method or scope exits.

Any similarity to an ordinary return from a method ends here, because *where* you return is someplace completely different from where you return for a normal method call. (You end up in an appropriate exception handler that might be miles away—many levels lower on the call stack—from where the exception was thrown.)

In addition, you can throw any type of **Throwable** object that you want. Typically, you'll throw a different class of exception for each different type of error. The information about the error is represented both inside the exception object and implicitly in the type of exception object chosen, so someone in the bigger context can figure out what to do with your exception. (Often, the only information is the type of exception object, and nothing meaningful is stored within the exception object.)

Catching an exception

If a method throws an exception, it must assume that exception is "caught" and dealt with. One of the advantages of Java exception handling is that it allows you to concentrate on the problem you're trying to solve in one place, and then deal with the errors from that code in another place.

To see how an exception is caught, you must first understand the concept of a *guarded region,* which is a section of code that might produce exceptions, and which is followed by the code to handle those exceptions.

The **try** block

If you're inside a method and you throw an exception (or another method you call within this method throws an exception), that method will exit in the process of throwing. If you don't want a **throw** to exit the method, you can set up a special block within that method to capture the exception. This is called the *try block* because you "try" your various method calls there. The try block is an ordinary scope, preceded by the keyword **try**:

```
try {
  // Code that might generate exceptions
}
```

If you were checking for errors carefully in a programming language that didn't support exception handling, you'd have to surround every method call with setup and error testing code, even if you call the same method several times. With exception handling, you put everything in a try block and capture all the exceptions in one place. This means your code is a lot easier to write and easier to read because the goal of the code is not confused with the error checking.

Exception handlers

Of course, the thrown exception must end up someplace. This "place" is the *exception handler,* and there's one for every exception type you want to catch. Exception handlers immediately follow the try block and are denoted by the keyword **catch**:

```
try {
  // Code that might generate exceptions
} catch(Type1 id1) {
  // Handle exceptions of Type1
} catch(Type2 id2) {
  // Handle exceptions of Type2
} catch(Type3 id3) {
  // Handle exceptions of Type3
```

```
}
// etc...
```

Each catch clause (exception handler) is like a little method that takes one and only one argument of a particular type. The identifier (**id1**, **id2**, and so on) can be used inside the handler, just like a method argument. Sometimes you never use the identifier because the type of the exception gives you enough information to deal with the exception, but the identifier must still be there.

The handlers must appear directly after the try block. If an exception is thrown, the exception handling mechanism goes hunting for the first handler with an argument that matches the type of the exception. Then it enters that catch clause, and the exception is considered handled. The search for handlers stops once the catch clause is finished. Only the matching catch clause executes; it's not like a **switch** statement in which you need a **break** after each **case** to prevent the remaining ones from executing.

Note that, within the try block, a number of different method calls might generate the same exception, but you need only one handler.

Termination vs. resumption

There are two basic models in exception handling theory. In *termination* (which is what Java and C++ support), you assume the error is so critical that there's no way to get back to where the exception occurred. Whoever threw the exception decided that there was no way to salvage the situation, and they don't *want* to come back.

The alternative is called *resumption*. It means that the exception handler is expected to do something to rectify the situation, and then the faulting method is retried, presuming success the second time. If you want resumption, it means you still hope to continue execution after the exception is handled. In this case, your exception is more like a method call—which is how you should set up situations in Java in which you want resumption-like behavior. (That is, don't throw an exception; call a method that fixes the problem.) Alternatively, place your **try** block inside a **while** loop that keeps reentering the **try** block until the result is satisfactory.

Historically, programmers using operating systems that supported resumptive exception handling eventually ended up using termination-like code and skipping resumption. So although resumption sounds attractive at first, it isn't quite so useful in practice. The dominant reason is probably the *coupling* that results: your handler must often be aware of where the exception is thrown from and contain nongeneric code specific to the throwing location. This makes the code difficult to write and maintain, especially for large systems where the exception can be generated from many points.

Creating your own exceptions

You're not stuck using the existing Java exceptions. This is important because you'll often need to create your own exceptions to denote a special error that your library is capable of creating, but which was not foreseen when the Java exception hierarchy was created.

To create your own exception class, you're forced to inherit from an existing type of exception, preferably one that is close in meaning to your new exception (this is often not possible, however). The most trivial way to create a new type of exception is just to let the compiler create the default constructor for you, so it requires almost no code at all:

```java
//: c10:SimpleExceptionDemo.java
// Inheriting your own exceptions.
class SimpleException extends Exception {}

public class SimpleExceptionDemo {
  public void f() throws SimpleException {
    System.out.println(
      "Throwing SimpleException from f()");
    throw new SimpleException ();
  }
  public static void main(String[] args) {
```

```
      SimpleExceptionDemo sed =
        new SimpleExceptionDemo();
      try {
        sed.f();
      } catch(SimpleException e) {
        System.err.println("Caught it!");
      }
    }
  }
} ///:~
```

When the compiler creates the default constructor, it which automatically (and invisibly) calls the base-class default constructor. Of course, in this case you don't get a **SimpleException(String)** constructor, but in practice that isn't used much. As you'll see, the most important thing about an exception is the class name, so most of the time an exception like the one shown above is satisfactory.

Here, the result is printed to the console *standard error* stream by writing to **System.err**. This is usually a better place to send error information than **System.out**, which may be redirected. If you send output to **System.err** it will not be redirected along with **System.out** so the user is more likely to notice it.

Creating an exception class that also has a constructor that takes a **String** is also quite simple:

```
//: c10:FullConstructors.java
// Inheriting your own exceptions.

class MyException extends Exception {
  public MyException() {}
  public MyException(String msg) {
    super(msg);
  }
}

public class FullConstructors {
  public static void f() throws MyException {
    System.out.println(
      "Throwing MyException from f()");
    throw new MyException();
```

```
    }
    public static void g() throws MyException {
      System.out.println(
        "Throwing MyException from g()");
      throw new MyException("Originated in g()");
    }
    public static void main(String[] args) {
      try {
        f();
      } catch(MyException e) {
        e.printStackTrace(System.err);
      }
      try {
        g();
      } catch(MyException e) {
        e.printStackTrace(System.err);
      }
    }
} ///:~
```

The added code is small—the addition of two constructors that define the way **MyException** is created. In the second constructor, the base-class constructor with a **String** argument is explicitly invoked by using the **super** keyword.

The stack trace information is sent to **System.err** so that it's more likely it will be noticed in the event that **System.out** has been redirected.

The output of the program is:

```
Throwing MyException from f()
MyException
        at FullConstructors.f(FullConstructors.java:16)
        at FullConstructors.main(FullConstructors.java:24)
Throwing MyException from g()
MyException: Originated in g()
        at FullConstructors.g(FullConstructors.java:20)
        at FullConstructors.main(FullConstructors.java:29)
```

You can see the absence of the detail message in the **MyException** thrown from **f( )**.

The process of creating your own exceptions can be taken further. You can add extra constructors and members:

```
//: c10:ExtraFeatures.java
// Further embellishment of exception classes.

class MyException2 extends Exception {
  public MyException2() {}
  public MyException2(String msg) {
    super(msg);
  }
  public MyException2(String msg, int x) {
    super(msg);
    i = x;
  }
  public int val() { return i; }
  private int i;
}

public class ExtraFeatures {
  public static void f() throws MyException2 {
    System.out.println(
      "Throwing MyException2 from f()");
    throw new MyException2();
  }
  public static void g() throws MyException2 {
    System.out.println(
      "Throwing MyException2 from g()");
    throw new MyException2("Originated in g()");
  }
  public static void h() throws MyException2 {
    System.out.println(
      "Throwing MyException2 from h()");
    throw new MyException2(
      "Originated in h()", 47);
  }
  public static void main(String[] args) {
    try {
      f();
    } catch(MyException2 e) {
      e.printStackTrace(System.err);
```

```
    }
    try {
      g();
    } catch(MyException2 e) {
      e.printStackTrace(System.err);
    }
    try {
      h();
    } catch(MyException2 e) {
      e.printStackTrace(System.err);
      System.err.println("e.val() = " + e.val());
    }
  }
} ///:~
```

A data member **i** has been added, along with a method that reads that value and an additional constructor that sets it. The output is:

```
Throwing MyException2 from f()
MyException2
        at ExtraFeatures.f(ExtraFeatures.java:22)
        at ExtraFeatures.main(ExtraFeatures.java:34)
Throwing MyException2 from g()
MyException2: Originated in g()
        at ExtraFeatures.g(ExtraFeatures.java:26)
        at ExtraFeatures.main(ExtraFeatures.java:39)
Throwing MyException2 from h()
MyException2: Originated in h()
        at ExtraFeatures.h(ExtraFeatures.java:30)
        at ExtraFeatures.main(ExtraFeatures.java:44)
e.val() = 47
```

Since an exception is just another kind of object, you can continue this process of embellishing the power of your exception classes. Keep in mind, however, that all this dressing-up might be lost on the client programmers using your packages, since they might simply look for the exception to be thrown and nothing more. (That's the way most of the Java library exceptions are used.)

The exception specification

In Java, you're required to inform the client programmer, who calls your method, of the exceptions that might be thrown from your method. This is civilized, because the caller can know exactly what code to write to catch all potential exceptions. Of course, if source code is available, the client programmer could hunt through and look for **throw** statements, but often a library doesn't come with sources. To prevent this from being a problem, Java provides syntax (and *forces* you to use that syntax) to allow you to politely tell the client programmer what exceptions this method throws, so the client programmer can handle them. This is the *exception specification,* and it's part of the method declaration, appearing after the argument list.

The exception specification uses an additional keyword, **throws**, followed by a list of all the potential exception types. So your method definition might look like this:

```
void f() throws TooBig, TooSmall, DivZero { //...
```

If you say

```
void f() { // ...
```

it means that no exceptions are thrown from the method. (*Except* for the exceptions of type **RuntimeException**, which can reasonably be thrown anywhere—this will be described later.)

You can't lie about an exception specification—if your method causes exceptions and doesn't handle them, the compiler will detect this and tell you that you must either handle the exception or indicate with an exception specification that it may be thrown from your method. By enforcing exception specifications from top to bottom, Java guarantees that exception correctness can be ensured *at compile-time*[2].

---

[2] This is a significant improvement over C++ exception handling, which doesn't catch violations of exception specifications until run time, when it's not very useful.

There is one place you can lie: you can claim to throw an exception that you really don't. The compiler takes your word for it, and forces the users of your method to treat it as if it really does throw that exception. This has the beneficial effect of being a placeholder for that exception, so you can actually start throwing the exception later without requiring changes to existing code. It's also important for creating **abstract** base classes and **interface**s whose derived classes or implementations may need to throw exceptions.

Catching any exception

It is possible to create a handler that catches any type of exception. You do this by catching the base-class exception type **Exception** (there are other types of base exceptions, but **Exception** is the base that's pertinent to virtually all programming activities):

```
catch(Exception e) {
  System.err.println("Caught an exception");
}
```

This will catch any exception, so if you use it you'll want to put it at the *end* of your list of handlers to avoid preempting any exception handlers that might otherwise follow it.

Since the **Exception** class is the base of all the exception classes that are important to the programmer, you don't get much specific information about the exception, but you can call the methods that come from *its* base type **Throwable**:

String getMessage( )
String getLocalizedMessage( )
Gets the detail message, or a message adjusted for this particular locale.

String toString( )
Returns a short description of the Throwable, including the detail message if there is one.

void printStackTrace( )
void printStackTrace(PrintStream)
void printStackTrace(PrintWriter)
Prints the Throwable and the Throwable's call stack trace. The call stack

---

shows the sequence of method calls that brought you to the point at which the exception was thrown. The first version prints to standard error, the second and third prints to a stream of your choice (in Chapter 11, you'll understand why there are two types of streams).

Throwable fillInStackTrace( )
Records information within this **Throwable** object about the current state of the stack frames. Useful when an application is rethrowing an error or exception (more about this shortly).

In addition, you get some other methods from **Throwable**'s base type **Object** (everybody's base type). The one that might come in handy for exceptions is **getClass( )**, which returns an object representing the class of this object. You can in turn query this **Class** object for its name with **getName( )** or **toString( )**. You can also do more sophisticated things with **Class** objects that aren't necessary in exception handling. **Class** objects will be studied later in this book.

Here's an example that shows the use of the basic **Exception** methods:

```
//: c10:ExceptionMethods.java
// Demonstrating the Exception Methods.

public class ExceptionMethods {
  public static void main(String[] args) {
    try {
      throw new Exception("Here's my Exception");
    } catch(Exception e) {
      System.err.println("Caught Exception");
      System.err.println(
        "e.getMessage(): " + e.getMessage());
      System.err.println(
        "e.getLocalizedMessage(): " +
        e.getLocalizedMessage());
      System.err.println("e.toString(): " + e);
      System.err.println("e.printStackTrace():");
      e.printStackTrace(System.err);
    }
  }
} ///:~
```

The output for this program is:

```
Caught Exception
e.getMessage(): Here's my Exception
e.getLocalizedMessage(): Here's my Exception
e.toString(): java.lang.Exception:
    Here's my Exception
e.printStackTrace():
java.lang.Exception: Here's my Exception
 at ExceptionMethods.main(ExceptionMethods.java:7)
java.lang.Exception:
    Here's my Exception
 at ExceptionMethods.main(ExceptionMethods.java:7)
```

You can see that the methods provide successively more information—
each is effectively a superset of the previous one.

Rethrowing an exception

Sometimes you'll want to rethrow the exception that you just caught,
particularly when you use **Exception** to catch any exception. Since you
already have the reference to the current exception, you can simply
rethrow that reference:

```
catch(Exception e) {
  System.err.println("An exception was thrown");
  throw e;
}
```

Rethrowing an exception causes the exception to go to the exception
handlers in the next-higher context. Any further **catch** clauses for the
same **try** block are still ignored. In addition, everything about the
exception object is preserved, so the handler at the higher context that
catches the specific exception type can extract all the information from
that object.

If you simply rethrow the current exception, the information that you
print about that exception in **printStackTrace( )** will pertain to the
exception's origin, not the place where you rethrow it. If you want to
install new stack trace information, you can do so by calling
fillInStackTrace( ), which returns an exception object that it creates by

---

Chapter 10: Error Handling with Exceptions   545 stuffing the current stack information into the old exception object. Here's what it looks like:

```
//: c10:Rethrowing.java
// Demonstrating fillInStackTrace()

public class Rethrowing {
  public static void f() throws Exception {
    System.out.println(
      "originating the exception in f()");
    throw new Exception("thrown from f()");
  }
  public static void g() throws Throwable {
    try {
      f();
    } catch(Exception e) {
      System.err.println(
        "Inside g(), e.printStackTrace()");
      e.printStackTrace(System.err);
      throw e; // 17
      // throw e.fillInStackTrace(); // 18
    }
  }
  public static void
  main(String[] args) throws Throwable {
    try {
      g();
    } catch(Exception e) {
      System.err.println(
        "Caught in main, e.printStackTrace()");
      e.printStackTrace(System.err);
    }
  }
} ///:~
```

The important line numbers are marked as comments. With line 17 uncommented (as shown), the output is:

```
originating the exception in f()
Inside g(), e.printStackTrace()
java.lang.Exception: thrown from f()
        at Rethrowing.f(Rethrowing.java:8)
```

```
        at Rethrowing.g(Rethrowing.java:12)
        at Rethrowing.main(Rethrowing.java:24)
Caught in main, e.printStackTrace()
java.lang.Exception: thrown from f()
        at Rethrowing.f(Rethrowing.java:8)
        at Rethrowing.g(Rethrowing.java:12)
        at Rethrowing.main(Rethrowing.java:24)
```

So the exception stack trace always remembers its true point of origin, no matter how many times it gets rethrown.

With line 17 commented and line 18 uncommented, **fillInStackTrace( )** is used instead, and the result is:

```
originating the exception in f()
Inside g(), e.printStackTrace()
java.lang.Exception: thrown from f()
        at Rethrowing.f(Rethrowing.java:8)
        at Rethrowing.g(Rethrowing.java:12)
        at Rethrowing.main(Rethrowing.java:24)
Caught in main, e.printStackTrace()
java.lang.Exception: thrown from f()
        at Rethrowing.g(Rethrowing.java:18)
        at Rethrowing.main(Rethrowing.java:24)
```

Because of **fillInStackTrace( )**, line 18 becomes the new point of origin of the exception.

The class **Throwable** must appear in the exception specification for **g( )** and **main( )** because **fillInStackTrace( )** produces a reference to a **Throwable** object. Since **Throwable** is a base class of **Exception**, it's possible to get an object that's a **Throwable** but *not* an **Exception**, so the handler for **Exception** in **main( )** might miss it. To make sure everything is in order, the compiler forces an exception specification for **Throwable**. For example, the exception in the following program is *not* caught in **main( )**:

```
//: c10:ThrowOut.java
public class ThrowOut {
  public static void
  main(String[] args) throws Throwable {
    try {
```

```
      throw new Throwable();
    } catch(Exception e) {
      System.err.println("Caught in main()");
    }
  }
} ///:~
```

It's also possible to rethrow a different exception from the one you caught. If you do this, you get a similar effect as when you use **fillInStackTrace( )**—the information about the original site of the exception is lost, and what you're left with is the information pertaining to the new **throw**:

```
//: c10:RethrowNew.java
// Rethrow a different object
// from the one that was caught.

class OneException extends Exception {
  public OneException(String s) { super(s); }
}

class TwoException extends Exception {
  public TwoException(String s) { super(s); }
}

public class RethrowNew {
  public static void f() throws OneException {
    System.out.println(
      "originating the exception in f()");
    throw new OneException("thrown from f()");
  }
  public static void main(String[] args)
  throws TwoException {
    try {
      f();
    } catch(OneException e) {
      System.err.println(
        "Caught in main, e.printStackTrace()");
      e.printStackTrace(System.err);
      throw new TwoException("from main()");
    }
```

```
    }
} ///:~
```

The output is:

```
originating the exception in f()
Caught in main, e.printStackTrace()
OneException: thrown from f()
        at RethrowNew.f(RethrowNew.java:17)
        at RethrowNew.main(RethrowNew.java:22)
Exception in thread "main" TwoException: from main()
        at RethrowNew.main(RethrowNew.java:27)
```

The final exception knows only that it came from **main( )**, and not from **f( )**.

You never have to worry about cleaning up the previous exception, or any exceptions for that matter. They're all heap-based objects created with **new**, so the garbage collector automatically cleans them all up.

Standard Java exceptions

The Java class **Throwable** describes anything that can be thrown as an exception. There are two general types of **Throwable** objects ("types of" = "inherited from"). **Error** represents compile-time and system errors that you don't worry about catching (except in special cases). **Exception** is the basic type that can be thrown from any of the standard Java library class methods and from your methods and run-time accidents. So the Java programmer's base type of interest is **Exception**.

The best way to get an overview of the exceptions is to browse the HTML Java documentation that you can download from *java.sun.com*. It's worth doing this once just to get a feel for the various exceptions, but you'll soon see that there isn't anything special between one exception and the next except for the name. Also, the number of exceptions in Java keeps expanding; basically it's pointless to print them in a book. Any new library you get from a third-party vendor will probably have its own exceptions as well. The important thing to understand is the concept and what you should do with the exceptions.

The basic idea is that the name of the exception represents the problem that occurred, and the exception name is intended to be relatively self-explanatory. The exceptions are not all defined in **java.lang**; some are created to support other libraries such as **util**, **net,** and **io**, which you can see from their full class names or what they are inherited from. For example, all I/O exceptions are inherited from **java.io.IOException**.

The special case of RuntimeException

The first example in this chapter was

```
if(t == null)
  throw new NullPointerException();
```

It can be a bit horrifying to think that you must check for **null** on every reference that is passed into a method (since you can't know if the caller has passed you a valid reference). Fortunately, you don't—this is part of the standard run-time checking that Java performs for you, and if any call is made to a **null** reference, Java will automatically throw a **NullPointerException**. So the above bit of code is always superfluous.

There's a whole group of exception types that are in this category. They're always thrown automatically by Java and you don't need to include them in your exception specifications. Conveniently enough, they're all grouped together by putting them under a single base class called **RuntimeException**, which is a perfect example of inheritance: it establishes a family of types that have some characteristics and behaviors in common. Also, you never need to write an exception specification saying that a method might throw a **RuntimeException**, since that's just assumed. Because they indicate bugs, you virtually never catch a **RuntimeException**—it's dealt with automatically. If you were forced to check for **RuntimeException**s your code could get messy. Even though you don't typically catch **RuntimeExceptions**, in your own packages you might choose to throw some of the **RuntimeException**s.

What happens when you don't catch such exceptions? Since the compiler doesn't enforce exception specifications for these, it's quite plausible that a **RuntimeException** could percolate all the way out to your **main( )**

method without being caught. To see what happens in this case, try the following example:

```
//: c10:NeverCaught.java
// Ignoring RuntimeExceptions.

public class NeverCaught {
  static void f() {
    throw new RuntimeException("From f()");
  }
  static void g() {
    f();
  }
  public static void main(String[] args) {
    g();
  }
} ///:~
```

You can already see that a **RuntimeException** (or anything inherited from it) is a special case, since the compiler doesn't require an exception specification for these types.

The output is:

```
Exception in thread "main"
java.lang.RuntimeException: From f()
        at NeverCaught.f(NeverCaught.java:9)
        at NeverCaught.g(NeverCaught.java:12)
        at NeverCaught.main(NeverCaught.java:15)
```

So the answer is: If a **RuntimeException** gets all the way out to **main( )** without being caught, **printStackTrace( )** is called for that exception as the program exits.

Keep in mind that you can only ignore **RuntimeException**s in your coding, since all other handling is carefully enforced by the compiler. The reasoning is that a **RuntimeException** represents a programming error:

1.   An error you cannot catch (receiving a **null** reference handed to your method by a client programmer, for example) .

2. An error that you, as a programmer, should have checked for in your code (such as **ArrayIndexOutOfBoundsException** where you should have paid attention to the size of the array).

You can see what a tremendous benefit it is to have exceptions in this case, since they help in the debugging process.

It's interesting to notice that you cannot classify Java exception handling as a single-purpose tool. Yes, it is designed to handle those pesky run-time errors that will occur because of forces outside your code's control, but it's also essential for certain types of programming bugs that the compiler cannot detect.

Performing cleanup with finally

There's often some piece of code that you want to execute whether or not an exception is thrown within a **try** block. This usually pertains to some operation other than memory recovery (since that's taken care of by the garbage collector). To achieve this effect, you use a **finally** clause[3] at the end of all the exception handlers. The full picture of an exception handling section is thus:

```
try {
  // The guarded region: Dangerous activities
  // that might throw A, B, or C
} catch(A a1) {
  // Handler for situation A
} catch(B b1) {
  // Handler for situation B
} catch(C c1) {
  // Handler for situation C
} finally {
  // Activities that happen every time
```

---

[3] C++ exception handling does not have the **finally** clause because it relies on destructors to accomplish this sort of cleanup.

```
        }
```

To demonstrate that the **finally** clause always runs, try this program:

```
//: c10:FinallyWorks.java
// The finally clause is always executed.

class ThreeException extends Exception {}

public class FinallyWorks {
  static int count = 0;
  public static void main(String[] args) {
    while(true) {
      try {
        // Post-increment is zero first time:
        if(count++ == 0)
          throw new ThreeException();
        System.out.println("No exception");
      } catch(ThreeException e) {
        System.err.println("ThreeException");
      } finally {
        System.err.println("In finally clause");
        if(count == 2) break; // out of "while"
      }
    }
  }
} ///:~
```

This program also gives a hint for how you can deal with the fact that exceptions in Java (like exceptions in C++) do not allow you to resume back to where the exception was thrown, as discussed earlier. If you place your **try** block in a loop, you can establish a condition that must be met before you continue the program. You can also add a **static** counter or some other device to allow the loop to try several different approaches before giving up. This way you can build a greater level of robustness into your programs.

The output is:

```
ThreeException
In finally clause
No exception
```

Whether an exception is thrown or not, the **finally** clause is always executed.

What's **finally** for?

In a language without garbage collection *and* without automatic destructor calls[4], **finally** is important because it allows the programmer to guarantee the release of memory regardless of what happens in the **try** block. But Java has garbage collection, so releasing memory is virtually never a problem. Also, it has no destructors to call. So when do you need to use **finally** in Java?

finally is necessary when you need to set something *other* than memory back to its original state. This is some kind of cleanup like an open file or network connection, something you've drawn on the screen, or even a switch in the outside world, as modeled in the following example:

```
//: c10:OnOffSwitch.java
// Why use finally?

class Switch {
  boolean state = false;
  boolean read() { return state; }
  void on() { state = true; }
  void off() { state = false; }
}
class OnOffException1 extends Exception {}
class OnOffException2 extends Exception {}

public class OnOffSwitch {
  static Switch sw = new Switch();
  static void f() throws
    OnOffException1, OnOffException2 {}
  public static void main(String[] args) {
```

---

[4] A destructor is a function that's always called when an object becomes unused. You always know exactly where and when the destructor gets called. C++ has automatic destructor calls, but Delphi's Object Pascal versions 1 and 2 do not (which changes the meaning and use of the concept of a destructor for that language).

```
      try {
        sw.on();
        // Code that can throw exceptions...
        f();
        sw.off();
      } catch(OnOffException1 e) {
        System.err.println("OnOffException1");
        sw.off();
      } catch(OnOffException2 e) {
        System.err.println("OnOffException2");
        sw.off();
      }
    }
} ///:~
```

The goal here is to make sure that the switch is off when **main( )** is completed, so **sw.off( )** is placed at the end of the try block and at the end of each exception handler. But it's possible that an exception could be thrown that isn't caught here, so **sw.off( )** would be missed. However, with **finally** you can place the cleanup code from a try block in just one place:

```
//: c10:WithFinally.java
// Finally Guarantees cleanup.

public class WithFinally {
  static Switch sw = new Switch();
  public static void main(String[] args) {
    try {
      sw.on();
      // Code that can throw exceptions...
      OnOffSwitch.f();
    } catch(OnOffException1 e) {
      System.err.println("OnOffException1");
    } catch(OnOffException2 e) {
      System.err.println("OnOffException2");
    } finally {
      sw.off();
    }
  }
} ///:~
```

Here the **sw.off( )** has been moved to just one place, where it's guaranteed to run no matter what happens.

Even in cases in which the exception is not caught in the current set of **catch** clauses, **finally** will be executed before the exception handling mechanism continues its search for a handler at the next higher level:

```
//: c10:AlwaysFinally.java
// Finally is always executed.

class FourException extends Exception {}

public class AlwaysFinally {
  public static void main(String[] args) {
    System.out.println(
      "Entering first try block");
    try {
      System.out.println(
        "Entering second try block");
      try {
        throw new FourException();
      } finally {
        System.out.println(
          "finally in 2nd try block");
      }
    } catch(FourException e) {
      System.err.println(
        "Caught FourException in 1st try block");
    } finally {
      System.err.println(
        "finally in 1st try block");
    }
  }
} ///:~
```

The output for this program shows you what happens:

```
Entering first try block
Entering second try block
finally in 2nd try block
Caught FourException in 1st try block
finally in 1st try block
```

The **finally** statement will also be executed in situations in which **break** and **continue** statements are involved. Note that, along with the labeled **break** and labeled **continue**, **finally** eliminates the need for a **goto** statement in Java.

Pitfall: the lost exception

In general, Java's exception implementation is quite outstanding, but unfortunately there's a flaw. Although exceptions are an indication of a crisis in your program and should never be ignored, it's possible for an exception to simply be lost. This happens with a particular configuration using a **finally** clause:

```
//: c10:LostMessage.java
// How an exception can be lost.

class VeryImportantException extends Exception {
  public String toString() {
    return "A very important exception!";
  }
}

class HoHumException extends Exception {
  public String toString() {
    return "A trivial exception";
  }
}

public class LostMessage {
  void f() throws VeryImportantException {
    throw new VeryImportantException();
  }
  void dispose() throws HoHumException {
    throw new HoHumException();
  }
  public static void main(String[] args)
      throws Exception {
    LostMessage lm = new LostMessage();
    try {
      lm.f();
```

```
    } finally {
      lm.dispose();
    }
  }
} ///:~
```

The output is:

```
Exception in thread "main" A trivial exception
    at LostMessage.dispose(LostMessage.java:21)
    at LostMessage.main(LostMessage.java:29)
```

You can see that there's no evidence of the **VeryImportantException**, which is simply replaced by the **HoHumException** in the **finally** clause. This is a rather serious pitfall, since it means that an exception can be completely lost, and in a far more subtle and difficult-to-detect fashion than the example above. In contrast, C++ treats the situation in which a second exception is thrown before the first one is handled as a dire programming error. Perhaps a future version of Java will repair this problem (on the other hand, you will typically wrap any method that throws an exception, such as **dispose( )**, inside a **try-catch** clause).

Exception restrictions

When you override a method, you can throw only the exceptions that have been specified in the base-class version of the method. This is a useful restriction, since it means that code that works with the base class will automatically work with any object derived from the base class (a fundamental OOP concept, of course), including exceptions.

This example demonstrates the kinds of restrictions imposed (at compile-time) for exceptions:

```
//: c10:StormyInning.java
// Overridden methods may throw only the
// exceptions specified in their base-class
// versions, or exceptions derived from the
// base-class exceptions.

class BaseballException extends Exception {}
class Foul extends BaseballException {}
```

```
class Strike extends BaseballException {}

abstract class Inning {
  Inning() throws BaseballException {}
  void event () throws BaseballException {
   // Doesn't actually have to throw anything
  }
  abstract void atBat() throws Strike, Foul;
  void walk() {} // Throws nothing
}

class StormException extends Exception {}
class RainedOut extends StormException {}
class PopFoul extends Foul {}

interface Storm {
  void event() throws RainedOut;
  void rainHard() throws RainedOut;
}

public class StormyInning extends Inning
    implements Storm {
  // OK to add new exceptions for
  // constructors, but you must deal
  // with the base constructor exceptions:
  StormyInning() throws RainedOut,
    BaseballException {}
  StormyInning(String s) throws Foul,
    BaseballException {}
  // Regular methods must conform to base class:
//! void walk() throws PopFoul {} //Compile error
  // Interface CANNOT add exceptions to existing
  // methods from the base class:
//! public void event() throws RainedOut {}
  // If the method doesn't already exist in the
  // base class, the exception is OK:
  public void rainHard() throws RainedOut {}
  // You can choose to not throw any exceptions,
  // even if base version does:
  public void event() {}
  // Overridden methods can throw
```

```
    // inherited exceptions:
    void atBat() throws PopFoul {}
    public static void main(String[] args) {
      try {
        StormyInning si = new StormyInning();
        si.atBat();
      } catch(PopFoul e) {
        System.err.println("Pop foul");
      } catch(RainedOut e) {
        System.err.println("Rained out");
      } catch(BaseballException e) {
        System.err.println("Generic error");
      }
      // Strike not thrown in derived version.
      try {
        // What happens if you upcast?
        Inning i = new StormyInning();
        i.atBat();
        // You must catch the exceptions from the
        // base-class version of the method:
      } catch(Strike e) {
        System.err.println("Strike");
      } catch(Foul e) {
        System.err.println("Foul");
      } catch(RainedOut e) {
        System.err.println("Rained out");
      } catch(BaseballException e) {
        System.err.println(
          "Generic baseball exception");
      }
    }
} ///:~
```

In **Inning**, you can see that both the constructor and the **event( )** method say they will throw an exception, but they never do. This is legal because it allows you to force the user to catch any exceptions that might be added in overridden versions of **event( )**. The same idea holds for **abstract** methods, as seen in **atBat( )**.

The **interface Storm** is interesting because it contains one method (**event( )**) that is defined in **Inning**, and one method that isn't. Both methods throw a new type of exception, **RainedOut**. When **StormyInning extends Inning** and **implements Storm**, you'll see that the **event( )** method in **Storm** *cannot* change the exception interface of **event( )** in **Inning**. Again, this makes sense because otherwise you'd never know if you were catching the correct thing when working with the base class. Of course, if a method described in an **interface** is not in the base class, such as **rainHard( )**, then there's no problem if it throws exceptions.

The restriction on exceptions does not apply to constructors. You can see in **StormyInning** that a constructor can throw anything it wants, regardless of what the base-class constructor throws. However, since a base-class constructor must always be called one way or another (here, the default constructor is called automatically), the derived-class constructor must declare any base-class constructor exceptions in its exception specification. Note that a derived-class constructor cannot catch exceptions thrown by its base-class constructor.

The reason **StormyInning.walk( )** will not compile is that it throws an exception, while **Inning.walk( )** does not. If this was allowed, then you could write code that called **Inning.walk( )** and that didn't have to handle any exceptions, but then when you substituted an object of a class derived from **Inning**, exceptions would be thrown so your code would break. By forcing the derived-class methods to conform to the exception specifications of the base-class methods, substitutability of objects is maintained.

The overridden **event( )** method shows that a derived-class version of a method may choose not to throw any exceptions, even if the base-class version does. Again, this is fine since it doesn't break any code that is written—assuming the base-class version throws exceptions. Similar logic applies to **atBat( )**, which throws **PopFoul**, an exception that is derived from **Foul** thrown by the base-class version of **atBat( )**. This way, if someone writes code that works with **Inning** and calls **atBat( )**, they must catch the **Foul** exception. Since **PopFoul** is derived from **Foul**, the exception handler will also catch **PopFoul**.

The last point of interest is in **main( )**. Here you can see that if you're dealing with exactly a **StormyInning** object, the compiler forces you to catch only the exceptions that are specific to that class, but if you upcast to the base type then the compiler (correctly) forces you to catch the exceptions for the base type. All these constraints produce much more robust exception-handling code[5].

It's useful to realize that although exception specifications are enforced by the compiler during inheritance, the exception specifications are not part of the type of a method, which is comprised of only the method name and argument types. Therefore, you cannot overload methods based on exception specifications. In addition, just because an exception specification exists in a base-class version of a method doesn't mean that it must exist in the derived-class version of the method. This is quite different from inheritance rules, where a method in the base class must also exist in the derived class. Put another way, the "exception specification interface" for a particular method may narrow during inheritance and overriding, but it may not widen—this is precisely the opposite of the rule for the class interface during inheritance.

Constructors

When writing code with exceptions, it's particularly important that you always ask, "If an exception occurs, will this be properly cleaned up?" Most of the time you're fairly safe, but in constructors there's a problem. The constructor puts the object into a safe starting state, but it might perform some operation—such as opening a file—that doesn't get cleaned up until the user is finished with the object and calls a special cleanup method. If you throw an exception from inside a constructor, these cleanup behaviors might not occur properly. This means that you must be especially diligent while you write your constructor.

Since you've just learned about **finally**, you might think that it is the correct solution. But it's not quite that simple, because **finally** performs the cleanup code *every time,* even in the situations in which you don't want the cleanup code executed until the cleanup method runs. Thus, if

---

[5] ISO C++ added similar constraints that require derived-method exceptions to be the same as, or derived from, the exceptions thrown by the base-class method. This is one case in which C++ is actually able to check exception specifications at compile-time.

you do perform cleanup in **finally**, you must set some kind of flag when the constructor finishes normally so that you don't do anything in the **finally** block if the flag is set. Because this isn't particularly elegant (you are coupling your code from one place to another), it's best if you try to avoid performing this kind of cleanup in **finally** unless you are forced to.

In the following example, a class called **InputFile** is created that opens a file and allows you to read it one line (converted into a **String**) at a time. It uses the classes **FileReader** and **BufferedReader** from the Java standard I/O library that will be discussed in Chapter 11, but which are simple enough that you probably won't have any trouble understanding their basic use:

```java
//: c10:Cleanup.java
// Paying attention to exceptions
// in constructors.
import java.io.*;

class InputFile {
  private BufferedReader in;
  InputFile(String fname) throws Exception {
    try {
      in =
        new BufferedReader(
          new FileReader(fname));
      // Other code that might throw exceptions
    } catch(FileNotFoundException e) {
      System.err.println(
        "Could not open " + fname);
      // Wasn't open, so don't close it
      throw e;
    } catch(Exception e) {
      // All other exceptions must close it
      try {
        in.close();
      } catch(IOException e2) {
        System.err.println(
          "in.close() unsuccessful");
      }
      throw e; // Rethrow
    } finally {
```

```
      // Don't close it here!!!
    }
  }
  String getLine() {
    String s;
    try {
      s = in.readLine();
    } catch(IOException e) {
      System.err.println(
        "readLine() unsuccessful");
      s = "failed";
    }
    return s;
  }
  void cleanup() {
    try {
      in.close();
    } catch(IOException e2) {
      System.err.println(
        "in.close() unsuccessful");
    }
  }
}

public class Cleanup {
  public static void main(String[] args) {
    try {
      InputFile in =
        new InputFile("Cleanup.java");
      String s;
      int i = 1;
      while((s = in.getLine()) != null)
        System.out.println(""+ i++ + ": " + s);
      in.cleanup();
    } catch(Exception e) {
      System.err.println(
        "Caught in main, e.printStackTrace()");
      e.printStackTrace(System.err);
    }
  }
} ///:~
```

The constructor for **InputFile** takes a **String** argument, which is the name of the file you want to open. Inside a **try** block, it creates a **FileReader** using the file name. A **FileReader** isn't particularly useful until you turn around and use it to create a **BufferedReader** that you can actually talk to—notice that one of the benefits of **InputFile** is that it combines these two actions.

If the **FileReader** constructor is unsuccessful, it throws a **FileNotFoundException**, which must be caught separately because that's the one case in which you don't want to close the file since it wasn't successfully opened. Any *other* catch clauses must close the file because it *was* opened by the time those catch clauses are entered. (Of course, this is trickier if more than one method can throw a **FileNotFoundException**. In that case, you might want to break things into several **try** blocks.) The **close( )** method might throw an exception so it is tried and caught even though it's within the block of another **catch** clause—it's just another pair of curly braces to the Java compiler. After performing local operations, the exception is rethrown, which is appropriate because this constructor failed, and you wouldn't want the calling method to assume that the object had been properly created and was valid.

In this example, which doesn't use the aforementioned flagging technique, the **finally** clause is definitely *not* the place to **close( )** the file, since that would close it every time the constructor completed. Since we want the file to be open for the useful lifetime of the **InputFile** object this would not be appropriate.

The **getLine( )** method returns a **String** containing the next line in the file. It calls **readLine( ),** which can throw an exception, but that exception is caught so **getLine( )** doesn't throw any exceptions. One of the design issues with exceptions is whether to handle an exception completely at this level, to handle it partially and pass the same exception (or a different one) on, or whether to simply pass it on. Passing it on, when appropriate, can certainly simplify coding. The **getLine( )** method becomes:

```
String getLine() throws IOException {
  return in.readLine();
}
```

But of course, the caller is now responsible for handling any **IOException** that might arise.

The **cleanup( )** method must be called by the user when finished using the **InputFile** object. This will release the system resources (such as file handles) that are used by the **BufferedReader** and/or **FileReader** objects[6]. You don't want to do this until you're finished with the **InputFile** object, at the point you're going to let it go. You might think of putting such functionality into a **finalize( )** method, but as mentioned in Chapter 4 you can't always be sure that **finalize( )** will be called (even if you *can* be sure that it will be called, you don't know *when*). This is one of the downsides to Java: all cleanup—other than memory cleanup—doesn't happen automatically, so you must inform the client programmer that they are responsible, and possibly guarantee that cleanup occurs using **finalize( )**.

In **Cleanup.java** an **InputFile** is created to open the same source file that creates the program, the file is read in a line at a time, and line numbers are added. All exceptions are caught generically in **main( )**, although you could choose greater granularity.

One of the benefits of this example is to show you why exceptions are introduced at this point in the book—you can't do basic I/O without using exceptions. Exceptions are so integral to programming in Java, especially because the compiler enforces them, that you can accomplish only so much without knowing how to work with them.

Exception matching

When an exception is thrown, the exception handling system looks through the "nearest" handlers in the order they are written. When it finds a match, the exception is considered handled, and no further searching occurs.

---

[6] In C++, a *destructor* would handle this for you.

Matching an exception doesn't require a perfect match between the exception and its handler. A derived-class object will match a handler for the base class, as shown in this example:

```
//: c10:Human.java
// Catching exception hierarchies.

class Annoyance extends Exception {}
class Sneeze extends Annoyance {}

public class Human {
  public static void main(String[] args) {
    try {
      throw new Sneeze();
    } catch(Sneeze s) {
      System.err.println("Caught Sneeze");
    } catch(Annoyance a) {
      System.err.println("Caught Annoyance");
    }
  }
} ///:~
```

The **Sneeze** exception will be caught by the first **catch** clause that it matches—which is the first one, of course. However, if you remove the first catch clause, leaving only:

```
try {
  throw new Sneeze();
} catch(Annoyance a) {
  System.err.println("Caught Annoyance");
}
```

The code will still work because it's catching the base class of **Sneeze**. Put another way, **catch(Annoyance e)** will catch an **Annoyance** *or any class derived from it*. This is useful because if you decide to add more derived exceptions to a method, then the client programmer's code will not need changing as long as the client catches the base class exceptions.

If you try to "mask" the derived-class exceptions by putting the base-class catch clause first, like this:

```
try {
```

```
    throw new Sneeze();
  } catch(Annoyance a) {
    System.err.println("Caught Annoyance");
  } catch(Sneeze s) {
    System.err.println("Caught Sneeze");
  }
```

the compiler will give you an error message, since it sees that the **Sneeze** catch-clause can never be reached.

Exception guidelines

Use exceptions to:

1. Fix the problem and call the method that caused the exception again.

2. Patch things up and continue without retrying the method.

3. Calculate some alternative result instead of what the method was supposed to produce.

4. Do whatever you can in the current context and rethrow the *same* exception to a higher context.

5. Do whatever you can in the current context and throw a *different* exception to a higher context.

6. Terminate the program.

7. Simplify. (If your exception scheme makes things more complicated, then it is painful and annoying to use.)

8. Make your library and program safer. (This is a short-term investment for debugging, and a long-term investment (for application robustness.)

Summary

Improved error recovery is one of the most powerful ways that you can increase the robustness of your code. Error recovery is a fundamental concern for every program you write, but it's especially important in Java, where one of the primary goals is to create program components for others to use. *To create a robust system, each component must be robust.*

The goals for exception handling in Java are to simplify the creation of large, reliable programs using less code than currently possible, and with more confidence that your application doesn't have an unhandled error.

Exceptions are not terribly difficult to learn, and are one of those features that provide immediate and significant benefits to your project. Fortunately, Java enforces all aspects of exceptions so it's guaranteed that they will be used consistently by both library designers and client programmers.

Exercises

Solutions to selected exercises can be found in the electronic document *The Thinking in Java Annotated Solution Guide*, available for a small fee from *www.BruceEckel.com*.

1. Create a class with a **main( )** that throws an object of class **Exception** inside a **try** block. Give the constructor for **Exception** a **String** argument. Catch the exception inside a **catch** clause and print the **String** argument. Add a **finally** clause and print a message to prove you were there.

2. Create your own exception class using the **extends** keyword. Write a constructor for this class that takes a **String** argument and stores it inside the object with a **String** reference. Write a method that prints out the stored **String**. Create a **try-catch** clause to exercise your new exception.

3. Write a class with a method that throws an exception of the type created in Exercise 2. Try compiling it without an exception specification to see what the compiler says. Add the appropriate exception specification. Try out your class and its exception inside a try-catch clause.

4. Define an object reference and initialize it to **null**. Try to call a method through this reference. Now wrap the code in a **try-catch** clause to catch the exception.

5. Create a class with two methods, **f( )** and **g( )**. In **g( )**, throw an exception of a new type that you define. In **f( )**, call **g( )**, catch its exception and, in the **catch** clause, throw a different exception (of a second type that you define). Test your code in **main( )**.

6. Create three new types of exceptions. Write a class with a method that throws all three. In **main( )**, call the method but only use a single **catch** clause that will catch all three types of exceptions.

7. Write code to generate and catch an **ArrayIndexOutOfBoundsException**.

8. Create your own resumption-like behavior using a **while** loop that repeats until an exception is no longer thrown.

9. Create a three-level hierarchy of exceptions. Now create a base-class **A** with a method that throws an exception at the base of your hierarchy. Inherit **B** from **A** and override the method so it throws an exception at level two of your hierarchy. Repeat by inheriting class **C** from **B**. In **main( )**, create a **C** and upcast it to **A**, then call the method.

10. Demonstrate that a derived-class constructor cannot catch exceptions thrown by its base-class constructor.

11. Show that **OnOffSwitch.java** can fail by throwing a **RuntimeException** inside the **try** block.

12. Show that **WithFinally.java** doesn't fail by throwing a **RuntimeException** inside the **try** block.

13. Modify Exercise 6 by adding a **finally** clause. Verify your **finally** clause is executed, even if a **NullPointerException** is thrown.

14. Create an example where you use a flag to control whether cleanup code is called, as described in the second paragraph after the heading "Constructors."

15. Modify **StormyInning.java** by adding an **UmpireArgument** exception type, and methods that throw this exception. Test the modified hierarchy.

16. Remove the first catch clause in **Human.java** and verify that the code still compiles and runs properly.

17. Add a second level of exception loss to **LostMessage.java** so that the **HoHumException** is itself replaced by a third exception.

18. In Chapter 5, find the two programs called **Assert.java** and modify these to throw their own type of exception instead of printing to **System.err**. This exception should be an inner class that extends **RuntimeException**.

19. Add an appropriate set of exceptions to **c08:GreenhouseControls.java**.

11: The Java I/O System

Creating a good input/output (I/O) system is one of the more difficult tasks for the language designer.

This is evidenced by the number of different approaches. The challenge seems to be in covering all eventualities. Not only are there different sources and sinks of I/O that you want to communicate with (files, the console, network connections), but you need to talk to them in a wide variety of ways (sequential, random-access, buffered, binary, character, by lines, by words, etc.).

The Java library designers attacked this problem by creating lots of classes. In fact, there are so many classes for Java's I/O system that it can be intimidating at first (ironically, the Java I/O design actually prevents an explosion of classes). There was also a significant change in the I/O library after Java 1.0, when the original **byte**-oriented library was supplemented with **char**-oriented, Unicode-based I/O classes. As a result there are a fair number of classes to learn before you understand enough of Java's I/O picture that you can use it properly. In addition, it's rather important to understand the evolution history of the I/O library, even if your first reaction is "don't bother me with history, just show me how to use it!" The problem is that without the historical perspective you will rapidly become confused with some of the classes and when you should and shouldn't use them.

This chapter will give you an introduction to the variety of I/O classes in the standard Java library and how to use them.

The **File** class

Before getting into the classes that actually read and write data to streams, we'll look a utility provided with the library to assist you in handling file directory issues.

The **File** class has a deceiving name—you might think it refers to a file, but it doesn't. It can represent either the *name* of a particular file or the *names* of a set of files in a directory. If it's a set of files, you can ask for the set with the **list( )** method, and this returns an array of **String**. It makes sense to return an array rather than one of the flexible container classes because the number of elements is fixed, and if you want a different directory listing you just create a different **File** object. In fact, "FilePath" would have been a better name for the class. This section shows an example of the use of this class, including the associated **FilenameFilter interface**.

A directory lister

Suppose you'd like to see a directory listing. The **File** object can be listed in two ways. If you call **list( )** with no arguments, you'll get the full list that the **File** object contains. However, if you want a restricted list—for example, if you want all of the files with an extension of **.java**—then you use a "directory filter," which is a class that tells how to select the **File** objects for display.

Here's the code for the example. Note that the result has been effortlessly sorted (alphabetically) using the **java.utils.Array.sort( )** method and the **AlphabeticComparator** defined in Chapter 9:

```
//: c11:DirList.java
// Displays directory listing.
import java.io.*;
import java.util.*;
import com.bruceeckel.util.*;

public class DirList {
  public static void main(String[] args) {
    File path = new File(".");
    String[] list;
```

```
       if(args.length == 0)
         list = path.list();
       else
         list = path.list(new DirFilter(args[0]));
       Arrays.sort(list,
         new AlphabeticComparator());
       for(int i = 0; i < list.length; i++)
         System.out.println(list[i]);
     }
   }

   class DirFilter implements FilenameFilter {
     String afn;
     DirFilter(String afn) { this.afn = afn; }
     public boolean accept(File dir, String name) {
       // Strip path information:
       String f = new File(name).getName();
       return f.indexOf(afn) != -1;
     }
   } ///:~
```

The **DirFilter** class "implements" the **interface FilenameFilter**. It's useful to see how simple the **FilenameFilter interface** is:

```
public interface FilenameFilter {
   boolean accept(File dir, String name);
}
```

It says all that this type of object does is provide a method called **accept( )**. The whole reason behind the creation of this class is to provide the **accept( )** method to the **list( )** method so that **list( )** can "call back" **accept( )** to determine which file names should be included in the list. Thus, this technique is often referred to as a *callback* or sometimes a *functor* (that is, **DirFilter** is a functor because its only job is to hold a method) or the *Command Pattern*. Because **list( )** takes a **FilenameFilter** object as its argument, it means that you can pass an object of any class that implements **FilenameFilter** to choose (even at run-time) how the **list( )** method will behave. The purpose of a callback is to provide flexibility in the behavior of code.

DirFilter shows that just because an **interface** contains only a set of methods, you're not restricted to writing only those methods. (You must at least provide definitions for all the methods in an interface, however.) In this case, the **DirFilter** constructor is also created.

The **accept( )** method must accept a **File** object representing the directory that a particular file is found in, and a **String** containing the name of that file. You might choose to use or ignore either of these arguments, but you will probably at least use the file name. Remember that the **list( )** method is calling **accept( )** for each of the file names in the directory object to see which one should be included—this is indicated by the **boolean** result returned by **accept( )**.

To make sure the element you're working with is only the file name and contains no path information, all you have to do is take the **String** object and create a **File** object out of it, then call **getName( )**, which strips away all the path information (in a platform-independent way). Then **accept( )** uses the **String** class **indexOf( )** method to see if the search string **afn** appears anywhere in the name of the file. If **afn** is found within the string, the return value is the starting index of **afn**, but if it's not found the return value is -1. Keep in mind that this is a simple string search and does not have "glob" expression wildcard matching—such as "fo?.b?r*"—which is much more difficult to implement.

The **list( )** method returns an array. You can query this array for its length and then move through it selecting the array elements. This ability to easily pass an array in and out of a method is a tremendous improvement over the behavior of C and C++.

Anonymous inner classes

This example is ideal for rewriting using an anonymous inner class (described in Chapter 8). As a first cut, a method **filter( )** is created that returns a reference to a **FilenameFilter**:

```
//: c11:DirList2.java
// Uses anonymous inner classes.
import java.io.*;
import java.util.*;
import com.bruceeckel.util.*;
```

```
public class DirList2 {
  public static FilenameFilter
  filter(final String afn) {
    // Creation of anonymous inner class:
    return new FilenameFilter() {
      String fn = afn;
      public boolean accept(File dir, String n) {
        // Strip path information:
        String f = new File(n).getName();
        return f.indexOf(fn) != -1;
      }
    }; // End of anonymous inner class
  }
  public static void main(String[] args) {
    File path = new File(".");
    String[] list;
    if(args.length == 0)
      list = path.list();
    else
      list = path.list(filter(args[0]));
    Arrays.sort(list,
      new AlphabeticComparator());
    for(int i = 0; i < list.length; i++)
      System.out.println(list[i]);
  }
} ///:~
```

Note that the argument to **filter( )** must be **final**. This is required by the anonymous inner class so that it can use an object from outside its scope.

This design is an improvement because the **FilenameFilter** class is now tightly bound to **DirList2**. However, you can take this approach one step further and define the anonymous inner class as an argument to **list( )**, in which case it's even smaller:

```
//: c11:DirList3.java
// Building the anonymous inner class "in-place."
import java.io.*;
import java.util.*;
import com.bruceeckel.util.*;

public class DirList3 {
```

```
public static void main(final String[] args) {
  File path = new File(".");
  String[] list;
  if(args.length == 0)
    list = path.list();
  else
    list = path.list(new FilenameFilter() {
      public boolean
      accept(File dir, String n) {
        String f = new File(n).getName();
        return f.indexOf(args[0]) != -1;
      }
    });
  Arrays.sort(list,
    new AlphabeticComparator());
  for(int i = 0; i < list.length; i++)
    System.out.println(list[i]);
  }
} ///:~
```

The argument to **main( )** is now **final**, since the anonymous inner class uses **args[0]** directly.

This shows you how anonymous inner classes allow the creation of quick-and-dirty classes to solve problems. Since everything in Java revolves around classes, this can be a useful coding technique. One benefit is that it keeps the code that solves a particular problem isolated together in one spot. On the other hand, it is not always as easy to read, so you must use it judiciously.

Checking for and creating directories

The **File** class is more than just a representation for an existing file or directory. You can also use a **File** object to create a new directory or an entire directory path if it doesn't exist. You can also look at the characteristics of files (size, last modification date, read/write), see whether a **File** object represents a file or a directory, and delete a file. This program shows some of the other methods available with the **File** class (see the HTML documentation from *java.sun.com* for the full set):

```
//: c11:MakeDirectories.java
// Demonstrates the use of the File class to
// create directories and manipulate files.
import java.io.*;

public class MakeDirectories {
  private final static String usage =
    "Usage:MakeDirectories path1 ...\n" +
    "Creates each path\n" +
    "Usage:MakeDirectories -d path1 ...\n" +
    "Deletes each path\n" +
    "Usage:MakeDirectories -r path1 path2\n" +
    "Renames from path1 to path2\n";
  private static void usage() {
    System.err.println(usage);
    System.exit(1);
  }
  private static void fileData(File f) {
    System.out.println(
      "Absolute path: " + f.getAbsolutePath() +
      "\n Can read: " + f.canRead() +
      "\n Can write: " + f.canWrite() +
      "\n getName: " + f.getName() +
      "\n getParent: " + f.getParent() +
      "\n getPath: " + f.getPath() +
      "\n length: " + f.length() +
      "\n lastModified: " + f.lastModified());
    if(f.isFile())
      System.out.println("it's a file");
    else if(f.isDirectory())
      System.out.println("it's a directory");
  }
  public static void main(String[] args) {
    if(args.length < 1) usage();
    if(args[0].equals("-r")) {
      if(args.length != 3) usage();
      File
        old = new File(args[1]),
        rname = new File(args[2]);
      old.renameTo(rname);
      fileData(old);
```

```
      fileData(rname);
      return; // Exit main
    }
    int count = 0;
    boolean del = false;
    if(args[0].equals("-d")) {
      count++;
      del = true;
    }
    for( ; count < args.length; count++) {
      File f = new File(args[count]);
      if(f.exists()) {
        System.out.println(f + " exists");
        if(del) {
          System.out.println("deleting..." + f);
          f.delete();
        }
      }
      else { // Doesn't exist
        if(!del) {
          f.mkdirs();
          System.out.println("created " + f);
        }
      }
      fileData(f);
    }
  }
} ///:~
```

In **fileData( )** you can see various file investigation methods used to display information about the file or directory path.

The first method that's exercised by **main( )** is **renameTo( )**, which allows you to rename (or move) a file to an entirely new path represented by the argument, which is another **File** object. This also works with directories of any length.

If you experiment with the above program, you'll find that you can make a directory path of any complexity because **mkdirs( )** will do all the work for you.

Input and output

I/O libraries often use the abstraction of a *stream*, which represents any data source or sink as an object capable of producing or receiving pieces of data. The stream hides the details of what happens to the data inside the actual I/O device.

The Java library classes for I/O are divided by input and output, as you can see by looking at the online Java class hierarchy with your Web browser. By inheritance, everything derived from the **InputStream** or **Reader** classes have basic methods called **read( )** for reading a single byte or array of bytes. Likewise, everything derived from **OutputStream** or **Writer** classes have basic methods called **write( )** for writing a single byte or array of bytes. However, you won't generally use these methods; they exist so that other classes can use them—these other classes provide a more useful interface. Thus, you'll rarely create your stream object by using a single class, but instead will layer multiple objects together to provide your desired functionality. The fact that you create more than one object to create a single resulting stream is the primary reason that Java's stream library is confusing.

It's helpful to categorize the classes by their functionality. In Java 1.0, the library designers started by deciding that all classes that had anything to do with input would be inherited from **InputStream** and all classes that were associated with output would be inherited from **OutputStream**.

Types of **InputStream**

InputStream's job is to represent classes that produce input from different sources. These sources can be:

1.   An array of bytes.

2.   A **String** object.

3.   A file.

4.   A "pipe," which works like a physical pipe: you put things in one end and they come out the other.

---

5. A sequence of other streams, so you can collect them together into a single stream.

6. Other sources, such as an Internet connection. (This will be discussed in a later chapter.)

Each of these has an associated subclass of **InputStream**. In addition, the **FilterInputStream** is also a type of **InputStream**, to provide a base class for "decorator" classes that attach attributes or useful interfaces to input streams. This is discussed later.

Table 11-1. Types of InputStream

Class	Function	Constructor Arguments
		How to use it
ByteArray-InputStream	Allows a buffer in memory to be used as an **InputStream**	The buffer from which to extract the bytes.
		As a source of data. Connect it to a **FilterInputStream** object to provide a useful interface.
StringBuffer-InputStream	Converts a **String** into an **InputStream**	A **String**. The underlying implementation actually uses a **StringBuffer**.
		As a source of data. Connect it to a **FilterInputStream** object to provide a useful interface.
File-InputStream	For reading information from a file	A **String** representing the file name, or a **File** or **FileDescriptor** object.
		As a source of data. Connect it to a **FilterInputStream** object to provide a useful interface.
Piped-InputStream	Produces the data that's being written to the	**PipedOutputStream**

Class	Function	Constructor Arguments
		How to use it
	associated **PipedOutputStream**. Implements the "piping" concept.	As a source of data in multithreading. Connect it to a **FilterInputStream** object to provide a useful interface.
Sequence-InputStream	Converts two or more **InputStream** objects into a single **InputStream**.	Two **InputStream** objects or an **Enumeration** for a container of **InputStream** objects.
		As a source of data. Connect it to a **FilterInputStream** object to provide a useful interface.
Filter-InputStream	Abstract class which is an interface for decorators that provide useful functionality to the other **InputStream** classes. See Table 11-3.	See Table 11-3.
		See Table 11-3.

Types of **OutputStream**

This category includes the classes that decide where your output will go: an array of bytes (no **String**, however; presumably you can create one using the array of bytes), a file, or a "pipe."

In addition, the **FilterOutputStream** provides a base class for "decorator" classes that attach attributes or useful interfaces to output streams. This is discussed later.

Table 11-2. Types of OutputStream

Class	Function	Constructor Arguments

		How to use it
ByteArray-OutputStream	Creates a buffer in memory. All the data that you send to the stream is placed in this buffer.	Optional initial size of the buffer.
		To designate the destination of your data. Connect it to a **FilterOutputStream** object to provide a useful interface.
File-OutputStream	For sending information to a file.	A String representing the file name, or a **File** or **FileDescriptor** object.
		To designate the destination of your data. Connect it to a **FilterOutputStream** object to provide a useful interface.
Piped-OutputStream	Any information you write to this automatically ends up as input for the associated **PipedInput-Stream**. Implements the "piping" concept.	**PipedInputStream**
		To designate the destination of your data for multithreading. Connect it to a **FilterOutputStream** object to provide a useful interface.
Filter-OutputStream	Abstract class which is an interface for decorators that provide useful functionality to the other **OutputStream** classes. See Table 11-4.	See Table 11-4.
		See Table 11-4.

Adding attributes
and useful interfaces

The use of layered objects to dynamically and transparently add responsibilities to individual objects is referred to as the *Decorator* pattern. (Patterns[1] are the subject of *Thinking in Patterns with Java*, downloadable at *www.BruceEckel.com*.) The decorator pattern specifies that all objects that wrap around your initial object have the same interface. This makes the basic use of the decorators transparent—you send the same message to an object whether it's been decorated or not. This is the reason for the existence of the "filter" classes in the Java I/O library: the abstract "filter" class is the base class for all the decorators. (A decorator must have the same interface as the object it decorates, but the decorator can also extend the interface, which occurs in several of the "filter" classes).

Decorators are often used when simple subclassing results in a large number of subclasses in order to satisfy every possible combination that is needed—so many subclasses that it becomes impractical. The Java I/O library requires many different combinations of features, which is why the decorator pattern is used. There is a drawback to the decorator pattern, however. Decorators give you much more flexibility while you're writing a program (since you can easily mix and match attributes), but they add complexity to your code. The reason that the Java I/O library is awkward to use is that you must create many classes—the "core" I/O type plus all the decorators—in order to get the single I/O object that you want.

The classes that provide the decorator interface to control a particular **InputStream** or **OutputStream** are the **FilterInputStream** and **FilterOutputStream**—which don't have very intuitive names. **FilterInputStream** and **FilterOutputStream** are abstract classes that are derived from the base classes of the I/O library, **InputStream** and **OutputStream**, which is the key requirement of the decorator (so that it

---

[1] *Design Patterns*, Erich Gamma *et al.*, Addison-Wesley 1995.

provides the common interface to all the objects that are being decorated).

Reading from an **InputStream** with **FilterInputStream**

The **FilterInputStream** classes accomplish two significantly different things. **DataInputStream** allows you to read different types of primitive data as well as **String** objects. (All the methods start with "read," such as **readByte( )**, **readFloat( )**, etc.) This, along with its companion **DataOutputStream**, allows you to move primitive data from one place to another via a stream. These "places" are determined by the classes in Table 11-1.

The remaining classes modify the way an **InputStream** behaves internally: whether it's buffered or unbuffered, if it keeps track of the lines it's reading (allowing you to ask for line numbers or set the line number), and whether you can push back a single character. The last two classes look a lot like support for building a compiler (that is, they were added to support the construction of the Java compiler), so you probably won't use them in general programming.

You'll probably need to buffer your input almost every time, regardless of the I/O device you're connecting to, so it would have made more sense for the I/O library to make a special case (or simply a method call) for unbuffered input rather than buffered input.

Table 11-3. Types of FilterInputStream

Class	Function	Constructor Arguments
		How to use it
Data-InputStream	Used in concert with **DataOutputStream**, so you can read primitives (**int, char, long**, etc.) from a stream in a portable fashion.	**InputStream**
		Contains a full interface to allow you to read primitive types.

Buffered-InputStream	Use this to prevent a physical read every time you want more data. You're saying "Use a buffer."	**InputStream**, with optional buffer size.
		This doesn't provide an interface *per se*, just a requirement that a buffer be used. Attach an interface object.
LineNumber-InputStream	Keeps track of line numbers in the input stream; you can call **getLineNumber( )** and **setLineNumber(int)**.	**InputStream**
		This just adds line numbering, so you'll probably attach an interface object.
Pushback-InputStream	Has a one byte push-back buffer so that you can push back the last character read.	**InputStream**
		Generally used in the scanner for a compiler and probably included because the Java compiler needed it. You probably won't use this.

Writing to an **OutputStream** with **FilterOutputStream**

The complement to **DataInputStream** is **DataOutputStream**, which formats each of the primitive types and **String** objects onto a stream in such a way that any **DataInputStream**, on any machine, can read them. All the methods start with "write," such as **writeByte( )**, **writeFloat( )**, etc.

The original intent of **PrintStream** was to print all of the primitive data types and **String** objects in a viewable format. This is different from **DataOutputStream**, whose goal is to put data elements on a stream in a way that **DataInputStream** can portably reconstruct them.

The two important methods in **PrintStream** are **print( )** and **println( )**, which are overloaded to print all the various types. The difference between **print( )** and **println( )** is that the latter adds a newline when it's done.

PrintStream can be problematic because it traps all **IOException**s (You must explicitly test the error status with **checkError( )**, which returns **true** if an error has occurred). Also, **PrintStream** doesn't internationalize properly and doesn't handle line breaks in a platform independent way (these problems are solved with **PrintWriter**).

BufferedOutputStream is a modifier and tells the stream to use buffering so you don't get a physical write every time you write to the stream. You'll probably always want to use this with files, and possibly console I/O.

Table 11-4. Types of FilterOutputStream

Class	Function	Constructor Arguments
		How to use it
Data-OutputStream	Used in concert with **DataInputStream** so you can write primitives (int, char, long, etc.) to a stream in a portable fashion.	**OutputStream**
		Contains full interface to allow you to write primitive types.
PrintStream	For producing formatted output. While **DataOutputStream** handles the *storage* of data, **PrintStream** handles *display*.	**OutputStream**, with optional **boolean** indicating that the buffer is flushed with every newline.
		Should be the "final" wrapping for your **OutputStream** object. You'll probably use this a lot.

Class	Function	Constructor Arguments
		How to use it
Buffered-OutputStream	Use this to prevent a physical write every time you send a piece of data. You're saying "Use a buffer." You can call **flush( )** to flush the buffer.	**OutputStream**, with optional buffer size.
		This doesn't provide an interface *per se*, just a requirement that a buffer is used. Attach an interface object.

Readers & Writers

Java 1.1 made some significant modifications to the fundamental I/O stream library (Java 2, however, did not make fundamental modifications). When you see the **Reader** and **Writer** classes your first thought (like mine) might be that these were meant to replace the **InputStream** and **OutputStream** classes. But that's not the case. Although some aspects of the original streams library are deprecated (if you use them you will receive a warning from the compiler), the **InputStream** and **OutputStream** classes still provide valuable functionality in the form of **byte**-oriented I/O, while the **Reader** and **Writer** classes provide Unicode-compliant, character-based I/O. In addition:

1.   Java 1.1 added new classes into the **InputStream** and **OutputStream** hierarchy, so it's obvious those classes weren't being replaced.

2.   There are times when you must use classes from the "byte" hierarchy *in combination* with classes in the "character" hierarchy. To accomplish this there are "bridge" classes: **InputStreamReader** converts an **InputStream** to a **Reader** and **OutputStreamWriter** converts an **OutputStream** to a **Writer**.

The most important reason for the **Reader** and **Writer** hierarchies is for internationalization. The old I/O stream hierarchy supports only 8-bit byte streams and doesn't handle the 16-bit Unicode characters well. Since Unicode is used for internationalization (and Java's native **char** is 16-bit Unicode), the **Reader** and **Writer** hierarchies were added to support Unicode in all I/O operations. In addition, the new libraries are designed for faster operations than the old.

As is the practice in this book, I will attempt to provide an overview of the classes, but assume that you will use online documentation to determine all the details, such as the exhaustive list of methods.

Sources and sinks of data

Almost all of the original Java I/O stream classes have corresponding **Reader** and **Writer** classes to provide native Unicode manipulation. However, there are some places where the **byte**-oriented **InputStream**s and **OutputStream**s are the correct solution; in particular, the **java.util.zip** libraries are **byte**-oriented rather than **char**-oriented. So the most sensible approach to take is to *try* to use the **Reader** and **Writer** classes whenever you can, and you'll discover the situations when you have to use the **byte**-oriented libraries because your code won't compile.

Here is a table that shows the correspondence between the sources and sinks of information (that is, where the data physically comes from or goes to) in the two hierarchies.

Sources & Sinks: Java 1.0 class	Corresponding Java 1.1 class
InputStream	**Reader** converter: **InputStreamReader**
OutputStream	**Writer** converter: **OutputStreamWriter**
FileInputStream	**FileReader**
FileOutputStream	**FileWriter**
StringBufferInputStream	**StringReader**

(no corresponding class)	StringWriter
ByteArrayInputStream	CharArrayReader
ByteArrayOutputStream	CharArrayWriter
PipedInputStream	PipedReader
PipedOutputStream	PipedWriter

In general, you'll find that the interfaces for the two different hierarchies are similar if not identical.

Modifying stream behavior

For **InputStream**s and **OutputStream**s, streams were adapted for particular needs using "decorator" subclasses of **FilterInputStream** and **FilterOutputStream**. The **Reader** and **Writer** class hierarchies continue the use of this idea—but not exactly.

In the following table, the correspondence is a rougher approximation than in the previous table. The difference is because of the class organization: while **BufferedOutputStream** is a subclass of **FilterOutputStream**, **BufferedWriter** is *not* a subclass of **FilterWriter** (which, even though it is **abstract**, has no subclasses and so appears to have been put in either as a placeholder or simply so you wouldn't wonder where it was). However, the interfaces to the classes are quite a close match.

Filters: Java 1.0 class	Corresponding Java 1.1 class
FilterInputStream	FilterReader
FilterOutputStream	FilterWriter (abstract class with no subclasses)
BufferedInputStream	BufferedReader (also has readLine( ))
BufferedOutputStream	BufferedWriter
DataInputStream	Use DataInputStream (Except when you need to use readLine( ), when you should use a BufferedReader)

Filters: Java 1.0 class	Corresponding Java 1.1 class
PrintStream	**PrintWriter**
LineNumberInputStream	**LineNumberReader**
StreamTokenizer	**StreamTokenizer** (use constructor that takes a **Reader** instead)
PushBackInputStream	**PushBackReader**

There's one direction that's quite clear: Whenever you want to use **readLine( )**, you shouldn't do it with a **DataInputStream** any more (this is met with a deprecation message at compile-time), but instead use a **BufferedReader**. Other than this, **DataInputStream** is still a "preferred" member of the I/O library.

To make the transition to using a **PrintWriter** easier, it has constructors that take any **OutputStream** object, as well as **Writer** objects. However, **PrintWriter** has no more support for formatting than **PrintStream** does; the interfaces are virtually the same.

The **PrintWriter** constructor also has an option to perform automatic flushing, which happens after every **println( )** if the constructor flag is set.

Unchanged Classes

Some classes were left unchanged between Java 1.0 and Java 1.1:

Java 1.0 classes without corresponding Java 1.1 classes
DataOutputStream
File
RandomAccessFile
SequenceInputStream

DataOutputStream, in particular, is used without change, so for storing and retrieving data in a transportable format you use the **InputStream** and **OutputStream** hierarchies.

Off by itself: RandomAccessFile

RandomAccessFile is used for files containing records of known size so that you can move from one record to another using **seek( )**, then read or change the records. The records don't have to be the same size; you just have to be able to determine how big they are and where they are placed in the file.

At first it's a little bit hard to believe that **RandomAccessFile** is not part of the **InputStream** or **OutputStream** hierarchy. However, it has no association with those hierarchies other than that it happens to implement the **DataInput** and **DataOutput** interfaces (which are also implemented by **DataInputStream** and **DataOutputStream**). It doesn't even use any of the functionality of the existing **InputStream** or **OutputStream** classes—it's a completely separate class, written from scratch, with all of its own (mostly native) methods. The reason for this may be that **RandomAccessFile** has essentially different behavior than the other I/O types, since you can move forward and backward within a file. In any event, it stands alone, as a direct descendant of **Object**.

Essentially, a **RandomAccessFile** works like a **DataInputStream** pasted together with a **DataOutputStream**, along with the methods **getFilePointer( )** to find out where you are in the file, **seek( )** to move to a new point in the file, and **length( )** to determine the maximum size of the file. In addition, the constructors require a second argument (identical to **fopen( )** in C) indicating whether you are just randomly reading (**"r"**) or reading and writing (**"rw"**). There's no support for write-only files, which could suggest that **RandomAccessFile** might have worked well if it were inherited from **DataInputStream**.

The seeking methods are available only in **RandomAccessFile**, which works for files only. **BufferedInputStream** does allow you to **mark( )** a position (whose value is held in a single internal variable) and **reset( )** to that position, but this is limited and not very useful.

Typical uses of I/O streams

Although you can combine the I/O stream classes in many different ways, you'll probably just use a few combinations. The following example can be used as a basic reference; it shows the creation and use of typical I/O configurations. Note that each configuration begins with a commented number and title that corresponds to the heading for the appropriate explanation that follows in the text.

```java
//: c11:IOStreamDemo.java
// Typical I/O stream configurations.
import java.io.*;

public class IOStreamDemo {
  // Throw exceptions to console:
  public static void main(String[] args)
  throws IOException {
    // 1. Reading input by lines:
    BufferedReader in =
      new BufferedReader(
        new FileReader("IOStreamDemo.java"));
    String s, s2 = new String();
    while((s = in.readLine())!= null)
      s2 += s + "\n";
    in.close();

    // 1b. Reading standard input:
    BufferedReader stdin =
      new BufferedReader(
        new InputStreamReader(System.in));
    System.out.print("Enter a line:");
    System.out.println(stdin.readLine());

    // 2. Input from memory
    StringReader in2 = new StringReader(s2);
    int c;
    while((c = in2.read()) != -1)
```

```java
    System.out.print((char)c);

// 3. Formatted memory input
try {
  DataInputStream in3 =
    new DataInputStream(
      new ByteArrayInputStream(s2.getBytes()));
  while(true)
    System.out.print((char)in3.readByte());
} catch(EOFException e) {
  System.err.println("End of stream");
}

// 4. File output
try {
  BufferedReader in4 =
    new BufferedReader(
      new StringReader(s2));
  PrintWriter out1 =
    new PrintWriter(
      new BufferedWriter(
        new FileWriter("IODemo.out")));
  int lineCount = 1;
  while((s = in4.readLine()) != null )
    out1.println(lineCount++ + ": " + s);
  out1.close();
} catch(EOFException e) {
  System.err.println("End of stream");
}

// 5. Storing & recovering data
try {
  DataOutputStream out2 =
    new DataOutputStream(
      new BufferedOutputStream(
        new FileOutputStream("Data.txt")));
  out2.writeDouble(3.14159);
  out2.writeChars("That was pi\n");
  out2.writeBytes("That was pi\n");
  out2.close();
  DataInputStream in5 =
```

```
        new DataInputStream(
          new BufferedInputStream(
            new FileInputStream("Data.txt")));
      BufferedReader in5br =
        new BufferedReader(
          new InputStreamReader(in5));
      // Must use DataInputStream for data:
      System.out.println(in5.readDouble());
      // Can now use the "proper" readLine():
      System.out.println(in5br.readLine());
      // But the line comes out funny.
      // The one created with writeBytes is OK:
      System.out.println(in5br.readLine());
    } catch(EOFException e) {
      System.err.println("End of stream");
    }

    // 6. Reading/writing random access files
    RandomAccessFile rf =
      new RandomAccessFile("rtest.dat", "rw");
    for(int i = 0; i < 10; i++)
      rf.writeDouble(i*1.414);
    rf.close();

    rf =
      new RandomAccessFile("rtest.dat", "rw");
    rf.seek(5*8);
    rf.writeDouble(47.0001);
    rf.close();

    rf =
      new RandomAccessFile("rtest.dat", "r");
    for(int i = 0; i < 10; i++)
      System.out.println(
        "Value " + i + ": " +
        rf.readDouble());
    rf.close();
  }
} ///:~
```

Here are the descriptions for the numbered sections of the program:

Input streams

Parts 1 through 4 demonstrate the creation and use of input streams. Part 4 also shows the simple use of an output stream.

1. Buffered input file

To open a file for character input, you use a **FileInputReader** with a **String** or a **File** object as the file name. For speed, you'll want that file to be buffered so you give the resulting reference to the constructor for a **BufferedReader**. Since **BufferedReader** also provides the **readLine( )** method, this is your final object and the interface you read from. When you reach the end of the file, **readLine( )** returns **null** so that is used to break out of the **while** loop.

The **String s2** is used to accumulate the entire contents of the file (including newlines that must be added since **readLine( )** strips them off). **s2** is then used in the later portions of this program. Finally, **close( )** is called to close the file. Technically, **close( )** will be called when **finalize( )** runs, and this is supposed to happen (whether or not garbage collection occurs) as the program exits. However, this has been inconsistently implemented, so the only safe approach is to explicitly call **close( )** for files.

Section 1b shows how you can wrap **System.in** for reading console input. **System.in** is a **DataInputStream** and **BufferedReader** needs a **Reader** argument, so **InputStreamReader** is brought in to perform the translation.

2. Input from memory

This section takes the **String s2** that now contains the entire contents of the file and uses it to create a **StringReader**. Then **read( )** is used to read each character one at a time and send it out to the console. Note that **read( )** returns the next byte as an **int** and thus it must be cast to a **char** to print properly.

3. Formatted memory input

To read "formatted" data, you use a **DataInputStream**, which is a **byte**-oriented I/O class (rather than **char** oriented). Thus you must use all

---

InputStream classes rather than **Reader** classes. Of course, you can read anything (such as a file) as bytes using **InputStream** classes, but here a **String** is used. To convert the **String** to an array of bytes, which is what is appropriate for a **ByteArrayInputStream**, **String** has a **getBytes( )** method to do the job. At that point, you have an appropriate **InputStream** to hand to **DataInputStream**.

If you read the characters from a **DataInputStream** one byte at a time using **readByte( )**, any byte value is a legitimate result so the return value cannot be used to detect the end of input. Instead, you can use the **available( )** method to find out how many more characters are available. Here's an example that shows how to read a file one byte at a time:

```
//: c11:TestEOF.java
// Testing for the end of file
// while reading a byte at a time.
import java.io.*;

public class TestEOF {
  // Throw exceptions to console:
  public static void main(String[] args)
  throws IOException {
    DataInputStream in =
      new DataInputStream(
       new BufferedInputStream(
        new FileInputStream("TestEof.java")));
    while(in.available() != 0)
      System.out.print((char)in.readByte());
  }
} ///:~
```

Note that **available( )** works differently depending on what sort of medium you're reading from; it's literally "the number of bytes that can be read *without blocking*." With a file this means the whole file, but with a different kind of stream this might not be true, so use it thoughtfully.

You could also detect the end of input in cases like these by catching an exception. However, the use of exceptions for control flow is considered a misuse of that feature.

4. File output

This example also shows how to write data to a file. First, a **FileWriter** is created to connect to the file. You'll virtually always want to buffer the output by wrapping it in a **BufferedWriter** (try removing this wrapping to see the impact on the performance—buffering tends to dramatically increase performance of I/O operations). Then for the formatting it's turned into a **PrintWriter**. The data file created this way is readable as an ordinary text file.

As the lines are written to the file, line numbers are added. Note that **LineNumberInputStream** is *not* used, because it's a silly class and you don't need it. As shown here, it's trivial to keep track of your own line numbers.

When the input stream is exhausted, **readLine( )** returns **null**. You'll see an explicit **close( )** for **out1**, because if you don't call **close( )** for all your output files, you might discover that the buffers don't get flushed so they're incomplete.

Output streams

The two primary kinds of output streams are separated by the way they write data: one writes it for human consumption, and the other writes it to be reacquired by a **DataInputStream**. The **RandomAccessFile** stands alone, although its data format is compatible with the **DataInputStream** and **DataOutputStream**.

5. Storing and recovering data

A **PrintWriter** formats data so it's readable by a human. However, to output data so that it can be recovered by another stream, you use a **DataOutputStream** to write the data and a **DataInputStream** to recover the data. Of course, these streams could be anything, but here a file is used, buffered for both reading and writing. **DataOutputStream** and **DataInputStream** are **byte**-oriented and thus require the **InputStream**s and **OutputStream**s.

If you use a **DataOutputStream** to write the data, then Java guarantees that you can accurately recover the data using a **DataInputStream**—

---

regardless of what different platforms write and read the data. This is incredibly valuable, as anyone knows who has spent time worrying about platform-specific data issues. That problem vanishes if you have Java on both platforms[2].

Note that the character string is written using both **writeChars( )** and **writeBytes( )**. When you run the program, you'll discover that **writeChars( )** outputs 16-bit Unicode characters. When you read the line using **readLine( )**, you'll see that there is a space between each character, because of the extra byte inserted by Unicode. Since there is no complementary "readChars" method in **DataInputStream**, you're stuck pulling these characters off one at a time with **readChar( )**. So for ASCII, it's easier to write the characters as bytes followed by a newline; then use **readLine( )** to read back the bytes as a regular ASCII line.

The **writeDouble( )** stores the **double** number to the stream and the complementary **readDouble( )** recovers it (there are similar methods for reading and writing the other types). But for any of the reading methods to work correctly, you must know the exact placement of the data item in the stream, since it would be equally possible to read the stored **double** as a simple sequence of bytes, or as a **char**, etc. So you must either have a fixed format for the data in the file or extra information must be stored in the file that you parse to determine where the data is located.

6. Reading and writing random access files

As previously noted, the **RandomAccessFile** is almost totally isolated from the rest of the I/O hierarchy, save for the fact that it implements the **DataInput** and **DataOutput** interfaces. So you cannot combine it with any of the aspects of the **InputStream** and **OutputStream** subclasses. Even though it might make sense to treat a **ByteArrayInputStream** as a random access element, you can use **RandomAccessFile** to only open a file. You must assume a **RandomAccessFile** is properly buffered since you cannot add that.

---

[2] XML is another way to solve the problem of moving data across different computing platforms, and does not depend on having Java on all platforms. However, Java tools exist that support XML.

The one option you have is in the second constructor argument: you can open a **RandomAccessFile** to read (**"r"**) or read and write (**"rw"**).

Using a **RandomAccessFile** is like using a combined **DataInputStream** and **DataOutputStream** (because it implements the equivalent interfaces). In addition, you can see that **seek( )** is used to move about in the file and change one of the values.

A bug?

If you look at section 5, you'll see that the data is written *before* the text. That's because a problem was introduced in Java 1.1 (and persists in Java 2) that sure seems like a bug to me, but I reported it and the bug people at JavaSoft said that this is the way it is supposed to work (however, the problem did *not* occur in Java 1.0, which makes me suspicious). The problem is shown in the following code:

```
//: c11:IOProblem.java
// Java 1.1 and higher I/O Problem.
import java.io.*;

public class IOProblem {
  // Throw exceptions to console:
  public static void main(String[] args)
  throws IOException {
    DataOutputStream out =
      new DataOutputStream(
        new BufferedOutputStream(
          new FileOutputStream("Data.txt")));
    out.writeDouble(3.14159);
    out.writeBytes("That was the value of pi\n");
    out.writeBytes("This is pi/2:\n");
    out.writeDouble(3.14159/2);
    out.close();

    DataInputStream in =
      new DataInputStream(
        new BufferedInputStream(
          new FileInputStream("Data.txt")));
    BufferedReader inbr =
      new BufferedReader(
```

```
      new InputStreamReader(in));
    // The doubles written BEFORE the line of text
    // read back correctly:
    System.out.println(in.readDouble());
    // Read the lines of text:
    System.out.println(inbr.readLine());
    System.out.println(inbr.readLine());
    // Trying to read the doubles after the line
    // produces an end-of-file exception:
    System.out.println(in.readDouble());
  }
} ///:~
```

It appears that anything you write after a call to **writeBytes( )** is not recoverable. The answer is apparently the same as the answer to the old vaudeville joke: "Doc, it hurts when I do this!" "Don't do that!"

Piped streams

The **PipedInputStream**, **PipedOutputStream**, **PipedReader** and **PipedWriter** have been mentioned only briefly in this chapter. This is not to suggest that they aren't useful, but their value is not apparent until you begin to understand multithreading, since the piped streams are used to communicate between threads. This is covered along with an example in Chapter 14.

Standard I/O

The term *standard I/O* refers to the Unix concept (which is reproduced in some form in Windows and many other operating systems) of a single stream of information that is used by a program. All the program's input can come from *standard input*, all its output can go to *standard output*, and all of its error messages can be sent to *standard error*. The value of standard I/O is that programs can easily be chained together and one program's standard output can become the standard input for another program. This is a powerful tool.

Reading from standard input

Following the standard I/O model, Java has **System.in**, **System.out**, and **System.err**. Throughout this book you've seen how to write to standard output using **System.out,** which is already prewrapped as a **PrintStream** object. **System.err** is likewise a **PrintStream**, but **System.in** is a raw **InputStream**, with no wrapping. This means that while you can use **System.out** and **System.err** right away, **System.in** must be wrapped before you can read from it.

Typically, you'll want to read input a line at a time using **readLine( )**, so you'll want to wrap **System.in** in a **BufferedReader**. To do this, you must convert **System.in** to a **Reader** using **InputStreamReader**. Here's an example that simply echoes each line that you type in:

```
//: c11:Echo.java
// How to read from standard input.
import java.io.*;

public class Echo {
  public static void main(String[] args)
  throws IOException {
    BufferedReader in =
        new BufferedReader(
          new InputStreamReader(System.in));
    String s;
    while((s = in.readLine()).length() != 0)
      System.out.println(s);
    // An empty line terminates the program
  }
} ///:~
```

The reason for the exception specification is that **readLine( )** can throw an **IOException**. Note that **System.in** should usually be buffered, as with most streams.

Changing **System.out** to a **PrintWriter**

System.out is a **PrintStream**, which is an **OutputStream**. **PrintWriter** has a constructor that takes an **OutputStream** as an argument. Thus, if you want you can convert **System.out** into a **PrintWriter** using that constructor:

```
//: c11:ChangeSystemOut.java
// Turn System.out into a PrintWriter.
import java.io.*;

public class ChangeSystemOut {
  public static void main(String[] args) {
    PrintWriter out =
      new PrintWriter(System.out, true);
    out.println("Hello, world");
  }
} ///:~
```

It's important to use the two-argument version of the **PrintWriter** constructor and to set the second argument to **true** in order to enable automatic flushing, otherwise you may not see the output.

Redirecting standard I/O

The Java **System** class allows you to redirect the standard input, output, and error I/O streams using simple static method calls:

setIn(InputStream)
setOut(PrintStream)
setErr(PrintStream)

Redirecting output is especially useful if you suddenly start creating a large amount of output on your screen and it's scrolling past faster than you can read it.[3] Redirecting input is valuable for a command-line

---

[3] Chapter 13 shows an even more convenient solution for this: a GUI program with a scrolling text area.

program in which you want to test a particular user-input sequence repeatedly. Here's a simple example that shows the use of these methods:

```
//: c11:Redirecting.java
// Demonstrates standard I/O redirection.
import java.io.*;

class Redirecting {
  // Throw exceptions to console:
  public static void main(String[] args)
  throws IOException {
    BufferedInputStream in =
      new BufferedInputStream(
        new FileInputStream(
          "Redirecting.java"));
    PrintStream out =
      new PrintStream(
        new BufferedOutputStream(
          new FileOutputStream("test.out")));
    System.setIn(in);
    System.setOut(out);
    System.setErr(out);

    BufferedReader br =
      new BufferedReader(
        new InputStreamReader(System.in));
    String s;
    while((s = br.readLine()) != null)
      System.out.println(s);
    out.close(); // Remember this!
  }
} ///:~
```

This program attaches standard input to a file, and redirects standard output and standard error to another file.

I/O redirection manipulates streams of bytes, not streams of characters, thus **InputStream**s and **OutputStream**s are used rather than **Reader**s and **Writer**s.

Compression

The Java I/O library contains classes to support reading and writing streams in a compressed format. These are wrapped around existing I/O classes to provide compression functionality.

These classes are not derived from the **Reader** and **Writer** classes, but instead are part of the **InputStream** and **OutputStream** hierarchies. This is because the compression library works with bytes, not characters. However, you might sometimes be forced to mix the two types of streams. (Remember that you can use **InputStreamReader** and **OutputStreamWriter** to provide easy conversion between one type and another.)

Compression class	Function
CheckedInputStream	**GetCheckSum( )** produces checksum for any **InputStream** (not just decompression).
CheckedOutputStream	**GetCheckSum( )** produces checksum for any **OutputStream** (not just compression).
DeflaterOutputStream	Base class for compression classes.
ZipOutputStream	A **DeflaterOutputStream** that compresses data into the Zip file format.
GZIPOutputStream	A **DeflaterOutputStream** that compresses data into the GZIP file format.
InflaterInputStream	Base class for decompression classes.
ZipInputStream	An **InflaterInputStream** that decompresses data that has been stored in the Zip file format.
GZIPInputStream	An **InflaterInputStream** that decompresses data that has been stored in the GZIP file format.

Although there are many compression algorithms, Zip and GZIP are possibly the most commonly used. Thus you can easily manipulate your compressed data with the many tools available for reading and writing these formats.

Simple compression with GZIP

The GZIP interface is simple and thus is probably more appropriate when you have a single stream of data that you want to compress (rather than a container of dissimilar pieces of data). Here's an example that compresses a single file:

```
//: c11:GZIPcompress.java
// Uses GZIP compression to compress a file
// whose name is passed on the command line.
import java.io.*;
import java.util.zip.*;

public class GZIPcompress {
  // Throw exceptions to console:
  public static void main(String[] args)
  throws IOException {
    BufferedReader in =
      new BufferedReader(
        new FileReader(args[0]));
    BufferedOutputStream out =
      new BufferedOutputStream(
        new GZIPOutputStream(
          new FileOutputStream("test.gz")));
    System.out.println("Writing file");
    int c;
    while((c = in.read()) != -1)
      out.write(c);
    in.close();
    out.close();
    System.out.println("Reading file");
    BufferedReader in2 =
      new BufferedReader(
        new InputStreamReader(
          new GZIPInputStream(
            new FileInputStream("test.gz"))));
    String s;
    while((s = in2.readLine()) != null)
```

```
      System.out.println(s);
    }
  } ///:~
```

The use of the compression classes is straightforward—you simply wrap your output stream in a **GZIPOutputStream** or **ZipOutputStream** and your input stream in a **GZIPInputStream** or **ZipInputStream**. All else is ordinary I/O reading and writing. This is an example of mixing the **char**-oriented streams with the **byte**-oriented streams: **in** uses the **Reader** classes, whereas **GZIPOutputStream**'s constructor can accept only an **OutputStream** object, not a **Writer** object. When the file is opened, the **GZIPInputStream** is converted to a **Reader**.

Multifile storage with Zip

The library that supports the Zip format is much more extensive. With it you can easily store multiple files, and there's even a separate class to make the process of reading a Zip file easy. The library uses the standard Zip format so that it works seamlessly with all the tools currently downloadable on the Internet. The following example has the same form as the previous example, but it handles as many command-line arguments as you want. In addition, it shows the use of the **Checksum** classes to calculate and verify the checksum for the file. There are two **Checksum** types: **Adler32** (which is faster) and **CRC32** (which is slower but slightly more accurate).

```
//: c11:ZipCompress.java
// Uses Zip compression to compress any
// number of files given on the command line.
import java.io.*;
import java.util.*;
import java.util.zip.*;

public class ZipCompress {
  // Throw exceptions to console:
  public static void main(String[] args)
  throws IOException {
    FileOutputStream f =
      new FileOutputStream("test.zip");
    CheckedOutputStream csum =
      new CheckedOutputStream(
```

```
        f, new Adler32());
    ZipOutputStream out =
      new ZipOutputStream(
        new BufferedOutputStream(csum));
    out.setComment("A test of Java Zipping");
    // No corresponding getComment(), though.
    for(int i = 0; i < args.length; i++) {
      System.out.println(
        "Writing file " + args[i]);
      BufferedReader in =
        new BufferedReader(
          new FileReader(args[i]));
      out.putNextEntry(new ZipEntry(args[i]));
      int c;
      while((c = in.read()) != -1)
        out.write(c);
      in.close();
    }
    out.close();
    // Checksum valid only after the file
    // has been closed!
    System.out.println("Checksum: " +
      csum.getChecksum().getValue());
    // Now extract the files:
    System.out.println("Reading file");
    FileInputStream fi =
      new FileInputStream("test.zip");
    CheckedInputStream csumi =
      new CheckedInputStream(
        fi, new Adler32());
    ZipInputStream in2 =
      new ZipInputStream(
        new BufferedInputStream(csumi));
    ZipEntry ze;
    while((ze = in2.getNextEntry()) != null) {
      System.out.println("Reading file " + ze);
      int x;
      while((x = in2.read()) != -1)
        System.out.write(x);
    }
    System.out.println("Checksum: " +
```

```
        csumi.getChecksum().getValue());
    in2.close();
    // Alternative way to open and read
    // zip files:
    ZipFile zf = new ZipFile("test.zip");
    Enumeration e = zf.entries();
    while(e.hasMoreElements()) {
      ZipEntry ze2 = (ZipEntry)e.nextElement();
      System.out.println("File: " + ze2);
      // ... and extract the data as before
    }
  }
} ///:~
```

For each file to add to the archive, you must call **putNextEntry( )** and pass it a **ZipEntry** object. The **ZipEntry** object contains an extensive interface that allows you to get and set all the data available on that particular entry in your Zip file: name, compressed and uncompressed sizes, date, CRC checksum, extra field data, comment, compression method, and whether it's a directory entry. However, even though the Zip format has a way to set a password, this is not supported in Java's Zip library. And although **CheckedInputStream** and **CheckedOutputStream** support both **Adler32** and **CRC32** checksums, the **ZipEntry** class supports only an interface for CRC. This is a restriction of the underlying Zip format, but it might limit you from using the faster **Adler32**.

To extract files, **ZipInputStream** has a **getNextEntry( )** method that returns the next **ZipEntry** if there is one. As a more succinct alternative, you can read the file using a **ZipFile** object, which has a method **entries( )** to return an **Enumeration** to the **ZipEntries**.

In order to read the checksum you must somehow have access to the associated **Checksum** object. Here, a reference to the **CheckedOutputStream** and **CheckedInputStream** objects is retained, but you could also just hold onto a reference to the **Checksum** object.

A baffling method in Zip streams is **setComment( )**. As shown above, you can set a comment when you're writing a file, but there's no way to recover the comment in the **ZipInputStream**. Comments appear to be supported fully on an entry-by-entry basis only via **ZipEntry**.

Of course, you are not limited to files when using the **GZIP** or **Zip** libraries—you can compress anything, including data to be sent through a network connection.

Java ARchives (JARs)

The Zip format is also used in the JAR (Java ARchive) file format, which is a way to collect a group of files into a single compressed file, just like Zip. However, like everything else in Java, JAR files are cross-platform so you don't need to worry about platform issues. You can also include audio and image files as well as class files.

JAR files are particularly helpful when you deal with the Internet. Before JAR files, your Web browser would have to make repeated requests of a Web server in order to download all of the files that make up an applet. In addition, each of these files was uncompressed. By combining all of the files for a particular applet into a single JAR file, only one server request is necessary and the transfer is faster because of compression. And each entry in a JAR file can be digitally signed for security (refer to the Java documentation for details).

A JAR file consists of a single file containing a collection of zipped files along with a "manifest" that describes them. (You can create your own manifest file; otherwise the **jar** program will do it for you.) You can find out more about JAR manifests in the JDK HTML documentation.

The **jar** utility that comes with Sun's JDK automatically compresses the files of your choice. You invoke it on the command line:

```
jar [options] destination [manifest] inputfile(s)
```

The options are simply a collection of letters (no hyphen or any other indicator is necessary). Unix/Linux users will note the similarity to the **tar** options. These are:

c	Creates a new or empty archive.
t	Lists the table of contents.

---

x	Extracts all files.
x file	Extracts the named file.
f	Says: "I'm going to give you the name of the file." If you don't use this, jar assumes that its input will come from standard input, or, if it is creating a file, its output will go to standard output.
m	Says that the first argument will be the name of the user-created manifest file.
v	Generates verbose output describing what jar is doing.
0	Only store the files; doesn't compress the files (use to create a JAR file that you can put in your classpath).
M	Don't automatically create a manifest file.

If a subdirectory is included in the files to be put into the JAR file, that subdirectory is automatically added, including all of its subdirectories, etc. Path information is also preserved.

Here are some typical ways to invoke **jar**:

```
jar cf myJarFile.jar *.class
```

This creates a JAR file called **myJarFile.jar** that contains all of the class files in the current directory, along with an automatically generated manifest file.

```
jar cmf myJarFile.jar myManifestFile.mf *.class
```

Like the previous example, but adding a user-created manifest file called **myManifestFile.mf**.

```
jar tf myJarFile.jar
```

Produces a table of contents of the files in **myJarFile.jar**.

```
jar tvf myJarFile.jar
```

Adds the "verbose" flag to give more detailed information about the files in **myJarFile.jar**.

```
jar cvf myApp.jar audio classes image
```

Assuming **audio**, **classes**, and **image** are subdirectories, this combines all of the subdirectories into the file **myApp.jar**. The "verbose" flag is also included to give extra feedback while the **jar** program is working.

If you create a JAR file using the **0** option, that file can be placed in your CLASSPATH:

```
CLASSPATH="lib1.jar;lib2.jar;"
```

Then Java can search **lib1.jar** and **lib2.jar** for class files.

The **jar** tool isn't as useful as a **zip** utility. For example, you can't add or update files to an existing JAR file; you can create JAR files only from scratch. Also, you can't move files into a JAR file, erasing them as they are moved. However, a JAR file created on one platform will be transparently readable by the **jar** tool on any other platform (a problem that sometimes plagues **zip** utilities).

As you will see in Chapter 13, JAR files are also used to package JavaBeans.

Object serialization

Java's *object serialization* allows you to take any object that implements the **Serializable** interface and turn it into a sequence of bytes that can later be fully restored to regenerate the original object. This is even true across a network, which means that the serialization mechanism automatically compensates for differences in operating systems. That is, you can create an object on a Windows machine, serialize it, and send it across the network to a Unix machine where it will be correctly reconstructed. You don't have to worry about the data representations on the different machines, the byte ordering, or any other details.

By itself, object serialization is interesting because it allows you to implement *lightweight persistence*. Remember that persistence means an object's lifetime is not determined by whether a program is executing—the object lives *in between* invocations of the program. By taking a serializable object and writing it to disk, then restoring that object when the program is reinvoked, you're able to produce the effect of persistence. The reason it's called "lightweight" is that you can't simply define an object using some kind of "persistent" keyword and let the system take care of the details (although this might happen in the future). Instead, you must explicitly serialize and deserialize the objects in your program.

Object serialization was added to the language to support two major features. Java's *remote method invocation* (RMI) allows objects that live on other machines to behave as if they live on your machine. When sending messages to remote objects, object serialization is necessary to transport the arguments and return values. RMI is discussed in Chapter 15.

Object serialization is also necessary for JavaBeans, described in Chapter 13. When a Bean is used, its state information is generally configured at design-time. This state information must be stored and later recovered when the program is started; object serialization performs this task.

Serializing an object is quite simple, as long as the object implements the **Serializable** interface (this interface is just a flag and has no methods). When serialization was added to the language, many standard library classes were changed to make them serializable, including all of the wrappers for the primitive types, all of the container classes, and many others. Even **Class** objects can be serialized. (See Chapter 12 for the implications of this.)

To serialize an object, you create some sort of **OutputStream** object and then wrap it inside an **ObjectOutputStream** object. At this point you need only call **writeObject( )** and your object is serialized and sent to the **OutputStream**. To reverse the process, you wrap an **InputStream** inside an **ObjectInputStream** and call **readObject( )**. What comes back is, as usual, a reference to an upcast **Object**, so you must downcast to set things straight.

A particularly clever aspect of object serialization is that it not only saves an image of your object but it also follows all the references contained in your object and saves *those* objects, and follows all the references in each of those objects, etc. This is sometimes referred to as the "web of objects" that a single object can be connected to, and it includes arrays of references to objects as well as member objects. If you had to maintain your own object serialization scheme, maintaining the code to follow all these links would be a bit mind-boggling. However, Java object serialization seems to pull it off flawlessly, no doubt using an optimized algorithm that traverses the web of objects. The following example tests the serialization mechanism by making a "worm" of linked objects, each of which has a link to the next segment in the worm as well as an array of references to objects of a different class, **Data**:

```
//: c11:Worm.java
// Demonstrates object serialization.
import java.io.*;

class Data implements Serializable {
  private int i;
  Data(int x) { i = x; }
  public String toString() {
    return Integer.toString(i);
  }
}

public class Worm implements Serializable {
  // Generate a random int value:
  private static int r() {
    return (int)(Math.random() * 10);
  }
  private Data[] d = {
    new Data(r()), new Data(r()), new Data(r())
  };
  private Worm next;
  private char c;
  // Value of i == number of segments
  Worm(int i, char x) {
    System.out.println(" Worm constructor: " + i);
    c = x;
    if(--i > 0)
      next = new Worm(i, (char)(x + 1));
  }
  Worm() {
    System.out.println("Default constructor");
  }
  public String toString() {
    String s = ":" + c + "(";
    for(int i = 0; i < d.length; i++)
```

```java
      s += d[i].toString();
    s += ")";
    if(next != null)
      s += next.toString();
    return s;
  }
  // Throw exceptions to console:
  public static void main(String[] args)
  throws ClassNotFoundException, IOException {
    Worm w = new Worm(6, 'a');
    System.out.println("w = " + w);
    ObjectOutputStream out =
      new ObjectOutputStream(
        new FileOutputStream("worm.out"));
    out.writeObject("Worm storage");
    out.writeObject(w);
    out.close(); // Also flushes output
    ObjectInputStream in =
      new ObjectInputStream(
        new FileInputStream("worm.out"));
    String s = (String)in.readObject();
    Worm w2 = (Worm)in.readObject();
    System.out.println(s + ", w2 = " + w2);
    ByteArrayOutputStream bout =
      new ByteArrayOutputStream();
    ObjectOutputStream out2 =
      new ObjectOutputStream(bout);
    out2.writeObject("Worm storage");
    out2.writeObject(w);
    out2.flush();
    ObjectInputStream in2 =
      new ObjectInputStream(
        new ByteArrayInputStream(
          bout.toByteArray()));
    s = (String)in2.readObject();
    Worm w3 = (Worm)in2.readObject();
    System.out.println(s + ", w3 = " + w3);
  }
} ///:~
```

To make things interesting, the array of **Data** objects inside **Worm** are initialized with random numbers. (This way you don't suspect the compiler of keeping some kind of meta-information.) Each **Worm** segment is labeled with a **char** that's automatically generated in the process of recursively generating the linked list of **Worm**s. When you create a **Worm**, you tell the constructor how long you want it to be. To make the **next** reference it calls the **Worm** constructor with a length of one less, etc. The final **next** reference is left as **null**, indicating the end of the **Worm**.

The point of all this was to make something reasonably complex that couldn't easily be serialized. The act of serializing, however, is quite simple. Once the **ObjectOutputStream** is created from some other stream, **writeObject( )** serializes the object. Notice the call to **writeObject( )** for a **String**, as well. You can also write all the primitive data types using the same methods as **DataOutputStream** (they share the same interface).

There are two separate code sections that look similar. The first writes and reads a file and the second, for variety, writes and reads a **ByteArray**. You can read and write an object using serialization to any **DataInputStream** or **DataOutputStream** including, as you will see in the Chapter 15, a network. The output from one run was:

```
Worm constructor:  6
Worm constructor:  5
Worm constructor:  4
Worm constructor:  3
Worm constructor:  2
Worm constructor:  1
w = :a(262):b(100):c(396):d(480):e(316):f(398)
Worm storage, w2 =
:a(262):b(100):c(396):d(480):e(316):f(398)
Worm storage, w3 =
:a(262):b(100):c(396):d(480):e(316):f(398)
```

You can see that the deserialized object really does contain all of the links that were in the original object.

Note that no constructor, not even the default constructor, is called in the process of deserializing a **Serializable** object. The entire object is restored by recovering data from the **InputStream**.

Object serialization is **byte**-oriented, and thus uses the **InputStream** and **OutputStream** hierarchies.

Finding the class

You might wonder what's necessary for an object to be recovered from its serialized state. For example, suppose you serialize an object and send it as a file or through a network to another machine. Could a program on the other machine reconstruct the object using only the contents of the file?

The best way to answer this question is (as usual) by performing an experiment. The following file goes in the subdirectory for this chapter:

```
//: c11:Alien.java
// A serializable class.
import java.io.*;

public class Alien implements Serializable {
} ///:~
```

The file that creates and serializes an **Alien** object goes in the same directory:

```
//: c11:FreezeAlien.java
// Create a serialized output file.
import java.io.*;

public class FreezeAlien {
  // Throw exceptions to console:
  public static void main(String[] args)
  throws IOException {
    ObjectOutput out =
      new ObjectOutputStream(
        new FileOutputStream("X.file"));
    Alien zorcon = new Alien();
    out.writeObject(zorcon);
  }
} ///:~
```

Rather than catching and handling exceptions, this program takes the quick and dirty approach of passing the exceptions out of **main( )**, so they'll be reported on the command line.

Once the program is compiled and run, copy the resulting **X.file** to a subdirectory called **xfiles**, where the following code goes:

```
//: c11:xfiles:ThawAlien.java
// Try to recover a serialized file without the
// class of object that's stored in that file.
import java.io.*;

public class ThawAlien {
  public static void main(String[] args)
  throws IOException, ClassNotFoundException {
    ObjectInputStream in =
      new ObjectInputStream(
        new FileInputStream("X.file"));
    Object mystery = in.readObject();
    System.out.println(mystery.getClass());
  }
} ///:~
```

This program opens the file and reads in the object **mystery** successfully. However, as soon as you try to find out anything about the object—which requires the **Class** object for **Alien**—the Java Virtual Machine (JVM) cannot find **Alien.class** (unless it happens to be in the Classpath, which it shouldn't be in this example). You'll get a **ClassNotFoundException.** (Once again, all evidence of alien life vanishes before proof of its existence can be verified!)

If you expect to do much after you've recovered an object that has been serialized, you must make sure that the JVM can find the associated **.class** file either in the local class path or somewhere on the Internet.

Controlling serialization

As you can see, the default serialization mechanism is trivial to use. But what if you have special needs? Perhaps you have special security issues and you don't want to serialize portions of your object, or perhaps it just

---

doesn't make sense for one subobject to be serialized if that part needs to be created anew when the object is recovered.

You can control the process of serialization by implementing the **Externalizable** interface instead of the **Serializable** interface. The **Externalizable** interface extends the **Serializable** interface and adds two methods, **writeExternal( )** and **readExternal( ),** that are automatically called for your object during serialization and deserialization so that you can perform your special operations.

The following example shows simple implementations of the **Externalizable** interface methods. Note that **Blip1** and **Blip2** are nearly identical except for a subtle difference (see if you can discover it by looking at the code):

```
//: c11:Blips.java
// Simple use of Externalizable & a pitfall.
import java.io.*;
import java.util.*;

class Blip1 implements Externalizable {
  public Blip1() {
    System.out.println("Blip1 Constructor");
  }
  public void writeExternal(ObjectOutput out)
      throws IOException {
    System.out.println("Blip1.writeExternal");
  }
  public void readExternal(ObjectInput in)
     throws IOException, ClassNotFoundException {
    System.out.println("Blip1.readExternal");
  }
}

class Blip2 implements Externalizable {
  Blip2() {
    System.out.println("Blip2 Constructor");
  }
  public void writeExternal(ObjectOutput out)
      throws IOException {
    System.out.println("Blip2.writeExternal");
```

```
    }
  public void readExternal(ObjectInput in)
     throws IOException, ClassNotFoundException {
    System.out.println("Blip2.readExternal");
  }
}

public class Blips {
  // Throw exceptions to console:
  public static void main(String[] args)
  throws IOException, ClassNotFoundException {
    System.out.println("Constructing objects:");
    Blip1 b1 = new Blip1();
    Blip2 b2 = new Blip2();
    ObjectOutputStream o =
      new ObjectOutputStream(
        new FileOutputStream("Blips.out"));
    System.out.println("Saving objects:");
    o.writeObject(b1);
    o.writeObject(b2);
    o.close();
    // Now get them back:
    ObjectInputStream in =
      new ObjectInputStream(
        new FileInputStream("Blips.out"));
    System.out.println("Recovering b1:");
    b1 = (Blip1)in.readObject();
    // OOPS! Throws an exception:
//! System.out.println("Recovering b2:");
//! b2 = (Blip2)in.readObject();
  }
} ///:~
```

The output for this program is:

```
Constructing objects:
Blip1 Constructor
Blip2 Constructor
Saving objects:
Blip1.writeExternal
Blip2.writeExternal
Recovering b1:
```

```
Blip1 Constructor
Blip1.readExternal
```

The reason that the **Blip2** object is not recovered is that trying to do so causes an exception. Can you see the difference between **Blip1** and **Blip2**? The constructor for **Blip1** is **public**, while the constructor for **Blip2** is not, and that causes the exception upon recovery. Try making **Blip2**'s constructor **public** and removing the //! comments to see the correct results.

When **b1** is recovered, the **Blip1** default constructor is called. This is different from recovering a **Serializable** object, in which the object is constructed entirely from its stored bits, with no constructor calls. With an **Externalizable** object, all the normal default construction behavior occurs (including the initializations at the point of field definition), and *then* **readExternal( )** is called. You need to be aware of this—in particular, the fact that all the default construction always takes place—to produce the correct behavior in your **Externalizable** objects.

Here's an example that shows what you must do to fully store and retrieve an **Externalizable** object:

```
//: c11:Blip3.java
// Reconstructing an externalizable object.
import java.io.*;
import java.util.*;

class Blip3 implements Externalizable {
  int i;
  String s; // No initialization
  public Blip3() {
    System.out.println("Blip3 Constructor");
    // s, i not initialized
  }
  public Blip3(String x, int a) {
    System.out.println("Blip3(String x, int a)");
    s = x;
    i = a;
    // s & i initialized only in nondefault
    // constructor.
  }
```

```java
    public String toString() { return s + i; }
    public void writeExternal(ObjectOutput out)
    throws IOException {
      System.out.println("Blip3.writeExternal");
      // You must do this:
      out.writeObject(s);
      out.writeInt(i);
    }
    public void readExternal(ObjectInput in)
    throws IOException, ClassNotFoundException {
      System.out.println("Blip3.readExternal");
      // You must do this:
      s = (String)in.readObject();
      i =in.readInt();
    }
    public static void main(String[] args)
    throws IOException, ClassNotFoundException {
      System.out.println("Constructing objects:");
      Blip3 b3 = new Blip3("A String ", 47);
      System.out.println(b3);
      ObjectOutputStream o =
        new ObjectOutputStream(
          new FileOutputStream("Blip3.out"));
      System.out.println("Saving object:");
      o.writeObject(b3);
      o.close();
      // Now get it back:
      ObjectInputStream in =
        new ObjectInputStream(
          new FileInputStream("Blip3.out"));
      System.out.println("Recovering b3:");
      b3 = (Blip3)in.readObject();
      System.out.println(b3);
    }
} ///:~
```

The fields **s** and **i** are initialized only in the second constructor, but not in the default constructor. This means that if you don't initialize **s** and **i** in **readExternal( )**, it will be **null** (since the storage for the object gets wiped to zero in the first step of object creation). If you comment out the two lines of code following the phrases "You must do this" and run the program, you'll see that when the object is recovered, **s** is **null** and **i** is zero.

If you are inheriting from an **Externalizable** object, you'll typically call the base-class versions of **writeExternal( )** and **readExternal( )** to provide proper storage and retrieval of the base-class components.

So to make things work correctly you must not only write the important data from the object during the **writeExternal( )** method (there is no default behavior that writes any of the member objects for an **Externalizable** object), but you must also recover that data in the **readExternal( )** method. This can be a bit confusing at first because the default construction behavior for an **Externalizable** object can make it seem like some kind of storage and retrieval takes place automatically. It does not.

The transient keyword

When you're controlling serialization, there might be a particular subobject that you don't want Java's serialization mechanism to automatically save and restore. This is commonly the case if that subobject represents sensitive information that you don't want to serialize, such as a password. Even if that information is **private** in the object, once it's serialized it's possible for someone to access it by reading a file or intercepting a network transmission.

One way to prevent sensitive parts of your object from being serialized is to implement your class as **Externalizable**, as shown previously. Then nothing is automatically serialized and you can explicitly serialize only the necessary parts inside **writeExternal( )**.

If you're working with a **Serializable** object, however, all serialization happens automatically. To control this, you can turn off serialization on a field-by-field basis using the **transient** keyword, which says "Don't bother saving or restoring this—I'll take care of it."

For example, consider a **Login** object that keeps information about a particular login session. Suppose that, once you verify the login, you want to store the data, but without the password. The easiest way to do this is by implementing **Serializable** and marking the **password** field as **transient**. Here's what it looks like:

```
//: c11:Logon.java
// Demonstrates the "transient" keyword.
import java.io.*;
import java.util.*;

class Logon implements Serializable {
  private Date date = new Date();
  private String username;
  private transient String password;
  Logon(String name, String pwd) {
    username = name;
    password = pwd;
  }
  public String toString() {
    String pwd =
      (password == null) ? "(n/a)" : password;
    return "logon info: \n    " +
      "username: " + username +
      "\n    date: " + date +
      "\n    password: " + pwd;
  }
  public static void main(String[] args)
  throws IOException, ClassNotFoundException {
    Logon a = new Logon("Hulk", "myLittlePony");
    System.out.println( "logon a = " + a);
      ObjectOutputStream o =
        new ObjectOutputStream(
          new FileOutputStream("Logon.out"));
    o.writeObject(a);
    o.close();
    // Delay:
    int seconds = 5;
    long t = System.currentTimeMillis()
          + seconds * 1000;
    while(System.currentTimeMillis() < t)
      ;
    // Now get them back:
    ObjectInputStream in =
```

```
            new ObjectInputStream(
                new FileInputStream("Logon.out"));
          System.out.println(
            "Recovering object at " + new Date());
          a = (Logon)in.readObject();
          System.out.println( "logon a = " + a);
      }
   } ///:~
```

You can see that the **date** and **username** fields are ordinary (not
transient), and thus are automatically serialized. However, the
password is **transient**, and so is not stored to disk; also the
serialization mechanism makes no attempt to recover it. The output is:

```
logon a = logon info:
    username: Hulk
    date: Sun Mar 23 18:25:53 PST 1997
    password: myLittlePony
Recovering object at Sun Mar 23 18:25:59 PST 1997
logon a = logon info:
    username: Hulk
    date: Sun Mar 23 18:25:53 PST 1997
    password: (n/a)
```

When the object is recovered, the **password** field is **null**. Note that
toString( ) must check for a **null** value of **password** because if you try
to assemble a **String** object using the overloaded '+' operator, and that
operator encounters a **null** reference, you'll get a
NullPointerException. (Newer versions of Java might contain code to
avoid this problem.)

You can also see that the **date** field is stored to and recovered from disk
and not generated anew.

Since **Externalizable** objects do not store any of their fields by default,
the **transient** keyword is for use with **Serializable** objects only.

An alternative to **Externalizable**

If you're not keen on implementing the **Externalizable** interface, there's
another approach. You can implement the **Serializable** interface and
add (notice I say "add" and not "override" or "implement") methods

called **writeObject( )** and **readObject( )** that will automatically be called when the object is serialized and deserialized, respectively. That is, if you provide these two methods they will be used instead of the default serialization.

The methods must have these exact signatures:

```
private void
  writeObject(ObjectOutputStream stream)
    throws IOException;

private void
  readObject(ObjectInputStream stream)
    throws IOException, ClassNotFoundException
```

From a design standpoint, things get really weird here. First of all, you might think that because these methods are not part of a base class or the **Serializable** interface, they ought to be defined in their own interface(s). But notice that they are defined as **private**, which means they are to be called only by other members of this class. However, you don't actually call them from other members of this class, but instead the **writeObject( )** and **readObject( )** methods of the **ObjectOutputStream** and **ObjectInputStream** objects call your object's **writeObject( )** and **readObject( )** methods. (Notice my tremendous restraint in not launching into a long diatribe about using the same method names here. In a word: confusing.) You might wonder how the **ObjectOutputStream** and **ObjectInputStream** objects have access to **private** methods of your class. We can only assume that this is part of the serialization magic.

In any event, anything defined in an **interface** is automatically **public** so if **writeObject( )** and **readObject( )** must be **private**, then they can't be part of an **interface**. Since you must follow the signatures exactly, the effect is the same as if you're implementing an **interface**.

It would appear that when you call **ObjectOutputStream.writeObject( )**, the **Serializable** object that you pass it to is interrogated (using reflection, no doubt) to see if it implements its own **writeObject( )**. If so, the normal serialization process is skipped and the **writeObject( )** is called. The same sort of situation exists for **readObject( )**.

There's one other twist. Inside your **writeObject( )**, you can choose to perform the default **writeObject( )** action by calling **defaultWriteObject( )**. Likewise, inside **readObject( )** you can call **defaultReadObject( )**. Here is a simple example that demonstrates how you can control the storage and retrieval of a **Serializable** object:

```
//: c11:SerialCtl.java
// Controlling serialization by adding your own
// writeObject() and readObject() methods.
import java.io.*;

public class SerialCtl implements Serializable {
  String a;
  transient String b;
  public SerialCtl(String aa, String bb) {
    a = "Not Transient: " + aa;
    b = "Transient: " + bb;
  }
  public String toString() {
    return a + "\n" + b;
  }
  private void
    writeObject(ObjectOutputStream stream)
      throws IOException {
    stream.defaultWriteObject();
    stream.writeObject(b);
  }
  private void
    readObject(ObjectInputStream stream)
      throws IOException, ClassNotFoundException {
    stream.defaultReadObject();
    b = (String)stream.readObject();
  }
  public static void main(String[] args)
  throws IOException, ClassNotFoundException {
    SerialCtl sc =
      new SerialCtl("Test1", "Test2");
    System.out.println("Before:\n" + sc);
```

```
    ByteArrayOutputStream buf =
      new ByteArrayOutputStream();
    ObjectOutputStream o =
      new ObjectOutputStream(buf);
    o.writeObject(sc);
    // Now get it back:
    ObjectInputStream in =
      new ObjectInputStream(
        new ByteArrayInputStream(
          buf.toByteArray()));
    SerialCtl sc2 = (SerialCtl)in.readObject();
    System.out.println("After:\n" + sc2);
  }
} ///:~
```

In this example, one **String** field is ordinary and the other is **transient**, to prove that the non-**transient** field is saved by the **defaultWriteObject( )** method and the **transient** field is saved and restored explicitly. The fields are initialized inside the constructor rather than at the point of definition to prove that they are not being initialized by some automatic mechanism during deserialization.

If you are going to use the default mechanism to write the non-**transient** parts of your object, you must call **defaultWriteObject( )** as the first operation in **writeObject( )** and **defaultReadObject( )** as the first operation in **readObject( )**. These are strange method calls. It would appear, for example, that you are calling **defaultWriteObject( )** for an **ObjectOutputStream** and passing it no arguments, and yet it somehow turns around and knows the reference to your object and how to write all the non-**transient** parts. Spooky.

The storage and retrieval of the **transient** objects uses more familiar code. And yet, think about what happens here. In **main( )**, a **SerialCtl** object is created, and then it's serialized to an **ObjectOutputStream.** (Notice in this case that a buffer is used instead of a file—it's all the same to the **ObjectOutputStream.**) The serialization occurs in the line:

```
o.writeObject(sc);
```

The **writeObject( )** method must be examining **sc** to see if it has its own **writeObject( )** method. (Not by checking the interface—there isn't one—

---

or the class type, but by actually hunting for the method using reflection.) If it does, it uses that. A similar approach holds true for **readObject( )**. Perhaps this was the only practical way that they could solve the problem, but it's certainly strange.

Versioning

It's possible that you might want to change the version of a serializable class (objects of the original class might be stored in a database, for example). This is supported but you'll probably do it only in special cases, and it requires an extra depth of understanding that we will not attempt to achieve here. The JDK HTML documents downloadable from *java.sun.com* cover this topic quite thoroughly.

You will also notice in the JDK HTML documentation many comments that begin with:

> **Warning:** *Serialized objects of this class will not be compatible with future Swing releases. The current serialization support is appropriate for short term storage or RMI between applications. ...*

This is because the versioning mechanism is too simple to work reliably in all situations, especially with JavaBeans. They're working on a correction for the design, and that's what the warning is about.

Using persistence

It's quite appealing to use serialization technology to store some of the state of your program so that you can easily restore the program to the current state later. But before you can do this, some questions must be answered. What happens if you serialize two objects that both have a reference to a third object? When you restore those two objects from their serialized state, do you get only one occurrence of the third object? What if you serialize your two objects to separate files and deserialize them in different parts of your code?

Here's an example that shows the problem:

```
//: c11:MyWorld.java
import java.io.*;
import java.util.*;
```

```java
class House implements Serializable {}

class Animal implements Serializable {
  String name;
  House preferredHouse;
  Animal(String nm, House h) {
    name = nm;
    preferredHouse = h;
  }
  public String toString() {
    return name + "[" + super.toString() +
      "], " + preferredHouse + "\n";
  }
}

public class MyWorld {
  public static void main(String[] args)
  throws IOException, ClassNotFoundException {
    House house = new House();
    ArrayList  animals = new ArrayList();
    animals.add(
      new Animal("Bosco the dog", house));
    animals.add(
      new Animal("Ralph the hamster", house));
    animals.add(
      new Animal("Fronk the cat", house));
    System.out.println("animals: " + animals);

    ByteArrayOutputStream buf1 =
      new ByteArrayOutputStream();
    ObjectOutputStream o1 =
      new ObjectOutputStream(buf1);
    o1.writeObject(animals);
    o1.writeObject(animals); // Write a 2nd set
    // Write to a different stream:
    ByteArrayOutputStream buf2 =
      new ByteArrayOutputStream();
    ObjectOutputStream o2 =
      new ObjectOutputStream(buf2);
    o2.writeObject(animals);
```

```
      // Now get them back:
      ObjectInputStream in1 =
        new ObjectInputStream(
          new ByteArrayInputStream(
            buf1.toByteArray()));
      ObjectInputStream in2 =
        new ObjectInputStream(
          new ByteArrayInputStream(
            buf2.toByteArray()));
      ArrayList animals1 =
        (ArrayList)in1.readObject();
      ArrayList animals2 =
        (ArrayList)in1.readObject();
      ArrayList animals3 =
        (ArrayList)in2.readObject();
      System.out.println("animals1: " + animals1);
      System.out.println("animals2: " + animals2);
      System.out.println("animals3: " + animals3);
  }
} ///:~
```

One thing that's interesting here is that it's possible to use object serialization to and from a byte array as a way of doing a "deep copy" of any object that's **Serializable.** (A deep copy means that you're duplicating the entire web of objects, rather than just the basic object and its references.) Copying is covered in depth in Appendix A.

Animal objects contain fields of type **House**. In **main( )**, an **ArrayList** of these **Animals** is created and it is serialized twice to one stream and then again to a separate stream. When these are deserialized and printed, you see the following results for one run (the objects will be in different memory locations each run):

```
animals: [Bosco the dog[Animal@1cc76c], House@1cc769
, Ralph the hamster[Animal@1cc76d], House@1cc769
, Fronk the cat[Animal@1cc76e], House@1cc769
]
animals1: [Bosco the dog[Animal@1cca0c], House@1cca16
, Ralph the hamster[Animal@1cca17], House@1cca16
, Fronk the cat[Animal@1cca1b], House@1cca16
]
```

```
animals2: [Bosco the dog[Animal@1cca0c], House@1cca16
, Ralph the hamster[Animal@1cca17], House@1cca16
, Fronk the cat[Animal@1cca1b], House@1cca16
]
animals3: [Bosco the dog[Animal@1cca52], House@1cca5c
, Ralph the hamster[Animal@1cca5d], House@1cca5c
, Fronk the cat[Animal@1cca61], House@1cca5c
]
```

Of course you expect that the deserialized objects have different addresses from their originals. But notice that in **animals1** and **animals2** the same addresses appear, including the references to the **House** object that both share. On the other hand, when **animals3** is recovered the system has no way of knowing that the objects in this other stream are aliases of the objects in the first stream, so it makes a completely different web of objects.

As long as you're serializing everything to a single stream, you'll be able to recover the same web of objects that you wrote, with no accidental duplication of objects. Of course, you can change the state of your objects in between the time you write the first and the last, but that's your responsibility—the objects will be written in whatever state they are in (and with whatever connections they have to other objects) at the time you serialize them.

The safest thing to do if you want to save the state of a system is to serialize as an "atomic" operation. If you serialize some things, do some other work, and serialize some more, etc., then you will not be storing the system safely. Instead, put all the objects that comprise the state of your system in a single container and simply write that container out in one operation. Then you can restore it with a single method call as well.

The following example is an imaginary computer-aided design (CAD) system that demonstrates the approach. In addition, it throws in the issue of **static** fields—if you look at the documentation you'll see that **Class** is **Serializable**, so it should be easy to store the **static** fields by simply serializing the **Class** object. That seems like a sensible approach, anyway.

```
//: c11:CADState.java
// Saving and restoring the state of a
// pretend CAD system.
```

```
import java.io.*;
import java.util.*;

abstract class Shape implements Serializable {
  public static final int
    RED = 1, BLUE = 2, GREEN = 3;
  private int xPos, yPos, dimension;
  private static Random r = new Random();
  private static int counter = 0;
  abstract public void setColor(int newColor);
  abstract public int getColor();
  public Shape(int xVal, int yVal, int dim) {
    xPos = xVal;
    yPos = yVal;
    dimension = dim;
  }
  public String toString() {
    return getClass() +
      " color[" + getColor() +
      "] xPos[" + xPos +
      "] yPos[" + yPos +
      "] dim[" + dimension + "]\n";
  }
  public static Shape randomFactory() {
    int xVal = r.nextInt() % 100;
    int yVal = r.nextInt() % 100;
    int dim = r.nextInt() % 100;
    switch(counter++ % 3) {
      default:
      case 0: return new Circle(xVal, yVal, dim);
      case 1: return new Square(xVal, yVal, dim);
      case 2: return new Line(xVal, yVal, dim);
    }
  }
}

class Circle extends Shape {
  private static int color = RED;
  public Circle(int xVal, int yVal, int dim) {
    super(xVal, yVal, dim);
  }
```

```
    public void setColor(int newColor) {
      color = newColor;
    }
    public int getColor() {
      return color;
    }
}

class Square extends Shape {
  private static int color;
  public Square(int xVal, int yVal, int dim) {
    super(xVal, yVal, dim);
    color = RED;
  }
  public void setColor(int newColor) {
    color = newColor;
  }
  public int getColor() {
    return color;
  }
}

class Line extends Shape {
  private static int color = RED;
  public static void
  serializeStaticState(ObjectOutputStream os)
      throws IOException {
    os.writeInt(color);
  }
  public static void
  deserializeStaticState(ObjectInputStream os)
      throws IOException {
    color = os.readInt();
  }
  public Line(int xVal, int yVal, int dim) {
    super(xVal, yVal, dim);
  }
  public void setColor(int newColor) {
    color = newColor;
  }
  public int getColor() {
```

```
      return color;
    }
  }

public class CADState {
  public static void main(String[] args)
  throws Exception {
    ArrayList shapeTypes, shapes;
    if(args.length == 0) {
      shapeTypes = new ArrayList();
      shapes = new ArrayList();
      // Add references to the class objects:
      shapeTypes.add(Circle.class);
      shapeTypes.add(Square.class);
      shapeTypes.add(Line.class);
      // Make some shapes:
      for(int i = 0; i < 10; i++)
        shapes.add(Shape.randomFactory());
      // Set all the static colors to GREEN:
      for(int i = 0; i < 10; i++)
        ((Shape)shapes.get(i))
          .setColor(Shape.GREEN);
      // Save the state vector:
      ObjectOutputStream out =
        new ObjectOutputStream(
          new FileOutputStream("CADState.out"));
      out.writeObject(shapeTypes);
      Line.serializeStaticState(out);
      out.writeObject(shapes);
    } else { // There's a command-line argument
      ObjectInputStream in =
        new ObjectInputStream(
          new FileInputStream(args[0]));
      // Read in the same order they were written:
      shapeTypes = (ArrayList)in.readObject();
      Line.deserializeStaticState(in);
      shapes = (ArrayList)in.readObject();
    }
    // Display the shapes:
    System.out.println(shapes);
  }
```

```
} ///:~
```

The **Shape** class **implements Serializable**, so anything that is inherited from **Shape** is automatically **Serializable** as well. Each **Shape** contains data, and each derived **Shape** class contains a **static** field that determines the color of all of those types of **Shape**s. (Placing a **static** field in the base class would result in only one field, since **static** fields are not duplicated in derived classes.) Methods in the base class can be overridden to set the color for the various types (**static** methods are not dynamically bound, so these are normal methods). The **randomFactory( )** method creates a different **Shape** each time you call it, using random values for the **Shape** data.

Circle and **Square** are straightforward extensions of **Shape**; the only difference is that **Circle** initializes **color** at the point of definition and **Square** initializes it in the constructor. We'll leave the discussion of **Line** for later.

In **main( )**, one **ArrayList** is used to hold the **Class** objects and the other to hold the shapes. If you don't provide a command line argument the **shapeTypes ArrayList** is created and the **Class** objects are added, and then the **shapes ArrayList** is created and **Shape** objects are added. Next, all the **static color** values are set to **GREEN**, and everything is serialized to the file **CADState.out**.

If you provide a command line argument (presumably **CADState.out**), that file is opened and used to restore the state of the program. In both situations, the resulting **ArrayList** of **Shape**s is printed. The results from one run are:

```
>java CADState
[class Circle color[3] xPos[-51] yPos[-99] dim[38]
, class Square color[3] xPos[2] yPos[61] dim[-46]
, class Line color[3] xPos[51] yPos[73] dim[64]
, class Circle color[3] xPos[-70] yPos[1] dim[16]
, class Square color[3] xPos[3] yPos[94] dim[-36]
, class Line color[3] xPos[-84] yPos[-21] dim[-35]
, class Circle color[3] xPos[-75] yPos[-43] dim[22]
, class Square color[3] xPos[81] yPos[30] dim[-45]
, class Line color[3] xPos[-29] yPos[92] dim[17]
, class Circle color[3] xPos[17] yPos[90] dim[-76]
```

```
]

>java CADState CADState.out
[class Circle color[1] xPos[-51] yPos[-99] dim[38]
, class Square color[0] xPos[2] yPos[61] dim[-46]
, class Line color[3] xPos[51] yPos[73] dim[64]
, class Circle color[1] xPos[-70] yPos[1] dim[16]
, class Square color[0] xPos[3] yPos[94] dim[-36]
, class Line color[3] xPos[-84] yPos[-21] dim[-35]
, class Circle color[1] xPos[-75] yPos[-43] dim[22]
, class Square color[0] xPos[81] yPos[30] dim[-45]
, class Line color[3] xPos[-29] yPos[92] dim[17]
, class Circle color[1] xPos[17] yPos[90] dim[-76]
]
```

You can see that the values of **xPos**, **yPos,** and **dim** were all stored and recovered successfully, but there's something wrong with the retrieval of the **static** information. It's all "3" going in, but it doesn't come out that way. **Circle**s have a value of 1 (**RED**, which is the definition), and **Square**s have a value of 0 (remember, they are initialized in the constructor). It's as if the **static**s didn't get serialized at all! That's right— even though class **Class** is **Serializable**, it doesn't do what you expect. So if you want to serialize **statics**, you must do it yourself.

This is what the **serializeStaticState( )** and **deserializeStaticState( )** **static** methods in **Line** are for. You can see that they are explicitly called as part of the storage and retrieval process. (Note that the order of writing to the serialize file and reading back from it must be maintained.) Thus to make **CADState.java** run correctly you must:

1.   Add a **serializeStaticState( )** and **deserializeStaticState( )** to the shapes.

2.   Remove the **ArrayList shapeTypes** and all code related to it.

3.   Add calls to the new serialize and deserialize static methods in the shapes.

Another issue you might have to think about is security, since serialization also saves **private** data. If you have a security issue, those fields should be marked as **transient**. But then you have to design a secure way to store that information so that when you do a restore you can reset those **private** variables.

Tokenizing input

Tokenizing is the process of breaking a sequence of characters into a sequence of "tokens," which are bits of text delimited by whatever you choose. For example, your tokens could be words, and then they would be delimited by white space and punctuation. There are two classes provided in the standard Java library that can be used for tokenization: **StreamTokenizer** and **StringTokenizer**.

StreamTokenizer

Although **StreamTokenizer** is not derived from **InputStream** or **OutputStream**, it works only with **InputStream** objects, so it rightfully belongs in the I/O portion of the library.

Consider a program to count the occurrence of words in a text file:

```
//: c11:WordCount.java
// Counts words from a file, outputs
// results in sorted form.
import java.io.*;
import java.util.*;

class Counter {
  private int i = 1;
  int read() { return i; }
  void increment() { i++; }
}

public class WordCount {
  private FileReader file;
  private StreamTokenizer st;
  // A TreeMap keeps keys in sorted order:
  private TreeMap counts = new TreeMap();
  WordCount(String filename)
    throws FileNotFoundException {
    try {
```

```java
      file = new FileReader(filename);
      st = new StreamTokenizer(
        new BufferedReader(file));
      st.ordinaryChar('.');
      st.ordinaryChar('-');
    } catch(FileNotFoundException e) {
      System.err.println(
        "Could not open " + filename);
      throw e;
    }
  }
  void cleanup() {
    try {
      file.close();
    } catch(IOException e) {
      System.err.println(
        "file.close() unsuccessful");
    }
  }
  void countWords() {
    try {
      while(st.nextToken() !=
        StreamTokenizer.TT_EOF) {
        String s;
        switch(st.ttype) {
          case StreamTokenizer.TT_EOL:
            s = new String("EOL");
            break;
          case StreamTokenizer.TT_NUMBER:
            s = Double.toString(st.nval);
            break;
          case StreamTokenizer.TT_WORD:
            s = st.sval; // Already a String
            break;
          default: // single character in ttype
            s = String.valueOf((char)st.ttype);
        }
        if(counts.containsKey(s))
          ((Counter)counts.get(s)).increment();
        else
          counts.put(s, new Counter());
```

```
      }
    } catch(IOException e) {
      System.err.println(
        "st.nextToken() unsuccessful");
    }
  }
  Collection values() {
    return counts.values();
  }
  Set keySet() { return counts.keySet(); }
  Counter getCounter(String s) {
    return (Counter)counts.get(s);
  }
  public static void main(String[] args)
  throws FileNotFoundException {
    WordCount wc =
      new WordCount(args[0]);
    wc.countWords();
    Iterator keys = wc.keySet().iterator();
    while(keys.hasNext()) {
      String key = (String)keys.next();
      System.out.println(key + ": "
                + wc.getCounter(key).read());
    }
    wc.cleanup();
  }
} ///:~
```

Presenting the words in sorted form is easy to do by storing the data in a **TreeMap**, which automatically organizes its keys in sorted order (see Chapter 9). When you get a set of keys using **keySet( )**, they will also be in sorted order.

To open the file, a **FileReader** is used, and to turn the file into words a **StreamTokenizer** is created from the **FileReader** wrapped in a **BufferedReader**. In **StreamTokenizer**, there is a default list of separators, and you can add more with a set of methods. Here, **ordinaryChar( )** is used to say "This character has no significance that I'm interested in," so the parser doesn't include it as part of any of the words that it creates. For example, saying **st.ordinaryChar('.')** means that periods will not be included as parts of the words that are parsed. You can find more information in the JDK HTML documentation from *java.sun.com*.

In **countWords( )**, the tokens are pulled one at a time from the stream, and the **ttype** information is used to determine what to do with each token, since a token can be an end-of-line, a number, a string, or a single character.

Once a token is found, the **TreeMap counts** is queried to see if it already contains the token as a key. If it does, the corresponding **Counter** object is incremented to indicate that another instance of this word has been found. If not, a new **Counter** is created—since the **Counter** constructor initializes its value to one, this also acts to count the word.

WordCount is not a type of **TreeMap**, so it wasn't inherited. It performs a specific type of functionality, so even though the **keys( )** and **values( )** methods must be reexposed, that still doesn't mean that inheritance should be used since a number of **TreeMap** methods are inappropriate here. In addition, other methods like **getCounter( )**, which get the **Counter** for a particular **String**, and **sortedKeys( )**, which produces an **Iterator**, finish the change in the shape of **WordCount**'s interface.

In **main( )** you can see the use of a **WordCount** to open and count the words in a file—it just takes two lines of code. Then an Iterator to a sorted list of keys (words) is extracted, and this is used to pull out each key and associated **Count**. The call to **cleanup( )** is necessary to ensure that the file is closed.

StringTokenizer

Although it isn't part of the I/O library, the **StringTokenizer** has sufficiently similar functionality to **StreamTokenizer** that it will be described here.

The **StringTokenizer** returns the tokens within a string one at a time. These tokens are consecutive characters delimited by tabs, spaces, and newlines. Thus, the tokens of the string "Where is my cat?" are "Where", "is", "my", and "cat?" Like the **StreamTokenizer**, you can tell the **StringTokenizer** to break up the input in any way that you want, but

---

with **StringTokenizer** you do this by passing a second argument to the constructor, which is a **String** of the delimiters you wish to use. In general, if you need more sophistication, use a **StreamTokenizer**.

You ask a **StringTokenizer** object for the next token in the string using the **nextToken( )** method, which either returns the token or an empty string to indicate that no tokens remain.

As an example, the following program performs a limited analysis of a sentence, looking for key phrase sequences to indicate whether happiness or sadness is implied.

```
//: c11:AnalyzeSentence.java
// Look for particular sequences in sentences.
import java.util.*;

public class AnalyzeSentence {
  public static void main(String[] args) {
    analyze("I am happy about this");
    analyze("I am not happy about this");
    analyze("I am not! I am happy");
    analyze("I am sad about this");
    analyze("I am not sad about this");
    analyze("I am not! I am sad");
    analyze("Are you happy about this?");
    analyze("Are you sad about this?");
    analyze("It's you! I am happy");
    analyze("It's you! I am sad");
  }
  static StringTokenizer st;
  static void analyze(String s) {
    prt("\nnew sentence >> " + s);
    boolean sad = false;
    st = new StringTokenizer(s);
    while (st.hasMoreTokens()) {
      String token = next();
      // Look until you find one of the
      // two starting tokens:
      if (!token.equals("I") &&
          !token.equals("Are"))
        continue; // Top of while loop
```

```
        if(token.equals("I")) {
          String tk2 = next();
          if(!tk2.equals("am")) // Must be after I
            break; // Out of while loop
          else {
            String tk3 = next();
            if(tk3.equals("sad")) {
              sad = true;
              break; // Out of while loop
            }
            if (tk3.equals("not")) {
              String tk4 = next();
              if(tk4.equals("sad"))
                break; // Leave sad false
              if(tk4.equals("happy")) {
                sad = true;
                break;
              }
            }
          }
        }
        if(token.equals("Are")) {
          String tk2 = next();
          if(!tk2.equals("you"))
            break; // Must be after Are
          String tk3 = next();
          if(tk3.equals("sad"))
            sad = true;
          break; // Out of while loop
        }
      }
      if(sad) prt("Sad detected");
    }
    static String next() {
      if(st.hasMoreTokens()) {
        String s = st.nextToken();
        prt(s);
        return s;
      }
      else
        return "";
```

```
    }
  static void prt(String s) {
    System.out.println(s);
  }
} ///:~
```

For each string being analyzed, a **while** loop is entered and tokens are
pulled off the string. Notice the first **if** statement, which says to **continue**
(go back to the beginning of the loop and start again) if the token is
neither an "I" nor an "Are." This means that it will get tokens until an "I"
or an "Are" is found. You might think to use the == instead of the
equals( ) method, but that won't work correctly, since == compares
reference values while **equals( )** compares contents.

The logic of the rest of the **analyze( )** method is that the pattern that's
being searched for is "I am sad," "I am not happy," or "Are you sad?"
Without the **break** statement, the code for this would be even messier
than it is. You should be aware that a typical parser (this is a primitive
example of one) normally has a table of these tokens and a piece of code
that moves through the states in the table as new tokens are read.

You should think of the **StringTokenizer** only as shorthand for a simple
and specific kind of **StreamTokenizer**. However, if you have a **String**
that you want to tokenize and **StringTokenizer** is too limited, all you
have to do is turn it into a stream with **StringBufferInputStream** and
then use that to create a much more powerful **StreamTokenizer**.

Checking capitalization style

In this section we'll look at a more complete example of the use of Java
I/O, which also uses tokenization. This project is directly useful because it
performs a style check to make sure that your capitalization conforms to
the Java style as found at *java.sun.com/docs/codeconv/index.html*. It
opens each **.java** file in the current directory and extracts all the class
names and identifiers, then shows you if any of them don't meet the Java
style.

For the program to operate correctly, you must first build a class name
repository to hold all the class names in the standard Java library. You do
this by moving into all the source code subdirectories for the standard

---

Java library and running **ClassScanner** in each subdirectory. Provide as arguments the name of the repository file (using the same path and name each time) and the **-a** command-line option to indicate that the class names should be added to the repository.

To use the program to check your code, hand it the path and name of the repository to use. It will check all the classes and identifiers in the current directory and tell you which ones don't follow the typical Java capitalization style.

You should be aware that the program isn't perfect; there are a few times when it will point out what it thinks is a problem but on looking at the code you'll see that nothing needs to be changed. This is a little annoying, but it's still much easier than trying to find all these cases by staring at your code.

```
//: c11:ClassScanner.java
// Scans all files in directory for classes
// and identifiers, to check capitalization.
// Assumes properly compiling code listings.
// Doesn't do everything right, but is a
// useful aid.
import java.io.*;
import java.util.*;

class MultiStringMap extends HashMap {
  public void add(String key, String value) {
    if(!containsKey(key))
      put(key, new ArrayList());
    ((ArrayList)get(key)).add(value);
  }
  public ArrayList getArrayList(String key) {
    if(!containsKey(key)) {
      System.err.println(
        "ERROR: can't find key: " + key);
      System.exit(1);
    }
    return (ArrayList)get(key);
  }
  public void printValues(PrintStream p) {
    Iterator k = keySet().iterator();
```

```java
    while(k.hasNext()) {
      String oneKey = (String)k.next();
      ArrayList val = getArrayList(oneKey);
      for(int i = 0; i < val.size(); i++)
        p.println((String)val.get(i));
    }
  }
}

public class ClassScanner {
  private File path;
  private String[] fileList;
  private Properties classes = new Properties();
  private MultiStringMap
    classMap = new MultiStringMap(),
    identMap = new MultiStringMap();
  private StreamTokenizer in;
  public ClassScanner() throws IOException {
    path = new File(".");
    fileList = path.list(new JavaFilter());
    for(int i = 0; i < fileList.length; i++) {
      System.out.println(fileList[i]);
      try {
        scanListing(fileList[i]);
      } catch(FileNotFoundException e) {
        System.err.println("Could not open " +
          fileList[i]);
      }
    }
  }
  void scanListing(String fname)
  throws IOException {
    in = new StreamTokenizer(
        new BufferedReader(
          new FileReader(fname)));
    // Doesn't seem to work:
    // in.slashStarComments(true);
    // in.slashSlashComments(true);
    in.ordinaryChar('/');
    in.ordinaryChar('.');
    in.wordChars('_', '_');
```

```
      in.eolIsSignificant(true);
      while(in.nextToken() !=
            StreamTokenizer.TT_EOF) {
        if(in.ttype == '/')
          eatComments();
        else if(in.ttype ==
              StreamTokenizer.TT_WORD) {
          if(in.sval.equals("class") ||
             in.sval.equals("interface")) {
            // Get class name:
              while(in.nextToken() !=
                    StreamTokenizer.TT_EOF
                    && in.ttype !=
                    StreamTokenizer.TT_WORD)
                ;
              classes.put(in.sval, in.sval);
              classMap.add(fname, in.sval);
          }
          if(in.sval.equals("import") ||
             in.sval.equals("package"))
            discardLine();
          else // It's an identifier or keyword
            identMap.add(fname, in.sval);
        }
      }
    }
    void discardLine() throws IOException {
      while(in.nextToken() !=
            StreamTokenizer.TT_EOF
            && in.ttype !=
            StreamTokenizer.TT_EOL)
        ; // Throw away tokens to end of line
    }
    // StreamTokenizer's comment removal seemed
    // to be broken. This extracts them:
    void eatComments() throws IOException {
      if(in.nextToken() !=
         StreamTokenizer.TT_EOF) {
        if(in.ttype == '/')
          discardLine();
        else if(in.ttype != '*')
```

```
          in.pushBack();
        else
          while(true) {
            if(in.nextToken() ==
              StreamTokenizer.TT_EOF)
              break;
            if(in.ttype == '*')
              if(in.nextToken() !=
                StreamTokenizer.TT_EOF
                && in.ttype == '/')
                break;
          }
      }
  }
  public String[] classNames() {
    String[] result = new String[classes.size()];
    Iterator e = classes.keySet().iterator();
    int i = 0;
    while(e.hasNext())
      result[i++] = (String)e.next();
    return result;
  }
  public void checkClassNames() {
    Iterator files = classMap.keySet().iterator();
    while(files.hasNext()) {
      String file = (String)files.next();
      ArrayList cls = classMap.getArrayList(file);
      for(int i = 0; i < cls.size(); i++) {
        String className = (String)cls.get(i);
        if(Character.isLowerCase(
            className.charAt(0)))
          System.out.println(
            "class capitalization error, file: "
            + file + ", class: "
            + className);
      }
    }
  }
  public void checkIdentNames() {
    Iterator files = identMap.keySet().iterator();
    ArrayList reportSet = new ArrayList();
```

```java
      while(files.hasNext()) {
        String file = (String)files.next();
        ArrayList ids = identMap.getArrayList(file);
        for(int i = 0; i < ids.size(); i++) {
          String id = (String)ids.get(i);
          if(!classes.contains(id)) {
            // Ignore identifiers of length 3 or
            // longer that are all uppercase
            // (probably static final values):
            if(id.length() >= 3 &&
               id.equals(
                 id.toUpperCase()))
              continue;
            // Check to see if first char is upper:
            if(Character.isUpperCase(id.charAt(0))){
              if(reportSet.indexOf(file + id)
                  == -1){ // Not reported yet
                reportSet.add(file + id);
                System.out.println(
                  "Ident capitalization error in:"
                  + file + ", ident: " + id);
              }
            }
          }
        }
      }
    }
    static final String usage =
      "Usage: \n" +
      "ClassScanner classnames -a\n" +
      "\tAdds all the class names in this \n" +
      "\tdirectory to the repository file \n" +
      "\tcalled 'classnames'\n" +
      "ClassScanner classnames\n" +
      "\tChecks all the java files in this \n" +
      "\tdirectory for capitalization errors, \n" +
      "\tusing the repository file 'classnames'";
    private static void usage() {
      System.err.println(usage);
      System.exit(1);
    }
```

```java
public static void main(String[] args)
throws IOException {
  if(args.length < 1 || args.length > 2)
    usage();
  ClassScanner c = new ClassScanner();
  File old = new File(args[0]);
  if(old.exists()) {
    try {
      // Try to open an existing
      // properties file:
      InputStream oldlist =
        new BufferedInputStream(
          new FileInputStream(old));
      c.classes.load(oldlist);
      oldlist.close();
    } catch(IOException e) {
      System.err.println("Could not open "
        + old + " for reading");
      System.exit(1);
    }
  }
  if(args.length == 1) {
    c.checkClassNames();
    c.checkIdentNames();
  }
  // Write the class names to a repository:
  if(args.length == 2) {
    if(!args[1].equals("-a"))
      usage();
    try {
      BufferedOutputStream out =
        new BufferedOutputStream(
          new FileOutputStream(args[0]));
      c.classes.store(out,
        "Classes found by ClassScanner.java");
      out.close();
    } catch(IOException e) {
      System.err.println(
        "Could not write " + args[0]);
      System.exit(1);
    }
```

```
        }
      }
    }

class JavaFilter implements FilenameFilter {
  public boolean accept(File dir, String name) {
    // Strip path information:
    String f = new File(name).getName();
    return f.trim().endsWith(".java");
  }
} ///:~
```

The class **MultiStringMap** is a tool that allows you to map a group of strings onto each key entry. It uses a **HashMap** (this time with inheritance) with the key as the single string that's mapped onto the **ArrayList** value. The **add( )** method simply checks to see if there's a key already in the **HashMap**, and if not it puts one there. The **getArrayList( )** method produces an **ArrayList** for a particular key, and **printValues( )**, which is primarily useful for debugging, prints out all the values **ArrayList** by **ArrayList**.

To keep life simple, the class names from the standard Java libraries are all put into a **Properties** object (from the standard Java library). Remember that a **Properties** object is a **HashMap** that holds only **String** objects for both the key and value entries. However, it can be saved to disk and restored from disk in one method call, so it's ideal for the repository of names. Actually, we need only a list of names, and a **HashMap** can't accept **null** for either its key or its value entry. So the same object will be used for both the key and the value.

For the classes and identifiers that are discovered for the files in a particular directory, two **MultiStringMap**s are used: **classMap** and **identMap**. Also, when the program starts up it loads the standard class name repository into the **Properties** object called **classes**, and when a new class name is found in the local directory that is also added to **classes** as well as to **classMap**. This way, **classMap** can be used to step through all the classes in the local directory, and **classes** can be used to see if the current token is a class name (which indicates a definition of an object or method is beginning, so grab the next tokens—until a semicolon—and put them into **identMap**).

The default constructor for **ClassScanner** creates a list of file names, using the **JavaFilter** implementation of **FilenameFilter**, shown at the end of the file. Then it calls **scanListing( )** for each file name.

Inside **scanListing( )** the source code file is opened and turned into a **StreamTokenizer**. In the documentation, passing **true** to **slashStarComments( )** and **slashSlashComments( )** is supposed to strip those comments out, but this seems to be a bit flawed, as it doesn't quite work. Instead, those lines are commented out and the comments are extracted by another method. To do this, the "/" must be captured as an ordinary character rather than letting the **StreamTokenizer** absorb it as part of a comment, and the **ordinaryChar( )** method tells the **StreamTokenizer** to do this. This is also true for dots ("**.**"), since we want to have the method calls pulled apart into individual identifiers. However, the underscore, which is ordinarily treated by **StreamTokenizer** as an individual character, should be left as part of identifiers since it appears in such **static final** values as **TT_EOF**, etc., used in this very program. The **wordChars( )** method takes a range of characters you want to add to those that are left inside a token that is being parsed as a word. Finally, when parsing for one-line comments or discarding a line we need to know when an end-of-line occurs, so by calling **eolIsSignificant(true)** the EOL will show up rather than being absorbed by the **StreamTokenizer**.

The rest of **scanListing( )** reads and reacts to tokens until the end of the file, signified when **nextToken( )** returns the **final static** value **StreamTokenizer.TT_EOF**.

If the token is a "/" it is potentially a comment, so **eatComments( )** is called to deal with it. The only other situation we're interested in here is if it's a word, of which there are some special cases.

If the word is **class** or **interface** then the next token represents a class or interface name, and it is put into **classes** and **classMap**. If the word is **import** or **package**, then we don't want the rest of the line. Anything else must be an identifier (which we're interested in) or a keyword (which we're not, but they're all lowercase anyway so it won't spoil things to put those in). These are added to **identMap**.

The **discardLine( )** method is a simple tool that looks for the end of a line. Note that any time you get a new token, you must check for the end of the file.

The **eatComments( )** method is called whenever a forward slash is encountered in the main parsing loop. However, that doesn't necessarily mean a comment has been found, so the next token must be extracted to see if it's another forward slash (in which case the line is discarded) or an asterisk. But if it's neither of those, it means the token you've just pulled out is needed back in the main parsing loop! Fortunately, the **pushBack( )** method allows you to "push back" the current token onto the input stream so that when the main parsing loop calls **nextToken( )** it will get the one you just pushed back.

For convenience, the **classNames( )** method produces an array of all the names in the **classes** container. This method is not used in the program but is helpful for debugging.

The next two methods are the ones in which the actual checking takes place. In **checkClassNames( )**, the class names are extracted from the **classMap** (which, remember, contains only the names in this directory, organized by file name so the file name can be printed along with the errant class name). This is accomplished by pulling each associated **ArrayList** and stepping through that, looking to see if the first character is lowercase. If so, the appropriate error message is printed.

In **checkIdentNames( )**, a similar approach is taken: each identifier name is extracted from **identMap**. If the name is not in the **classes** list, it's assumed to be an identifier or keyword. A special case is checked: if the identifier length is three or more *and* all the characters are uppercase, this identifier is ignored because it's probably a **static final** value such as **TT_EOF**. Of course, this is not a perfect algorithm, but it assumes that you'll eventually notice any all-uppercase identifiers that are out of place.

Instead of reporting every identifier that starts with an uppercase character, this method keeps track of which ones have already been reported in an **ArrayList** called **reportSet( )**. This treats the **ArrayList** as a "set" that tells you whether an item is already in the set. The item is produced by concatenating the file name and identifier. If the element isn't in the set, it's added and then the report is made.

The rest of the listing is comprised of **main( )**, which busies itself by handling the command line arguments and figuring out whether you're building a repository of class names from the standard Java library or checking the validity of code you've written. In both cases it makes a **ClassScanner** object.

Whether you're building a repository or using one, you must try to open the existing repository. By making a **File** object and testing for existence, you can decide whether to open the file and **load( )** the **Properties** list **classes** inside **ClassScanner**. (The classes from the repository add to, rather than overwrite, the classes found by the **ClassScanner** constructor.) If you provide only one command-line argument it means that you want to perform a check of the class names and identifier names, but if you provide two arguments (the second being "**-a**") you're building a class name repository. In this case, an output file is opened and the method **Properties.save( )** is used to write the list into a file, along with a string that provides header file information.

Summary

The Java I/O stream library does satisfy the basic requirements: you can perform reading and writing with the console, a file, a block of memory, or even across the Internet (as you will see in Chapter 15). With inheritance, you can create new types of input and output objects. And you can even add a simple extensibility to the kinds of objects a stream will accept by redefining the **toString( )** method that's automatically called when you pass an object to a method that's expecting a **String** (Java's limited "automatic type conversion").

There are questions left unanswered by the documentation and design of the I/O stream library. For example, it would have been nice if you could say that you want an exception thrown if you try to overwrite a file when opening it for output—some programming systems allow you to specify that you want to open an output file, but only if it doesn't already exist. In Java, it appears that you are supposed to use a **File** object to determine whether a file exists, because if you open it as a **FileOutputStream** or **FileWriter** it will always get overwritten.

The I/O stream library brings up mixed feelings; it does much of the job and it's portable. But if you don't already understand the decorator pattern, the design is nonintuitive, so there's extra overhead in learning and teaching it. It's also incomplete: there's no support for the kind of output formatting that almost every other language's I/O package supports.

However, once you *do* understand the decorator pattern and begin using the library in situations that require its flexibility, you can begin to benefit from this design, at which point its cost in extra lines of code may not bother you as much.

If you do not find what you're looking for in this chapter (which has only been an introduction, and is not meant to be comprehensive), you can find in-depth coverage in *Java I/O*, by Elliotte Rusty Harold (O'Reilly, 1999).

Exercises

Solutions to selected exercises can be found in the electronic document *The Thinking in Java Annotated Solution Guide*, available for a small fee from *www.BruceEckel.com*.

1. Open a text file so that you can read the file one line at a time. Read each line as a **String** and place that **String** object into a **LinkedList**. Print all of the lines in the **LinkedList** in reverse order.

2. Modify Exercise 1 so that the name of the file you read is provided as a command-line argument.

3. Modify Exercise 2 to also open a text file so you can write text into it. Write the lines in the **ArrayList**, along with line numbers (do not attempt to use the "LineNumber" classes), out to the file.

4. Modify Exercise 2 to force all the lines in the **ArrayList** to upper case and send the results to **System.out**.

5. Modify Exercise 2 to take additional command-line arguments of words to find in the file. Print any lines in which the words match.

6. Modify **DirList.java** so that the **FilenameFilter** actually opens each file and accepts the file based on whether any of the trailing arguments on the command line exist in that file.

7. Create a class called **SortedDirList** with a constructor that takes file path information and builds a sorted directory list from the files at that path. Create two overloaded **list( )** methods that will either produce the whole list or a subset of the list based on an argument. Add a **size( )** method that takes a file name and produces the size of that file.

8. Modify **WordCount.java** so that it produces an alphabetic sort instead, using the tool from Chapter 9.

9. Modify **WordCount.java** so that it uses a class containing a **String** and a count value to store each different word, and a **Set** of these objects to maintain the list of words.

10. Modify **IOStreamDemo.java** so that it uses **LineNumberInputStream** to keep track of the line count. Note that it's much easier to just keep track programmatically.

11. Starting with section 4 of **IOStreamDemo.java**, write a program that compares the performance of writing to a file when using buffered and unbuffered I/O.

12. Modify section 5 of **IOStreamDemo.java** to eliminate the spaces in the line produced by the first call to **in5br.readLine( )**. Do this using a **while** loop and **readChar( )**.

13. Repair the program **CADState.java** as described in the text.

14. In **Blips.java**, copy the file and rename it to **BlipCheck.java** and rename the class **Blip2** to **BlipCheck** (making it **public** and removing the public scope from the class **Blips** in the process). Remove the //! marks in the file and execute the program including the offending lines. Next, comment out the default constructor for **BlipCheck**. Run it and explain why it works. Note that after compiling, you must execute the program with "**java Blips**" because the **main( )** method is still in class **Blips**.

15.　In **Blip3.java**, comment out the two lines after the phrases "You must do this:" and run the program. Explain the result and why it differs from when the two lines are in the program.

16.　(Intermediate) In Chapter 8, locate the **GreenhouseControls.java** example, which consists of three files. In **GreenhouseControls.java**, the **Restart( )** inner class has a hard-coded set of events. Change the program so that it reads the events and their relative times from a text file. (Challenging: Use a design patterns *factory method* to build the events—see *Thinking in Patterns with Java*, downloadable at *www.BruceEckel.com*.)

12: Run-time Type Identification

The idea of run-time type identification (RTTI) seems fairly simple at first: it lets you find the exact type of an object when you only have a reference to the base type.

However, the *need* for RTTI uncovers a whole plethora of interesting (and often perplexing) OO design issues, and raises fundamental questions of how you should structure your programs.

This chapter looks at the ways that Java allows you to discover information about objects and classes at run-time. This takes two forms: "traditional" RTTI, which assumes that you have all the types available at compile-time and run-time, and the "reflection" mechanism, which allows you to discover class information solely at run-time. The "traditional" RTTI will be covered first, followed by a discussion of reflection.

The need for RTTI

Consider the now familiar example of a class hierarchy that uses polymorphism. The generic type is the base class **Shape**, and the specific derived types are **Circle**, **Square**, and **Triangle**:

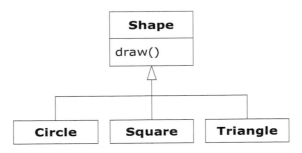

This is a typical class hierarchy diagram, with the base class at the top and the derived classes growing downward. The normal goal in object-oriented programming is for the bulk of your code to manipulate references to the base type (**Shape**, in this case), so if you decide to extend the program by adding a new class (**Rhomboid**, derived from **Shape**, for example), the bulk of the code is not affected. In this example, the dynamically bound method in the **Shape** interface is **draw( )**, so the intent is for the client programmer to call **draw( )** through a generic **Shape** reference. **draw( )** is overridden in all of the derived classes, and because it is a dynamically bound method, the proper behavior will occur even though it is called through a generic **Shape** reference. That's polymorphism.

Thus, you generally create a specific object (**Circle**, **Square**, or **Triangle**), upcast it to a **Shape** (forgetting the specific type of the object), and use that anonymous **Shape** reference in the rest of the program.

As a brief review of polymorphism and upcasting, you might code the above example as follows:

```
//: c12:Shapes.java
import java.util.*;

class Shape {
  void draw() {
    System.out.println(this + ".draw()");
  }
}

class Circle extends Shape {
  public String toString() { return "Circle"; }
}

class Square extends Shape {
  public String toString() { return "Square"; }
}

class Triangle extends Shape {
  public String toString() { return "Triangle"; }
}
```

```
public class Shapes {
  public static void main(String[] args) {
    ArrayList s = new ArrayList();
    s.add(new Circle());
    s.add(new Square());
    s.add(new Triangle());
    Iterator e = s.iterator();
    while(e.hasNext())
      ((Shape)e.next()).draw();
  }
} ///:~
```

The base class contains a **draw( )** method that indirectly uses **toString( )** to print an identifier for the class by passing **this** to **System.out.println( )**. If that function sees an object, it automatically calls the **toString( )** method to produce a **String** representation.

Each of the derived classes overrides the **toString( )** method (from **Object**) so that **draw( )** ends up printing something different in each case. In **main( )**, specific types of **Shape** are created and then added to an **ArrayList**. This is the point at which the upcast occurs because the **ArrayList** holds only **Object**s. Since everything in Java (with the exception of primitives) is an **Object**, an **ArrayList** can also hold **Shape** objects. But during an upcast to **Object**, it also loses any specific information, including the fact that the objects are **Shape**s. To the **ArrayList**, they are just **Object**s.

At the point you fetch an element out of the **ArrayList** with **next( )**, things get a little busy. Since **ArrayList** holds only **Object**s, **next( )** naturally produces an **Object reference**. But we know it's really a **Shape** reference, and we want to send **Shape** messages to that object. So a cast to **Shape** is necessary using the traditional "**(Shape)**" cast. This is the most basic form of RTTI, since in Java all casts are checked at run-time for correctness. That's exactly what RTTI means: at run-time, the type of an object is identified.

In this case, the RTTI cast is only partial: the **Object** is cast to a **Shape**, and not all the way to a **Circle**, **Square**, or **Triangle**. That's because the only thing we *know* at this point is that the **ArrayList** is full of **Shape**s.

At compile-time, this is enforced only by your own self-imposed rules, but at run-time the cast ensures it.

Now polymorphism takes over and the exact method that's called for the **Shape** is determined by whether the reference is for a **Circle**, **Square**, or **Triangle**. And in general, this is how it should be; you want the bulk of your code to know as little as possible about *specific* types of objects, and to just deal with the general representation of a family of objects (in this case, **Shape**). As a result, your code will be easier to write, read, and maintain, and your designs will be easier to implement, understand, and change. So polymorphism is the general goal in object-oriented programming.

But what if you have a special programming problem that's easiest to solve if you know the exact type of a generic reference? For example, suppose you want to allow your users to highlight all the shapes of any particular type by turning them purple. This way, they can find all the triangles on the screen by highlighting them. This is what RTTI accomplishes: you can ask a **Shape** reference the exact type that it's referring to.

The **Class** object

To understand how RTTI works in Java, you must first know how type information is represented at run-time. This is accomplished through a special kind of object called the *Class object,* which contains information about the class. (This is sometimes called a *meta-class.*) In fact, the **Class** object is used to create all of the "regular" objects of your class.

There's a **Class** object for each class that is part of your program. That is, each time you write and compile a new class, a single **Class** object is also created (and stored, appropriately enough, in an identically named **.class** file). At run-time, when you want to make an object of that class, the Java Virtual Machine (JVM) that's executing your program first checks to see if the **Class** object for that type is loaded. If not, the JVM loads it by finding the **.class** file with that name. Thus, a Java program isn't completely loaded before it begins, which is different from many traditional languages.

Once the **Class** object for that type is in memory, it is used to create all objects of that type.

If this seems shadowy or if you don't really believe it, here's a demonstration program to prove it:

```
//: c12:SweetShop.java
// Examination of the way the class loader works.

class Candy {
  static {
    System.out.println("Loading Candy");
  }
}

class Gum {
  static {
    System.out.println("Loading Gum");
  }
}

class Cookie {
  static {
    System.out.println("Loading Cookie");
  }
}

public class SweetShop {
  public static void main(String[] args) {
    System.out.println("inside main");
    new Candy();
    System.out.println("After creating Candy");
    try {
      Class.forName("Gum");
    } catch(ClassNotFoundException e) {
      e.printStackTrace(System.err);
    }
    System.out.println(
      "After Class.forName(\"Gum\")");
    new Cookie();
    System.out.println("After creating Cookie");
```

```
    }
} ///:~
```

Each of the classes **Candy**, **Gum**, and **Cookie** have a **static** clause that is executed as the class is loaded for the first time. Information will be printed to tell you when loading occurs for that class. In **main( )**, the object creations are spread out between print statements to help detect the time of loading.

A particularly interesting line is:

```
Class.forName("Gum");
```

This method is a **static** member of **Class** (to which all **Class** objects belong). A **Class** object is like any other object and so you can get and manipulate a reference to it. (That's what the loader does.) One of the ways to get a reference to the **Class** object is **forName( )**, which takes a **String** containing the textual name (watch the spelling and capitalization!) of the particular class you want a reference for. It returns a **Class** reference.

The output of this program for one JVM is:

```
inside main
Loading Candy
After creating Candy
Loading Gum
After Class.forName("Gum")
Loading Cookie
After creating Cookie
```

You can see that each **Class** object is loaded only when it's needed, and the **static** initialization is performed upon class loading.

Class literals

Java provides a second way to produce the reference to the **Class** object, using a *class literal*. In the above program this would look like:

```
Gum.class;
```

which is not only simpler, but also safer since it's checked at compile-time. Because it eliminates the method call, it's also more efficient.

Class literals work with regular classes as well as interfaces, arrays, and primitive types. In addition, there's a standard field called **TYPE** that exists for each of the primitive wrapper classes. The **TYPE** field produces a reference to the **Class** object for the associated primitive type, such that:

... is equivalent to ...	
boolean.class	**Boolean.TYPE**
char.class	**Character.TYPE**
byte.class	**Byte.TYPE**
short.class	**Short.TYPE**
int.class	**Integer.TYPE**
long.class	**Long.TYPE**
float.class	**Float.TYPE**
double.class	**Double.TYPE**
void.class	**Void.TYPE**

My preference is to use the ".**class**" versions if you can, since they're more consistent with regular classes.

Checking before a cast

So far, you've seen RTTI forms including:

1. The classic cast; e.g., "**(Shape),**" which uses RTTI to make sure the cast is correct and throws a **ClassCastException** if you've performed a bad cast.

2. The **Class** object representing the type of your object. The **Class** object can be queried for useful run-time information.

In C++, the classic cast "**(Shape)**" does *not* perform RTTI. It simply tells the compiler to treat the object as the new type. In Java, which does perform the type check, this cast is often called a "type safe downcast."

The reason for the term "downcast" is the historical arrangement of the class hierarchy diagram. If casting a **Circle** to a **Shape** is an upcast, then casting a **Shape** to a **Circle** is a downcast. However, you know a **Circle** is also a **Shape**, and the compiler freely allows an upcast assignment, but you *don't* know that a **Shape** is necessarily a **Circle**, so the compiler doesn't allow you to perform a downcast assignment without using an explicit cast.

There's a third form of RTTI in Java. This is the keyword **instanceof** that tells you if an object is an instance of a particular type. It returns a **boolean** so you use it in the form of a question, like this:

```
if(x instanceof Dog)
  ((Dog)x).bark();
```

The above **if** statement checks to see if the object **x** belongs to the class **Dog** *before* casting **x** to a **Dog**. It's important to use **instanceof** before a downcast when you don't have other information that tells you the type of the object; otherwise you'll end up with a **ClassCastException**.

Ordinarily, you might be hunting for one type (triangles to turn purple, for example), but you can easily tally *all* of the objects using **instanceof**. Suppose you have a family of **Pet** classes:

```
//: c12:Pets.java
class Pet {}
class Dog extends Pet {}
class Pug extends Dog {}
class Cat extends Pet {}
class Rodent extends Pet {}
class Gerbil extends Rodent {}
class Hamster extends Rodent {}

class Counter { int i; } ///:~
```

The **Counter** class is used to keep track of the number of any particular type of **Pet**. You could think of it as an **Integer** that can be modified.

Using **instanceof**, all the pets can be counted:

```
//: c12:PetCount.java
// Using instanceof.
```

```
import java.util.*;

public class PetCount {
  static String[] typenames = {
    "Pet", "Dog", "Pug", "Cat",
    "Rodent", "Gerbil", "Hamster",
  };
  // Exceptions thrown out to console:
  public static void main(String[] args)
  throws Exception {
    ArrayList pets = new ArrayList();
    try {
      Class[] petTypes = {
        Class.forName("Dog"),
        Class.forName("Pug"),
        Class.forName("Cat"),
        Class.forName("Rodent"),
        Class.forName("Gerbil"),
        Class.forName("Hamster"),
      };
      for(int i = 0; i < 15; i++)
        pets.add(
          petTypes[
            (int)(Math.random()*petTypes.length)]
            .newInstance());
    } catch(InstantiationException e) {
      System.err.println("Cannot instantiate");
      throw e;
    } catch(IllegalAccessException e) {
      System.err.println("Cannot access");
      throw e;
    } catch(ClassNotFoundException e) {
      System.err.println("Cannot find class");
      throw e;
    }
    HashMap h = new HashMap();
    for(int i = 0; i < typenames.length; i++)
      h.put(typenames[i], new Counter());
    for(int i = 0; i < pets.size(); i++) {
      Object o = pets.get(i);
      if(o instanceof Pet)
```

```
        ((Counter)h.get("Pet")).i++;
      if(o instanceof Dog)
        ((Counter)h.get("Dog")).i++;
      if(o instanceof Pug)
        ((Counter)h.get("Pug")).i++;
      if(o instanceof Cat)
        ((Counter)h.get("Cat")).i++;
      if(o instanceof Rodent)
        ((Counter)h.get("Rodent")).i++;
      if(o instanceof Gerbil)
        ((Counter)h.get("Gerbil")).i++;
      if(o instanceof Hamster)
        ((Counter)h.get("Hamster")).i++;
    }
    for(int i = 0; i < pets.size(); i++)
      System.out.println(pets.get(i).getClass());
    for(int i = 0; i < typenames.length; i++)
      System.out.println(
        typenames[i] + " quantity: " +
        ((Counter)h.get(typenames[i])).i);
  }
} ///:~
```

There's a rather narrow restriction on **instanceof**: you can compare it to
a named type only, and not to a **Class** object. In the example above you
might feel that it's tedious to write out all of those **instanceof**
expressions, and you're right. But there is no way to cleverly automate
instanceof by creating an **ArrayList** of **Class** objects and comparing it
to those instead (stay tuned—you'll see an alternative). This isn't as great
a restriction as you might think, because you'll eventually understand that
your design is probably flawed if you end up writing a lot of **instanceof**
expressions.

Of course this example is contrived—you'd probably put a **static** data
member in each type and increment it in the constructor to keep track of
the counts. You would do something like that *if* you had control of the
source code for the class and could change it. Since this is not always the
case, RTTI can come in handy.

Using class literals

It's interesting to see how the **PetCount.java** example can be rewritten using class literals. The result is cleaner in many ways:

```java
//: c12:PetCount2.java
// Using class literals.
import java.util.*;

public class PetCount2 {
  public static void main(String[] args)
  throws Exception {
    ArrayList pets = new ArrayList();
    Class[] petTypes = {
      // Class literals:
      Pet.class,
      Dog.class,
      Pug.class,
      Cat.class,
      Rodent.class,
      Gerbil.class,
      Hamster.class,
    };
    try {
      for(int i = 0; i < 15; i++) {
        // Offset by one to eliminate Pet.class:
        int rnd = 1 + (int)(
          Math.random() * (petTypes.length - 1));
        pets.add(
          petTypes[rnd].newInstance());
      }
    } catch(InstantiationException e) {
      System.err.println("Cannot instantiate");
      throw e;
    } catch(IllegalAccessException e) {
      System.err.println("Cannot access");
      throw e;
    }
    HashMap h = new HashMap();
    for(int i = 0; i < petTypes.length; i++)
      h.put(petTypes[i].toString(),
```

```
      new Counter());
    for(int i = 0; i < pets.size(); i++) {
      Object o = pets.get(i);
      if(o instanceof Pet)
        ((Counter)h.get("class Pet")).i++;
      if(o instanceof Dog)
        ((Counter)h.get("class Dog")).i++;
      if(o instanceof Pug)
        ((Counter)h.get("class Pug")).i++;
      if(o instanceof Cat)
        ((Counter)h.get("class Cat")).i++;
      if(o instanceof Rodent)
        ((Counter)h.get("class Rodent")).i++;
      if(o instanceof Gerbil)
        ((Counter)h.get("class Gerbil")).i++;
      if(o instanceof Hamster)
        ((Counter)h.get("class Hamster")).i++;
    }
    for(int i = 0; i < pets.size(); i++)
      System.out.println(pets.get(i).getClass());
    Iterator keys = h.keySet().iterator();
    while(keys.hasNext()) {
      String nm = (String)keys.next();
      Counter cnt = (Counter)h.get(nm);
      System.out.println(
        nm.substring(nm.lastIndexOf('.') + 1) +
        " quantity: " + cnt.i);
    }
  }
} ///:~
```

Here, the **typenames** array has been removed in favor of getting the type
name strings from the **Class** object. Notice that the system can
distinguish between classes and interfaces.

You can also see that the creation of **petTypes** does not need to be
surrounded by a **try** block since it's evaluated at compile-time and thus
won't throw any exceptions, unlike **Class.forName( )**.

When the **Pet** objects are dynamically created, you can see that the
random number is restricted so it is between one and **petTypes.length**

and does not include zero. That's because zero refers to **Pet.class**, and presumably a generic **Pet** object is not interesting. However, since **Pet.class** is part of **petTypes** the result is that all of the pets get counted.

A dynamic **instanceof**

The **Class isInstance** method provides a way to dynamically call the **instanceof** operator. Thus, all those tedious **instanceof** statements can be removed in the **PetCount** example:

```
//: c12:PetCount3.java
// Using isInstance().
import java.util.*;

public class PetCount3 {
  public static void main(String[] args)
  throws Exception {
    ArrayList pets = new ArrayList();
    Class[] petTypes = {
      Pet.class,
      Dog.class,
      Pug.class,
      Cat.class,
      Rodent.class,
      Gerbil.class,
      Hamster.class,
    };
    try {
      for(int i = 0; i < 15; i++) {
        // Offset by one to eliminate Pet.class:
        int rnd = 1 + (int)(
          Math.random() * (petTypes.length - 1));
        pets.add(
          petTypes[rnd].newInstance());
      }
    } catch(InstantiationException e) {
      System.err.println("Cannot instantiate");
      throw e;
    } catch(IllegalAccessException e) {
      System.err.println("Cannot access");
      throw e;
```

```
    }
    HashMap h = new HashMap();
    for(int i = 0; i < petTypes.length; i++)
      h.put(petTypes[i].toString(),
        new Counter());
    for(int i = 0; i < pets.size(); i++) {
      Object o = pets.get(i);
      // Using isInstance to eliminate individual
      // instanceof expressions:
      for (int j = 0; j < petTypes.length; ++j)
        if (petTypes[j].isInstance(o)) {
          String key = petTypes[j].toString();
          ((Counter)h.get(key)).i++;
        }
    }
    for(int i = 0; i < pets.size(); i++)
      System.out.println(pets.get(i).getClass());
    Iterator keys = h.keySet().iterator();
    while(keys.hasNext()) {
      String nm = (String)keys.next();
      Counter cnt = (Counter)h.get(nm);
      System.out.println(
        nm.substring(nm.lastIndexOf('.') + 1) +
        " quantity: " + cnt.i);
    }
  }
} ///:~
```

You can see that the **isInstance( )** method has eliminated the need for the **instanceof** expressions. In addition, this means that you can add new types of pets simply by changing the **petTypes** array; the rest of the program does not need modification (as it did when using the **instanceof** expressions).

instanceof vs. Class equivalence

When querying for type information, there's an important difference between either form of **instanceof** (that is, **instanceof** or **isInstance( )**, which produce equivalent results) and the direct comparison of the **Class** objects. Here's an example that demonstrates the difference:

```
//: c12:FamilyVsExactType.java
// The difference between instanceof and class

class Base {}
class Derived extends Base {}

public class FamilyVsExactType {
  static void test(Object x) {
    System.out.println("Testing x of type " +
      x.getClass());
    System.out.println("x instanceof Base " +
      (x instanceof Base));
    System.out.println("x instanceof Derived " +
      (x instanceof Derived));
    System.out.println("Base.isInstance(x) " +
      Base.class.isInstance(x));
    System.out.println("Derived.isInstance(x) " +
      Derived.class.isInstance(x));
    System.out.println(
      "x.getClass() == Base.class " +
      (x.getClass() == Base.class));
    System.out.println(
      "x.getClass() == Derived.class " +
      (x.getClass() == Derived.class));
    System.out.println(
      "x.getClass().equals(Base.class)) " +
      (x.getClass().equals(Base.class)));
    System.out.println(
      "x.getClass().equals(Derived.class)) " +
      (x.getClass().equals(Derived.class)));
  }
  public static void main(String[] args) {
    test(new Base());
    test(new Derived());
  }
} ///:~
```

The **test( )** method performs type checking with its argument using both forms of **instanceof**. It then gets the **Class** reference and uses == and **equals( )** to test for equality of the **Class** objects. Here is the output:

```
Testing x of type class Base
```

```
x instanceof Base true
x instanceof Derived false
Base.isInstance(x) true
Derived.isInstance(x) false
x.getClass() == Base.class true
x.getClass() == Derived.class false
x.getClass().equals(Base.class)) true
x.getClass().equals(Derived.class)) false
Testing x of type class Derived
x instanceof Base true
x instanceof Derived true
Base.isInstance(x) true
Derived.isInstance(x) true
x.getClass() == Base.class false
x.getClass() == Derived.class true
x.getClass().equals(Base.class)) false
x.getClass().equals(Derived.class)) true
```

Reassuringly, **instanceof** and **isInstance( )** produce exactly the same results, as do **equals( )** and ==. But the tests themselves draw different conclusions. In keeping with the concept of type, **instanceof** says "are you this class, or a class derived from this class?" On the other hand, if you compare the actual **Class** objects using ==, there is no concern with inheritance—it's either the exact type or it isn't.

RTTI syntax

Java performs its RTTI using the **Class** object, even if you're doing something like a cast. The class **Class** also has a number of other ways you can use RTTI.

First, you must get a reference to the appropriate **Class** object. One way to do this, as shown in the previous example, is to use a string and the **Class.forName( )** method. This is convenient because you don't need an object of that type in order to get the **Class** reference. However, if you do already have an object of the type you're interested in, you can fetch the **Class** reference by calling a method that's part of the **Object** root class: **getClass( )**. This returns the **Class** reference representing the actual type of the object. **Class** has many interesting methods, demonstrated in the following example:

```
//: c12:ToyTest.java
// Testing class Class.

interface HasBatteries {}
interface Waterproof {}
interface ShootsThings {}
class Toy {
  // Comment out the following default
  // constructor to see
  // NoSuchMethodError from (*1*)
  Toy() {}
  Toy(int i) {}
}

class FancyToy extends Toy
    implements HasBatteries,
      Waterproof, ShootsThings {
  FancyToy() { super(1); }
}

public class ToyTest {
  public static void main(String[] args)
  throws Exception {
    Class c = null;
    try {
      c = Class.forName("FancyToy");
    } catch(ClassNotFoundException e) {
      System.err.println("Can't find FancyToy");
      throw e;
    }
    printInfo(c);
    Class[] faces = c.getInterfaces();
    for(int i = 0; i < faces.length; i++)
      printInfo(faces[i]);
    Class cy = c.getSuperclass();
    Object o = null;
    try {
      // Requires default constructor:
      o = cy.newInstance(); // (*1*)
    } catch(InstantiationException e) {
      System.err.println("Cannot instantiate");
```

```
      throw e;
    } catch(IllegalAccessException e) {
      System.err.println("Cannot access");
      throw e;
    }
    printInfo(o.getClass());
  }
  static void printInfo(Class cc) {
    System.out.println(
      "Class name: " + cc.getName() +
      " is interface? [" +
      cc.isInterface() + "]");
  }
} ///:~
```

You can see that **class FancyToy** is quite complicated, since it inherits from **Toy** and **implements** the **interface**s of **HasBatteries**, **Waterproof**, and **ShootsThings**. In **main( )**, a **Class** reference is created and initialized to the **FancyToy Class** using **forName( )** inside an appropriate **try** block.

The **Class.getInterfaces( )** method returns an array of **Class** objects representing the interfaces that are contained in the **Class** object of interest.

If you have a **Class** object you can also ask it for its direct base class using **getSuperclass( )**. This, of course, returns a **Class** reference that you can further query. This means that, at run-time, you can discover an object's entire class hierarchy.

The **newInstance( )** method of **Class** can, at first, seem like just another way to **clone( )** an object. However, you can create a new object with **newInstance( )** *without* an existing object, as seen here, because there is no **Toy** object—only **cy**, which is a reference to **y**'s **Class** object. This is a way to implement a "virtual constructor," which allows you to say "I don't know exactly what type you are, but create yourself properly anyway." In the example above, **cy** is just a **Class** reference with no further type information known at compile-time. And when you create a new instance, you get back an **Object reference**. But that reference is pointing to a **Toy** object. Of course, before you can send any messages other than those accepted by **Object**, you have to investigate it a bit and do some casting. In addition, the class that's being created with **newInstance( )** must have a default constructor. In the next section, you'll see how to dynamically create objects of classes using any constructor, with the Java *reflection* API.

The final method in the listing is **printInfo( )**, which takes a **Class** reference and gets its name with **getName( )**, and finds out whether it's an interface with **isInterface( )**.

The output from this program is:

```
Class name: FancyToy is interface? [false]
Class name: HasBatteries is interface? [true]
Class name: Waterproof is interface? [true]
Class name: ShootsThings is interface? [true]
Class name: Toy is interface? [false]
```

Thus, with the **Class** object you can find out just about everything you want to know about an object.

Reflection: run-time class information

If you don't know the precise type of an object, RTTI will tell you. However, there's a limitation: the type must be known at compile-time in order for you to be able to detect it using RTTI and do something useful with the information. Put another way, the compiler must know about all the classes you're working with for RTTI.

This doesn't seem like that much of a limitation at first, but suppose you're given a reference to an object that's not in your program space. In fact, the class of the object isn't even available to your program at compile-time. For example, suppose you get a bunch of bytes from a disk file or from a network connection and you're told that those bytes represent a class. Since the compiler can't know about the class while it's compiling the code, how can you possibly use such a class?

In a traditional programming environment this seems like a far-fetched scenario. But as we move into a larger programming world there are

---

important cases in which this happens. The first is component-based programming, in which you build projects using *Rapid Application Development* (RAD) in an application builder tool. This is a visual approach to creating a program (which you see on the screen as a "form") by moving icons that represent components onto the form. These components are then configured by setting some of their values at program time. This design-time configuration requires that any component be instantiable, that it exposes parts of itself, and that it allows its values to be read and set. In addition, components that handle GUI events must expose information about appropriate methods so that the RAD environment can assist the programmer in overriding these event-handling methods. Reflection provides the mechanism to detect the available methods and produce the method names. Java provides a structure for component-based programming through JavaBeans (described in Chapter 13).

Another compelling motivation for discovering class information at run-time is to provide the ability to create and execute objects on remote platforms across a network. This is called *Remote Method Invocation* (RMI) and it allows a Java program to have objects distributed across many machines. This distribution can happen for a number of reasons: for example, perhaps you're doing a computation-intensive task and you want to break it up and put pieces on machines that are idle in order to speed things up. In some situations you might want to place code that handles particular types of tasks (e.g., "Business Rules" in a multitier client/server architecture) on a particular machine, so that machine becomes a common repository describing those actions and it can be easily changed to affect everyone in the system. (This is an interesting development, since the machine exists solely to make software changes easy!) Along these lines, distributed computing also supports specialized hardware that might be good at a particular task—matrix inversions, for example—but inappropriate or too expensive for general purpose programming.

The class **Class** (described previously in this chapter) supports the concept of *reflection*, and there's an additional library, **java.lang.reflect,** with classes **Field**, **Method**, and **Constructor** (each of which implement the **Member interface**). Objects of these types are created by the JVM at run-time to represent the corresponding member in the unknown class. You can then use the **Constructor**s to create new objects, the **get( )** and **set( )** methods to read and modify the fields associated with **Field** objects, and the **invoke( )** method to call a method associated with a **Method** object. In addition, you can call the convenience methods **getFields( )**, **getMethods( )**, **getConstructors( )**, etc., to return arrays of the objects representing the fields, methods, and constructors. (You can find out more by looking up the class **Class** in your online documentation.) Thus, the class information for anonymous objects can be completely determined at run-time, and nothing need be known at compile-time.

It's important to realize that there's nothing magic about reflection. When you're using reflection to interact with an object of an unknown type, the JVM will simply look at the object and see that it belongs to a particular class (just like ordinary RTTI) but then, before it can do anything else, the **Class** object must be loaded. Thus, the **.class** file for that particular type must still be available to the JVM, either on the local machine or across the network. So the true difference between RTTI and reflection is that with RTTI, the compiler opens and examines the **.class** file at compile-time. Put another way, you can call all the methods of an object in the "normal" way. With reflection, the **.class** file is unavailable at compile-time; it is opened and examined by the run-time environment.

A class method extractor

You'll rarely need to use the reflection tools directly; they're in the language to support other Java features, such as object serialization (Chapter 11), JavaBeans (Chapter 13), and RMI (Chapter 15). However, there are times when it's quite useful to be able to dynamically extract information about a class. One extremely useful tool is a class method extractor. As mentioned before, looking at a class definition source code or online documentation shows only the methods that are defined or overridden *within that class definition*. But there could be dozens more available to you that have come from base classes. To locate these is both tedious and time consuming[1]. Fortunately, reflection provides a way to

---

[1] Especially in the past. However, Sun has greatly improved its HTML Java documentation so that it's easier to see base-class methods.

write a simple tool that will automatically show you the entire interface. Here's the way it works:

```
//: c12:ShowMethods.java
// Using reflection to show all the methods of
// a class, even if the methods are defined in
// the base class.
import java.lang.reflect.*;

public class ShowMethods {
  static final String usage =
    "usage: \n" +
    "ShowMethods qualified.class.name\n" +
    "To show all methods in class or: \n" +
    "ShowMethods qualified.class.name word\n" +
    "To search for methods involving 'word'";
  public static void main(String[] args) {
    if(args.length < 1) {
      System.out.println(usage);
      System.exit(0);
    }
    try {
      Class c = Class.forName(args[0]);
      Method[] m = c.getMethods();
      Constructor[] ctor = c.getConstructors();
      if(args.length == 1) {
        for (int i = 0; i < m.length; i++)
          System.out.println(m[i]);
        for (int i = 0; i < ctor.length; i++)
          System.out.println(ctor[i]);
      } else {
        for (int i = 0; i < m.length; i++)
          if(m[i].toString()
             .indexOf(args[1]) != -1)
            System.out.println(m[i]);
        for (int i = 0; i < ctor.length; i++)
          if(ctor[i].toString()
             .indexOf(args[1]) != -1)
          System.out.println(ctor[i]);
      }
    } catch(ClassNotFoundException e) {
```

```
         System.err.println("No such class: " + e);
    }
  }
} ///:~
```

The **Class** methods **getMethods( )** and **getConstructors( )** return an array of **Method** and **Constructor**, respectively. Each of these classes has further methods to dissect the names, arguments, and return values of the methods they represent. But you can also just use **toString( )**, as is done here, to produce a **String** with the entire method signature. The rest of the code is just for extracting command line information, determining if a particular signature matches with your target string (using **indexOf( )**), and printing the results.

This shows reflection in action, since the result produced by **Class.forName( )** cannot be known at compile-time, and therefore all the method signature information is being extracted at run-time. If you investigate your online documentation on reflection, you'll see that there is enough support to actually set up and make a method call on an object that's totally unknown at compile-time (there will be examples of this later in this book). Again, this is something you may never need to do yourself—the support is there for RMI and so a programming environment can manipulate JavaBeans—but it's interesting.

An interesting experiment is to run

```
java ShowMethods ShowMethods
```

This produces a listing that includes a **public** default constructor, even though you can see from the code that no constructor was defined. The constructor you see is the one that's automatically synthesized by the compiler. If you then make **ShowMethods** a non-**public** class (that is, friendly), the synthesized default constructor no longer shows up in the output. The synthesized default constructor is automatically given the same access as the class.

The output for **ShowMethods** is still a little tedious. For example, here's a portion of the output produced by invoking **java ShowMethods java.lang.String**:

```
public boolean
```

```
  java.lang.String.startsWith(java.lang.String,int)
public boolean
  java.lang.String.startsWith(java.lang.String)
public boolean
  java.lang.String.endsWith(java.lang.String)
```

It would be even nicer if the qualifiers like **java.lang** could be stripped off. The **StreamTokenizer** class introduced in the previous chapter can help create a tool to solve this problem:

```
//: com:bruceeckel:util:StripQualifiers.java
package com.bruceeckel.util;
import java.io.*;

public class StripQualifiers {
  private StreamTokenizer st;
  public StripQualifiers(String qualified) {
    st = new StreamTokenizer(
      new StringReader(qualified));
    st.ordinaryChar(' '); // Keep the spaces
  }
  public String getNext() {
    String s = null;
    try {
      int token = st.nextToken();
      if(token != StreamTokenizer.TT_EOF) {
        switch(st.ttype) {
          case StreamTokenizer.TT_EOL:
            s = null;
            break;
          case StreamTokenizer.TT_NUMBER:
            s = Double.toString(st.nval);
            break;
          case StreamTokenizer.TT_WORD:
            s = new String(st.sval);
            break;
          default: // single character in ttype
            s = String.valueOf((char)st.ttype);
        }
      }
    } catch(IOException e) {
```

```
        System.err.println("Error fetching token");
      }
      return s;
    }
    public static String strip(String qualified) {
      StripQualifiers sq =
        new StripQualifiers(qualified);
      String s = "", si;
      while((si = sq.getNext()) != null) {
        int lastDot = si.lastIndexOf('.');
        if(lastDot != -1)
          si = si.substring(lastDot + 1);
        s += si;
      }
      return s;
    }
} ///:~
```

To facilitate reuse, this class is placed in **com.bruceeckel.util**. As you can see, this uses the **StreamTokenizer** and **String** manipulation to do its work.

The new version of the program uses the above class to clean up the output:

```
//: c12:ShowMethodsClean.java
// ShowMethods with the qualifiers stripped
// to make the results easier to read.
import java.lang.reflect.*;
import com.bruceeckel.util.*;

public class ShowMethodsClean {
  static final String usage =
    "usage: \n" +
    "ShowMethodsClean qualified.class.name\n" +
    "To show all methods in class or: \n" +
    "ShowMethodsClean qualif.class.name word\n" +
    "To search for methods involving 'word'";
  public static void main(String[] args) {
    if(args.length < 1) {
      System.out.println(usage);
      System.exit(0);
```

```
    }
    try {
      Class c = Class.forName(args[0]);
      Method[] m = c.getMethods();
      Constructor[] ctor = c.getConstructors();
      // Convert to an array of cleaned Strings:
      String[] n =
        new String[m.length + ctor.length];
      for(int i = 0; i < m.length; i++) {
        String s = m[i].toString();
        n[i] = StripQualifiers.strip(s);
      }
      for(int i = 0; i < ctor.length; i++) {
        String s = ctor[i].toString();
        n[i + m.length] =
          StripQualifiers.strip(s);
      }
      if(args.length == 1)
        for (int i = 0; i < n.length; i++)
          System.out.println(n[i]);
      else
        for (int i = 0; i < n.length; i++)
          if(n[i].indexOf(args[1]) != -1)
            System.out.println(n[i]);
    } catch(ClassNotFoundException e) {
      System.err.println("No such class: " + e);
    }
  }
} ///:~
```

The class **ShowMethodsClean** is quite similar to the previous **ShowMethods**, except that it takes the arrays of **Method** and **Constructor** and converts them into a single array of **String**. Each of these **String** objects is then passed through **StripQualifiers.Strip( )** to remove all the method qualification.

This tool can be a real time-saver while you're programming, when you can't remember if a class has a particular method and you don't want to go walking through the class hierarchy in the online documentation, or if you don't know whether that class can do anything with, for example, **Color** objects.

Chapter 13 contains a GUI version of this program (customized to extract information for Swing components) so you can leave it running while you're writing code, to allow quick lookups.

Summary

RTTI allows you to discover type information from an anonymous base-class reference. Thus, it's ripe for misuse by the novice since it might make sense before polymorphic method calls do. For many people coming from a procedural background, it's difficult not to organize their programs into sets of **switch** statements. They could accomplish this with RTTI and thus lose the important value of polymorphism in code development and maintenance. The intent of Java is that you use polymorphic method calls throughout your code, and you use RTTI only when you must.

However, using polymorphic method calls as they are intended requires that you have control of the base-class definition because at some point in the extension of your program you might discover that the base class doesn't include the method you need. If the base class comes from a library or is otherwise controlled by someone else, a solution to the problem is RTTI: You can inherit a new type and add your extra method. Elsewhere in the code you can detect your particular type and call that special method. This doesn't destroy the polymorphism and extensibility of the program because adding a new type will not require you to hunt for switch statements in your program. However, when you add new code in your main body that requires your new feature, you must use RTTI to detect your particular type.

Putting a feature in a base class might mean that, for the benefit of one particular class, all of the other classes derived from that base require some meaningless stub of a method. This makes the interface less clear and annoys those who must override abstract methods when they derive from that base class. For example, consider a class hierarchy representing musical instruments. Suppose you wanted to clear the spit valves of all the appropriate instruments in your orchestra. One option is to put a **clearSpitValve( )** method in the base class **Instrument**, but this is confusing because it implies that **Percussion** and **Electronic** instruments also have spit valves. RTTI provides a much more reasonable solution in this case because you can place the method in the specific class (**Wind** in this case), where it's appropriate. However, a more appropriate solution is to put a **prepareInstrument( )** method in the base class, but you might not see this when you're first solving the problem and could mistakenly assume that you must use RTTI.

Finally, RTTI will sometimes solve efficiency problems. If your code nicely uses polymorphism, but it turns out that one of your objects reacts to this general purpose code in a horribly inefficient way, you can pick out that type using RTTI and write case-specific code to improve the efficiency. Be wary, however, of programming for efficiency too soon. It's a seductive trap. It's best to get the program working *first*, then decide if it's running fast enough, and only then should you attack efficiency issues—with a profiler.

Exercises

Solutions to selected exercises can be found in the electronic document *The Thinking in Java Annotated Solution Guide*, available for a small fee from *www.BruceEckel.com*.

1. Add **Rhomboid** to **Shapes.java**. Create a **Rhomboid**, upcast it to a **Shape**, then downcast it back to a **Rhomboid**. Try downcasting to a **Circle** and see what happens.

2. Modify Exercise 1 so that it uses **instanceof** to check the type before performing the downcast.

3. Modify **Shapes.java** so that it can "highlight" (set a flag) in all shapes of a particular type. The **toString( )** method for each derived **Shape** should indicate whether that **Shape** is "highlighted."

4. Modify **SweetShop.java** so that each type of object creation is controlled by a command-line argument. That is, if your command line is "**java SweetShop Candy**," then only the **Candy** object is created. Notice how you can control which **Class** objects are loaded via the command-line argument.

5. Add a new type of **Pet** to **PetCount3.java**. Verify that it is created and counted correctly in **main( )**.

6. Write a method that takes an object and recursively prints all the classes in that object's hierarchy.

7. Modify Exercise 6 so that it uses **Class.getDeclaredFields( )** to also display information about the fields in a class.

8. In **ToyTest.java**, comment out **Toy**'s default constructor and explain what happens.

9. Incorporate a new kind of **interface** into **ToyTest.java** and verify that it is detected and displayed properly.

10. Create a new type of container that uses a **private ArrayList** to hold the objects. Capture the type of the first object you put in it, and then allow the user to insert objects of only that type from then on.

11. Write a program to determine whether an array of **char** is a primitive type or a true object.

12. Implement **clearSpitValve( )** as described in the summary.

13. Implement the **rotate(Shape)** method described in this chapter, such that it checks to see if it is rotating a **Circle** (and, if so, doesn't perform the operation).

14. Modify Exercise 6 so that it uses reflection instead of RTTI.

15. Modify Exercise 7 so that it uses reflection instead of RTTI.

16. In **ToyTest.java**, use reflection to create a **Toy** object using the nondefault constructor.

17. Look up the interface for **java.lang.Class** in the HTML Java documentation from *java.sun.com*. Write a program that takes the name of a class as a command-line argument, then uses the **Class** methods to dump all the information available for that class. Test your program with a standard library class and a class you create.

13: Creating Windows & Applets

A fundamental design guideline is "make simple things easy, and difficult things possible."[1]

The original design goal of the graphical user interface (GUI) library in Java 1.0 was to allow the programmer to build a GUI that looks good on all platforms. That goal was not achieved. Instead, the Java 1.0 *Abstract Window Toolkit* (AWT) produces a GUI that looks equally mediocre on all systems. In addition, it's restrictive: you can use only four fonts and you cannot access any of the more sophisticated GUI elements that exist in your operating system. The Java 1.0 AWT programming model is also awkward and non-object-oriented. A student in one of my seminars (who had been at Sun during the creation of Java) explained why: the original AWT had been conceptualized, designed, and implemented in a month. Certainly a marvel of productivity, and also an object lesson in why design is important.

The situation improved with the Java 1.1 AWT event model, which takes a much clearer, object-oriented approach, along with the addition of JavaBeans, a component programming model that is oriented toward the easy creation of visual programming environments. Java 2 finishes the transformation away from the old Java 1.0 AWT by essentially replacing everything with the *Java Foundation Classes* (JFC), the GUI portion of which is called "Swing." These are a rich set of easy-to-use, easy-to-

---

[1] A variation on this is called "the principle of least astonishment," which essentially says: "don't surprise the user."

understand JavaBeans that can be dragged and dropped (as well as hand programmed) to create a GUI that you can (finally) be satisfied with. The "revision 3" rule of the software industry (a product isn't good until revision 3) seems to hold true with programming languages as well.

This chapter does not cover anything but the modern, Java 2 Swing library, and makes the reasonable assumption that Swing is the final destination GUI library for Java. If for some reason you need to use the original "old" AWT (because you're supporting old code or you have browser limitations), you can find that introduction in the first edition of this book, downloadable at *www.BruceEckel.com* (also included on the CD ROM bound with this book).

Early in this chapter, you'll see how things are different when you want to create an applet vs. a regular application using Swing, and how to create programs that are both applets and applications so they can be run either inside a browser or from the command line. Almost all the GUI examples in this book will be executable as either applets or applications.

Please be aware that this is not a comprehensive glossary of either all the Swing components, or all the methods for the described classes. What you see here is intended to be simple. The Swing library is vast, and the goal of this chapter is only to get you started with the essentials and comfortable with the concepts. If you need to do more, then Swing can probably give you what you want if you're willing to do the research.

I assume here that you have downloaded and installed the (free) Java library documents in HTML format from *java.sun.com* and will browse the **javax.swing** classes in that documentation to see the full details and methods of the Swing library. Because of the simplicity of the Swing design, this will often be enough information to solve your problem. There are numerous (rather thick) books dedicated solely to Swing and you'll want to go to those if you need more depth, or if you want to modify the default Swing behavior.

As you learn about Swing you'll discover:

1.   Swing is a much better programming model than you've probably seen in other languages and development environments.

JavaBeans (which will be introduced toward the end of this chapter) is the framework for that library.

2. "GUI builders" (visual programming environments) are a *de rigueur* aspect of a complete Java development environment. JavaBeans and Swing allow the GUI builder to write code for you as you place components onto forms using graphical tools. This not only rapidly speeds development during GUI building, but it allows for greater experimentation and thus the ability to try out more designs and presumably come up with a better one.

3. The simplicity and well-designed nature of Swing means that even if you do use a GUI builder rather than coding by hand, the resulting code will still be comprehensible—this solves a big problem with GUI builders from the past, which could easily generate unreadable code.

Swing contains all the components that you expect to see in a modern UI, everything from buttons that contain pictures to trees and tables. It's a big library, but it's designed to have appropriate complexity for the task at hand—if something is simple, you don't have to write much code but as you try to do more complex things, your code becomes proportionally more complex. This means an easy entry point, but you've got the power if you need it.

Much of what you'll like about Swing could be called "orthogonality of use." That is, once you pick up the general ideas about the library you can apply them everywhere. Primarily because of the standard naming conventions, much of the time that I was writing these examples I could guess at the method names and get it right the first time, without looking anything up. This is certainly the hallmark of a good library design. In addition, you can generally plug components into other components and things will work correctly.

For speed, all the components are "lightweight," and Swing is written entirely in Java for portability.

Keyboard navigation is automatic—you can run a Swing application without using the mouse, and this doesn't require any extra programming. Scrolling support is effortless—you simply wrap your component in a **JScrollPane** as you add it to your form. Features such as tool tips typically require a single line of code to use.

Swing also supports a rather radical feature called "pluggable look and feel," which means that the appearance of the UI can be dynamically changed to suit the expectations of users working under different platforms and operating systems. It's even possible (albeit difficult) to invent your own look and feel.

The basic applet

One of Java's design goals is to create *applets*, which are little programs that run inside a Web browser. Because they must be safe, applets are limited in what they can accomplish. However, applets are a powerful tool that support client-side programming, a major issue for the Web.

Applet restrictions

Programming within an applet is so restrictive that it's often referred to as being "inside the sandbox," since you always have someone—that is, the Java run-time security system—watching over you.

However, you can also step outside the sandbox and write regular applications rather than applets, in which case you can access the other features of your OS. We've been writing regular applications all along in this book, but they've been *console applications* without any graphical components. Swing can also be used to build GUI interfaces for regular applications.

You can generally answer the question of what an applet is able to do by looking at what it is *supposed* to do: extend the functionality of a Web page in a browser. Since, as a Net surfer, you never really know if a Web page is from a friendly place or not, you want any code that it runs to be safe. So the biggest restrictions you'll notice are probably:

1. *An applet can't touch the local disk.* This means writing *or* reading, since you wouldn't want an applet to read and transmit private information over the Internet without your permission. Writing is prevented, of course, since that would be an open invitation to a virus. Java offers *digital signing* for applets. Many applet

restrictions are relaxed when you choose to allow *trusted applets* (those signed by a trusted source) to have access to your machine.

2.   *Applets can take longer to display,* since you must download the whole thing every time, including a separate server hit for each different class. Your browser can cache the applet, but there are no guarantees. Because of this, you should always package your applets in a JAR (Java ARchive) file that combines all the applet components (including other **.class** files as well as images and sounds) together into a single compressed file that can be downloaded in a single server transaction. "Digital signing" is available for each individual entry in the JAR file.

Applet advantages

If you can live within the restrictions, applets have definite advantages, especially when building client/server or other networked applications:

1.   *There is no installation issue.* An applet has true platform independence (including the ability to easily play audio files, etc.) so you don't need to make any changes in your code for different platforms nor does anyone have to perform any "tweaking" on installation. In fact, installation is automatic every time the user loads the Web page that contains applets, so updates happen silently and automatically. In traditional client/server systems, building and installing a new version of the client software is often a nightmare.

2.   *You don't have to worry about bad code causing damage to someone's system,* because of the security built into the core Java language and applet structure. This, along with the previous point, makes Java popular for so-called *intranet* client/server applications that live only within a company or restricted arena of operation where the user environment (Web browser and add-ins) can be specified and/or controlled.

Because applets are automatically integrated with HTML, you have a built-in platform-independent documentation system to support the applet. It's an interesting twist, since we're used to having the documentation part of the program rather than vice versa.

Application frameworks

Libraries are often grouped according to their functionality. Some libraries, for example, are used as is, off the shelf. The standard Java library **String** and **ArrayList** classes are examples of these. Other libraries are designed specifically as building blocks to create other classes. A certain category of library is the *application framework*, whose goal is to help you build applications by providing a class or set of classes that produces the basic behavior that you need in every application of a particular type. Then, to customize the behavior to your own needs, you inherit from the application class and override the methods of interest. The application framework's default control mechanism will call your overridden methods at the appropriate time. An application framework is a good example of "separating the things that change from the things that stay the same," since it attempts to localize all the unique parts of a program in the overridden methods[2].

Applets are built using an application framework. You inherit from class **JApplet** and override the appropriate methods. There are a few methods that control the creation and execution of an applet on a Web page:

Method	Operation
init( )	Automatically called to perform first-time initialization of the applet, including component layout. You'll always override this method.
start( )	Called every time the applet moves into sight on the Web browser to allow the applet to start up its normal operations (especially those that are shut off by **stop( )**). Also called after **init( )**.
stop( )	Called every time the applet moves out of sight on the Web browser to allow the applet to shut off expensive operations. Also called right before **destroy( )**.
destroy( )	Called when the applet is being unloaded from the page to perform final release of resources when the applet is no longer used

---

[2] This is an example of the design pattern called the *template method*.

With this information you are ready to create a simple applet:

```
//: c13:Applet1.java
// Very simple applet.
import javax.swing.*;
import java.awt.*;

public class Applet1 extends JApplet {
  public void init() {
    getContentPane().add(new JLabel("Applet!"));
  }
} ///:~
```

Note that applets are not required to have a **main( )**. That's all wired into the application framework; you put any startup code in **init( )**.

In this program, the only activity is putting a text label on the applet, via the **JLabel** class (the old AWT appropriated the name **Label** as well as other names of components, so you will often see a leading "**J**" used with Swing components). The constructor for this class takes a **String** and uses it to create the label. In the above program this label is placed on the form.

The **init( )** method is responsible for putting all the components on the form using the **add( )** method. You might think that you ought to be able to simply call **add( )** by itself, and in fact that's the way it used to be in the old AWT. However, Swing requires you to add all components to the "content pane" of a form, and so you must call **getContentPane( )** as part of the **add( )** process.

Running applets inside a Web browser

To run this program you must place it inside a Web page and view that page inside your Java-enabled Web browser. To place an applet inside a

Web page you put a special tag inside the HTML source for that Web page[3] to tell the page how to load and run the applet.

This process used to be very simple, when Java itself was simple and everyone was on the same bandwagon and incorporated the same Java support inside their Web browsers. Then you might have been able to get away with a very simple bit of HTML inside your Web page, like this:

```
<applet code=Applet1 width=100 height=50>
</applet>
```

Then along came the browser and language wars, and we (programmers and end users alike) lost. After awhile, JavaSoft realized that we could no longer expect browsers to support the correct flavor of Java, and the only solution was to provide some kind of add-on that would conform to a browser's extension mechanism. By using the extension mechanism (which a browser vendor cannot disable—in an attempt to gain competitive advantage—without breaking all the third-party extensions), JavaSoft guarantees that Java cannot be shut out of the Web browser by an antagonistic vendor.

With Internet Explorer, the extension mechanism is the ActiveX control, and with Netscape it is the plug-in. In your HTML code, you must provide tags to support both. Here's what the simplest resulting HTML page looks like for **Applet1**:[4]

```
//:! c13:Applet1.html
<html><head><title>Applet1</title></head><hr>
<OBJECT
   classid="clsid:8AD9C840-044E-11D1-B3E9-00805F499D93"
   width="100" height="50" align="baseline"
codebase="http://java.sun.com/products/plugin/1.2.2/ji
nstall-1_2_2-win.cab#Version=1,2,2,0">
<PARAM NAME="code" VALUE="Applet1.class">
```

---

[3] It is assumed that the reader is familiar with the basics of HTML. It's not too hard to figure out, and there are lots of books and resources.

[4] This page—in particular, the 'clsid' portion—seemed to work fine with both JDK1.2.2 and JDK1.3 rc-1. However, you may find that you have to change the tag sometime in the future. Details can be found at *java.sun.com*.

```
<PARAM NAME="codebase" VALUE=".">
<PARAM NAME="type" VALUE="application/x-java-
applet;version=1.2.2">
<COMMENT>
  <EMBED type=
    "application/x-java-applet;version=1.2.2"
    width="200" height="200" align="baseline"
    code="Applet1.class" codebase="."
pluginspage="http://java.sun.com/products/plugin/1.2/p
lugin-install.html">
  <NOEMBED>
</COMMENT>
  No Java 2 support for APPLET!!
  </NOEMBED>
</EMBED>
</OBJECT>
<hr></body></html>
///:~
```

Some of these lines were too long and had to be wrapped to fit on the page. The code in this book's source code (on the book's CD ROM, and downloadable from *www.BruceEckel.com*) will work without having to worry about correcting line wraps.

The **code** value gives the name of the **.class** file where the applet resides. The **width** and **height** specify the initial size of the applet (in pixels, as before). There are other items you can place within the applet tag: a place to find other **.class** files on the Internet (**codebase**), alignment information (**align**), a special identifier that makes it possible for applets to communicate with each other (**name**), and applet parameters to provide information that the applet can retrieve. Parameters are in the form:

```
<param name="identifier" value = "information">
```

and there can be as many as you want.

The source code package for this book provides an HTML page for each of the applets in this book, and thus many examples of the applet tag. You can find a full and current description of the details of placing applets in Web pages at *java.sun.com*.

Using *Appletviewer*

Sun's JDK (freely downloadable from *java.sun.com*) contains a tool called the *Appletviewer* that picks the **<applet>** tags out of the HTML file and runs the applets without displaying the surrounding HTML text. Because the Appletviewer ignores everything but APPLET tags, you can put those tags in the Java source file as comments:

```
// <applet code=MyApplet width=200 height=100>
// </applet>
```

This way, you can run "**appletviewer MyApplet.java**" and you don't need to create tiny HTML files to run tests. For example, you can add the commented HTML tags to **Applet1.java**:

```
//: c13:Applet1b.java
// Embedding the applet tag for Appletviewer.
// <applet code=Applet1b width=100 height=50>
// </applet>
import javax.swing.*;
import java.awt.*;

public class Applet1b extends JApplet {
  public void init() {
    getContentPane().add(new JLabel("Applet!"));
  }
} ///:~
```

Now you can invoke the applet with the command

```
appletviewer Applet1b.java
```

In this book, this form will be used for easy testing of applets. Shortly, you'll see another coding approach which will allow you to execute applets from the command line without the Appletviewer.

Testing applets

You can perform a simple test without any network connection by starting up your Web browser and opening the HTML file containing the applet tag. As the HTML file is loaded, the browser will discover the applet tag and go hunt for the **.class** file specified by the **code** value. Of course, it looks at the CLASSPATH to find out where to hunt, and if your **.class** file isn't in the CLASSPATH then it will give an error message on the status line of the browser to the effect that it couldn't find that **.class** file.

When you want to try this out on your Web site things are a little more complicated. First of all, you must *have* a Web site, which for most people means a third-party Internet Service Provider (ISP) at a remote location. Since the applet is just a file or set of files, the ISP does not have to provide any special support for Java. You must also have a way to move the HTML files and the **.class** files from your site to the correct directory on the ISP machine. This is typically done with a File Transfer Protocol (FTP) program, of which there are many different types available for free or as shareware. So it would seem that all you need to do is move the files to the ISP machine with FTP, then connect to the site and HTML file using your browser; if the applet comes up and works, then everything checks out, right?

Here's where you can get fooled. If the browser on the client machine cannot locate the **.class** file on the server, it will hunt through the CLASSPATH on your *local* machine. Thus, the applet might not be loading properly from the server, but to you it looks fine during your testing process because the browser finds it on your machine. When someone else connects, however, his or her browser can't find it. So when you're testing, make sure you erase the relevant **.class** files (or **.jar** file) on your local machine to verify that they exist in the proper location on the server.

One of the most insidious places where this happened to me is when I innocently placed an applet inside a **package**. After uploading the HTML file and applet, it turned out that the server path to the applet was confused because of the package name. However, my browser found it in the local CLASSPATH. So I was the only one who could properly load the applet. It took some time to discover that the **package** statement was the culprit. In general, you'll want to leave the **package** statement out of an applet.

Running applets from the command line

There are times when you'd like to make a windowed program do something else other than sit on a Web page. Perhaps you'd also like it to do some of the things a "regular" application can do but still have the vaunted instant portability provided by Java. In previous chapters in this book we've made command-line applications, but in some operating environments (the Macintosh, for example) there isn't a command line. So for any number of reasons you'd like to build a windowed, non-applet program using Java. This is certainly a reasonable desire.

The Swing library allows you to make an application that preserves the look and feel of the underlying operating environment. If you want to build windowed applications, it makes sense to do so[5] only if you can use the latest version of Java and associated tools so you can deliver applications that won't confound your users. If for some reason you're forced to use an older version of Java, think hard before committing to building a significant windowed application.

Often you'll want to be able to create a class that can be invoked as either a window or an applet. This is especially convenient when you're testing the applets, since it's typically much faster and easier to run the resulting applet-application from the command line than it is to start up a Web browser or the Appletviewer.

To create an applet that can be run from the console command line, you simply add a **main( )** to your applet that builds an instance of the applet inside a **JFrame**.[6] As a simple example, let's look at **Applet1b.java** modified to work as both an application and an applet:

```
//: c13:Applet1c.java
```

---

[5] In my opinion. And after you learn about Swing, you won't want to waste your time on the earlier stuff.

[6] As described earlier, "Frame" was already taken by the AWT, so Swing uses JFrame.

```
// An application and an applet.
// <applet code=Applet1c width=100 height=50>
// </applet>
import javax.swing.*;
import java.awt.*;
import com.bruceeckel.swing.*;

public class Applet1c extends JApplet {
  public void init() {
    getContentPane().add(new JLabel("Applet!"));
  }
  // A main() for the application:
  public static void main(String[] args) {
    JApplet applet = new Applet1c();
    JFrame frame = new JFrame("Applet1c");
    // To close the application:
    Console.setupClosing(frame);
    frame.getContentPane().add(applet);
    frame.setSize(100,50);
    applet.init();
    applet.start();
    frame.setVisible(true);
  }
} ///:~
```

main( ) is the only element added to the applet, and the rest of the applet is untouched. The applet is created and added to a **JFrame** so that it can be displayed.

The line:

```
Console.setupClosing(frame);
```

Causes the window to be properly closed. **Console** comes from **com.bruceeckel.swing** and will be explained a little later.

You can see that in **main( )**, the applet is explicitly initialized and started since in this case the browser isn't available to do it for you. Of course, this doesn't provide the full behavior of the browser, which also calls

stop( ) and **destroy( )**, but for most situations it's acceptable. If it's a problem, you can force the calls yourself.[7]

Notice the last line:

```
frame.setVisible(true);
```

Without this, you won't see anything on the screen.

A display framework

Although the code that turns programs into both applets and applications produces valuable results, if used everywhere it becomes distracting and wastes paper. Instead, the following display framework will be used for the Swing examples in the rest of this book:

```
//: com:bruceeckel:swing:Console.java
// Tool for running Swing demos from the
// console, both applets and JFrames.
package com.bruceeckel.swing;
import javax.swing.*;
import java.awt.event.*;

public class Console {
  // Create a title string from the class name:
  public static String title(Object o) {
    String t = o.getClass().toString();
    // Remove the word "class":
    if(t.indexOf("class") != -1)
      t = t.substring(6);
    return t;
  }
  public static void setupClosing(JFrame frame) {
    // The JDK 1.2 Solution as an
    // anonymous inner class:
    frame.addWindowListener(new WindowAdapter() {
```

---

[7] This will make sense after you've read further in this chapter. First, make the reference **JApplet** a **static** member of the class (instead of a local variable of **main( )**), and then call **applet.stop( )** and **applet.destroy( )** inside **WindowAdapter.windowClosing( )** before you call **System.exit( )**.

```
      public void windowClosing(WindowEvent e) {
        System.exit(0);
      }
    });
    // The improved solution in JDK 1.3:
    // frame.setDefaultCloseOperation(
    //     EXIT_ON_CLOSE);
  }
  public static void
  run(JFrame frame, int width, int height) {
    setupClosing(frame);
    frame.setSize(width, height);
    frame.setVisible(true);
  }
  public static void
  run(JApplet applet, int width, int height) {
    JFrame frame = new JFrame(title(applet));
    setupClosing(frame);
    frame.getContentPane().add(applet);
    frame.setSize(width, height);
    applet.init();
    applet.start();
    frame.setVisible(true);
  }
  public static void
  run(JPanel panel, int width, int height) {
    JFrame frame = new JFrame(title(panel));
    setupClosing(frame);
    frame.getContentPane().add(panel);
    frame.setSize(width, height);
    frame.setVisible(true);
  }
} ///:~
```

This is a tool you may want to use yourself, so it's placed in the library
com.bruceeckel.swing. The **Console** class consists entirely of **static**
methods. The first is used to extract the class name (using RTTI) from any
object and to remove the word "class," which is typically prepended by
getClass( ). This uses the **String** methods **indexOf( )** to determine
whether the word "class" is there, and **substring( )** to produce the new

string without "class" or the trailing space. This name is used to label the window that is displayed by the **run( )** methods.

setupClosing( ) is used to hide the code that causes a **JFrame** to exit a program when that **JFrame** is closed. The default behavior is to do nothing, so if you don't call **setupClosing( )** or write the equivalent code for your **JFrame**, the application won't close. The reason this code is hidden rather than placing it directly in the subsequent **run( )** methods is partly because it allows you to use the method by itself when what you want to do is more complicated than what **run( )** provides. However, it also isolates a change factor: Java 2 has two ways of causing certain types of windows to close. In JDK 1.2, the solution is to create a new **WindowAdapter** class and implement **windowClosing( )**, as seen above (the meaning of this will be fully explained later in this chapter). However, during the creation of JDK 1.3 the library designers observed that you typically need to close windows whenever you're creating a non-applet, and so they added the **setDefaultCloseOperation( )** to **JFrame** and **JDialog**. From the standpoint of writing code, the new method is much nicer to use but this book was written while there was still no JDK 1.3 implemented on Linux and other platforms, so in the interest of cross-version portability the change was isolated inside **setupClosing( )**.

The **run( )** method is overloaded to work with **JApplet**s, **JPanel**s, and **JFrame**s. Note that only if it's a **JApplet** are **init( )** and **start( )** called.

Now any applet can be run from the console by creating a **main( )** containing a line like this:

```
Console.run(new MyClass(), 500, 300);
```

in which the last two arguments are the display width and height. Here's **Applet1c.java** modified to use **Console**:

```
//: c13:Applet1d.java
// Console runs applets from the command line.
// <applet code=Applet1d width=100 height=50>
// </applet>
import javax.swing.*;
import java.awt.*;
import com.bruceeckel.swing.*;
```

```
public class Applet1d extends JApplet {
  public void init() {
    getContentPane().add(new JLabel("Applet!"));
  }
  public static void main(String[] args) {
    Console.run(new Applet1d(), 100, 50);
  }
} ///:~
```

This allows the elimination of repeated code while providing the greatest flexibility in running the examples.

Using the Windows Explorer

If you're using Windows, you can simplify the process of running a command-line Java program by configuring the Windows Explorer—the file browser in Windows, *not* the Internet Explorer—so that you can simply double-click on a **.class** file to execute it. There are several steps in this process.

First, download and install the Perl programming language from *www.Perl.org*. You'll find the instructions and language documentation on that site.

Next, create the following script without the first and last lines (this script is part of this book's source-code package):

```
//:! c13:RunJava.bat
@rem = '--*-Perl-*--
@echo off
perl -x -S "%0" %1 %2 %3 %4 %5 %6 %7 %8 %9
goto endofperl
@rem ';
#!perl
$file = $ARGV[0];
$file =~ s/(.*)\..*/\1/;
$file =~ s/(.*\\)*(.*)/$+/;
`java $file`;
__END__
:endofperl
///:~
```

Now, open the Windows Explorer, select "View," "Folder Options," then click on the "File Types" tab. Press the "New Type" button. For "Description of Type" enter "Java class file." For "Associated Extension," enter "class." Under "Actions" press the "New" button. For "Action" enter "Open," and for "Application used to perform action" enter a line like this:

```
"c:\aaa\Perl\RunJava.bat" "%L"
```

You must customize the path before "RunJava.bat" to conform to the location where you placed the batch file.

Once you perform this installation, you may run any Java program by simply double-clicking on the **.class** file containing a **main( )**.

Making a button

Making a button is quite simple: you just call the **JButton** constructor with the label you want on the button. You'll see later that you can do fancier things, like putting graphic images on buttons.

Usually you'll want to create a field for the button inside your class so that you can refer to it later.

The **JButton** is a component—its own little window—that will automatically get repainted as part of an update. This means that you don't explicitly paint a button or any other kind of control; you simply place them on the form and let them automatically take care of painting themselves. So to place a button on a form, you do it inside **init( )**:

```
//: c13:Button1.java
// Putting buttons on an applet.
// <applet code=Button1 width=200 height=50>
// </applet>
import javax.swing.*;
import java.awt.*;
import com.bruceeckel.swing.*;

public class Button1 extends JApplet {
  JButton
    b1 = new JButton("Button 1"),
    b2 = new JButton("Button 2");
```

```
public void init() {
    Container cp = getContentPane();
    cp.setLayout(new FlowLayout());
    cp.add(b1);
    cp.add(b2);
}
public static void main(String[] args) {
    Console.run(new Button1(), 200, 50);
}
} ///:~
```

Something new has been added here: before any elements are placed on the content pane, it is given a new "layout manager," of type **FlowLayout**. The layout manager is the way that the pane implicitly decides where to place the control on the form. The normal behavior of an applet is to use the **BorderLayout**, but that won't work here because (as you will learn later in this chapter when controlling the layout of a form is examined in more detail) it defaults to covering each control entirely with every new one that is added. However, **FlowLayout** causes the controls to flow evenly onto the form, left to right and top to bottom.

Capturing an event

You'll notice that if you compile and run the applet above, nothing happens when you press the buttons. This is where you must step in and write some code to determine what will happen. The basis of event-driven programming, which comprises a lot of what a GUI is about, is tying events to code that responds to those events.

The way that this is accomplished in Swing is by cleanly separating the interface (the graphical components) and the implementation (the code that you want to run when an event happens to a component). Each Swing component can report all the events that might happen to it, and it can report each kind of event individually. So if you're not interested in, for example, whether the mouse is being moved over your button, you don't register your interest in that event. It's a very straightforward and elegant way to handle event-driven programming, and once you understand the basic concepts you can easily use Swing components that you haven't seen before—in fact, this model extends to anything that can be classified as a JavaBean (which you'll learn about later in the chapter).

At first, we will just focus on the main event of interest for the components being used. In the case of a **JButton**, this "event of interest" is that the button is pressed. To register your interest in when a button is pressed, you call the **JButton**'s **addActionListener( )** method. This method expects an argument that is an object that implements the **ActionListener** interface, which contains a single method called **actionPerformed( )**. So all you have to do to attach code to a **JButton** is to implement the **ActionListener** interface in a class, and register an object of that class with the **JButton** via **addActionListener( )**. The method will be called when the button is pressed (this is normally referred to as a *callback*).

But what should the result of pressing that button be? We'd like to see something change on the screen, so a new Swing component will be introduced: the **JTextField**. This is a place where text can be typed, or in this case modified by the program. Although there are a number of ways to create a **JTextField**, the simplest is just to tell the constructor how wide you want that field to be. Once the **JTextField** is placed on the form, you can modify its contents by using the **setText( )** method (there are many other methods in **JTextField**, but you must look these up in the HTML documentation for the JDK from *java.sun.com*). Here is what it looks like:

```
//: c13:Button2.java
// Responding to button presses.
// <applet code=Button2 width=200 height=75>
// </applet>
import javax.swing.*;
import java.awt.event.*;
import java.awt.*;
import com.bruceeckel.swing.*;

public class Button2 extends JApplet {
  JButton
    b1 = new JButton("Button 1"),
    b2 = new JButton("Button 2");
  JTextField txt = new JTextField(10);
```

```
class BL implements ActionListener {
  public void actionPerformed(ActionEvent e){
    String name =
      ((JButton)e.getSource()).getText();
    txt.setText(name);
  }
}
BL al = new BL();
public void init() {
  b1.addActionListener(al);
  b2.addActionListener(al);
  Container cp = getContentPane();
  cp.setLayout(new FlowLayout());
  cp.add(b1);
  cp.add(b2);
  cp.add(txt);
}
public static void main(String[] args) {
  Console.run(new Button2(), 200, 75);
}
} ///:~
```

Creating a **JTextField** and placing it on the canvas takes the same steps as for **JButton**s, or for any Swing component. The difference in the above program is in the creation of the aforementioned **ActionListener** class **BL**. The argument to **actionPerformed( )** is of type **ActionEvent**, which contains all the information about the event and where it came from. In this case, I wanted to describe the button that was pressed: **getSource( )** produces the object where the event originated, and I assumed that is a **JButton**. **getText( )** returns the text that's on the button, and this is placed in the **JTextField** to prove that the code was actually called when the button was pressed.

In **init( )**, **addActionListener( )** is used to register the **BL** object with both the buttons.

It is often more convenient to code the **ActionListener** as an anonymous inner class, especially since you tend to only use a single instance of each listener class. **Button2.java** can be modified to use an anonymous inner class as follows:

```
//: c13:Button2b.java
// Using anonymous inner classes.
// <applet code=Button2b width=200 height=75>
// </applet>
import javax.swing.*;
import java.awt.event.*;
import java.awt.*;
import com.bruceeckel.swing.*;

public class Button2b extends JApplet {
  JButton
    b1 = new JButton("Button 1"),
    b2 = new JButton("Button 2");
  JTextField txt = new JTextField(10);
  ActionListener al = new ActionListener() {
    public void actionPerformed(ActionEvent e){
      String name =
        ((JButton)e.getSource()).getText();
      txt.setText(name);
    }
  };
  public void init() {
    b1.addActionListener(al);
    b2.addActionListener(al);
    Container cp = getContentPane();
    cp.setLayout(new FlowLayout());
    cp.add(b1);
    cp.add(b2);
    cp.add(txt);
  }
  public static void main(String[] args) {
    Console.run(new Button2b(), 200, 75);
  }
} ///:~
```

The approach of using an anonymous inner class will be preferred (when possible) for the examples in this book.

Text areas

A **JTextArea** is like a **JTextField** except that it can have multiple lines and has more functionality. A particularly useful method is **append( )**; with this you can easily pour output into the **JTextArea**, thus making a Swing program an improvement (since you can scroll backward) over what has been accomplished thus far using command-line programs that print to standard output. As an example, the following program fills a **JTextArea** with the output from the **geography** generator in Chapter 9:

```
//: c13:TextArea.java
// Using the JTextArea control.
// <applet code=TextArea width=475 height=425>
// </applet>
import javax.swing.*;
import java.awt.event.*;
import java.awt.*;
import java.util.*;
import com.bruceeckel.swing.*;
import com.bruceeckel.util.*;

public class TextArea extends JApplet {
  JButton
    b = new JButton("Add Data"),
    c = new JButton("Clear Data");
  JTextArea t = new JTextArea(20, 40);
  Map m = new HashMap();
  public void init() {
    // Use up all the data:
    Collections2.fill(m,
      Collections2.geography,
      CountryCapitals.pairs.length);
    b.addActionListener(new ActionListener() {
      public void actionPerformed(ActionEvent e){
        for(Iterator it= m.entrySet().iterator();
            it.hasNext();){
          Map.Entry me = (Map.Entry)(it.next());
          t.append(me.getKey() + ": "
            + me.getValue() + "\n");
        }
```

```
      }
    });
    c.addActionListener(new ActionListener() {
      public void actionPerformed(ActionEvent e){
        t.setText("");
      }
    });
    Container cp = getContentPane();
    cp.setLayout(new FlowLayout());
    cp.add(new JScrollPane(t));
    cp.add(b);
    cp.add(c);
  }
  public static void main(String[] args) {
    Console.run(new TextArea(), 475, 425);
  }
} ///:~
```

In **init( )**, the **Map** is filled with all the countries and their capitals. Note that for both buttons the **ActionListener** is created and added without defining an intermediate variable, since you never need to refer to that listener again during the program. The "Add Data" button formats and appends all the data, while the "Clear Data" button uses **setText( )** to remove all the text from the **JTextArea**.

As the **JTextArea** is added to the applet, it is wrapped in a **JScrollPane**, to control scrolling when too much text is placed on the screen. That's all you must do in order to produce full scrolling capabilities. Having tried to figure out how to do the equivalent in some other GUI programming environments, I am very impressed with the simplicity and good design of components like **JScrollPane**.

Controlling layout

The way that you place components on a form in Java is probably different from any other GUI system you've used. First, it's all code; there are no "resources" that control placement of components. Second, the way components are placed on a form is controlled not by absolute positioning but by a "layout manager" that decides how the components lie based on the order that you **add( )** them. The size, shape, and placement of components will be remarkably different from one layout manager to another. In addition, the layout managers adapt to the dimensions of your applet or application window, so if the window dimension is changed, the size, shape, and placement of the components can change in response.

JApplet, JFrame JWindow, and **JDialog** can all produce a **Container** with **getContentPane( )** that can contain and display **Component**s. In **Container,** there's a method called **setLayout( )** that allows you to choose a different layout manager. Other classes, such as **JPanel**, contain and display components directly and so you also set the layout manager directly, without using the content pane.

In this section we'll explore the various layout managers by placing buttons in them (since that's the simplest thing to do). There won't be any capturing of button events since these examples are just intended to show how the buttons are laid out.

BorderLayout

The applet uses a default layout scheme: the **BorderLayout** (a number of the previous example have changed the layout manager to **FlowLayout**). Without any other instruction, this takes whatever you **add( )** to it and places it in the center, stretching the object all the way out to the edges.

However, there's more to the **BorderLayout**. This layout manager has the concept of four border regions and a center area. When you add something to a panel that's using a **BorderLayout** you can use the overloaded **add( )** method that takes a constant value as its first argument. This value can be any of the following:

> **BorderLayout. NORTH** (top)
> **BorderLayout. SOUTH** (bottom)
> **BorderLayout. EAST** (right)
> **BorderLayout. WEST** (left)
> **BorderLayout.CENTER** (fill the middle, up to the other components or to the edges)

If you don't specify an area to place the object, it defaults to **CENTER**.

Here's a simple example. The default layout is used, since **JApplet** defaults to **BorderLayout**:

```
//: c13:BorderLayout1.java
// Demonstrates BorderLayout.
// <applet code=BorderLayout1
// width=300 height=250> </applet>
import javax.swing.*;
import java.awt.*;
import com.bruceeckel.swing.*;

public class BorderLayout1 extends JApplet {
  public void init() {
    Container cp = getContentPane();
    cp.add(BorderLayout.NORTH,
      new JButton("North"));
    cp.add(BorderLayout.SOUTH,
      new JButton("South"));
    cp.add(BorderLayout.EAST,
      new JButton("East"));
    cp.add(BorderLayout.WEST,
      new JButton("West"));
    cp.add(BorderLayout.CENTER,
      new JButton("Center"));
  }
  public static void main(String[] args) {
    Console.run(new BorderLayout1(), 300, 250);
  }
} ///:~
```

For every placement but **CENTER**, the element that you add is compressed to fit in the smallest amount of space along one dimension while it is stretched to the maximum along the other dimension. **CENTER**, however, spreads out in both dimensions to occupy the middle.

FlowLayout

This simply "flows" the components onto the form, from left to right until the top space is full, then moves down a row and continues flowing.

Here's an example that sets the layout manager to **FlowLayout** and then places buttons on the form. You'll notice that with **FlowLayout** the components take on their "natural" size. A **JButton**, for example, will be the size of its string.

```
//: c13:FlowLayout1.java
// Demonstrates FlowLayout.
// <applet code=FlowLayout1
// width=300 height=250> </applet>
import javax.swing.*;
import java.awt.*;
import com.bruceeckel.swing.*;

public class FlowLayout1 extends JApplet {
  public void init() {
    Container cp = getContentPane();
    cp.setLayout(new FlowLayout());
    for(int i = 0; i < 20; i++)
      cp.add(new JButton("Button " + i));
  }
  public static void main(String[] args) {
    Console.run(new FlowLayout1(), 300, 250);
  }
} ///:~
```

All components will be compacted to their smallest size in a **FlowLayout**, so you might get a little bit of surprising behavior. For example, because a **JLabel** will be the size of its string, attempting to right-justify its text yields an unchanged display when using **FlowLayout**.

GridLayout

A **GridLayout** allows you to build a table of components, and as you add them they are placed left-to-right and top-to-bottom in the grid. In the constructor you specify the number of rows and columns that you need and these are laid out in equal proportions.

```
//: c13:GridLayout1.java
// Demonstrates GridLayout.
// <applet code=GridLayout1
```

```
// width=300 height=250> </applet>
import javax.swing.*;
import java.awt.*;
import com.bruceeckel.swing.*;

public class GridLayout1 extends JApplet {
  public void init() {
    Container cp = getContentPane();
    cp.setLayout(new GridLayout(7,3));
    for(int i = 0; i < 20; i++)
      cp.add(new JButton("Button " + i));
  }
  public static void main(String[] args) {
    Console.run(new GridLayout1(), 300, 250);
  }
} ///:~
```

In this case there are 21 slots but only 20 buttons. The last slot is left empty because no "balancing" goes on with a **GridLayout**.

GridBagLayout

The **GridBagLayout** provides you with tremendous control in deciding exactly how the regions of your window will lay themselves out and reformat themselves when the window is resized. However, it's also the most complicated layout manager, and quite difficult to understand. It is intended primarily for automatic code generation by a GUI builder (good GUI builders will use **GridBagLayout** instead of absolute placement). If your design is so complicated that you feel you need to use **GridBagLayout**, then you should be using a GUI builder tool to generate that design. If you feel you must know the intricate details, I'll refer you to *Core Java 2* by Horstmann & Cornell (Prentice-Hall, 1999), or a dedicated Swing book, as a starting point.

Absolute positioning

It is also possible to set the absolute position of the graphical components in this way:

1.   Set a **null** layout manager for your **Container**: **setLayout(null)**.

2.	Call **setBounds( )** or **reshape( )** (depending on the language version) for each component, passing a bounding rectangle in pixel coordinates. You can do this in the constructor, or in **paint( )**, depending on what you want to achieve.

Some GUI builders use this approach extensively, but this is usually not the best way to generate code. More useful GUI builders will use **GridBagLayout** instead.

BoxLayout

Because people had so much trouble understanding and working with **GridBagLayout**, Swing also includes the **BoxLayout**, which gives you many of the benefits of **GridBagLayout** without the complexity, so you can often use it when you need to do hand-coded layouts (again, if your design becomes too complex, use a GUI builder that generates **GridBagLayout**s for you). **BoxLayout** allows you to control the placement of components either vertically or horizontally, and to control the space between the components using something called "struts and glue." First, let's see how to use the **BoxLayout** directly, in the same way that the other layout managers have been demonstrated:

```
//: c13:BoxLayout1.java
// Vertical and horizontal BoxLayouts.
// <applet code=BoxLayout1
// width=450 height=200> </applet>
import javax.swing.*;
import java.awt.*;
import com.bruceeckel.swing.*;

public class BoxLayout1 extends JApplet {
  public void init() {
    JPanel jpv = new JPanel();
    jpv.setLayout(
      new BoxLayout(jpv, BoxLayout.Y_AXIS));
    for(int i = 0; i < 5; i++)
      jpv.add(new JButton("" + i));
    JPanel jph = new JPanel();
    jph.setLayout(
      new BoxLayout(jph, BoxLayout.X_AXIS));
    for(int i = 0; i < 5; i++)
```

```
      jph.add(new JButton("" + i));
    Container cp = getContentPane();
    cp.add(BorderLayout.EAST, jpv);
    cp.add(BorderLayout.SOUTH, jph);
  }
  public static void main(String[] args) {
    Console.run(new BoxLayout1(), 450, 200);
  }
} ///:~
```

The constructor for **BoxLayout** is a bit different than the other layout managers—you provide the **Container** that is to be controlled by the **BoxLayout** as the first argument, and the direction of the layout as the second argument.

To simplify matters, there's a special container called **Box** that uses **BoxLayout** as its native manager. The following example lays out components horizontally and vertically using **Box**, which has two **static** methods to create boxes with vertical and horizontal alignment:

```
//: c13:Box1.java
// Vertical and horizontal BoxLayouts.
// <applet code=Box1
// width=450 height=200> </applet>
import javax.swing.*;
import java.awt.*;
import com.bruceeckel.swing.*;

public class Box1 extends JApplet {
  public void init() {
    Box bv = Box.createVerticalBox();
    for(int i = 0; i < 5; i++)
      bv.add(new JButton("" + i));
    Box bh = Box.createHorizontalBox();
    for(int i = 0; i < 5; i++)
      bh.add(new JButton("" + i));
    Container cp = getContentPane();
    cp.add(BorderLayout.EAST, bv);
    cp.add(BorderLayout.SOUTH, bh);
  }
  public static void main(String[] args) {
```

```
      Console.run(new Box1(), 450, 200);
  }
} ///:~
```

Once you have a **Box**, you pass it as a second argument when adding
components to the content pane.

Struts add space between components, measured in pixels. To use a strut,
you simply add it in between the addition of the components that you
want spaced apart:

```
//: c13:Box2.java
// Adding struts.
// <applet code=Box2
// width=450 height=300> </applet>
import javax.swing.*;
import java.awt.*;
import com.bruceeckel.swing.*;

public class Box2 extends JApplet {
  public void init() {
    Box bv = Box.createVerticalBox();
    for(int i = 0; i < 5; i++) {
      bv.add(new JButton("" + i));
      bv.add(Box.createVerticalStrut(i*10));
    }
    Box bh = Box.createHorizontalBox();
    for(int i = 0; i < 5; i++) {
      bh.add(new JButton("" + i));
      bh.add(Box.createHorizontalStrut(i*10));
    }
    Container cp = getContentPane();
    cp.add(BorderLayout.EAST, bv);
    cp.add(BorderLayout.SOUTH, bh);
  }
  public static void main(String[] args) {
    Console.run(new Box2(), 450, 300);
  }
} ///:~
```

Struts separate components by a fixed amount, but glue is the opposite: it
separates components by as much as possible. Thus it's more of a "spring"

than "glue" (and the design on which this was based was called "springs and struts" so the choice of the term is a bit mysterious).

```
//: c13:Box3.java
// Using Glue.
// <applet code=Box3
// width=450 height=300> </applet>
import javax.swing.*;
import java.awt.*;
import com.bruceeckel.swing.*;

public class Box3 extends JApplet {
  public void init() {
    Box bv = Box.createVerticalBox();
    bv.add(new JLabel("Hello"));
    bv.add(Box.createVerticalGlue());
    bv.add(new JLabel("Applet"));
    bv.add(Box.createVerticalGlue());
    bv.add(new JLabel("World"));
    Box bh = Box.createHorizontalBox();
    bh.add(new JLabel("Hello"));
    bh.add(Box.createHorizontalGlue());
    bh.add(new JLabel("Applet"));
    bh.add(Box.createHorizontalGlue());
    bh.add(new JLabel("World"));
    bv.add(Box.createVerticalGlue());
    bv.add(bh);
    bv.add(Box.createVerticalGlue());
    getContentPane().add(bv);
  }
  public static void main(String[] args) {
    Console.run(new Box3(), 450, 300);
  }
} ///:~
```

A strut works in one direction, but a rigid area fixes the spacing between components in both directions:

```
//: c13:Box4.java
// Rigid Areas are like pairs of struts.
// <applet code=Box4
// width=450 height=300> </applet>
```

```
import javax.swing.*;
import java.awt.*;
import com.bruceeckel.swing.*;

public class Box4 extends JApplet {
  public void init() {
    Box bv = Box.createVerticalBox();
    bv.add(new JButton("Top"));
    bv.add(Box.createRigidArea(
      new Dimension(120, 90)));
    bv.add(new JButton("Bottom"));
    Box bh = Box.createHorizontalBox();
    bh.add(new JButton("Left"));
    bh.add(Box.createRigidArea(
      new Dimension(160, 80)));
    bh.add(new JButton("Right"));
    bv.add(bh);
    getContentPane().add(bv);
  }
  public static void main(String[] args) {
    Console.run(new Box4(), 450, 300);
  }
} ///:~
```

You should be aware that rigid areas are a bit controversial. Since they use absolute values, some people feel that they cause more trouble than they are worth.

The best approach?

Swing is powerful; it can get a lot done with a few lines of code. The examples shown in this book are reasonably simple, and for learning purposes it makes sense to write them by hand. You can actually accomplish quite a bit by combining simple layouts. At some point, however, it stops making sense to hand-code GUI forms—it becomes too complicated and is not a good use of your programming time. The Java and Swing designers oriented the language and libraries to support GUI building tools, which have been created for the express purpose of making your programming experience easier. As long as you understand what's going on with layouts and how to deal with the events (described next), it's not particularly important that you actually know the details of how to

---

lay out components by hand—let the appropriate tool do that for you (Java is, after all, designed to increase programmer productivity).

The Swing event model

In the Swing event model a component can initiate ("fire") an event. Each type of event is represented by a distinct class. When an event is fired, it is received by one or more "listeners," which act on that event. Thus, the source of an event and the place where the event is handled can be separate. Since you typically use Swing components as they are, but need to write code that is called when the components receive an event, this is an excellent example of the separation of interface and implementation.

Each event listener is an object of a class that implements a particular type of listener **interface**. So as a programmer, all you do is create a listener object and register it with the component that's firing the event. This registration is performed by calling an **addXXXListener( )** method in the event-firing component, in which "**XXX**" represents the type of event listened for. You can easily know what types of events can be handled by noticing the names of the "addListener" methods, and if you try to listen for the wrong events you'll discover your mistake at compile-time. You'll see later in the chapter that JavaBeans also use the names of the "addListener" methods to determine what events a Bean can handle.

All of your event logic, then, will go inside a listener class. When you create a listener class, the sole restriction is that it must implement the appropriate interface. You can create a global listener class, but this is a situation in which inner classes tend to be quite useful, not only because they provide a logical grouping of your listener classes inside the UI or business logic classes they are serving, but because (as you shall see later) the fact that an inner class object keeps a reference to its parent object provides a nice way to call across class and subsystem boundaries.

All the examples so far in this chapter have been using the Swing event model, but the remainder of this section will fill out the details of that model.

Event and listener types

All Swing components include **addXXXListener( )** and **removeXXXListener( )** methods so that the appropriate types of listeners can be added and removed from each component. You'll notice that the "**XXX**" in each case also represents the argument for the method, for example: **addMyListener(MyListener m)**. The following table includes the basic associated events, listeners, and methods, along with the basic components that support those particular events by providing the **addXXXListener( )** and **removeXXXListener( )** methods. You should keep in mind that the event model is designed to be extensible, so you may encounter other events and listener types that are not covered in this table.

Event, listener interface and add- and remove-methods	Components supporting this event
ActionEvent **ActionListener** **addActionListener( )** **removeActionListener( )**	**JButton, JList, JTextField, JMenuItem** and its derivatives including **JCheckBoxMenuItem, JMenu,** and **JpopupMenu.**
AdjustmentEvent **AdjustmentListener** **addAdjustmentListener( )** **removeAdjustmentListener( )**	**JScrollbar** and anything you create that implements the **Adjustable interface.**
ComponentEvent **ComponentListener** **addComponentListener( )** **removeComponentListener( )**	*****Component** and its derivatives, including **JButton, JCanvas, JCheckBox, JComboBox, Container, JPanel, JApplet, JScrollPane, Window, JDialog, JFileDialog, JFrame, JLabel, JList, JScrollbar, JTextArea,** and **JTextField.**
ContainerEvent **ContainerListener** **addContainerListener( )** **removeContainerListener( )**	**Container** and its derivatives, including **JPanel, JApplet, JScrollPane, Window, JDialog, JFileDialog,** and **JFrame.**
FocusEvent **FocusListener** **addFocusListener( )** **removeFocusListener( )**	**Component** and **derivatives*.**
KeyEvent	**Component** and **derivatives*.**

Event, listener interface and add- and remove-methods	Components supporting this event
KeyListener **addKeyListener( )** **removeKeyListener( )**	
MouseEvent (for both clicks and motion) **MouseListener** **addMouseListener( )** **removeMouseListener( )**	**Component** and **derivatives***.
MouseEvent[8] (for both clicks and motion) **MouseMotionListener** **addMouseMotionListener( )** **removeMouseMotionListener( )**	**Component** and **derivatives***.
WindowEvent **WindowListener** **addWindowListener( )** **removeWindowListener( )**	**Window** and its derivatives, including **JDialog, JFileDialog, and JFrame.**
ItemEvent **ItemListener** **addItemListener( )** **removeItemListener( )**	**JCheckBox, JCheckBoxMenuItem, JComboBox, JList,** and anything that implements the **ItemSelectable interface.**
TextEvent **TextListener** **addTextListener( )** **removeTextListener( )**	Anything derived from **JTextComponent**, including **JTextArea** and **JTextField.**

You can see that each type of component supports only certain types of events. It turns out to be rather difficult to look up all the events supported by each component. A simpler approach is to modify the **ShowMethodsClean.java** program from Chapter 12 so that it displays all the event listeners supported by any Swing component that you enter.

Chapter 12 introduced *reflection* and used that feature to look up methods for a particular class—either the entire list of methods or a subset of those

---

[8] There is no **MouseMotionEvent** even though it seems like there ought to be. Clicking and motion is combined into **MouseEvent**, so this second appearance of **MouseEvent** in the table is not an error.

whose names match a keyword that you provide. The magic of this is that it can automatically show you *all* the methods for a class without forcing you to walk up the inheritance hierarchy examining the base classes at each level. Thus, it provides a valuable timesaving tool for programming: because the names of most Java methods are made nicely verbose and descriptive, you can search for the method names that contain a particular word of interest. When you find what you think you're looking for, check the online documentation.

However, by Chapter 12 you hadn't seen Swing, so the tool in that chapter was developed as a command-line application. Here is the more useful GUI version, specialized to look for the "addListener" methods in Swing components:

```
//: c13:ShowAddListeners.java
// Display the "addXXXListener" methods of any
// Swing class.
// <applet code = ShowAddListeners
// width=500 height=400></applet>
import javax.swing.*;
import javax.swing.event.*;
import java.awt.*;
import java.awt.event.*;
import java.lang.reflect.*;
import java.io.*;
import com.bruceeckel.swing.*;
import com.bruceeckel.util.*;

public class ShowAddListeners extends JApplet {
  Class cl;
  Method[] m;
  Constructor[] ctor;
  String[] n = new String[0];
  JTextField name = new JTextField(25);
  JTextArea results = new JTextArea(40, 65);
  class NameL implements ActionListener {
    public void actionPerformed(ActionEvent e) {
      String nm = name.getText().trim();
      if(nm.length() == 0) {
        results.setText("No match");
        n = new String[0];
```

```
        return;
      }
      try {
        cl = Class.forName("javax.swing." + nm);
      } catch(ClassNotFoundException ex) {
        results.setText("No match");
        return;
      }
      m = cl.getMethods();
      // Convert to an array of Strings:
      n = new String[m.length];
      for(int i = 0; i < m.length; i++)
        n[i] = m[i].toString();
      reDisplay();
    }
  }
  void reDisplay() {
    // Create the result set:
    String[] rs = new String[n.length];
    int j = 0;
    for (int i = 0; i < n.length; i++)
      if(n[i].indexOf("add") != -1 &&
        n[i].indexOf("Listener") != -1)
          rs[j++] =
            n[i].substring(n[i].indexOf("add"));
    results.setText("");
    for (int i = 0; i < j; i++)
      results.append(
        StripQualifiers.strip(rs[i]) + "\n");
  }
  public void init() {
    name.addActionListener(new NameL());
    JPanel top = new JPanel();
    top.add(new JLabel(
      "Swing class name (press ENTER):"));
    top.add(name);
    Container cp = getContentPane();
    cp.add(BorderLayout.NORTH, top);
    cp.add(new JScrollPane(results));
  }
  public static void main(String[] args) {
```

```
      Console.run(new ShowAddListeners(), 500,400);
  }
} ///:~
```

The **StripQualifiers** class defined in Chapter 12 is reused here by importing the **com.bruceeckel.util** library.

The GUI contains a **JTextField name** in which you can enter the Swing class name you want to look up. The results are displayed in a **JTextArea**.

You'll notice that there are no buttons or other components by which to indicate that you want the search to begin. That's because the **JTextField** is monitored by an **ActionListener**. Whenever you make a change and press ENTER, the list is immediately updated. If the text isn't empty, it is used inside **Class.forName( )** to try to look up the class. If the name is incorrect, **Class.forName( )** will fail, which means that it throws an exception. This is trapped and the **JTextArea** is set to "No match." But if you type in a correct name (capitalization counts), **Class.forName( )** is successful and **getMethods( )** will return an array of **Method** objects. Each of the objects in the array is turned into a **String** via **toString( )** (this produces the complete method signature) and added to **n**, a **String** array. The array **n** is a member of **class ShowAddListeners** and is used in updating the display whenever **reDisplay( )** is called.

reDisplay( ) creates an array of **String** called **rs** (for "result set"). The result set is conditionally copied from the **String**s in **n** that contain "add" and "Listener." **indexOf( )** and **substring( )** are then used to remove the qualifiers like **public**, **static**, etc. Finally, **StripQualifiers.strip( )** removes the extra name qualifiers.

This program is a convenient way to investigate the capabilities of a Swing component. Once you know which events a particular component supports, you don't need to look anything up to react to that event. You simply:

1. Take the name of the event class and remove the word "**Event**." Add the word "**Listener**" to what remains. This is the listener interface you must implement in your inner class.

2. Implement the interface above and write out the methods for the events you want to capture. For example, you might be looking for mouse movements, so you write code for the **mouseMoved( )** method of the **MouseMotionListener** interface. (You must implement the other methods, of course, but there's often a shortcut for that which you'll see soon.)

3. Create an object of the listener class in Step 2. Register it with your component with the method produced by prefixing "**add**" to your listener name. For example, **addMouseMotionListener( )**.

Here are some of the listener interfaces:

Listener interface w/ adapter	Methods in interface
ActionListener	actionPerformed(ActionEvent)
AdjustmentListener	adjustmentValueChanged(AdjustmentEvent)
ComponentListener ComponentAdapter	componentHidden(ComponentEvent) componentShown(ComponentEvent) componentMoved(ComponentEvent) componentResized(ComponentEvent)
ContainerListener ContainerAdapter	componentAdded(ContainerEvent) componentRemoved(ContainerEvent)
FocusListener FocusAdapter	focusGained(FocusEvent) focusLost(FocusEvent)
KeyListener KeyAdapter	keyPressed(KeyEvent) keyReleased(KeyEvent) keyTyped(KeyEvent)
MouseListener MouseAdapter	mouseClicked(MouseEvent) mouseEntered(MouseEvent) mouseExited(MouseEvent) mousePressed(MouseEvent) mouseReleased(MouseEvent)
MouseMotionListener MouseMotionAdapter	mouseDragged(MouseEvent) mouseMoved(MouseEvent)
WindowListener WindowAdapter	windowOpened(WindowEvent) windowClosing(WindowEvent)

Listener interface w/ adapter	Methods in interface
	windowClosed(WindowEvent) windowActivated(WindowEvent) windowDeactivated(WindowEvent) windowIconified(WindowEvent) windowDeiconified(WindowEvent)
ItemListener	itemStateChanged(ItemEvent)

This is not an exhaustive listing, partly because the event model allows you to create your own event types and associated listeners. Thus, you'll regularly come across libraries that have invented their own events, and the knowledge gained in this chapter will allow you to figure out how to use these events.

Using listener adapters for simplicity

In the table above, you can see that some listener interfaces have only one method. These are trivial to implement since you'll implement them only when you want to write that particular method. However, the listener interfaces that have multiple methods can be less pleasant to use. For example, something you must always do when creating an application is provide a **WindowListener** to the **JFrame** so that when you get the **windowClosing( )** event you can call **System.exit( )** to exit the application. But since **WindowListener** is an **interface**, you must implement all of the other methods even if they don't do anything. This can be annoying.

To solve the problem, some (but not all) of the listener interfaces that have more than one method are provided with *adapters*, the names of which you can see in the table above. Each adapter provides default empty methods for each of the interface methods. Then all you need to do is inherit from the adapter and override only the methods you need to change. For example, the typical **WindowListener** you'll use looks like this (remember that this has been wrapped inside the **Console** class in **com.bruceeckel.swing**):

```
class MyWindowListener extends WindowAdapter {
  public void windowClosing(WindowEvent e) {
    System.exit(0);
```

```
      }
   }
```

The whole point of the adapters is to make the creation of listener classes easy.

There is a downside to adapters, however, in the form of a pitfall. Suppose you write a **WindowAdapter** like the one above:

```
class MyWindowListener extends WindowAdapter {
  public void WindowClosing(WindowEvent e) {
    System.exit(0);
  }
}
```

This doesn't work, but it will drive you crazy trying to figure out why, since everything will compile and run fine—except that closing the window won't exit the program. Can you see the problem? It's in the name of the method: **WindowClosing( )** instead of **windowClosing( )**. A simple slip in capitalization results in the addition of a completely new method. However, this is not the method that's called when the window is closing, so you don't get the desired results. Despite the inconvenience, an **interface** will guarantee that the methods are properly implemented.

Tracking multiple events

To prove to yourself that these events are in fact being fired, and as an interesting experiment, it's worth creating an applet that tracks extra behavior in a **JButton** (other than just whether it's pressed or not). This example also shows you how to inherit your own button object because that's what is used as the target of all the events of interest. To do so, you can just inherit from **JButton**.[9]

The **MyButton** class is an inner class of **TrackEvent**, so **MyButton** can reach into the parent window and manipulate its text fields, which is what's necessary to be able to write the status information into the fields of the parent. Of course this is a limited solution, since **myButton** can be

---

[9] In Java 1.0/1.1 you could *not* usefully inherit from the button object. This was only one of numerous fundamental design flaws.

used only in conjunction with **TrackEvent**. This kind of code is sometimes called "highly coupled":

```
//: c13:TrackEvent.java
// Show events as they happen.
// <applet code=TrackEvent
//   width=700 height=500></applet>
import javax.swing.*;
import java.awt.*;
import java.awt.event.*;
import java.util.*;
import com.bruceeckel.swing.*;

public class TrackEvent extends JApplet {
  HashMap h = new HashMap();
  String[] event = {
    "focusGained", "focusLost", "keyPressed",
    "keyReleased", "keyTyped", "mouseClicked",
    "mouseEntered", "mouseExited","mousePressed",
    "mouseReleased", "mouseDragged", "mouseMoved"
  };
  MyButton
    b1 = new MyButton(Color.blue, "test1"),
    b2 = new MyButton(Color.red, "test2");
  class MyButton extends JButton {
    void report(String field, String msg) {
      ((JTextField)h.get(field)).setText(msg);
    }
    FocusListener fl = new FocusListener() {
      public void focusGained(FocusEvent e) {
        report("focusGained", e.paramString());
      }
      public void focusLost(FocusEvent e) {
        report("focusLost", e.paramString());
      }
    };
    KeyListener kl = new KeyListener() {
      public void keyPressed(KeyEvent e) {
        report("keyPressed", e.paramString());
      }
      public void keyReleased(KeyEvent e) {
```

```java
        report("keyReleased", e.paramString());
      }
      public void keyTyped(KeyEvent e) {
        report("keyTyped", e.paramString());
      }
    };
    MouseListener ml = new MouseListener() {
      public void mouseClicked(MouseEvent e) {
        report("mouseClicked", e.paramString());
      }
      public void mouseEntered(MouseEvent e) {
        report("mouseEntered", e.paramString());
      }
      public void mouseExited(MouseEvent e) {
        report("mouseExited", e.paramString());
      }
      public void mousePressed(MouseEvent e) {
        report("mousePressed", e.paramString());
      }
      public void mouseReleased(MouseEvent e) {
        report("mouseReleased", e.paramString());
      }
    };
    MouseMotionListener mml =
      new MouseMotionListener() {
      public void mouseDragged(MouseEvent e) {
        report("mouseDragged", e.paramString());
      }
      public void mouseMoved(MouseEvent e) {
        report("mouseMoved", e.paramString());
      }
    };
    public MyButton(Color color, String label) {
      super(label);
      setBackground(color);
      addFocusListener(fl);
      addKeyListener(kl);
      addMouseListener(ml);
      addMouseMotionListener(mml);
    }
  }
```

```
    public void init() {
      Container c = getContentPane();
      c.setLayout(new GridLayout(event.length+1,2));
      for(int i = 0; i < event.length; i++) {
        JTextField t = new JTextField();
        t.setEditable(false);
        c.add(new JLabel(event[i], JLabel.RIGHT));
        c.add(t);
        h.put(event[i], t);
      }
      c.add(b1);
      c.add(b2);
    }
    public static void main(String[] args) {
      Console.run(new TrackEvent(), 700, 500);
    }
} ///:~
```

In the **MyButton** constructor, the button's color is set with a call to **SetBackground( )**. The listeners are all installed with simple method calls.

The **TrackEvent** class contains a **HashMap** to hold the strings representing the type of event and **JTextField**s where information about that event is held. Of course, these could have been created statically rather than putting them in a **HashMap**, but I think you'll agree that it's a lot easier to use and change. In particular, if you need to add or remove a new type of event in **TrackEvent**, you simply add or remove a string in the **event** array—everything else happens automatically.

When **report( )** is called it is given the name of the event and the parameter string from the event. It uses the **HashMap h** in the outer class to look up the actual **JTextField** associated with that event name, and then places the parameter string into that field.

This example is fun to play with since you can really see what's going on with the events in your program.

A catalog of Swing components

Now that you understand layout managers and the event model, you're ready to see how Swing components can be used. This section is a nonexhaustive tour of the Swing components and features that you'll probably use most of the time. Each example is intended to be reasonably small so that you can easily lift the code and use it in your own programs.

You can easily see what each of these examples looks like while running by viewing the HTML pages in the downloadable source code for this chapter.

Keep in mind:

1.   The HTML documentation from *java.sun.com* contains all of the Swing classes and methods (only a few are shown here).

2.   Because of the naming convention used for Swing events, it's fairly easy to guess how to write and install a handler for a particular type of event. Use the lookup program **ShowAddListeners.java** from earlier in this chapter to aid in your investigation of a particular component.

3.   When things start to get complicated you should graduate to a GUI builder.

Buttons

Swing includes a number of different types of buttons. All buttons, check boxes, radio buttons, and even menu items are inherited from **AbstractButton** (which, since menu items are included, would probably have been better named "AbstractChooser" or something equally general). You'll see the use of menu items shortly, but the following example shows the various types of buttons available:

```
//: c13:Buttons.java
// Various Swing buttons.
// <applet code=Buttons
```

```
//   width=350 height=100></applet>
import javax.swing.*;
import java.awt.*;
import java.awt.event.*;
import javax.swing.plaf.basic.*;
import javax.swing.border.*;
import com.bruceeckel.swing.*;

public class Buttons extends JApplet {
  JButton jb = new JButton("JButton");
  BasicArrowButton
    up = new BasicArrowButton(
      BasicArrowButton.NORTH),
    down = new BasicArrowButton(
      BasicArrowButton.SOUTH),
    right = new BasicArrowButton(
      BasicArrowButton.EAST),
    left = new BasicArrowButton(
      BasicArrowButton.WEST);
  public void init() {
    Container cp = getContentPane();
    cp.setLayout(new FlowLayout());
    cp.add(jb);
    cp.add(new JToggleButton("JToggleButton"));
    cp.add(new JCheckBox("JCheckBox"));
    cp.add(new JRadioButton("JRadioButton"));
    JPanel jp = new JPanel();
    jp.setBorder(new TitledBorder("Directions"));
    jp.add(up);
    jp.add(down);
    jp.add(left);
    jp.add(right);
    cp.add(jp);
  }
  public static void main(String[] args) {
    Console.run(new Buttons(), 350, 100);
  }
} ///:~
```

This begins with the **BasicArrowButton** from
javax.swing.plaf.basic, then continues with the various specific types

---

of buttons. When you run the example, you'll see that the toggle button holds its last position, in or out. But the check boxes and radio buttons behave identically to each other, just clicking on or off (they are inherited from **JToggleButton**).

Button groups

If you want radio buttons to behave in an "exclusive or" fashion, you must add them to a "button group." But, as the example below demonstrates, any **AbstractButton** can be added to a **ButtonGroup**.

To avoid repeating a lot of code, this example uses reflection to generate the groups of different types of buttons. This is seen in **makeBPanel( )**, which creates a button group and a **JPanel**. The second argument to **makeBPanel( )** is an array of **String**. For each **String**, a button of the class represented by the first argument is added to the **JPanel**:

```
//: c13:ButtonGroups.java
// Uses reflection to create groups
// of different types of AbstractButton.
// <applet code=ButtonGroups
//   width=500 height=300></applet>
import javax.swing.*;
import java.awt.*;
import java.awt.event.*;
import javax.swing.border.*;
import java.lang.reflect.*;
import com.bruceeckel.swing.*;

public class ButtonGroups extends JApplet {
  static String[] ids = {
    "June", "Ward", "Beaver",
    "Wally", "Eddie", "Lumpy",
  };
  static JPanel
  makeBPanel(Class bClass, String[] ids) {
    ButtonGroup bg = new ButtonGroup();
    JPanel jp = new JPanel();
    String title = bClass.getName();
    title = title.substring(
      title.lastIndexOf('.') + 1);
```

```
      jp.setBorder(new TitledBorder(title));
      for(int i = 0; i < ids.length; i++) {
        AbstractButton ab = new JButton("failed");
        try {
          // Get the dynamic constructor method
          // that takes a String argument:
          Constructor ctor = bClass.getConstructor(
            new Class[] { String.class });
          // Create a new object:
          ab = (AbstractButton)ctor.newInstance(
            new Object[]{ids[i]});
        } catch(Exception ex) {
          System.err.println("can't create " +
            bClass);
        }
        bg.add(ab);
        jp.add(ab);
      }
      return jp;
    }
    public void init() {
      Container cp = getContentPane();
      cp.setLayout(new FlowLayout());
      cp.add(makeBPanel(JButton.class, ids));
      cp.add(makeBPanel(JToggleButton.class, ids));
      cp.add(makeBPanel(JCheckBox.class, ids));
      cp.add(makeBPanel(JRadioButton.class, ids));
    }
    public static void main(String[] args) {
      Console.run(new ButtonGroups(), 500, 300);
    }
  } ///:~
```

The title for the border is taken from the name of the class, stripping off
all the path information. The **AbstractButton** is initialized to a
JButton that has the label "Failed" so if you ignore the exception
message, you'll still see the problem on screen. The **getConstructor( )**
method produces a **Constructor** object that takes the array of arguments
of the types in the **Class** array passed to **getConstructor( )**. Then all
you do is call **newInstance( )**, passing it an array of **Object** containing
your actual arguments—in this case, just the **String** from the **ids** array.

This adds a little complexity to what is a simple process. To get "exclusive or" behavior with buttons, you create a button group and add each button for which you want that behavior to the group. When you run the program, you'll see that all the buttons except **JButton** exhibit this "exclusive or" behavior.

Icons

You can use an **Icon** inside a **JLabel** or anything that inherits from **AbstractButton** (including **JButton, JCheckBox, JRadioButton,** and the different kinds of **JMenuItem**). Using **Icon**s with **JLabel**s is quite straightforward (you'll see an example later). The following example explores all the additional ways you can use **Icon**s with buttons and their descendants.

You can use any **gif** files you want, but the ones used in this example are part of this book's code distribution, available at *www.BruceEckel.com*. To open a file and bring in the image, simply create an **ImageIcon** and hand it the file name. From then on, you can use the resulting **Icon** in your program.

Note that path information is hard-coded into this example; you will need to change the path to correspond to the location of the image files.

```
//: c13:Faces.java
// Icon behavior in Jbuttons.
// <applet code=Faces
//   width=250 height=100></applet>
import javax.swing.*;
import java.awt.*;
import java.awt.event.*;
import com.bruceeckel.swing.*;

public class Faces extends JApplet {
  // The following path information is necessary
  // to run via an applet directly from the disk:
  static String path =
    "C:/aaa-TIJ2-distribution/code/c13/";
  static Icon[] faces = {
    new ImageIcon(path + "face0.gif"),
    new ImageIcon(path + "face1.gif"),
```

```
          new ImageIcon(path + "face2.gif"),
          new ImageIcon(path + "face3.gif"),
          new ImageIcon(path + "face4.gif"),
  };
  JButton
    jb = new JButton("JButton", faces[3]),
    jb2 = new JButton("Disable");
  boolean mad = false;
  public void init() {
    Container cp = getContentPane();
    cp.setLayout(new FlowLayout());
    jb.addActionListener(new ActionListener() {
      public void actionPerformed(ActionEvent e){
        if(mad) {
          jb.setIcon(faces[3]);
          mad = false;
        } else {
          jb.setIcon(faces[0]);
          mad = true;
        }
        jb.setVerticalAlignment(JButton.TOP);
        jb.setHorizontalAlignment(JButton.LEFT);
      }
    });
    jb.setRolloverEnabled(true);
    jb.setRolloverIcon(faces[1]);
    jb.setPressedIcon(faces[2]);
    jb.setDisabledIcon(faces[4]);
    jb.setToolTipText("Yow!");
    cp.add(jb);
    jb2.addActionListener(new ActionListener() {
      public void actionPerformed(ActionEvent e){
        if(jb.isEnabled()) {
          jb.setEnabled(false);
          jb2.setText("Enable");
        } else {
          jb.setEnabled(true);
          jb2.setText("Disable");
        }
      }
    });
```

```
      cp.add(jb2);
   }
   public static void main(String[] args) {
     Console.run(new Faces(), 400, 200);
   }
} ///:~
```

An **Icon** can be used in many constructors, but you can also use **setIcon( )** to add or change an **Icon**. This example also shows how a **JButton** (or any **AbstractButton**) can set the various different sorts of icons that appear when things happen to that button: when it's pressed, disabled, or "rolled over" (the mouse moves over it without clicking). You'll see that this gives the button a nice animated feel.

Tool tips

The previous example added a "tool tip" to the button. Almost all of the classes that you'll be using to create your user interfaces are derived from **JComponent**, which contains a method called **setToolTipText(String)**. So, for virtually anything you place on your form, all you need to do is say (for an object **jc** of any **JComponent**-derived class):

```
jc.setToolTipText("My tip");
```

and when the mouse stays over that **JComponent** for a predetermined period of time, a tiny box containing your text will pop up next to the mouse.

Text fields

This example shows the extra behavior that **JTextField**s are capable of:

```
//: c13:TextFields.java
// Text fields and Java events.
// <applet code=TextFields width=375
// height=125></applet>
import javax.swing.*;
import javax.swing.event.*;
import javax.swing.text.*;
import java.awt.*;
import java.awt.event.*;
```

```
import com.bruceeckel.swing.*;

public class TextFields extends JApplet {
  JButton
    b1 = new JButton("Get Text"),
    b2 = new JButton("Set Text");
  JTextField
    t1 = new JTextField(30),
    t2 = new JTextField(30),
    t3 = new JTextField(30);
  String s = new String();
  UpperCaseDocument
    ucd = new UpperCaseDocument();
  public void init() {
    t1.setDocument(ucd);
    ucd.addDocumentListener(new T1());
    b1.addActionListener(new B1());
    b2.addActionListener(new B2());
    DocumentListener dl = new T1();
    t1.addActionListener(new T1A());
    Container cp = getContentPane();
    cp.setLayout(new FlowLayout());
    cp.add(b1);
    cp.add(b2);
    cp.add(t1);
    cp.add(t2);
    cp.add(t3);
  }
  class T1 implements DocumentListener {
    public void changedUpdate(DocumentEvent e){}
    public void insertUpdate(DocumentEvent e){
      t2.setText(t1.getText());
      t3.setText("Text: "+ t1.getText());
    }
    public void removeUpdate(DocumentEvent e){
      t2.setText(t1.getText());
    }
  }
  class T1A implements ActionListener {
    private int count = 0;
    public void actionPerformed(ActionEvent e) {
```

```java
          t3.setText("t1 Action Event " + count++);
      }
    }
    class B1 implements ActionListener {
      public void actionPerformed(ActionEvent e) {
        if(t1.getSelectedText() == null)
          s = t1.getText();
        else
          s = t1.getSelectedText();
        t1.setEditable(true);
      }
    }
    class B2 implements ActionListener {
      public void actionPerformed(ActionEvent e) {
        ucd.setUpperCase(false);
        t1.setText("Inserted by Button 2: " + s);
        ucd.setUpperCase(true);
        t1.setEditable(false);
      }
    }
    public static void main(String[] args) {
      Console.run(new TextFields(), 375, 125);
    }
}

class UpperCaseDocument extends PlainDocument {
  boolean upperCase = true;
  public void setUpperCase(boolean flag) {
    upperCase = flag;
  }
  public void insertString(int offset,
    String string, AttributeSet attributeSet)
    throws BadLocationException {
      if(upperCase)
        string = string.toUpperCase();
      super.insertString(offset,
        string, attributeSet);
  }
} ///:~
```

The **JTextField t3** is included as a place to report when the action listener for the **JTextField t1** is fired. You'll see that the action listener for a **JTextField** is fired only when you press the "enter" key.

The **JTextField t1** has several listeners attached to it. The **T1** listener is a **DocumentListener** that responds to any change in the "document" (the contents of the **JTextField**, in this case). It automatically copies all text from **t1** into **t2**. In addition, **t1**'s document is set to a derived class of **PlainDocument**, called **UpperCaseDocument**, which forces all characters to uppercase. It automatically detects backspaces and performs the deletion, adjusting the caret and handling everything as you would expect.

Borders

JComponent contains a method called **setBorder( )**, which allows you to place various interesting borders on any visible component. The following example demonstrates a number of the different borders that are available, using a method called **showBorder( )** that creates a **JPanel** and puts on the border in each case. Also, it uses RTTI to find the name of the border that you're using (stripping off all the path information), then puts that name in a **JLabel** in the middle of the panel:

```
//: c13:Borders.java
// Different Swing borders.
// <applet code=Borders
//  width=500 height=300></applet>
import javax.swing.*;
import java.awt.*;
import java.awt.event.*;
import javax.swing.border.*;
import com.bruceeckel.swing.*;

public class Borders extends JApplet {
  static JPanel showBorder(Border b) {
    JPanel jp = new JPanel();
    jp.setLayout(new BorderLayout());
    String nm = b.getClass().toString();
    nm = nm.substring(nm.lastIndexOf('.') + 1);
    jp.add(new JLabel(nm, JLabel.CENTER),
```

```
      BorderLayout.CENTER);
    jp.setBorder(b);
    return jp;
  }
  public void init() {
    Container cp = getContentPane();
    cp.setLayout(new FlowLayout());
    cp.setLayout(new GridLayout(2,4));
    cp.add(showBorder(new TitledBorder("Title")));
    cp.add(showBorder(new EtchedBorder()));
    cp.add(showBorder(new LineBorder(Color.blue)));
    cp.add(showBorder(
      new MatteBorder(5,5,30,30,Color.green)));
    cp.add(showBorder(
      new BevelBorder(BevelBorder.RAISED)));
    cp.add(showBorder(
      new SoftBevelBorder(BevelBorder.LOWERED)));
    cp.add(showBorder(new CompoundBorder(
      new EtchedBorder(),
      new LineBorder(Color.red))));
  }
  public static void main(String[] args) {
    Console.run(new Borders(), 500, 300);
  }
} ///:~
```

You can also create your own borders and put them inside buttons, labels, etc.—anything derived from **JComponent**.

JScrollPanes

Most of the time you'll just want to let a **JScrollPane** do it's job, but you can also control which scroll bars are allowed—vertical, horizontal, both, or neither:

```
//: c13:JScrollPanes.java
// Controlling the scrollbars in a JScrollPane.
// <applet code=JScrollPanes width=300 height=725>
// </applet>
import javax.swing.*;
import java.awt.*;
import java.awt.event.*;
```

```
import javax.swing.border.*;
import com.bruceeckel.swing.*;

public class JScrollPanes extends JApplet {
  JButton
    b1 = new JButton("Text Area 1"),
    b2 = new JButton("Text Area 2"),
    b3 = new JButton("Replace Text"),
    b4 = new JButton("Insert Text");
  JTextArea
    t1 = new JTextArea("t1", 1, 20),
    t2 = new JTextArea("t2", 4, 20),
    t3 = new JTextArea("t3", 1, 20),
    t4 = new JTextArea("t4", 10, 10),
    t5 = new JTextArea("t5", 4, 20),
    t6 = new JTextArea("t6", 10, 10);
  JScrollPane
    sp3 = new JScrollPane(t3,
      JScrollPane.VERTICAL_SCROLLBAR_NEVER,
      JScrollPane.HORIZONTAL_SCROLLBAR_NEVER),
    sp4 = new JScrollPane(t4,
      JScrollPane.VERTICAL_SCROLLBAR_ALWAYS,
      JScrollPane.HORIZONTAL_SCROLLBAR_NEVER),
    sp5 = new JScrollPane(t5,
      JScrollPane.VERTICAL_SCROLLBAR_NEVER,
      JScrollPane.HORIZONTAL_SCROLLBAR_ALWAYS),
    sp6 = new JScrollPane(t6,
      JScrollPane.VERTICAL_SCROLLBAR_ALWAYS,
      JScrollPane.HORIZONTAL_SCROLLBAR_ALWAYS);
  class B1L implements ActionListener {
    public void actionPerformed(ActionEvent e) {
      t5.append(t1.getText() + "\n");
    }
  }
  class B2L implements ActionListener {
    public void actionPerformed(ActionEvent e) {
      t2.setText("Inserted by Button 2");
      t2.append(": " + t1.getText());
      t5.append(t2.getText() + "\n");
    }
  }
```

```java
class B3L implements ActionListener {
  public void actionPerformed(ActionEvent e) {
    String s = " Replacement ";
    t2.replaceRange(s, 3, 3 + s.length());
  }
}
class B4L implements ActionListener {
  public void actionPerformed(ActionEvent e) {
    t2.insert(" Inserted ", 10);
  }
}
public void init() {
  Container cp = getContentPane();
  cp.setLayout(new FlowLayout());
  // Create Borders for components:
  Border brd = BorderFactory.createMatteBorder(
    1, 1, 1, 1, Color.black);
  t1.setBorder(brd);
  t2.setBorder(brd);
  sp3.setBorder(brd);
  sp4.setBorder(brd);
  sp5.setBorder(brd);
  sp6.setBorder(brd);
  // Initialize listeners and add components:
  b1.addActionListener(new B1L());
  cp.add(b1);
  cp.add(t1);
  b2.addActionListener(new B2L());
  cp.add(b2);
  cp.add(t2);
  b3.addActionListener(new B3L());
  cp.add(b3);
  b4.addActionListener(new B4L());
  cp.add(b4);
  cp.add(sp3);
  cp.add(sp4);
  cp.add(sp5);
  cp.add(sp6);
}
public static void main(String[] args) {
  Console.run(new JScrollPanes(), 300, 725);
```

```
    }
} ///:~
```

Using different arguments in the **JScrollPane** constructor controls the
scrollbars that are available. This example also dresses things up a bit
using borders.

A mini-editor

The **JTextPane** control provides a great deal of support for editing,
without much effort. The following example makes very simple use of this,
ignoring the bulk of the functionality of the class:

```
//: c13:TextPane.java
// The JTextPane control is a little editor.
// <applet code=TextPane width=475 height=425>
// </applet>
import javax.swing.*;
import java.awt.*;
import java.awt.event.*;
import com.bruceeckel.swing.*;
import com.bruceeckel.util.*;

public class TextPane extends JApplet {
  JButton b = new JButton("Add Text");
  JTextPane tp = new JTextPane();
  static Generator sg =
    new Arrays2.RandStringGenerator(7);
  public void init() {
    b.addActionListener(new ActionListener() {
      public void actionPerformed(ActionEvent e){
        for(int i = 1; i < 10; i++)
          tp.setText(tp.getText() +
            sg.next() + "\n");
      }
    });
    Container cp = getContentPane();
    cp.add(new JScrollPane(tp));
    cp.add(BorderLayout.SOUTH, b);
  }
  public static void main(String[] args) {
```

```
    Console.run(new TextPane(), 475, 425);
  }
} ///:~
```

The button just adds randomly generated text. The intent of the
JTextPane is to allow text to be edited in place, so you will see that there
is no **append( )** method. In this case (admittedly, a poor use of the
capabilities of **JTextPane**), the text must be captured, modified, and
placed back into the pane using **setText( )**.

As mentioned before, the default layout behavior of an applet is to use the
BorderLayout. If you add something to the pane without specifying any
details, it just fills the center of the pane out to the edges. However, if you
specify one of the surrounding regions (NORTH, SOUTH, EAST, or
WEST) as is done here, the component will fit itself into that region—in
this case, the button will nest down at the bottom of the screen.

Notice the built-in features of **JTextPane**, such as automatic line
wrapping. There are lots of other features that you can look up using the
JDK documentation.

Check boxes

A check box provides a way to make a single on/off choice; it consists of a
tiny box and a label. The box typically holds a little "x" (or some other
indication that it is set) or is empty, depending on whether that item was
selected.

You'll normally create a **JCheckBox** using a constructor that takes the
label as an argument. You can get and set the state, and also get and set
the label if you want to read or change it after the **JCheckBox** has been
created.

Whenever a **JCheckBox** is set or cleared, an event occurs, which you can
capture the same way you do a button, by using an **ActionListener**. The
following example uses a **JTextArea** to enumerate all the check boxes
that have been checked:

```
//: c13:CheckBoxes.java
// Using JCheckBoxes.
// <applet code=CheckBoxes width=200 height=200>
```

```
// </applet>
import javax.swing.*;
import java.awt.event.*;
import java.awt.*;
import com.bruceeckel.swing.*;

public class CheckBoxes extends JApplet {
  JTextArea t = new JTextArea(6, 15);
  JCheckBox
    cb1 = new JCheckBox("Check Box 1"),
    cb2 = new JCheckBox("Check Box 2"),
    cb3 = new JCheckBox("Check Box 3");
  public void init() {
    cb1.addActionListener(new ActionListener() {
      public void actionPerformed(ActionEvent e){
        trace("1", cb1);
      }
    });
    cb2.addActionListener(new ActionListener() {
      public void actionPerformed(ActionEvent e){
        trace("2", cb2);
      }
    });
    cb3.addActionListener(new ActionListener() {
      public void actionPerformed(ActionEvent e){
        trace("3", cb3);
      }
    });
    Container cp = getContentPane();
    cp.setLayout(new FlowLayout());
    cp.add(new JScrollPane(t));
    cp.add(cb1);
    cp.add(cb2);
    cp.add(cb3);
  }
  void trace(String b, JCheckBox cb) {
    if(cb.isSelected())
      t.append("Box " + b + " Set\n");
    else
      t.append("Box " + b + " Cleared\n");
  }
```

```
  public static void main(String[] args) {
    Console.run(new CheckBoxes(), 200, 200);
  }
} ///:~
```

The **trace( )** method sends the name of the selected **JCheckBox** and its current state to the **JTextArea** using **append( )**, so you'll see a cumulative list of the checkboxes that were selected and what their state is.

Radio buttons

The concept of a radio button in GUI programming comes from pre-electronic car radios with mechanical buttons: when you push one in, any other button that was pressed pops out. Thus, it allows you to force a single choice among many.

All you need to do to set up an associated group of **JRadioButton**s is to add them to a **ButtonGroup** (you can have any number of **ButtonGroup**s on a form). One of the buttons can optionally have its starting state set to **true** (using the second argument in the constructor). If you try to set more than one radio button to **true** then only the final one set will be **true**.

Here's a simple example of the use of radio buttons. Note that you capture radio button events like all others:

```
//: c13:RadioButtons.java
// Using JRadioButtons.
// <applet code=RadioButtons
// width=200 height=100> </applet>
import javax.swing.*;
import java.awt.event.*;
import java.awt.*;
import com.bruceeckel.swing.*;

public class RadioButtons extends JApplet {
  JTextField t = new JTextField(15);
  ButtonGroup g = new ButtonGroup();
  JRadioButton
    rb1 = new JRadioButton("one", false),
```

```
      rb2 = new JRadioButton("two", false),
      rb3 = new JRadioButton("three", false);
   ActionListener al = new ActionListener() {
      public void actionPerformed(ActionEvent e) {
        t.setText("Radio button " +
          ((JRadioButton)e.getSource()).getText());
      }
   };
   public void init() {
      rb1.addActionListener(al);
      rb2.addActionListener(al);
      rb3.addActionListener(al);
      g.add(rb1); g.add(rb2); g.add(rb3);
      t.setEditable(false);
      Container cp = getContentPane();
      cp.setLayout(new FlowLayout());
      cp.add(t);
      cp.add(rb1);
      cp.add(rb2);
      cp.add(rb3);
   }
   public static void main(String[] args) {
      Console.run(new RadioButtons(), 200, 100);
   }
} ///:~
```

To display the state, a text field is used. This field is set to noneditable because it's used only to display data, not to collect it. Thus it is an alternative to using a **JLabel**.

Combo boxes (drop-down lists)

Like a group of radio buttons, a drop-down list is a way to force the user to select only one element from a group of possibilities. However, it's a more compact way to accomplish this, and it's easier to change the elements of the list without surprising the user. (You can change radio buttons dynamically, but that tends to be visibly jarring).

Java's **JComboBox** box is not like the combo box in Windows, which lets you select from a list *or* type in your own selection. With a **JComboBox** box you choose one and only one element from the list. In the following

---

example, the **JComboBox** box starts with a certain number of entries
and then new entries are added to the box when a button is pressed.

```
//: c13:ComboBoxes.java
// Using drop-down lists.
// <applet code=ComboBoxes
// width=200 height=100> </applet>
import javax.swing.*;
import java.awt.event.*;
import java.awt.*;
import com.bruceeckel.swing.*;

public class ComboBoxes extends JApplet {
  String[] description = { "Ebullient", "Obtuse",
    "Recalcitrant", "Brilliant", "Somnescent",
    "Timorous", "Florid", "Putrescent" };
  JTextField t = new JTextField(15);
  JComboBox c = new JComboBox();
  JButton b = new JButton("Add items");
  int count = 0;
  public void init() {
    for(int i = 0; i < 4; i++)
      c.addItem(description[count++]);
    t.setEditable(false);
    b.addActionListener(new ActionListener() {
      public void actionPerformed(ActionEvent e){
        if(count < description.length)
          c.addItem(description[count++]);
      }
    });
    c.addActionListener(new ActionListener() {
      public void actionPerformed(ActionEvent e){
        t.setText("index: "+ c.getSelectedIndex()
          + "    " + ((JComboBox)e.getSource())
          .getSelectedItem());
      }
    });
    Container cp = getContentPane();
    cp.setLayout(new FlowLayout());
    cp.add(t);
    cp.add(c);
```

```
    cp.add(b);
  }
  public static void main(String[] args) {
    Console.run(new ComboBoxes(), 200, 100);
  }
} ///:~
```

The **JTextField** displays the "selected index," which is the sequence
number of the currently selected element, as well as the label on the radio
button.

List boxes

List boxes are significantly different from **JComboBox** boxes, and not
just in appearance. While a **JComboBox** box drops down when you
activate it, a **JList** occupies some fixed number of lines on a screen all the
time and doesn't change. If you want to see the items in a list, you simply
call **getSelectedValues( )**, which produces an array of **String** of the
items that have been selected.

A **JList** allows multiple selection: if you control-click on more than one
item (holding down the "control" key while performing additional mouse
clicks) the original item stays highlighted and you can select as many as
you want. If you select an item, then shift-click on another item, all the
items in the span between the two are selected. To remove an item from a
group you can control-click it.

```
//: c13:List.java
// <applet code=List width=250
// height=375> </applet>
import javax.swing.*;
import javax.swing.event.*;
import java.awt.*;
import java.awt.event.*;
import javax.swing.border.*;
import com.bruceeckel.swing.*;

public class List extends JApplet {
  String[] flavors = { "Chocolate", "Strawberry",
    "Vanilla Fudge Swirl", "Mint Chip",
    "Mocha Almond Fudge", "Rum Raisin",
```

```
      "Praline Cream", "Mud Pie" };
  DefaultListModel lItems=new DefaultListModel();
  JList lst = new JList(lItems);
  JTextArea t = new JTextArea(flavors.length,20);
  JButton b = new JButton("Add Item");
  ActionListener bl = new ActionListener() {
    public void actionPerformed(ActionEvent e) {
      if(count < flavors.length) {
        lItems.add(0, flavors[count++]);
      } else {
        // Disable, since there are no more
        // flavors left to be added to the List
        b.setEnabled(false);
      }
    }
  };
  ListSelectionListener ll =
    new ListSelectionListener() {
      public void valueChanged(
        ListSelectionEvent e) {
          t.setText("");
          Object[] items=lst.getSelectedValues();
          for(int i = 0; i < items.length; i++)
            t.append(items[i] + "\n");
      }
    };
  int count = 0;
  public void init() {
    Container cp = getContentPane();
    t.setEditable(false);
    cp.setLayout(new FlowLayout());
    // Create Borders for components:
    Border brd = BorderFactory.createMatteBorder(
      1, 1, 2, 2, Color.black);
    lst.setBorder(brd);
    t.setBorder(brd);
    // Add the first four items to the List
    for(int i = 0; i < 4; i++)
      lItems.addElement(flavors[count++]);
    // Add items to the Content Pane for Display
    cp.add(t);
```

```
      cp.add(lst);
      cp.add(b);
      // Register event listeners
      lst.addListSelectionListener(ll);
      b.addActionListener(bl);
  }
  public static void main(String[] args) {
    Console.run(new List(), 250, 375);
  }
} ///:~
```

When you press the button it adds items to the *top* of the list (because
addItem( )'s second argument is 0).

You can see that borders have also been added to the lists.

If you just want to put an array of **String**s into a **JList**, there's a much
simpler solution: you pass the array to the **JList** constructor, and it builds
the list automatically. The only reason for using the "list model" in the
above example is so that the list could be manipulated during the
execution of the program.

JLists do not automatically provide direct support for scrolling. Of
course, all you need to do is wrap the **JList** in a **JScrollPane** and all the
details are automatically managed for you.

Tabbed panes

The **JTabbedPane** allows you to create a "tabbed dialog," which has file-
folder tabs running across one edge, and all you have to do is press a tab
to bring forward a different dialog.

```
//: c13:TabbedPane1.java
// Demonstrates the Tabbed Pane.
// <applet code=TabbedPane1
// width=350 height=200> </applet>
import javax.swing.*;
import javax.swing.event.*;
import java.awt.*;
import com.bruceeckel.swing.*;

public class TabbedPane1 extends JApplet {
```

```
    String[] flavors = { "Chocolate", "Strawberry",
      "Vanilla Fudge Swirl", "Mint Chip",
      "Mocha Almond Fudge", "Rum Raisin",
      "Praline Cream", "Mud Pie" };
    JTabbedPane tabs = new JTabbedPane();
    JTextField txt = new JTextField(20);
    public void init() {
      for(int i = 0; i < flavors.length; i++)
        tabs.addTab(flavors[i],
          new JButton("Tabbed pane " + i));
      tabs.addChangeListener(new ChangeListener() {
        public void stateChanged(ChangeEvent e) {
          txt.setText("Tab selected: " +
            tabs.getSelectedIndex());
        }
      });
      Container cp = getContentPane();
      cp.add(BorderLayout.SOUTH, txt);
      cp.add(tabs);
    }
    public static void main(String[] args) {
      Console.run(new TabbedPane1(), 350, 200);
    }
} ///:~
```

In Java, the use of some sort of "tabbed panel" mechanism is quite
important because in applet programming the use of pop-up dialogs is
discouraged by automatically adding a little warning to any dialog that
pops up out of an applet.

When you run the program you'll see that the **JTabbedPane**
automatically stacks the tabs if there are too many of them to fit on one
row. You can see this by resizing the window when you run the program
from the console command line.

Message boxes

Windowing environments commonly contain a standard set of message
boxes that allow you to quickly post information to the user or to capture
information from the user. In Swing, these message boxes are contained
in **JOptionPane**. You have many different possibilities (some quite

sophisticated), but the ones you'll most commonly use are probably the message dialog and confirmation dialog, invoked using the **static JOptionPane.showMessageDialog( )** and **JOptionPane. showConfirmDialog( )**. The following example shows a subset of the message boxes available with **JOptionPane**:

```
//: c13:MessageBoxes.java
// Demonstrates JoptionPane.
// <applet code=MessageBoxes
// width=200 height=150> </applet>
import javax.swing.*;
import java.awt.event.*;
import java.awt.*;
import com.bruceeckel.swing.*;

public class MessageBoxes extends JApplet {
  JButton[] b = { new JButton("Alert"),
    new JButton("Yes/No"), new JButton("Color"),
    new JButton("Input"), new JButton("3 Vals")
  };
  JTextField txt = new JTextField(15);
  ActionListener al = new ActionListener() {
    public void actionPerformed(ActionEvent e){
      String id =
        ((JButton)e.getSource()).getText();
      if(id.equals("Alert"))
        JOptionPane.showMessageDialog(null,
          "There's a bug on you!", "Hey!",
          JOptionPane.ERROR_MESSAGE);
      else if(id.equals("Yes/No"))
        JOptionPane.showConfirmDialog(null,
          "or no", "choose yes",
          JOptionPane.YES_NO_OPTION);
      else if(id.equals("Color")) {
        Object[] options = { "Red", "Green" };
        int sel = JOptionPane.showOptionDialog(
          null, "Choose a Color!", "Warning",
          JOptionPane.DEFAULT_OPTION,
          JOptionPane.WARNING_MESSAGE, null,
          options, options[0]);
        if(sel != JOptionPane.CLOSED_OPTION)
```

```
        txt.setText(
          "Color Selected: " + options[sel]);
    } else if(id.equals("Input")) {
      String val = JOptionPane.showInputDialog(
        "How many fingers do you see?");
      txt.setText(val);
    } else if(id.equals("3 Vals")) {
      Object[] selections = {
        "First", "Second", "Third" };
      Object val = JOptionPane.showInputDialog(
        null, "Choose one", "Input",
        JOptionPane.INFORMATION_MESSAGE,
        null, selections, selections[0]);
      if(val != null)
        txt.setText(
          val.toString());
    }
  }
};
public void init() {
  Container cp = getContentPane();
  cp.setLayout(new FlowLayout());
  for(int i = 0; i < b.length; i++) {
    b[i].addActionListener(al);
    cp.add(b[i]);
  }
  cp.add(txt);
}
public static void main(String[] args) {
  Console.run(new MessageBoxes(), 200, 200);
}
} ///:~
```

To be able to write a single **ActionListener**, I've used the somewhat risky approach of checking the **String** labels on the buttons. The problem with this is that it's easy to get the label a little bit wrong, typically in capitalization, and this bug can be hard to spot.

Note that **showOptionDialog( )** and **showInputDialog( )** provide return objects that contain the value entered by the user.

Menus

Each component capable of holding a menu, including **JApplet**, **JFrame**, **JDialog**, and their descendants, has a **setJMenuBar( )** method that accepts a **JMenuBar** (you can have only one **JMenuBar** on a particular component). You add **JMenu**s to the **JMenuBar**, and **JMenuItem**s to the **JMenu**s. Each **JMenuItem** can have an **ActionListener** attached to it, to be fired when that menu item is selected.

Unlike a system that uses resources, with Java and Swing you must hand assemble all the menus in source code. Here is a very simple menu example:

```
//: c13:SimpleMenus.java
// <applet code=SimpleMenus
// width=200 height=75> </applet>
import javax.swing.*;
import java.awt.event.*;
import java.awt.*;
import com.bruceeckel.swing.*;

public class SimpleMenus extends JApplet {
  JTextField t = new JTextField(15);
  ActionListener al = new ActionListener() {
    public void actionPerformed(ActionEvent e){
      t.setText(
        ((JMenuItem)e.getSource()).getText());
    }
  };
  JMenu[] menus = { new JMenu("Winken"),
    new JMenu("Blinken"), new JMenu("Nod") };
  JMenuItem[] items = {
    new JMenuItem("Fee"), new JMenuItem("Fi"),
    new JMenuItem("Fo"),  new JMenuItem("Zip"),
    new JMenuItem("Zap"), new JMenuItem("Zot"),
    new JMenuItem("Olly"), new JMenuItem("Oxen"),
    new JMenuItem("Free") };
  public void init() {
    for(int i = 0; i < items.length; i++) {
      items[i].addActionListener(al);
```

```
        menus[i%3].add(items[i]);
    }
    JMenuBar mb = new JMenuBar();
    for(int i = 0; i < menus.length; i++)
      mb.add(menus[i]);
    setJMenuBar(mb);
    Container cp = getContentPane();
    cp.setLayout(new FlowLayout());
    cp.add(t);
  }
  public static void main(String[] args) {
    Console.run(new SimpleMenus(), 200, 75);
  }
} ///:~
```

The use of the modulus operator in "**i%3**" distributes the menu items among the three **JMenu**s. Each **JMenuItem** must have an **ActionListener** attached to it; here, the same **ActionListener** is used everywhere but you'll usually need an individual one for each **JMenuItem**.

JMenuItem inherits **AbstractButton**, so it has some buttonlike behaviors. By itself, it provides an item that can be placed on a drop-down menu. There are also three types inherited from **JMenuItem**: **JMenu** to hold other **JMenuItem**s (so you can have cascading menus), **JCheckBoxMenuItem**, which produces a checkmark to indicate whether that menu item is selected, and **JRadioButtonMenuItem**, which contains a radio button.

As a more sophisticated example, here are the ice cream flavors again, used to create menus. This example also shows cascading menus, keyboard mnemonics, **JCheckBoxMenuItem**s, and the way you can dynamically change menus:

```
//: c13:Menus.java
// Submenus, checkbox menu items, swapping menus,
// mnemonics (shortcuts) and action commands.
// <applet code=Menus width=300
// height=100> </applet>
import javax.swing.*;
import java.awt.*;
```

```
import java.awt.event.*;
import com.bruceeckel.swing.*;

public class Menus extends JApplet {
  String[] flavors = { "Chocolate", "Strawberry",
    "Vanilla Fudge Swirl", "Mint Chip",
    "Mocha Almond Fudge", "Rum Raisin",
    "Praline Cream", "Mud Pie" };
  JTextField t = new JTextField("No flavor", 30);
  JMenuBar mb1 = new JMenuBar();
  JMenu
    f = new JMenu("File"),
    m = new JMenu("Flavors"),
    s = new JMenu("Safety");
  // Alternative approach:
  JCheckBoxMenuItem[] safety = {
    new JCheckBoxMenuItem("Guard"),
    new JCheckBoxMenuItem("Hide")
  };
  JMenuItem[] file = {
    new JMenuItem("Open"),
  };
  // A second menu bar to swap to:
  JMenuBar mb2 = new JMenuBar();
  JMenu fooBar = new JMenu("fooBar");
  JMenuItem[] other = {
    // Adding a menu shortcut (mnemonic) is very
    // simple, but only JMenuItems can have them
    // in their constructors:
    new JMenuItem("Foo", KeyEvent.VK_F),
    new JMenuItem("Bar", KeyEvent.VK_A),
    // No shortcut:
    new JMenuItem("Baz"),
  };
  JButton b = new JButton("Swap Menus");
  class BL implements ActionListener {
    public void actionPerformed(ActionEvent e) {
      JMenuBar m = getJMenuBar();
      setJMenuBar(m == mb1 ? mb2 : mb1);
      validate(); // Refresh the frame
    }
```

```java
  }
class ML implements ActionListener {
  public void actionPerformed(ActionEvent e) {
    JMenuItem target = (JMenuItem)e.getSource();
    String actionCommand =
      target.getActionCommand();
    if(actionCommand.equals("Open")) {
      String s = t.getText();
      boolean chosen = false;
      for(int i = 0; i < flavors.length; i++)
        if(s.equals(flavors[i])) chosen = true;
      if(!chosen)
        t.setText("Choose a flavor first!");
      else
        t.setText("Opening "+ s +". Mmm, mm!");
    }
  }
}
class FL implements ActionListener {
  public void actionPerformed(ActionEvent e) {
    JMenuItem target = (JMenuItem)e.getSource();
    t.setText(target.getText());
  }
}
// Alternatively, you can create a different
// class for each different MenuItem. Then you
// Don't have to figure out which one it is:
class FooL implements ActionListener {
  public void actionPerformed(ActionEvent e) {
    t.setText("Foo selected");
  }
}
class BarL implements ActionListener {
  public void actionPerformed(ActionEvent e) {
    t.setText("Bar selected");
  }
}
class BazL implements ActionListener {
  public void actionPerformed(ActionEvent e) {
    t.setText("Baz selected");
  }
```

```
    }
class CMIL implements ItemListener {
  public void itemStateChanged(ItemEvent e) {
    JCheckBoxMenuItem target =
      (JCheckBoxMenuItem)e.getSource();
    String actionCommand =
      target.getActionCommand();
    if(actionCommand.equals("Guard"))
      t.setText("Guard the Ice Cream! " +
        "Guarding is " + target.getState());
    else if(actionCommand.equals("Hide"))
      t.setText("Hide the Ice Cream! " +
        "Is it cold? " + target.getState());
  }
}
public void init() {
  ML ml = new ML();
  CMIL cmil = new CMIL();
  safety[0].setActionCommand("Guard");
  safety[0].setMnemonic(KeyEvent.VK_G);
  safety[0].addItemListener(cmil);
  safety[1].setActionCommand("Hide");
  safety[0].setMnemonic(KeyEvent.VK_H);
  safety[1].addItemListener(cmil);
  other[0].addActionListener(new FooL());
  other[1].addActionListener(new BarL());
  other[2].addActionListener(new BazL());
  FL fl = new FL();
  for(int i = 0; i < flavors.length; i++) {
    JMenuItem mi = new JMenuItem(flavors[i]);
    mi.addActionListener(fl);
    m.add(mi);
    // Add separators at intervals:
    if((i+1) % 3 == 0)
      m.addSeparator();
  }
  for(int i = 0; i < safety.length; i++)
    s.add(safety[i]);
  s.setMnemonic(KeyEvent.VK_A);
  f.add(s);
  f.setMnemonic(KeyEvent.VK_F);
```

```
      for(int i = 0; i < file.length; i++) {
        file[i].addActionListener(fl);
        f.add(file[i]);
      }
    mb1.add(f);
    mb1.add(m);
    setJMenuBar(mb1);
    t.setEditable(false);
    Container cp = getContentPane();
    cp.add(t, BorderLayout.CENTER);
    // Set up the system for swapping menus:
    b.addActionListener(new BL());
    b.setMnemonic(KeyEvent.VK_S);
    cp.add(b, BorderLayout.NORTH);
    for(int i = 0; i < other.length; i++)
      fooBar.add(other[i]);
    fooBar.setMnemonic(KeyEvent.VK_B);
    mb2.add(fooBar);
  }
  public static void main(String[] args) {
    Console.run(new Menus(), 300, 100);
  }
} ///:~
```

In this program I placed the menu items into arrays and then stepped through each array calling **add( )** for each **JMenuItem**. This makes adding or subtracting a menu item somewhat less tedious.

This program creates not one but two **JMenuBar**s to demonstrate that menu bars can be actively swapped while the program is running. You can see how a **JMenuBar** is made up of **JMenus**, and each **JMenu** is made up of **JMenuItems**, **JCheckBoxMenuItem**s, or even other **JMenu**s (which produce submenus). When a **JMenuBar** is assembled it can be installed into the current program with the **setJMenuBar( )** method. Note that when the button is pressed, it checks to see which menu is currently installed by calling **getJMenuBar( )**, then it puts the other menu bar in its place.

When testing for "Open," notice that spelling and capitalization are critical, but Java signals no error if there is no match with "Open." This kind of string comparison is a source of programming errors.

The checking and unchecking of the menu items is taken care of automatically. The code handling the **JCheckBoxMenuItem**s shows two different ways to determine what was checked: string matching (which, as mentioned above, isn't a very safe approach although you'll see it used) and matching on the event target object. As shown, the **getState( )** method can be used to reveal the state. You can also change the state of a **JCheckBoxMenuItem** with **setState( )**.

The events for menus are a bit inconsistent and can lead to confusion: **JMenuItem**s use **ActionListener**s, but **JCheckboxMenuItem**s use **ItemListener**s. The **JMenu** objects can also support **ActionListener**s, but that's not usually helpful. In general, you'll attach listeners to each **JMenuItem**, **JCheckBoxMenuItem**, or **JRadioButtonMenuItem**, but the example shows **ItemListener**s and **ActionListener**s attached to the various menu components.

Swing supports mnemonics, or "keyboard shortcuts," so you can select anything derived from **AbstractButton** (button, menu item, etc.) using the keyboard instead of the mouse. These are quite simple: for **JMenuItem** you can use the overloaded constructor that takes as a second argument the identifier for the key. However, most **AbstractButton**s do not have constructors like this so the more general way to solve the problem is to use the **setMnemonic( )** method. The example above adds mnemonics to the button and some of the menu items; shortcut indicators automatically appear on the components.

You can also see the use of **setActionCommand( )**. This seems a bit strange because in each case the "action command" is exactly the same as the label on the menu component. Why not just use the label instead of this alternative string? The problem is internationalization. If you retarget this program to another language, you want to change only the label in the menu, and not change the code (which would no doubt introduce new errors). So to make this easy for code that checks the text string associated with a menu component, the "action command" can be immutable while the menu label can change. All the code works with the "action command," so it's unaffected by changes to the menu labels. Note that in this program, not all the menu components are examined for their action commands, so those that aren't don't have their action command set.

The bulk of the work happens in the listeners. **BL** performs the **JMenuBar** swapping. In **ML**, the "figure out who rang" approach is taken by getting the source of the **ActionEvent** and casting it to a **JMenuItem**, then getting the action command string to pass it through a cascaded **if** statement.

The **FL** listener is simple even though it's handling all the different flavors in the flavor menu. This approach is useful if you have enough simplicity in your logic, but in general, you'll want to take the approach used with **FooL**, **BarL**, and **BazL**, in which they are each attached to only a single menu component so no extra detection logic is necessary and you know exactly who called the listener. Even with the profusion of classes generated this way, the code inside tends to be smaller and the process is more foolproof.

You can see that menu code quickly gets long-winded and messy. This is another case where the use of a GUI builder is the appropriate solution. A good tool will also handle the maintenance of the menus.

Pop-up menus

The most straightforward way to implement a **JPopupMenu** is to create an inner class that extends **MouseAdapter**, then add an object of that inner class to each component that you want to produce pop-up behavior:

```
//: c13:Popup.java
// Creating popup menus with Swing.
// <applet code=Popup
//  width=300 height=200></applet>
import javax.swing.*;
import java.awt.*;
import java.awt.event.*;
import com.bruceeckel.swing.*;

public class Popup extends JApplet {
  JPopupMenu popup = new JPopupMenu();
  JTextField t = new JTextField(10);
  public void init() {
    Container cp = getContentPane();
    cp.setLayout(new FlowLayout());
    cp.add(t);
```

```java
    ActionListener al = new ActionListener() {
      public void actionPerformed(ActionEvent e){
        t.setText(
          ((JMenuItem)e.getSource()).getText());
      }
    };
    JMenuItem m = new JMenuItem("Hither");
    m.addActionListener(al);
    popup.add(m);
    m = new JMenuItem("Yon");
    m.addActionListener(al);
    popup.add(m);
    m = new JMenuItem("Afar");
    m.addActionListener(al);
    popup.add(m);
    popup.addSeparator();
    m = new JMenuItem("Stay Here");
    m.addActionListener(al);
    popup.add(m);
    PopupListener pl = new PopupListener();
    addMouseListener(pl);
    t.addMouseListener(pl);
  }
  class PopupListener extends MouseAdapter {
    public void mousePressed(MouseEvent e) {
      maybeShowPopup(e);
    }
    public void mouseReleased(MouseEvent e) {
      maybeShowPopup(e);
    }
    private void maybeShowPopup(MouseEvent e) {
      if(e.isPopupTrigger()) {
        popup.show(
          e.getComponent(), e.getX(), e.getY());
      }
    }
  }
  public static void main(String[] args) {
    Console.run(new Popup(), 300, 200);
  }
} ///:~
```

The same **ActionListener** is added to each **JMenuItem**, so that it fetches the text from the menu label and inserts it into the **JTextField**.

Drawing

In a good GUI framework, drawing should be reasonably easy—and it is, in the Swing library. The problem with any drawing example is that the calculations that determine where things go are typically a lot more complicated that the calls to the drawing routines, and these calculations are often mixed together with the drawing calls so it can seem that the interface is more complicated than it actually is.

For simplicity, consider the problem of representing data on the screen—here, the data will be provided by the built-in **Math.sin( )** method which is a mathematical sine function. To make things a little more interesting, and to further demonstrate how easy it is to use Swing components, a slider will be placed at the bottom of the form to dynamically control the number of sine wave cycles that are displayed. In addition, if you resize the window, you'll see that the sine wave refits itself to the new window size.

Although any **JComponent** may be painted and thus used as a canvas, if you just want a straightforward drawing surface you will typically inherit from a **JPanel**. The only method you need to override is **paintComponent( )**, which is called whenever that component must be repainted (you normally don't need to worry about this, as the decision is managed by Swing). When it is called, Swing passes a **Graphics** object to the method, and you can then use this object to draw or paint on the surface.

In the following example, all the intelligence concerning painting is in the **SineDraw** class; the **SineWave** class simply configures the program and the slider control. Inside **SineDraw**, the **setCycles( )** method provides a hook to allow another object—the slider control, in this case—to control the number of cycles.

```
//: c13:SineWave.java
// Drawing with Swing, using a JSlider.
// <applet code=SineWave
//  width=700 height=400></applet>
```

```java
import javax.swing.*;
import javax.swing.event.*;
import java.awt.*;
import com.bruceeckel.swing.*;

class SineDraw extends JPanel {
  static final int SCALEFACTOR = 200;
  int cycles;
  int points;
  double[] sines;
  int[] pts;
  SineDraw() { setCycles(5); }
  public void setCycles(int newCycles) {
    cycles = newCycles;
    points = SCALEFACTOR * cycles * 2;
    sines = new double[points];
    pts = new int[points];
    for(int i = 0; i < points; i++) {
      double radians = (Math.PI/SCALEFACTOR) * i;
      sines[i] = Math.sin(radians);
    }
    repaint();
  }
  public void paintComponent(Graphics g) {
    super.paintComponent(g);
    int maxWidth = getWidth();
    double hstep = (double)maxWidth/(double)points;
    int maxHeight = getHeight();
    for(int i = 0; i < points; i++)
      pts[i] = (int)(sines[i] * maxHeight/2 * .95
                     + maxHeight/2);
    g.setColor(Color.red);
    for(int i = 1; i < points; i++) {
      int x1 = (int)((i - 1) * hstep);
      int x2 = (int)(i * hstep);
      int y1 = pts[i-1];
      int y2 = pts[i];
      g.drawLine(x1, y1, x2, y2);
    }
  }
}
```

```
public class SineWave extends JApplet {
  SineDraw sines = new SineDraw();
  JSlider cycles = new JSlider(1, 30, 5);
  public void init() {
    Container cp = getContentPane();
    cp.add(sines);
    cycles.addChangeListener(new ChangeListener(){
      public void stateChanged(ChangeEvent e) {
        sines.setCycles(
          ((JSlider)e.getSource()).getValue());
      }
    });
    cp.add(BorderLayout.SOUTH, cycles);
  }
  public static void main(String[] args) {
    Console.run(new SineWave(), 700, 400);
  }
} ///:~
```

All of the data members and arrays are used in the calculation of the sine wave points: **cycles** indicates the number of complete sine waves desired, **points** contains the total number of points that will be graphed, **sines** contains the sine function values, and **pts** contains the y-coordinates of the points that will be drawn on the **JPanel**. The **setCycles( )** method creates the arrays according to the number of points needed and fills the **sines** array with numbers. By calling **repaint( )** , **setCycles( )** forces **paintComponent( )** to be called so the rest of the calculation and redraw will take place.

The first thing you must do when you override **paintComponent( )** is to call the base-class version of the method. Then you are free to do whatever you like; normally, this means using the **Graphics** methods that you can find in the documentation for **java.awt.Graphics** (in the HTML documentation from *java.sun.com*) to draw and paint pixels onto the **JPanel**. Here, you can see that almost all the code is involved in performing the calculations; the only two method calls that actually manipulate the screen are **setColor( )** and **drawLine( )**. You will probably have a similar experience when creating your own program that displays graphical data—you'll spend most of your time figuring out what it is you want to draw, but the actual drawing process will be quite simple.

When I created this program, the bulk of my time was spent in getting the sine wave to display. Once I did that, I thought it would be nice to be able to dynamically change the number of cycles. My programming experiences when trying to do such things in other languages made me a bit reluctant to try this, but it turned out to be the easiest part of the project. I created a **JSlider** (the arguments are the left-most value of the **JSlider**, the right-most value, and the starting value, respectively, but there are other constructors as well) and dropped it into the **JApplet**. Then I looked at the HTML documentation and noticed that the only listener was the **addChangeListener**, which was triggered whenever the slider was changed enough for it to produce a different value. The only method for this was the obviously named **stateChanged( )**, which provided a **ChangeEvent** object so that I could look backward to the source of the change and find the new value. By calling the **sines** object's **setCycles( )**, the new value was incorporated and the **JPanel** redrawn.

In general, you will find that most of your Swing problems can be solved by following a similar process, and you'll find that it's generally quite simple, even if you haven't used a particular component before.

If your problem is more complex, there are other more sophisticated alternatives for drawing, including third-party JavaBeans components and the Java 2D API. These solutions are beyond the scope of this book, but you should look them up if your drawing code becomes too onerous.

Dialog Boxes

A dialog box is a window that pops up out of another window. Its purpose is to deal with some specific issue without cluttering the original window with those details. Dialog boxes are heavily used in windowed programming environments, but less frequently used in applets.

To create a dialog box, you inherit from **JDialog**, which is just another kind of **Window**, like a **JFrame**. A **JDialog** has a layout manager (which defaults to **BorderLayout**) and you add event listeners to deal with events. One significant difference when **windowClosing( )** is called is that you don't want to shut down the application. Instead, you release the resources used by the dialog's window by calling **dispose( )**. Here's a very simple example:

```
//: c13:Dialogs.java
// Creating and using Dialog Boxes.
// <applet code=Dialogs width=125 height=75>
// </applet>
import javax.swing.*;
import java.awt.event.*;
import java.awt.*;
import com.bruceeckel.swing.*;

class MyDialog extends JDialog {
  public MyDialog(JFrame parent) {
    super(parent, "My dialog", true);
    Container cp = getContentPane();
    cp.setLayout(new FlowLayout());
    cp.add(new JLabel("Here is my dialog"));
    JButton ok = new JButton("OK");
    ok.addActionListener(new ActionListener() {
      public void actionPerformed(ActionEvent e){
        dispose(); // Closes the dialog
      }
    });
    cp.add(ok);
    setSize(150,125);
  }
}

public class Dialogs extends JApplet {
  JButton b1 = new JButton("Dialog Box");
  MyDialog dlg = new MyDialog(null);
  public void init() {
    b1.addActionListener(new ActionListener() {
      public void actionPerformed(ActionEvent e){
        dlg.show();
      }
    });
    getContentPane().add(b1);
  }
  public static void main(String[] args) {
```

```
    Console.run(new Dialogs(), 125, 75);
  }
} ///:~
```

Once the **JDialog** is created, the **show( )** method must be called to display and activate it. For the dialog to close, it must call **dispose( )**.

You'll see that anything that pops up out of an applet, including dialog boxes, is "untrusted." That is, you get a warning in the window that's been popped up. This is because, in theory, it would be possible to fool the user into thinking that they're dealing with a regular native application and to get them to type in their credit card number, which then goes across the Web. An applet is always attached to a Web page and visible within your Web browser, while a dialog box is detached—so in theory, it could be possible. As a result it is not so common to see an applet that uses a dialog box.

The following example is more complex; the dialog box is made up of a grid (using **GridLayout**) of a special kind of button that is defined here as class **ToeButton**. This button draws a frame around itself and, depending on its state, a blank, an "x," or an "o" in the middle. It starts out blank, and then depending on whose turn it is, changes to an "x" or an "o." However, it will also flip back and forth between "x" and "o" when you click on the button. (This makes the tic-tac-toe concept only slightly more annoying than it already is.) In addition, the dialog box can be set up for any number of rows and columns by changing numbers in the main application window.

```
//: c13:TicTacToe.java
// Demonstration of dialog boxes
// and creating your own components.
// <applet code=TicTacToe
//  width=200 height=100></applet>
import javax.swing.*;
import java.awt.*;
import java.awt.event.*;
import com.bruceeckel.swing.*;

public class TicTacToe extends JApplet {
  JTextField
    rows = new JTextField("3"),
```

```
    cols = new JTextField("3");
  static final int BLANK = 0, XX = 1, OO = 2;
  class ToeDialog extends JDialog {
    int turn = XX; // Start with x's turn
    // w = number of cells wide
    // h = number of cells high
    public ToeDialog(int w, int h) {
      setTitle("The game itself");
      Container cp = getContentPane();
      cp.setLayout(new GridLayout(w, h));
      for(int i = 0; i < w * h; i++)
        cp.add(new ToeButton());
      setSize(w * 50, h * 50);
      // JDK 1.3 close dialog:
      //#setDefaultCloseOperation(
      //#  DISPOSE_ON_CLOSE);
      // JDK 1.2 close dialog:
      addWindowListener(new WindowAdapter() {
        public void windowClosing(WindowEvent e){
          dispose();
        }
      });
    }
    class ToeButton extends JPanel {
      int state = BLANK;
      public ToeButton() {
        addMouseListener(new ML());
      }
      public void paintComponent(Graphics g) {
        super.paintComponent(g);
        int x1 = 0;
        int y1 = 0;
        int x2 = getSize().width - 1;
        int y2 = getSize().height - 1;
        g.drawRect(x1, y1, x2, y2);
        x1 = x2/4;
        y1 = y2/4;
        int wide = x2/2;
        int high = y2/2;
        if(state == XX) {
          g.drawLine(x1, y1,
```

```
                  x1 + wide, y1 + high);
              g.drawLine(x1, y1 + high,
                x1 + wide, y1);
          }
          if(state == OO) {
            g.drawOval(x1, y1,
              x1 + wide/2, y1 + high/2);
          }
        }
      }
      class ML extends MouseAdapter {
        public void mousePressed(MouseEvent e) {
          if(state == BLANK) {
            state = turn;
            turn = (turn == XX ? OO : XX);
          }
          else
            state = (state == XX ? OO : XX);
          repaint();
        }
      }
    }
  }
  class BL implements ActionListener {
    public void actionPerformed(ActionEvent e) {
      JDialog d = new ToeDialog(
        Integer.parseInt(rows.getText()),
        Integer.parseInt(cols.getText()));
      d.setVisible(true);
    }
  }
  public void init() {
    JPanel p = new JPanel();
    p.setLayout(new GridLayout(2,2));
    p.add(new JLabel("Rows", JLabel.CENTER));
    p.add(rows);
    p.add(new JLabel("Columns", JLabel.CENTER));
    p.add(cols);
    Container cp = getContentPane();
    cp.add(p, BorderLayout.NORTH);
    JButton b = new JButton("go");
    b.addActionListener(new BL());
```

```
      cp.add(b, BorderLayout.SOUTH);
    }
  public static void main(String[] args) {
    Console.run(new TicTacToe(), 200, 100);
  }
} ///:~
```

Because **static**s can only be at the outer level of the class, inner classes cannot have **static** data or **static** inner classes.

The **paintComponent( )** method draws the square around the panel, and the "x" or the "o." This is full of tedious calculations, but it's straightforward.

A mouse click is captured by the **MouseListener**, which first checks to see if the panel has anything written on it. If not, the parent window is queried to find out whose turn it is and that is used to establish the state of the **ToeButton**. Via the inner class mechanism, the **ToeButton** then reaches back into the parent and changes the turn. If the button is already displaying an "x" or an "o" then that is flopped. You can see in these calculations the convenient use of the ternary if-else described in Chapter 3. After a state change, the **ToeButton** is repainted.

The constructor for **ToeDialog** is quite simple: it adds into a **GridLayout** as many buttons as you request, then resizes it for 50 pixels on a side for each button.

TicTacToe sets up the whole application by creating the **JTextField**s (for inputting the rows and columns of the button grid) and the "go" button with its **ActionListener**. When the button is pressed, the data in the **JTextField**s must be fetched, and, since they are in **String** form, turned into **int**s using the **static Integer.parseInt( )** method.

File dialogs

Some operating systems have a number of special built-in dialog boxes to handle the selection of things such as fonts, colors, printers, and the like. Virtually all graphical operating systems support the opening and saving of files, however, and so Java's **JFileChooser** encapsulates these for easy use.

The following application exercises two forms of **JFileChooser** dialogs, one for opening and one for saving. Most of the code should by now be familiar, and all the interesting activities happen in the action listeners for the two different button clicks:

```
//: c13:FileChooserTest.java
// Demonstration of File dialog boxes.
import javax.swing.*;
import java.awt.*;
import java.awt.event.*;
import com.bruceeckel.swing.*;

public class FileChooserTest extends JFrame {
  JTextField
    filename = new JTextField(),
    dir = new JTextField();
  JButton
    open = new JButton("Open"),
    save = new JButton("Save");
  public FileChooserTest() {
    JPanel p = new JPanel();
    open.addActionListener(new OpenL());
    p.add(open);
    save.addActionListener(new SaveL());
    p.add(save);
    Container cp = getContentPane();
    cp.add(p, BorderLayout.SOUTH);
    dir.setEditable(false);
    filename.setEditable(false);
    p = new JPanel();
    p.setLayout(new GridLayout(2,1));
    p.add(filename);
    p.add(dir);
    cp.add(p, BorderLayout.NORTH);
  }
  class OpenL implements ActionListener {
    public void actionPerformed(ActionEvent e) {
      JFileChooser c = new JFileChooser();
      // Demonstrate "Open" dialog:
      int rVal =
        c.showOpenDialog(FileChooserTest.this);
```

```
      if(rVal == JFileChooser.APPROVE_OPTION) {
        filename.setText(
          c.getSelectedFile().getName());
          dir.setText(
            c.getCurrentDirectory().toString());
      }
      if(rVal == JFileChooser.CANCEL_OPTION) {
        filename.setText("You pressed cancel");
        dir.setText("");
      }
    }
  }
  class SaveL implements ActionListener {
    public void actionPerformed(ActionEvent e) {
      JFileChooser c = new JFileChooser();
      // Demonstrate "Save" dialog:
      int rVal =
        c.showSaveDialog(FileChooserTest.this);
      if(rVal == JFileChooser.APPROVE_OPTION) {
        filename.setText(
          c.getSelectedFile().getName());
          dir.setText(
            c.getCurrentDirectory().toString());
      }
      if(rVal == JFileChooser.CANCEL_OPTION) {
        filename.setText("You pressed cancel");
        dir.setText("");
      }
    }
  }
  public static void main(String[] args) {
    Console.run(new FileChooserTest(), 250, 110);
  }
} ///:~
```

Note that there are many variations you can apply to **JFileChooser**,
including filters to narrow the file names that you will allow.

For an "open file" dialog, you call **showOpenDialog( )**, and for a "save
file" dialog you call **showSaveDialog( )**. These commands don't return
until the dialog is closed. The **JFileChooser** object still exists, so you can

read data from it. The methods **getSelectedFile( )** and **getCurrentDirectory( )** are two ways you can interrogate the results of the operation. If these return **null** it means the user canceled out of the dialog.

HTML on Swing components

Any component that can take text can also take HTML text, which it will reformat according to HTML rules. This means you can very easily add fancy text to a Swing component. For example,

```
//: c13:HTMLButton.java
// Putting HTML text on Swing components.
// <applet code=HTMLButton width=200 height=500>
// </applet>
import javax.swing.*;
import java.awt.event.*;
import java.awt.*;
import com.bruceeckel.swing.*;

public class HTMLButton extends JApplet {
  JButton b = new JButton("<html><b><font size=+2>" +
    "<center>Hello!<br><i>Press me now!");
  public void init() {
    b.addActionListener(new ActionListener() {
      public void actionPerformed(ActionEvent e){
        getContentPane().add(new JLabel("<html>"+
          "<i><font size=+4>Kapow!"));
        // Force a re-layout to
        // include the new label:
        validate();
      }
    });
    Container cp = getContentPane();
    cp.setLayout(new FlowLayout());
    cp.add(b);
  }
  public static void main(String[] args) {
    Console.run(new HTMLButton(), 200, 500);
  }
} ///:~
```

You must start the text with "<html>," and then you can use normal HTML tags. Note that you are not forced to include the normal closing tags.

The **ActionListener** adds a new **JLabel** to the form, which also contains HTML text. However, this label is not added during **init( )** so you must call the container's **validate( )** method in order to force a re-layout of the components (and thus the display of the new label).

You can also use HTML text for **JTabbedPane**, **JMenuItem**, **JToolTip**, **JRadioButton** and **JCheckBox**.

Sliders and progress bars

A slider (which has already been used in the sine wave example) allows the user to input data by moving a point back and forth, which is intuitive in some situations (volume controls, for example). A progress bar displays data in a relative fashion from "full" to "empty" so the user gets a perspective. My favorite example for these is to simply hook the slider to the progress bar so when you move the slider the progress bar changes accordingly:

```
//: c13:Progress.java
// Using progress bars and sliders.
// <applet code=Progress
//   width=300 height=200></applet>
import javax.swing.*;
import java.awt.*;
import java.awt.event.*;
import javax.swing.event.*;
import javax.swing.border.*;
import com.bruceeckel.swing.*;

public class Progress extends JApplet {
  JProgressBar pb = new JProgressBar();
  JSlider sb =
    new JSlider(JSlider.HORIZONTAL, 0, 100, 60);
  public void init() {
    Container cp = getContentPane();
    cp.setLayout(new GridLayout(2,1));
    cp.add(pb);
```

```
      sb.setValue(0);
      sb.setPaintTicks(true);
      sb.setMajorTickSpacing(20);
      sb.setMinorTickSpacing(5);
      sb.setBorder(new TitledBorder("Slide Me"));
      pb.setModel(sb.getModel()); // Share model
      cp.add(sb);
    }
  public static void main(String[] args) {
    Console.run(new Progress(), 300, 200);
    }
} ///:~
```

The key to hooking the two components together is in sharing their model, in the line:

```
pb.setModel(sb.getModel());
```

Of course, you could also control the two using a listener, but this is more straightforward for simple situations.

The **JProgressBar** is fairly straightforward, but the **JSlider** has a lot of options, such as the orientation and major and minor tick marks. Notice how straightforward it is to add a titled border.

Trees

Using a **JTree** can be as simple as saying:

```
add(new JTree(
  new Object[] {"this", "that", "other"}));
```

This displays a primitive tree. The API for trees is vast, however—certainly one of the largest in Swing. It appears that you can do just about anything with trees, but more sophisticated tasks might require quite a bit of research and experimentation.

Fortunately, there is a middle ground provided in the library: the "default" tree components, which generally do what you need. So most of the time you can use these components, and only in special cases will you need to delve in and understand trees more deeply.

The following example uses the "default" tree components to display a tree in an applet. When you press the button, a new subtree is added under the currently selected node (if no node is selected, the root node is used):

```
//: c13:Trees.java
// Simple Swing tree example. Trees can
// be made vastly more complex than this.
// <applet code=Trees
//   width=250 height=250></applet>
import javax.swing.*;
import java.awt.*;
import java.awt.event.*;
import javax.swing.tree.*;
import com.bruceeckel.swing.*;

// Takes an array of Strings and makes the first
// element a node and the rest leaves:
class Branch {
  DefaultMutableTreeNode r;
  public Branch(String[] data) {
    r = new DefaultMutableTreeNode(data[0]);
    for(int i = 1; i < data.length; i++)
      r.add(new DefaultMutableTreeNode(data[i]));
  }
  public DefaultMutableTreeNode node() {
    return r;
  }
}

public class Trees extends JApplet {
  String[][] data = {
    { "Colors", "Red", "Blue", "Green" },
    { "Flavors", "Tart", "Sweet", "Bland" },
    { "Length", "Short", "Medium", "Long" },
    { "Volume", "High", "Medium", "Low" },
    { "Temperature", "High", "Medium", "Low" },
    { "Intensity", "High", "Medium", "Low" },
  };
  static int i = 0;
  DefaultMutableTreeNode root, child, chosen;
```

```
  JTree tree;
  DefaultTreeModel model;
  public void init() {
    Container cp = getContentPane();
    root = new DefaultMutableTreeNode("root");
    tree = new JTree(root);
    // Add it and make it take care of scrolling:
    cp.add(new JScrollPane(tree),
      BorderLayout.CENTER);
    // Capture the tree's model:
    model =(DefaultTreeModel)tree.getModel();
    JButton test = new JButton("Press me");
    test.addActionListener(new ActionListener() {
      public void actionPerformed(ActionEvent e){
        if(i < data.length) {
          child = new Branch(data[i++]).node();
          // What's the last one you clicked?
          chosen = (DefaultMutableTreeNode)
            tree.getLastSelectedPathComponent();
          if(chosen == null) chosen = root;
          // The model will create the
          // appropriate event. In response, the
          // tree will update itself:
          model.insertNodeInto(child, chosen, 0);
          // This puts the new node on the
          // currently chosen node.
        }
      }
    });
    // Change the button's colors:
    test.setBackground(Color.blue);
    test.setForeground(Color.white);
    JPanel p = new JPanel();
    p.add(test);
    cp.add(p, BorderLayout.SOUTH);
  }
  public static void main(String[] args) {
    Console.run(new Trees(), 250, 250);
  }
} ///:~
```

The first class, **Branch**, is a tool to take an array of **String** and build a **DefaultMutableTreeNode** with the first **String** as the root and the rest of the **String**s in the array as leaves. Then **node( )** can be called to produce the root of this "branch."

The **Trees** class contains a two-dimensional array of **String**s from which **Branch**es can be made and a **static int i** to count through this array. The **DefaultMutableTreeNode** objects hold the nodes, but the physical representation on screen is controlled by the **JTree** and its associated model, the **DefaultTreeModel**. Note that when the **JTree** is added to the applet, it is wrapped in a **JScrollPane**—this is all it takes to provide automatic scrolling.

The **JTree** is controlled through its *model*. When you make a change to the model, the model generates an event that causes the **JTree** to perform any necessary updates to the visible representation of the tree. In **init( )**, the model is captured by calling **getModel( )**. When the button is pressed, a new "branch" is created. Then the currently selected component is found (or the root is used if nothing is selected) and the model's **insertNodeInto( )** method does all the work of changing the tree and causing it to be updated.

An example like the one above may give you what you need in a tree. However, trees have the power to do just about anything you can imagine—everywhere you see the word "default" in the example above, you can substitute your own class to get different behavior. But beware: almost all of these classes have a large interface, so you could spend a lot of time struggling to understand the intricacies of trees. Despite this, it's a good design and the alternatives are usually much worse.

Tables

Like trees, tables in Swing are vast and powerful. They are primarily intended to be the popular "grid" interface to databases via Java Database Connectivity (JDBC, discussed in Chapter 15) and thus they have a tremendous amount of flexibility, which you pay for in complexity. There's easily enough here to be the basis of a full-blown spreadsheet and could probably justify an entire book. However, it is also possible to create a relatively simple **JTable** if you understand the basics.

The **JTable** controls how the data is displayed, but the **TableModel** controls the data itself. So to create a **JTable** you'll typically create a **TableModel** first. You can fully implement the **TableModel** interface, but it's usually simpler to inherit from the helper class **AbstractTableModel**:

```
//: c13:Table.java
// Simple demonstration of JTable.
// <applet code=Table
//   width=350 height=200></applet>
import javax.swing.*;
import java.awt.*;
import java.awt.event.*;
import javax.swing.table.*;
import javax.swing.event.*;
import com.bruceeckel.swing.*;

public class Table extends JApplet {
  JTextArea txt = new JTextArea(4, 20);
  // The TableModel controls all the data:
  class DataModel extends AbstractTableModel {
    Object[][] data = {
      {"one", "two", "three", "four"},
      {"five", "six", "seven", "eight"},
      {"nine", "ten", "eleven", "twelve"},
    };
    // Prints data when table changes:
    class TML implements TableModelListener {
      public void tableChanged(TableModelEvent e){
        txt.setText(""); // Clear it
        for(int i = 0; i < data.length; i++) {
          for(int j = 0; j < data[0].length; j++)
            txt.append(data[i][j] + " ");
          txt.append("\n");
        }
      }
    }
    public DataModel() {
      addTableModelListener(new TML());
    }
    public int getColumnCount() {
```

```
        return data[0].length;
      }
      public int getRowCount() {
        return data.length;
      }
      public Object getValueAt(int row, int col) {
        return data[row][col];
      }
      public void
      setValueAt(Object val, int row, int col) {
        data[row][col] = val;
        // Indicate the change has happened:
        fireTableDataChanged();
      }
      public boolean
      isCellEditable(int row, int col) {
        return true;
      }
    }
  public void init() {
    Container cp = getContentPane();
    JTable table = new JTable(new DataModel());
    cp.add(new JScrollPane(table));
    cp.add(BorderLayout.SOUTH, txt);
  }
  public static void main(String[] args) {
    Console.run(new Table(), 350, 200);
  }
} ///:~
```

DataModel contains an array of data, but you could also get the data
from some other source such as a database. The constructor adds a
TableModelListener that prints the array every time the table is
changed. The rest of the methods follow the Beans naming convention,
and are used by **JTable** when it wants to present the information in
DataModel. **AbstractTableModel** provides default methods for
setValueAt( ) and **isCellEditable( )** that prevent changes to the data,
so if you want to be able to edit the data, you must override these
methods.

Once you have a **TableModel**, you only need to hand it to the **JTable** constructor. All the details of displaying, editing, and updating will be taken care of for you. This example also puts the **JTable** in a **JScrollPane**.

Selecting Look & Feel

One of the very interesting aspects of Swing is the "Pluggable Look & Feel." This allows your program to emulate the look and feel of various operating environments. You can even do all sorts of fancy things like dynamically changing the look and feel while the program is executing. However, you generally just want to do one of two things, either select the "cross platform" look and feel (which is Swing's "metal"), or select the look and feel for the system you are currently on, so your Java program looks like it was created specifically for that system. The code to select either of these behaviors is quite simple—but you must execute it *before* you create any visual components, because the components will be made based on the current look and feel and will not be changed just because you happen to change the look and feel midway during the program (that process is more complicated and uncommon, and is relegated to Swing-specific books).

Actually, if you want to use the cross-platform ("metal") look and feel that is characteristic of Swing programs, you don't have to do anything—it's the default. But if you want instead to use the current operating environment's look and feel, you just insert the following code, typically at the beginning of your **main( )** but somehow before any components are added:

```
try {
  UIManager.setLookAndFeel(UIManager.
    getSystemLookAndFeelClassName());
} catch(Exception e) {}
```

You don't need anything in the **catch** clause because the **UIManager** will default to the cross-platform look and feel if your attempts to set up any of the alternatives fail. However, during debugging the exception can be quite useful so you may at least want to put a print statement in the catch clause.

Here is a program that takes a command-line argument to select a look and feel, and shows how several different components look under the chosen look and feel:

```
//: c13:LookAndFeel.java
// Selecting different looks & feels.
import javax.swing.*;
import java.awt.*;
import java.awt.event.*;
import java.util.*;
import com.bruceeckel.swing.*;

public class LookAndFeel extends JFrame {
  String[] choices = {
    "eeny", "meeny", "minie", "moe", "toe", "you"
  };
  Component[] samples = {
    new JButton("JButton"),
    new JTextField("JTextField"),
    new JLabel("JLabel"),
    new JCheckBox("JCheckBox"),
    new JRadioButton("Radio"),
    new JComboBox(choices),
    new JList(choices),
  };
  public LookAndFeel() {
    super("Look And Feel");
    Container cp = getContentPane();
    cp.setLayout(new FlowLayout());
    for(int i = 0; i < samples.length; i++)
      cp.add(samples[i]);
  }
  private static void usageError() {
    System.out.println(
      "Usage:LookAndFeel [cross|system|motif]");
    System.exit(1);
  }
  public static void main(String[] args) {
    if(args.length == 0) usageError();
    if(args[0].equals("cross")) {
      try {
```

```
        UIManager.setLookAndFeel(UIManager.
          getCrossPlatformLookAndFeelClassName());
      } catch(Exception e) {
          e.printStackTrace(System.err);
      }
    } else if(args[0].equals("system")) {
      try {
        UIManager.setLookAndFeel(UIManager.
          getSystemLookAndFeelClassName());
      } catch(Exception e) {
          e.printStackTrace(System.err);
      }
    } else if(args[0].equals("motif")) {
      try {
        UIManager.setLookAndFeel("com.sun.java."+
          "swing.plaf.motif.MotifLookAndFeel");
      } catch(Exception e) {
          e.printStackTrace(System.err);
      }
    } else usageError();
    // Note the look & feel must be set before
    // any components are created.
    Console.run(new LookAndFeel(), 300, 200);
  }
} ///:~
```

You can see that one option is to explicitly specify a string for a look and feel, as seen with **MotifLookAndFeel**. However, that one and the default "metal" look and feel are the only ones that can legally be used on any platform; even though there are strings for Windows and Macintosh look and feels, those can only be used on their respective platforms (these are produced when you call **getSystemLookAndFeelClassName( )** and you're on that particular platform).

It is also possible to create a custom look and feel package, for example, if you are building a framework for a company that wants a distinctive appearance. This is a big job and is far beyond the scope of this book (in fact, you'll discover it is beyond the scope of many dedicated Swing books!).

The clipboard

The JFC supports limited operations with the system clipboard (in the **java.awt.datatransfer** package). You can copy **String** objects to the clipboard as text, and you can paste text from the clipboard into **String** objects. Of course, the clipboard is designed to hold any type of data, but how this data is represented on the clipboard is up to the program doing the cutting and pasting. The Java clipboard API provides for extensibility through the concept of a "flavor." When data comes off the clipboard, it has an associated set of flavors that it can be converted to (for example, a graph might be represented as a string of numbers or as an image) and you can see if that particular clipboard data supports the flavor you're interested in.

The following program is a simple demonstration of cut, copy, and paste with **String** data in a **JTextArea**. One thing you'll notice is that the keyboard sequences you normally use for cutting, copying, and pasting also work. But if you look at any **JTextField** or **JTextArea** in any other program you'll find that they also automatically support the clipboard key sequences. This example simply adds programmatic control of the clipboard, and you could use these techniques if you want to capture clipboard text into something other than a **JTextComponent**.

```
//: c13:CutAndPaste.java
// Using the clipboard.
import javax.swing.*;
import java.awt.*;
import java.awt.event.*;
import java.awt.datatransfer.*;
import com.bruceeckel.swing.*;

public class CutAndPaste extends JFrame  {
  JMenuBar mb = new JMenuBar();
  JMenu edit = new JMenu("Edit");
  JMenuItem
    cut = new JMenuItem("Cut"),
    copy = new JMenuItem("Copy"),
    paste = new JMenuItem("Paste");
  JTextArea text = new JTextArea(20, 20);
  Clipboard clipbd =
```

```
        getToolkit().getSystemClipboard();
    public CutAndPaste()  {
      cut.addActionListener(new CutL());
      copy.addActionListener(new CopyL());
      paste.addActionListener(new PasteL());
      edit.add(cut);
      edit.add(copy);
      edit.add(paste);
      mb.add(edit);
      setJMenuBar(mb);
      getContentPane().add(text);
    }
    class CopyL implements ActionListener {
      public void actionPerformed(ActionEvent e) {
        String selection = text.getSelectedText();
        if (selection == null)
          return;
        StringSelection clipString =
          new StringSelection(selection);
        clipbd.setContents(clipString,clipString);
      }
    }
    class CutL implements ActionListener {
      public void actionPerformed(ActionEvent e) {
        String selection = text.getSelectedText();
        if (selection == null)
          return;
        StringSelection clipString =
          new StringSelection(selection);
        clipbd.setContents(clipString, clipString);
        text.replaceRange("",
          text.getSelectionStart(),
          text.getSelectionEnd());
      }
    }
    class PasteL implements ActionListener {
      public void actionPerformed(ActionEvent e) {
        Transferable clipData =
          clipbd.getContents(CutAndPaste.this);
        try {
          String clipString =
```

```
          (String)clipData.
            getTransferData(
              DataFlavor.stringFlavor);
        text.replaceRange(clipString,
          text.getSelectionStart(),
          text.getSelectionEnd());
      } catch(Exception ex) {
        System.err.println("Not String flavor");
      }
    }
  }
  public static void main(String[] args) {
    Console.run(new CutAndPaste(), 300, 200);
  }
} ///:~
```

The creation and addition of the menu and **JTextArea** should by now seem a pedestrian activity. What's different is the creation of the **Clipboard** field **clipbd**, which is done through the **Toolkit**.

All the action takes place in the listeners. The **CopyL** and **CutL** listeners are the same except for the last line of **CutL**, which erases the line that's been copied. The special two lines are the creation of a **StringSelection** object from the **String** and the call to **setContents( )** with this **StringSelection**. That's all there is to putting a **String** on the clipboard.

In **PasteL,** data is pulled off the clipboard using **getContents( )**. What comes back is a fairly anonymous **Transferable** object, and you don't really know what it contains. One way to find out is to call **getTransferDataFlavors( )**, which returns an array of **DataFlavor** objects indicating which flavors are supported by this particular object. You can also ask it directly with **isDataFlavorSupported( )**, passing in the flavor you're interested in. Here, however, the bold approach is taken: **getTransferData( )** is called assuming that the contents supports the **String** flavor, and if it doesn't the problem is sorted out in the exception handler.

In the future you can expect more data flavors to be supported.

Packaging an applet into a JAR file

An important use of the JAR utility is to optimize applet loading. In Java 1.0, people tended to try to cram all their code into a single applet class so the client would need only a single server hit to download the applet code. Not only did this result in messy, hard to read (and maintain) programs, but the **.class** file was still uncompressed so downloading wasn't as fast as it could have been.

JAR files solve the problem by compressing all of your **.class** files into a single file that is downloaded by the browser. Now you can create the right design without worrying about how many **.class** files it will generate, and the user will get a much faster download time.

Consider **TicTacToe.java**. It looks like a single class, but in fact it contains five inner classes, so that's six in all. Once you've compiled the program, you package it into a JAR file with the line:

```
jar cf TicTacToe.jar *.class
```

This assumes that the only **.class** files in the current directory are the ones from **TicTacToe.java** (otherwise you'll get extra baggage).

Now you can create an HTML page with the new **archive** tag to indicate the name of the JAR file. Here is the tag using the old form of the HTML tag, as an illustration:

```
<head><title>TicTacToe Example Applet
</title></head>
<body>
<applet code=TicTacToe.class
        archive=TicTacToe.jar
        width=200 height=100>
</applet>
</body>
```

You'll need to put it into the new (messy, complicated) form shown earlier in the chapter in order to get it to work.

Programming techniques

Because GUI programming in Java has been an evolving technology with some very significant changes between Java 1.0/1.1 and the Swing library in Java 2, there have been some old programming idioms that have seeped through to examples that you might see given for Swing. In addition, Swing allows you to program in more and better ways than were allowed by the old models. In this section, some of these issues will be demonstrated by introducing and examining some programming idioms.

Binding events dynamically

One of the benefits of the Swing event model is flexibility. You can add and remove event behavior with single method calls. The following example demonstrates this:

```
//: c13:DynamicEvents.java
// You can change event behavior dynamically.
// Also shows multiple actions for an event.
// <applet code=DynamicEvents
//   width=250 height=400></applet>
import javax.swing.*;
import java.awt.*;
import java.awt.event.*;
import java.util.*;
import com.bruceeckel.swing.*;

public class DynamicEvents extends JApplet {
  ArrayList v = new ArrayList();
  int i = 0;
  JButton
    b1 = new JButton("Button1"),
    b2 = new JButton("Button2");
  JTextArea txt = new JTextArea();
  class B implements ActionListener {
    public void actionPerformed(ActionEvent e) {
      txt.append("A button was pressed\n");
    }
  }
  class CountListener implements ActionListener {
```

```
      int index;
      public CountListener(int i) { index = i; }
      public void actionPerformed(ActionEvent e) {
        txt.append("Counted Listener "+index+"\n");
      }
    }
    class B1 implements ActionListener {
      public void actionPerformed(ActionEvent e) {
        txt.append("Button 1 pressed\n");
        ActionListener a = new CountListener(i++);
        v.add(a);
        b2.addActionListener(a);
      }
    }
    class B2 implements ActionListener {
      public void actionPerformed(ActionEvent e) {
        txt.append("Button2 pressed\n");
        int end = v.size() - 1;
        if(end >= 0) {
          b2.removeActionListener(
            (ActionListener)v.get(end));
          v.remove(end);
        }
      }
    }
    public void init() {
      Container cp = getContentPane();
      b1.addActionListener(new B());
      b1.addActionListener(new B1());
      b2.addActionListener(new B());
      b2.addActionListener(new B2());
      JPanel p = new JPanel();
      p.add(b1);
      p.add(b2);
      cp.add(BorderLayout.NORTH, p);
      cp.add(new JScrollPane(txt));
    }
    public static void main(String[] args) {
      Console.run(new DynamicEvents(), 250, 400);
    }
  } ///:~
```

The new twists in this example are:

1. There is more than one listener attached to each **Button**. Usually, components handle events as *multicast*, meaning that you can register many listeners for a single event. In the special components in which an event is handled as *unicast*, you'll get a **TooManyListenersException**.

2. During the execution of the program, listeners are dynamically added and removed from the **Button b2**. Adding is accomplished in the way you've seen before, but each component also has a **removeXXXListener( )** method to remove each type of listener.

This kind of flexibility provides much greater power in your programming.

You should notice that event listeners are not guaranteed to be called in the order they are added (although most implementations do in fact work that way).

Separating business logic from UI logic

In general you'll want to design your classes so that each one does "only one thing." This is particularly important when user-interface code is concerned, since it's easy to tie up "what you're doing" with "how you're displaying it." This kind of coupling prevents code reuse. It's much more desirable to separate your "business logic" from the GUI. This way, you can not only reuse the business logic more easily, it's also easier to reuse the GUI.

Another issue is *multitiered* systems, where the "business objects" reside on a completely separate machine. This central location of the business rules allows changes to be instantly effective for all new transactions, and is thus a compelling way to set up a system. However, these business objects can be used in many different applications and so should not be tied to any particular mode of display. They should just perform the business operations and nothing more.

The following example shows how easy it is to separate the business logic from the GUI code:

```
//: c13:Separation.java
// Separating GUI logic and business objects.
// <applet code=Separation
// width=250 height=150> </applet>
import javax.swing.*;
import java.awt.*;
import javax.swing.event.*;
import java.awt.event.*;
import java.applet.*;
import com.bruceeckel.swing.*;

class BusinessLogic {
  private int modifier;
  public BusinessLogic(int mod) {
    modifier = mod;
  }
  public void setModifier(int mod) {
    modifier = mod;
  }
  public int getModifier() {
    return modifier;
  }
  // Some business operations:
  public int calculation1(int arg) {
    return arg * modifier;
  }
  public int calculation2(int arg) {
    return arg + modifier;
  }
}

public class Separation extends JApplet {
  JTextField
    t = new JTextField(15),
    mod = new JTextField(15);
  BusinessLogic bl = new BusinessLogic(2);
  JButton
    calc1 = new JButton("Calculation 1"),
```

```java
      calc2 = new JButton("Calculation 2");
    static int getValue(JTextField tf) {
      try {
        return Integer.parseInt(tf.getText());
      } catch(NumberFormatException e) {
        return 0;
      }
    }
    class Calc1L implements ActionListener {
      public void actionPerformed(ActionEvent e) {
        t.setText(Integer.toString(
          bl.calculation1(getValue(t))));
      }
    }
    class Calc2L implements ActionListener {
      public void actionPerformed(ActionEvent e) {
        t.setText(Integer.toString(
          bl.calculation2(getValue(t))));
      }
    }
    // If you want something to happen whenever
    // a JTextField changes, add this listener:
    class ModL implements DocumentListener {
      public void changedUpdate(DocumentEvent e) {}
      public void insertUpdate(DocumentEvent e) {
        bl.setModifier(getValue(mod));
      }
      public void removeUpdate(DocumentEvent e) {
        bl.setModifier(getValue(mod));
      }
    }
    public void init() {
      Container cp = getContentPane();
      cp.setLayout(new FlowLayout());
      cp.add(t);
      calc1.addActionListener(new Calc1L());
      calc2.addActionListener(new Calc2L());
      JPanel p1 = new JPanel();
      p1.add(calc1);
      p1.add(calc2);
      cp.add(p1);
```

```
      mod.getDocument().
        addDocumentListener(new ModL());
      JPanel p2 = new JPanel();
      p2.add(new JLabel("Modifier:"));
      p2.add(mod);
      cp.add(p2);
    }
    public static void main(String[] args) {
      Console.run(new Separation(), 250, 100);
    }
  } ///:~
```

You can see that **BusinessLogic** is a straightforward class that performs its operations without even a hint that it might be used in a GUI environment. It just does its job.

Separation keeps track of all the UI details, and it talks to **BusinessLogic** only through its **public** interface. All the operations are centered around getting information back and forth through the UI and the **BusinessLogic** object. So **Separation**, in turn, just does its job. Since **Separation** knows only that it's talking to a **BusinessLogic** object (that is, it isn't highly coupled), it could be massaged into talking to other types of objects without much trouble.

Thinking in terms of separating UI from business logic also makes life easier when you're adapting legacy code to work with Java.

A canonical form

Inner classes, the Swing event model, and the fact that the old event model is still supported along with new library features that rely on old-style programming has added a new element of confusion to the code design process. Now there are even more different ways for people to write unpleasant code.

Except in extenuating circumstances you can always use the simplest and clearest approach: listener classes (typically written as inner classes) to solve your event-handling needs. This is the form used in most of the examples in this chapter.

By following this model you should be able to reduce the statements in your programs that say: "I wonder what caused this event." Each piece of code is concerned with *doing*, not type-checking. This is the best way to write your code; not only is it easier to conceptualize, but much easier to read and maintain.

Visual programming and Beans

So far in this book you've seen how valuable Java is for creating reusable pieces of code. The "most reusable" unit of code has been the class, since it comprises a cohesive unit of characteristics (fields) and behaviors (methods) that can be reused either directly via composition or through inheritance.

Inheritance and polymorphism are essential parts of object-oriented programming, but in the majority of cases when you're putting together an application, what you really want is components that do exactly what you need. You'd like to drop these parts into your design like the electronic engineer puts together chips on a circuit board. It seems, too, that there should be some way to accelerate this "modular assembly" style of programming.

"Visual programming" first became successful—*very* successful—with Microsoft's Visual Basic (VB), followed by a second-generation design in Borland's Delphi (the primary inspiration for the JavaBeans design). With these programming tools the components are represented visually, which makes sense since they usually display some kind of visual component such as a button or a text field. The visual representation, in fact, is often exactly the way the component will look in the running program. So part of the process of visual programming involves dragging a component from a palette and dropping it onto your form. The application builder tool writes code as you do this, and that code will cause the component to be created in the running program.

Simply dropping the component onto a form is usually not enough to complete the program. Often, you must change the characteristics of a component, such as what color it is, what text is on it, what database it's connected to, etc. Characteristics that can be modified at design time are referred to as *properties*. You can manipulate the properties of your component inside the application builder tool, and when you create the program this configuration data is saved so that it can be rejuvenated when the program is started.

By now you're probably used to the idea that an object is more than characteristics; it's also a set of behaviors. At design-time, the behaviors of a visual component are partially represented by *events*, meaning "Here's something that can happen to the component." Ordinarily, you decide what you want to happen when an event occurs by tying code to that event.

Here's the critical part: the application builder tool uses reflection to dynamically interrogate the component and find out which properties and events the component supports. Once it knows what they are, it can display the properties and allow you to change those (saving the state when you build the program), and also display the events. In general, you do something like double-clicking on an event and the application builder tool creates a code body and ties it to that particular event. All you have to do at that point is write the code that executes when the event occurs.

All this adds up to a lot of work that's done for you by the application builder tool. As a result you can focus on what the program looks like and what it is supposed to do, and rely on the application builder tool to manage the connection details for you. The reason that visual programming tools have been so successful is that they dramatically speed up the process of building an application—certainly the user interface, but often other portions of the application as well.

What is a Bean?

After the dust settles, then, a component is really just a block of code, typically embodied in a class. The key issue is the ability for the application builder tool to discover the properties and events for that component. To create a VB component, the programmer had to write a fairly complicated piece of code following certain conventions to expose the properties and events. Delphi was a second-generation visual programming tool and the language was actively designed around visual

---

programming so it is much easier to create a visual component. However, Java has brought the creation of visual components to its most advanced state with JavaBeans, because a Bean is just a class. You don't have to write any extra code or use special language extensions in order to make something a Bean. The only thing you need to do, in fact, is slightly modify the way that you name your methods. It is the method name that tells the application builder tool whether this is a property, an event, or just an ordinary method.

In the Java documentation, this naming convention is mistakenly termed a "design pattern." This is unfortunate, since design patterns (see *Thinking in Patterns with Java*, downloadable at *www.BruceEckel.com*) are challenging enough without this sort of confusion. It's not a design pattern, it's just a naming convention and it's fairly simple:

1. For a property named **xxx**, you typically create two methods: **getXxx( )** and **setXxx( )**. Note that the first letter after "get" or "set" is automatically lowercased to produce the property name. The type produced by the "get" method is the same as the type of the argument to the "set" method. The name of the property and the type for the "get" and "set" are not related.

2. For a **boolean** property, you can use the "get" and "set" approach above, but you can also use "is" instead of "get."

3. Ordinary methods of the Bean don't conform to the above naming convention, but they're **public**.

4. For events, you use the Swing "listener" approach. It's exactly the same as you've been seeing: **addFooBarListener(FooBarListener)** and **removeFooBarListener(FooBarListener)** to handle a **FooBarEvent**. Most of the time the built-in events and listeners will satisfy your needs, but you can also create your own events and listener interfaces.

Point 1 above answers a question about something you might have noticed when looking at older code vs. newer code: a number of method names have had small, apparently meaningless name changes. Now you can see that most of those changes had to do with adapting to the "get" and "set" naming conventions in order to make that particular component into a Bean.

We can use these guidelines to create a simple Bean:

```
//: frogbean:Frog.java
// A trivial JavaBean.
package frogbean;
import java.awt.*;
import java.awt.event.*;

class Spots {}

public class Frog {
  private int jumps;
  private Color color;
  private Spots spots;
  private boolean jmpr;
  public int getJumps() { return jumps; }
  public void setJumps(int newJumps) {
    jumps = newJumps;
  }
  public Color getColor() { return color; }
  public void setColor(Color newColor) {
    color = newColor;
  }
  public Spots getSpots() { return spots; }
  public void setSpots(Spots newSpots) {
    spots = newSpots;
  }
  public boolean isJumper() { return jmpr; }
  public void setJumper(boolean j) { jmpr = j; }
  public void addActionListener(
      ActionListener l) {
    //...
  }
  public void removeActionListener(
      ActionListener l) {
    // ...
  }
  public void addKeyListener(KeyListener l) {
```

```
    // ...
  }
  public void removeKeyListener(KeyListener l) {
    // ...
  }
  // An "ordinary" public method:
  public void croak() {
    System.out.println("Ribbet!");
  }
} ///:~
```

First, you can see that it's just a class. Usually, all your fields will be **private**, and accessible only through methods. Following the naming convention, the properties are **jumps**, **color**, **spots**, and **jumper** (notice the case change of the first letter in the property name). Although the name of the internal identifier is the same as the name of the property in the first three cases, in **jumper** you can see that the property name does not force you to use any particular identifier for internal variables (or, indeed, to even *have* any internal variables for that property).

The events this Bean handles are **ActionEvent** and **KeyEvent**, based on the naming of the "add" and "remove" methods for the associated listener. Finally, you can see that the ordinary method **croak( )** is still part of the Bean simply because it's a **public** method, not because it conforms to any naming scheme.

Extracting **BeanInfo** with the **Introspector**

One of the most critical parts of the Bean scheme occurs when you drag a Bean off a palette and plop it onto a form. The application builder tool must be able to create the Bean (which it can do if there's a default constructor) and then, without access to the Bean's source code, extract all the necessary information to create the property sheet and event handlers.

Part of the solution is already evident from the end of Chapter 12: Java *reflection* allows all the methods of an anonymous class to be discovered. This is perfect for solving the Bean problem without requiring you to use any extra language keywords like those required in other visual programming languages. In fact, one of the prime reasons that reflection was added to Java was to support Beans (although reflection also supports object serialization and remote method invocation). So you might expect that the creator of the application builder tool would have to reflect each Bean and hunt through its methods to find the properties and events for that Bean.

This is certainly possible, but the Java designers wanted to provide a standard tool, not only to make Beans simpler to use but also to provide a standard gateway to the creation of more complex Beans. This tool is the **Introspector** class, and the most important method in this class is the **static getBeanInfo( )**. You pass a **Class** reference to this method and it fully interrogates that class and returns a **BeanInfo** object that you can then dissect to find properties, methods, and events.

Usually you won't care about any of this—you'll probably get most of your Beans off the shelf from vendors, and you don't need to know all the magic that's going on underneath. You'll simply drag your Beans onto your form, then configure their properties and write handlers for the events you're interested in. However, it's an interesting and educational exercise to use the **Introspector** to display information about a Bean, so here's a tool that does it:

```
//: c13:BeanDumper.java
// Introspecting a Bean.
// <applet code=BeanDumper width=600 height=500>
// </applet>
import java.beans.*;
import java.lang.reflect.*;
import javax.swing.*;
import java.awt.*;
import java.awt.event.*;
import com.bruceeckel.swing.*;

public class BeanDumper extends JApplet {
  JTextField query =
    new JTextField(20);
  JTextArea results = new JTextArea();
  public void prt(String s) {
    results.append(s + "\n");
```

```
    }
    public void dump(Class bean){
      results.setText("");
      BeanInfo bi = null;
      try {
        bi = Introspector.getBeanInfo(
          bean, java.lang.Object.class);
      } catch(IntrospectionException e) {
        prt("Couldn't introspect " +
          bean.getName());
        return;
      }
      PropertyDescriptor[] properties =
        bi.getPropertyDescriptors();
      for(int i = 0; i < properties.length; i++) {
        Class p = properties[i].getPropertyType();
        prt("Property type:\n  " + p.getName() +
          "Property name:\n  " +
          properties[i].getName());
        Method readMethod =
          properties[i].getReadMethod();
        if(readMethod != null)
          prt("Read method:\n  " + readMethod);
        Method writeMethod =
          properties[i].getWriteMethod();
        if(writeMethod != null)
          prt("Write method:\n  " + writeMethod);
        prt("====================");
      }
      prt("Public methods:");
      MethodDescriptor[] methods =
        bi.getMethodDescriptors();
      for(int i = 0; i < methods.length; i++)
        prt(methods[i].getMethod().toString());
      prt("======================");
      prt("Event support:");
      EventSetDescriptor[] events =
        bi.getEventSetDescriptors();
      for(int i = 0; i < events.length; i++) {
        prt("Listener type:\n  " +
          events[i].getListenerType().getName());
```

```
          Method[] lm =
            events[i].getListenerMethods();
          for(int j = 0; j < lm.length; j++)
            prt("Listener method:\n   " +
              lm[j].getName());
          MethodDescriptor[] lmd =
            events[i].getListenerMethodDescriptors();
          for(int j = 0; j < lmd.length; j++)
            prt("Method descriptor:\n   " +
              lmd[j].getMethod());
          Method addListener =
            events[i].getAddListenerMethod();
          prt("Add Listener Method:\n   " +
              addListener);
          Method removeListener =
            events[i].getRemoveListenerMethod();
          prt("Remove Listener Method:\n   " +
            removeListener);
          prt("====================");
        }
      }
    class Dumper implements ActionListener {
      public void actionPerformed(ActionEvent e) {
        String name = query.getText();
        Class c = null;
        try {
          c = Class.forName(name);
        } catch(ClassNotFoundException ex) {
          results.setText("Couldn't find " + name);
          return;
        }
        dump(c);
      }
    }
    public void init() {
      Container cp = getContentPane();
      JPanel p = new JPanel();
      p.setLayout(new FlowLayout());
      p.add(new JLabel("Qualified bean name:"));
      p.add(query);
      cp.add(BorderLayout.NORTH, p);
```

```
    cp.add(new JScrollPane(results));
    Dumper dmpr = new Dumper();
    query.addActionListener(dmpr);
    query.setText("frogbean.Frog");
    // Force evaluation
    dmpr.actionPerformed(
      new ActionEvent(dmpr, 0, ""));
  }
  public static void main(String[] args) {
    Console.run(new BeanDumper(), 600, 500);
  }
} ///:~
```

BeanDumper.dump( ) is the method that does all the work. First it
tries to create a **BeanInfo** object, and if successful calls the methods of
BeanInfo that produce information about properties, methods, and
events. In **Introspector.getBeanInfo( )**, you'll see there is a second
argument. This tells the **Introspector** where to stop in the inheritance
hierarchy. Here, it stops before it parses all the methods from **Object**,
since we're not interested in seeing those.

For properties, **getPropertyDescriptors( )** returns an array of
PropertyDescriptors. For each **PropertyDescriptor** you can call
getPropertyType( ) to find the class of object that is passed in and out
via the property methods. Then, for each property you can get its
pseudonym (extracted from the method names) with **getName( )**, the
method for reading with **getReadMethod( )**, and the method for writing
with **getWriteMethod( )**. These last two methods return a **Method**
object that can actually be used to invoke the corresponding method on
the object (this is part of reflection).

For the **public** methods (including the property methods),
getMethodDescriptors( ) returns an array of **MethodDescriptor**s.
For each one you can get the associated **Method** object and print its
name.

For the events, **getEventSetDescriptors( )** returns an array of (what
else?) **EventSetDescriptor**s. Each of these can be queried to find out
the class of the listener, the methods of that listener class, and the add-

and remove-listener methods. The **BeanDumper** program prints out all of this information.

Upon startup, the program forces the evaluation of **frogbean.Frog**. The output, after removing extra details that are unnecessary here, is:

```
class name: Frog
Property type:
  Color
Property name:
  color
Read method:
  public Color getColor()
Write method:
  public void setColor(Color)
====================
Property type:
  Spots
Property name:
  spots
Read method:
  public Spots getSpots()
Write method:
  public void setSpots(Spots)
====================
Property type:
  boolean
Property name:
  jumper
Read method:
  public boolean isJumper()
Write method:
  public void setJumper(boolean)
====================
Property type:
  int
Property name:
  jumps
Read method:
  public int getJumps()
Write method:
```

```
    public void setJumps(int)
=====================
Public methods:
public void setJumps(int)
public void croak()
public void removeActionListener(ActionListener)
public void addActionListener(ActionListener)
public int getJumps()
public void setColor(Color)
public void setSpots(Spots)
public void setJumper(boolean)
public boolean isJumper()
public void addKeyListener(KeyListener)
public Color getColor()
public void removeKeyListener(KeyListener)
public Spots getSpots()
=====================
Event support:
Listener type:
  KeyListener
Listener method:
  keyTyped
Listener method:
  keyPressed
Listener method:
  keyReleased
Method descriptor:
  public void keyTyped(KeyEvent)
Method descriptor:
  public void keyPressed(KeyEvent)
Method descriptor:
  public void keyReleased(KeyEvent)
Add Listener Method:
  public void addKeyListener(KeyListener)
Remove Listener Method:
  public void removeKeyListener(KeyListener)
====================
Listener type:
  ActionListener
Listener method:
  actionPerformed
```

```
Method descriptor:
  public void actionPerformed(ActionEvent)
Add Listener Method:
  public void addActionListener(ActionListener)
Remove Listener Method:
  public void removeActionListener(ActionListener)
====================
```

This reveals most of what the **Introspector** sees as it produces a
BeanInfo object from your Bean. You can see that the type of the
property and its name are independent. Notice the lowercasing of the
property name. (The only time this doesn't occur is when the property
name begins with more than one capital letter in a row.) And remember
that the method names you're seeing here (such as the read and write
methods) are actually produced from a **Method** object that can be used
to invoke the associated method on the object.

The **public** method list includes the methods that are not associated with
a property or event, such as **croak( )**, as well as those that are. These are
all the methods that you can call programmatically for a Bean, and the
application builder tool can choose to list all of these while you're making
method calls, to ease your task.

Finally, you can see that the events are fully parsed out into the listener,
its methods, and the add- and remove-listener methods. Basically, once
you have the **BeanInfo**, you can find out everything of importance for
the Bean. You can also call the methods for that Bean, even though you
don't have any other information except the object (again, a feature of
reflection).

A more sophisticated Bean

This next example is slightly more sophisticated, albeit frivolous. It's a
JPanel that draws a little circle around the mouse whenever the mouse is
moved. When you press the mouse, the word "Bang!" appears in the
middle of the screen, and an action listener is fired.

The properties you can change are the size of the circle as well as the
color, size, and text of the word that is displayed when you press the
mouse. A **BangBean** also has its own **addActionListener( )** and

---

removeActionListener( ) so you can attach your own listener that will be fired when the user clicks on the **BangBean**. You should be able to recognize the property and event support:

```
//: bangbean:BangBean.java
// A graphical Bean.
package bangbean;
import javax.swing.*;
import java.awt.*;
import java.awt.event.*;
import java.io.*;
import java.util.*;
import com.bruceeckel.swing.*;

public class BangBean extends JPanel
      implements Serializable {
  protected int xm, ym;
  protected int cSize = 20; // Circle size
  protected String text = "Bang!";
  protected int fontSize = 48;
  protected Color tColor = Color.red;
  protected ActionListener actionListener;
  public BangBean() {
    addMouseListener(new ML());
    addMouseMotionListener(new MML());
  }
  public int getCircleSize() { return cSize; }
  public void setCircleSize(int newSize) {
    cSize = newSize;
  }
  public String getBangText() { return text; }
  public void setBangText(String newText) {
    text = newText;
  }
  public int getFontSize() { return fontSize; }
  public void setFontSize(int newSize) {
    fontSize = newSize;
  }
  public Color getTextColor() { return tColor; }
  public void setTextColor(Color newColor) {
    tColor = newColor;
```

```java
    }
    public void paintComponent(Graphics g) {
      super.paintComponent(g);
      g.setColor(Color.black);
      g.drawOval(xm - cSize/2, ym - cSize/2,
        cSize, cSize);
    }
    // This is a unicast listener, which is
    // the simplest form of listener management:
    public void addActionListener (
        ActionListener l)
          throws TooManyListenersException {
      if(actionListener != null)
        throw new TooManyListenersException();
      actionListener = l;
    }
    public void removeActionListener(
        ActionListener l) {
      actionListener = null;
    }
    class ML extends MouseAdapter {
      public void mousePressed(MouseEvent e) {
        Graphics g = getGraphics();
        g.setColor(tColor);
        g.setFont(
          new Font(
            "TimesRoman", Font.BOLD, fontSize));
        int width =
          g.getFontMetrics().stringWidth(text);
        g.drawString(text,
          (getSize().width - width) /2,
          getSize().height/2);
        g.dispose();
        // Call the listener's method:
        if(actionListener != null)
          actionListener.actionPerformed(
            new ActionEvent(BangBean.this,
              ActionEvent.ACTION_PERFORMED, null));
      }
    }
    class MML extends MouseMotionAdapter {
```

```
    public void mouseMoved(MouseEvent e) {
      xm = e.getX();
      ym = e.getY();
      repaint();
    }
  }
  public Dimension getPreferredSize() {
    return new Dimension(200, 200);
  }
} ///:~
```

The first thing you'll notice is that **BangBean** implements the
Serializable interface. This means that the application builder tool can
"pickle" all the information for the **BangBean** using serialization after
the program designer has adjusted the values of the properties. When the
Bean is created as part of the running application, these "pickled"
properties are restored so that you get exactly what you designed.

You can see that all the fields are **private**, which is what you'll usually do
with a Bean—allow access only through methods, usually using the
"property" scheme.

When you look at the signature for **addActionListener( )**, you'll see
that it can throw a **TooManyListenersException**. This indicates that it
is *unicast*, which means it notifies only one listener when the event
occurs. Ordinarily, you'll use *multicast* events so that many listeners can
be notified of an event. However, that runs into issues that you won't be
ready for until the next chapter, so it will be revisited there (under the
heading "JavaBeans revisited"). A unicast event sidesteps the problem.

When you click the mouse, the text is put in the middle of the **BangBean**,
and if the **actionListener** field is not **null**, its **actionPerformed( )** is
called, creating a new **ActionEvent** object in the process. Whenever the
mouse is moved, its new coordinates are captured and the canvas is
repainted (erasing any text that's on the canvas, as you'll see).

Here is the **BangBeanTest** class to allow you to test the bean as either an
applet or an application:

```
//: c13:BangBeanTest.java
// <applet code=BangBeanTest
```

```
// width=400 height=500></applet>
import bangbean.*;
import javax.swing.*;
import java.awt.*;
import java.awt.event.*;
import java.util.*;
import com.bruceeckel.swing.*;

public class BangBeanTest extends JApplet {
  JTextField txt = new JTextField(20);
  // During testing, report actions:
  class BBL implements ActionListener {
    int count = 0;
    public void actionPerformed(ActionEvent e){
      txt.setText("BangBean action "+ count++);
    }
  }
  public void init() {
    BangBean bb = new BangBean();
    try {
      bb.addActionListener(new BBL());
    } catch(TooManyListenersException e) {
      txt.setText("Too many listeners");
    }
    Container cp = getContentPane();
    cp.add(bb);
    cp.add(BorderLayout.SOUTH, txt);
  }
  public static void main(String[] args) {
    Console.run(new BangBeanTest(), 400, 500);
  }
} ///:~
```

When a Bean is in a development environment, this class will not be used, but it's helpful to provide a rapid testing method for each of your Beans. **BangBeanTest** places a **BangBean** within the applet, attaching a simple **ActionListener** to the **BangBean** to print an event count to the **JTextField** whenever an **ActionEvent** occurs. Usually, of course, the application builder tool would create most of the code that uses the Bean.

When you run the **BangBean** through **BeanDumper** or put the **BangBean** inside a Bean-enabled development environment, you'll notice that there are many more properties and actions than are evident from the above code. That's because **BangBean** is inherited from **JPanel**, and **JPanel** is also Bean, so you're seeing its properties and events as well.

Packaging a Bean

Before you can bring a Bean into a Bean-enabled visual builder tool, it must be put into the standard Bean container, which is a JAR file that includes all the Bean classes as well as a "manifest" file that says "This is a Bean." A manifest file is simply a text file that follows a particular form. For the **BangBean**, the manifest file looks like this (without the first and last lines):

```
//:! :BangBean.mf
Manifest-Version: 1.0

Name: bangbean/BangBean.class
Java-Bean: True
///:~
```

The first line indicates the version of the manifest scheme, which until further notice from Sun is 1.0. The second line (empty lines are ignored) names the **BangBean.class** file, and the third says, "It's a Bean." Without the third line, the program builder tool will not recognize the class as a Bean.

The only tricky part is that you must make sure that you get the proper path in the "Name:" field. If you look back at **BangBean.java**, you'll see it's in **package bangbean** (and thus in a subdirectory called "bangbean" that's off of the classpath), and the name in the manifest file must include this package information. In addition, you must place the manifest file in the directory *above* the root of your package path, which in this case means placing the file in the directory above the "bangbean" subdirectory. Then you must invoke **jar** from the same directory as the manifest file, as follows:

```
jar cfm BangBean.jar BangBean.mf bangbean
```

This assumes that you want the resulting JAR file to be named **BangBean.jar** and that you've put the manifest in a file called **BangBean.mf**.

You might wonder "What about all the other classes that were generated when I compiled **BangBean.java**?" Well, they all ended up inside the **bangbean** subdirectory, and you'll see that the last argument for the above **jar** command line is the **bangbean** subdirectory. When you give **jar** the name of a subdirectory, it packages that entire subdirectory into the jar file (including, in this case, the original **BangBean.java** source-code file—you might not choose to include the source with your own Beans). In addition, if you turn around and unpack the JAR file you've just created, you'll discover that your manifest file isn't inside, but that **jar** has created its own manifest file (based partly on yours) called **MANIFEST.MF** and placed it inside the subdirectory **META-INF** (for "meta-information"). If you open this manifest file you'll also notice that digital signature information has been added by **jar** for each file, of the form:

```
Digest-Algorithms: SHA MD5
SHA-Digest: pDpEAG9NaeCx8aFtqPI4udSX/OO=
MD5-Digest: O4NcS1hE3Smnzlp2hj6qeg==
```

In general, you don't need to worry about any of this, and if you make changes you can just modify your original manifest file and reinvoke **jar** to create a new JAR file for your Bean. You can also add other Beans to the JAR file simply by adding their information to your manifest.

One thing to notice is that you'll probably want to put each Bean in its own subdirectory, since when you create a JAR file you hand the **jar** utility the name of a subdirectory and it puts everything in that subdirectory into the JAR file. You can see that both **Frog** and **BangBean** are in their own subdirectories.

Once you have your Bean properly inside a JAR file you can bring it into a Beans-enabled program-builder environment. The way you do this varies from one tool to the next, but Sun provides a freely available test bed for JavaBeans in their "Beans Development Kit" (BDK) called the "beanbox." (Download the BDK from *java.sun.com/beans*.) To place your Bean in the beanbox, copy the JAR file into the BDK's "jars" subdirectory before you start up the beanbox.

More complex Bean support

You can see how remarkably simple it is to make a Bean. But you aren't limited to what you've seen here. The JavaBeans architecture provides a simple point of entry but can also scale to more complex situations. These situations are beyond the scope of this book, but they will be briefly introduced here. You can find more details at *java.sun.com/beans*.

One place where you can add sophistication is with properties. The examples above have shown only single properties, but it's also possible to represent multiple properties in an array. This is called an *indexed property*. You simply provide the appropriate methods (again following a naming convention for the method names) and the **Introspector** recognizes an indexed property so your application builder tool can respond appropriately.

Properties can be *bound*, which means that they will notify other objects via a **PropertyChangeEvent**. The other objects can then choose to change themselves based on the change to the Bean.

Properties can be *constrained*, which means that other objects can veto a change to that property if it is unacceptable. The other objects are notified using a **PropertyChangeEvent**, and they can throw a **PropertyVetoException** to prevent the change from happening and to restore the old values.

You can also change the way your Bean is represented at design time:

1. You can provide a custom property sheet for your particular Bean. The ordinary property sheet will be used for all other Beans, but yours is automatically invoked when your Bean is selected.

2. You can create a custom editor for a particular property, so the ordinary property sheet is used, but when your special property is being edited, your editor will automatically be invoked.

3. You can provide a custom **BeanInfo** class for your Bean that produces information that's different from the default created by the **Introspector**.

4. It's also possible to turn "expert" mode on and off in all **FeatureDescriptor**s to distinguish between basic features and more complicated ones.

More to Beans

There's another issue that couldn't be addressed here. Whenever you create a Bean, you should expect that it will be run in a multithreaded environment. This means that you must understand the issues of threading, which will be introduced in Chapter 14. You'll find a section there called "JavaBeans revisited" that will look at the problem and its solution.

There are a number of books about JavaBeans; for example, *JavaBeans* by Elliotte Rusty Harold (IDG, 1998).

Summary

Of all the libraries in Java, the GUI library has seen the most dramatic changes from Java 1.0 to Java 2. The Java 1.0 AWT was roundly criticized as being one of the worst designs seen, and while it would allow you to create portable programs, the resulting GUI was "equally mediocre on all platforms." It was also limiting, awkward, and unpleasant to use compared with the native application development tools available on a particular platform.

When Java 1.1 introduced the new event model and JavaBeans, the stage was set—now it was possible to create GUI components that could be easily dragged and dropped inside visual application builder tools. In addition, the design of the event model and Beans clearly shows strong consideration for ease of programming and maintainable code (something that was not evident in the 1.0 AWT). But it wasn't until the JFC/Swing classes appeared that the job was finished. With the Swing components, cross-platform GUI programming can be a civilized experience.

Actually, the only thing that's missing is the application builder tool, and this is where the real revolution lies. Microsoft's Visual Basic and Visual C++ require Microsoft's application builder tools, as does Borland's Delphi and C++ Builder. If you want the application builder tool to get better, you have to cross your fingers and hope the vendor will give you what you want. But Java is an open environment, and so not only does it allow for competing application builder environments, it encourages them. And for these tools to be taken seriously, they must support JavaBeans. This means a leveled playing field: if a better application builder tool comes along, you're not tied to the one you've been using—you can pick up and move to the new one and increase your productivity. This kind of competitive environment for GUI application builder tools has not been seen before, and the resulting marketplace can generate only positive results for the productivity of the programmer.

This chapter was meant only to give you an introduction to the power of Swing and to get you started so you could see how relatively simple it is to feel your way through the libraries. What you've seen so far will probably suffice for a good portion of your UI design needs. However, there's a lot more to Swing—it's intended to be a fully powered UI design tool kit. There's probably a way to accomplish just about everything you can imagine.

If you don't see what you need here, delve into the online documentation from Sun and search the Web, and if that's not enough then find a dedicated Swing book—a good place to start is *The JFC Swing Tutorial*, by Walrath & Campione (Addison Wesley, 1999).

Exercises

1. Create an applet/application using the **Console** class as shown in this chapter. Include a text field and three buttons. When you press each button, make some different text appear in the text field.

2. Add a check box to the applet created in Exercise 1, capture the event, and insert different text into the text field.

3. Create an applet/application using **Console**. In the HTML documentation from *java.sun.com*, find the **JPasswordField** and add this to the program. If the user types in the correct password, use **Joptionpane** to provide a success message to the user.

4. Create an applet/application using **Console**, and add all the components that have an **addActionListener( )** method. (Look these up in the HTML documentation from *java.sun.com*. Hint: use the index.) Capture their events and display an appropriate message for each inside a text field.

5. Create an applet/application using **Console**, with a **JButton** and a **JTextField**. Write and attach the appropriate listener so that if the button has the focus, characters typed into it will appear in the **JTextField**.

6. Create an applet/application using **Console**. Add to the main frame all the components described in this chapter, including menus and a dialog box.

7. Modify **TextFields.java** so that the characters in **t2** retain the original case that they were typed in, instead of automatically being forced to upper case.

8. Locate and download one or more of the free GUI builder development environments available on the Internet, or buy a commercial product. Discover what is necessary to add **BangBean** to this environment and to use it.

9. Add **Frog.class** to the manifest file as shown in this chapter and run **jar** to create a JAR file containing both **Frog** and **BangBean**. Now either download and install the BDK from Sun or use your own Beans-enabled program builder tool and add the JAR file to your environment so you can test the two Beans.

10. Create your own JavaBean called **Valve** that contains two properties: a **boolean** called "on" and an **int** called "level." Create a manifest file, use **jar** to package your Bean, then load it into the

---

beanbox or into a Beans-enabled program builder tool so that you can test it.

11. Modify **MessageBoxes.java** so that it has an individual **ActionListener** for each button (instead of matching the button text).

12. Monitor a new type of event in **TrackEvent.java** by adding the new event handling code. You'll need to discover on your own the type of event that you want to monitor.

13. Inherit a new type of button from **JButton**. Each time you press this button, it should change its color to a randomly-selected value. See **ColorBoxes.java** in Chapter 14 for an example of how to generate a random color value.

14. Modify **TextPane.java** to use a **JTextArea** instead of a **JTextPane**.

15. Modify **Menus.java** to use radio buttons instead of check boxes on the menus.

16. Simplify **List.java** by passing the array to the constructor and eliminating the dynamic addition of elements to the list.

17. Modify **SineWave.java** to turn **SineDraw** into a JavaBean by adding "getter" and "setter" methods.

18. Remember the "sketching box" toy with two knobs, one that controls the vertical movement of the drawing point, and one that controls the horizontal movement? Create one of those, using **SineWave.java** to get you started. Instead of knobs, use sliders. Add a button that will erase the entire sketch.

19. Create an "asymptotic progress indicator" that gets slower and slower as it approaches the finish point. Add random erratic behavior so it will periodically look like it's starting to speed up.

20. Modify **Progress.java** so that it does not share models, but instead uses a listener to connect the slider and progress bar.

21.   Follow the instructions in the section titled "Packaging an applet into a JAR file" to place **TicTacToe.java** into a JAR file. Create an HTML page with the (messy, complicated) version of the applet tag, and modify it to use the archive tag so as to use the JAR file. (Hint: start with the HTML page for **TicTacToe.java** that comes with this book's source-code distribution.)

22.   Create an applet/application using **Console**. This should have three sliders, one each for the red, green, and blue values in **java.awt.Color**. The rest of the form should be a **JPanel** that displays the color determined by the three sliders. Also include non-editable text fields that show the current RGB values.

23.   In the HTML documentation for **javax.swing**, look up the **JColorChooser**. Write a program with a button that brings up the color chooser as a dialog.

24.   Almost every Swing component is derived from **Component**, which has a **setCursor( )** method. Look this up in the Java HTML documentation. Create an applet and change the cursor to one of the stock cursors in the **Cursor** class.

25.   Starting with **ShowAddListeners.java**, create a program with the full functionality of **ShowMethodsClean.java** from Chapter 12.

14: Multiple Threads

Objects provide a way to divide a program into independent sections. Often, you also need to turn a program into separate, independently running subtasks.

Each of these independent subtasks is called a *thread*, and you program as if each thread runs by itself and has the CPU to itself. Some underlying mechanism is actually dividing up the CPU time for you, but in general, you don't have to think about it, which makes programming with multiple threads a much easier task.

A *process* is a self-contained running program with its own address space. A *multitasking* operating system is capable of running more than one process (program) at a time, while making it look like each one is chugging along on its own, by periodically providing CPU cycles to each process. A thread is a single sequential flow of control within a process. A single process can thus have multiple concurrently executing threads.

There are many possible uses for multithreading, but in general, you'll have some part of your program tied to a particular event or resource, and you don't want to hang up the rest of your program because of that. So you create a thread associated with that event or resource and let it run independently of the main program. A good example is a "quit" button—you don't want to be forced to poll the quit button in every piece of code you write in your program and yet you want the quit button to be responsive, as if you *were* checking it regularly. In fact, one of the most immediately compelling reasons for multithreading is to produce a responsive user interface.

Responsive user interfaces

As a starting point, consider a program that performs some CPU-intensive operation and thus ends up ignoring user input and being unresponsive. This one, a combined applet/application, will simply display the result of a running counter:

```
//: c14:Counter1.java
// A non-responsive user interface.
// <applet code=Counter1 width=300 height=100>
// </applet>
import javax.swing.*;
import java.awt.event.*;
import java.awt.*;
import com.bruceeckel.swing.*;

public class Counter1 extends JApplet {
  private int count = 0;
  private JButton
    start = new JButton("Start"),
    onOff = new JButton("Toggle");
  private JTextField t = new JTextField(10);
  private boolean runFlag = true;
  public void init() {
    Container cp = getContentPane();
    cp.setLayout(new FlowLayout());
    cp.add(t);
    start.addActionListener(new StartL());
    cp.add(start);
    onOff.addActionListener(new OnOffL());
    cp.add(onOff);
  }
  public void go() {
    while (true) {
      try {
        Thread.sleep(100);
      } catch(InterruptedException e) {
        System.err.println("Interrupted");
      }
      if (runFlag)
```

```
      t.setText(Integer.toString(count++));
    }
  }
  class StartL implements ActionListener {
    public void actionPerformed(ActionEvent e) {
      go();
    }
  }
  class OnOffL implements ActionListener {
    public void actionPerformed(ActionEvent e) {
      runFlag = !runFlag;
    }
  }
  public static void main(String[] args) {
    Console.run(new Counter1(), 300, 100);
  }
} ///:~
```

At this point, the Swing and applet code should be reasonably familiar from Chapter 13. The **go( )** method is where the program stays busy: it puts the current value of **count** into the **JTextField t**, then increments **count**.

Part of the infinite loop inside **go( )** is to call **sleep( )**. **sleep( )** must be associated with a **Thread** object, and it turns out that every application has *some* thread associated with it. (Indeed, Java is based on threads and there are always some running along with your application.) So regardless of whether you're explicitly using threads, you can produce the current thread used by your program with **Thread** and the static **sleep( )** method.

Note that **sleep( )** can throw an **InterruptedException**, although throwing such an exception is considered a hostile way to break from a thread and should be discouraged. (Once again, exceptions are for exceptional conditions, not normal flow of control.) Interrupting a sleeping thread is included to support a future language feature.

When the **start** button is pressed, **go( )** is invoked. On examining **go( )**, you might naively think (as I did) that it should allow multithreading because it goes to sleep. That is, while the method is asleep, it seems like the CPU could be busy monitoring other button presses. But it turns out that the real problem is that **go( )** never returns, since it's in an infinite loop, and this means that **actionPerformed( )** never returns. Since you're stuck inside **actionPerformed( )** for the first keypress, the program can't handle any other events. (To get out, you must somehow kill the process; the easiest way to do this is to press Control-C in the console window, if you started it from the console. If you start it via the browser, you have to kill the browser window.)

The basic problem here is that **go( )** needs to continue performing its operations, and at the same time it needs to return so that **actionPerformed( )** can complete and the user interface can continue responding to the user. But in a conventional method like **go( )** it cannot continue *and* at the same time return control to the rest of the program. This sounds like an impossible thing to accomplish, as if the CPU must be in two places at once, but this is precisely the illusion that threading provides.

The thread model (and its programming support in Java) is a programming convenience to simplify juggling several operations at the same time within a single program. With threads, the CPU will pop around and give each thread some of its time. Each thread has the consciousness of constantly having the CPU to itself, but the CPU's time is actually sliced between all the threads. The exception to this is if your program is running on multiple CPUs. But one of the great things about threading is that you are abstracted away from this layer, so your code does not need to know whether it is actually running on a single CPU or many. Thus, threads are a way to create transparently scalable programs.

Threading reduces computing efficiency somewhat, but the net improvement in program design, resource balancing, and user convenience is often quite valuable. Of course, if you have more than one CPU, then the operating system can dedicate each CPU to a set of threads or even a single thread and the whole program can run much faster. Multitasking and multithreading tend to be the most reasonable ways to utilize multiprocessor systems.

Inheriting from **Thread**

The simplest way to create a thread is to inherit from class **Thread**, which has all the wiring necessary to create and run threads. The most important method for **Thread** is **run( )**, which you must override to make the thread do your bidding. Thus, **run( )** is the code that will be executed "simultaneously" with the other threads in a program.

The following example creates any number of threads that it keeps track of by assigning each thread a unique number, generated with a **static** variable. The **Thread**'s **run( )** method is overridden to count down each time it passes through its loop and to finish when the count is zero (at the point when **run( )** returns, the thread is terminated).

```java
//: c14:SimpleThread.java
// Very simple Threading example.

public class SimpleThread extends Thread {
  private int countDown = 5;
  private static int threadCount = 0;
  private int threadNumber = ++threadCount;
  public SimpleThread() {
    System.out.println("Making " + threadNumber);
  }
  public void run() {
    while(true) {
      System.out.println("Thread " +
        threadNumber + "(" + countDown + ")");
      if(--countDown == 0) return;
    }
  }
  public static void main(String[] args) {
    for(int i - 0; i < 5; i++)
      new SimpleThread().start();
    System.out.println("All Threads Started");
  }
} ///:~
```

A **run( )** method virtually always has some kind of loop that continues until the thread is no longer necessary, so you must establish the condition on which to break out of this loop (or, in the case above, simply **return** from **run( )**). Often, **run( )** is cast in the form of an infinite loop, which means that, barring some external factor that causes **run( )** to terminate, it will continue forever.

In **main( )** you can see a number of threads being created and run. The **start( )** method in the **Thread** class performs special initialization for the thread and then calls **run( )**. So the steps are: the constructor is called to build the object, then **start( )** configures the thread and calls **run( )**. If you don't call **start( )** (which you can do in the constructor, if that's appropriate) the thread will never be started.

The output for one run of this program (it will be different from one run to another) is:

```
Making 1
Making 2
Making 3
Making 4
Making 5
Thread 1(5)
Thread 1(4)
Thread 1(3)
Thread 1(2)
Thread 2(5)
Thread 2(4)
Thread 2(3)
Thread 2(2)
Thread 2(1)
Thread 1(1)
All Threads Started
Thread 3(5)
Thread 4(5)
Thread 4(4)
Thread 4(3)
Thread 4(2)
Thread 4(1)
Thread 5(5)
Thread 5(4)
Thread 5(3)
Thread 5(2)
Thread 5(1)
Thread 3(4)
Thread 3(3)
Thread 3(2)
Thread 3(1)
```

You'll notice that nowhere in this example is **sleep( )** called, and yet the output indicates that each thread gets a portion of the CPU's time in which to execute. This shows that **sleep( )**, while it relies on the existence of a thread in order to execute, is not involved with either enabling or disabling threading. It's simply another method.

You can also see that the threads are not run in the order that they're created. In fact, the order that the CPU attends to an existing set of threads is indeterminate, unless you go in and adjust the priorities using **Thread**'s **setPriority( )** method.

When **main( )** creates the **Thread** objects it isn't capturing the references for any of them. An ordinary object would be fair game for garbage collection, but not a **Thread**. Each **Thread** "registers" itself so there is actually a reference to it someplace and the garbage collector can't clean it up.

Threading for a responsive interface

Now it's possible to solve the problem in **Counter1.java** with a thread. The trick is to place the subtask—that is, the loop that's inside **go( )**—inside the **run( )** method of a thread. When the user presses the **start** button, the thread is started, but then the *creation* of the thread completes, so even though the thread is running, the main job of the program (watching for and responding to user-interface events) can continue. Here's the solution:

```
//: c14:Counter2.java
// A responsive user interface with threads.
// <applet code=Counter2 width=300 height=100>
// </applet>
import javax.swing.*;
import java.awt.*;
import java.awt.event.*;
import com.bruceeckel.swing.*;

public class Counter2 extends JApplet {
  private class SeparateSubTask extends Thread {
```

```java
      private int count = 0;
      private boolean runFlag = true;
      SeparateSubTask() { start(); }
      void invertFlag() { runFlag = !runFlag; }
      public void run() {
        while (true) {
         try {
           sleep(100);
         } catch(InterruptedException e) {
           System.err.println("Interrupted");
         }
          if(runFlag)
            t.setText(Integer.toString(count++));
        }
      }
    }
    private SeparateSubTask sp = null;
    private JTextField t = new JTextField(10);
    private JButton
      start = new JButton("Start"),
      onOff = new JButton("Toggle");
    class StartL implements ActionListener {
      public void actionPerformed(ActionEvent e) {
        if(sp == null)
          sp = new SeparateSubTask();
      }
    }
    class OnOffL implements ActionListener {
      public void actionPerformed(ActionEvent e) {
        if(sp != null)
          sp.invertFlag();
      }
    }
    public void init() {
      Container cp = getContentPane();
      cp.setLayout(new FlowLayout());
      cp.add(t);
      start.addActionListener(new StartL());
      cp.add(start);
      onOff.addActionListener(new OnOffL());
      cp.add(onOff);
```

```
    }
    public static void main(String[] args) {
      Console.run(new Counter2 (), 300, 100);
    }
} ///:~
```

Counter2 is a straightforward program, whose only job is to set up and maintain the user interface. But now, when the user presses the **start** button, the event-handling code does not call a method. Instead a thread of class **SeparateSubTask** is created, and then the **Counter2** event loop continues.

The class **SeparateSubTask** is a simple extension of **Thread** with a constructor that runs the thread by calling **start( )**, and a **run( )** that essentially contains the "**go( )**" code from **Counter1.java**.

Because **SeparateSubTask** is an inner class, it can directly access the **JTextField t** in **Counter2**; you can see this happening inside **run( )**. The **t** field in the outer class is **private** since **SeparateSubTask** can access it without getting any special permission—and it's always good to make fields "as **private** as possible" so they cannot be accidentally changed by forces outside your class.

When you press the **onOff** button it toggles the **runFlag** inside the **SeparateSubTask** object. That thread (when it looks at the flag) can then start and stop itself. Pressing the **onOff** button produces an apparently instant response. Of course, the response isn't really instant, not like that of a system that's driven by interrupts. The counter stops only when the thread has the CPU and notices that the flag has changed.

You can see that the inner class **SeparateSubTask** is **private**, which means that its fields and methods can be given default access (except for **run( )**, which must be **public** since it is **public** in the base class). The **private** inner class is not accessible to anyone but **Counter2**, and the two classes are tightly coupled. Anytime you notice classes that appear to have high coupling with each other, consider the coding and maintenance improvements you might get by using inner classes.

Combining the thread
with the main class

In the example above you can see that the thread class is separate from the program's main class. This makes a lot of sense and is relatively easy to understand. There is, however, an alternate form that you will often see used that is not so clear but is usually more concise (which probably accounts for its popularity). This form combines the main program class with the thread class by making the main program class a thread. Since for a GUI program the main program class must be inherited from either **Frame** or **Applet**, an interface must be used to paste on the additional functionality. This interface is called **Runnable**, and it contains the same basic method that **Thread** does. In fact, **Thread** also implements **Runnable**, which specifies only that there be a **run( )** method.

The *use* of the combined program/thread is not quite so obvious. When you start the program, you create an object that's **Runnable**, but you don't start the thread. This must be done explicitly. You can see this in the following program, which reproduces the functionality of **Counter2**:

```
//: c14:Counter3.java
// Using the Runnable interface to turn the
// main class into a thread.
// <applet code=Counter3 width=300 height=100>
// </applet>
import javax.swing.*;
import java.awt.*;
import java.awt.event.*;
import com.bruceeckel.swing.*;

public class Counter3
    extends JApplet implements Runnable {
  private int count = 0;
  private boolean runFlag = true;
  private Thread selfThread = null;
  private JButton
    start = new JButton("Start"),
    onOff = new JButton("Toggle");
  private JTextField t = new JTextField(10);
  public void run() {
```

```
      while (true) {
        try {
          selfThread.sleep(100);
        } catch(InterruptedException e) {
          System.err.println("Interrupted");
        }
        if(runFlag)
          t.setText(Integer.toString(count++));
      }
    }
    class StartL implements ActionListener {
      public void actionPerformed(ActionEvent e) {
        if(selfThread == null) {
          selfThread = new Thread(Counter3.this);
          selfThread.start();
        }
      }
    }
    class OnOffL implements ActionListener {
      public void actionPerformed(ActionEvent e) {
        runFlag = !runFlag;
      }
    }
    public void init() {
      Container cp = getContentPane();
      cp.setLayout(new FlowLayout());
      cp.add(t);
      start.addActionListener(new StartL());
      cp.add(start);
      onOff.addActionListener(new OnOffL());
      cp.add(onOff);
    }
    public static void main(String[] args) {
      Console.run(new Counter3(), 300, 100);
    }
} ///:~
```

Now the **run( )** is inside the class, but it's still dormant after **init( )** completes. When you press the **start** button, the thread is created (if it doesn't already exist) in the somewhat obscure expression:

```
new Thread(Counter3.this);
```

When something has a **Runnable** interface, it simply means that it has a **run( )** method, but there's nothing special about that—it doesn't produce any innate threading abilities, like those of a class inherited from **Thread**. So to produce a thread from a **Runnable** object, you must create a separate **Thread** object as shown above, handing the **Runnable** object to the special **Thread** constructor. You can then call **start( )** for that thread:

```
selfThread.start();
```

This performs the usual initialization and then calls **run( )**.

The convenient aspect about the **Runnable interface** is that everything belongs to the same class. If you need to access something, you simply do it without going through a separate object. However, as you saw in the previous example, this access is just as easy using an inner class[1].

Making many threads

Consider the creation of many different threads. You can't do this with the previous example, so you must go back to having separate classes inherited from **Thread** to encapsulate the **run( )**. But this is a more general solution and easier to understand, so while the previous example shows a coding style you'll often see, I can't recommend it for most cases because it's just a little bit more confusing and less flexible.

The following example repeats the form of the examples above with counters and toggle buttons. But now all the information for a particular counter, including the button and text field, is inside its own object that is inherited from **Thread**. All the fields in **Ticker** are **private**, which means that the **Ticker** implementation can be changed at will, including the quantity and type of data components to acquire and display

---

[1] **Runnable** was in Java 1.0, while inner classes were not introduced until Java 1.1, which may partially account for the existence of **Runnable**. Also, traditional multithreading architectures focused on a function to be run rather than an object. My preference is always to inherit from **Thread** if I can; it seems cleaner and more flexible to me.

information. When a **Ticker** object is created, the constructor adds its visual components to the content pane of the outer object:

```
//: c14:Counter4.java
// By keeping your thread as a distinct class,
// you can have as many threads as you want.
// <applet code=Counter4 width=200 height=600>
// <param name=size value="12"></applet>
import javax.swing.*;
import java.awt.*;
import java.awt.event.*;
import com.bruceeckel.swing.*;

public class Counter4 extends JApplet {
  private JButton start = new JButton("Start");
  private boolean started = false;
  private Ticker[] s;
  private boolean isApplet = true;
  private int size = 12;
  class Ticker extends Thread {
    private JButton b = new JButton("Toggle");
    private JTextField t = new JTextField(10);
    private int count = 0;
    private boolean runFlag = true;
    public Ticker() {
      b.addActionListener(new ToggleL());
      JPanel p = new JPanel();
      p.add(t);
      p.add(b);
      // Calls JApplet.getContentPane().add():
      getContentPane().add(p);
    }
    class ToggleL implements ActionListener {
      public void actionPerformed(ActionEvent e) {
        runFlag = !runFlag;
      }
    }
    public void run() {
      while (true) {
        if (runFlag)
          t.setText(Integer.toString(count++));
```

```java
        try {
          sleep(100);
        } catch(InterruptedException e) {
          System.err.println("Interrupted");
        }
      }
    }
  }
  class StartL implements ActionListener {
    public void actionPerformed(ActionEvent e) {
      if(!started) {
        started = true;
        for (int i = 0; i < s.length; i++)
          s[i].start();
      }
    }
  }
  public void init() {
    Container cp = getContentPane();
    cp.setLayout(new FlowLayout());
    // Get parameter "size" from Web page:
    if (isApplet) {
      String sz = getParameter("size");
      if(sz != null)
        size = Integer.parseInt(sz);
    }
    s = new Ticker[size];
    for (int i = 0; i < s.length; i++)
      s[i] = new Ticker();
    start.addActionListener(new StartL());
    cp.add(start);
  }
  public static void main(String[] args) {
    Counter4 applet = new Counter4();
    // This isn't an applet, so set the flag and
    // produce the parameter values from args:
    applet.isApplet = false;
    if(args.length != 0)
      applet.size = Integer.parseInt(args[0]);
    Console.run(applet, 200, applet.size * 50);
  }
```

```
} ///:~
```

Ticker contains not only its threading equipment but also the way to control and display the thread. You can create as many threads as you want without explicitly creating the windowing components.

In **Counter4** there's an array of **Ticker** objects called **s**. For maximum flexibility, the size of this array is initialized by reaching out into the Web page using applet parameters. Here's what the size parameter looks like on the page, embedded inside the applet tag:

```
<param name=size value="20">
```

The **param**, **name**, and **value** are all HTML keywords. **name** is what you'll be referring to in your program, and **value** can be any string, not just something that resolves to a number.

You'll notice that the determination of the size of the array **s** is done inside **init( )**, and not as part of an inline definition of **s**. That is, you *cannot* say as part of the class definition (outside of any methods):

```
int size = Integer.parseInt(getParameter("size"));
Ticker[] s = new Ticker[size];
```

You can compile this, but you'll get a strange "null-pointer exception" at run-time. It works fine if you move the **getParameter( )** initialization inside of **init( )**. The applet framework performs the necessary startup to grab the parameters before entering **init( )**.

In addition, this code is set up to be either an applet or an application. When it's an application the **size** argument is extracted from the command line (or a default value is provided).

Once the size of the array is established, new **Ticker** objects are created; as part of the **Ticker** constructor the button and text field for each **Ticker** is added to the applet.

Pressing the **start** button means looping through the entire array of **Ticker**s and calling **start( )** for each one. Remember, **start( )** performs necessary thread initialization and then calls **run( )** for that thread.

The **ToggleL** listener simply inverts the flag in **Ticker** and when the associated thread next takes note it can react accordingly.

One value of this example is that it allows you to easily create large sets of independent subtasks and to monitor their behavior. In this case, you'll see that as the number of subtasks gets larger, your machine will probably show more divergence in the displayed numbers because of the way that the threads are served.

You can also experiment to discover how important the **sleep(100)** is inside **Ticker.run( )**. If you remove the **sleep( )**, things will work fine until you press a toggle button. Then that particular thread has a false **runFlag** and the **run( )** is just tied up in a tight infinite loop, which appears difficult to break during multithreading, so the responsiveness and speed of the program really bogs down.

Daemon threads

A "daemon" thread is one that is supposed to provide a general service in the background as long as the program is running, but is not part of the essence of the program. Thus, when all of the non-daemon threads complete, the program is terminated. Conversely, if there are any non-daemon threads still running, the program doesn't terminate. (There is, for instance, a thread that runs **main( )**.)

You can find out if a thread is a daemon by calling **isDaemon( )**, and you can turn the "daemonhood" of a thread on and off with **setDaemon( )**. If a thread is a daemon, then any threads it creates will automatically be daemons.

The following example demonstrates daemon threads:

```
//: c14:Daemons.java
// Daemonic behavior.
import java.io.*;

class Daemon extends Thread {
  private static final int SIZE = 10;
  private Thread[] t = new Thread[SIZE];
  public Daemon() {
    setDaemon(true);
    start();
  }
  public void run() {
```

```
    for(int i = 0; i < SIZE; i++)
      t[i] = new DaemonSpawn(i);
    for(int i = 0; i < SIZE; i++)
      System.out.println(
        "t[" + i + "].isDaemon() = "
        + t[i].isDaemon());
    while(true)
      yield();
  }
}

class DaemonSpawn extends Thread {
  public DaemonSpawn(int i) {
    System.out.println(
      "DaemonSpawn " + i + " started");
    start();
  }
  public void run() {
    while(true)
      yield();
  }
}

public class Daemons {
  public static void main(String[] args)
  throws IOException {
    Thread d = new Daemon();
    System.out.println(
      "d.isDaemon() = " + d.isDaemon());
    // Allow the daemon threads to
    // finish their startup processes:
    System.out.println("Press any key");
    System.in.read();
  }
} ///:~
```

The **Daemon** thread sets its daemon flag to "true" and then spawns a
bunch of other threads to show that they are also daemons. Then it goes
into an infinite loop that calls **yield( )** to give up control to the other
processes. In an earlier version of this program, the infinite loops would

increment **int** counters, but this seemed to bring the whole program to a stop. Using **yield( )** makes the program quite peppy.

There's nothing to keep the program from terminating once **main( )** finishes its job, since there are nothing but daemon threads running. So that you can see the results of starting all the daemon threads, **System.in** is set up to read so the program waits for a keypress before terminating. Without this you see only some of the results from the creation of the daemon threads. (Try replacing the **read( )** code with **sleep( )** calls of various lengths to see this behavior.)

Sharing limited resources

You can think of a single-threaded program as one lonely entity moving around through your problem space and doing one thing at a time. Because there's only one entity, you never have to think about the problem of two entities trying to use the same resource at the same time, like two people trying to park in the same space, walk through a door at the same time, or even talk at the same time.

With multithreading, things aren't lonely anymore, but you now have the possibility of two or more threads trying to use the same limited resource at once. Colliding over a resource must be prevented or else you'll have two threads trying to access the same bank account at the same time, print to the same printer, or adjust the same valve, etc.

Improperly accessing resources

Consider a variation on the counters that have been used so far in this chapter. In the following example, each thread contains two counters that are incremented and displayed inside **run( )**. In addition, there's another thread of class **Watcher** that is watching the counters to see if they're always equivalent. This seems like a needless activity, since looking at the code it appears obvious that the counters will always be the same. But that's where the surprise comes in. Here's the first version of the program:

```
//: c14:Sharing1.java
// Problems with resource sharing while threading.
// <applet code=Sharing1 width=350 height=500>
```

```
// <param name=size value="12">
// <param name=watchers value="15">
// </applet>
import javax.swing.*;
import java.awt.*;
import java.awt.event.*;
import com.bruceeckel.swing.*;

public class Sharing1 extends JApplet {
  private static int accessCount = 0;
  private static JTextField aCount =
    new JTextField("0", 7);
  public static void incrementAccess() {
    accessCount++;
    aCount.setText(Integer.toString(accessCount));
  }
  private JButton
    start = new JButton("Start"),
    watcher = new JButton("Watch");
  private boolean isApplet = true;
  private int numCounters = 12;
  private int numWatchers = 15;
  private TwoCounter[] s;
  class TwoCounter extends Thread {
    private boolean started = false;
    private JTextField
      t1 = new JTextField(5),
      t2 = new JTextField(5);
    private JLabel l =
      new JLabel("count1 == count2");
    private int count1 = 0, count2 = 0;
    // Add the display components as a panel:
    public TwoCounter() {
      JPanel p = new JPanel();
      p.add(t1);
      p.add(t2);
      p.add(l);
      getContentPane().add(p);
    }
    public void start() {
      if(!started) {
```

```
        started = true;
        super.start();
      }
    }
    public void run() {
      while (true) {
        t1.setText(Integer.toString(count1++));
        t2.setText(Integer.toString(count2++));
        try {
          sleep(500);
        } catch(InterruptedException e) {
          System.err.println("Interrupted");
        }
      }
    }
    public void synchTest() {
      Sharing1.incrementAccess();
      if(count1 != count2)
        l.setText("Unsynched");
    }
  }
  class Watcher extends Thread {
    public Watcher() { start(); }
    public void run() {
      while(true) {
        for(int i = 0; i < s.length; i++)
          s[i].synchTest();
        try {
          sleep(500);
        } catch(InterruptedException e) {
          System.err.println("Interrupted");
        }
      }
    }
  }
  class StartL implements ActionListener {
    public void actionPerformed(ActionEvent e) {
      for(int i = 0; i < s.length; i++)
        s[i].start();
    }
  }
```

```
class WatcherL implements ActionListener {
  public void actionPerformed(ActionEvent e) {
    for(int i = 0; i < numWatchers; i++)
      new Watcher();
  }
}
public void init() {
  if(isApplet) {
    String counters = getParameter("size");
    if(counters != null)
      numCounters = Integer.parseInt(counters);
    String watchers = getParameter("watchers");
    if(watchers != null)
      numWatchers = Integer.parseInt(watchers);
  }
  s = new TwoCounter[numCounters];
  Container cp = getContentPane();
  cp.setLayout(new FlowLayout());
  for(int i = 0; i < s.length; i++)
    s[i] = new TwoCounter();
  JPanel p = new JPanel();
  start.addActionListener(new StartL());
  p.add(start);
  watcher.addActionListener(new WatcherL());
  p.add(watcher);
  p.add(new JLabel("Access Count"));
  p.add(aCount);
  cp.add(p);
}
public static void main(String[] args) {
  Sharing1 applet = new Sharing1();
  // This isn't an applet, so set the flag and
  // produce the parameter values from args:
  applet.isApplet = false;
  applet.numCounters =
    (args.length == 0 ? 12 :
      Integer.parseInt(args[0]));
  applet.numWatchers =
    (args.length < 2 ? 15 :
      Integer.parseInt(args[1]));
  Console.run(applet, 350,
```

```
        applet.numCounters * 50);
    }
} ///:~
```

As before, each counter contains its own display components: two text fields and a label that initially indicates that the counts are equivalent. These components are added to the content pane of the outer class object in the **TwoCounter** constructor.

Because a **TwoCounter** thread is started via a keypress by the user, it's possible that **start( )** could be called more than once. It's illegal for **Thread.start( )** to be called more than once for a thread (an exception is thrown). You can see the machinery to prevent this in the **started** flag and the overridden **start( )** method.

In **run( )**, **count1** and **count2** are incremented and displayed in a manner that would seem to keep them identical. Then **sleep( )** is called; without this call the program balks because it becomes hard for the CPU to swap tasks.

The **synchTest( )** method performs the apparently useless activity of checking to see if **count1** is equivalent to **count2**; if they are not equivalent it sets the label to "Unsynched" to indicate this. But first, it calls a static member of the class **Sharing1** that increments and displays an access counter to show how many times this check has occurred successfully. (The reason for this will become apparent in later variations of this example.)

The **Watcher** class is a thread whose job is to call **synchTest( )** for all of the **TwoCounter** objects that are active. It does this by stepping through the array that's kept in the **Sharing1** object. You can think of the **Watcher** as constantly peeking over the shoulders of the **TwoCounter** objects.

Sharing1 contains an array of **TwoCounter** objects that it initializes in **init( )** and starts as threads when you press the "start" button. Later, when you press the "Watch" button, one or more watchers are created and freed upon the unsuspecting **TwoCounter** threads.

Note that to run this as an applet in a browser, your applet tag will need to contain the lines:

```
<param name=size value="20">
<param name=watchers value="1">
```

You can experiment by changing the width, height, and parameters to suit your tastes. By changing the **size** and **watchers** you'll change the behavior of the program. This program is set up to run as a stand-alone application by pulling the arguments from the command line (or providing defaults).

Here's the surprising part. In **TwoCounter.run( )**, the infinite loop is just repeatedly passing over the adjacent lines:

```
t1.setText(Integer.toString(count1++));
t2.setText(Integer.toString(count2++));
```

(as well as sleeping, but that's not important here). When you run the program, however, you'll discover that **count1** and **count2** will be observed (by the **Watcher**s) to be unequal at times! This is because of the nature of threads—they can be suspended at any time. So at times, the suspension occurs *between* the execution of the above two lines, and the **Watcher** thread happens to come along and perform the comparison at just this moment, thus finding the two counters to be different.

This example shows a fundamental problem with using threads. You never know when a thread might be run. Imagine sitting at a table with a fork, about to spear the last piece of food on your plate and as your fork reaches for it, the food suddenly vanishes (because your thread was suspended and another thread came in and stole the food). That's the problem that you're dealing with.

Sometimes you don't care if a resource is being accessed at the same time you're trying to use it (the food is on some other plate). But for multithreading to work, you need some way to prevent two threads from accessing the same resource, at least during critical periods.

Preventing this kind of collision is simply a matter of putting a lock on a resource when one thread is using it. The first thread that accesses a resource locks it, and then the other threads cannot access that resource until it is unlocked, at which time another thread locks and uses it, etc. If the front seat of the car is the limited resource, the child who shouts "Dibs!" asserts the lock.

How Java shares resources

Java has built-in support to prevent collisions over one kind of resource: the memory in an object. Since you typically make the data elements of a class **private** and access that memory only through methods, you can prevent collisions by making a particular method **synchronized**. Only one thread at a time can call a **synchronized** method for a particular object (although that thread can call more than one of the object's synchronized methods). Here are simple **synchronized** methods:

```
synchronized void f() { /* ... */ }
synchronized void g(){ /* ... */ }
```

Each object contains a single lock (also called a *monitor*) that is automatically part of the object (you don't have to write any special code). When you call any **synchronized** method, that object is locked and no other **synchronized** method of that object can be called until the first one finishes and releases the lock. In the example above, if **f( )** is called for an object, **g( )** cannot be called for the same object until **f( )** is completed and releases the lock. Thus, there's a single lock that's shared by all the **synchronized** methods of a particular object, and this lock prevents common memory from being written by more than one method at a time (i.e., more than one thread at a time).

There's also a single lock per class (as part of the **Class** object for the class), so that **synchronized static** methods can lock each other out from simultaneous access of **static** data on a class-wide basis.

Note that if you want to guard some other resource from simultaneous access by multiple threads, you can do so by forcing access to that resource through **synchronized** methods.

Synchronizing the counters

Armed with this new keyword it appears that the solution is at hand: we'll simply use the **synchronized** keyword for the methods in **TwoCounter**. The following example is the same as the previous one, with the addition of the new keyword:

```
//: c14:Sharing2.java
// Using the synchronized keyword to prevent
```

```
// multiple access to a particular resource.
// <applet code=Sharing2 width=350 height=500>
// <param name=size value="12">
// <param name=watchers value="15">
// </applet>
import javax.swing.*;
import java.awt.*;
import java.awt.event.*;
import com.bruceeckel.swing.*;

public class Sharing2 extends JApplet {
  TwoCounter[] s;
  private static int accessCount = 0;
  private static JTextField aCount =
    new JTextField("0", 7);
  public static void incrementAccess() {
    accessCount++;
    aCount.setText(Integer.toString(accessCount));
  }
  private JButton
    start = new JButton("Start"),
    watcher = new JButton("Watch");
  private boolean isApplet = true;
  private int numCounters = 12;
  private int numWatchers = 15;

  class TwoCounter extends Thread {
    private boolean started = false;
    private JTextField
      t1 = new JTextField(5),
      t2 = new JTextField(5);
    private JLabel l =
      new JLabel("count1 == count2");
    private int count1 = 0, count2 = 0;
    public TwoCounter() {
      JPanel p = new JPanel();
      p.add(t1);
      p.add(t2);
      p.add(l);
      getContentPane().add(p);
    }
```

```java
  public void start() {
    if(!started) {
      started = true;
      super.start();
    }
  }
  public synchronized void run() {
    while (true) {
      t1.setText(Integer.toString(count1++));
      t2.setText(Integer.toString(count2++));
      try {
        sleep(500);
      } catch(InterruptedException e) {
        System.err.println("Interrupted");
      }
    }
  }
  public synchronized void synchTest() {
    Sharing2.incrementAccess();
    if(count1 != count2)
      l.setText("Unsynched");
  }
}

class Watcher extends Thread {
  public Watcher() { start(); }
  public void run() {
    while(true) {
      for(int i = 0; i < s.length; i++)
        s[i].synchTest();
      try {
        sleep(500);
      } catch(InterruptedException e) {
        System.err.println("Interrupted");
      }
    }
  }
}
class StartL implements ActionListener {
  public void actionPerformed(ActionEvent e) {
    for(int i = 0; i < s.length; i++)
```

```
        s[i].start();
    }
  }
  class WatcherL implements ActionListener {
    public void actionPerformed(ActionEvent e) {
      for(int i = 0; i < numWatchers; i++)
        new Watcher();
    }
  }
  public void init() {
    if(isApplet) {
      String counters = getParameter("size");
      if(counters != null)
        numCounters = Integer.parseInt(counters);
      String watchers = getParameter("watchers");
      if(watchers != null)
        numWatchers = Integer.parseInt(watchers);
    }
    s = new TwoCounter[numCounters];
    Container cp = getContentPane();
    cp.setLayout(new FlowLayout());
    for(int i = 0; i < s.length; i++)
      s[i] = new TwoCounter();
    JPanel p = new JPanel();
    start.addActionListener(new StartL());
    p.add(start);
    watcher.addActionListener(new WatcherL());
    p.add(watcher);
    p.add(new Label("Access Count"));
    p.add(aCount);
    cp.add(p);
  }
  public static void main(String[] args) {
    Sharing2 applet = new Sharing2();
    // This isn't an applet, so set the flag and
    // produce the parameter values from args:
    applet.isApplet = false;
    applet.numCounters =
      (args.length == 0 ? 12 :
        Integer.parseInt(args[0]));
    applet.numWatchers =
```

```
      (args.length < 2 ? 15 :
        Integer.parseInt(args[1]));
    Console.run(applet, 350,
      applet.numCounters * 50);
  }
} ///:~
```

You'll notice that *both* **run( )** and **synchTest( )** are **synchronized**. If you synchronize only one of the methods, then the other is free to ignore the object lock and can be called with impunity. This is an important point: Every method that accesses a critical shared resource must be **synchronized** or it won't work right.

Now a new issue arises. The **Watcher** can never get a peek at what's going on because the entire **run( )** method has been **synchronized**, and since **run( )** is always running for each object the lock is always tied up and **synchTest( )** can never be called. You can see this because the **accessCount** never changes.

What we'd like for this example is a way to isolate only *part* of the code inside **run( )**. The section of code you want to isolate this way is called a *critical section* and you use the **synchronized** keyword in a different way to set up a critical section. Java supports critical sections with the *synchronized block;* this time **synchronized** is used to specify the object whose lock is being used to synchronize the enclosed code:

```
synchronized(syncObject) {
  // This code can be accessed
  // by only one thread at a time
}
```

Before the synchronized block can be entered, the lock must be acquired on **syncObject**. If some other thread already has this lock, then the block cannot be entered until the lock is given up.

The **Sharing2** example can be modified by removing the **synchronized** keyword from the entire **run( )** method and instead putting a **synchronized** block around the two critical lines. But what object should be used as the lock? The one that is already respected by **synchTest( )**, which is the current object (**this**)! So the modified **run( )** looks like this:

```
public void run() {
  while (true) {
    synchronized(this) {
      t1.setText(Integer.toString(count1++));
      t2.setText(Integer.toString(count2++));
    }
    try {
      sleep(500);
    } catch(InterruptedException e) {
      System.err.println("Interrupted");
    }
  }
}
```

This is the only change that must be made to **Sharing2.java**, and you'll see that while the two counters are never out of synch (according to when the **Watcher** is allowed to look at them), there is still adequate access provided to the **Watcher** during the execution of **run( )**.

Of course, all synchronization depends on programmer diligence: every piece of code that can access a shared resource must be wrapped in an appropriate synchronized block.

Synchronized efficiency

Since having two methods write to the same piece of data *never* sounds like a particularly good idea, it might seem to make sense for all methods to be automatically **synchronized** and eliminate the **synchronized** keyword altogether. (Of course, the example with a **synchronized run( )** shows that this wouldn't work either.) But it turns out that acquiring a lock is not a cheap operation—it multiplies the cost of a method call (that is, entering and exiting from the method, not executing the body of the method) by a minimum of four times, and could be much more depending on your implementation. So if you know that a particular method will not cause contention problems it is expedient to leave off the **synchronized** keyword. On the other hand, leaving off the **synchronized** keyword because you think it is a performance bottleneck, and hoping that there aren't any collisions is an invitation to disaster.

JavaBeans revisited

Now that you understand synchronization, you can take another look at JavaBeans. Whenever you create a Bean, you must assume that it will run in a multithreaded environment. This means that:

1. Whenever possible, all the **public** methods of a Bean should be **synchronized**. Of course, this incurs the **synchronized** run-time overhead. If that's a problem, methods that will not cause problems in critical sections can be left un-**synchronized**, but keep in mind that this is not always obvious. Methods that qualify tend to be small (such as **getCircleSize( )** in the following example) and/or "atomic," that is, the method call executes in such a short amount of code that the object cannot be changed during execution. Making such methods un-**synchronized** might not have a significant effect on the execution speed of your program. You might as well make all **public** methods of a Bean **synchronized** and remove the **synchronized** keyword only when you know for sure that it's necessary and that it makes a difference.

2. When firing a multicast event to a bunch of listeners interested in that event, you must assume that listeners might be added or removed while moving through the list.

The first point is fairly easy to deal with, but the second point requires a little more thought. Consider the **BangBean.java** example presented in the last chapter. That ducked out of the multithreading question by ignoring the **synchronized** keyword (which hadn't been introduced yet) and making the event unicast. Here's that example modified to work in a multithreaded environment and to use multicasting for events:

```
//: c14:BangBean2.java
// You should write your Beans this way so they
// can run in a multithreaded environment.
import javax.swing.*;
import java.awt.*;
import java.awt.event.*;
import java.util.*;
import java.io.*;
```

```
import com.bruceeckel.swing.*;

public class BangBean2 extends JPanel
    implements Serializable {
  private int xm, ym;
  private int cSize = 20; // Circle size
  private String text = "Bang!";
  private int fontSize = 48;
  private Color tColor = Color.red;
  private ArrayList actionListeners =
    new ArrayList();
  public BangBean2() {
    addMouseListener(new ML());
    addMouseMotionListener(new MM());
  }
  public synchronized int getCircleSize() {
    return cSize;
  }
  public synchronized void
  setCircleSize(int newSize) {
    cSize = newSize;
  }
  public synchronized String getBangText() {
    return text;
  }
  public synchronized void
  setBangText(String newText) {
    text = newText;
  }
  public synchronized int getFontSize() {
    return fontSize;
  }
  public synchronized void
  setFontSize(int newSize) {
    fontSize = newSize;
  }
  public synchronized Color getTextColor() {
    return tColor;
  }
  public synchronized void
  setTextColor(Color newColor) {
```

```
      tColor = newColor;
    }
    public void paintComponent(Graphics g) {
      super.paintComponent(g);
      g.setColor(Color.black);
      g.drawOval(xm - cSize/2, ym - cSize/2,
        cSize, cSize);
    }
    // This is a multicast listener, which is
    // more typically used than the unicast
    // approach taken in BangBean.java:
    public synchronized void
      addActionListener(ActionListener l) {
      actionListeners.add(l);
    }
    public synchronized void
      removeActionListener(ActionListener l) {
      actionListeners.remove(l);
    }
    // Notice this isn't synchronized:
    public void notifyListeners() {
      ActionEvent a =
        new ActionEvent(BangBean2.this,
          ActionEvent.ACTION_PERFORMED, null);
      ArrayList lv = null;
      // Make a shallow copy of the List in case
      // someone adds a listener while we're
      // calling listeners:
      synchronized(this) {
        lv = (ArrayList)actionListeners.clone();
      }
      // Call all the listener methods:
      for(int i = 0; i < lv.size(); i++)
        ((ActionListener)lv.get(i))
          .actionPerformed(a);
    }
    class ML extends MouseAdapter {
      public void mousePressed(MouseEvent e) {
        Graphics g = getGraphics();
        g.setColor(tColor);
        g.setFont(
```

```
          new Font(
            "TimesRoman", Font.BOLD, fontSize));
        int width =
          g.getFontMetrics().stringWidth(text);
        g.drawString(text,
          (getSize().width - width) /2,
          getSize().height/2);
        g.dispose();
        notifyListeners();
      }
    }
  class MM extends MouseMotionAdapter {
    public void mouseMoved(MouseEvent e) {
      xm = e.getX();
      ym = e.getY();
      repaint();
    }
  }
  public static void main(String[] args) {
    BangBean2 bb = new BangBean2();
    bb.addActionListener(new ActionListener() {
      public void actionPerformed(ActionEvent e){
        System.out.println("ActionEvent" + e);
      }
    });
    bb.addActionListener(new ActionListener() {
      public void actionPerformed(ActionEvent e){
        System.out.println("BangBean2 action");
      }
    });
    bb.addActionListener(new ActionListener() {
      public void actionPerformed(ActionEvent e){
        System.out.println("More action");
      }
    });
    Console.run(bb, 300, 300);
  }
} ///:~
```

Adding **synchronized** to the methods is an easy change. However, notice in **addActionListener( )** and **removeActionListener( )** that the **ActionListener**s are now added to and removed from an **ArrayList**, so you can have as many as you want.

You can see that the method **notifyListeners( )** is *not* **synchronized**. It can be called from more than one thread at a time. It's also possible for **addActionListener( )** or **removeActionListener( )** to be called in the middle of a call to **notifyListeners( )**, which is a problem since it traverses the **ArrayList actionListeners**. To alleviate the problem, the **ArrayList** is cloned inside a **synchronized** clause and the clone is traversed (see Appendix A for details of cloning). This way the original **ArrayList** can be manipulated without impact on **notifyListeners( )**.

The **paintComponent( )** method is also not **synchronized**. Deciding whether to synchronize overridden methods is not as clear as when you're just adding your own methods. In this example it turns out that **paint( )** seems to work OK whether it's **synchronized** or not. But the issues you must consider are:

1. Does the method modify the state of "critical" variables within the object? To discover whether the variables are "critical" you must determine whether they will be read or set by other threads in the program. (In this case, the reading or setting is virtually always accomplished via **synchronized** methods, so you can just examine those.) In the case of **paint( )**, no modification takes place.

2. Does the method depend on the state of these "critical" variables? If a **synchronized** method modifies a variable that your method uses, then you might very well want to make your method **synchronized** as well. Based on this, you might observe that **cSize** is changed by **synchronized** methods and therefore **paint( )** should be **synchronized**. Here, however, you can ask "What's the worst thing that will happen if **cSize** is changed during a **paint( )**?" When you see that it's nothing too bad, and a transient effect at that, you can decide to leave **paint( )** un-**synchronized** to prevent the extra overhead from the **synchronized** method call.

3. A third clue is to notice whether the base-class version of **paint( )** is **synchronized**, which it isn't. This isn't an airtight argument,

just a clue. In this case, for example, a field that *is* changed via **synchronized** methods (that is **cSize**) has been mixed into the **paint( )** formula and might have changed the situation. Notice, however, that **synchronized** doesn't inherit—that is, if a method is **synchronized** in the base class then it *is not* automatically **synchronized** in the derived class overridden version.

The test code in **TestBangBean2** has been modified from that in the previous chapter to demonstrate the multicast ability of **BangBean2** by adding extra listeners.

Blocking

A thread can be in any one of four states:

1. *New*: The thread object has been created but it hasn't been started yet so it cannot run.

2. *Runnable*: This means that a thread *can* be run when the time-slicing mechanism has CPU cycles available for the thread. Thus, the thread might or might not be running, but there's nothing to prevent it from being run if the scheduler can arrange it; it's not dead or blocked.

3. *Dead*: The normal way for a thread to die is by returning from its **run( )** method. You can also call **stop( )**, but this throws an exception that's a subclass of **Error** (which means you aren't forced to put the call in a **try** block). Remember that throwing an exception should be a special event and not part of normal program execution; thus the use of **stop( )** is deprecated in Java 2. There's also a **destroy( )** method (which has never been implemented) that you should never call if you can avoid it since it's drastic and doesn't release object locks.

4. *Blocked*: The thread could be run but there's something that prevents it. While a thread is in the blocked state the scheduler will simply skip over it and not give it any CPU time. Until a thread reenters the runnable state it won't perform any operations.

Becoming blocked

The blocked state is the most interesting one, and is worth further examination. A thread can become blocked for five reasons:

1. You've put the thread to sleep by calling **sleep(milliseconds),** in which case it will not be run for the specified time.

2. You've suspended the execution of the thread with **suspend( )**. It will not become runnable again until the thread gets the **resume( )** message (these are deprecated in Java 2, and will be examined further).

3. You've suspended the execution of the thread with **wait( )**. It will not become runnable again until the thread gets the **notify( )** or **notifyAll( )** message. (Yes, this looks just like number 2, but there's a distinct difference that will be revealed.)

4. The thread is waiting for some I/O to complete.

5. The thread is trying to call a **synchronized** method on another object, and that object's lock is not available.

You can also call **yield( )** (a method of the **Thread** class) to voluntarily give up the CPU so that other threads can run. However, the same thing happens if the scheduler decides that your thread has had enough time and jumps to another thread. That is, nothing prevents the scheduler from moving your thread and giving time to some other thread. When a thread is blocked, there's some reason that it cannot continue running.

The following example shows all five ways of becoming blocked. It all exists in a single file called **Blocking.java,** but it will be examined here in discrete pieces. (You'll notice the "Continued" and "Continuing" tags that allow the code extraction tool to piece everything together.)

Because this example demonstrates some deprecated methods, you *will* get deprecation messages when it is compiled.

First, the basic framework:

```
//: c14:Blocking.java
// Demonstrates the various ways a thread
```

```
// can be blocked.
// <applet code=Blocking width=350 height=550>
// </applet>
import javax.swing.*;
import java.awt.*;
import java.awt.event.*;
import java.io.*;
import com.bruceeckel.swing.*;

/////////// The basic framework ///////////
class Blockable extends Thread {
  private Peeker peeker;
  protected JTextField state = new JTextField(30);
  protected int i;
  public Blockable(Container c) {
    c.add(state);
    peeker = new Peeker(this, c);
  }
  public synchronized int read() { return i; }
  protected synchronized void update() {
    state.setText(getClass().getName()
      + " state: i = " + i);
  }
  public void stopPeeker() {
    // peeker.stop(); Deprecated in Java 1.2
    peeker.terminate(); // The preferred approach
  }
}

class Peeker extends Thread {
  private Blockable b;
  private int session;
  private JTextField status = new JTextField(30);
  private boolean stop = false;
  public Peeker(Blockable b, Container c) {
    c.add(status);
    this.b = b;
    start();
  }
  public void terminate() { stop = true; }
  public void run() {
```

```
    while (!stop) {
      status.setText(b.getClass().getName()
        + " Peeker " + (++session)
        + "; value = " + b.read());
       try {
        sleep(100);
      } catch(InterruptedException e) {
        System.err.println("Interrupted");
      }
    }
  }
} ///:Continued
```

The **Blockable** class is meant to be a base class for all the classes in this example that demonstrate blocking. A **Blockable** object contains a **JTextField** called **state** that is used to display information about the object. The method that displays this information is **update( )**. You can see it uses **getClass( ).getName( )** to produce the name of the class instead of just printing it out; this is because **update( )** cannot know the exact name of the class it is called for, since it will be a class derived from **Blockable**.

The indicator of change in **Blockable** is an **int i,** which will be incremented by the **run( )** method of the derived class.

There's a thread of class **Peeker** that is started for each **Blockable** object, and the **Peeker**'s job is to watch its associated **Blockable** object to see changes in **i** by calling **read( )** and reporting them in its **status JTextField**. This is important: Note that **read( )** and **update( )** are both **synchronized**, which means they require that the object lock be free.

Sleeping

The first test in this program is with **sleep( ):**

```
///:Continuing
/////////////// Blocking via sleep() //////////////
class Sleeper1 extends Blockable {
  public Sleeper1(Container c) { super(c); }
  public synchronized void run() {
```

```
      while(true) {
        i++;
        update();
         try {
          sleep(1000);
        } catch(InterruptedException e) {
          System.err.println("Interrupted");
        }
      }
    }
  }
}

class Sleeper2 extends Blockable {
  public Sleeper2(Container c) { super(c); }
  public void run() {
    while(true) {
      change();
       try {
        sleep(1000);
      } catch(InterruptedException e) {
        System.err.println("Interrupted");
      }
    }
  }
  public synchronized void change() {
      i++;
      update();
  }
} ///:Continued
```

In **Sleeper1** the entire **run( )** method is **synchronized**. You'll see that
the **Peeker** associated with this object will run along merrily *until* you
start the thread, and then the **Peeker** stops cold. This is one form of
blocking: since **Sleeper1.run( )** is **synchronized**, and once the thread
starts it's always inside **run( )**, the method never gives up the object lock
and the **Peeker** is blocked.

Sleeper2 provides a solution by making **run( )** un-**synchronized**. Only
the **change( )** method is **synchronized**, which means that while **run( )**
is in **sleep( )**, the **Peeker** can access the **synchronized** method it

needs, namely **read( )**. Here you'll see that the **Peeker** continues
running when you start the **Sleeper2** thread.

Suspending and resuming

The next part of the example introduces the concept of suspension. The
Thread class has a method **suspend( )** to temporarily stop the thread
and **resume( )** that restarts it at the point it was halted. **resume( )** must
be called by some thread outside the suspended one, and in this case
there's a separate class called **Resumer** that does just that. Each of the
classes demonstrating suspend/resume has an associated resumer:

```
///:Continuing
////////// Blocking via suspend() //////////
class SuspendResume extends Blockable {
  public SuspendResume(Container c) {
    super(c);
    new Resumer(this);
  }
}

class SuspendResume1 extends SuspendResume {
  public SuspendResume1(Container c) { super(c); }
  public synchronized void run() {
    while(true) {
      i++;
      update();
      suspend(); // Deprecated in Java 1.2
    }
  }
}

class SuspendResume2 extends SuspendResume {
  public SuspendResume2(Container c) { super(c); }
  public void run() {
    while(true) {
      change();
      suspend(); // Deprecated in Java 1.2
    }
  }
  public synchronized void change() {
```

```
        i++;
        update();
    }
}

class Resumer extends Thread {
  private SuspendResume sr;
  public Resumer(SuspendResume sr) {
    this.sr = sr;
    start();
  }
  public void run() {
    while(true) {
       try {
         sleep(1000);
       } catch(InterruptedException e) {
         System.err.println("Interrupted");
       }
       sr.resume(); // Deprecated in Java 1.2
    }
  }
} ///:Continued
```

SuspendResume1 also has a **synchronized run( )** method. Again, when you start this thread you'll see that its associated **Peeker** gets blocked waiting for the lock to become available, which never happens. This is fixed as before in **SuspendResume2**, which does not **synchronize** the entire **run( )** method but instead uses a separate **synchronized change( )** method.

You should be aware that Java 2 deprecates the use of **suspend( )** and **resume( )**, because **suspend( )** holds the object's lock and is thus deadlock-prone. That is, you can easily get a number of locked objects waiting on each other, and this will cause your program to freeze. Although you might see them used in older programs you should not use **suspend( )** and **resume( )**. The proper solution is described later in this chapter.

Wait and notify

In the first two examples, it's important to understand that both **sleep( )** and **suspend( )** *do not* release the lock as they are called. You must be aware of this when working with locks. On the other hand, the method **wait( )** *does* release the lock when it is called, which means that other **synchronized** methods in the thread object could be called during a **wait( )**. In the following two classes, you'll see that the **run( )** method is fully **synchronized** in both cases, however, the **Peeker** still has full access to the **synchronized** methods during a **wait( )**. This is because **wait( )** releases the lock on the object as it suspends the method it's called within.

You'll also see that there are two forms of **wait( )**. The first takes an argument in milliseconds that has the same meaning as in **sleep( )**: pause for this period of time. The difference is that in **wait( )**, the object lock is released *and* you can come out of the **wait( )** because of a **notify( )** as well as having the clock run out.

The second form takes no arguments, and means that the **wait( )** will continue until a **notify( )** comes along and will not automatically terminate after a time.

One fairly unique aspect of **wait( )** and **notify( )** is that both methods are part of the base class **Object** and not part of **Thread** as are **sleep( )**, **suspend( )**, and **resume( )**. Although this seems a bit strange at first—to have something that's exclusively for threading as part of the universal base class—it's essential because they manipulate the lock that's also part of every object. As a result, you can put a **wait( )** inside any **synchronized** method, regardless of whether there's any threading going on inside that particular class. In fact, the *only* place you can call **wait( )** is within a **synchronized** method or block. If you call **wait( )** or **notify( )** within a method that's not **synchronized,** the program will compile, but when you run it you'll get an **IllegalMonitorStateException** with the somewhat nonintuitive message "current thread not owner." Note that **sleep( )**, **suspend( )**, and **resume( )** can all be called within non-**synchronized** methods since they don't manipulate the lock.

You can call **wait( )** or **notify( )** only for your own lock. Again, you can compile code that tries to use the wrong lock, but it will produce the same **IllegalMonitorStateException** message as before. You can't fool with someone else's lock, but you can ask another object to perform an operation that manipulates its own lock. So one approach is to create a **synchronized** method that calls **notify( )** for its own object. However, in **Notifier** you'll see the **notify( )** call inside a **synchronized** block:

```
synchronized(wn2) {
  wn2.notify();
}
```

where **wn2** is the object of type **WaitNotify2**. This method, which is not part of **WaitNotify2**, acquires the lock on the **wn2** object, at which point it's legal for it to call **notify( )** for **wn2** and you won't get the **IllegalMonitorStateException**.

```
///:Continuing
////////// Blocking via wait() //////////
class WaitNotify1 extends Blockable {
  public WaitNotify1(Container c) { super(c); }
  public synchronized void run() {
    while(true) {
      i++;
      update();
       try {
        wait(1000);
      } catch(InterruptedException e) {
        System.err.println("Interrupted");
      }
    }
  }
}

class WaitNotify2 extends Blockable {
  public WaitNotify2(Container c) {
    super(c);
    new Notifier(this);
  }
  public synchronized void run() {
    while(true) {
```

```
      i++;
      update();
       try {
        wait();
      } catch(InterruptedException e) {
        System.err.println("Interrupted");
      }
    }
  }
}

class Notifier extends Thread {
  private WaitNotify2 wn2;
  public Notifier(WaitNotify2 wn2) {
    this.wn2 = wn2;
    start();
  }
  public void run() {
    while(true) {
      try {
        sleep(2000);
      } catch(InterruptedException e) {
        System.err.println("Interrupted");
      }
      synchronized(wn2) {
        wn2.notify();
      }
    }
  }
} ///:Continued
```

wait( ) is typically used when you've gotten to the point where you're
waiting for some other condition, under the control of forces outside your
thread, to change and you don't want to idly wait by inside the thread. So
wait( ) allows you to put the thread to sleep while waiting for the world to
change, and only when a **notify( )** or **notifyAll( )** occurs does the thread
wake up and check for changes. Thus, it provides a way to synchronize
between threads.

Blocking on I/O

If a stream is waiting for some I/O activity, it will automatically block. In the following portion of the example, the two classes work with generic **Reader** and **Writer** objects, but in the test framework a piped stream will be set up to allow the two threads to safely pass data to each other (which is the purpose of piped streams).

The **Sender** puts data into the **Writer** and sleeps for a random amount of time. However, **Receiver** has no **sleep( )**, **suspend( )**, or **wait( )**. But when it does a **read( )** it automatically blocks when there is no more data.

```
///:Continuing
class Sender extends Blockable { // send
  private Writer out;
  public Sender(Container c, Writer out) {
    super(c);
    this.out = out;
  }
  public void run() {
    while(true) {
      for(char c = 'A'; c <= 'z'; c++) {
        try {
          i++;
          out.write(c);
          state.setText("Sender sent: "
            + (char)c);
          sleep((int)(3000 * Math.random()));
        } catch(InterruptedException e) {
          System.err.println("Interrupted");
        } catch(IOException e) {
          System.err.println("IO problem");
        }
      }
    }
  }
}

class Receiver extends Blockable {
  private Reader in;
```

```
    public Receiver(Container c, Reader in) {
      super(c);
      this.in = in;
    }
    public void run() {
      try {
        while(true) {
          i++; // Show peeker it's alive
          // Blocks until characters are there:
          state.setText("Receiver read: "
            + (char)in.read());
        }
      } catch(IOException e) {
        System.err.println("IO problem");
      }
    }
} ///:Continued
```

Both classes also put information into their **state** fields and change **i** so the **Peeker** can see that the thread is running.

Testing

The main applet class is surprisingly simple because most of the work has been put into the **Blockable** framework. Basically, an array of **Blockable** objects is created, and since each one is a thread, they perform their own activities when you press the "start" button. There's also a button and **actionPerformed( )** clause to stop all of the **Peeker** objects, which provides a demonstration of the alternative to the deprecated (in Java 2) **stop( )** method of **Thread**.

To set up a connection between the **Sender** and **Receiver** objects, a **PipedWriter** and **PipedReader** are created. Note that the **PipedReader in** must be connected to the **PipedWriter out** via a constructor argument. After that, anything that's placed in **out** can later be extracted from **in**, as if it passed through a pipe (hence the name). The **in** and **out** objects are then passed to the **Receiver** and **Sender** constructors, respectively, which treat them as **Reader** and **Writer** objects of any type (that is, they are upcast).

The array of **Blockable** references **b** is not initialized at its point of definition because the piped streams cannot be set up before that definition takes place (the need for the **try** block prevents this).

```
///:Continuing
////////// Testing Everything //////////
public class Blocking extends JApplet {
  private JButton
    start = new JButton("Start"),
    stopPeekers = new JButton("Stop Peekers");
  private boolean started = false;
  private Blockable[] b;
  private PipedWriter out;
  private PipedReader in;
  class StartL implements ActionListener {
    public void actionPerformed(ActionEvent e) {
      if(!started) {
        started = true;
        for(int i = 0; i < b.length; i++)
          b[i].start();
      }
    }
  }
  class StopPeekersL implements ActionListener {
    public void actionPerformed(ActionEvent e) {
      // Demonstration of the preferred
      // alternative to Thread.stop():
      for(int i = 0; i < b.length; i++)
        b[i].stopPeeker();
    }
  }
  public void init() {
    Container cp = getContentPane();
    cp.setLayout(new FlowLayout());
    out = new PipedWriter();
    try {
      in = new PipedReader(out);
    } catch(IOException e) {
      System.err.println("PipedReader problem");
    }
    b = new Blockable[] {
```

```
      new Sleeper1(cp),
      new Sleeper2(cp),
      new SuspendResume1(cp),
      new SuspendResume2(cp),
      new WaitNotify1(cp),
      new WaitNotify2(cp),
      new Sender(cp, out),
      new Receiver(cp, in)
    };
    start.addActionListener(new StartL());
    cp.add(start);
    stopPeekers.addActionListener(
      new StopPeekersL());
    cp.add(stopPeekers);
  }
  public static void main(String[] args) {
    Console.run(new Blocking(), 350, 550);
  }
} ///:~
```

In **init( )**, notice the loop that moves through the entire array and adds the **state** and **peeker.status** text fields to the page.

When the **Blockable** threads are initially created, each one automatically creates and starts its own **Peeker**. So you'll see the **Peeker**s running before the **Blockable** threads are started. This is important, as some of the **Peeker**s will get blocked and stop when the **Blockable** threads start, and it's essential to see this to understand that particular aspect of blocking.

Deadlock

Because threads can become blocked *and* because objects can have **synchronized** methods that prevent threads from accessing that object until the synchronization lock is released, it's possible for one thread to get stuck waiting for another thread, which in turn waits for another thread, etc., until the chain leads back to a thread waiting on the first one. You get a continuous loop of threads waiting on each other and no one can move. This is called *deadlock*. The claim is that it doesn't happen that often, but when it happens to you it's frustrating to debug.

There is no language support to help prevent deadlock; it's up to you to avoid it by careful design. These are not comforting words to the person who's trying to debug a deadlocking program.

The deprecation of **stop( )**, **suspend( )**, **resume( )**, and **destroy( )** in Java 2

One change that has been made in Java 2 to reduce the possibility of deadlock is the deprecation of **Thread**'s **stop( )**, **suspend( )**, **resume( )**, and **destroy( )** methods.

The reason that the **stop( )** method is deprecated is because it doesn't release the locks that the thread has acquired, and if the objects are in an inconsistent state ("damaged") other threads can view and modify them in that state. The resulting problems can be subtle and difficult to detect. Instead of using **stop( )**, you should follow the example in **Blocking.java** and use a flag to tell the thread when to terminate itself by exiting its **run( )** method.

There are times when a thread blocks—such as when it is waiting for input—and it cannot poll a flag as it does in **Blocking.java**. In these cases, you still shouldn't use **stop( )**, but instead you can use the **interrupt( )** method in **Thread** to break out of the blocked code:

```
//: c14:Interrupt.java
// The alternative approach to using
// stop() when a thread is blocked.
// <applet code=Interrupt width=200 height=100>
// </applet>
import javax.swing.*;
import java.awt.*;
import java.awt.event.*;
import com.bruceeckel.swing.*;

class Blocked extends Thread {
  public synchronized void run() {
    try {
      wait(); // Blocks
    } catch(InterruptedException e) {
      System.err.println("Interrupted");
    }
```

```
        System.out.println("Exiting run()");
    }
}

public class Interrupt extends JApplet {
  private JButton
    interrupt = new JButton("Interrupt");
  private Blocked blocked = new Blocked();
  public void init() {
    Container cp = getContentPane();
    cp.setLayout(new FlowLayout());
    cp.add(interrupt);
    interrupt.addActionListener(
      new ActionListener() {
        public
        void actionPerformed(ActionEvent e) {
          System.out.println("Button pressed");
          if(blocked == null) return;
          Thread remove = blocked;
          blocked = null; // to release it
          remove.interrupt();
        }
      });
    blocked.start();
  }
  public static void main(String[] args) {
    Console.run(new Interrupt(), 200, 100);
  }
} ///:~
```

The **wait( )** inside **Blocked.run( )** produces the blocked thread. When you press the button, the **blocked** reference is set to **null** so the garbage collector will clean it up, and then the object's **interrupt( )** method is called. The first time you press the button you'll see that the thread quits, but after that there's no thread to kill so you just see that the button has been pressed.

The **suspend( )** and **resume( )** methods turn out to be inherently deadlock-prone. When you call **suspend( )**, the target thread stops but it still holds any locks that it has acquired up to that point. So no other thread can access the locked resources until the thread is resumed. Any thread that wants to resume the target thread and also tries to use any of the locked resources produces deadlock. You should not use **suspend( )** and **resume( )**, but instead put a flag in your **Thread** class to indicate whether the thread should be active or suspended. If the flag indicates that the thread is suspended, the thread goes into a wait using **wait( )**. When the flag indicates that the thread should be resumed the thread is restarted with **notify( )**. An example can be produced by modifying **Counter2.java**. Although the effect is similar, you'll notice that the code organization is quite different—anonymous inner classes are used for all of the listeners and the **Thread** is an inner class, which makes programming slightly more convenient since it eliminates some of the extra bookkeeping necessary in **Counter2.java**:

```
//: c14:Suspend.java
// The alternative approach to using suspend()
// and resume(), which are deprecated in Java 2.
// <applet code=Suspend width=300 height=100>
// </applet>
import javax.swing.*;
import java.awt.*;
import java.awt.event.*;
import com.bruceeckel.swing.*;

public class Suspend extends JApplet {
  private JTextField t = new JTextField(10);
  private JButton
    suspend = new JButton("Suspend"),
    resume = new JButton("Resume");
  private Suspendable ss = new Suspendable();
  class Suspendable extends Thread {
    private int count = 0;
    private boolean suspended = false;
    public Suspendable() { start(); }
    public void fauxSuspend() {
      suspended = true;
    }
    public synchronized void fauxResume() {
      suspended = false;
      notify();
    }
```

```java
    public void run() {
      while (true) {
        try {
          sleep(100);
          synchronized(this) {
            while(suspended)
              wait();
          }
        } catch(InterruptedException e) {
          System.err.println("Interrupted");
        }
        t.setText(Integer.toString(count++));
      }
    }
  public void init() {
    Container cp = getContentPane();
    cp.setLayout(new FlowLayout());
    cp.add(t);
    suspend.addActionListener(
      new ActionListener() {
        public
        void actionPerformed(ActionEvent e) {
          ss.fauxSuspend();
        }
      });
    cp.add(suspend);
    resume.addActionListener(
      new ActionListener() {
        public
        void actionPerformed(ActionEvent e) {
          ss.fauxResume();
        }
      });
    cp.add(resume);
  }
  public static void main(String[] args) {
    Console.run(new Suspend(), 300, 100);
  }
} ///:~
```

The flag **suspended** inside **Suspendable** is used to turn suspension on and off. To suspend, the flag is set to **true** by calling **fauxSuspend( )** and this is detected inside **run( )**. The **wait( )**, as described earlier in this chapter, must be **synchronized** so that it has the object lock. In **fauxResume( )**, the **suspended** flag is set to **false** and **notify( )** is called—since this wakes up **wait( )** inside a **synchronized** clause the **fauxResume( )** method must also be **synchronized** so that it acquires the lock before calling **notify( )** (thus the lock is available for the **wait( )** to wake up with). If you follow the style shown in this program you can avoid using **suspend( )** and **resume( )**.

The **destroy( )** method of **Thread** has never been implemented; it's like a **suspend( )** that cannot resume, so it has the same deadlock issues as **suspend( )**. However, this is not a deprecated method and it might be implemented in a future version of Java (after 2) for special situations in which the risk of a deadlock is acceptable.

You might wonder why these methods, now deprecated, were included in Java in the first place. It seems an admission of a rather significant mistake to simply remove them outright (and pokes yet another hole in the arguments for Java's exceptional design and infallibility touted by Sun marketing people). The heartening part about the change is that it clearly indicates that the technical people and not the marketing people are running the show—they discovered a problem and they are fixing it. I find this much more promising and hopeful than leaving the problem in because "fixing it would admit an error." It means that Java will continue to improve, even if it means a little discomfort on the part of Java programmers. I'd rather deal with the discomfort than watch the language stagnate.

Priorities

The *priority* of a thread tells the scheduler how important this thread is. If there are a number of threads blocked and waiting to be run, the scheduler will run the one with the highest priority first. However, this doesn't mean that threads with lower priority don't get run (that is, you can't get deadlocked because of priorities). Lower priority threads just tend to run less often.

Although priorities are interesting to know about and to play with, in practice you almost never need to set priorities yourself. So feel free to skip the rest of this section if priorities aren't interesting to you.

Reading and setting priorities

You can read the priority of a thread with **getPriority( )** and change it with **setPriority( )**. The form of the prior "counter" examples can be used to show the effect of changing the priorities. In this applet you'll see that the counters slow down as the associated threads have their priorities lowered:

```
//: c14:Counter5.java
// Adjusting the priorities of threads.
// <applet code=Counter5 width=450 height=600>
// </applet>
import javax.swing.*;
import java.awt.*;
import java.awt.event.*;
import com.bruceeckel.swing.*;

class Ticker2 extends Thread {
  private JButton
    b = new JButton("Toggle"),
    incPriority = new JButton("up"),
    decPriority = new JButton("down");
  private JTextField
    t = new JTextField(10),
    pr = new JTextField(3); // Display priority
  private int count = 0;
  private boolean runFlag = true;
  public Ticker2(Container c) {
    b.addActionListener(new ToggleL());
    incPriority.addActionListener(new UpL());
    decPriority.addActionListener(new DownL());
    JPanel p = new JPanel();
    p.add(t);
    p.add(pr);
    p.add(b);
    p.add(incPriority);
    p.add(decPriority);
```

```
      c.add(p);
    }
    class ToggleL implements ActionListener {
      public void actionPerformed(ActionEvent e) {
        runFlag = !runFlag;
      }
    }
    class UpL implements ActionListener {
      public void actionPerformed(ActionEvent e) {
        int newPriority = getPriority() + 1;
        if(newPriority > Thread.MAX_PRIORITY)
          newPriority = Thread.MAX_PRIORITY;
        setPriority(newPriority);
      }
    }
    class DownL implements ActionListener {
      public void actionPerformed(ActionEvent e) {
        int newPriority = getPriority() - 1;
        if(newPriority < Thread.MIN_PRIORITY)
          newPriority = Thread.MIN_PRIORITY;
        setPriority(newPriority);
      }
    }
    public void run() {
      while (true) {
        if(runFlag) {
          t.setText(Integer.toString(count++));
          pr.setText(
            Integer.toString(getPriority()));
        }
        yield();
      }
    }
  }

public class Counter5 extends JApplet {
  private JButton
    start = new JButton("Start"),
    upMax = new JButton("Inc Max Priority"),
    downMax = new JButton("Dec Max Priority");
  private boolean started = false;
```

```
private static final int SIZE = 10;
private Ticker2[] s = new Ticker2[SIZE];
private JTextField mp = new JTextField(3);
public void init() {
  Container cp = getContentPane();
  cp.setLayout(new FlowLayout());
  for(int i = 0; i < s.length; i++)
    s[i] = new Ticker2(cp);
  cp.add(new JLabel(
    "MAX_PRIORITY = " + Thread.MAX_PRIORITY));
  cp.add(new JLabel("MIN_PRIORITY = "
    + Thread.MIN_PRIORITY));
  cp.add(new JLabel("Group Max Priority = "));
  cp.add(mp);
  cp.add(start);
  cp.add(upMax);
  cp.add(downMax);
  start.addActionListener(new StartL());
  upMax.addActionListener(new UpMaxL());
  downMax.addActionListener(new DownMaxL());
  showMaxPriority();
  // Recursively display parent thread groups:
  ThreadGroup parent =
    s[0].getThreadGroup().getParent();
  while(parent != null) {
    cp.add(new Label(
      "Parent threadgroup max priority = "
      + parent.getMaxPriority()));
    parent = parent.getParent();
  }
}
public void showMaxPriority() {
  mp.setText(Integer.toString(
    s[0].getThreadGroup().getMaxPriority()));
}
class StartL implements ActionListener {
  public void actionPerformed(ActionEvent e) {
    if(!started) {
      started = true;
      for(int i = 0; i < s.length; i++)
        s[i].start();
```

```
        }
      }
    }
    class UpMaxL implements ActionListener {
      public void actionPerformed(ActionEvent e) {
        int maxp =
          s[0].getThreadGroup().getMaxPriority();
        if(++maxp > Thread.MAX_PRIORITY)
          maxp = Thread.MAX_PRIORITY;
        s[0].getThreadGroup().setMaxPriority(maxp);
        showMaxPriority();
      }
    }
    class DownMaxL implements ActionListener {
      public void actionPerformed(ActionEvent e) {
        int maxp =
          s[0].getThreadGroup().getMaxPriority();
        if(--maxp < Thread.MIN_PRIORITY)
          maxp = Thread.MIN_PRIORITY;
        s[0].getThreadGroup().setMaxPriority(maxp);
        showMaxPriority();
      }
    }
    public static void main(String[] args) {
      Console.run(new Counter5(), 450, 600);
    }
} ///:~
```

Ticker2 follows the form established earlier in this chapter, but there's an extra **JTextField** for displaying the priority of the thread and two more buttons for incrementing and decrementing the priority.

Also notice the use of **yield( )**, which voluntarily hands control back to the scheduler. Without this the multithreading mechanism still works, but you'll notice it runs slowly (try removing the call to **yield( )** to see this). You could also call **sleep( )**, but then the rate of counting would be controlled by the **sleep( )** duration instead of the priority.

The **init( )** in **Counter5** creates an array of ten **Ticker2**s; their buttons and fields are placed on the form by the **Ticker2** constructor. **Counter5** adds buttons to start everything up as well as increment and decrement the maximum priority of the thread group. In addition, there are labels that display the maximum and minimum priorities possible for a thread and a **JTextField** to show the thread group's maximum priority. (The next section will describe thread groups.) Finally, the priorities of the parent thread groups are also displayed as labels.

When you press an "up" or "down" button, that **Ticker2**'s priority is fetched and incremented or decremented accordingly.

When you run this program, you'll notice several things. First of all, the thread group's default priority is five. Even if you decrement the maximum priority below five before starting the threads (or before creating the threads, which requires a code change), each thread will have a default priority of five.

The simple test is to take one counter and decrement its priority to one, and observe that it counts much slower. But now try to increment it again. You can get it back up to the thread group's priority, but no higher. Now decrement the thread group's priority a couple of times. The thread priorities are unchanged, but if you try to modify them either up or down you'll see that they'll automatically pop to the priority of the thread group. Also, new threads will still be given a default priority, even if that's higher than the group priority. (Thus the group priority is not a way to prevent new threads from having higher priorities than existing ones.)

Finally, try to increment the group maximum priority. It can't be done. You can only reduce thread group maximum priorities, not increase them.

Thread groups

All threads belong to a thread group. This can be either the default thread group or a group you explicitly specify when you create the thread. At creation, the thread is bound to a group and cannot change to a different group. Each application has at least one thread that belongs to the system thread group. If you create more threads without specifying a group, they will also belong to the system thread group.

Thread groups must also belong to other thread groups. The thread group that a new one belongs to must be specified in the constructor. If you create a thread group without specifying a thread group for it to belong to, it will be placed under the system thread group. Thus, all thread groups in your application will ultimately have the system thread group as the parent.

The reason for the existence of thread groups is hard to determine from the literature, which tends to be confusing on this subject. It's often cited as "security reasons." According to Arnold & Gosling,[2] "Threads within a thread group can modify the other threads in the group, including any farther down the hierarchy. A thread cannot modify threads outside of its own group or contained groups." It's hard to know what "modify" is supposed to mean here. The following example shows a thread in a "leaf" subgroup modifying the priorities of all the threads in its tree of thread groups as well as calling a method for all the threads in its tree.

```java
//: c14:TestAccess.java
// How threads can access other threads
// in a parent thread group.

public class TestAccess {
  public static void main(String[] args) {
    ThreadGroup
      x = new ThreadGroup("x"),
      y = new ThreadGroup(x, "y"),
      z = new ThreadGroup(y, "z");
    Thread
      one = new TestThread1(x, "one"),
      two = new TestThread2(z, "two");
  }
}

class TestThread1 extends Thread {
  private int i;
  TestThread1(ThreadGroup g, String name) {
    super(g, name);
  }
  void f() {
```

---

[2] *The Java Programming Language*, by Ken Arnold and James Gosling, Addison-Wesley 1996 pp 179.

```
      i++; // modify this thread
      System.out.println(getName() + " f()");
    }
  }
}

class TestThread2 extends TestThread1 {
  TestThread2(ThreadGroup g, String name) {
    super(g, name);
    start();
  }
  public void run() {
    ThreadGroup g =
      getThreadGroup().getParent().getParent();
    g.list();
    Thread[] gAll = new Thread[g.activeCount()];
    g.enumerate(gAll);
    for(int i = 0; i < gAll.length; i++) {
      gAll[i].setPriority(Thread.MIN_PRIORITY);
      ((TestThread1)gAll[i]).f();
    }
    g.list();
  }
} ///:~
```

In **main( )**, several **ThreadGroup**s are created, leafing off from each other: **x** has no argument but its name (a **String**), so it is automatically placed in the "system" thread group, while **y** is under **x** and **z** is under **y**. Note that initialization happens in textual order so this code is legal.

Two threads are created and placed in different thread groups. **TestThread1** doesn't have a **run( )** method but it does have an **f( )** that modifies the thread and prints something so you can see it was called. **TestThread2** is a subclass of **TestThread1** and its **run( )** is fairly elaborate. It first gets the thread group of the current thread, then moves up the heritage tree by two levels using **getParent( )**. (This is contrived since I purposely place the **TestThread2** object two levels down in the hierarchy.) At this point, an array of references to **Thread**s is created using the method **activeCount( )** to ask how many threads are in this thread group and all the child thread groups. The **enumerate( )** method places references to all of these threads in the array **gAll**, then I simply move through the entire array calling the **f( )** method for each thread, as well as modifying the priority. Thus, a thread in a "leaf" thread group modifies threads in parent thread groups.

The debugging method **list( )** prints all the information about a thread group to standard output and is helpful when investigating thread group behavior. Here's the output of the program:

```
java.lang.ThreadGroup[name=x,maxpri=10]
    Thread[one,5,x]
    java.lang.ThreadGroup[name=y,maxpri=10]
        java.lang.ThreadGroup[name=z,maxpri=10]
            Thread[two,5,z]
one f()
two f()
java.lang.ThreadGroup[name=x,maxpri=10]
    Thread[one,1,x]
    java.lang.ThreadGroup[name=y,maxpri=10]
        java.lang.ThreadGroup[name=z,maxpri=10]
            Thread[two,1,z]
```

Not only does **list( )** print the class name of **ThreadGroup** or **Thread**, but it also prints the thread group name and its maximum priority. For threads, the thread name is printed, followed by the thread priority and the group that it belongs to. Note that **list( )** indents the threads and thread groups to indicate that they are children of the unindented thread group.

You can see that **f( )** is called by the **TestThread2 run( )** method, so it's obvious that all threads in a group are vulnerable. However, you can access only the threads that branch off from your own **system** thread group tree, and perhaps this is what is meant by "safety." You cannot access anyone else's system thread group tree.

Controlling thread groups

Putting aside the safety issue, one thing thread groups seem to be useful for is control: you can perform certain operations on an entire thread group with a single command. The following example demonstrates this, and the restrictions on priorities within thread groups. The commented numbers in parentheses provide a reference to compare to the output.

```
//: c14:ThreadGroup1.java
// How thread groups control priorities
// of the threads inside them.

public class ThreadGroup1 {
  public static void main(String[] args) {
    // Get the system thread & print its Info:
    ThreadGroup sys =
      Thread.currentThread().getThreadGroup();
    sys.list(); // (1)
    // Reduce the system thread group priority:
    sys.setMaxPriority(Thread.MAX_PRIORITY - 1);
    // Increase the main thread priority:
    Thread curr = Thread.currentThread();
    curr.setPriority(curr.getPriority() + 1);
    sys.list(); // (2)
    // Attempt to set a new group to the max:
    ThreadGroup g1 = new ThreadGroup("g1");
    g1.setMaxPriority(Thread.MAX_PRIORITY);
    // Attempt to set a new thread to the max:
    Thread t = new Thread(g1, "A");
    t.setPriority(Thread.MAX_PRIORITY);
    g1.list(); // (3)
    // Reduce g1's max priority, then attempt
    // to increase it:
    g1.setMaxPriority(Thread.MAX_PRIORITY - 2);
    g1.setMaxPriority(Thread.MAX_PRIORITY);
    g1.list(); // (4)
    // Attempt to set a new thread to the max:
    t = new Thread(g1, "B");
    t.setPriority(Thread.MAX_PRIORITY);
    g1.list(); // (5)
    // Lower the max priority below the default
    // thread priority:
    g1.setMaxPriority(Thread.MIN_PRIORITY + 2);
    // Look at a new thread's priority before
    // and after changing it:
    t = new Thread(g1, "C");
    g1.list(); // (6)
    t.setPriority(t.getPriority() -1);
    g1.list(); // (7)
```

```
    // Make g2 a child Threadgroup of g1 and
    // try to increase its priority:
    ThreadGroup g2 = new ThreadGroup(g1, "g2");
    g2.list(); // (8)
    g2.setMaxPriority(Thread.MAX_PRIORITY);
    g2.list(); // (9)
    // Add a bunch of new threads to g2:
    for (int i = 0; i < 5; i++)
      new Thread(g2, Integer.toString(i));
    // Show information about all threadgroups
    // and threads:
    sys.list(); // (10)
    System.out.println("Starting all threads:");
    Thread[] all = new Thread[sys.activeCount()];
    sys.enumerate(all);
    for(int i = 0; i < all.length; i++)
      if(!all[i].isAlive())
        all[i].start();
    // Suspends & Stops all threads in
    // this group and its subgroups:
    System.out.println("All threads started");
    sys.suspend(); // Deprecated in Java 2
    // Never gets here...
    System.out.println("All threads suspended");
    sys.stop(); // Deprecated in Java 2
    System.out.println("All threads stopped");
  }
} ///:~
```

The output that follows has been edited to allow it to fit on the page (the **java.lang.** has been removed) and to add numbers to correspond to the commented numbers in the listing above.

```
(1)  ThreadGroup[name=system,maxpri=10]
        Thread[main,5,system]
(2)  ThreadGroup[name=system,maxpri=9]
        Thread[main,6,system]
(3)  ThreadGroup[name=g1,maxpri=9]
        Thread[A,9,g1]
(4)  ThreadGroup[name=g1,maxpri=8]
        Thread[A,9,g1]
```

```
(5)  ThreadGroup[name=g1,maxpri=8]
         Thread[A,9,g1]
         Thread[B,8,g1]
(6)  ThreadGroup[name=g1,maxpri=3]
         Thread[A,9,g1]
         Thread[B,8,g1]
         Thread[C,6,g1]
(7)  ThreadGroup[name=g1,maxpri=3]
         Thread[A,9,g1]
         Thread[B,8,g1]
         Thread[C,3,g1]
(8)  ThreadGroup[name=g2,maxpri=3]
(9)  ThreadGroup[name=g2,maxpri=3]
(10) ThreadGroup[name=system,maxpri=9]
         Thread[main,6,system]
         ThreadGroup[name=g1,maxpri=3]
            Thread[A,9,g1]
            Thread[B,8,g1]
            Thread[C,3,g1]
            ThreadGroup[name=g2,maxpri=3]
               Thread[0,6,g2]
               Thread[1,6,g2]
               Thread[2,6,g2]
               Thread[3,6,g2]
               Thread[4,6,g2]
Starting all threads:
All threads started
```

All programs have at least one thread running, and the first action in
main( ) is to call the **static** method of **Thread** called
currentThread( ). From this thread, the thread group is produced and
list( ) is called for the result. The output is:

```
(1)  ThreadGroup[name=system,maxpri=10]
         Thread[main,5,system]
```

You can see that the name of the main thread group is **system**, and the
name of the main thread is **main**, and it belongs to the **system** thread
group.

The second exercise shows that the **system** group's maximum priority
can be reduced and the **main** thread can have its priority increased:

```
(2)  ThreadGroup[name=system,maxpri=9]
        Thread[main,6,system]
```

The third exercise creates a new thread group, **g1**, which automatically belongs to the **system** thread group since it isn't otherwise specified. A new thread **A** is placed in **g1**. After attempting to set this group's maximum priority to the highest level and **A**'s priority to the highest level, the result is:

```
(3)  ThreadGroup[name=g1,maxpri=9]
        Thread[A,9,g1]
```

Thus, it's not possible to change the thread group's maximum priority to be higher than its parent thread group.

The fourth exercise reduces **g1**'s maximum priority by two and then tries to increase it up to **Thread.MAX_PRIORITY**. The result is:

```
(4)  ThreadGroup[name=g1,maxpri=8]
        Thread[A,9,g1]
```

You can see that the increase in maximum priority didn't work. You can only decrease a thread group's maximum priority, not increase it. Also, notice that thread **A**'s priority didn't change, and now it is higher than the thread group's maximum priority. Changing a thread group's maximum priority doesn't affect existing threads.

The fifth exercise attempts to set a new thread to maximum priority:

```
(5)  ThreadGroup[name=g1,maxpri=8]
        Thread[A,9,g1]
        Thread[B,8,g1]
```

The new thread cannot be changed to anything higher than the maximum thread group priority.

The default thread priority for this program is six; that's the priority a new thread will be created at and where it will stay if you don't manipulate the priority. Exercise 6 lowers the maximum thread group priority below the default thread priority to see what happens when you create a new thread under this condition:

```
(6)  ThreadGroup[name=g1,maxpri=3]
```

```
Thread[A,9,g1]
Thread[B,8,g1]
Thread[C,6,g1]
```

Even though the maximum priority of the thread group is three, the new thread is still created using the default priority of six. Thus, maximum thread group priority does not affect default priority. (In fact, there appears to be no way to set the default priority for new threads.)

After changing the priority, attempting to decrement it by one, the result is:

```
(7)  ThreadGroup[name=g1,maxpri=3]
        Thread[A,9,g1]
        Thread[B,8,g1]
        Thread[C,3,g1]
```

Only when you attempt to change the priority is the thread group's maximum priority enforced.

A similar experiment is performed in (8) and (9), in which a new thread group **g2** is created as a child of **g1** and its maximum priority is changed. You can see that it's impossible for **g2**'s maximum to go higher than **g1**'s:

```
(8)  ThreadGroup[name=g2,maxpri=3]
(9)  ThreadGroup[name=g2,maxpri=3]
```

Also notice that **g2** is automatically set to the thread group maximum priority of **g1** as **g2** is created.

After all of these experiments, the entire system of thread groups and threads is printed:

```
(10) ThreadGroup[name=system,maxpri=9]
        Thread[main,6,system]
        ThreadGroup[name=g1,maxpri=3]
          Thread[A,9,g1]
          Thread[B,8,g1]
          Thread[C,3,g1]
          ThreadGroup[name=g2,maxpri=3]
            Thread[0,6,g2]
            Thread[1,6,g2]
            Thread[2,6,g2]
```

```
Thread[3,6,g2]
Thread[4,6,g2]
```

So because of the rules of thread groups, a child group must always have a maximum priority that's less than or equal to its parent's maximum priority.

The last part of this program demonstrates methods for an entire group of threads. First the program moves through the entire tree of threads and starts each one that hasn't been started. For drama, the **system** group is then suspended and finally stopped. (Although it's interesting to see that **suspend( )** and **stop( )** work on entire thread groups, you should keep in mind that these methods are deprecated in Java 2.) But when you suspend the **system** group you also suspend the **main** thread and the whole program shuts down, so it never gets to the point where the threads are stopped. Actually, if you do stop the **main** thread it throws a **ThreadDeath** exception, so this is not a typical thing to do. Since **ThreadGroup** is inherited from **Object,** which contains the **wait( )** method, you can also choose to suspend the program for any number of seconds by calling **wait(seconds * 1000)**. This must acquire the lock inside a synchronized block, of course.

The **ThreadGroup** class also has **suspend( )** and **resume( )** methods so you can stop and start an entire thread group and all of its threads and subgroups with a single command. (Again, **suspend( )** and **resume( )** are deprecated in Java 2.)

Thread groups can seem a bit mysterious at first, but keep in mind that you probably won't be using them directly very often.

Runnable revisited

Earlier in this chapter, I suggested that you think carefully before making an applet or main **Frame** as an implementation of **Runnable**. Of course, if you must inherit from a class *and* you want to add threading behavior to the class, **Runnable** is the correct solution. The final example in this chapter exploits this by making a **Runnable JPanel** class that paints different colors on itself. This application is set up to take values from the command line to determine how big the grid of colors is and how long to

---

sleep( ) between color changes. By playing with these values you'll discover some interesting and possibly inexplicable features of threads:

```java
//: c14:ColorBoxes.java
// Using the Runnable interface.
// <applet code=ColorBoxes width=500 height=400>
// <param name=grid value="12">
// <param name=pause value="50">
// </applet>
import javax.swing.*;
import java.awt.*;
import java.awt.event.*;
import com.bruceeckel.swing.*;

class CBox extends JPanel implements Runnable {
  private Thread t;
  private int pause;
  private static final Color[] colors = {
    Color.black, Color.blue, Color.cyan,
    Color.darkGray, Color.gray, Color.green,
    Color.lightGray, Color.magenta,
    Color.orange, Color.pink, Color.red,
    Color.white, Color.yellow
  };
  private Color cColor = newColor();
  private static final Color newColor() {
    return colors[
      (int)(Math.random() * colors.length)
    ];
  }
  public void paintComponent(Graphics  g) {
    super.paintComponent(g);
    g.setColor(cColor);
    Dimension s = getSize();
    g.fillRect(0, 0, s.width, s.height);
  }
  public CBox(int pause) {
    this.pause = pause;
    t = new Thread(this);
    t.start();
  }
```

```
  public void run() {
    while(true) {
      cColor = newColor();
      repaint();
      try {
        t.sleep(pause);
      } catch(InterruptedException e) {
        System.err.println("Interrupted");
      }
    }
  }
}

public class ColorBoxes extends JApplet {
  private boolean isApplet = true;
  private int grid = 12;
  private int pause = 50;
  public void init() {
    // Get parameters from Web page:
    if (isApplet) {
      String gsize = getParameter("grid");
      if(gsize != null)
        grid = Integer.parseInt(gsize);
      String pse = getParameter("pause");
      if(pse != null)
        pause = Integer.parseInt(pse);
    }
    Container cp = getContentPane();
    cp.setLayout(new GridLayout(grid, grid));
    for (int i = 0; i < grid * grid; i++)
      cp.add(new CBox(pause));
  }
  public static void main(String[] args) {
    ColorBoxes applet = new ColorBoxes();
    applet.isApplet = false;
    if(args.length > 0)
      applet.grid = Integer.parseInt(args[0]);
    if(args.length > 1)
      applet.pause = Integer.parseInt(args[1]);
    Console.run(applet, 500, 400);
  }
```

```
} ///:~
```

ColorBoxes is the usual applet/application with an **init( )** that sets up the GUI. This sets up the **GridLayout** so that it has **grid** cells in each dimension. Then it adds the appropriate number of **CBox** objects to fill the grid, passing the **pause** value to each one. In **main( )** you can see how **pause** and **grid** have default values that can be changed if you pass in command-line arguments, or by using applet parameters.

CBox is where all the work takes place. This is inherited from **JPanel** and it implements the **Runnable** interface so each **JPanel** can also be a **Thread**. Remember that when you implement **Runnable**, you don't make a **Thread** object, just a class that has a **run( )** method. Thus, you must explicitly create a **Thread** object and hand the **Runnable** object to the constructor, then call **start( )** (this happens in the constructor). In **CBox** this thread is called **t**.

Notice the array **colors**, which is an enumeration of all the colors in class **Color**. This is used in **newColor( )** to produce a randomly selected color. The current cell color is **cColor**.

paintComponent( ) is quite simple—it just sets the color to **cColor** and fills the entire **JPanel** with that color.

In **run( )**, you see the infinite loop that sets the **cColor** to a new random color and then calls **repaint( )** to show it. Then the thread goes to **sleep( )** for the amount of time specified on the command line.

Precisely because this design is flexible and threading is tied to each **JPanel** element, you can experiment by making as many threads as you want. (In reality, there is a restriction imposed by the number of threads your JVM can comfortably handle.)

This program also makes an interesting benchmark, since it can show dramatic performance differences between one JVM threading implementation and another.

Too many threads

At some point, you'll find that **ColorBoxes** bogs down. On my machine, this occurred somewhere after a 10 x 10 grid. Why does this happen?

You're naturally suspicious that Swing might have something to do with it, so here's an example that tests that premise by making fewer threads. The following code is reorganized so that an **ArrayList implements Runnable** and that **ArrayList** holds a number of color blocks and randomly chooses ones to update. Then a number of these **ArrayList** objects are created, depending roughly on the grid dimension you choose. As a result, you have far fewer threads than color blocks, so if there's a speedup we'll know it was because there were too many threads in the previous example:

```
//: c14:ColorBoxes2.java
// Balancing thread use.
// <applet code=ColorBoxes2 width=600 height=500>
// <param name=grid value="12">
// <param name=pause value="50">
// </applet>
import javax.swing.*;
import java.awt.*;
import java.awt.event.*;
import java.util.*;
import com.bruceeckel.swing.*;

class CBox2 extends JPanel {
  private static final Color[] colors = {
    Color.black, Color.blue, Color.cyan,
    Color.darkGray, Color.gray, Color.green,
    Color.lightGray, Color.magenta,
    Color.orange, Color.pink, Color.red,
    Color.white, Color.yellow
  };
  private Color cColor = newColor();
  private static final Color newColor() {
    return colors[
      (int)(Math.random() * colors.length)
    ];
  }
  void nextColor() {
    cColor = newColor();
    repaint();
  }
  public void paintComponent(Graphics g) {
```

```
      super.paintComponent(g);
      g.setColor(cColor);
      Dimension s = getSize();
      g.fillRect(0, 0, s.width, s.height);
    }
  }

class CBoxList
  extends ArrayList implements Runnable {
  private Thread t;
  private int pause;
  public CBoxList(int pause) {
    this.pause = pause;
    t = new Thread(this);
  }
  public void go() { t.start(); }
  public void run() {
    while(true) {
      int i = (int)(Math.random() * size());
      ((CBox2)get(i)).nextColor();
      try {
        t.sleep(pause);
      } catch(InterruptedException e) {
        System.err.println("Interrupted");
      }
    }
  }
  public Object last() { return get(size() - 1);}
}

public class ColorBoxes2 extends JApplet {
  private boolean isApplet = true;
  private int grid = 12;
  // Shorter default pause than ColorBoxes:
  private int pause = 50;
  private CBoxList[] v;
  public void init() {
    // Get parameters from Web page:
    if (isApplet) {
      String gsize = getParameter("grid");
      if(gsize != null)
```

```
        grid = Integer.parseInt(gsize);
      String pse = getParameter("pause");
      if(pse != null)
        pause = Integer.parseInt(pse);
    }
    Container cp = getContentPane();
    cp.setLayout(new GridLayout(grid, grid));
    v = new CBoxList[grid];
    for(int i = 0; i < grid; i++)
      v[i] = new CBoxList(pause);
    for (int i = 0; i < grid * grid; i++) {
      v[i % grid].add(new CBox2());
      cp.add((CBox2)v[i % grid].last());
    }
    for(int i = 0; i < grid; i++)
      v[i].go();
  }
  public static void main(String[] args) {
    ColorBoxes2 applet = new ColorBoxes2();
    applet.isApplet = false;
    if(args.length > 0)
      applet.grid = Integer.parseInt(args[0]);
    if(args.length > 1)
      applet.pause = Integer.parseInt(args[1]);
    Console.run(applet, 500, 400);
  }
} ///:~
```

In **ColorBoxes2** an array of **CBoxList** is created and initialized to hold
grid CBoxLists, each of which knows how long to sleep. An equal
number of **CBox2** objects is then added to each **CBoxList**, and each list
is told to **go( )**, which starts its thread.

CBox2 is similar to **CBox**: it paints itself with a randomly chosen color.
But that's *all* a **CBox2** does. All of the threading has been moved into
CBoxList.

The **CBoxList** could also have inherited **Thread** and had a member
object of type **ArrayList**. That design has the advantage that the **add( )**
and **get( )** methods could then be given specific argument and return
value types instead of generic **Object**s. (Their names could also be

---

changed to something shorter.) However, the design used here seemed at first glance to require less code. In addition, it automatically retains all the other behaviors of an **ArrayList**. With all the casting and parentheses necessary for **get( )**, this might not be the case as your body of code grows.

As before, when you implement **Runnable** you don't get all of the equipment that comes with **Thread**, so you have to create a new **Thread** and hand yourself to its constructor in order to have something to **start( )**, as you can see in the **CBoxList** constructor and in **go( )**. The **run( )** method simply chooses a random element number within the list and calls **nextColor( )** for that element to cause it to choose a new randomly selected color.

Upon running this program, you see that it does indeed run faster and respond more quickly (for instance, when you interrupt it, it stops more quickly), and it doesn't seem to bog down as much at higher grid sizes. Thus, a new factor is added into the threading equation: you must watch to see that you don't have "too many threads" (whatever that turns out to mean for your particular program and platform—here, the slowdown in **ColorBoxes** appears to be caused by the fact that there's only one thread that is responsible for all painting, and it gets bogged down by too many requests). If you have too many threads, you must try to use techniques like the one above to "balance" the number of threads in your program. If you see performance problems in a multithreaded program you now have a number of issues to examine:

1.   Do you have enough calls to **sleep( )**, **yield( )**, and/or **wait( )**?

2.   Are calls to **sleep( )** long enough?

3.   Are you running too many threads?

4.   Have you tried different platforms and JVMs?

Issues like this are one reason that multithreaded programming is often considered an art.

Summary

It is vital to learn when to use multithreading and when to avoid it. The main reason to use it is to manage a number of tasks whose intermingling will make more efficient use of the computer (including the ability to transparently distribute the tasks across multiple CPUs) or be more convenient for the user. The classic example of resource balancing is using the CPU during I/O waits. The classic example of user convenience is monitoring a "stop" button during long downloads.

The main drawbacks to multithreading are:

1. Slowdown while waiting for shared resources

2. Additional CPU overhead required to manage threads

3. Unrewarded complexity, such as the silly idea of having a separate thread to update each element of an array

4. Pathologies including starving, racing, and deadlock

An additional advantage to threads is that they substitute "light" execution context switches (of the order of 100 instructions) for "heavy" process context switches (of the order of 1000s of instructions). Since all threads in a given process share the same memory space, a light context switch changes only program execution and local variables. On the other hand, a process change—the heavy context switch—must exchange the full memory space.

Threading is like stepping into an entirely new world and learning a whole new programming language, or at least a new set of language concepts. With the appearance of thread support in most microcomputer operating systems, extensions for threads have also been appearing in programming languages or libraries. In all cases, thread programming (1) seems mysterious and requires a shift in the way you think about programming; and (2) looks similar to thread support in other languages, so when you understand threads, you understand a common tongue. And although support for threads can make Java seem like a more complicated language, don't blame Java. Threads are tricky.

One of the biggest difficulties with threads occurs because more than one thread might be sharing a resource—such as the memory in an object—and you must make sure that multiple threads don't try to read and change that resource at the same time. This requires judicious use of the **synchronized** keyword, which is a helpful tool but must be understood thoroughly because it can quietly introduce deadlock situations.

In addition, there's a certain art to the application of threads. Java is designed to allow you to create as many objects as you need to solve your problem—at least in theory. (Creating millions of objects for an engineering finite-element analysis, for example, might not be practical in Java.) However, it seems that there is an upper bound to the number of threads you'll want to create, because at some point a large number of threads seems to become unwieldy. This critical point is not in the many thousands as it might be with objects, but rather in the low hundreds, sometimes less than 100. As you often create only a handful of threads to solve a problem, this is typically not much of a limit, yet in a more general design it becomes a constraint.

A significant nonintuitive issue in threading is that, because of thread scheduling, you can typically make your applications run *faster* by inserting calls to **sleep( )** inside **run( )**'s main loop. This definitely makes it feel like an art, in particular when the longer delays seem to speed up performance. Of course, the reason this happens is that shorter delays can cause the end-of-**sleep( )** scheduler interrupt to happen before the running thread is ready to go to sleep, forcing the scheduler to stop it and restart it later so it can finish what it was doing and then go to sleep. It takes extra thought to realize how messy things can get.

One thing you might notice missing in this chapter is an animation example, which is one of the most popular things to do with applets. However, a complete solution (with sound) to this problem comes with the Java JDK (available at *java.sun.com*) in the demo section. In addition, we can expect better animation support to become part of future versions of Java, while completely different non-Java, non-programming solutions to animation for the Web are appearing that will probably be superior to traditional approaches. For explanations about how Java animation works, see *Core Java 2* by Horstmann & Cornell, Prentice-Hall, 1997. For more advanced discussions of threading, see *Concurrent Programming in Java* by Doug Lea, Addison-Wesley, 1997, or *Java Threads* by Oaks & Wong, O'Reilly, 1997.

Exercises

Solutions to selected exercises can be found in the electronic document *The Thinking in Java Annotated Solution Guide*, available for a small fee from *www.BruceEckel.com*.

1. Inherit a class from **Thread** and override the **run( )** method. Inside **run( )**, print a message, and then call **sleep( )**. Repeat this three times, then return from **run( )**. Put a start-up message in the constructor and override **finalize( )** to print a shut-down message. Make a separate thread class that calls **System.gc( )** and **System.runFinalization( )** inside **run( )**, printing a message as it does so. Make several thread objects of both types and run them to see what happens.

2. Modify **Sharing2.java** to add a **synchronized** block inside the **run( )** method of **TwoCounter** instead of synchronizing the entire **run( )** method.

3. Create two **Thread** subclasses, one with a **run( )** that starts up, captures the reference of the second **Thread** object and then calls **wait( )**. The other class' **run( )** should call **notifyAll( )** for the first thread after some number of seconds have passed, so the first thread can print a message.

4. In **Counter5.java** inside **Ticker2**, remove the **yield( )** and explain the results. Replace the **yield( )** with a **sleep( )** and explain the results.

5. In **ThreadGroup1.java**, replace the call to **sys.suspend( )** with a call to **wait( )** for the thread group, causing it to wait for two seconds. For this to work correctly you must acquire the lock for **sys** inside a **synchronized** block.

6. Change **Daemons.java** so that **main( )** has a **sleep( )** instead of a **readLine( )**. Experiment with different sleep times to see what happens.

---

7.   In Chapter 8, locate the **GreenhouseControls.java** example, which consists of three files. In **Event.java**, the class **Event** is based on watching the time. Change **Event** so that it is a **Thread**, and change the rest of the design so that it works with this new **Thread**-based **Event**.

8.   Modify Exercise 7 so that the **java.util.Timer** class found in JDK 1.3 is used to run the system.

9.   Starting with **SineWave.java** from Chapter 13, create a program (an applet/application using the **Console** class) that draws an animated sine wave that appears to scrolls past the viewing window like an oscilloscope, driving the animation with a **Thread**. The speed of the animation should be controlled with a **java.swing.JSlider** control.

10.   Modify Exercise 9 so that multiple sine wave panels are created within the application. The number of sine wave panels should be controlled by HTML tags or command-line parameters.

11.   Modify Exercise 9 so that the **java.swing.Timer** class is used to drive the animation. Note the difference between this and **java.util.Timer**.

15: Distributed Computing

Historically, programming across multiple machines has been error-prone, difficult, and complex.

The programmer had to know many details about the network and sometimes even the hardware. You usually needed to understand the various "layers" of the networking protocol, and there were a lot of different functions in each different networking library concerned with connecting, packing, and unpacking blocks of information; shipping those blocks back and forth; and handshaking. It was a daunting task.

However, the basic idea of distributed computing is not so difficult, and is abstracted very nicely in the Java libraries. You want to:

> ➤ Get some information from that machine over there and move it to this machine here, or vice versa. This is accomplished with basic network programming.

> ➤ Connect to a database, which may live across a network. This is accomplished with *Java DataBase Connectivity* (JDBC), which is an abstraction away from the messy, platform-specific details of SQL (the *structured query language* used for most database transactions).

> ➤ Provide services via a Web server. This is accomplished with Java's *servlets* and *Java Server Pages* (JSPs).

> ➤ Execute methods on Java objects that live on remote machines transparently, as if those objects were resident on local machines. This is accomplished with Java's *Remote Method Invocation* (RMI).

> ➢ Use code written in other languages, running on other architectures. This is accomplished using the *Common Object Request Broker Architecture* (CORBA), which is directly supported by Java.

> ➢ Isolate business logic from connectivity issues, especially connections with databases including transaction management and security. This is accomplished using *Enterprise JavaBeans* (EJBs). EJBs are not actually a distributed architecture, but the resulting applications are usually used in a networked client-server system.

> ➢ Easily, dynamically, add and remove devices from a network representing a local system. This is accomplished with Java's Jini.

Each topic will be given a light introduction in this chapter. Please note that each subject is voluminous and by itself the subject of entire books, so this chapter is only meant to familiarize you with the topics, not make you an expert (however, you can go a long way with the information presented here on network programming, servlets and JSPs).

Network programming

One of Java's great strengths is painless networking. The Java network library designers have made it quite similar to reading and writing files, except that the "file" exists on a remote machine and the remote machine can decide exactly what it wants to do about the information you're requesting or sending. As much as possible, the underlying details of networking have been abstracted away and taken care of within the JVM and local machine installation of Java. The programming model you use is that of a file; in fact, you actually wrap the network connection (a "socket") with stream objects, so you end up using the same method calls as you do with all other streams. In addition, Java's built-in multithreading is exceptionally handy when dealing with another networking issue: handling multiple connections at once.

This section introduces Java's networking support using easy-to-understand examples.

Identifying a machine

Of course, in order to tell one machine from another and to make sure that you are connected with a particular machine, there must be some way of uniquely identifying machines on a network. Early networks were satisfied to provide unique names for machines within the local network. However, Java works within the Internet, which requires a way to uniquely identify a machine from all the others *in the world*. This is accomplished with the IP (Internet Protocol) address which can exist in two forms:

1. The familiar DNS (*Domain Name System*) form. My domain name is **bruceeckel.com**, and if I have a computer called **Opus** in my domain, its domain name would be **Opus.bruceeckel.com**. This is exactly the kind of name that you use when you send email to people, and is often incorporated into a World Wide Web address.

2. Alternatively, you can use the "dotted quad" form, which is four numbers separated by dots, such as **123.255.28.120**.

In both cases, the IP address is represented internally as a 32-bit number[1] (so each of the quad numbers cannot exceed 255), and you can get a special Java object to represent this number from either of the forms above by using the **static InetAddress.getByName( )** method that's in **java.net**. The result is an object of type **InetAddress** that you can use to build a "socket," as you will see later.

As a simple example of using **InetAddress.getByName( )**, consider what happens if you have a dial-up Internet service provider (ISP). Each time you dial up, you are assigned a temporary IP address. But while you're connected, your IP address has the same validity as any other IP address on the Internet. If someone connects to your machine using your IP address then they can connect to a Web server or FTP server that you have running on your machine. Of course, they need to know your IP

---

[1] This means a maximum of just over four billion numbers, which is rapidly running out. The new standard for IP addresses will use a 128-bit number, which should produce enough unique IP addresses for the foreseeable future.

address, and since a new one is assigned each time you dial up, how can you find out what it is?

The following program uses **InetAddress.getByName( )** to produce your IP address. To use it, you must know the name of your computer. On Windows 95/98, go to "Settings," "Control Panel," "Network," and then select the "Identification" tab. "Computer name" is the name to put on the command line.

```
//: c15:WhoAmI.java
// Finds out your network address when
// you're connected to the Internet.
import java.net.*;

public class WhoAmI {
  public static void main(String[] args)
      throws Exception {
    if(args.length != 1) {
      System.err.println(
        "Usage: WhoAmI MachineName");
      System.exit(1);
    }
    InetAddress a =
      InetAddress.getByName(args[0]);
    System.out.println(a);
  }
} ///:~
```

In this case, the machine is called "peppy." So, once I've connected to my ISP I run the program:

```
java WhoAmI peppy
```

I get back a message like this (of course, the address is different each time):

```
peppy/199.190.87.75
```

If I tell my friend this address and I have a Web server running on my computer, he can connect to it by going to the URL *http://199.190.87.75* (only as long as I continue to stay connected during that session). This can sometimes be a handy way to distribute information to someone else, or to test out a Web site configuration before posting it to a "real" server.

Servers and clients

The whole point of a network is to allow two machines to connect and talk to each other. Once the two machines have found each other they can have a nice, two-way conversation. But how do they find each other? It's like getting lost in an amusement park: one machine has to stay in one place and listen while the other machine says, "Hey, where are you?"

The machine that "stays in one place" is called the *server*, and the one that seeks is called the *client*. This distinction is important only while the client is trying to connect to the server. Once they've connected, it becomes a two-way communication process and it doesn't matter anymore that one happened to take the role of server and the other happened to take the role of the client.

So the job of the server is to listen for a connection, and that's performed by the special server object that you create. The job of the client is to try to make a connection to a server, and this is performed by the special client object you create. Once the connection is made, you'll see that at both server and client ends, the connection is magically turned into an I/O stream object, and from then on you can treat the connection as if you were reading from and writing to a file. Thus, after the connection is made you will just use the familiar I/O commands from Chapter 11. This is one of the nice features of Java networking.

Testing programs without a network

For many reasons, you might not have a client machine, a server machine, and a network available to test your programs. You might be performing exercises in a classroom situation, or you could be writing programs that aren't yet stable enough to put onto the network. The creators of the Internet Protocol were aware of this issue, and they created a special address called **localhost** to be the "local loopback" IP address for testing without a network. The generic way to produce this address in Java is:

```
InetAddress addr = InetAddress.getByName(null);
```

If you hand **getByName( )** a **null**, it defaults to using the **localhost**. The **InetAddress** is what you use to refer to the particular machine, and you must produce this before you can go any further. You can't manipulate the contents of an **InetAddress** (but you can print them out, as you'll see in the next example). The only way you can create an **InetAddress** is through one of that class's overloaded **static** member methods **getByName( )** (which is what you'll usually use), **getAllByName( )**, or **getLocalHost( )**.

You can also produce the local loopback address by handing it the string **localhost**:

```
InetAddress.getByName("localhost");
```

(assuming "localhost" is configured in your machine's "hosts" table), or by using its dotted quad form to name the reserved IP number for the loopback:

```
InetAddress.getByName("127.0.0.1");
```

All three forms produce the same result.

Port: a unique place within the machine

An IP address isn't enough to identify a unique server, since many servers can exist on one machine. Each IP machine also contains *ports*, and when you're setting up a client or a server you must choose a port where both client and server agree to connect; if you're meeting someone, the IP address is the neighborhood and the port is the bar.

The port is not a physical location in a machine, but a software abstraction (mainly for bookkeeping purposes). The client program knows how to connect to the machine via its IP address, but how does it connect to a desired service (potentially one of many on that machine)? That's where the port numbers come in as a second level of addressing. The idea is that if you ask for a particular port, you're requesting the service that's associated with the port number. The time of day is a simple example of a service. Typically, each service is associated with a unique port number on a given server machine. It's up to the client to know ahead of time which port number the desired service is running on.

The system services reserve the use of ports 1 through 1024, so you shouldn't use those or any other port that you know to be in use. The first choice for examples in this book will be port 8080 (in memory of the venerable old 8-bit Intel 8080 chip in my first computer, a CP/M machine).

Sockets

The *socket* is the software abstraction used to represent the "terminals" of a connection between two machines. For a given connection, there's a socket on each machine, and you can imagine a hypothetical "cable" running between the two machines with each end of the "cable" plugged into a socket. Of course, the physical hardware and cabling between machines is completely unknown. The whole point of the abstraction is that we don't have to know more than is necessary.

In Java, you create a socket to make the connection to the other machine, then you get an **InputStream** and **OutputStream** (or, with the appropriate converters, **Reader** and **Writer**) from the socket in order to be able to treat the connection as an I/O stream object. There are two stream-based socket classes: a **ServerSocket** that a server uses to "listen" for incoming connections and a **Socket** that a client uses in order to initiate a connection. Once a client makes a socket connection, the **ServerSocket** returns (via the **accept( )** method) a corresponding **Socket** through which communications will take place on the server side. From then on, you have a true **Socket** to **Socket** connection and you treat both ends the same way because they *are* the same. At this point, you use the methods **getInputStream( )** and **getOutputStream( )** to produce the corresponding **InputStream** and **OutputStream** objects from each **Socket**. These must be wrapped inside buffers and formatting classes just like any other stream object described in Chapter 11.

The use of the term **ServerSocket** would seem to be another example of a confusing naming scheme in the Java libraries. You might think **ServerSocket** would be better named "ServerConnector" or something without the word "Socket" in it. You might also think that **ServerSocket** and **Socket** should both be inherited from some common base class. Indeed, the two classes do have several methods in common, but not enough to give them a common base class. Instead, **ServerSocket**'s job is to wait until some other machine connects to it, then to return an actual **Socket**. This is why **ServerSocket** seems to be a bit misnamed, since its job isn't really to be a socket but instead to make a **Socket** object when someone else connects to it.

However, the **ServerSocket** does create a physical "server" or listening socket on the host machine. This socket listens for incoming connections and then returns an "established" socket (with the local and remote endpoints defined) via the **accept( )** method. The confusing part is that both of these sockets (listening and established) are associated with the same server socket. The listening socket can accept only new connection requests and not data packets. So while **ServerSocket** doesn't make much sense programmatically, it does "physically."

When you create a **ServerSocket**, you give it only a port number. You don't have to give it an IP address because it's already on the machine it represents. When you create a **Socket**, however, you must give both the IP address and the port number where you're trying to connect. (However, the **Socket** that comes back from **ServerSocket.accept( )** already contains all this information.)

A simple server and client

This example makes the simplest use of servers and clients using sockets. All the server does is wait for a connection, then uses the **Socket** produced by that connection to create an **InputStream** and **OutputStream**. These are converted to a **Reader** and a **Writer**, then wrapped in a **BufferedReader** and a **PrintWriter**. After that, everything it reads from the **BufferedReader** it echoes to the **PrintWriter** until it receives the line "END," at which time it closes the connection.

The client makes the connection to the server, then creates an **OutputStream** and performs the same wrapping as in the server. Lines of text are sent through the resulting **PrintWriter**. The client also creates an **InputStream** (again, with appropriate conversions and wrapping) to hear what the server is saying (which, in this case, is just the words echoed back).

Both the server and client use the same port number and the client uses the local loopback address to connect to the server on the same machine so you don't have to test it over a network. (For some configurations, you might need to be *connected* to a network for the programs to work, even if you aren't *communicating* over that network.)

Here is the server:

```
//: c15:JabberServer.java
// Very simple server that just
// echoes whatever the client sends.
import java.io.*;
import java.net.*;

public class JabberServer {
  // Choose a port outside of the range 1-1024:
  public static final int PORT = 8080;
  public static void main(String[] args)
      throws IOException {
    ServerSocket s = new ServerSocket(PORT);
    System.out.println("Started: " + s);
    try {
      // Blocks until a connection occurs:
      Socket socket = s.accept();
      try {
        System.out.println(
          "Connection accepted: "+ socket);
        BufferedReader in =
          new BufferedReader(
            new InputStreamReader(
              socket.getInputStream()));
        // Output is automatically flushed
        // by PrintWriter:
        PrintWriter out =
          new PrintWriter(
            new BufferedWriter(
              new OutputStreamWriter(
                socket.getOutputStream())),true);
        while (true) {
          String str = in.readLine();
          if (str.equals("END")) break;
```

```
          System.out.println("Echoing: " + str);
          out.println(str);
        }
      // Always close the two sockets...
      } finally {
        System.out.println("closing...");
        socket.close();
      }
    } finally {
      s.close();
    }
  }
} ///:~
```

You can see that the **ServerSocket** just needs a port number, not an IP address (since it's running on *this* machine!). When you call **accept( )**, the method *blocks* until some client tries to connect to it. That is, it's there waiting for a connection, but other processes can run (see Chapter 14). When a connection is made, **accept( )** returns with a **Socket** object representing that connection.

The responsibility for cleaning up the sockets is crafted carefully here. If the **ServerSocket** constructor fails, the program just quits (notice we must assume that the constructor for **ServerSocket** doesn't leave any open network sockets lying around if it fails). For this case, **main( ) throws IOException** so a **try** block is not necessary. If the **ServerSocket** constructor is successful then all other method calls must be guarded in a **try-finally** block to ensure that, no matter how the block is left, the **ServerSocket** is properly closed.

The same logic is used for the **Socket** returned by **accept( )**. If **accept( )** fails, then we must assume that the **Socket** doesn't exist or hold any resources, so it doesn't need to be cleaned up. If it's successful, however, the following statements must be in a **try-finally** block so that if they fail the **Socket** will still be cleaned up. Care is required here because sockets use important nonmemory resources, so you must be diligent in order to clean them up (since there is no destructor in Java to do it for you).

Both the **ServerSocket** and the **Socket** produced by **accept( )** are printed to **System.out**. This means that their **toString( )** methods are automatically called. These produce:

```
ServerSocket[addr=0.0.0.0,PORT=0,localport=8080]
Socket[addr=127.0.0.1,PORT=1077,localport=8080]
```

Shortly, you'll see how these fit together with what the client is doing.

The next part of the program looks just like opening files for reading and writing except that the **InputStream** and **OutputStream** are created from the **Socket** object. Both the **InputStream** and **OutputStream** objects are converted to **Reader** and **Writer** objects using the "converter" classes **InputStreamReader** and **OutputStreamWriter**, respectively. You could also have used the Java 1.0 **InputStream** and **OutputStream** classes directly, but with output there's a distinct advantage to using the **Writer** approach. This appears with **PrintWriter**, which has an overloaded constructor that takes a second argument, a **boolean** flag that indicates whether to automatically flush the output at the end of each **println( )** (but *not* **print( )**) statement. Every time you write to **out**, its buffer must be flushed so the information goes out over the network. Flushing is important for this particular example because the client and server each wait for a line from the other party before proceeding. If flushing doesn't occur, the information will not be put onto the network until the buffer is full, which causes lots of problems in this example.

When writing network programs you need to be careful about using automatic flushing. Every time you flush the buffer a packet must be created and sent. In this case, that's exactly what we want, since if the packet containing the line isn't sent then the handshaking back and forth between server and client will stop. Put another way, the end of a line is the end of a message. But in many cases, messages aren't delimited by lines so it's much more efficient to not use auto flushing and instead let the built-in buffering decide when to build and send a packet. This way, larger packets can be sent and the process will be faster.

Note that, like virtually all streams you open, these are buffered. There's an exercise at the end of this chapter to show you what happens if you don't buffer the streams (things get slow).

The infinite **while** loop reads lines from the **BufferedReader in** and writes information to **System.out** and to the **PrintWriter out**. Note that **in** and **out** could be any streams, they just happen to be connected to the network.

When the client sends the line consisting of "END," the program breaks out of the loop and closes the **Socket**.

Here's the client:

```
//: c15:JabberClient.java
// Very simple client that just sends
// lines to the server and reads lines
// that the server sends.
import java.net.*;
import java.io.*;

public class JabberClient {
  public static void main(String[] args)
      throws IOException {
    // Passing null to getByName() produces the
    // special "Local Loopback" IP address, for
    // testing on one machine w/o a network:
    InetAddress addr =
      InetAddress.getByName(null);
    // Alternatively, you can use
    // the address or name:
    // InetAddress addr =
    //     InetAddress.getByName("127.0.0.1");
    // InetAddress addr =
    //     InetAddress.getByName("localhost");
    System.out.println("addr = " + addr);
    Socket socket =
      new Socket(addr, JabberServer.PORT);
    // Guard everything in a try-finally to make
    // sure that the socket is closed:
    try {
      System.out.println("socket = " + socket);
      BufferedReader in =
        new BufferedReader(
          new InputStreamReader(
```

```
        socket.getInputStream()));
    // Output is automatically flushed
    // by PrintWriter:
    PrintWriter out =
      new PrintWriter(
        new BufferedWriter(
          new OutputStreamWriter(
            socket.getOutputStream())),true);
    for(int i = 0; i < 10; i ++) {
      out.println("howdy " + i);
      String str = in.readLine();
      System.out.println(str);
    }
    out.println("END");
  } finally {
    System.out.println("closing...");
    socket.close();
  }
 }
} ///:~
```

In **main( )** you can see all three ways to produce the **InetAddress** of the local loopback IP address: using **null**, **localhost**, or the explicit reserved address **127.0.0.1**. Of course, if you want to connect to a machine across a network you substitute that machine's IP address. When the **InetAddress addr** is printed (via the automatic call to its **toString( )** method) the result is:

```
localhost/127.0.0.1
```

By handing **getByName( )** a **null**, it defaulted to finding the **localhost**, and that produced the special address **127.0.0.1**.

Note that the **Socket** called **socket** is created with both the **InetAddress** and the port number. To understand what it means when you print one of these **Socket** objects, remember that an Internet connection is determined uniquely by these four pieces of data: **clientHost**, **clientPortNumber**, **serverHost**, and **serverPortNumber**. When the server comes up, it takes up its assigned port (8080) on the localhost (127.0.0.1). When the client comes up, it is allocated to the next available port on its machine, 1077 in this case, which also happens to be on the same machine (127.0.0.1) as the server. Now, in order for data to move between the client and server, each side has to know where to send it. Therefore, during the process of connecting to the "known" server, the client sends a "return address" so the server knows where to send its data. This is what you see in the example output for the server side:

```
Socket[addr=127.0.0.1,port=1077,localport=8080]
```

This means that the server just accepted a connection from 127.0.0.1 on port 1077 while listening on its local port (8080). On the client side:

```
Socket[addr=localhost/127.0.0.1,PORT=8080,localport=1077]
```

which means that the client made a connection to 127.0.0.1 on port 8080 using the local port 1077.

You'll notice that every time you start up the client anew, the local port number is incremented. It starts at 1025 (one past the reserved block of ports) and keeps going up until you reboot the machine, at which point it starts at 1025 again. (On UNIX machines, once the upper limit of the socket range is reached, the numbers will wrap around to the lowest available number again.)

Once the **Socket** object has been created, the process of turning it into a **BufferedReader** and **PrintWriter** is the same as in the server (again, in both cases you start with a **Socket**). Here, the client initiates the conversation by sending the string "howdy" followed by a number. Note that the buffer must again be flushed (which happens automatically via the second argument to the **PrintWriter** constructor). If the buffer isn't flushed, the whole conversation will hang because the initial "howdy" will never get sent (the buffer isn't full enough to cause the send to happen automatically). Each line that is sent back from the server is written to **System.out** to verify that everything is working correctly. To terminate the conversation, the agreed-upon "END" is sent. If the client simply hangs up, then the server throws an exception.

You can see that the same care is taken here to ensure that the network resources represented by the **Socket** are properly cleaned up, using a **try-finally** block.

Sockets produce a "dedicated" connection that persists until it is explicitly disconnected. (The dedicated connection can still be disconnected unexplicitly if one side, or an intermediary link, of the connection crashes.) This means the two parties are locked in communication and the connection is constantly open. This seems like a logical approach to networking, but it puts an extra load on the network. Later in this chapter you'll see a different approach to networking, in which the connections are only temporary.

Serving multiple clients

The **JabberServer** works, but it can handle only one client at a time. In a typical server, you'll want to be able to deal with many clients at once. The answer is multithreading, and in languages that don't directly support multithreading this means all sorts of complications. In Chapter 14 you saw that multithreading in Java is about as simple as possible, considering that multithreading is a rather complex topic. Because threading in Java is reasonably straightforward, making a server that handles multiple clients is relatively easy.

The basic scheme is to make a single **ServerSocket** in the server and call **accept( )** to wait for a new connection. When **accept( )** returns, you take the resulting **Socket** and use it to create a new thread whose job is to serve that particular client. Then you call **accept( )** again to wait for a new client.

In the following server code, you can see that it looks similar to the **JabberServer.java** example except that all of the operations to serve a particular client have been moved inside a separate thread class:

```
//: c15:MultiJabberServer.java
// A server that uses multithreading
// to handle any number of clients.
import java.io.*;
import java.net.*;

class ServeOneJabber extends Thread {
  private Socket socket;
  private BufferedReader in;
  private PrintWriter out;
```

```java
  public ServeOneJabber(Socket s)
      throws IOException {
    socket = s;
    in =
      new BufferedReader(
        new InputStreamReader(
          socket.getInputStream()));
    // Enable auto-flush:
    out =
      new PrintWriter(
        new BufferedWriter(
          new OutputStreamWriter(
            socket.getOutputStream())), true);
    // If any of the above calls throw an
    // exception, the caller is responsible for
    // closing the socket. Otherwise the thread
    // will close it.
    start(); // Calls run()
  }
  public void run() {
    try {
      while (true) {
        String str = in.readLine();
        if (str.equals("END")) break;
        System.out.println("Echoing: " + str);
        out.println(str);
      }
      System.out.println("closing...");
    } catch(IOException e) {
      System.err.println("IO Exception");
    } finally {
      try {
        socket.close();
      } catch(IOException e) {
        System.err.println("Socket not closed");
      }
    }
  }
}

public class MultiJabberServer {
```

```
   static final int PORT = 8080;
   public static void main(String[] args)
       throws IOException {
     ServerSocket s = new ServerSocket(PORT);
     System.out.println("Server Started");
     try {
       while(true) {
         // Blocks until a connection occurs:
         Socket socket = s.accept();
         try {
           new ServeOneJabber(socket);
         } catch(IOException e) {
           // If it fails, close the socket,
           // otherwise the thread will close it:
           socket.close();
         }
       }
     } finally {
       s.close();
     }
   }
} ///:~
```

The **ServeOneJabber** thread takes the **Socket** object that's produced
by **accept( )** in **main( )** every time a new client makes a connection.
Then, as before, it creates a **BufferedReader** and auto-flushed
PrintWriter object using the **Socket**. Finally, it calls the special
Thread method **start( )**, which performs thread initialization and then
calls **run( )**. This performs the same kind of action as in the previous
example: reading something from the socket and then echoing it back
until it reads the special "END" signal.

The responsibility for cleaning up the socket must again be carefully
designed. In this case, the socket is created outside of the
ServeOneJabber so the responsibility can be shared. If the
ServeOneJabber constructor fails, it will just throw the exception to the
caller, who will then clean up the thread. But if the constructor succeeds,
then the **ServeOneJabber** object takes over responsibility for cleaning
up the thread, in its **run( )**.

Notice the simplicity of the **MultiJabberServer**. As before, a **ServerSocket** is created and **accept( )** is called to allow a new connection. But this time, the return value of **accept( )** (a **Socket**) is passed to the constructor for **ServeOneJabber,** which creates a new thread to handle that connection. When the connection is terminated, the thread simply goes away.

If the creation of the **ServerSocket** fails, the exception is again thrown through **main( )**. But if the creation succeeds, the outer **try-finally** guarantees its cleanup. The inner **try-catch** guards only against the failure of the **ServeOneJabber** constructor; if the constructor succeeds, then the **ServeOneJabber** thread will close the associated socket.

To test that the server really does handle multiple clients, the following program creates many clients (using threads) that connect to the same server. The maximum number of threads allowed is determined by the **final int MAX_THREADS**.

```
//: c15:MultiJabberClient.java
// Client that tests the MultiJabberServer
// by starting up multiple clients.
import java.net.*;
import java.io.*;

class JabberClientThread extends Thread {
  private Socket socket;
  private BufferedReader in;
  private PrintWriter out;
  private static int counter = 0;
  private int id = counter++;
  private static int threadcount = 0;
  public static int threadCount() {
    return threadcount;
  }
  public JabberClientThread(InetAddress addr) {
    System.out.println("Making client " + id);
    threadcount++;
    try {
      socket =
        new Socket(addr, MultiJabberServer.PORT);
    } catch(IOException e) {
```

```
        System.err.println("Socket failed");
        // If the creation of the socket fails,
        // nothing needs to be cleaned up.
      }
      try {
        in =
          new BufferedReader(
            new InputStreamReader(
              socket.getInputStream()));
        // Enable auto-flush:
        out =
          new PrintWriter(
            new BufferedWriter(
              new OutputStreamWriter(
                socket.getOutputStream())), true);
        start();
      } catch(IOException e) {
        // The socket should be closed on any
        // failures other than the socket
        // constructor:
        try {
          socket.close();
        } catch(IOException e2) {
          System.err.println("Socket not closed");
        }
      }
      // Otherwise the socket will be closed by
      // the run() method of the thread.
    }
    public void run() {
      try {
        for(int i = 0; i < 25; i++) {
          out.println("Client " + id + ": " + i);
          String str = in.readLine();
          System.out.println(str);
        }
        out.println("END");
      } catch(IOException e) {
        System.err.println("IO Exception");
      } finally {
        // Always close it:
```

```
      try {
        socket.close();
      } catch(IOException e) {
        System.err.println("Socket not closed");
      }
      threadcount--; // Ending this thread
    }
  }
}

public class MultiJabberClient {
  static final int MAX_THREADS = 40;
  public static void main(String[] args)
      throws IOException, InterruptedException {
    InetAddress addr =
      InetAddress.getByName(null);
    while(true) {
      if(JabberClientThread.threadCount()
          < MAX_THREADS)
        new JabberClientThread(addr);
      Thread.currentThread().sleep(100);
    }
  }
} ///:~
```

The **JabberClientThread** constructor takes an **InetAddress** and uses it to open a **Socket**. You're probably starting to see the pattern: the **Socket** is always used to create some kind of **Reader** and/or **Writer** (or **InputStream** and/or **OutputStream**) object, which is the only way that the **Socket** can be used. (You can, of course, write a class or two to automate this process instead of doing all the typing if it becomes painful.) Again, **start( )** performs thread initialization and calls **run( )**. Here, messages are sent to the server and information from the server is echoed to the screen. However, the thread has a limited lifetime and eventually completes. Note that the socket is cleaned up if the constructor fails after the socket is created but before the constructor completes. Otherwise the responsibility for calling **close( )** for the socket is relegated to the **run( )** method.

The **threadcount** keeps track of how many **JabberClientThread** objects currently exist. It is incremented as part of the constructor and decremented as **run( )** exits (which means the thread is terminating). In **MultiJabberClient.main( ),** you can see that the number of threads is tested, and if there are too many, no more are created. Then the method sleeps. This way, some threads will eventually terminate and more can be created. You can experiment with **MAX_THREADS** to see where your particular system begins to have trouble with too many connections.

Datagrams

The examples you've seen so far use the *Transmission Control Protocol* (TCP, also known as *stream-based sockets*), which is designed for ultimate reliability and guarantees that the data will get there. It allows retransmission of lost data, it provides multiple paths through different routers in case one goes down, and bytes are delivered in the order they are sent. All this control and reliability comes at a cost: TCP has a high overhead.

There's a second protocol, called *User Datagram Protocol* (UDP), which doesn't guarantee that the packets will be delivered and doesn't guarantee that they will arrive in the order they were sent. It's called an "unreliable protocol" (TCP is a "reliable protocol"), which sounds bad, but because it's much faster it can be useful. There are some applications, such as an audio signal, in which it isn't so critical if a few packets are dropped here or there but speed is vital. Or consider a time-of-day server, where it really doesn't matter if one of the messages is lost. Also, some applications might be able to fire off a UDP message to a server and can then assume, if there is no response in a reasonable period of time, that the message was lost.

Typically, you'll do most of your direct network programming with TCP, and only occasionally will you use UDP. There's a more complete treatment of UDP, including an example, in the first edition of this book (available on the CD ROM bound into this book, or as a free download from *www.BruceEckel.com*).

Using URLs from within an applet

It's possible for an applet to cause the display of any URL through the Web browser the applet is running within. You can do this with the following line:

```
getAppletContext().showDocument(u);
```

in which **u** is the **URL** object. Here's a simple example that redirects you
to another Web page. Although you're just redirected to an HTML page,
you could also redirect to the output of a CGI program.

```
//: c15:ShowHTML.java
// <applet code=ShowHTML width=100 height=50>
// </applet>
import javax.swing.*;
import java.awt.*;
import java.awt.event.*;
import java.net.*;
import java.io.*;
import com.bruceeckel.swing.*;

public class ShowHTML extends JApplet {
  JButton send = new JButton("Go");
  JLabel l = new JLabel();
  public void init() {
    Container cp = getContentPane();
    cp.setLayout(new FlowLayout());
    send.addActionListener(new Al());
    cp.add(send);
    cp.add(l);
  }
  class Al implements ActionListener {
    public void actionPerformed(ActionEvent ae) {
      try {
        // This could be a CGI program instead of
        // an HTML page.
        URL u = new URL(getDocumentBase(),
          "FetcherFrame.html");
        // Display the output of the URL using
        // the Web browser, as an ordinary page:
        getAppletContext().showDocument(u);
      } catch(Exception e) {
        l.setText(e.toString());
      }
    }
  }
}
```

```
   public static void main(String[] args) {
      Console.run(new ShowHTML(), 100, 50);
   }
} ///:~
```

The beauty of the **URL** class is how much it shields you from. You can connect to Web servers without knowing much at all about what's going on under the covers.

Reading a file from the server

A variation on the above program reads a file located on the server. In this case, the file is specified by the client:

```
//: c15:Fetcher.java
// <applet code=Fetcher width=500 height=300>
// </applet>
import javax.swing.*;
import java.awt.*;
import java.awt.event.*;
import java.net.*;
import java.io.*;
import com.bruceeckel.swing.*;

public class Fetcher extends JApplet {
  JButton fetchIt= new JButton("Fetch the Data");
  JTextField f =
    new JTextField("Fetcher.java", 20);
  JTextArea t = new JTextArea(10,40);
  public void init() {
    Container cp = getContentPane();
    cp.setLayout(new FlowLayout());
    fetchIt.addActionListener(new FetchL());
    cp.add(new JScrollPane(t));
    cp.add(f); cp.add(fetchIt);
  }
  public class FetchL implements ActionListener {
    public void actionPerformed(ActionEvent e) {
      try {
        URL url = new URL(getDocumentBase(),
          f.getText());
        t.setText(url + "\n");
```

```
        InputStream is = url.openStream();
        BufferedReader in = new BufferedReader(
          new InputStreamReader(is));
        String line;
        while ((line = in.readLine()) != null)
          t.append(line + "\n");
      } catch(Exception ex) {
        t.append(ex.toString());
      }
    }
  }
  public static void main(String[] args) {
    Console.run(new Fetcher(), 500, 300);
  }
} ///:~
```

The creation of the **URL** object is similar to the previous example—
getDocumentBase( ) is the starting point as before, but this time the
name of the file is read from the **JTextField**. Once the **URL** object is
created, its **String** version is placed in the **JTextArea** so we can see what
it looks like. Then an **InputStream** is procured from the **URL**, which in
this case will simply produce a stream of the characters in the file. After
converting to a **Reader** and buffering, each line is read and appended to
the **JTextArea**. Note that the **JTextArea** has been placed inside a
JScrollPane so that scrolling is handled automatically.

More to networking

There's actually a lot more to networking than can be covered in this
introductory treatment. Java networking also provides fairly extensive
support for URLs, including protocol handlers for different types of
content that can be discovered at an Internet site. You can find other Java
networking features fully and carefully described in *Java Network
Programming* by Elliotte Rusty Harold (O'Reilly, 1997).

Java Database Connectivity (JDBC)

It has been estimated that half of all software development involves client/server operations. A great promise of Java has been the ability to build platform-independent client/server database applications. This has come to fruition with Java DataBase Connectivity (JDBC).

One of the major problems with databases has been the feature wars between the database companies. There is a "standard" database language, Structured Query Language (SQL-92), but you must usually know which database vendor you're working with despite the standard. JDBC is designed to be platform-independent, so you don't need to worry about the database you're using while you're programming. However, it's still possible to make vendor-specific calls from JDBC so you aren't restricted from doing what you must.

One place where programmers may need to use SQL type names is in the SQL `TABLE CREATE` statement when they are creating a new database table and defining the SQL type for each column. Unfortunately there are significant variations between SQL types supported by different database products. Different databases that support SQL types with the same semantics and structure may give those types different names. Most major databases support an SQL data type for large binary values: in Oracle this type is called a `LONG RAW`, Sybase calls it `IMAGE`, Informix calls it `BYTE`, and DB2 calls it `LONG VARCHAR FOR BIT DATA`. Therefore, if database portability is a goal you should try to use only generic SQL type identifiers.

Portability is an issue when writing for a book where readers may be testing the examples with all kinds of unknown data stores. I have tried to write these examples to be as portable as possible. You should also notice that the database-specific code has been isolated in order to centralize any changes that you may need to perform to get the examples operational in your environment.

JDBC, like many of the APIs in Java, is designed for simplicity. The method calls you make correspond to the logical operations you'd think of doing when gathering data from a database: connect to the database, create a statement and execute the query, and look at the result set.

To allow this platform independence, JDBC provides a *driver manager* that dynamically maintains all the driver objects that your database queries will need. So if you have three different kinds of vendor databases to connect to, you'll need three different driver objects. The driver objects register themselves with the driver manager at the time of loading, and you can force the loading using **Class.forName( )**.

To open a database, you must create a "database URL" that specifies:

1.   That you're using JDBC with "jdbc."

2.   The "subprotocol": the name of the driver or the name of a database connectivity mechanism. Since the design of JDBC was inspired by ODBC, the first subprotocol available is the "jdbc-odbc bridge," specified by "odbc."

3.   The database identifier. This varies with the database driver used, but it generally provides a logical name that is mapped by the database administration software to a physical directory where the database tables are located. For your database identifier to have any meaning, you must register the name using your database administration software. (The process of registration varies from platform to platform.)

All this information is combined into one string, the "database URL." For example, to connect through the ODBC subprotocol to a database identified as "people," the database URL could be:

```
String dbUrl = "jdbc:odbc:people";
```

If you're connecting across a network, the database URL will contain the connection information identifying the remote machine and can become a bit intimidating. Here is an example of a CloudScape database being called from a remote client utilizing RMI:

```
jdbc:rmi://192.168.170.27:1099/jdbc:cloudscape:db
```

This database URL is really two jdbc calls in one. The first part "`jdbc:rmi://192.168.170.27:1099/`" uses RMI to make the connection to the remote database engine listening on port 1099 at IP Address 192.168.170.27. The second part of the URL, "`jdbc:cloudscape:db`" conveys the more typical settings using the subprotocol and database name but this will only happen after the first section has made the connection via RMI to the remote machine.

When you're ready to connect to the database, call the **static** method **DriverManager.getConnection( )** and pass it the database URL, the user name, and a password to get into the database. You get back a **Connection** object that you can then use to query and manipulate the database.

The following example opens a database of contact information and looks for a person's last name as given on the command line. It selects only the names of people that have email addresses, then prints out all the ones that match the given last name:

```java
//: c15:jdbc:Lookup.java
// Looks up email addresses in a
// local database using JDBC.
import java.sql.*;

public class Lookup {
  public static void main(String[] args)
  throws SQLException, ClassNotFoundException {
    String dbUrl = "jdbc:odbc:people";
    String user = "";
    String password = "";
    // Load the driver (registers itself)
    Class.forName(
      "sun.jdbc.odbc.JdbcOdbcDriver");
    Connection c = DriverManager.getConnection(
      dbUrl, user, password);
    Statement s = c.createStatement();
    // SQL code:
    ResultSet r =
      s.executeQuery(
        "SELECT FIRST, LAST, EMAIL " +
        "FROM people.csv people " +
```

```
      "WHERE " +
      "(LAST='" + args[0] + "') " +
      " AND (EMAIL Is Not Null) " +
      "ORDER BY FIRST");
    while(r.next()) {
      // Capitalization doesn't matter:
      System.out.println(
        r.getString("Last") + ", "
        + r.getString("fIRST")
        + ": " + r.getString("EMAIL") );
    }
    s.close(); // Also closes ResultSet
  }
} ///:~
```

You can see the creation of the database URL as previously described. In this example, there is no password protection on the database so the user name and password are empty strings.

Once the connection is made with **DriverManager.getConnection( )**, you can use the resulting **Connection** object to create a **Statement** object using the **createStatement( )** method. With the resulting **Statement**, you can call **executeQuery( )**, passing in a string containing an SQL-92 standard SQL statement. (You'll see shortly how you can generate this statement automatically, so you don't have to know much about SQL.)

The **executeQuery( )** method returns a **ResultSet** object, which is an iterator: the **next( )** method moves the iterator to the next record in the statement, or returns **false** if the end of the result set has been reached. You'll always get a **ResultSet** object back from **executeQuery( )** even if a query results in an empty set (that is, an exception is not thrown). Note that you must call **next( )** once before trying to read any record data. If the result set is empty, this first call to **next( )** will return **false**. For each record in the result set, you can select the fields using (among other approaches) the field name as a string. Also note that the capitalization of the field name is ignored—it doesn't matter with an SQL database. You determine the type you'll get back by calling **getInt( )**, **getString( )**, **getFloat( )**, etc. At this point, you've got your database data in Java native format and can do whatever you want with it using ordinary Java code.

Getting the example to work

With JDBC, understanding the code is relatively simple. The confusing part is making it work on your particular system. The reason this is confusing is that it requires you to figure out how to get your JDBC driver to load properly, and how to set up a database using your database administration software.

Of course, this process can vary radically from machine to machine, but the process I used to make it work under 32-bit Windows might give you clues to help you attack your own situation.

Step 1: Find the JDBC Driver

The program above contains the statement:

```
Class.forName("sun.jdbc.odbc.JdbcOdbcDriver");
```

This implies a directory structure, which is deceiving. With this particular installation of JDK 1.1, there was no file called **JdbcOdbcDriver.class**, so if you looked at this example and went searching for it you'd be frustrated. Other published examples use a pseudo name, such as "myDriver.ClassName," which is less than helpful. In fact, the load statement above for the jdbc-odbc driver (the only one that actually comes with the JDK) appears in only a few places in the online documentation (in particular, a page labeled "JDBC-ODBC Bridge Driver"). If the load statement above doesn't work, then the name might have been changed as part of a Java version change, so you should hunt through the documentation again.

If the load statement is wrong, you'll get an exception at this point. To test whether your driver load statement is working correctly, comment out the code after the statement and up to the **catch** clause; if the program throws no exceptions it means that the driver is loading properly.

Step 2: Configure the database

Again, this is specific to 32-bit Windows; you might need to do some research to figure it out for your own platform.

First, open the control panel. You might find two icons that say "ODBC." You must use the one that says "32bit ODBC," since the other one is for backward compatibility with 16-bit ODBC software and will produce no results for JDBC. When you open the "32bit ODBC" icon, you'll see a tabbed dialog with a number of tabs, including "User DSN," "System DSN," "File DSN," etc., in which "DSN" means "Data Source Name." It turns out that for the JDBC-ODBC bridge, the only place where it's important to set up your database is "System DSN," but you'll also want to test your configuration and create queries, and for that you'll also need to set up your database in "File DSN." This will allow the Microsoft Query tool (that comes with Microsoft Office) to find the database. Note that other query tools are also available from other vendors.

The most interesting database is one that you're already using. Standard ODBC supports a number of different file formats including such venerable workhorses as DBase. However, it also includes the simple "comma-separated ASCII" format, which virtually every data tool has the ability to write. In my case, I just took my "people" database that I've been maintaining for years using various contact-management tools and exported it as a comma-separated ASCII file (these typically have an extension of **.csv**). In the "System DSN" section I chose "Add," chose the text driver to handle my comma-separated ASCII file, and then unchecked "use current directory" to allow me to specify the directory where I exported the data file.

You'll notice when you do this that you don't actually specify a file, only a directory. That's because a database is typically represented as a collection of files under a single directory (although it could be represented in other forms as well). Each file usually contains a single table, and the SQL statements can produce results that are culled from multiple tables in the database (this is called a *join*). A database that contains only a single table (like my "people" database) is usually called a *flat-file database*. Most problems that go beyond the simple storage and retrieval of data generally require multiple tables that must be related by joins to produce the desired results, and these are called *relational* databases.

Step 3: Test the configuration

To test the configuration you'll need a way to discover whether the database is visible from a program that queries it. Of course, you can simply run the JDBC program example above, up to and including the statement:

```
Connection c = DriverManager.getConnection(
  dbUrl, user, password);
```

If an exception is thrown, your configuration was incorrect.

However, it's useful to get a query-generation tool involved at this point. I used Microsoft Query that came with Microsoft Office, but you might prefer something else. The query tool must know where the database is, and Microsoft Query required that I go to the ODBC Administrator's "File DSN" tab and add a new entry there, again specifying the text driver and the directory where my database lives. You can name the entry anything you want, but it's helpful to use the same name you used in "System DSN."

Once you've done this, you will see that your database is available when you create a new query using your query tool.

Step 4: Generate your SQL query

The query that I created using Microsoft Query not only showed me that my database was there and in good order, but it also automatically created the SQL code that I needed to insert into my Java program. I wanted a query that would search for records that had the last name that was typed on the command line when starting the Java program. So as a starting point, I searched for a specific last name, "Eckel." I also wanted to display only those names that had email addresses associated with them. The steps I took to create this query were:

1.   Start a new query and use the Query Wizard. Select the "people" database. (This is the equivalent of opening the database connection using the appropriate database URL.)

2.   Select the "people" table within the database. From within the table, choose the columns FIRST, LAST, and EMAIL.

3.   Under "Filter Data," choose LAST and select "equals" with an argument of "Eckel." Click the "And" radio button.

4.   Choose EMAIL and select "Is not Null."

5.   Under "Sort By," choose FIRST.

The result of this query will show you whether you're getting what you want.

Now you can press the SQL button and without any research on your part, up will pop the correct SQL code, ready for you to cut and paste. For this query, it looked like this:

```
SELECT people.FIRST, people.LAST, people.EMAIL
FROM people.csv people
WHERE (people.LAST='Eckel') AND
(people.EMAIL Is Not Null)
ORDER BY people.FIRST
```

Especially with more complicated queries it's easy to get things wrong, but by using a query tool you can interactively test your queries and automatically generate the correct code. It's hard to argue the case for doing this by hand.

Step 5: Modify and paste in your query

You'll notice that the code above looks different from what's used in the program. That's because the query tool uses full qualification for all of the names, even when there's only one table involved. (When more than one table is involved, the qualification prevents collisions between columns from different tables that have the same names.) Since this query involves only one table, you can optionally remove the "people" qualifier from most of the names, like this:

```
SELECT FIRST, LAST, EMAIL
FROM people.csv people
WHERE (LAST='Eckel') AND
(EMAIL Is Not Null)
```

```
ORDER BY FIRST
```

In addition, you don't want this program to be hard coded to look for only one name. Instead, it should hunt for the name given as the command-line argument. Making these changes and turning the SQL statement into a dynamically-created **String** produces:

```
"SELECT FIRST, LAST, EMAIL " +
"FROM people.csv people " +
"WHERE " +
"(LAST='" + args[0] + "') " +
" AND (EMAIL Is Not Null) " +
"ORDER BY FIRST");
```

SQL has another way to insert names into a query called *stored procedures*, which is used for speed. But for much of your database experimentation and for your first cut, building your own query strings in Java is fine.

You can see from this example that by using the tools currently available—in particular the query-building tool—database programming with SQL and JDBC can be quite straightforward.

A GUI version of the lookup program

It's more useful to leave the lookup program running all the time and simply switch to it and type in a name whenever you want to look someone up. The following program creates the lookup program as an application/applet, and it also adds name completion so the data will show up without forcing you to type the entire last name:

```
//: c15:jdbc:VLookup.java
// GUI version of Lookup.java.
// <applet code=VLookup
// width=500 height=200></applet>
import javax.swing.*;
import java.awt.*;
import java.awt.event.*;
import javax.swing.event.*;
import java.sql.*;
```

```java
import com.bruceeckel.swing.*;

public class VLookup extends JApplet {
  String dbUrl = "jdbc:odbc:people";
  String user = "";
  String password = "";
  Statement s;
  JTextField searchFor = new JTextField(20);
  JLabel completion =
    new JLabel("                              ");
  JTextArea results = new JTextArea(40, 20);
  public void init() {
    searchFor.getDocument().addDocumentListener(
      new SearchL());
    JPanel p = new JPanel();
    p.add(new Label("Last name to search for:"));
    p.add(searchFor);
    p.add(completion);
    Container cp = getContentPane();
    cp.add(p, BorderLayout.NORTH);
    cp.add(results, BorderLayout.CENTER);
    try {
      // Load the driver (registers itself)
      Class.forName(
        "sun.jdbc.odbc.JdbcOdbcDriver");
      Connection c = DriverManager.getConnection(
        dbUrl, user, password);
      s = c.createStatement();
    } catch(Exception e) {
      results.setText(e.toString());
    }
  }
  class SearchL implements DocumentListener {
    public void changedUpdate(DocumentEvent e){}
    public void insertUpdate(DocumentEvent e){
      textValueChanged();
    }
    public void removeUpdate(DocumentEvent e){
      textValueChanged();
    }
```

```
public void textValueChanged() {
  ResultSet r;
  if(searchFor.getText().length() == 0) {
    completion.setText("");
    results.setText("");
    return;
  }
  try {
    // Name completion:
    r = s.executeQuery(
      "SELECT LAST FROM people.csv people " +
      "WHERE (LAST Like '" +
      searchFor.getText()  +
      "%') ORDER BY LAST");
    if(r.next())
      completion.setText(
        r.getString("last"));
    r = s.executeQuery(
      "SELECT FIRST, LAST, EMAIL " +
      "FROM people.csv people " +
      "WHERE (LAST='" +
      completion.getText() +
      "') AND (EMAIL Is Not Null) " +
      "ORDER BY FIRST");
  } catch(Exception e) {
    results.setText(
      searchFor.getText() + "\n");
    results.append(e.toString());
    return;
  }
  results.setText("");
  try {
    while(r.next()) {
      results.append(
        r.getString("Last") + ", "
        + r.getString("fIRST") +
        ": " + r.getString("EMAIL") + "\n");
    }
  } catch(Exception e) {
    results.setText(e.toString());
  }
```

```
    }
  public static void main(String[] args) {
    Console.run(new VLookup(), 500, 200);
  }
} ///:~
```

Much of the database logic is the same, but you can see that a
DocumentListener is added to listen to the **JTextField** (see the
javax.swing.JTextField entry in the Java HTML documentation from
java.sun.com for details), so that whenever you type a new character it
first tries to do a name completion by looking up the last name in the
database and using the first one that shows up. (It places it in the
completion JLabel, and uses that as the lookup text.) This way, as soon
as you've typed enough characters for the program to uniquely find the
name you're looking for, you can stop.

Why the JDBC API
seems so complex

When you browse the online documentation for JDBC it can seem
daunting. In particular, in the **DatabaseMetaData** interface—which is
just huge, contrary to most of the interfaces you see in Java—there are
methods such as **dataDefinitionCausesTransactionCommit( )**,
getMaxColumnNameLength( ), **getMaxStatementLength( )**,
storesMixedCaseQuotedIdentifiers( ),
supportsANSI92IntermediateSQL( ),
supportsLimitedOuterJoins( ), and so on. What's this all about?

As mentioned earlier, databases have seemed from their inception to be in
a constant state of turmoil, primarily because the demand for database
applications, and thus database tools, is so great. Only recently has there
been any convergence on the common language of SQL (and there are
plenty of other database languages in common use). But even with an SQL
"standard" there are so many variations on that theme that JDBC must
provide the large **DatabaseMetaData** interface so that your code can
discover the capabilities of the particular "standard" SQL database that
it's currently connected to. In short, you can write simple, transportable
SQL, but if you want to optimize speed your coding will multiply

tremendously as you investigate the capabilities of a particular vendor's database.

This, of course, is not Java's fault. The discrepancies between database products are just something that JDBC tries to help compensate for. But bear in mind that your life will be easier if you can either write generic queries and not worry quite as much about performance, or, if you must tune for performance, know the platform you're writing for so you don't need to write all that investigation code.

A more sophisticated example

A more interesting example[2] involves a multitable database that resides on a server. Here, the database is meant to provide a repository for community activities and to allow people to sign up for these events, so it is called the *Community Interests Database* (CID). This example will only provide an overview of the database and its implementation, and is not intended to be an in-depth tutorial on database development. There are numerous books, seminars, and software packages that will help you in the design and development of a database.

In addition, this example presumes the prior installation of an SQL database on a server (although it could also be run on a local machine), and the interrogation and discovery of an appropriate JDBC driver for that database. Several free SQL databases are available, and some are even automatically installed with various flavors of Linux. You are responsible for making the choice of database and locating the JDBC driver; the example here is based on an SQL database system called "Cloudscape."

To keep changes in the connection information simple, the database driver, database URL, user name, and password are placed in a separate class:

```
//: c15:jdbc:CIDConnect.java
// Database connection information for
// the community interests database (CID).
```

---

[2] Created by Dave Bartlett.

```
public class CIDConnect {
  // All the information specific to CloudScape:
  public static String dbDriver =
    "COM.cloudscape.core.JDBCDriver";
  public static String dbURL =
    "jdbc:cloudscape:d:/docs/_work/JSapienDB";
  public static String user = "";
  public static String password = "";
} ///:~
```

In this example, there is no password protection on the database so the user name and password are empty strings.

The database consists of a set of tables that have a structure as shown here:

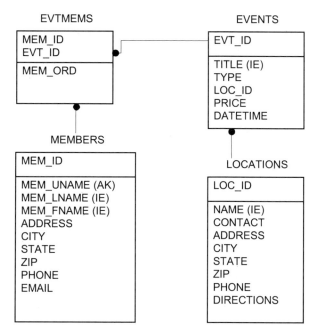

"Members" contains community member information, "Events" and "Locations" contain information about the activities and where they take place, and "Evtmems" connects events and members that would like to attend that event. You can see that a data member in one table produces a key in another table.

The following class contains the SQL strings that will create these database tables (refer to an SQL guide for an explanation of the SQL code):

```
//: c15:jdbc:CIDSQL.java
// SQL strings to create the tables for the CID.

public class CIDSQL {
  public static String[] sql = {
    // Create the MEMBERS table:
    "drop table MEMBERS",
    "create table MEMBERS " +
    "(MEM_ID INTEGER primary key, " +
    "MEM_UNAME VARCHAR(12) not null unique, "+
    "MEM_LNAME VARCHAR(40), " +
    "MEM_FNAME VARCHAR(20), " +
    "ADDRESS VARCHAR(40), " +
    "CITY VARCHAR(20), " +
    "STATE CHAR(4), " +
    "ZIP CHAR(5), " +
    "PHONE CHAR(12), " +
    "EMAIL VARCHAR(30))",
    "create unique index " +
    "LNAME_IDX on MEMBERS(MEM_LNAME)",
    // Create the EVENTS table
    "drop table EVENTS",
    "create table EVENTS " +
    "(EVT_ID INTEGER primary key, " +
    "EVT_TITLE VARCHAR(30) not null, " +
    "EVT_TYPE VARCHAR(20), " +
    "LOC_ID INTEGER, " +
    "PRICE DECIMAL, " +
    "DATETIME TIMESTAMP)",
    "create unique index " +
    "TITLE_IDX on EVENTS(EVT_TITLE)",
    // Create the EVTMEMS table
    "drop table EVTMEMS",
    "create table EVTMEMS " +
    "(MEM_ID INTEGER not null, " +
    "EVT_ID INTEGER not null, " +
    "MEM_ORD INTEGER)",
```

```
    "create unique index " +
    "EVTMEM_IDX on EVTMEMS(MEM_ID, EVT_ID)",
    // Create the LOCATIONS table
    "drop table LOCATIONS",
    "create table LOCATIONS " +
    "(LOC_ID INTEGER primary key, " +
    "LOC_NAME VARCHAR(30) not null, " +
    "CONTACT VARCHAR(50), " +
    "ADDRESS VARCHAR(40), " +
    "CITY VARCHAR(20), " +
    "STATE VARCHAR(4), " +
    "ZIP VARCHAR(5), " +
    "PHONE CHAR(12), " +
    "DIRECTIONS VARCHAR(4096))",
    "create unique index " +
    "NAME_IDX on LOCATIONS(LOC_NAME)",
  };
} ///:~
```

The following program uses the **CIDConnect** and **CIDSQL** information
to load the JDBC driver, make a connection to the database, and then
create the table structure diagrammed above. To connect with the
database, you call the **static** method
DriverManager.getConnection( ), passing it the database URL, the
user name, and a password to get into the database. You get back a
Connection object that you can use to query and manipulate the
database. Once the connection is made you can simply push the SQL to
the database, in this case by marching through the **CIDSQL** array.
However, the first time this program is run, the "drop table" command
will fail, causing an exception, which is caught, reported, and then
ignored. The reason for the "drop table" command is to allow easy
experimentation: you can modify the SQL that defines the tables and then
rerun the program, causing the old tables to be replaced by the new.

In this example, it makes sense to let the exceptions be thrown out to the
console:

```
//: c15:jdbc:CIDCreateTables.java
// Creates database tables for the
// community interests database.
import java.sql.*;
```

```java
public class CIDCreateTables {
  public static void main(String[] args)
  throws SQLException, ClassNotFoundException,
  IllegalAccessException {
    // Load the driver (registers itself)
    Class.forName(CIDConnect.dbDriver);
    Connection c = DriverManager.getConnection(
      CIDConnect.dbURL, CIDConnect.user,
      CIDConnect.password);
    Statement s = c.createStatement();
    for(int i = 0; i < CIDSQL.sql.length; i++) {
      System.out.println(CIDSQL.sql[i]);
      try {
        s.executeUpdate(CIDSQL.sql[i]);
      } catch(SQLException sqlEx) {
        System.err.println(
          "Probably a 'drop table' failed");
      }
    }
    s.close();
    c.close();
  }
} ///:~
```

Note that all changes in the database can be controlled by changing **String**s in the **CIDSQL** table, without modifying **CIDCreateTables**.

executeUpdate( ) will usually return the number of rows that were affected by the SQL statement. **executeUpdate( )** is more commonly used to execute INSERT, UPDATE, or DELETE statements that modify one or more rows. For statements such as CREATE TABLE, DROP TABLE, and CREATE INDEX, **executeUpdate( )** always returns zero.

To test the database, it is loaded with some sample data. This requires a series of INSERTs followed by a SELECT to produce result set. To make additions and changes to the test data easy, the test data is set up as a two-dimensional array of **Object**s, and the **executeInsert( )** method can then use the information in one row of the table to create the appropriate SQL command.

```
//: c15:jdbc:LoadDB.java
// Loads and tests the database.
import java.sql.*;

class TestSet {
  Object[][] data = {
    { "MEMBERS", new Integer(1),
      "dbartlett", "Bartlett", "David",
      "123 Mockingbird Lane",
      "Gettysburg", "PA", "19312",
      "123.456.7890", "bart@you.net" },
    { "MEMBERS", new Integer(2),
      "beckel", "Eckel", "Bruce",
      "123 Over Rainbow Lane",
      "Crested Butte", "CO", "81224",
      "123.456.7890", "beckel@you.net" },
    { "MEMBERS", new Integer(3),
      "rcastaneda", "Castaneda", "Robert",
      "123 Downunder Lane",
      "Sydney", "NSW", "12345",
      "123.456.7890", "rcastaneda@you.net" },
    { "LOCATIONS", new Integer(1),
      "Center for Arts",
      "Betty Wright", "123 Elk Ave.",
      "Crested Butte", "CO", "81224",
      "123.456.7890",
      "Go this way then that." },
    { "LOCATIONS", new Integer(2),
      "Witts End Conference Center",
      "John Wittig", "123 Music Drive",
      "Zoneville", "PA", "19123",
      "123.456.7890",
      "Go that way then this." },
    { "EVENTS", new Integer(1),
      "Project Management Myths",
      "Software Development",
      new Integer(1), new Float(2.50),
      "2000-07-17 19:30:00" },
    { "EVENTS", new Integer(2),
      "Life of the Crested Dog",
      "Archeology",
```

```
          new Integer(2), new Float(0.00),
          "2000-07-19 19:00:00" },
      // Match some people with events
      {  "EVTMEMS",
         new Integer(1),  // Dave is going to
         new Integer(1),  // the Software event.
         new Integer(0) },
      { "EVTMEMS",
         new Integer(2),  // Bruce is going to
         new Integer(2),  // the Archeology event.
         new Integer(0) },
      { "EVTMEMS",
         new Integer(3),  // Robert is going to
         new Integer(1),  // the Software event.
         new Integer(1) },
      { "EVTMEMS",
         new Integer(3), // ... and
         new Integer(2), // the Archeology event.
         new Integer(1) },
    };
    // Use the default data set:
    public TestSet() {}
    // Use a different data set:
    public TestSet(Object[][] dat) { data = dat; }
}

public class LoadDB {
    Statement statement;
    Connection connection;
    TestSet tset;
    public LoadDB(TestSet t) throws SQLException {
      tset = t;
      try {
        // Load the driver (registers itself)
        Class.forName(CIDConnect.dbDriver);
      } catch(java.lang.ClassNotFoundException e) {
        e.printStackTrace(System.err);
      }
      connection = DriverManager.getConnection(
        CIDConnect.dbURL, CIDConnect.user,
        CIDConnect.password);
```

```java
    statement = connection.createStatement();
  }
  public void cleanup() throws SQLException {
    statement.close();
    connection.close();
  }
  public void executeInsert(Object[] data) {
    String sql = "insert into "
      + data[0] + " values(";
    for(int i = 1; i < data.length; i++) {
      if(data[i] instanceof String)
        sql += "'" + data[i] + "'";
      else
        sql += data[i];
      if(i < data.length - 1)
        sql += ", ";
    }
    sql += ')';
    System.out.println(sql);
    try {
      statement.executeUpdate(sql);
    } catch(SQLException sqlEx) {
      System.err.println("Insert failed.");
      while (sqlEx != null) {
        System.err.println(sqlEx.toString());
        sqlEx = sqlEx.getNextException();
      }
    }
  }
  public void load() {
    for(int i = 0; i< tset.data.length; i++)
      executeInsert(tset.data[i]);
  }
  // Throw exceptions out to console:
  public static void main(String[] args)
  throws SQLException {
    LoadDB db = new LoadDB(new TestSet());
    db.load();
    try {
      // Get a ResultSet from the loaded database:
      ResultSet rs = db.statement.executeQuery(
```

```
        "select " +
        "e.EVT_TITLE, m.MEM_LNAME, m.MEM_FNAME "+
        "from EVENTS e, MEMBERS m, EVTMEMS em " +
        "where em.EVT_ID = 2 " +
        "and e.EVT_ID = em.EVT_ID " +
        "and m.MEM_ID = em.MEM_ID");
    while (rs.next())
      System.out.println(
        rs.getString(1) + "   " +
        rs.getString(2) + ",  " +
        rs.getString(3));
  } finally {
    db.cleanup();
  }
 }
} ///:~
```

The **TestSet** class contains a default set of data that is produced if you use the default constructor; however, you can also create a **TestSet** object using an alternate data set with the second constructor. The set of data is held in a two-dimensional array of **Object** because it can be any type, including **String** or numerical types. The **executeInsert( )** method uses RTTI to distinguish between **String** data (which must be quoted) and non-**String** data as it builds the SQL command from the data. After printing this command to the console, **executeUpdate( )** is used to send it to the database.

The constructor for **LoadDB** makes the connection, and **load( )** steps through the data and calls **executeInsert( )** for each record. **cleanup( )** closes the statement and the connection; to guarantee that this is called, it is placed inside a finally clause.

Once the database is loaded, an **executeQuery( )** statement produces a sample result set. Since the query combines several tables, it is an example of a join.

There is more JDBC information available in the electronic documents that come as part of the Java distribution from Sun. In addition, you can find more in the book *JDBC Database Access with Java* (Hamilton, Cattel, and Fisher, Addison-Wesley, 1997). Other JDBC books appear regularly.

Servlets

Client access from the Internet or corporate intranets is a sure way to allow many users to access data and resources easily[3]. This type of access is based on clients using the World Wide Web standards of Hypertext Markup Language (HTML) and Hypertext Transfer Protocol (HTTP). The Servlet API set abstracts a common solution framework for responding to HTTP requests.

Traditionally, the way to handle a problem such as allowing an Internet client to update a database is to create an HTML page with text fields and a "submit" button. The user types the appropriate information into the text fields and presses the "submit" button. The data is submitted along with a URL that tells the server what to do with the data by specifying the location of a Common Gateway Interface (CGI) program that the server runs, providing the program with the data as it is invoked. The CGI program is typically written in Perl, Python, C, C++, or any language that can read from standard input and write to standard output. That's all that is provided by the Web server: the CGI program is invoked, and standard streams (or, optionally for input, an environment variable) are used for input and output. The CGI program is responsible for everything else. First it looks at the data and decides whether the format is correct. If not, the CGI program must produce HTML to describe the problem; this page is handed to the Web server (via standard output from the CGI program), which sends it back to the user. The user must usually back up a page and try again. If the data is correct, the CGI program processes the data in an appropriate way, perhaps adding it to a database. It must then produce an appropriate HTML page for the Web server to return to the user.

It would be ideal to go to a completely Java-based solution to this problem—an applet on the client side to validate and send the data, and a servlet on the server side to receive and process the data. Unfortunately, although applets are a proven technology with plenty of support, they have been problematic to use on the Web because you cannot rely on a

---

[3] Dave Bartlett was instrumental in the development of this material, and also the JSP section.

particular version of Java being available on a client's Web browser; in fact, you can't rely on a Web browser supporting Java at all! In an intranet, you can require that certain support be available, which allows a lot more flexibility in what you can do, but on the Web the safest approach is to handle all the processing on the server side and deliver plain HTML to the client. That way, no client will be denied the use of your site because they do not have the proper software installed.

Because servlets provide an excellent solution for server-side programming support, they are one of the most popular reasons for moving to Java. Not only do they provide a framework that replaces CGI programming (and eliminates a number of thorny CGI problems), but all your code has the platform portability gained from using Java, and you have access to all the Java APIs (except, of course, the ones that produce GUIs, like Swing).

The basic servlet

The architecture of the servlet API is that of a classic service provider with a **service( )** method through which all client requests will be sent by the servlet container software, and life cycle methods **init( )** and **destroy( )**, which are called only when the servlet is loaded and unloaded (this happens rarely).

```
public interface Servlet {
  public void init(ServletConfig config)
    throws ServletException;
  public ServletConfig getServletConfig();
  public void service(ServletRequest req,
    ServletResponse res)
    throws ServletException, IOException;
  public String getServletInfo();
  public void destroy();
}
```

getServletConfig( )'s sole purpose is to return a **ServletConfig** object that contains initialization and startup parameters for this servlet. **getServletInfo( )** returns a string containing information about the servlet, such as author, version, and copyright.

The **GenericServlet** class is a shell implementation of this interface and is typically not used. The **HttpServlet** class is an extension of **GenericServlet** and is designed specifically to handle the HTTP protocol— **HttpServlet** is the one that you'll use most of the time.

The most convenient attribute of the servlet API is the auxiliary objects that come along with the HttpServlet class to support it. If you look at the **service( )** method in the **Servlet** interface, you'll see it has two parameters: **ServletRequest** and **ServletResponse**. With the **HttpServlet** class these two object are extended for HTTP: **HttpServletRequest** and **HttpServletResponse**. Here's a simple example that shows the use of **HttpServletResponse**:

```
//: c15:servlets:ServletsRule.java
import javax.servlet.*;
import javax.servlet.http.*;
import java.io.*;

public class ServletsRule extends HttpServlet {
  int i = 0; // Servlet "persistence"
  public void service(HttpServletRequest req,
  HttpServletResponse res) throws IOException {
    res.setContentType("text/html");
    PrintWriter out = res.getWriter();
    out.print("<HEAD><TITLE>");
    out.print("A server-side strategy");
    out.print("</TITLE></HEAD><BODY>");
    out.print("<h1>Servlets Rule! " + i++);
    out.print("</h1></BODY>");
    out.close();
  }
} ///:~
```

ServletsRule is about as simple as a servlet can get. The servlet is initialized only once by calling its **init( )** method, on loading the servlet after the servlet container is first booted up. When a client makes a request to a URL that happens to represent a servlet, the servlet container intercepts this request and makes a call to the **service( )** method, after setting up the **HttpServletRequest** and **HttpServletResponse** objects.

The main responsibility of the **service( )** method is to interact with the HTTP request that the client has sent, and to build an HTTP response based on the attributes contained within the request. **ServletsRule** only manipulates the response object without looking at what the client may have sent.

After setting the content type of the response (which must always be done before the **Writer** or **OutputStream** is procured), the **getWriter( )** method of the response object produces a **PrintWriter** object, which is used for writing character-based response data (alternatively, **getOutputStream( )** produces an **OutputStream**, used for binary response, which is only utilized in more specialized solutions).

The rest of the program simply sends HTML back to the client (it's assumed you understand HTML, so that part is not explained) as a sequence of **String**s. However, notice the inclusion of the "hit counter" represented by the variable **i**. This is automatically converted to a **String** in the **print( )** statement.

When you run the program, you'll notice that the value of **i** is retained between requests to the servlet. This is an essential property of servlets: since only one servlet of a particular class is loaded into the container, and it is never unloaded (unless the servlet container is terminated, which is something that only normally happens if you reboot the server computer), any fields of that servlet class effectively become persistent objects! This means that you can effortlessly maintain values between servlet requests, whereas with CGI you had to write values to disk in order to preserve them, which required a fair amount of fooling around to get it right, and resulted in a non-cross-platform solution.

Of course, sometimes the Web server, and thus the servlet container, must be rebooted as part of maintenance or during a power failure. To avoid losing any persistent information, the servlet's **init( )** and **destroy( )** methods are automatically called whenever the servlet is loaded or unloaded, giving you the opportunity to save data during shutdown, and restore it after rebooting. The servlet container calls the **destroy( )** method as it is terminating itself, so you always get an opportunity to save valuable data as long as the server machine is configured in an intelligent way.

There's one other issue when using **HttpServlet**. This class provides **doGet( )** and **doPost( )** methods that differentiate between a CGI "GET" submission from the client, and a CGI "POST." GET and POST vary only in the details of the way that they submit the data, which is something that I personally would prefer to ignore. However, most published information that I've seen seems to favor the creation of separate **doGet( )** and **doPost( )** methods instead of a single generic **service( )** method, which handles both cases. This favoritism seems quite common, but I've never seen it explained in a fashion that leads me to believe that it's anything more than inertia from CGI programmers who are used to paying attention to whether a GET or POST is being used. So in the spirit of "doing the simplest thing that could possibly work,"[4] I will just use the **service( )** method in these examples, and let it care about GETs vs. POSTs. However, keep in mind that I might have missed something and so there may in fact be a good reason to use **doGet( )** and **doPost( )** instead.

Whenever a form is submitted to a servlet, the **HttpServletRequest** comes preloaded with all the form data, stored as key-value pairs. If you know the names of the fields, you can just use them directly with the **getParameter( )** method to look up the values. You can also get an **Enumeration** (the old form of the **Iterator**) to the field names, as is shown in the following example. This example also demonstrates how a single servlet can be used to produce the page that contains the form, and to respond to the page (a better solution will be seen later, with JSPs). If the **Enumeration** is empty, there are no fields; this means no form was submitted. In this case, the form is produced, and the submit button will re-call the same servlet. If fields do exist, however, they are displayed.

```
//: c15:servlets:EchoForm.java
// Dumps the name-value pairs of any HTML form
import javax.servlet.*;
import javax.servlet.http.*;
import java.io.*;
import java.util.*;
```

---

[4] A primary tenet of Extreme Programming (XP). See *www.xprogramming.com*.

```java
public class EchoForm extends HttpServlet {
  public void service(HttpServletRequest req,
    HttpServletResponse res) throws IOException {
    res.setContentType("text/html");
    PrintWriter out = res.getWriter();
    Enumeration flds = req.getParameterNames();
    if(!flds.hasMoreElements()) {
      // No form submitted -- create one:
      out.print("<html>");
      out.print("<form method=\"POST\"" +
        " action=\"EchoForm\">");
      for(int i = 0; i < 10; i++)
        out.print("<b>Field" + i + "</b> " +
          "<input type=\"text\""+
          " size=\"20\" name=\"Field" + i +
          "\" value=\"Value" + i + "\"><br>");
      out.print("<INPUT TYPE=submit name=submit"+
      " Value=\"Submit\"></form></html>");
    } else {
      out.print("<h1>Your form contained:</h1>");
      while(flds.hasMoreElements()) {
        String field= (String)flds.nextElement();
        String value= req.getParameter(field);
        out.print(field + " = " + value+ "<br>");
      }
    }
    out.close();
  }
} ///:~
```

One drawback you'll notice here is that Java does not seem to be designed with string processing in mind—the formatting of the return page is painful because of line breaks, escaping quote marks, and the "+" signs necessary to build **String** objects. With a larger HTML page it becomes unreasonable to code it directly into Java. One solution is to keep the page as a separate text file, then open it and hand it to the Web server. If you have to perform any kind of substitution to the contents of the page, it's not much better since Java has treated string processing so poorly. In these cases you're probably better off using a more appropriate solution (Python would be my choice; there's a version that embeds itself in Java called JPython) to generate the response page.

Servlets and multithreading

The servlet container has a pool of threads that it will dispatch to handle client requests. It is quite likely that two clients arriving at the same time could be processing through your **service( )** at the same time. Therefore the **service( )** method must written in a thread-safe manner. Any access to common resources (files, databases) will need to be guarded by using the **synchronized** keyword.

The following simple example puts a **synchronized** clause around the thread's **sleep( )** method. This will block all other threads until the allotted time (five seconds) is all used up. When testing this you should start several browser instances and hit this servlet as quickly as possible in each one—you'll see that each one has to wait until its turn comes up.

```
//: c15:servlets:ThreadServlet.java
import javax.servlet.*;
import javax.servlet.http.*;
import java.io.*;

public class ThreadServlet extends HttpServlet {
  int i;
  public void service(HttpServletRequest req,
    HttpServletResponse res) throws IOException {
    res.setContentType("text/html");
    PrintWriter out = res.getWriter();
    synchronized(this) {
      try {
        Thread.currentThread().sleep(5000);
      } catch(InterruptedException e) {
        System.err.println("Interrupted");
      }
    }
    out.print("<h1>Finished " + i++ + "</h1>");
    out.close();
  }
} ///:~
```

It is also possible to synchronize the entire servlet by putting the **synchronized** keyword in front of the **service( )** method. In fact, the only reason to use the **synchronized** clause instead is if the critical section is in an execution path that might not get executed. In that case, you might as well avoid the overhead of synchronizing every time by using a **synchronized** clause. Otherwise, all the threads will have to wait anyway so you might as well **synchronize** the whole method.

Handling sessions with servlets

HTTP is a "sessionless" protocol, so you cannot tell from one server hit to another if you've got the same person repeatedly querying your site, or if it is a completely different person. A great deal of effort has gone into mechanisms that will allow Web developers to track sessions. Companies could not do e-commerce without keeping track of a client and the items they have put into their shopping cart, for example.

There are several methods of session tracking, but the most common method is with persistent "cookies," which are an integral part of the Internet standards. The HTTP Working Group of the Internet Engineering Task Force has written cookies into the official standard in RFC 2109 (*ds.internic.net/rfc/rfc2109.txt* or check *www.cookiecentral.com*).

A cookie is nothing more than a small piece of information sent by a Web server to a browser. The browser stores the cookie on the local disk, and whenever another call is made to the URL that the cookie is associated with, the cookie is quietly sent along with the call, thus providing the desired information back to that server (generally, providing some way that the server can be told that it's you calling). Clients can, however, turn off the browser's ability to accept cookies. If your site must track a client who has turned off cookies, then another method of session tracking (URL rewriting or hidden form fields) must be incorporated by hand, since the session tracking capabilities built into the servlet API are designed around cookies.

The **Cookie** class

The servlet API (version 2.0 and up) provides the **Cookie** class. This class incorporates all the HTTP header details and allows the setting of various cookie attributes. Using the cookie is simply a matter of adding it to the response object. The constructor takes a cookie name as the first argument and a value as the second. Cookies are added to the response object before you send any content.

```
Cookie oreo = new Cookie("TIJava", "2000");
res.addCookie(cookie);
```

Cookies are recovered by calling the **getCookies( )** method of the **HttpServletRequest** object, which returns an array of cookie objects.

```
Cookie[] cookies = req.getCookies();
```

You can then call **getValue( )** for each cookie, to produce a **String** containing the cookie contents. In the above example, **getValue("TIJava")** will produce a **String** containing "2000."

The **Session** class

A session is one or more page requests by a client to a Web site during a defined period of time. If you buy groceries online, for example, you want a session to be confined to the period from when you first add an item to "my shopping cart" to the point where you check out. Each item you add to the shopping cart will result in a new HTTP connection, which has no knowledge of previous connections or items in the shopping cart. To compensate for this lack of information, the mechanics supplied by the cookie specification allow your servlet to perform session tracking.

A servlet **Session** object lives on the server side of the communication channel; its goal is to capture useful data about this client as the client moves through and interacts with your Web site. This data may be pertinent for the present session, such as items in the shopping cart, or it may be data such as authentication information that was entered when the client first entered your Web site, and which should not have to be reentered during a particular set of transactions.

The **Session** class of the servlet API uses the **Cookie** class to do its work. However, all the **Session** object needs is some kind of unique identifier stored on the client and passed to the server. Web sites may also use the other types of session tracking but these mechanisms will be more difficult to implement as they are not encapsulated into the servlet API (that is, you must write them by hand to deal with the situation when the client has disabled cookies).

Here's an example that implements session tracking with the servlet API:

```
//: c15:servlets:SessionPeek.java
// Using the HttpSession class.
import java.io.*;
import java.util.*;
import javax.servlet.*;
import javax.servlet.http.*;

public class SessionPeek extends HttpServlet {
  public void service(HttpServletRequest req,
  HttpServletResponse res)
  throws ServletException, IOException {
    // Retrieve Session Object before any
    // output is sent to the client.
    HttpSession session = req.getSession();
    res.setContentType("text/html");
    PrintWriter out = res.getWriter();
    out.println("<HEAD><TITLE> SessionPeek ");
    out.println(" </TITLE></HEAD><BODY>");
    out.println("<h1> SessionPeek </h1>");
    // A simple hit counter for this session.
    Integer ival = (Integer)
      session.getAttribute("sesspeek.cntr");
    if(ival==null)
      ival = new Integer(1);
    else
      ival = new Integer(ival.intValue() + 1);
    session.setAttribute("sesspeek.cntr", ival);
    out.println("You have hit this page <b>"
      + ival + "</b> times.<p>");
    out.println("<h2>");
    out.println("Saved Session Data </h2>");
    // Loop through all data in the session:
    Enumeration sesNames =
      session.getAttributeNames();
    while(sesNames.hasMoreElements()) {
      String name =
        sesNames.nextElement().toString();
      Object value = session.getAttribute(name);
      out.println(name + " = " + value + "<br>");
```

```
        }
        out.println("<h3> Session Statistics </h3>");
        out.println("Session ID: "
            + session.getId() + "<br>");
        out.println("New Session: " + session.isNew()
            + "<br>");
        out.println("Creation Time: "
            + session.getCreationTime());
        out.println("<I>(" +
            new Date(session.getCreationTime())
            + ")</I><br>");
        out.println("Last Accessed Time: " +
            session.getLastAccessedTime());
        out.println("<I>(" +
            new Date(session.getLastAccessedTime())
            + ")</I><br>");
        out.println("Session Inactive Interval: "
            + session.getMaxInactiveInterval());
        out.println("Session ID in Request: "
            + req.getRequestedSessionId() + "<br>");
        out.println("Is session id from Cookie: "
            + req.isRequestedSessionIdFromCookie()
            + "<br>");
        out.println("Is session id from URL: "
            + req.isRequestedSessionIdFromURL()
            + "<br>");
        out.println("Is session id valid: "
            + req.isRequestedSessionIdValid()
            + "<br>");
        out.println("</BODY>");
        out.close();
    }
    public String getServletInfo() {
        return "A session tracking servlet";
    }
} ///:~
```

Inside the **service( )** method, **getSession( )** is called for the request object, which returns the **Session** object associated with this request. The **Session** object does not travel across the network, but instead it lives on the server and is associated with a client and its requests.

getSession( ) comes in two versions: no parameter, as used here, and **getSession(boolean)**. **getSession(true)** is equivalent to **getSession( )**. The only reason for the **boolean** is to state whether you want the session object created if it is not found. **getSession(true)** is the most likely call, hence **getSession( )**.

The **Session** object, if it is not new, will give us details about the client from previous visits. If the **Session** object is new then the program will start to gather information about this client's activities on this visit. Capturing this client information is done through the **setAttribute( )** and **getAttribute( )** methods of the session object.

```
java.lang.Object getAttribute(java.lang.String)
void setAttribute(java.lang.String name,
                  java.lang.Object value)
```

The **Session** object uses a simple name-value pairing for loading information. The name is a **String**, and the value can be any object derived from **java.lang.Object**. **SessionPeek** keeps track of how many times the client has been back during this session. This is done with an **Integer** object named **sesspeek.cntr**. If the name is not found an **Integer** is created with value of one, otherwise an **Integer** is created with the incremented value of the previously held **Integer**. The new **Integer** is placed into the **Session** object. If you use same key in a **setAttribute( )** call, then the new object overwrites the old one. The incremented counter is used to display the number of times that the client has visited during this session.

getAttributeNames( ) is related to **getAttribute( )** and **setAttribute( )**; it returns an enumeration of the names of the objects that are bound to the **Session** object. A **while** loop in **SessionPeek** shows this method in action.

You may wonder how long a **Session** object hangs around. The answer depends on the servlet container you are using; they usually default to 30 minutes (1800 seconds), which is what you should see from the **ServletPeek** call to **getMaxInactiveInterval( )**. Tests seem to produce mixed results between servlet containers. Sometimes the **Session** object can hang around overnight, but I have never seen a case where the **Session** object disappears in less than the time specified by the inactive interval. You can try this by setting the inactive interval with **setMaxInactiveInterval( )** to 5 seconds and see if your **Session** object hangs around or if it is cleaned up at the appropriate time. This may be an attribute you will want to investigate while choosing a servlet container.

Running the servlet examples

If you are not already working with an application server that handles Sun's servlet and JSP technologies for you, you may download the Tomcat implementation of Java servlets and JSPs, which is a free, open-source implementation of servlets, and is the official reference implementation sanctioned by Sun. It can be found at *jakarta.apache.org*.

Follow the instructions for installing the Tomcat implementation, then edit the **server.xml** file to point to the location in your directory tree where your servlets will be placed. Once you start up the Tomcat program you can test your servlet programs.

This has only been a brief introduction to servlets; there are entire books on the subject. However, this introduction should give you enough ideas to get you started. In addition, many of the ideas in the next section are backward compatible with servlets.

Java Server Pages

Java Server Pages (JSP) is a standard Java extension that is defined on top of the servlet Extensions. The goal of JSPs is the simplified creation and management of dynamic Web pages.

The previously mentioned, freely available Tomcat reference implementation from *jakarta.apache.org* automatically supports JSPs.

JSPs allow you to combine the HTML of a Web page with pieces of Java code in the same document. The Java code is surrounded by special tags that tell the JSP container that it should use the code to generate a servlet, or part of one. The benefit of JSPs is that you can maintain a single document that represents both the page and the Java code that enables it. The downside is that the maintainer of the JSP page must be skilled in both HTML and Java (however, GUI builder environments for JSPs should be forthcoming).

The first time a JSP is loaded by the JSP container (which is typically associated with, or even part of, a Web server), the servlet code necessary to fulfill the JSP tags is automatically generated, compiled, and loaded into the servlet container. The static portions of the HTML page are produced by sending static **String** objects to **write( )**. The dynamic portions are included directly into the servlet.

From then on, as long as the JSP source for the page is not modified, it behaves as if it were a static HTML page with associated servlets (all the HTML code is actually generated by the servlet, however). If you modify the source code for the JSP, it is automatically recompiled and reloaded the next time that page is requested. Of course, because of all this dynamism you'll see a slow response for the first-time access to a JSP. However, since a JSP is usually used much more than it is changed, you will normally not be affected by this delay.

The structure of a JSP page is a cross between a servlet and an HTML page. The JSP tags begin and end with angle brackets, just like HTML tags, but the tags also include percent signs, so all JSP tags are denoted by

```
<% JSP code here %>
```

The leading percent sign may be followed by other characters that determine the precise type of JSP code in the tag.

Here's an extremely simple JSP example that uses a standard Java library call to get the current time in milliseconds, which is then divided by 1000 to produce the time in seconds. Since a *JSP expression* (the **<%=**) is used, the result of the calculation is coerced into a **String** and placed on the generated Web page:

```
//:! c15:jsp:ShowSeconds.jsp
<html><body>
<H1>The time in seconds is:
<%= System.currentTimeMillis()/1000 %></H1>
</body></html>
///:~
```

In the JSP examples in this book, the first and last lines are not included in the actual code file that is extracted and placed in the book's source-code tree.

When the client creates a request for the JSP page, the Web server must have been configured to relay the request to the JSP container, which then invokes the page. As mentioned above, the first time the page is invoked, the components specified by the page are generated and compiled by the JSP container as one or more servlets. In the above example, the servlet will contain code to configure the **HttpServletResponse** object, produce a **PrintWriter** object (which is always named **out**), and then turn the time calculation into a **String** which is sent to **out**. As you can see, all this is accomplished with a very succinct statement, but the average HTML programmer/Web designer will not have the skills to write such code.

Implicit objects

Servlets include classes that provide convenient utilities, such as **HttpServletRequest**, **HttpServletResponse**, **Session**, etc. Objects of these classes are built into the JSP specification and automatically available for use in your JSP without writing any extra lines of code. The implicit objects in a JSP are detailed in the table below.

Implicit variable	Of Type (javax.servlet)	Description	Scope
request	protocol dependent subtype of **HttpServletRequest**	The request that triggers the service invocation.	request
response	protocol dependent subtype of **HttpServletResponse**	The response to the request.	page
pageContext	**jsp.PageContext**	The page context encapsulates implementation-dependent features and provides convenience methods and namespace access for this JSP.	page
session	Protocol dependent subtype of **http.HttpSession**	The session object created for the requesting client. See servlet Session object.	session
application	**ServletContext**	The servlet context obtained from the	app

		servlet configuration object (e.g., **getServletConfig()**, **getContext( )**.	
out	**jsp.JspWriter**	The object that writes into the output stream.	page
config	**ServletConfig**	The **ServletConfig** for this JSP.	page
page	**java.lang.Object**	The instance of this page's implementation class processing the current request.	page

The scope of each object can vary significantly. For example, the **session** object has a scope which exceeds that of a page, as it many span several client requests and pages. The **application** object can provide services to a group of JSP pages that together represent a Web application.

JSP directives

Directives are messages to the JSP container and are denoted by the "**@**":

```
<%@ directive {attr="value"}* %>
```

Directives do not send anything to the **out** stream, but they are important in setting up your JSP page's attributes and dependencies with the JSP container. For example, the line:

```
<%@ page language="java" %>
```

says that the scripting language being used within the JSP page is Java. In fact, the JSP specification *only* describes the semantics of scripts for the language attribute equal to "Java." The intent of this directive is to build flexibility into the JSP technology. In the future, if you were to choose another language, say Python (a good scripting choice), then that language would have to support the Java Run-time Environment by exposing the Java technology object model to the scripting environment, especially the implicit variables defined above, JavaBeans properties, and public methods.

The most important directive is the page directive. It defines a number of page dependent attributes and communicates these attributes to the JSP

---

container. These attributes include: **language**, **extends**, **import**, **session**, **buffer**, **autoFlush**, **isThreadSafe**, **info** and **errorPage**. For example:

```
<%@ page session="true" import="java.util.*" %>
```

This line first indicates that the page requires participation in an HTTP session. Since we have not set the language directive the JSP container defaults to using Java and the implicit script language variable named **session** is of type **javax.servlet.http.HttpSession**. If the directive had been false then the implicit variable **session** would be unavailable. If the **session** variable is not specified, then it defaults to "true."

The **import** attribute describes the types that are available to the scripting environment. This attribute is used just as it would be in the Java programming language, i.e., a comma-separated list of ordinary **import** expressions. This list is imported by the translated JSP page implementation and is available to the scripting environment. Again, this is currently only defined when the value of the language directive is "java."

JSP scripting elements

Once the directives have been used to set up the scripting environment you can utilize the scripting language elements. JSP 1.1 has three scripting language elements—*declarations*, *scriptlets*, and *expressions*. A declaration will declare elements, a scriptlet is a statement fragment, and an expression is a complete language expression. In JSP each scripting element begins with a "**<%**". The syntax for each is:

```
<%! declaration %>
<%  scriptlet   %>
<%= expression  %>
```

White space is optional after "<%!", "<%", "<%=", and before "%>."

All these tags are based upon XML; you could even say that a JSP page can be mapped to a XML document. The XML equivalent syntax for the scripting elements above would be:

```
<jsp:declaration> declaration </jsp:declaration>
<jsp:scriptlet>   scriptlet   </jsp:scriptlet>
```

```
<jsp:expression>  expression  </jsp:expression>
```

In addition, there are two types of comments:

```
<%-- jsp comment --%>
<!-- html comment -->
```

The first form allows you to add comments to JSP source pages that will not appear in any form in the HTML that is sent to the client. Of course, the second form of comment is not specific to JSPs—it's just an ordinary HTML comment. What's interesting is that you can insert JSP code inside an HTML comment and the comment will be produced in the resulting page, including the result from the JSP code.

Declarations are used to declare variables and methods in the scripting language (currently Java only) used in a JSP page. The declaration must be a complete Java statement and cannot produce any output in the **out** stream. In the **Hello.jsp** example below, the declarations for the variables **loadTime**, **loadDate** and **hitCount** are all complete Java statements that declare and initialize new variables.

```
//:! c15:jsp:Hello.jsp
<%-- This JSP comment will not appear in the
generated html --%>
<%-- This is a JSP directive: --%>
<%@ page import="java.util.*" %>
<%-- These are declarations: --%>
<%!
    long loadTime= System.currentTimeMillis();
    Date loadDate = new Date();
    int hitCount = 0;
%>
<html><body>
<%-- The next several lines are the result of a
JSP expression inserted in the generated html;
the '=' indicates a JSP expression --%>
<H1>This page was loaded at <%= loadDate %> </H1>
<H1>Hello, world! It's <%= new Date() %></H1>
<H2>Here's an object: <%= new Object() %></H2>
<H2>This page has been up
<%= (System.currentTimeMillis()-loadTime)/1000 %>
seconds</H2>
```

```
<H3>Page has been accessed <%= ++hitCount %>
times since <%= loadDate %></H3>
<%-- A "scriptlet" that writes to the server
console and to the client page.
Note that the ';' is required: --%>
<%
    System.out.println("Goodbye");
    out.println("Cheerio");
%>
</body></html>
///:~
```

When you run this program you'll see that the variables **loadTime**, **loadDate** and **hitCount** hold their values between hits to the page, so they are clearly fields and not local variables.

At the end of the example is a scriptlet that writes "Goodbye" to the Web server console and "Cheerio" to the implicit **JspWriter** object **out**. Scriptlets can contain any code fragments that are valid Java statements. Scriptlets are executed at request-processing time. When all the scriptlet fragments in a given JSP are combined in the order they appear in the JSP page, they should yield a valid statement as defined by the Java programming language. Whether or not they produce any output into the **out** stream depends upon the code in the scriptlet. You should be aware that scriptlets can produce side effects by modifying the objects that are visible to them.

JSP expressions can found intermingled with the HTML in the middle section of **Hello.jsp**. Expressions must be complete Java statements, which are evaluated, coerced to a **String**, and sent to **out**. If the result of the expression cannot be coerced to a **String** then a **ClassCastException** is thrown.

Extracting fields and values

The following example is similar to one shown earlier in the servlet section. The first time you hit the page it detects that you have no fields and returns a page containing a form, using the same code as in the servlet example, but in JSP format. When you submit the form with the filled-in fields to the same JSP URL, it detects the fields and displays them. This is a nice technique because it allows you to have both the page containing the form for the user to fill out and the response code for that page in a single file, thus making it easier to create and maintain.

```
//:! c15:jsp:DisplayFormData.jsp
<%-- Fetching the data from an HTML form. --%>
<%-- This JSP also generates the form. --%>
<%@ page import="java.util.*" %>
<html><body>
<H1>DisplayFormData</H1><H3>
<%
  Enumeration flds = request.getParameterNames();
  if(!flds.hasMoreElements()) { // No fields %>
    <form method="POST"
    action="DisplayFormData.jsp">
<%  for(int i = 0; i < 10; i++) {   %>
      Field<%=i%>: <input type="text" size="20"
      name="Field<%=i%>" value="Value<%=i%>"><br>
<%  } %>
    <INPUT TYPE=submit name=submit
    value="Submit"></form>
<%} else {
    while(flds.hasMoreElements()) {
      String field = (String)flds.nextElement();
      String value = request.getParameter(field);
%>
      <li><%= field %> = <%= value %></li>
<%  }
  } %>
</H3></body></html>
///:~
```

The most interesting feature of this example is that it demonstrates how scriptlet code can be intermixed with HTML code, even to the point of generating HTML within a Java **for** loop. This is especially convenient for building any kind of form where repetitive HTML code would otherwise be required.

JSP page attributes and scope

By poking around in the HTML documentation for servlets and JSPs, you will find features that report information about the servlet or JSP that is currently running. The following example displays a few of these pieces of data.

```
//:! c15:jsp:PageContext.jsp
<%--Viewing the attributes in the pageContext--%>
<%-- Note that you can include any amount of code
inside the scriptlet tags --%>
<%@ page import="java.util.*" %>
<html><body>
Servlet Name: <%= config.getServletName() %><br>
Servlet container supports servlet version:
<% out.print(application.getMajorVersion() + "."
+ application.getMinorVersion()); %><br>
<%
  session.setAttribute("My dog", "Ralph");
  for(int scope = 1; scope <= 4; scope++) {   %>
    <H3>Scope: <%= scope %> </H3>
<%   Enumeration e =
      pageContext.getAttributeNamesInScope(scope);
    while(e.hasMoreElements()) {
      out.println("\t<li>" +
        e.nextElement() + "</li>");
    }
  }
%>
</body></html>
///:~
```

This example also shows the use of both embedded HTML and writing to **out** in order to output to the resulting HTML page.

The first piece of information produced is the name of the servlet, which will probably just be "JSP" but it depends on your implementation. You can also discover the current version of the servlet container by using the application object. Finally, after setting a session attribute, the "attribute names" in a particular scope are displayed. You don't use the scopes very much in most JSP programming; they were just shown here to add interest to the example. There are four attribute scopes, as follows: The *page scope* (scope 1), the *request scope* (scope 2), the *session scope* (scope 3—here, the only element available in session scope is "My dog," added right before the **for** loop), and the *application scope* (scope 4), based upon the **ServletContext** object. There is one **ServletContext** per "Web application" per Java Virtual Machine. (A "Web application" is a collection of servlets and content installed under a specific subset of the server's URL namespace such as /catalog. This is generally set up using a configuration file.) At the application scope you will see objects that represent paths for the working directory and temporary directory.

Manipulating sessions in JSP

Sessions were introduced in the prior section on servlets, and are also available within JSPs. The following example exercises the **session** object and allows you to manipulate the amount of time before the session becomes invalid.

```
//:! c15:jsp:SessionObject.jsp
<%--Getting and setting session object values--%>
<html><body>
<H1>Session id: <%= session.getId() %></H1>
<H3><li>This session was created at
<%= session.getCreationTime() %></li></H1>
<H3><li>Old MaxInactiveInterval =
  <%= session.getMaxInactiveInterval() %></li>
<% session.setMaxInactiveInterval(5); %>
<li>New MaxInactiveInterval=
  <%= session.getMaxInactiveInterval() %></li>
</H3>
<H2>If the session object "My dog" is
still around, this value will be non-null:<H2>
<H3><li>Session value for "My dog" =
<%= session.getAttribute("My dog") %></li></H3>
<%-- Now add the session object "My dog" --%>
<% session.setAttribute("My dog",
                    new String("Ralph")); %>
<H1>My dog's name is
<%= session.getAttribute("My dog") %></H1>
<%-- See if "My dog" wanders to another form --%>
```

```
<FORM TYPE=POST ACTION=SessionObject2.jsp>
<INPUT TYPE=submit name=submit
Value="Invalidate"></FORM>
<FORM TYPE=POST ACTION=SessionObject3.jsp>
<INPUT TYPE=submit name=submit
Value="Keep Around"></FORM>
</body></html>
///:~
```

The **session** object is provided by default so it is available without any extra coding. The calls to **getID( )**, **getCreationTime( )** and **getMaxInactiveInterval( )** are used to display information about this session object.

When you first bring up this session you will see a **MaxInactiveInterval** of, for example, 1800 seconds (30 minutes). This will depend on the way your JSP/servlet container is configured. The **MaxInactiveInterval** is shortened to 5 seconds to make things interesting. If you refresh the page before the 5 second interval expires, then you'll see:

```
Session value for "My dog" = Ralph
```

But if you wait longer than that, "Ralph" will become **null**.

To see how the session information can be carried through to other pages, and also to see the effect of invalidating a session object versus just letting it expire, two other JSPs are created. The first one (reached by pressing the "invalidate" button in **SessionObject.jsp**) reads the session information and then explicitly invalidates that session:

```
//:! c15:jsp:SessionObject2.jsp
<%--The session object carries through--%>
<html><body>
<H1>Session id: <%= session.getId() %></H1>
<H1>Session value for "My dog"
<%= session.getValue("My dog") %></H1>
<% session.invalidate(); %>
</body></html>
///:~
```

To experiment with this, refresh **SessionObject.jsp**, then immediately click the "invalidate" button to bring you to **SessionObject2.jsp**. At this point you will still see "Ralph," and right away (before the 5-second interval has expired), refresh **SessionObject2.jsp** to see that the session has been forcefully invalidated and "Ralph" has disappeared.

If you go back to **SessionObject.jsp**, refresh the page so you have a new 5-second interval, then press the "Keep Around" button, it will take you to the following page, **SessionObject3.jsp**, which does NOT invalidate the session:

```
//:! c15:jsp:SessionObject3.jsp
<%--The session object carries through--%>
<html><body>
<H1>Session id: <%= session.getId() %></H1>
<H1>Session value for "My dog"
<%= session.getValue("My dog") %></H1>
<FORM TYPE=POST ACTION=SessionObject.jsp>
<INPUT TYPE=submit name=submit Value="Return">
</FORM>
</body></html>
///:~
```

Because this page doesn't invalidate the session, "Ralph" will hang around as long as you keep refreshing the page before the 5 second time interval expires. This is not unlike a "Tomagotchi" pet—as long as you play with "Ralph" he will stick around, otherwise he expires.

Creating and modifying cookies

Cookies were introduced in the prior section on servlets. Once again, the brevity of JSPs makes playing with cookies much simpler here than when using servlets. The following example shows this by fetching the cookies that come with the request, reading and modifying their maximum ages (expiration dates) and attaching a new cookie to the outgoing response:

```
//:! c15:jsp:Cookies.jsp
<%--This program has different behaviors under
  different browsers! --%>
<html><body>
<H1>Session id: <%= session.getId() %></H1>
<%
Cookie[] cookies = request.getCookies();
```

```
for(int i = 0; i < cookies.length; i++) { %>
  Cookie name: <%= cookies[i].getName() %> <br>
  value: <%= cookies[i].getValue() %><br>
  Old max age in seconds:
  <%= cookies[i].getMaxAge() %><br>
  <% cookies[i].setMaxAge(5); %>
  New max age in seconds:
  <%= cookies[i].getMaxAge() %><br>
<% } %>
<%! int count = 0; int dcount = 0; %>
<% response.addCookie(new Cookie(
    "Bob" + count++, "Dog" + dcount++)); %>
</body></html>
///:~
```

Since each browser stores cookies in its own way, you may see different behaviors with different browsers (not reassuring, but it might be some kind of bug that could be fixed by the time you read this). Also, you may experience different results if you shut down the browser and restart it, rather than just visiting a different page and then returning to **Cookies.jsp**. Note that using session objects seems to be more robust than directly using cookies.

After displaying the session identifier, each cookie in the array of cookies that comes in with the **request** object is displayed, along with its maximum age. The maximum age is changed and displayed again to verify the new value, then a new cookie is added to the response. However, your browser may seem to ignore the maximum age; it's worth playing with this program and modifying the maximum age value to see the behavior under different browsers.

JSP summary

This section has only been a brief coverage of JSPs, and yet even with what was covered here (along with the Java you've learned in the rest of the book, and your own knowledge of HTML) you can begin to write sophisticated web pages via JSPs. The JSP syntax isn't meant to be particularly deep or complicated, so if you understand what was presented in this section you're ready to be productive with JSPs. You can

find further information in most current books on servlets, or at
java.sun.com.

It's especially nice to have JSPs available, even if your goal is only to
produce servlets. You'll discover that if you have a question about the
behavior of a servlet feature, it's much easier and faster to write a JSP test
program to answer that question than it is to write a servlet. Part of the
benefit comes from having to write less code and being able to mix the
display HTML in with the Java code, but the leverage becomes especially
obvious when you see that the JSP Container handles all the
recompilation and reloading of the JSP for you whenever the source is
changed.

As terrific as JSPs are, however, it's worth keeping in mind that JSP
creation requires a higher level of skill than just programming in Java or
just creating Web pages. In addition, debugging a broken JSP page is not
as easy as debugging a Java program, as (currently) the error messages
are more obscure. This should change as development systems improve,
but we may also see other technologies built on top of Java and the Web
that are better adapted to the skills of the web site designer.

RMI (Remote Method Invocation)

Traditional approaches to executing code on other machines across a
network have been confusing as well as tedious and error-prone to
implement. The nicest way to think about this problem is that some object
happens to live on another machine, and that you can send a message to
the remote object and get a result as if the object lived on your local
machine. This simplification is exactly what Java *Remote Method
Invocation* (RMI) allows you to do. This section walks you through the
steps necessary to create your own RMI objects.

Remote interfaces

RMI makes heavy use of interfaces. When you want to create a remote
object, you mask the underlying implementation by passing around an
interface. Thus, when the client gets a reference to a remote object, what

---

they really get is an interface reference, which *happens* to connect to some local stub code that talks across the network. But you don't think about this, you just send messages via your interface reference.

When you create a remote interface, you must follow these guidelines:

1.   The remote interface must be **public** (it cannot have "package access," that is, it cannot be "friendly"). Otherwise, a client will get an error when attempting to load a remote object that implements the remote interface.

2.   The remote interface must extend the interface **java.rmi.Remote**.

3.   Each method in the remote interface must declare **java.rmi.RemoteException** in its **throws** clause in addition to any application-specific exceptions.

4.   A remote object passed as an argument or return value (either directly or embedded within a local object) must be declared as the remote interface, not the implementation class.

Here's a simple remote interface that represents an accurate time service:

```
//: c15:rmi:PerfectTimeI.java
// The PerfectTime remote interface.
package c15.rmi;
import java.rmi.*;

interface PerfectTimeI extends Remote {
  long getPerfectTime() throws RemoteException;
} ///:~
```

It looks like any other interface except that it extends **Remote** and all of its methods throw **RemoteException**. Remember that an **interface** and all of its methods are automatically **public**.

Implementing the remote interface

The server must contain a class that extends **UnicastRemoteObject** and implements the remote interface. This class can also have additional methods, but only the methods in the remote interface are available to the client, of course, since the client will get only a reference to the interface, not the class that implements it.

You must explicitly define the constructor for the remote object even if you're only defining a default constructor that calls the base-class constructor. You must write it out since it must throw **RemoteException**.

Here's the implementation of the remote interface **PerfectTimeI**:

```
//: c15:rmi:PerfectTime.java
// The implementation of
// the PerfectTime remote object.
package c15.rmi;
import java.rmi.*;
import java.rmi.server.*;
import java.rmi.registry.*;
import java.net.*;

public class PerfectTime
    extends UnicastRemoteObject
    implements PerfectTimeI {
  // Implementation of the interface:
  public long getPerfectTime()
      throws RemoteException {
    return System.currentTimeMillis();
  }
  // Must implement constructor
  // to throw RemoteException:
  public PerfectTime() throws RemoteException {
    // super(); // Called automatically
  }
  // Registration for RMI serving. Throw
  // exceptions out to the console.
  public static void main(String[] args)
  throws Exception {
    System.setSecurityManager(
    new RMISecurityManager());
    PerfectTime pt = new PerfectTime();
    Naming.bind(
      "//peppy:2005/PerfectTime", pt);
```

```
    System.out.println("Ready to do time");
  }
} ///:~
```

Here, **main( )** handles all the details of setting up the server. When you're serving RMI objects, at some point in your program you must:

1. Create and install a security manager that supports RMI. The only one available for RMI as part of the Java distribution is **RMISecurityManager**.

2. Create one or more instances of a remote object. Here, you can see the creation of the **PerfectTime** object.

3. Register at least one of the remote objects with the RMI remote object registry for bootstrapping purposes. One remote object can have methods that produce references to other remote objects. This allows you to set it up so the client must go to the registry only once, to get the first remote object.

Setting up the registry

Here, you see a call to the **static** method **Naming.bind( )**. However, this call requires that the registry be running as a separate process on the computer. The name of the registry server is **rmiregistry**, and under 32-bit Windows you say:

```
start rmiregistry
```

to start it in the background. On Unix, the command is:

```
rmiregistry &
```

Like many network programs, the **rmiregistry** is located at the IP address of whatever machine started it up, but it must also be listening at a port. If you invoke the **rmiregistry** as above, with no argument, the registry's port will default to 1099. If you want it to be at some other port, you add an argument on the command line to specify the port. For this example, the port is located at 2005, so the **rmiregistry** should be started like this under 32-bit Windows:

```
start rmiregistry 2005
```

or for Unix:

```
rmiregistry 2005 &
```

The information about the port must also be given to the **bind( )**
command, as well as the IP address of the machine where the registry is
located. But this brings up what can be a frustrating problem if you're
expecting to test RMI programs locally the way the network programs
have been tested so far in this chapter. In the JDK 1.1.1 release, there are a
couple of problems:[5]

1.   **localhost** does not work with RMI. Thus, to experiment with RMI
     on a single machine, you must provide the name of the machine. To
     find out the name of your machine under 32-bit Windows, go to the
     control panel and select "Network." Select the "Identification" tab,
     and you'll see your computer name. In my case, I called my
     computer "Peppy." It appears that capitalization is ignored.

2.   RMI will not work unless your computer has an active TCP/IP
     connection, even if all your components are just talking to each
     other on the local machine. This means that you must connect to
     your Internet service provider before trying to run the program or
     you'll get some obscure exception messages.

With all this in mind, the **bind( )** command becomes:

```
Naming.bind("//peppy:2005/PerfectTime", pt);
```

If you are using the default port 1099, you don't need to specify a port, so
you could say:

```
Naming.bind("//peppy/PerfectTime", pt);
```

You should be able to perform local testing by leaving off the IP address
and using only the identifier:

```
Naming.bind("PerfectTime", pt);
```

The name for the service is arbitrary; it happens to be PerfectTime here,
just like the name of the class, but you could call it anything you want. The

---

[5] Many brain cells died in agony to discover this information.

important thing is that it's a unique name in the registry that the client knows to look for to procure the remote object. If the name is already in the registry, you'll get an **AlreadyBoundException**. To prevent this, you can always use **rebind( )** instead of **bind( )**, since **rebind( )** either adds a new entry or replaces the one that's already there.

Even though **main( )** exits, your object has been created and registered so it's kept alive by the registry, waiting for a client to come along and request it. As long as the **rmiregistry** is running and you don't call **Naming.unbind( )** on your name, the object will be there. For this reason, when you're developing your code you need to shut down the **rmiregistry** and restart it when you compile a new version of your remote object.

You aren't forced to start up **rmiregistry** as an external process. If you know that your application is the only one that's going to use the registry, you can start it up inside your program with the line:

```
LocateRegistry.createRegistry(2005);
```

Like before, 2005 is the port number we happen to be using in this example. This is the equivalent of running **rmiregistry 2005** from a command line, but it can often be more convenient when you're developing RMI code since it eliminates the extra steps of starting and stopping the registry. Once you've executed this code, you can **bind( )** using **Naming** as before.

Creating stubs and skeletons

If you compile and run **PerfectTime.java**, it won't work even if you have the **rmiregistry** running correctly. That's because the framework for RMI isn't all there yet. You must first create the stubs and skeletons that provide the network connection operations and allow you to pretend that the remote object is just another local object on your machine.

What's going on behind the scenes is complex. Any objects that you pass into or return from a remote object must **implement Serializable** (if you want to pass remote references instead of the entire objects, the object arguments can **implement Remote**), so you can imagine that the stubs and skeletons are automatically performing serialization and deserialization as they "marshal" all of the arguments across the network and return the result. Fortunately, you don't have to know any of this, but you *do* have to create the stubs and skeletons. This is a simple process: you invoke the **rmic** tool on your compiled code, and it creates the necessary files. So the only requirement is that another step be added to your compilation process.

The **rmic** tool is particular about packages and classpaths, however. **PerfectTime.java** is in the **package c15.rmi**, and even if you invoke **rmic** in the same directory in which **PerfectTime.class** is located, **rmic** won't find the file, since it searches the classpath. So you must specify the location off the class path, like so:

```
rmic c15.rmi.PerfectTime
```

You don't have to be in the directory containing **PerfectTime.class** when you execute this command, but the results will be placed in the current directory.

When **rmic** runs successfully, you'll have two new classes in the directory:

```
PerfectTime_Stub.class
PerfectTime_Skel.class
```

corresponding to the stub and skeleton. Now you're ready to get the server and client to talk to each other.

Using the remote object

The whole point of RMI is to make the use of remote objects simple. The only extra thing that you must do in your client program is to look up and fetch the remote interface from the server. From then on, it's just regular Java programming: sending messages to objects. Here's the program that uses **PerfectTime**:

```
//: c15:rmi:DisplayPerfectTime.java
// Uses remote object PerfectTime.
package c15.rmi;
import java.rmi.*;
import java.rmi.registry.*;
```

```
public class DisplayPerfectTime {
  public static void main(String[] args)
  throws Exception {
    System.setSecurityManager(
      new RMISecurityManager());
    PerfectTimeI t =
      (PerfectTimeI)Naming.lookup(
        "//peppy:2005/PerfectTime");
    for(int i = 0; i < 10; i++)
      System.out.println("Perfect time = " +
        t.getPerfectTime());
  }
} ///:~
```

The ID string is the same as the one used to register the object with **Naming**, and the first part represents the URL and port number. Since you're using a URL, you can also specify a machine on the Internet.

What comes back from **Naming.lookup( )** must be cast to the remote interface, *not* to the class. If you use the class instead, you'll get an exception.

You can see in the method call

```
t.getPerfectTime()
```

that once you have a reference to the remote object, programming with it is indistinguishable from programming with a local object (with one difference: remote methods throw **RemoteException**).

CORBA

In large, distributed applications, your needs might not be satisfied by the preceding approaches. For example, you might want to interface with legacy data stores, or you might need services from a server object regardless of its physical location. These situations require some form of Remote Procedure Call (RPC), and possibly language independence. This is where CORBA can help.

CORBA is not a language feature; it's an integration technology. It's a specification that vendors can follow to implement CORBA-compliant integration products. CORBA is part of the OMG's effort to define a standard framework for distributed, language-independent object interoperability.

CORBA supplies the ability to make remote procedure calls into Java objects and non-Java objects, and to interface with legacy systems in a location-transparent way. Java adds networking support and a nice object-oriented language for building graphical and non-graphical applications. The Java and OMG object model map nicely to each other; for example, both Java and CORBA implement the interface concept and a reference object model.

CORBA fundamentals

The object interoperability specification developed by the OMG is commonly referred to as the Object Management Architecture (OMA). The OMA defines two components: the Core Object Model and the OMA Reference Architecture. The Core Object Model states the basic concepts of object, interface, operation, and so on. (CORBA is a refinement of the Core Object Model.) The OMA Reference Architecture defines an underlying infrastructure of services and mechanisms that allow objects to interoperate. The OMA Reference Architecture includes the Object Request Broker (ORB), Object Services (also known as CORBA services), and common facilities.

The ORB is the communication bus by which objects can request services from other objects, regardless of their physical location. This means that what looks like a method call in the client code is actually a complex operation. First, a connection with the server object must exist, and to create a connection the ORB must know where the server implementation code resides. Once the connection is established, the method arguments must be marshaled, i.e. converted in a binary stream to be sent across a network. Other information that must be sent are the server machine name, the server process, and the identity of the server object inside that process. Finally, this information is sent through a low-level wire protocol, the information is decoded on the server side, and the call is executed. The ORB hides all of this complexity from the programmer and makes the operation almost as simple as calling a method on local object.

There is no specification for how an ORB Core should be implemented, but to provide a basic compatibility among different vendors' ORBs, the OMG defines a set of services that are accessible through standard interfaces.

CORBA Interface Definition Language (IDL)

CORBA is designed for language transparency: a client object can call methods on a server object of different class, regardless of the language they are implemented with. Of course, the client object must know the names and signatures of methods that the server object exposes. This is where IDL comes in. The CORBA IDL is a language-neutral way to specify data types, attributes, operations, interfaces, and more. The IDL syntax is similar to the C++ or Java syntax. The following table shows the correspondence between some of the concepts common to three languages that can be specified through CORBA IDL:

CORBA IDL	Java	C++
Module	Package	Namespace
Interface	Interface	Pure abstract class
Method	Method	Member function

The inheritance concept is supported as well, using the colon operator as in C++. The programmer writes an IDL description of the attributes, methods, and interfaces that are implemented and used by the server and clients. The IDL is then compiled by a vendor-provided IDL/Java compiler, which reads the IDL source and generates Java code.

The IDL compiler is an extremely useful tool: it doesn't just generate a Java source equivalent of the IDL, it also generates the code that will be used to marshal method arguments and to make remote calls. This code, called the stub and skeleton code, is organized in multiple Java source files and is usually part of the same Java package.

The naming service

The naming service is one of the fundamental CORBA services. A CORBA object is accessed through a reference, a piece of information that's not meaningful for the human reader. But references can be assigned programmer-defined, string names. This operation is known as *stringifying the reference*, and one of the OMA components, the Naming Service, is devoted to performing string-to-object and object-to-string conversion and mapping. Since the Naming Service acts as a telephone directory that both servers and clients can consult and manipulate, it runs as a separate process. Creating an object-to-string mapping is called *binding an object*, and removing the mapping is called *unbinding*. Getting an object reference passing a string is called *resolving the name*.

For example, on startup, a server application could create a server object, bind the object into the name service, and then wait for clients to make requests. A client first obtains a server object reference, resolving the string name, and then can make calls into the server using the reference.

Again, the Naming Service specification is part of CORBA, but the application that implements it is provided by the ORB vendor. The way you get access to the Naming Service functionality can vary from vendor to vendor.

An example

The code shown here will not be elaborate because different ORBs have different ways to access CORBA services, so examples are vendor specific. (The example below uses JavaIDL, a free product from Sun that comes with a light-weight ORB, a naming service, and an IDL-to-Java compiler.) In addition, since Java is young and still evolving, not all CORBA features are present in the various Java/CORBA products.

We want to implement a server, running on some machine, that can be queried for the exact time. We also want to implement a client that asks for the exact time. In this case we'll be implementing both programs in Java, but we could also use two different languages (which often happens in real situations).

Writing the IDL source

The first step is to write an IDL description of the services provided. This is usually done by the server programmer, who is then free to implement the server in any language in which a CORBA IDL compiler exists. The

IDL file is distributed to the client side programmer and becomes the bridge between languages.

The example below shows the IDL description of our **ExactTime** server:

```
//: c15:corba:ExactTime.idl
//# You must install idltojava.exe from
//# java.sun.com and adjust the settings to use
//# your local C preprocessor in order to compile
//# This file. See docs at java.sun.com.
module remotetime {
    interface ExactTime {
        string getTime();
    };
}; ///:~
```

This is a declaration of the **ExactTime** interface inside the **remotetime** namespace. The interface is made up of one single method that gives back the current time in **string** format.

Creating stubs and skeletons

The second step is to compile the IDL to create the Java stub and skeleton code that we'll use for implementing the client and the server. The tool that comes with the JavaIDL product is **idltojava**:

```
idltojava remotetime.idl
```

This will automatically generate code for both the stub and the skeleton. **Idltojava** generates a Java **package** named after the IDL module, **remotetime**, and the generated Java files are put in the **remotetime** subdirectory. **_ExactTimeImplBase.java** is the skeleton that we'll use to implement the server object, and **_ExactTimeStub.java** will be used for the client. There are Java representations of the IDL interface in **ExactTime.java** and a couple of other support files used, for example, to facilitate access to the naming service operations.

Implementing the server and the client

Below you can see the code for the server side. The server object implementation is in the **ExactTimeServer** class. The **RemoteTimeServer** is the application that creates a server object, registers it with the ORB, gives a name to the object reference, and then sits quietly waiting for client requests.

```
//: c15:corba:RemoteTimeServer.java
import remotetime.*;
import org.omg.CosNaming.*;
import org.omg.CosNaming.NamingContextPackage.*;
import org.omg.CORBA.*;
import java.util.*;
import java.text.*;

// Server object implementation
class ExactTimeServer extends _ExactTimeImplBase {
  public String getTime(){
    return DateFormat.
        getTimeInstance(DateFormat.FULL).
          format(new Date(
              System.currentTimeMillis())));
  }
}

// Remote application implementation
public class RemoteTimeServer {
  // Throw exceptions to console:
  public static void main(String[] args)
  throws Exception {
    // ORB creation and initialization:
    ORB orb = ORB.init(args, null);
    // Create the server object and register it:
    ExactTimeServer timeServerObjRef =
      new ExactTimeServer();
    orb.connect(timeServerObjRef);
    // Get the root naming context:
    org.omg.CORBA.Object objRef =
      orb.resolve_initial_references(
        "NameService");
    NamingContext ncRef =
      NamingContextHelper.narrow(objRef);
    // Assign a string name to the
    // object reference (binding):
    NameComponent nc =
```

```
      new NameComponent("ExactTime", "");
    NameComponent[] path = { nc };
    ncRef.rebind(path, timeServerObjRef);
    // Wait for client requests:
    java.lang.Object sync =
      new java.lang.Object();
    synchronized(sync){
      sync.wait();
    }
  }
} ///:~
```

As you can see, implementing the server object is simple; it's a regular Java class that inherits from the skeleton code generated by the IDL compiler. Things get a bit more complicated when it comes to interacting with the ORB and other CORBA services.

Some CORBA services

This is a short description of what the JavaIDL-related code is doing (primarily ignoring the part of the CORBA code that is vendor dependent). The first line in **main( )** starts up the ORB, and of course, this is because our server object will need to interact with it. Right after the ORB initialization, a server object is created. Actually, the right term would be a *transient servant object*: an object that receives requests from clients, and whose lifetime is the same as the process that creates it. Once the transient servant object is created, it is registered with the ORB, which means that the ORB knows of its existence and can now forward requests to it.

Up to this point, all we have is **timeServerObjRef**, an object reference that is known only inside the current server process. The next step will be to assign a stringified name to this servant object; clients will use that name to locate the servant object. We accomplish this operation using the Naming Service. First, we need an object reference to the Naming Service; the call to **resolve_initial_references( )** takes the stringified object reference of the Naming Service that is "NameService," in JavaIDL, and returns an object reference. This is cast to a specific **NamingContext** reference using the **narrow( )** method. We can use now the naming services.

To bind the servant object with a stringified object reference, we first create a **NameComponent** object, initialized with "ExactTime," the name string we want to bind to the servant object. Then, using the **rebind( )** method, the stringified reference is bound to the object reference. We use **rebind( )** to assign a reference, even if it already exists, whereas **bind( )** raises an exception if the reference already exists. A name is made up in CORBA by a sequence of NameContexts—that's why we use an array to bind the name to the object reference.

The servant object is finally ready for use by clients. At this point, the server process enters a wait state. Again, this is because it is a transient servant, so its lifetime is confined to the server process. JavaIDL does not currently support persistent objects—objects that survive the execution of the process that creates them.

Now that we have an idea of what the server code is doing, let's look at the client code:

```
//: c15:corba:RemoteTimeClient.java
import remotetime.*;
import org.omg.CosNaming.*;
import org.omg.CORBA.*;

public class RemoteTimeClient {
  // Throw exceptions to console:
  public static void main(String[] args)
  throws Exception {
    // ORB creation and initialization:
    ORB orb = ORB.init(args, null);
    // Get the root naming context:
    org.omg.CORBA.Object objRef =
      orb.resolve_initial_references(
        "NameService");
    NamingContext ncRef =
      NamingContextHelper.narrow(objRef);
    // Get (resolve) the stringified object
    // reference for the time server:
    NameComponent nc =
      new NameComponent("ExactTime", "");
    NameComponent[] path = { nc };
    ExactTime timeObjRef =
```

```
    ExactTimeHelper.narrow(
      ncRef.resolve(path));
    // Make requests to the server object:
    String exactTime = timeObjRef.getTime();
    System.out.println(exactTime);
  }
} ///:~
```

The first few lines do the same as they do in the server process: the ORB is initialized and a reference to the naming service server is resolved. Next, we need an object reference for the servant object, so we pass the stringified object reference to the **resolve( )** method, and we cast the result into an **ExactTime** interface reference using the **narrow( )** method. Finally, we call **getTime( )**.

Activating the name service process

Finally we have a server and a client application ready to interoperate. You've seen that both need the naming service to bind and resolve stringified object references. You must start the naming service process before running either the server or the client. In JavaIDL, the naming service is a Java application that comes with the product package, but it can be different with other products. The JavaIDL naming service runs inside an instance of the JVM and listens by default to network port 900.

Activating the server and the client

Now you are ready to start your server and client application (in this order, since our server is transient). If everything is set up correctly, what you'll get is a single output line on the client console window, giving you the current time. Of course, this might be not very exciting by itself, but you should take one thing into account: even if they are on the same physical machine, the client and the server application are running inside different virtual machines and they can communicate via an underlying integration layer, the ORB and the Naming Service.

This is a simple example, designed to work without a network, but an ORB is usually configured for location transparency. When the server and the client are on different machines, the ORB can resolve remote stringified references using a component known as the *Implementation*

Repository. Although the Implementation Repository is part of CORBA, there is almost no specification, so it differs from vendor to vendor.

As you can see, there is much more to CORBA than what has been covered here, but you should get the basic idea. If you want more information about CORBA, the place to start is the OMG Web site, at *www.omg.org*. There you'll find documentation, white papers, proceedings, and references to other CORBA sources and products.

Java Applets and CORBA

Java applets can act as CORBA clients. This way, an applet can access remote information and services exposed as CORBA objects. But an applet can connect only with the server from which it was downloaded, so all the CORBA objects the applet interacts with must be on that server. This is the opposite of what CORBA tries to do: give you complete location transparency.

This is an issue of network security. If you're on an intranet, one solution is to loosen the security restrictions on the browser. Or, set up a firewall policy for connecting with external servers.

Some Java ORB products offer proprietary solutions to this problem. For example, some implement what is called HTTP Tunneling, while others have their special firewall features.

This is too complex a topic to be covered in an appendix, but it is definitely something you should be aware of.

CORBA vs. RMI

You saw that one of the main CORBA features is RPC support, which allows your local objects to call methods in remote objects. Of course, there already is a native Java feature that does exactly the same thing: RMI (see Chapter 15). While RMI makes RPC possible between Java objects, CORBA makes RPC possible between objects implemented in any language. It's a big difference.

However, RMI can be used to call services on remote, non-Java code. All you need is some kind of wrapper Java object around the non-Java code on the server side. The wrapper object connects externally to Java clients via RMI, and internally connects to the non-Java code using one of the techniques shown above, such as JNI or J/Direct.

This approach requires you to write a kind of integration layer, which is exactly what CORBA does for you, but then you don't need a third-party ORB.

Enterprise JavaBeans

Suppose[6] you need to develop a multi-tiered application to view and update records in a database through a Web interface. You can write a database application using JDBC, a Web interface using JSP/servlets, and a distributed system using CORBA/RMI. But what extra considerations must you make when developing a distributed object system rather than just knowing API's? Here are the issues:

Performance: The distributed objects you create must perform well, as they could potentially service many clients at a time. You'll need to use optimization techniques such as caching as well as pooling resources like database connections. You'll also have to manage the lifecycle of your distributed objects.

Scalability: The distributed objects must also be scalable. Scalability in a distributed application means that the number of instances of your distributed objects can be increased and moved onto additional machines without modifying any code.

Security: A distributed object must often manage the authorization of the clients that access it. Ideally, you can add new users and roles to it without recompilation.

Distributed Transactions: A distributed object should be able to reference distributed transactions transparently. For example, if you are working with two separated databases, you should be able to update them simultaneously within the same transaction and roll them both back if a certain criteria is not met.

---

[6] This section was contributed by Robert Castaneda, with help from Dave Bartlett.

Reusability: The ideal distributed object can be effortlessly moved onto another vendors' application server. It would be nice if you could resell a distributed object component without making special modifications, or buy someone else's component and use it without having to recompile or rewrite it.

Availability: If one of the machines in the system goes down, clients should automatically fail-over to backup copies of the objects running on other machines.

These considerations, in addition the business problem that you set out to solve, can make for a daunting development project. However, all the issues *except* for your business problem are redundant—solutions must be reinvented for every distributed business application.

Sun, along with other leading distributed object vendors, realized that sooner or later every development team would be reinventing these particular solutions, so they created the Enterprise JavaBeans specification (EJB). EJB describes a server-side component model that tackles all of the considerations mentioned above using a standard approach that allows developers to create business components called EJBs that are isolated from low-level "plumbing" code and that focus solely on providing business logic. Because EJB's are defined in a standard way, they can vendor independent.

JavaBeans vs. EJBs

Because of the similarity in names, there is much confusion about the relationship between the JavaBeans component model and the Enterprise JavaBeans specification. While both the JavaBeans and Enterprise JavaBeans specifications share the same objectives in promoting reuse and portability of Java code between development and deployment tools with the use of standard design patterns, the motives behind each specification are geared to solve different problems.

The standards defined in the JavaBeans component model are designed for creating reusable components that are typically used in IDE development tools and are commonly, although not exclusively, visual components.

The Enterprise JavaBeans specification defines a component model for developing server side java code. Because EJBs can potentially run on many different server-side platforms—including mainframes that do not have visual displays—An EJB cannot make use of graphical libraries such as AWT or Swing.

The EJB specification

The Enterprise JavaBeans specification describes a server-side component model. It defines six roles that are used to perform the tasks in development and deployment as well as defining the components of the system. These roles are used in the development, deployment and running of a distributed system. Vendors, administrators and developers play the various roles, to allow the partitioning of technical and domain knowledge. The vendor provides a technically sound framework and the developers create domain-specific components; for example, an "accounting" component. The same party can perform one or many roles. The roles defined in the EJB specification are summarized in the following table:

Role	Responsibility
Enterprise Bean Provider	The developer responsible for creating reusable EJB components. These components are packaged into a special jar file (ejb-jar file).
Application Assembler	Creates and assembles applications from a collection of ejb-jar files. This includes writing applications that utilize the collection of EJBs (e.g., servlets, JSP, Swing etc. etc.).
Deployer	Takes the collection of ejb-jar files from the Assembler and/or Bean Provider and deploys them into a run-time environment: one or more EJB Containers.
EJB Container/Server Provider	Provides a run-time environment and tools that are used to deploy, administer, and run EJB components.
System Administrator	Manages the different components and services so that they are configured and they interact correctly, as well as ensuring that the system is up and running.

EJB components

EJB components are elements of reusable business logic that adhere to strict standards and design patterns as defined in the EJB specification. This allows the components to be portable. It also allows other services—such as security, caching and distributed transactions—to be performed on behalf of the components. An Enterprise Bean Provider is responsible for developing EJB components.

EJB Container & Server

The *EJB Container* is a run-time environment that contains and runs EJB components and provides a set of standard services to those components. The EJB Container's responsibilities are tightly defined by the specification to allow for vendor neutrality. The EJB container provides the low-level "plumbing" of EJB, including distributed transactions, security, lifecycle management of beans, caching, threading and session management. The EJB Container Provider is responsible for providing an EJB Container.

An *EJB Server* is defined as an Application Server that contains and runs one or more EJB Containers. The EJB Server Provider is responsible for providing an EJB Server. You can generally assume that the EJB Container and EJB Server are the same.

Java Naming and Directory Interface (JNDI)

Java Naming and Directory Interface (JNDI) is used in Enterprise JavaBeans as the naming service for EJB Components on the network and other container services such as transactions. JNDI maps very closely to other naming and directory standards such as CORBA CosNaming and can actually be implemeted as a wrapper on top of it.

Java Transaction API/Java Transaction Service (JTA/JTS)

JTA/JTS is used in Enterprise JavaBeans as the transactional API. An Enterprise Bean Provider can use the JTS to create transaction code, although the EJB Container commonly implements transactions in EJB on the EJB components' behalf. The deployer can define the transactional attributes of an EJB component at deployment time. The EJB Container is responsible for handling the transaction whether it is local or distributed. The JTS specification is the Java mapping to the CORBA OTS (Object Transaction Service)

CORBA and RMI/IIOP

The EJB specification defines interoperability with CORBA through compatibility with CORBA protocols. This is achieved by mapping EJB services such as JTS and JNDI to corresponding CORBA services and the implementation of RMI on top of the CORBA protocol IIOP.

Use of CORBA and RMI/IIOP in Enterprise JavaBeans is implemented in the EJB Container and is the responsibility of the EJB Container provider. Use of CORBA and RMI/IIOP in the EJB Container is hidden from the EJB Component itself. This means that the Enterprise Bean Provider can write their EJB Component and deploy it into any EJB Container without any regard of which communication protocol is being used.

The pieces of an EJB component

An EJB consists of a number of pieces, including the Bean itself, the implementation of some interfaces, and an information file. Everything is packaged together into a special jar file.

Enterprise Bean

The Enterprise Bean is a Java class that the Enterprise Bean Provider develops. It implements an Enterprise Bean interface and provides the implementation of the business methods that the component is to perform. The class does not implement any authorization, authentication, multithreading, or transactional code.

Home interface

Every Enterprise Bean that is created must have an associated Home interface. The Home interface is used as a factory for your EJB. Clients use the Home interface to find an instance of your EJB or create a new instance of your EJB.

Remote interface

The Remote interface is a Java Interface that reflects the methods of your Enterprise Bean that you wish to expose to the outside world. The Remote interface plays a similar role to a CORBA IDL interface.

Deployment descriptor

The deployment descriptor is an XML file that contains information about your EJB. Using XML allows the deployer to easily change attributes about your EJB. The configurable attributes defined in the deployment descriptor include:

- The Home and Remote interface names that are required by your EJB

- The name to publish into JNDI for your EJBs Home interface

- Transactional attributes for each method of your EJB

- Access Control Lists for authentication

EJB-Jar file

The EJB-Jar file is a normal java jar file that contains your EJB, Home and Remote interfaces, as well as the deployment descriptor.

EJB operation

Once you have an EJB-Jar file containing the Bean, the Home and Remote interfaces, and the deployment descriptor, you can fit all of the pieces together and in the process understand why the Home and Remote interfaces are needed and how the EJB Container uses them.

The EJB Container implements the Home and Remote interfaces that are in the EJB-Jar file. As mentioned earlier, the Home interface provides methods to create and find your EJB. This means that the EJB Container is responsible for the lifecycle management of your EJB. This level of indirection allows for optimizations to occur. For example, 5 clients might simultaneously request the creation of an EJB through a Home Interface, and the EJB Container would respond by creating only one EJB and sharing it between all 5 clients. This is achieved through the Remote

Interface, which is also implemented by the EJB Container. The implemented Remote object plays the role of a proxy object to the EJB.

All calls to the EJB are 'proxied' through the EJB Container via the Home and Remote interfaces. This indirection is the reason why the EJB container can control security and transactional behavior.

Types of EJBs

The Enterprise JavaBeans specification defines different types of EJBs that have different characteristics and behaviors. Two categories of EJBs have been defined in the specification: *Session Beans* and *Entity Beans*, and each categoriy has variations.

Session Beans

Session Beans are used to represent Use-Cases or Workflow on behalf of a client. They represent operations on persistent data, but not the persistent data itself. There are two types of Session Beans, *Stateless* and *Stateful*. All Session Beans must implement the **javax.ejb.SessionBean** interface. The EJB Container governs the life of a Session Bean.

Stateless Session Beans are the simplest type of EJB component to implement. They do not maintain any conversational state with clients between method invocations so they are easily reusable on the server side and because they can be cached, they scale well on demand. When using Stateless Session Beans, all state must be stored outside of the EJB.

Stateful Session Beans maintain state between invocations. They have a one-to-one logical mapping to a client and can maintain state within themselves. The EJB Container is responsible for pooling and caching of Stateful Session Beans, which is achieved through *Passivation* and *Activation*. If the EJB Container crashes, data for all Stateful Session Beans could be lost. Some high-end EJB Containers provide recovery for Stateful Session Beans.

Entity Beans

Entity Beans are components that represent persistent data and behavior of this data. Entity Beans can be shared among multiple clients, the same way that data in a database can be shared. The EJB Container is responsible for caching Entity Beans and for maintaining the integrity of the Entity Beans. The life of an Entity Bean outlives the EJB Container, so if an EJB Container crashes, the Entity Bean is still expected to be available when the EJB Container again becomes available.

There are two types of Entity Beans: those with Container Managed persistence and those with Bean-Managed persistence.

Container Managed Persistence (CMP). A CMP Entity Bean has its persistence implemented on its behalf by the EJB Container. Through attributes specified in the deployment descriptor, the EJB Container will map the Entity Bean's attributes to some persistent store (usually—but not always—a database). CMP reduces the development time for the EJB, as well as dramatically reducing the amount of code required.

Bean Managed Persistence (BMP). A BMP Entity Bean has its persistence implemented by the Enterprise Bean Provider. The Enterprise Bean Provider is responsible for implementing the logic required to create a new EJB, update some attributes of the EJBS, delete an EJB and find an EJB from persistent store. This usually involves writing JDBC code to interact with a database or other persistent store. With BMP, the developer is in full control of how the Entity Bean persistence is managed.

BMP also gives flexibility where a CMP implementation may not be available. For example, if you wanted to create an EJB that wrapped some code on an existing mainframe system, you could write your persistence using CORBA.

Developing an EJB

As an example, the "Perfect Time" example from the previous RMI section will be implemented as an EJB component. The example will be a simple Stateless Session Bean.

As mentioned earlier, EJB components consist of at least one class (the EJB) and two interfaces: the Remote and Home interfaces. When you create a Remote interface for an EJB , you must follow these guidelines:

1.   The remote interface must be **public**.

2. The remote interface must extend the interface **javax.ejb.EJBObject**.

3. Each method in the remote interface must declare **java.rmi.RemoteException** in its **throws** clause in addition to any application-specific exceptions.

4. Any object passed as an argument or return value (either directly or embedded within a local object) must be a valid RMI-IIOP data type (this includes other EJB objects).

Here is the simple remote interface for the PerfectTime EJB:

```
//: c15:ejb:PerfectTime.java
//# You must install the J2EE Java Enterprise
//# Edition from java.sun.com and add j2ee.jar
//# to your CLASSPATH in order to compile
//# this file. See details at java.sun.com.
// Remote Interface of PerfectTimeBean
import java.rmi.*;
import javax.ejb.*;

public interface PerfectTime extends EJBObject {
  public long getPerfectTime()
    throws RemoteException;
} ///:~
```

The Home interface is the factory where the component will be created. It can define *create* methods, to create instances of EJBs, or *finder* methods, which locate existing EJBs and are used for Entity Beans only. When you create a Home interface for an EJB , you must follow these guidelines:

1. The Home interface must be **public**.

2. The Home interface must extend the interface **javax.ejb.EJBHome**.

3. Each *create* method in the Home interface must declare **java.rmi.RemoteException** in its **throws** clause as well as a **javax.ejb.CreateException**.

4. The return value of a *create* method must be a Remote Interface.

5. The return value of a *finder* method (Entity Beans only) must be a Remote Interface or **java.util.Enumeration** or **java.util.Collection**.

6. Any object passed as an argument (either directly or embedded within a local object) must be a valid RMI-IIOP data type (this includes other EJB objects)

The standard naming convention for Home interfaces is to take the Remote interface name and append "Home" to the end. Here is the Home interface for the PerfectTime EJB:

```
//: c15:ejb:PerfectTimeHome.java
// Home Interface of PerfectTimeBean.
import java.rmi.*;
import javax.ejb.*;

public interface PerfectTimeHome extends EJBHome {
  public PerfectTime create()
    throws CreateException, RemoteException;
} ///:~
```

You can now implement the business logic. When you create your EJB implementation class, you must follow these guidelines, (note that you should consult the EJB specification for a complete list of guidelines when developing Enterprise JavaBeans):

1. The class must be **public**.

2. The class must implement an EJB interface (either **javax.ejb.SessionBean** or **javax.ejb.EntityBean**).

3. The class should define methods that map directly to the methods in the Remote interface. Note that the class does not implement the Remote interface; it mirrors the methods in the Remote interface but does *not* throw **java.rmi.RemoteException**.

4. Define one or more **ejbCreate( )** methods to initialize your EJB.

5. The return value and arguments of all methods must be valid RMI-IIOP data types.

```
//: c15:ejb:PerfectTimeBean.java
// Simple Stateless Session Bean
// that returns current system time.
import java.rmi.*;
import javax.ejb.*;

public class PerfectTimeBean
  implements SessionBean {
  private SessionContext sessionContext;
  //return current time
  public long getPerfectTime() {
    return System.currentTimeMillis();
  }
  // EJB methods
  public void ejbCreate()
  throws CreateException {}
  public void ejbRemove() {}
  public void ejbActivate() {}
  public void ejbPassivate() {}
  public void
  setSessionContext(SessionContext ctx) {
    sessionContext = ctx;
  }
}///:~
```

Because this is a simple example, the EJB methods (**ejbCreate( )**, **ejbRemove( )**, **ejbActivate( )**, **ejbPassivate( )**) are all empty. These methods are invoked by the EJB Container and are used to control the state of the component. The **setSessionContext( )** method passes a **javax.ejb.SessionContext** object which contains information about the component's context, such as the current transaction and security information.

After we have created the Enterprise JavaBean, we then need to create a deployment descriptor. The deployment descriptor is an XML file that describes the EJB component. The deployment descriptor should be stored in a file called **ejb-jar.xml**.

```
//:! c15:ejb:ejb-jar.xml
<?xml version="1.0" encoding="Cp1252"?>
```

```
<!DOCTYPE ejb-jar PUBLIC '-//Sun Microsystems,
Inc.//DTD Enterprise JavaBeans 1.1//EN'
'http://java.sun.com/j2ee/dtds/ejb-jar_1_1.dtd'>

<ejb-jar>
  <description>Example for Chapter 15</description>
  <display-name></display-name>
  <small-icon></small-icon>
  <large-icon></large-icon>
  <enterprise-beans>
    <session>
      <ejb-name>PerfectTime</ejb-name>
      <home>PerfectTimeHome</home>
      <remote>PerfectTime</remote>
      <ejb-class>PerfectTimeBean</ejb-class>
      <session-type>Stateless</session-type>
      <transaction-type>Container</transaction-type>
    </session>
  </enterprise-beans>
  <ejb-client-jar></ejb-client-jar>
</ejb-jar>
///:~
```

You can see the Component, the Remote interface and the Home interface defined inside the **<session>** tag of this deployment descriptor. Deployment descriptors may be automatically generated using EJB development tools.

Along with the standard **ejb-jar.xml** deployment descriptor, the EJB specification states that any vendor specific tags should be stored in a separate file. This is to achieve high portability between components and different brands of EJB containers.

The files must be archived inside a standard Java Archive (JAR) file. The deployment descriptors should be placed inside the **/META-INF** sub-directory of the Jar file.

Once the EJB component is defined in the deployment descriptor, the deployer should then deploy the EJB component into the EJB Container. At the time of this writing, the deployment process was quite "GUI intensive" and specific to each individual EJB Container, so this overview does not document that process. Every EJB Container, however will have a documented process for deploying an EJB.

Because an EJB component is a distributed object, the deployment process should also create some client stubs for calling the EJB component. These classes should be placed on the classpath of the client application. Because EJB components can be implemented on top of RMI-IIOP (CORBA) or RMI-JRMP, the stubs generated could vary between EJB Containers; nevertheless they are generated classes.

When a client program wishes to invoke an EJB, it must look up the EJB component inside JNDI and obtain a reference to the home interface of the EJB component. The Home interface is used to create an instance of the EJB.

In this example the client program is a simple Java program, but you should remember that it could just as easily be a servlet, a JSP or even a CORBA or RMI distributed object.

```
//: c15:ejb:PerfectTimeClient.java
// Client program for PerfectTimeBean

public class PerfectTimeClient {
public static void main(String[] args)
throws Exception {
  // Get a JNDI context using
  // the JNDI Naming service:
  javax.naming.Context context =
    new javax.naming.InitialContext();
  // Look up the home interface in the
  // JNDI Naming service:
  Object ref = context.lookup("perfectTime");
  // Cast the remote object to the home interface:
  PerfectTimeHome home = (PerfectTimeHome)
    javax.rmi.PortableRemoteObject.narrow(
      ref, PerfectTimeHome.class);
  // Create a remote object from the home interface:
  PerfectTime pt = home.create();
  // Invoke  getPerfectTime()
  System.out.println(
    "Perfect Time EJB invoked, time is: " +
```

```
        pt.getPerfectTime() );
    }
} ///:~
```

The sequence of the example is explained in the comments. Note the use of the **narrow( )** method to perform a kind of casting of the object before a Java cast is performed. This is very similar to what happens in CORBA. Also note that the Home object becomes a factory for **PerfectTime** objects.

EJB summary

The Enterprise JavaBeans specification is a dramatic step forward in the standardization and simplification of distributed object computing. It is a major piece of the Java 2 Enterprise Edition (J2EE) platform and is receiving much support from the distributed object community. Many tools are currently available or will be available in the near future to help accelerate the development of EJB components.

This overview was only a brief tour of EJBs. For more information about the EJB specification you should see the official Enterprise JavaBeans home page at *java.sun.com/products/ejb/*, where you can download the latest specification and the J2EE reference implementation. These can be used to develop and deploy your own EJB components.

Jini: distributed services

This section[7] gives an overview of Sun Microsystems's Jini technology. It describes some Jini nuts and bolts and shows how Jini's architecture helps to raise the level of abstraction in distributed systems programming, effectively turning network programming into object-oriented programming.

Jini in context

Traditionally, operating systems have been designed with the assumption that a computer will have a processor, some memory, and a disk. When

---

[7] This section was contributed by Bill Venners (www.artima.com).

you boot a computer, the first thing it does is look for a disk. If it doesn't find a disk, it can't function as a computer. Increasingly, however, computers are appearing in a different guise: as embedded devices that have a processor, some memory, and a network connection—but no disk. The first thing a cell phone does when you boot it up, for example, is look for the telephone network. If it doesn't find the network, it can't function as a cell phone. This trend in the hardware environment, from disk-centric to network-centric, will affect how we organize the software—and that's where Jini comes in.

Jini is an attempt to rethink computer architecture, given the rising importance of the network and the proliferation of processors in devices that have no disk drive. These devices, which will come from many different vendors, will need to interact over a network. The network itself will be very dynamic—devices and services will be added and removed regularly. Jini provides mechanisms to enable smooth adding, removal, and finding of devices and services on the network. In addition, Jini provides a programming model that makes it easier for programmers to get their devices talking to each other.

Building on top of Java, object serialization, and RMI (which together enable objects to move around the network from virtual machine to virtual machine) Jini attempts to extend the benefits of object-oriented programming to the network. Instead of requiring device vendors to agree on the network protocols through which their devices can interact, Jini enables the devices to talk to each other through interfaces to objects.

What is Jini?

Jini is a set of APIs and network protocols that can help you build and deploy distributed systems that are organized as *federations of services*. A *service* can be anything that sits on the network and is ready to perform a useful function. Hardware devices, software, communications channels—even human users themselves—can be services. A Jini-enabled disk drive, for example, could offer a "storage" service. A Jini-enabled printer could offer a "printing" service. A federation of services, then, is a set of services, currently available on the network, that a client (meaning a program, service, or user) can bring together to help it accomplish some goal.

To perform a task, a client enlists the help of services. For example, a client program might upload pictures from the image storage service in a digital camera, download the pictures to a persistent storage service offered by a disk drive, and send a page of thumbnail-sized versions of the images to the printing service of a color printer. In this example, the client program builds a distributed system consisting of itself, the image storage service, the persistent storage service, and the color-printing service. The client and services of this distributed system work together to perform the task: to offload and store images from a digital camera and print a page of thumbnails.

The idea behind the word *federation* is that the Jini view of the network doesn't involve a central controlling authority. Because no one service is in charge, the set of all services available on the network form a federation—a group composed of equal peers. Instead of a central authority, Jini's run-time infrastructure merely provides a way for clients and services to find each other (via a lookup service, which stores a directory of currently available services). After services locate each other, they are on their own. The client and its enlisted services perform their task independently of the Jini run-time infrastructure. If the Jini lookup service crashes, any distributed systems brought together via the lookup service before it crashed can continue their work. Jini even includes a network protocol that clients can use to find services in the absence of a lookup service.

How Jini works

Jini defines a *run-time infrastructure* that resides on the network and provides mechanisms that enable you to add, remove, locate, and access services. The run-time infrastructure resides in three places: in lookup services that sit on the network, in the service providers (such as Jini-enabled devices), and in clients. *Lookup services* are the central organizing mechanism for Jini-based systems. When new services become available on the network, they register themselves with a lookup service. When clients wish to locate a service to assist with some task, they consult a lookup service.

The run-time infrastructure uses one network-level protocol, called *discovery*, and two object-level protocols, called *join* and *lookup*.

Discovery enables clients and services to locate lookup services. Join enables a service to register itself in a lookup service. Lookup enables a client to query for services that can help accomplish its goals.

The discovery process

Discovery works like this: Imagine you have a Jini-enabled disk drive that offers a persistent storage service. As soon as you connect the drive to the network, it broadcasts a *presence announcement* by dropping a multicast packet onto a well-known port. Included in the presence announcement is an IP address and port number where the disk drive can be contacted by a lookup service.

Lookup services monitor the well-known port for presence announcement packets. When a lookup service receives a presence announcement, it opens and inspects the packet. The packet contains information that enables the lookup service to determine whether or not it should contact the sender of the packet. If so, it contacts the sender directly by making a TCP connection to the IP address and port number extracted from the packet. Using RMI, the lookup service sends an object, called a *service registrar*, across the network to the originator of the packet. The purpose of the service registrar object is to facilitate further communication with the lookup service. By invoking methods on this object, the sender of the announcement packet can perform join and lookup on the lookup service. In the case of the disk drive, the lookup service would make a TCP connection to the disk drive and would send it a service registrar object, through which the disk drive would then register its persistent storage service via the join process.

The join process

Once a service provider has a service registrar object, the end product of discovery, it is ready to do a join—to become part of the federation of services that are registered in the lookup service. To do a join, the service provider invokes the **register( )** method on the service registrar object, passing as a parameter an object called a service item, a bundle of objects that describe the service. The **register( )** method sends a copy of the service item up to the lookup service, where the service item is stored.

Once this has completed, the service provider has finished the join process: its service has become registered in the lookup service.

The service item is a container for several objects, including an object called a *service object*, which clients can use to interact with the service. The service item can also include any number of *attributes*, which can be any object. Some potential attributes are icons, classes that provide GUIs for the service, and objects that give more information about the service.

Service objects usually implement one or more interfaces through which clients interact with the service. For example, a lookup service is a Jini service, and its service object is the service registrar. The **register( )** method invoked by service providers during join is declared in the **ServiceRegistrar** interface (a member of the **net.jini.core.lookup** package), which all service registrar objects implement. Clients and service providers talk to the lookup service through the service registrar object by invoking methods declared in the **ServiceRegistrar** interface. Likewise, a disk drive would provide a service object that implemented some well-known storage service interface. Clients would look up and interact with the disk drive by this storage service interface.

The lookup process

Once a service has registered with a lookup service via the join process, that service is available for use by clients who query that lookup service. To build a distributed system of services that will work together to perform some task, a client must locate and enlist the help of the individual services. To find a service, clients query lookup services via a process called *lookup*.

To perform a lookup, a client invokes the **lookup( )** method on a service registrar object. (A client, like a service provider, gets a service registrar through the previously-described process of discovery.) The client passes as an argument to **lookup( )** a *service template*, an object that serves as search criteria for the query. The service template can include a reference to an array of **Class** objects. These **Class** objects indicate to the lookup service the Java type (or types) of the service object desired by the client. The service template can also include a *service ID*, which uniquely identifies a service, and attributes, which must exactly match the attributes uploaded by the service provider in the service item. The service

---

template can also contain wildcards for any of these fields. A wildcard in the service ID field, for example, will match any service ID. The **lookup( )** method sends the service template to the lookup service, which performs the query and sends back zero to any matching service objects. The client gets a reference to the matching service objects as the return value of the **lookup( )** method.

In the general case, a client looks up a service by Java type, usually an interface. For example, if a client needed to use a printer, it would compose a service template that included a **Class** object for a well-known interface to printer services. All printer services would implement this well-known interface. The lookup service would return a service object (or objects) that implemented this interface. Attributes can be included in the service template to narrow the number of matches for such a type-based search. The client would use the printer service by invoking methods from the well-known printer service interface on the service object.

Separation of interface and implementation

Jini's architecture brings object-oriented programming to the network by enabling network services to take advantage of one of the fundamentals of objects: the separation of interface and implementation. For example, a service object can grant clients access to the service in many ways. The object can actually represent the entire service, which is downloaded to the client during lookup and then executed locally. Alternatively, the service object can serve merely as a proxy to a remote server. Then when the client invokes methods on the service object, it sends the requests across the network to the server, which does the real work. A third option is for the local service object and a remote server to each do part of the work.

One important consequence of Jini's architecture is that the network protocol used to communicate between a proxy service object and a remote server does not need to be known to the client. As illustrated in the figure below, the network protocol is part of the service's implementation. This protocol is a private matter decided upon by the developer of the service. The client can communicate with the service via this private protocol because the service injects some of its own code (the service object) into the client's address space. The injected service object could communicate with the service via RMI, CORBA, DCOM, some home-brewed protocol built on top of sockets and streams, or anything else. The client simply doesn't need to care about network protocols, because it can talk to the well-known interface that the service object implements. The service object takes care of any necessary communication on the network.

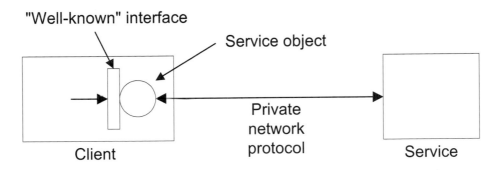

The client talks to the service through a well-known interface

Different implementations of the same service interface can use completely different approaches and network protocols. A service can use specialized hardware to fulfill client requests, or it can do all its work in software. In fact, the implementation approach taken by a single service can evolve over time. The client can be sure it has a service object that understands the current implementation of the service, because the client receives the service object (by way of the lookup service) from the service provider itself. To the client, a service looks like the well-known interface, regardless of how the service is implemented.

Abstracting distributed systems

Jini attempts to raise the level of abstraction for distributed systems programming, from the network protocol level to the object interface level. In the emerging proliferation of embedded devices connected to networks, many pieces of a distributed system may come from different vendors. Jini makes it unnecessary for vendors of devices to agree on network level protocols that allow their devices to interact. Instead, vendors must agree on Java interfaces through which their devices can

---

interact. The processes of discovery, join, and lookup, provided by the Jini run-time infrastructure, enable devices to locate each other on the network. Once they locate each other, devices can communicate with each other through Java interfaces.

Summary

Along with Jini for local device networks, this chapter has introduced some, but not all, of the components that Sun refers to as J2EE: the *Java 2 Enterprise Edition*. The goal of J2EE is to build a set of tools that allows the Java developer to build server-based applications much more quickly, and in a platform-independent way. It's not only difficult and time-consuming to build such applications, but it's especially hard to build them so that they can be easily ported to other platforms, and also to keep the business logic separated from the underlying details of the implementation. J2EE provides a framework to assist in creating server-based applications; these applications are in demand now, and that demand appears to be increasing.

Exercises

Solutions to selected exercises can be found in the electronic document *The Thinking in Java Annotated Solution Guide*, available for a small fee from *www.BruceEckel.com*.

1. Compile and run the **JabberServer** and **JabberClient** programs in this chapter. Now edit the files to remove all of the buffering for the input and output, then compile and run them again to observe the results.

2. Create a server that asks for a password, then opens a file and sends the file over the network connection. Create a client that connects to this server, gives the appropriate password, then captures and saves the file. Test the pair of programs on your machine using the **localhost** (the local loopback IP address **127.0.0.1** produced by calling **InetAddress.getByName(null)**).

3. Modify the server in Exercise 2 so that it uses multithreading to handle multiple clients.

4.   Modify **JabberClient.java** so that output flushing doesn't occur and observe the effect.

5.   Modify **MultiJabberServer** so that it uses *thread pooling*. Instead of throwing away a thread each time a client disconnects, the thread should put itself into an "available pool" of threads. When a new client wants to connect, the server will look in the available pool for a thread to handle the request, and if one isn't available, make a new one. This way the number of threads necessary will naturally grow to the required quantity. The value of thread pooling is that it doesn't require the overhead of creating and destroying a new thread for each new client.

6.   Starting with **ShowHTML.java**, create an applet that is a password-protected gateway to a particular portion of your Web site.

7.   Modify **CIDCreateTables.java** so that it reads the SQL strings from a text file instead of **CIDSQL**.

8.   Configure your system so that you can successfully execute **CIDCreateTables.java** and **LoadDB.java**.

9.   Modify **ServletsRule.java** by overriding the **destroy( )** method to save the value of **i** to a file, and and the **init( )** method to restore the value. Demonstrate that it works by rebooting the servlet container. If you do not have an existing servlet container, you will need to download, install, and run Tomcat from *jakarta.apache.org* in order to run servlets.

10.   Create a servlet that adds a cookie to the response object, thereby storing it on the client's site. Add code to the servlet that retrieves and displays the cookie. If you do not have an existing servlet container, you will need to download, install, and run Tomcat from *jakarta.apache.org* in order to run servlets.

11.   Create a servlet that uses a **Session** object to store session information of your choosing. In the same servlet, retrieve and display that session information. If you do not have an existing

servlet container, you will need to download, install, and run Tomcat from *jakarta.apache.org* in order to run servlets.

12.   Create a servlet that changes the inactive interval of a session to 5 seconds by calling **getMaxInactiveInterval( )**. Test to see that the session does indeed expire after 5 seconds. If you do not have an existing servlet container, you will need to download, install, and run Tomcat from *jakarta.apache.org* in order to run servlets.

13.   Create a JSP page that prints a line of text using the <H1> tag. Set the color of this text randomly, using Java code embedded in the JSP page. If you do not have an existing JSP container, you will need to download, install, and run Tomcat from *jakarta.apache.org* in order to run JSPs.

14.   Modify the maximum age value in **Cookies.jsp** and observe the behavior under two different browsers. Also note the difference between just re-visiting the page, and shutting down and restarting the browser. If you do not have an existing JSP container, you will need to download, install, and run Tomcat from *jakarta.apache.org* in order to run JSPs.

15.   Create a JSP with a field that allows the user to enter the session expiration time and and a second field that holds data that is stored in the session. The submit button refreshes the page and fetches the current expiration time and session data and puts them in as default values of the aforementioned fields. If you do not have an existing JSP container, you will need to download, install, and run Tomcat from *jakarta.apache.org* in order to run JSPs.

16.   (More challenging) Take the **VLookup.java** program and modify it so that when you click on the resulting name it automatically takes that name and copies it to the clipboard (so you can simply paste it into your email). You'll need to look back at Chapter 13 to remember how to use the clipboard in JFC.

A: Passing & Returning Objects

By now you should be reasonably comfortable with the idea that when you're "passing" an object, you're actually passing a reference.

In many programming languages you can use that language's "regular" way to pass objects around, and most of the time everything works fine. But it always seems that there comes a point at which you must do something irregular and suddenly things get a bit more complicated (or in the case of C++, quite complicated). Java is no exception, and it's important that you understand exactly what's happening as you pass objects around and manipulate them. This appendix will provide that insight.

Another way to pose the question of this appendix, if you're coming from a programming language so equipped, is "Does Java have pointers?" Some have claimed that pointers are hard and dangerous and therefore bad, and since Java is all goodness and light and will lift your earthly programming burdens, it cannot possibly contain such things. However, it's more accurate to say that Java has pointers; indeed, every object identifier in Java (except for primitives) is one of these pointers, but their use is restricted and guarded not only by the compiler but by the run-time system. Or to put it another way, Java has pointers, but no pointer arithmetic. These are what I've been calling "references," and you can think of them as "safety pointers," not unlike the safety scissors of elementary school—they aren't sharp, so you cannot hurt yourself without great effort, but they can sometimes be slow and tedious.

Passing references around

When you pass a reference into a method, you're still pointing to the same object. A simple experiment demonstrates this:

```
//: appendixa:PassReferences.java
// Passing references around.

public class PassReferences {
  static void f(PassReferences h) {
    System.out.println("h inside f(): " + h);
  }
  public static void main(String[] args) {
    PassReferences p = new PassReferences();
    System.out.println("p inside main(): " + p);
    f(p);
  }
} ///:~
```

The method **toString( )** is automatically invoked in the print statements, and **PassReferences** inherits directly from **Object** with no redefinition of **toString( )**. Thus, **Object**'s version of **toString( )** is used, which prints out the class of the object followed by the address where that object is located (not the reference, but the actual object storage). The output looks like this:

```
p inside main(): PassReferences@1653748
h inside f(): PassReferences@1653748
```

You can see that both **p** and **h** refer to the same object. This is far more efficient than duplicating a new **PassReferences** object just so that you can send an argument to a method. But it brings up an important issue.

Aliasing

Aliasing means that more than one reference is tied to the same object, as in the above example. The problem with aliasing occurs when someone *writes* to that object. If the owners of the other references aren't expecting that object to change, they'll be surprised. This can be demonstrated with a simple example:

```
//: appendixa:Alias1.java
// Aliasing two references to one object.

public class Alias1 {
  int i;
  Alias1(int ii) { i = ii; }
  public static void main(String[] args) {
    Alias1 x = new Alias1(7);
    Alias1 y = x; // Assign the reference
    System.out.println("x: " + x.i);
    System.out.println("y: " + y.i);
    System.out.println("Incrementing x");
    x.i++;
    System.out.println("x: " + x.i);
    System.out.println("y: " + y.i);
  }
} ///:~
```

In the line:

```
Alias1 y = x; // Assign the reference
```

a new **Alias1** reference is created, but instead of being assigned to a fresh object created with **new**, it's assigned to an existing reference. So the contents of reference **x**, which is the address of the object **x** is pointing to, is assigned to **y**, and thus both **x** and **y** are attached to the same object. So when **x**'s **i** is incremented in the statement:

```
x.i++;
```

y's **i** will be affected as well. This can be seen in the output:

```
x: 7
y: 7
Incrementing x
x: 8
y: 8
```

One good solution in this case is to simply not do it: don't consciously alias more than one reference to an object at the same scope. Your code will be much easier to understand and debug. However, when you're passing a reference in as an argument—which is the way Java is supposed to work—you automatically alias because the local reference that's created

---

can modify the "outside object" (the object that was created outside the scope of the method). Here's an example:

```
//: appendixa:Alias2.java
// Method calls implicitly alias their
// arguments.

public class Alias2 {
  int i;
  Alias2(int ii) { i = ii; }
  static void f(Alias2 reference) {
    reference.i++;
  }
  public static void main(String[] args) {
    Alias2 x = new Alias2(7);
    System.out.println("x: " + x.i);
    System.out.println("Calling f(x)");
    f(x);
    System.out.println("x: " + x.i);
  }
} ///:~
```

The output is:

```
x: 7
Calling f(x)
x: 8
```

The method is changing its argument, the outside object. When this kind of situation arises, you must decide whether it makes sense, whether the user expects it, and whether it's going to cause problems.

In general, you call a method in order to produce a return value and/or a change of state in the object *that the method is called for*. (A method is how you "send a message" to that object.) It's much less common to call a method in order to manipulate its arguments; this is referred to as "calling a method for its *side effects*." Thus, when you create a method that modifies its arguments the user must be clearly instructed and warned about the use of that method and its potential surprises. Because of the confusion and pitfalls, it's much better to avoid changing the argument.

If you need to modify an argument during a method call and you don't intend to modify the outside argument, then you should protect that argument by making a copy inside your method. That's the subject of much of this appendix.

Making local copies

To review: All argument passing in Java is performed by passing references. That is, when you pass "an object," you're really passing only a reference to an object that lives outside the method, so if you perform any modifications with that reference, you modify the outside object. In addition:

♦ Aliasing happens automatically during argument passing.

♦ There are no local objects, only local references.

♦ References have scopes, objects do not.

♦ Object lifetime is never an issue in Java.

♦ There is no language support (e.g., "const") to prevent objects from being modified (that is, to prevent the negative effects of aliasing).

If you're only reading information from an object and not modifying it, passing a reference is the most efficient form of argument passing. This is nice; the default way of doing things is also the most efficient. However, sometimes it's necessary to be able to treat the object as if it were "local" so that changes you make affect only a local copy and do not modify the outside object. Many programming languages support the ability to automatically make a local copy of the outside object, inside the method[1]. Java does not, but it allows you to produce this effect.

----

[1] In C, which generally handles small bits of data, the default is pass-by-value. C++ had to follow this form, but with objects pass-by-value isn't usually the most efficient way. In addition, coding classes to support pass-by-value in C++ is a big headache.

Pass by value

This brings up the terminology issue, which always seems good for an argument. The term is "pass by value," and the meaning depends on how you perceive the operation of the program. The general meaning is that you get a local copy of whatever you're passing, but the real question is how you think about what you're passing. When it comes to the meaning of "pass by value," there are two fairly distinct camps:

1. Java passes everything by value. When you're passing primitives into a method, you get a distinct copy of the primitive. When you're passing a reference into a method, you get a copy of the reference. Ergo, everything is pass-by-value. Of course, the assumption is that you're always thinking (and caring) that references are being passed, but it seems like the Java design has gone a long way toward allowing you to ignore (most of the time) that you're working with a reference. That is, it seems to allow you to think of the reference as "the object," since it implicitly dereferences it whenever you make a method call.

2. Java passes primitives by value (no argument there), but objects are passed by reference. This is the world view that the reference is an alias for the object, so you *don't* think about passing references, but instead say "I'm passing the object." Since you don't get a local copy of the object when you pass it into a method, objects are clearly not passed by value. There appears to be some support for this view within Sun, since one of the "reserved but not implemented" keywords was **byvalue**. (There's no knowing, however, whether that keyword will ever see the light of day.)

Having given both camps a good airing, and after saying "It depends on how you think of a reference," I will attempt to sidestep the issue. In the end, it isn't *that* important—what is important is that you understand that passing a reference allows the caller's object to be changed unexpectedly.

Cloning objects

The most likely reason for making a local copy of an object is if you're going to modify that object and you don't want to modify the caller's object. If you decide that you want to make a local copy, you simply use the **clone( )** method to perform the operation. This is a method that's defined as **protected** in the base class **Object**, and which you must override as **public** in any derived classes that you want to clone. For example, the standard library class **ArrayList** overrides **clone( )**, so we can call **clone( )** for **ArrayList**:

```
//: appendixa:Cloning.java
// The clone() operation works for only a few
// items in the standard Java library.
import java.util.*;

class Int {
  private int i;
  public Int(int ii) { i = ii; }
  public void increment() { i++; }
  public String toString() {
    return Integer.toString(i);
  }
}

public class Cloning {
  public static void main(String[] args) {
    ArrayList v = new ArrayList();
    for(int i = 0; i < 10; i++ )
      v.add(new Int(i));
    System.out.println("v: " + v);
    ArrayList v2 = (ArrayList)v.clone();
    // Increment all v2's elements:
    for(Iterator e = v2.iterator();
        e.hasNext(); )
      ((Int)e.next()).increment();
    // See if it changed v's elements:
    System.out.println("v: " + v);
  }
} ///:~
```

The **clone( )** method produces an **Object**, which must then be recast to the proper type. This example shows how **ArrayList**'s **clone( )** method *does not* automatically try to clone each of the objects that the **ArrayList** contains—the old **ArrayList** and the cloned **ArrayList** are aliased to the same objects. This is often called a *shallow copy,* since it's copying only the "surface" portion of an object. The actual object consists of this "surface," plus all the objects that the references are pointing to, plus all the objects *those* objects are pointing to, etc. This is often referred to as the "web of objects." Copying the entire mess is called a *deep copy*.

You can see the effect of the shallow copy in the output, where the actions performed on **v2** affect **v**:

```
v: [0, 1, 2, 3, 4, 5, 6, 7, 8, 9]
v: [1, 2, 3, 4, 5, 6, 7, 8, 9, 10]
```

Not trying to **clone( )** the objects contained in the **ArrayList** is probably a fair assumption because there's no guarantee that those objects *are* cloneable[2].

Adding cloneability to a class

Even though the clone method is defined in the base-of-all-classes **Object**, cloning is *not* automatically available in every class[3]. This would seem to be counterintuitive to the idea that base-class methods are always available in derived classes. Cloning in Java goes against this idea; if you want it to exist for a class, you must specifically add code to make cloning work.

---

[2] This is not the dictionary spelling of the word, but it's what is used in the Java library, so I've used it here, too, in some hopes of reducing confusion.

[3] You can apparently create a simple counter-example to this statement, like this:

```
public class Cloneit implements Cloneable {
  public static void main (String[] args)
  throws CloneNotSupportedException {
    Cloneit a = new Cloneit();
    Cloneit b = (Cloneit)a.clone();
  }
}
```

However, this only works because **main( )** is a method of **Cloneit** and thus has permission to call the **protected** base-class method **clone( )**. If you call it from a different class, it won't compile.

Using a trick with **protected**

To prevent default cloneability in every class you create, the **clone( )** method is **protected** in the base class **Object**. Not only does this mean that it's not available by default to the client programmer who is simply using the class (not subclassing it), but it also means that you cannot call **clone( )** via a reference to the base class. (Although that might seem to be useful in some situations, such as to polymorphically clone a bunch of **Object**s.) It is in effect a way to give you, at compile-time, the information that your object is not cloneable—and oddly enough most classes in the standard Java library are not cloneable. Thus, if you say:

```
Integer x = new Integer(1);
x = x.clone();
```

You will get, at compile-time, an error message that says **clone( )** is not accessible (since **Integer** doesn't override it and it defaults to the **protected** version).

If, however, you're in a class derived from **Object** (as all classes are), then you have permission to call **Object.clone( )** because it's **protected** and you're an inheritor. The base class **clone( )** has useful functionality—it performs the actual bitwise duplication *of the derived-class object*, thus acting as the common cloning operation. However, you then need to make *your* clone operation **public** for it to be accessible. So, two key issues when you clone are:

- Virtually always call **super.clone( )**

- Make your clone **public**

You'll probably want to override **clone( )** in any further derived classes, otherwise your (now **public**) **clone( )** will be used, and that might not do the right thing (although, since **Object.clone( )** makes a copy of the actual object, it might). The **protected** trick works only once—the first time you inherit from a class that has no cloneability and you want to make a class that's cloneable. In any classes inherited from your class the **clone( )** method is available since it's not possible in Java to reduce the access of a method during derivation. That is, once a class is cloneable, everything derived from it is cloneable unless you use provided mechanisms (described later) to "turn off" cloning.

Implementing the **Cloneable** interface

There's one more thing you need to do to complete the cloneability of an object: implement the **Cloneable interface**. This **interface** is a bit strange, because it's empty!

```
interface Cloneable {}
```

The reason for implementing this empty **interface** is obviously not because you are going to upcast to **Cloneable** and call one of its methods. The use of **interface** here is considered by some to be a "hack" because it's using a feature for something other than its original intent. Implementing the **Cloneable interface** acts as a kind of a flag, wired into the type of the class.

There are two reasons for the existence of the **Cloneable interface**. First, you might have an upcast reference to a base type and not know whether it's possible to clone that object. In this case, you can use the **instanceof** keyword (described in Chapter 12) to find out whether the reference is connected to an object that can be cloned:

```
if(myReference instanceof Cloneable) // ...
```

The second reason is that mixed into this design for cloneability was the thought that maybe you didn't want all types of objects to be cloneable. So **Object.clone( )** verifies that a class implements the **Cloneable** interface. If not, it throws a **CloneNotSupportedException** exception. So in general, you're forced to **implement Cloneable** as part of support for cloning.

Successful cloning

Once you understand the details of implementing the **clone( )** method, you're able to create classes that can be easily duplicated to provide a local copy:

```
//: appendixa:LocalCopy.java
// Creating local copies with clone().
import java.util.*;

class MyObject implements Cloneable {
  int i;
```

```java
  MyObject(int ii) { i = ii; }
  public Object clone() {
    Object o = null;
    try {
      o = super.clone();
    } catch(CloneNotSupportedException e) {
      System.err.println("MyObject can't clone");
    }
    return o;
  }
  public String toString() {
    return Integer.toString(i);
  }
}

public class LocalCopy {
  static MyObject g(MyObject v) {
    // Passing a reference, modifies outside object:
    v.i++;
    return v;
  }
  static MyObject f(MyObject v) {
    v = (MyObject)v.clone(); // Local copy
    v.i++;
    return v;
  }
  public static void main(String[] args) {
    MyObject a = new MyObject(11);
    MyObject b = g(a);
    // Testing reference equivalence,
    // not object equivalence:
    if(a == b)
      System.out.println("a == b");
    else
      System.out.println("a != b");
    System.out.println("a = " + a);
    System.out.println("b = " + b);
    MyObject c = new MyObject(47);
    MyObject d = f(c);
    if(c == d)
      System.out.println("c == d");
```

```
      else
        System.out.println("c != d");
      System.out.println("c = " + c);
      System.out.println("d = " + d);
    }
} ///:~
```

First of all, **clone( )** must be accessible so you must make it **public**. Second, for the initial part of your **clone( )** operation you should call the base-class version of **clone( )**. The **clone( )** that's being called here is the one that's predefined inside **Object**, and you can call it because it's **protected** and thereby accessible in derived classes.

Object.clone( ) figures out how big the object is, creates enough memory for a new one, and copies all the bits from the old to the new. This is called a *bitwise copy,* and is typically what you'd expect a **clone( )** method to do. But before **Object.clone( )** performs its operations, it first checks to see if a class is **Cloneable**—that is, whether it implements the **Cloneable** interface. If it doesn't, **Object.clone( )** throws a **CloneNotSupportedException** to indicate that you can't clone it. Thus, you've got to surround your call to **super.clone( )** with a try-catch block, to catch an exception that should never happen (because you've implemented the **Cloneable** interface).

In **LocalCopy**, the two methods **g( )** and **f( )** demonstrate the difference between the two approaches for argument passing. **g( )** shows passing by reference in which it modifies the outside object and returns a reference to that outside object, while **f( )** clones the argument, thereby decoupling it and leaving the original object alone. It can then proceed to do whatever it wants, and even to return a reference to this new object without any ill effects to the original. Notice the somewhat curious-looking statement:

```
v = (MyObject)v.clone();
```

This is where the local copy is created. To prevent confusion by such a statement, remember that this rather strange coding idiom is perfectly feasible in Java because every object identifier is actually a reference. So the reference **v** is used to **clone( )** a copy of what it refers to, and this returns a reference to the base type **Object** (because it's defined that way in **Object.clone( )**) that must then be cast to the proper type.

In **main( )**, the difference between the effects of the two different argument-passing approaches in the two different methods is tested. The output is:

```
a == b
a = 12
b = 12
c != d
c = 47
d = 48
```

It's important to notice that the equivalence tests in Java do not look inside the objects being compared to see if their values are the same. The == and != operators are simply comparing the *references*. If the addresses inside the references are the same, the references are pointing to the same object and are therefore "equal." So what the operators are really testing is whether the references are aliased to the same object!

The effect of **Object.clone( )**

What actually happens when **Object.clone( )** is called that makes it so essential to call **super.clone( )** when you override **clone( )** in your class? The **clone( )** method in the root class is responsible for creating the correct amount of storage and making the bitwise copy of the bits from the original object into the new object's storage. That is, it doesn't just make storage and copy an **Object**—it actually figures out the size of the precise object that's being copied and duplicates that. Since all this is happening from the code in the **clone( )** method defined in the root class (that has no idea what's being inherited from it), you can guess that the process involves RTTI to determine the actual object that's being cloned. This way, the **clone( )** method can create the proper amount of storage and do the correct bitcopy for that type.

Whatever you do, the first part of the cloning process should normally be a call to **super.clone( )**. This establishes the groundwork for the cloning operation by making an exact duplicate. At this point you can perform other operations necessary to complete the cloning.

To know for sure what those other operations are, you need to understand exactly what **Object.clone( )** buys you. In particular, does it automatically clone the destination of all the references? The following example tests this:

```java
//: appendixa:Snake.java
// Tests cloning to see if destination
// of references are also cloned.

public class Snake implements Cloneable {
  private Snake next;
  private char c;
  // Value of i == number of segments
  Snake(int i, char x) {
    c = x;
    if(--i > 0)
      next = new Snake(i, (char)(x + 1));
  }
  void increment() {
    c++;
    if(next != null)
      next.increment();
  }
  public String toString() {
    String s = ":" + c;
    if(next != null)
      s += next.toString();
    return s;
  }
  public Object clone() {
    Object o = null;
    try {
      o = super.clone();
    } catch(CloneNotSupportedException e) {
      System.err.println("Snake can't clone");
    }
    return o;
  }
  public static void main(String[] args) {
    Snake s = new Snake(5, 'a');
    System.out.println("s = " + s);
    Snake s2 = (Snake)s.clone();
    System.out.println("s2 = " + s2);
```

```
    s.increment();
    System.out.println(
       "after s.increment, s2 = " + s2);
   }
} ///:~
```

A **Snake** is made up of a bunch of segments, each of type **Snake**. Thus, it's a singly linked list. The segments are created recursively, decrementing the first constructor argument for each segment until zero is reached. To give each segment a unique tag, the second argument, a **char**, is incremented for each recursive constructor call.

The **increment( )** method recursively increments each tag so you can see the change, and the **toString( )** recursively prints each tag. The output is:

```
s = :a:b:c:d:e
s2 = :a:b:c:d:e
after s.increment, s2 = :a:c:d:e:f
```

This means that only the first segment is duplicated by **Object.clone( )**, therefore it does a shallow copy. If you want the whole snake to be duplicated—a deep copy—you must perform the additional operations inside your overridden **clone( )**.

You'll typically call **super.clone( )** in any class derived from a cloneable class to make sure that all of the base-class operations (including **Object.clone( )**) take place. This is followed by an explicit call to **clone( )** for every reference in your object; otherwise those references will be aliased to those of the original object. It's analogous to the way constructors are called—base-class constructor first, then the next-derived constructor, and so on to the most-derived constructor. The difference is that **clone( )** is not a constructor, so there's nothing to make it happen automatically. You must make sure to do it yourself.

Cloning a composed object

There's a problem you'll encounter when trying to deep copy a composed object. You must assume that the **clone( )** method in the member objects will in turn perform a deep copy on *their* references, and so on. This is quite a commitment. It effectively means that for a deep copy to work you must either control all of the code in all of the classes, or at least have

---

enough knowledge about all of the classes involved in the deep copy to
know that they are performing their own deep copy correctly.

This example shows what you must do to accomplish a deep copy when
dealing with a composed object:

```
//: appendixa:DeepCopy.java
// Cloning a composed object.

class DepthReading implements Cloneable {
  private double depth;
  public DepthReading(double depth) {
    this.depth = depth;
  }
  public Object clone() {
    Object o = null;
    try {
      o = super.clone();
    } catch(CloneNotSupportedException e) {
      e.printStackTrace(System.err);
    }
    return o;
  }
}

class TemperatureReading implements Cloneable {
  private long time;
  private double temperature;
  public TemperatureReading(double temperature) {
    time = System.currentTimeMillis();
    this.temperature = temperature;
  }
  public Object clone() {
    Object o = null;
    try {
      o = super.clone();
    } catch(CloneNotSupportedException e) {
      e.printStackTrace(System.err);
    }
    return o;
  }
```

```
    }

class OceanReading implements Cloneable {
  private DepthReading depth;
  private TemperatureReading temperature;
  public OceanReading(double tdata, double ddata){
    temperature = new TemperatureReading(tdata);
    depth = new DepthReading(ddata);
  }
  public Object clone() {
    OceanReading o = null;
    try {
      o = (OceanReading)super.clone();
    } catch(CloneNotSupportedException e) {
      e.printStackTrace(System.err);
    }
    // Must clone references:
    o.depth = (DepthReading)o.depth.clone();
    o.temperature =
      (TemperatureReading)o.temperature.clone();
    return o; // Upcasts back to Object
  }
}

public class DeepCopy {
  public static void main(String[] args) {
    OceanReading reading =
      new OceanReading(33.9, 100.5);
    // Now clone it:
    OceanReading r =
      (OceanReading)reading.clone();
  }
} ///:~
```

DepthReading and **TemperatureReading** are quite similar; they both contain only primitives. Therefore, the **clone( )** method can be quite simple: it calls **super.clone( )** and returns the result. Note that the **clone( )** code for both classes is identical.

OceanReading is composed of **DepthReading** and **TemperatureReading** objects and so, to produce a deep copy, its

---

clone( ) must clone the references inside **OceanReading**. To accomplish this, the result of **super.clone( )** must be cast to an **OceanReading** object (so you can access the **depth** and **temperature** references).

A deep copy with **ArrayList**

Let's revisit the **ArrayList** example from earlier in this appendix. This time the **Int2** class is cloneable, so the **ArrayList** can be deep copied:

```
//: appendixa:AddingClone.java
// You must go through a few gyrations
// to add cloning to your own class.
import java.util.*;

class Int2 implements Cloneable {
  private int i;
  public Int2(int ii) { i = ii; }
  public void increment() { i++; }
  public String toString() {
    return Integer.toString(i);
  }
  public Object clone() {
    Object o = null;
    try {
      o = super.clone();
    } catch(CloneNotSupportedException e) {
      System.err.println("Int2 can't clone");
    }
    return o;
  }
}

// Once it's cloneable, inheritance
// doesn't remove cloneability:
class Int3 extends Int2 {
  private int j; // Automatically duplicated
  public Int3(int i) { super(i); }
}

public class AddingClone {
```

```
  public static void main(String[] args) {
    Int2 x = new Int2(10);
    Int2 x2 = (Int2)x.clone();
    x2.increment();
    System.out.println(
      "x = " + x + ", x2 = " + x2);
    // Anything inherited is also cloneable:
    Int3 x3 = new Int3(7);
    x3 = (Int3)x3.clone();

    ArrayList v = new ArrayList();
    for(int i = 0; i < 10; i++ )
      v.add(new Int2(i));
    System.out.println("v: " + v);
    ArrayList v2 = (ArrayList)v.clone();
    // Now clone each element:
    for(int i = 0; i < v.size(); i++)
      v2.set(i, ((Int2)v2.get(i)).clone());
    // Increment all v2's elements:
    for(Iterator e = v2.iterator();
        e.hasNext(); )
      ((Int2)e.next()).increment();
    // See if it changed v's elements:
    System.out.println("v: " + v);
    System.out.println("v2: " + v2);
  }
} ///:~
```

Int3 is inherited from **Int2** and a new primitive member **int j** is added. You might think that you'd need to override **clone( )** again to make sure **j** is copied, but that's not the case. When **Int2**'s **clone( )** is called as **Int3**'s **clone( )**, it calls **Object.clone( ),** which determines that it's working with an **Int3** and duplicates all the bits in the **Int3**. As long as you don't add references that need to be cloned, the one call to **Object.clone( )** performs all of the necessary duplication, regardless of how far down in the hierarchy **clone( )** is defined.

You can see what's necessary in order to do a deep copy of an **ArrayList**: after the **ArrayList** is cloned, you have to step through and clone each one of the objects pointed to by the **ArrayList**. You'd have to do something similar to this to do a deep copy of a **HashMap**.

The remainder of the example shows that the cloning did happen by showing that, once an object is cloned, you can change it and the original object is left untouched.

Deep copy via serialization

When you consider Java's object serialization (introduced in Chapter 11), you might observe that an object that's serialized and then deserialized is, in effect, cloned.

So why not use serialization to perform deep copying? Here's an example that compares the two approaches by timing them:

```
//: appendixa:Compete.java
import java.io.*;

class Thing1 implements Serializable {}
class Thing2 implements Serializable {
  Thing1 o1 = new Thing1();
}

class Thing3 implements Cloneable {
  public Object clone() {
    Object o = null;
    try {
      o = super.clone();
    } catch(CloneNotSupportedException e) {
      System.err.println("Thing3 can't clone");
    }
    return o;
  }
}

class Thing4 implements Cloneable {
  Thing3 o3 = new Thing3();
  public Object clone() {
    Thing4 o = null;
    try {
      o = (Thing4)super.clone();
    } catch(CloneNotSupportedException e) {
      System.err.println("Thing4 can't clone");
```

```
      }
      // Clone the field, too:
      o.o3 = (Thing3)o3.clone();
      return o;
    }
  }

public class Compete {
  static final int SIZE = 5000;
  public static void main(String[] args)
  throws Exception {
    Thing2[] a = new Thing2[SIZE];
    for(int i = 0; i < a.length; i++)
      a[i] = new Thing2();
    Thing4[] b = new Thing4[SIZE];
    for(int i = 0; i < b.length; i++)
      b[i] = new Thing4();
    long t1 = System.currentTimeMillis();
    ByteArrayOutputStream buf =
      new ByteArrayOutputStream();
    ObjectOutputStream o =
      new ObjectOutputStream(buf);
    for(int i = 0; i < a.length; i++)
      o.writeObject(a[i]);
    // Now get copies:
    ObjectInputStream in =
      new ObjectInputStream(
        new ByteArrayInputStream(
          buf.toByteArray()));
    Thing2[] c = new Thing2[SIZE];
    for(int i = 0; i < c.length; i++)
      c[i] = (Thing2)in.readObject();
    long t2 = System.currentTimeMillis();
    System.out.println(
      "Duplication via serialization: " +
      (t2 - t1) + " Milliseconds");
    // Now try cloning:
    t1 = System.currentTimeMillis();
    Thing4[] d = new Thing4[SIZE];
    for(int i = 0; i < d.length; i++)
      d[i] = (Thing4)b[i].clone();
```

```
      t2 = System.currentTimeMillis();
      System.out.println(
        "Duplication via cloning: " +
        (t2 - t1) + " Milliseconds");
  }
} ///:~
```

Thing2 and **Thing4** contain member objects so that there's some deep copying going on. It's interesting to notice that while **Serializable** classes are easy to set up, there's much more work going on to duplicate them. Cloning involves a lot of work to set up the class, but the actual duplication of objects is relatively simple. The results really tell the tale. Here is the output from three different runs:

```
Duplication via serialization: 940 Milliseconds
Duplication via cloning: 50 Milliseconds

Duplication via serialization: 710 Milliseconds
Duplication via cloning: 60 Milliseconds

Duplication via serialization: 770 Milliseconds
Duplication via cloning: 50 Milliseconds
```

Despite the significant time difference between serialization and cloning, you'll also notice that the serialization technique seems to vary more in its duration, while cloning tends to be more stable.

Adding cloneability further down a hierarchy

If you create a new class, its base class defaults to **Object**, which defaults to noncloneability (as you'll see in the next section). As long as you don't explicitly add cloneability, you won't get it. But you can add it in at any layer and it will then be cloneable from that layer downward, like this:

```
//: appendixa:HorrorFlick.java
// You can insert Cloneability
// at any level of inheritance.
import java.util.*;

class Person {}
```

```
class Hero extends Person {}
class Scientist extends Person
    implements Cloneable {
  public Object clone() {
    try {
      return super.clone();
    } catch(CloneNotSupportedException e) {
      // this should never happen:
      // It's Cloneable already!
      throw new InternalError();
    }
  }
}
class MadScientist extends Scientist {}

public class HorrorFlick {
  public static void main(String[] args) {
    Person p = new Person();
    Hero h = new Hero();
    Scientist s = new Scientist();
    MadScientist m = new MadScientist();

    // p = (Person)p.clone(); // Compile error
    // h = (Hero)h.clone(); // Compile error
    s = (Scientist)s.clone();
    m = (MadScientist)m.clone();
  }
} ///:~
```

Before cloneability was added, the compiler stopped you from trying to clone things. When cloneability is added in **Scientist**, then **Scientist** and all its descendants are cloneable.

Why this strange design?

If all this seems to be a strange scheme, that's because it is. You might wonder why it worked out this way. What is the meaning behind this design?

Originally, Java was designed as a language to control hardware boxes, and definitely not with the Internet in mind. In a general-purpose language like this, it makes sense that the programmer be able to clone any object. Thus, **clone( )** was placed in the root class **Object**, *but* it was a **public** method so you could always clone any object. This seemed to be the most flexible approach, and after all, what could it hurt?

Well, when Java was seen as the ultimate Internet programming language, things changed. Suddenly, there are security issues, and of course, these issues are dealt with using objects, and you don't necessarily want anyone to be able to clone your security objects. So what you're seeing is a lot of patches applied on the original simple and straightforward scheme: **clone( )** is now **protected** in **Object**. You must override it *and* **implement Cloneable** *and* deal with the exceptions.

It's worth noting that you must use the **Cloneable** interface *only* if you're going to call **Object**'s **clone( )**, method, since that method checks at runtime to make sure that your class implements **Cloneable**. But for consistency (and since **Cloneable** is empty anyway) you should implement it.

Controlling cloneability

You might suggest that, to remove cloneability, the **clone( )** method simply be made **private**, but this won't work since you cannot take a base-class method and make it less accessible in a derived class. So it's not that simple. And yet, it's necessary to be able to control whether an object can be cloned. There are actually a number of attitudes you can take to this in a class that you design:

1. Indifference. You don't do anything about cloning, which means that your class can't be cloned but a class that inherits from you can add cloning if it wants. This works only if the default **Object.clone( )** will do something reasonable with all the fields in your class.

2. Support **clone( )**. Follow the standard practice of implementing **Cloneable** and overriding **clone( )**. In the overridden **clone( )**, you call **super.clone( )** and catch all exceptions (so your overridden **clone( )** doesn't throw any exceptions).

3.   Support cloning conditionally. If your class holds references to other objects that might or might not be cloneable (a container class, for example), your **clone( )** can try to clone all of the objects for which you have references, and if they throw exceptions just pass those exceptions out to the programmer. For example, consider a special sort of **ArrayList** that tries to clone all the objects it holds. When you write such an **ArrayList**, you don't know what sort of objects the client programmer might put into your **ArrayList**, so you don't know whether they can be cloned.

4.   Don't implement **Cloneable** but override **clone( )** as **protected**, producing the correct copying behavior for any fields. This way, anyone inheriting from this class can override **clone( )** and call **super.clone( )** to produce the correct copying behavior. Note that your implementation can and should invoke **super.clonc( )** even though that method expects a **Cloneable** object (it will throw an exception otherwise), because no one will directly invoke it on an object of your type. It will get invoked only through a derived class, which, if it is to work successfully, implements **Cloneable**.

5.   Try to prevent cloning by not implementing **Cloneable** and overriding **clone( )** to throw an exception. This is successful only if any class derived from this calls **super.clone( )** in its redefinition of **clone( )**. Otherwise, a programmer may be able to get around it.

6.   Prevent cloning by making your class **final**. If **clone( )** has not been overridden by any of your ancestor classes, then it can't be. If it has, then override it again and throw **CloneNotSupportedException**. Making the class **final** is the only way to guarantee that cloning is prevented. In addition, when dealing with security objects or other situations in which you want to control the number of objects created you should make all constructors **private** and provide one or more special methods for creating objects. That way, these methods can restrict the number of objects created and the conditions in which they're created. (A particular case of this is the *singleton* pattern shown in *Thinking in Patterns with Java*, downloadable at *www.BruceEckel.com*.)

Here's an example that shows the various ways cloning can be implemented and then, later in the hierarchy, "turned off":

```
//: appendixa:CheckCloneable.java
// Checking to see if a reference can be cloned.

// Can't clone this because it doesn't
// override clone():
class Ordinary {}

// Overrides clone, but doesn't implement
// Cloneable:
class WrongClone extends Ordinary {
  public Object clone()
      throws CloneNotSupportedException {
    return super.clone(); // Throws exception
  }
}

// Does all the right things for cloning:
class IsCloneable extends Ordinary
    implements Cloneable {
  public Object clone()
      throws CloneNotSupportedException {
    return super.clone();
  }
}

// Turn off cloning by throwing the exception:
class NoMore extends IsCloneable {
  public Object clone()
      throws CloneNotSupportedException {
    throw new CloneNotSupportedException();
  }
}

class TryMore extends NoMore {
  public Object clone()
      throws CloneNotSupportedException {
    // Calls NoMore.clone(), throws exception:
    return super.clone();
```

```
    }
  }

class BackOn extends NoMore {
  private BackOn duplicate(BackOn b) {
    // Somehow make a copy of b
    // and return that copy. This is a dummy
    // copy, just to make the point:
    return new BackOn();
  }
  public Object clone() {
    // Doesn't call NoMore.clone():
    return duplicate(this);
  }
}

// Can't inherit from this, so can't override
// the clone method like in BackOn:
final class ReallyNoMore extends NoMore {}

public class CheckCloneable {
  static Ordinary tryToClone(Ordinary ord) {
    String id = ord.getClass().getName();
    Ordinary x = null;
    if(ord instanceof Cloneable) {
      try {
        System.out.println("Attempting " + id);
        x = (Ordinary)((IsCloneable)ord).clone();
        System.out.println("Cloned " + id);
      } catch(CloneNotSupportedException e) {
        System.err.println("Could not clone "+id);
      }
    }
    return x;
  }
  public static void main(String[] args) {
    // Upcasting:
    Ordinary[] ord = {
      new IsCloneable(),
      new WrongClone(),
      new NoMore(),
```

```
    new TryMore(),
    new BackOn(),
    new ReallyNoMore(),
  };
  Ordinary x = new Ordinary();
  // This won't compile, since clone() is
  // protected in Object:
  //! x = (Ordinary)x.clone();
  // tryToClone() checks first to see if
  // a class implements Cloneable:
  for(int i = 0; i < ord.length; i++)
    tryToClone(ord[i]);
  }
} ///:~
```

The first class, **Ordinary**, represents the kinds of classes we've seen throughout this book: no support for cloning, but as it turns out, no prevention of cloning either. But if you have a reference to an **Ordinary** object that might have been upcast from a more derived class, you can't tell if it can be cloned or not.

The class **WrongClone** shows an incorrect way to implement cloning. It does override **Object.clone( )** and makes that method **public**, but it doesn't implement **Cloneable**, so when **super.clone( )** is called (which results in a call to **Object.clone( )**), **CloneNotSupportedException** is thrown so the cloning doesn't work.

In **IsCloneable** you can see all the right actions performed for cloning: **clone( )** is overridden and **Cloneable** is implemented. However, this **clone( )** method and several others that follow in this example *do not* catch **CloneNotSupportedException,** but instead pass it through to the caller, who must then put a try-catch block around it. In your own **clone( )** methods you will typically catch **CloneNotSupportedException** *inside* **clone( )** rather than passing it through. As you'll see, in this example it's more informative to pass the exceptions through.

Class **NoMore** attempts to "turn off" cloning in the way that the Java designers intended: in the derived class **clone( )**, you throw **CloneNotSupportedException**. The **clone( )** method in class

TryMore properly calls **super.clone( )**, and this resolves to **NoMore.clone( )**, which throws an exception and prevents cloning.

But what if the programmer doesn't follow the "proper" path of calling **super.clone( )** inside the overridden **clone( )** method? In **BackOn**, you can see how this can happen. This class uses a separate method **duplicate( )** to make a copy of the current object and calls this method inside **clone( )** *instead* of calling **super.clone( )**. The exception is never thrown and the new class is cloneable. You can't rely on throwing an exception to prevent making a cloneable class. The only sure-fire solution is shown in **ReallyNoMore**, which is **final** and thus cannot be inherited. That means if **clone( )** throws an exception in the **final** class, it cannot be modified with inheritance and the prevention of cloning is assured. (You cannot explicitly call **Object.clone( )** from a class that has an arbitrary level of inheritance; you are limited to calling **super.clone( )**, which has access to only the direct base class.) Thus, if you make any objects that involve security issues, you'll want to make those classes **final**.

The first method you see in class **CheckCloneable** is **tryToClone( )**, which takes any **Ordinary** object and checks to see whether it's cloneable with **instanceof**. If so, it casts the object to an **IsCloneable**, calls **clone( )** and casts the result back to **Ordinary**, catching any exceptions that are thrown. Notice the use of run-time type identification (see Chapter 12) to print the class name so you can see what's happening.

In **main( )**, different types of **Ordinary** objects are created and upcast to **Ordinary** in the array definition. The first two lines of code after that create a plain **Ordinary** object and try to clone it. However, this code will not compile because **clone( )** is a **protected** method in **Object**. The remainder of the code steps through the array and tries to clone each object, reporting the success or failure of each. The output is:

```
Attempting IsCloneable
Cloned IsCloneable
Attempting NoMore
Could not clone NoMore
Attempting TryMore
Could not clone TryMore
Attempting BackOn
```

```
Cloned BackOn
Attempting ReallyNoMore
Could not clone ReallyNoMore
```

So to summarize, if you want a class to be cloneable:

1.   Implement the **Cloneable** interface.

2.   Override **clone( )**.

3.   Call **super.clone( )** inside your **clone( )**.

4.   Capture exceptions inside your **clone( )**.

This will produce the most convenient effects.

The copy constructor

Cloning can seem to be a complicated process to set up. It might seem like there should be an alternative. One approach that might occur to you (especially if you're a C++ programmer) is to make a special constructor whose job it is to duplicate an object. In C++, this is called the *copy constructor*. At first, this seems like the obvious solution, but in fact it doesn't work. Here's an example:

```
//: appendixa:CopyConstructor.java
// A constructor for copying an object of the same
// type, as an attempt to create a local copy.

class FruitQualities {
  private int weight;
  private int color;
  private int firmness;
  private int ripeness;
  private int smell;
  // etc.
  FruitQualities() { // Default constructor
    // do something meaningful...
  }
  // Other constructors:
  // ...
  // Copy constructor:
  FruitQualities(FruitQualities f) {
```

```
      weight = f.weight;
      color = f.color;
      firmness = f.firmness;
      ripeness = f.ripeness;
      smell = f.smell;
      // etc.
  }
}

class Seed {
  // Members...
  Seed() { /* Default constructor */ }
  Seed(Seed s) { /* Copy constructor */ }
}

class Fruit {
  private FruitQualities fq;
  private int seeds;
  private Seed[] s;
  Fruit(FruitQualities q, int seedCount) {
    fq = q;
    seeds = seedCount;
    s = new Seed[seeds];
    for(int i = 0; i < seeds; i++)
      s[i] = new Seed();
  }
  // Other constructors:
  // ...
  // Copy constructor:
  Fruit(Fruit f) {
    fq = new FruitQualities(f.fq);
    seeds = f.seeds;
    // Call all Seed copy-constructors:
    for(int i = 0; i < seeds; i++)
      s[i] = new Seed(f.s[i]);
    // Other copy-construction activities...
  }
  // To allow derived constructors (or other
  // methods) to put in different qualities:
  protected void addQualities(FruitQualities q) {
    fq = q;
```

```
    }
    protected FruitQualities getQualities() {
      return fq;
    }
  }

class Tomato extends Fruit {
  Tomato() {
    super(new FruitQualities(), 100);
  }
  Tomato(Tomato t) { // Copy-constructor
    super(t); // Upcast for base copy-constructor
    // Other copy-construction activities...
  }
}

class ZebraQualities extends FruitQualities {
  private int stripedness;
  ZebraQualities() { // Default constructor
    // do something meaningful...
  }
  ZebraQualities(ZebraQualities z) {
    super(z);
    stripedness = z.stripedness;
  }
}

class GreenZebra extends Tomato {
  GreenZebra() {
    addQualities(new ZebraQualities());
  }
  GreenZebra(GreenZebra g) {
    super(g); // Calls Tomato(Tomato)
    // Restore the right qualities:
    addQualities(new ZebraQualities());
  }
  void evaluate() {
    ZebraQualities zq =
      (ZebraQualities)getQualities();
    // Do something with the qualities
    // ...
```

```
      }
  }

  public class CopyConstructor {
    public static void ripen(Tomato t) {
      // Use the "copy constructor":
      t = new Tomato(t);
      System.out.println("In ripen, t is a " +
        t.getClass().getName());
    }
    public static void slice(Fruit f) {
      f = new Fruit(f); // Hmmm... will this work?
      System.out.println("In slice, f is a " +
        f.getClass().getName());
    }
    public static void main(String[] args) {
      Tomato tomato = new Tomato();
      ripen(tomato); // OK
      slice(tomato); // OOPS!
      GreenZebra g = new GreenZebra();
      ripen(g); // OOPS!
      slice(g); // OOPS!
      g.evaluate();
    }
  } ///:~
```

This seems a bit strange at first. Sure, fruit has qualities, but why not just put data members representing those qualities directly into the **Fruit** class? There are two potential reasons. The first is that you might want to easily insert or change the qualities. Note that **Fruit** has a **protected addQualities( )** method to allow derived classes to do this. (You might think the logical thing to do is to have a **protected** constructor in **Fruit** that takes a **FruitQualities** argument, but constructors don't inherit so it wouldn't be available in second or greater level classes.) By making the fruit qualities into a separate class, you have greater flexibility, including the ability to change the qualities midway through the lifetime of a particular **Fruit** object.

The second reason for making **FruitQualities** a separate object is in case you want to add new qualities or to change the behavior via inheritance and polymorphism. Note that for **GreenZebra** (which *really is* a type of tomato—I've grown them and they're fabulous), the constructor calls **addQualities( )** and passes it a **ZebraQualities** object, which is derived from **FruitQualities** so it can be attached to the **FruitQualities** reference in the base class. Of course, when **GreenZebra** uses the **FruitQualities** it must downcast it to the correct type (as seen in **evaluate( )**), but it always knows that type is **ZebraQualities**.

You'll also see that there's a **Seed** class, and that **Fruit** (which by definition carries its own seeds)[4] contains an array of **Seed**s.

Finally, notice that each class has a copy constructor, and that each copy constructor must take care to call the copy constructors for the base class and member objects to produce a deep copy. The copy constructor is tested inside the class **CopyConstructor**. The method **ripen( )** takes a **Tomato** argument and performs copy-construction on it in order to duplicate the object:

```
t = new Tomato(t);
```

while **slice( )** takes a more generic **Fruit** object and also duplicates it:

```
f = new Fruit(f);
```

These are tested with different kinds of **Fruit** in **main( )**. Here's the output:

```
In ripen, t is a Tomato
In slice, f is a Fruit
In ripen, t is a Tomato
In slice, f is a Fruit
```

This is where the problem shows up. After the copy-construction that happens to the **Tomato** inside **slice( )**, the result is no longer a **Tomato** object, but just a **Fruit**. It has lost all of its tomato-ness. Further, when you take a **GreenZebra**, both **ripen( )** and **slice( )** turn it into a **Tomato** and a **Fruit**, respectively. Thus, unfortunately, the copy constructor scheme is no good to us in Java when attempting to make a local copy of an object.

---

[4] Except for the poor avocado, which has been reclassified to simply "fat."

Why does it work in C++ and not Java?

The copy constructor is a fundamental part of C++, since it automatically makes a local copy of an object. Yet the example above proves that it does not work for Java. Why? In Java everything that we manipulate is a reference, while in C++ you can have reference-like entities and you can *also* pass around the objects directly. That's what the C++ copy constructor is for: when you want to take an object and pass it in by value, thus duplicating the object. So it works fine in C++, but you should keep in mind that this scheme fails in Java, so don't use it.

Read-only classes

While the local copy produced by **clone( )** gives the desired results in the appropriate cases, it is an example of forcing the programmer (the author of the method) to be responsible for preventing the ill effects of aliasing. What if you're making a library that's so general purpose and commonly used that you cannot make the assumption that it will always be cloned in the proper places? Or more likely, what if you *want* to allow aliasing for efficiency—to prevent the needless duplication of objects—but you don't want the negative side effects of aliasing?

One solution is to create *immutable objects* which belong to read-only classes. You can define a class such that no methods in the class cause changes to the internal state of the object. In such a class, aliasing has no impact since you can read only the internal state, so if many pieces of code are reading the same object there's no problem.

As a simple example of immutable objects, Java's standard library contains "wrapper" classes for all the primitive types. You might have already discovered that, if you want to store an **int** inside a container such as an **ArrayList** (which takes only **Object reference**s), you can wrap your **int** inside the standard library **Integer** class:

```
//: appendixa:ImmutableInteger.java
// The Integer class cannot be changed.
import java.util.*;

public class ImmutableInteger {
```

```
  public static void main(String[] args) {
    ArrayList v = new ArrayList();
    for(int i = 0; i < 10; i++)
      v.add(new Integer(i));
    // But how do you change the int
    // inside the Integer?
  }
} ///:~
```

The **Integer** class (as well as all the primitive "wrapper" classes) implements immutability in a simple fashion: they have no methods that allow you to change the object.

If you do need an object that holds a primitive type that can be modified, you must create it yourself. Fortunately, this is trivial:

```
//: appendixa:MutableInteger.java
// A changeable wrapper class.
import java.util.*;

class IntValue {
  int n;
  IntValue(int x) { n = x; }
  public String toString() {
    return Integer.toString(n);
  }
}

public class MutableInteger {
  public static void main(String[] args) {
    ArrayList v = new ArrayList();
    for(int i = 0; i < 10; i++)
      v.add(new IntValue(i));
    System.out.println(v);
    for(int i = 0; i < v.size(); i++)
      ((IntValue)v.get(i)).n++;
    System.out.println(v);
  }
} ///:~
```

Note that **n** is friendly to simplify coding.

IntValue can be even simpler if the default initialization to zero is adequate (then you don't need the constructor) and you don't care about printing it out (then you don't need the **toString( )**):

```
class IntValue { int n; }
```

Fetching the element out and casting it is a bit awkward, but that's a feature of **ArrayList,** not of **IntValue.**

Creating read-only classes

It's possible to create your own read-only class. Here's an example:

```
//: appendixa:Immutable1.java
// Objects that cannot be modified
// are immune to aliasing.

public class Immutable1 {
  private int data;
  public Immutable1(int initVal) {
    data = initVal;
  }
  public int read() { return data; }
  public boolean nonzero() { return data != 0; }
  public Immutable1 quadruple() {
    return new Immutable1(data * 4);
  }
  static void f(Immutable1 i1) {
    Immutable1 quad = i1.quadruple();
    System.out.println("i1 = " + i1.read());
    System.out.println("quad = " + quad.read());
  }
  public static void main(String[] args) {
    Immutable1 x = new Immutable1(47);
    System.out.println("x = " + x.read());
    f(x);
    System.out.println("x = " + x.read());
  }
} ///:~
```

All data is **private**, and you'll see that none of the **public** methods modify that data. Indeed, the method that does appear to modify an

---

object is **quadruple( )**, but this creates a new **Immutable1** object and leaves the original one untouched.

The method **f( )** takes an **Immutable1** object and performs various operations on it, and the output of **main( )** demonstrates that there is no change to **x**. Thus, **x**'s object could be aliased many times without harm because the **Immutable1** class is designed to guarantee that objects cannot be changed.

The drawback to immutability

Creating an immutable class seems at first to provide an elegant solution. However, whenever you do need a modified object of that new type you must suffer the overhead of a new object creation, as well as potentially causing more frequent garbage collections. For some classes this is not a problem, but for others (such as the **String** class) it is prohibitively expensive.

The solution is to create a companion class that *can* be modified. Then, when you're doing a lot of modifications, you can switch to using the modifiable companion class and switch back to the immutable class when you're done.

The example above can be modified to show this:

```
//: appendixa:Immutable2.java
// A companion class for making
// changes to immutable objects.

class Mutable {
  private int data;
  public Mutable(int initVal) {
    data = initVal;
  }
  public Mutable add(int x) {
    data += x;
    return this;
  }
  public Mutable multiply(int x) {
    data *= x;
    return this;
```

```
    }
    public Immutable2 makeImmutable2() {
      return new Immutable2(data);
    }
}

public class Immutable2 {
  private int data;
  public Immutable2(int initVal) {
    data = initVal;
  }
  public int read() { return data; }
  public boolean nonzero() { return data != 0; }
  public Immutable2 add(int x) {
    return new Immutable2(data + x);
  }
  public Immutable2 multiply(int x) {
    return new Immutable2(data * x);
  }
  public Mutable makeMutable() {
    return new Mutable(data);
  }
  public static Immutable2 modify1(Immutable2 y){
    Immutable2 val = y.add(12);
    val = val.multiply(3);
    val = val.add(11);
    val = val.multiply(2);
    return val;
  }
  // This produces the same result:
  public static Immutable2 modify2(Immutable2 y){
    Mutable m = y.makeMutable();
    m.add(12).multiply(3).add(11).multiply(2);
    return m.makeImmutable2();
  }
  public static void main(String[] args) {
    Immutable2 i2 = new Immutable2(47);
    Immutable2 r1 = modify1(i2);
    Immutable2 r2 = modify2(i2);
    System.out.println("i2 = " + i2.read());
    System.out.println("r1 = " + r1.read());
```

```
      System.out.println("r2 = " + r2.read());
  }
} ///:~
```

Immutable2 contains methods that, as before, preserve the immutability of the objects by producing new objects whenever a modification is desired. These are the **add( )** and **multiply( )** methods. The companion class is called **Mutable**, and it also has **add( )** and **multiply( )** methods, but these modify the **Mutable** object rather than making a new one. In addition, **Mutable** has a method to use its data to produce an **Immutable2** object and vice versa.

The two static methods **modify1( )** and **modify2( )** show two different approaches to producing the same result. In **modify1( )**, everything is done within the **Immutable2** class and you can see that four new **Immutable2** objects are created in the process. (And each time **val** is reassigned, the previous object becomes garbage.)

In the method **modify2( )**, you can see that the first action is to take the **Immutable2 y** and produce a **Mutable** from it. (This is just like calling **clone( )** as you saw earlier, but this time a different type of object is created.) Then the **Mutable** object is used to perform a lot of change operations *without* requiring the creation of many new objects. Finally, it's turned back into an **Immutable2**. Here, two new objects are created (the **Mutable** and the result **Immutable2**) instead of four.

This approach makes sense, then, when:

1.   You need immutable objects and

2.   You often need to make a lot of modifications or

3.   It's expensive to create new immutable objects.

Immutable **String**s

Consider the following code:

```
//: appendixa:Stringer.java

public class Stringer {
  static String upcase(String s) {
```

```
    return s.toUpperCase();
  }
  public static void main(String[] args) {
    String q = new String("howdy");
    System.out.println(q); // howdy
    String qq = upcase(q);
    System.out.println(qq); // HOWDY
    System.out.println(q); // howdy
  }
} ///:~
```

When **q** is passed in to **upcase( )** it's actually a copy of the reference to **q**. The object this reference is connected to stays put in a single physical location. The references are copied as they are passed around.

Looking at the definition for **upcase( )**, you can see that the reference that's passed in has the name **s**, and it exists for only as long as the body of **upcase( )** is being executed. When **upcase( )** completes, the local reference **s** vanishes. **upcase( )** returns the result, which is the original string with all the characters set to uppercase. Of course, it actually returns a reference to the result. But it turns out that the reference that it returns is for a new object, and the original **q** is left alone. How does this happen?

Implicit constants

If you say:

```
String s = "asdf";
String x = Stringer.upcase(s);
```

do you really want the **upcase( )** method to *change* the argument? In general, you don't, because an argument usually looks to the reader of the code as a piece of information provided to the method, not something to be modified. This is an important guarantee, since it makes code easier to write and understand.

In C++, the availability of this guarantee was important enough to put in a special keyword, **const**, to allow the programmer to ensure that a reference (pointer or reference in C++) could not be used to modify the original object. But then the C++ programmer was required to be diligent and remember to use **const** everywhere. It can be confusing and easy to forget.

Overloading '+' and the **StringBuffer**

Objects of the **String** class are designed to be immutable, using the technique shown previously. If you examine the online documentation for the **String** class (which is summarized a little later in this appendix), you'll see that every method in the class that appears to modify a **String** really creates and returns a brand new **String** object containing the modification. The original **String** is left untouched. Thus, there's no feature in Java like C++'s **const** to make the compiler support the immutability of your objects. If you want it, you have to wire it in yourself, like **String** does.

Since **String** objects are immutable, you can alias to a particular **String** as many times as you want. Because it's read-only there's no possibility that one reference will change something that will affect the other references. So a read-only object solves the aliasing problem nicely.

It also seems possible to handle all the cases in which you need a modified object by creating a brand new version of the object with the modifications, as **String** does. However, for some operations this isn't efficient. A case in point is the operator '+' that has been overloaded for **String** objects. Overloading means that it has been given an extra meaning when used with a particular class. (The '+' and '+=' for **String** are the only operators that are overloaded in Java, and Java does not allow the programmer to overload any others)[5].

When used with **String** objects, the '+' allows you to concatenate **String**s together:

```
String s = "abc" + foo + "def" + Integer.toString(47);
```

---

[5] C++ allows the programmer to overload operators at will. Because this can often be a complicated process (see Chapter 10 of *Thinking in C++, 2nd edition,* Prentice-Hall, 2000), the Java designers deemed it a "bad" feature that shouldn't be included in Java. It wasn't so bad that they didn't end up doing it themselves, and ironically enough, operator overloading would be much easier to use in Java than in C++. This can be seen in Python (see www.Python.org) which has garbage collection and straightforward operator overloading.

You could imagine how this *might* work: the **String** "abc" could have a method **append( )** that creates a new **String** object containing "abc" concatenated with the contents of **foo**. The new **String** object would then create another new **String** that added "def," and so on.

This would certainly work, but it requires the creation of a lot of **String** objects just to put together this new **String**, and then you have a bunch of the intermediate **String** objects that need to be garbage-collected. I suspect that the Java designers tried this approach first (which is a lesson in software design—you don't really know anything about a system until you try it out in code and get something working). I also suspect they discovered that it delivered unacceptable performance.

The solution is a mutable companion class similar to the one shown previously. For **String**, this companion class is called **StringBuffer**, and the compiler automatically creates a **StringBuffer** to evaluate certain expressions, in particular when the overloaded operators + and += are used with **String** objects. This example shows what happens:

```
//: appendixa:ImmutableStrings.java
// Demonstrating StringBuffer.

public class ImmutableStrings {
  public static void main(String[] args) {
    String foo = "foo";
    String s = "abc" + foo +
      "def" + Integer.toString(47);
    System.out.println(s);
    // The "equivalent" using StringBuffer:
    StringBuffer sb =
      new StringBuffer("abc"); // Creates String!
    sb.append(foo);
    sb.append("def"); // Creates String!
    sb.append(Integer.toString(47));
    System.out.println(sb);
  }
} ///:~
```

In the creation of **String s**, the compiler is doing the rough equivalent of the subsequent code that uses **sb**: a **StringBuffer** is created and **append( )** is used to add new characters directly into the **StringBuffer** object (rather than making new copies each time). While this is more efficient, it's worth noting that each time you create a quoted character string such as **"abc"** and **"def"**, the compiler turns those into **String** objects. So there can be more objects created than you expect, despite the efficiency afforded through **StringBuffer**.

The **String** and **StringBuffer** classes

Here is an overview of the methods available for both **String** and **StringBuffer** so you can get a feel for the way they interact. These tables don't contain every single method, but rather the ones that are important to this discussion. Methods that are overloaded are summarized in a single row.

First, the **String** class:

Method	Arguments, Overloading	Use
Constructor	Overloaded: Default, **String**, **StringBuffer**, **char** arrays, **byte** arrays.	Creating **String** objects.
length( )		Number of characters in the **String**.
charAt()	**int** Index	The char at a location in the **String**.
getChars( ), **getBytes( )**	The beginning and end from which to copy, the array to copy into, an index into the destination array.	Copy **char**s or **byte**s into an external array.
toCharArray( )		Produces a **char[]** containing the characters in the **String**.
equals( ), **equals-IgnoreCase( )**	A **String** to compare with.	An equality check on the contents of the two

Method	Arguments, Overloading	Use
		Strings.
compareTo( )	A **String** to compare with.	Result is negative, zero, or positive depending on the lexicographical ordering of the **String** and the argument. Uppercase and lowercase are not equal!
regionMatches( )	Offset into this **String**, the other **String** and its offset and length to compare. Overload adds "ignore case."	**boolean** result indicates whether the region matches.
startsWith( )	**String** that it might start with. Overload adds offset into argument.	**boolean** result indicates whether the **String** starts with the argument.
endsWith( )	**String** that might be a suffix of this **String**.	**boolean** result indicates whether the argument is a suffix.
indexOf( ), lastIndexOf( )	Overloaded: **char**, **char** and starting index, **String**, **String**, and starting index.	Returns -1 if the argument is not found within this **String**, otherwise returns the index where the argument starts. **lastIndexOf( )** searches backward from end.
substring( )	Overloaded: Starting index, starting index, and ending index.	Returns a new **String** object containing the specified character set.
concat( )	The **String** to concatenate	Returns a new **String** object containing the original **String**'s characters followed by

Method	Arguments, Overloading	Use
		the characters in the argument.
replace( )	The old character to search for, the new character to replace it with.	Returns a new **String** object with the replacements made. Uses the old **String** if no match is found.
toLowerCase( ) **toUpperCase( )**		Returns a new **String** object with the case of all letters changed. Uses the old **String** if no changes need to be made.
trim( )		Returns a new **String** object with the white space removed from each end. Uses the old **String** if no changes need to be made.
valueOf( )	Overloaded: **Object**, **char[]**, **char[]** and offset and count, **boolean**, **char**, **int**, **long**, **float**, **double**.	Returns a **String** containing a character representation of the argument.
intern( )		Produces one and only one **String** ref per unique character sequence.

You can see that every **String** method carefully returns a new **String** object when it's necessary to change the contents. Also notice that if the contents don't need changing the method will just return a reference to the original **String**. This saves storage and overhead.

Here's the **StringBuffer** class:

Method	Arguments, overloading	Use

Method	Arguments, overloading	Use
Constructor	Overloaded: default, length of buffer to create, **String** to create from.	Create a new **StringBuffer** object.
toString( )		Creates a **String** from this **StringBuffer**.
length( )		Number of characters in the **StringBuffer**.
capacity( )		Returns current number of spaces allocated.
ensure-Capacity( )	Integer indicating desired capacity.	Makes the **StringBuffer** hold at least the desired number of spaces.
setLength( )	Integer indicating new length of character string in buffer.	Truncates or expands the previous character string. If expanding, pads with nulls.
charAt( )	Integer indicating the location of the desired element.	Returns the **char** at that location in the buffer.
setCharAt( )	Integer indicating the location of the desired element and the new **char** value for the element.	Modifies the value at that location.
getChars( )	The beginning and end from which to copy, the array to copy into, an index into the destination array.	Copy **char**s into an external array. There is no **getBytes( )** as in **String**.
append( )	Overloaded: **Object**, **String**, **char[]**, **char[]** with offset and length, **boolean**, **char**, **int**, **long**, **float**, **double**.	The argument is converted to a string and appended to the end of the current buffer, increasing the buffer if necessary.
insert( )	Overloaded, each with a first argument of the offset	The second argument is converted to a

Method	Arguments, overloading	Use
	at which to start inserting: **Object**, **String**, **char[]**, **boolean**, **char**, **int**, **long**, **float**, **double**.	string and inserted into the current buffer beginning at the offset. The buffer is increased if necessary.
reverse( )		The order of the characters in the buffer is reversed.

The most commonly used method is **append( )**, which is used by the compiler when evaluating **String** expressions that contain the '+' and '+=' operators. The **insert( )** method has a similar form, and both methods perform significant manipulations to the buffer instead of creating new objects.

Strings are special

By now you've seen that the **String** class is not just another class in Java. There are a lot of special cases in **String**, not the least of which is that it's a built-in class and fundamental to Java. Then there's the fact that a quoted character string is converted to a **String** by the compiler and the special overloaded operators + and +=. In this appendix you've seen the remaining special case: the carefully built immutability using the companion **StringBuffer** and some extra magic in the compiler.

Summary

Because everything is a reference in Java, and because every object is created on the heap and garbage-collected only when it is no longer used, the flavor of object manipulation changes, especially when passing and returning objects. For example, in C or C++, if you wanted to initialize some piece of storage in a method, you'd probably request that the user pass the address of that piece of storage into the method. Otherwise you'd have to worry about who was responsible for destroying that storage. Thus, the interface and understanding of such methods is more complicated. But in Java, you never have to worry about responsibility or whether an object will still exist when it is needed, since that is always taken care of for you. Your can create an object at the point that it is needed, and no sooner, and never worry about the mechanics of passing around responsibility for that object: you simply pass the reference. Sometimes the simplification that this provides is unnoticed, other times it is staggering.

The downside to all this underlying magic is twofold:

1. You always take the efficiency hit for the extra memory management (although this can be quite small), and there's always a slight amount of uncertainty about the time something can take to run (since the garbage collector can be forced into action whenever you get low on memory). For most applications, the benefits outweigh the drawbacks, and particularly time-critical sections can be written using **native** methods (see Appendix B).

2. Aliasing: sometimes you can accidentally end up with two references to the same object, which is a problem only if both references are assumed to point to a *distinct* object. This is where you need to pay a little closer attention and, when necessary, **clone( )** an object to prevent the other reference from being surprised by an unexpected change. Alternatively, you can support aliasing for efficiency by creating immutable objects whose operations can return a new object of the same type or some different type, but never change the original object so that anyone aliased to that object sees no change.

Some people say that cloning in Java is a botched design, and to heck with it, so they implement their own version of cloning[6] and never call the **Object.clone( )** method, thus eliminating the need to implement **Cloneable** and catch the **CloneNotSupportedException**. This is certainly a reasonable approach and since **clone( )** is supported so rarely within the standard Java library, it is apparently a safe one as well. But as long as you don't call **Object.clone( )** you don't need to implement **Cloneable** or catch the exception, so that would seem acceptable as well.

---

[6] Doug Lea, who was helpful in resolving this issue, suggested this to me, saying that he simply creates a function called **duplicate( )** for each class.

Exercises

Solutions to selected exercises can be found in the electronic document *The Thinking in Java Annotated Solution Guide*, available for a small fee from *www.BruceEckel.com*.

1. Demonstrate a second level of aliasing. Create a method that takes a reference to an object but doesn't modify that reference's object. However, the method calls a second method, passing it the reference, and this second method does modify the object.

2. Create a class **myString** containing a **String** object that you initialize in the constructor using the constructor's argument. Add a **toString( )** method and a method **concatenate( )** that appends a **String** object to your internal string. Implement **clone( )** in **myString**. Create two **static** methods that each take a **myString x** reference as an argument and call **x.concatenate("test")**, but in the second method call **clone( )** first. Test the two methods and show the different effects.

3. Create a class called **Battery** containing an **int** that is a battery number (as a unique identifier). Make it cloneable and give it a **toString( )** method. Now create a class called **Toy** that contains an array of **Battery** and a **toString( )** that prints out all the batteries. Write a **clone( )** for **Toy** that automatically clones all of its **Battery** objects. Test this by cloning **Toy** and printing the result.

4. Change **CheckCloneable.java** so that all of the **clone( )** methods catch the **CloneNotSupportedException** rather than passing it to the caller.

5. Using the mutable-companion-class technique, make an immutable class containing an **int**, a **double** and an array of **char**.

6. Modify **Compete.java** to add more member objects to classes **Thing2** and **Thing4** and see if you can determine how the timings vary with complexity—whether it's a simple linear relationship or if it seems more complicated.

7. Starting with **Snake.java**, create a deep-copy version of the snake.

8. Inherit an **ArrayList** and make its **clone( )** perform a deep copy.

B: The Java Native Interface (JNI)

The material in this appendix was contributed by and used with the permission of Andrea Provaglio (www.AndreaProvaglio.com).

The Java language and its standard API are rich enough to write full-fledged applications. But in some cases you must call non-Java code; for example, if you want to access operating-system-specific features, interface with special hardware devices, reuse a preexisting, non-Java code base, or implement time-critical sections of code.

Interfacing with non-Java code requires dedicated support in the compiler and in the Virtual Machine, and additional tools to map the Java code to the non-Java code. The standard solution for calling non-Java code that is provided by JavaSoft is called the *Java Native Interface*, which will be introduced in this appendix. This is not an in-depth treatment, and in some cases you're assumed to have partial knowledge of the related concepts and techniques.

JNI is a fairly rich programming interface that allows you to call native methods from a Java application. It was added in Java 1.1, maintaining a certain degree of compatibility with its Java 1.0 equivalent: the native method interface (NMI). NMI has design characteristics that make it unsuitable for adoption across all virtual machines. For this reason, future versions of the language might no longer support NMI, and it will not be covered here.

Currently, JNI is designed to interface with native methods written only in C or C++. Using JNI, your native methods can:

- Create, inspect, and update Java objects (including arrays and **String**s)
- Call Java methods

- Catch and throw exceptions

- Load classes and obtain class information

- Perform run-time type checking

Thus, virtually everything you can do with classes and objects in ordinary Java you can also do in native methods.

Calling a native method

We'll start with a simple example: a Java program that calls a native method, which in turn calls the standard C library function **printf( )**.

The first step is to write the Java code declaring a native method and its arguments:

```
//: appendixb:ShowMessage.java
public class ShowMessage {
  private native void ShowMessage(String msg);
  static {
    System.loadLibrary("MsgImpl");
    // Linux hack, if you can't get your library
    // path set in your environment:
    // System.load(
    //   "/home/bruce/tij2/appendixb/MsgImpl.so");
  }
  public static void main(String[] args) {
    ShowMessage app = new ShowMessage();
    app.ShowMessage("Generated with JNI");
  }
} ///:~
```

The native method declaration is followed by a **static** block that calls **System.loadLibrary( )** (which you could call at any time, but this style is more appropriate). **System.loadLibrary( )** loads a DLL in memory and links to it. The DLL must be in your system library path. The file name extension is automatically added by the JVM depending on the platform.

In the above code you can also see a call to the **System.load( )** method, which is commented out. The path specified here is an absolute path, rather than relying on an environment variable. Using an environment variable is naturally the better and more portable solution, but if you can't figure that out you can comment out the **loadLibrary( )** call and uncomment this one, adjusting the path to your own directory.

The header file generator: javah

Now compile your Java source file and run **javah** on the resulting **.class** file, specifying the **jni** switch (this is done automatically for you by the makefile in the source code distribution for this book):

```
javah -jni ShowMessage
```

javah reads the Java class file and for each native method declaration it generates a function prototype in a C or C++ header file. Here's the output: the **ShowMessage.h** source file (edited slightly to fit into this book):

```
/* DO NOT EDIT THIS FILE
   - it is machine generated */
#include <jni.h>
/* Header for class ShowMessage */

#ifndef _Included_ShowMessage
#define _Included_ShowMessage
#ifdef __cplusplus
extern "C" {
#endif
/*
 * Class:      ShowMessage
 * Method:     ShowMessage
 * Signature: (Ljava/lang/String;)V
 */
JNIEXPORT void JNICALL
Java_ShowMessage_ShowMessage
  (JNIEnv *, jobject, jstring);

#ifdef __cplusplus
}
```

```
#endif
#endif
```

As you can see by the **#ifdef __cplusplus** preprocessor directive, this file can be compiled either by a C or a C++ compiler. The first **#include** directive includes **jni.h**, a header file that, among other things, defines the types that you can see used in the rest of the file. **JNIEXPORT** and **JNICALL** are macros that expand to match platform-specific directives. **JNIEnv**, **jobject** and **jstring** are JNI data type definitions, which will be explained shortly.

Name mangling and function signatures

JNI imposes a naming convention (called *name mangling*) on native methods. This is important, since it's part of the mechanism by which the virtual machine links Java calls to native methods. Basically, all native methods start with the word "Java," followed by the name of the class in which the Java native declaration appears, followed by the name of the Java method. The underscore character is used as a separator. If the Java native method is overloaded, then the function signature is appended to the name as well; you can see the native signature in the comments preceding the prototype. For more information about name mangling and native method signatures, please refer to the JNI documentation.

Implementing your DLL

At this point, all you have to do is write a C or C++ source code file that includes the **javah**-generated header file and implements the native method, then compile it and generate a dynamic link library. This part is platform-dependent. The code below is compiled and linked into a file called **MsgImpl.dll** for Windows or **MsgImpl.so** for Unix/Linux (the makefile packaged with the code listings contains the commands to do this—it is available on the CD ROM bound into this book, or as a free download from *www.BruceEckel.com*):

```
//: appendixb:MsgImpl.cpp
//# Tested with VC++ & BC++. Include path must
//# be adjusted to find the JNI headers. See
```

```
//# the makefile for this chapter (in the
//# downloadable source code) for an example.
#include <jni.h>
#include <stdio.h>
#include "ShowMessage.h"

extern "C" JNIEXPORT void JNICALL
Java_ShowMessage_ShowMessage(JNIEnv* env,
jobject, jstring jMsg) {
  const char* msg=env->GetStringUTFChars(jMsg,0);
  printf("Thinking in Java, JNI: %s\n", msg);
  env->ReleaseStringUTFChars(jMsg, msg);
} ///:~
```

The arguments that are passed into the native method are the gateway
back into Java. The first, of type **JNIEnv**, contains all the hooks that
allow you to call back into the JVM. (We'll look at this in the next section.)
The second argument has a different meaning depending on the type of
method. For non-**static** methods like the example above, the second
argument is the equivalent of the "this" pointer in C++ and similar to **this**
in Java: it's a reference to the object that called the native method. For
static methods, it's a reference to the **Class** object where the method is
implemented.

The remaining arguments represent the Java objects passed into the
native method call. Primitives are also passed in this way, but they come
in by value.

In the following sections we'll explain this code by looking at the ways that
you access and control the JVM from inside a native method.

Accessing JNI functions: the **JNIEnv** argument

JNI functions are those that the programmer uses to interact with the
JVM from inside a native method. As you can see in the example above,
every JNI native method receives a special argument as its first
parameter: the **JNIEnv** argument, which is a pointer to a special JNI

---

data structure of type **JNIEnv_**. One element of the JNI data structure is a pointer to an array generated by the JVM. Each element of this array is a pointer to a JNI function. The JNI functions can be called from the native method by dereferencing these pointers (it's simpler than it sounds). Every JVM provides its own implementation of the JNI functions, but their addresses will always be at predefined offsets.

Through the **JNIEnv** argument, the programmer has access to a large set of functions. These functions can be grouped into the following categories:

♦ Obtaining version information

♦ Performing class and object operations

♦ Handling global and local references to Java objects

♦ Accessing instance fields and static fields

♦ Calling instance methods and static methods

♦ Performing string and array operations

♦ Generating and handling Java exceptions

The number of JNI functions is quite large and won't be covered here. Instead, I'll show the rationale behind the use of these functions. For more detailed information, consult your compiler's JNI documentation.

If you take a look at the **jni.h** header file, you'll see that inside the **#ifdef __cplusplus** preprocessor conditional, the **JNIEnv_** structure is defined as a class when compiled by a C++ compiler. This class contains a number of inline functions that let you access the JNI functions with an easy and familiar syntax. For example, the line of C++ code in the preceding example:

```
env->ReleaseStringUTFChars(jMsg, msg);
```

could also be called from C like this:

```
(*env)->ReleaseStringUTFChars(env, jMsg, msg);
```

You'll notice that the C style is (naturally) more complicated—you need a double dereferencing of the **env** pointer, and you must also pass the same pointer as the first parameter to the JNI function call. The examples in this appendix use the C++ style.

Accessing Java Strings

As an example of accessing a JNI function, consider the code in **MsgImpl.cpp**. Here, the **JNIEnv** argument **env** is used to access a Java **String**. Java **String**s are in Unicode format, so if you receive one and want to pass it to a non-Unicode function (**printf( )**, for example), you must first convert it into ASCII characters with the JNI function **GetStringUTFChars( )**. This function takes a Java **String** and converts it to UTF-8 characters. (These are 8 bits wide to hold ASCII values or 16 bits wide to hold Unicode. If the content of the original string was composed only of ASCII, the resulting string will be ASCII as well.)

GetStringUTFChars( ) is one of the member functions in **JNIEnv**. To access the JNI function, we use the typical C++ syntax for calling a member function though a pointer. You use the form above to access all of the JNI functions.

Passing and using Java objects

In the previous example we passed a **String** to the native method. You can also pass Java objects of your own creation to a native method. Inside your native method, you can access the fields and methods of the object that was received.

To pass objects, use the ordinary Java syntax when declaring the native method. In the example below, **MyJavaClass** has one **public** field and one **public** method. The class **UseObjects** declares a native method that takes an object of class **MyJavaClass**. To see if the native method manipulates its argument, the **public** field of the argument is set, the native method is called, and then the value of the **public** field is printed.

```
//: appendixb:UseObjects.java
```

```
class MyJavaClass {
  public int aValue;
  public void divByTwo() { aValue /= 2; }
}

public class UseObjects {
  private native void
    changeObject(MyJavaClass obj);
  static {
    System.loadLibrary("UseObjImpl");
    // Linux hack, if you can't get your library
    // path set in your environment:
    // System.load(
    //"/home/bruce/tij2/appendixb/UseObjImpl.so");
  }
  public static void main(String[] args) {
    UseObjects app = new UseObjects();
    MyJavaClass anObj = new MyJavaClass();
    anObj.aValue = 2;
    app.changeObject(anObj);
    System.out.println("Java: " + anObj.aValue);
  }
} ///:~
```

After compiling the code and running **javah**, you can implement the native method. In the example below, once the field and method ID are obtained, they are accessed through JNI functions.

```
//: appendixb:UseObjImpl.cpp
//# Tested with VC++ & BC++. Include path must
//# be adjusted to find the JNI headers. See
//# the makefile for this chapter (in the
//# downloadable source code) for an example.
#include <jni.h>
extern "C" JNIEXPORT void JNICALL
Java_UseObjects_changeObject(
JNIEnv* env, jobject, jobject obj) {
  jclass cls = env->GetObjectClass(obj);
  jfieldID fid = env->GetFieldID(
    cls, "aValue", "I");
  jmethodID mid = env->GetMethodID(
```

```
    cls, "divByTwo", "()V");
  int value = env->GetIntField(obj, fid);
  printf("Native: %d\n", value);
  env->SetIntField(obj, fid, 6);
  env->CallVoidMethod(obj, mid);
  value = env->GetIntField(obj, fid);
  printf("Native: %d\n", value);
} ///:~
```

Ignoring the "this" equivalent, the C++ function receives a **jobject**, which is the native side of the Java object reference we pass from the Java code. We simply read **aValue**, print it out, change the value, call the object's **divByTwo( )** method, and print the value out again.

To access a Java field or method, you must first obtain its identifier using **GetFieldID( )** for fields and **GetMethodID( )** for methods. These functions take the class object, a string containing the element name, and a string that gives type information: the data type of the field, or signature information for a method (details can be found in the JNI documentation). These functions return an identifier that you use to access the element. This approach might seem convoluted, but your native method has no knowledge of the internal layout of the Java object. Instead, it must access fields and methods through indexes returned by the JVM. This allows different JVMs to implement different internal object layouts with no impact on your native methods.

If you run the Java program, you'll see that the object that's passed from the Java side is manipulated by your native method. But what exactly is passed? A pointer or a Java reference? And what is the garbage collector doing during native method calls?

The garbage collector continues to operate during native method execution, but it's guaranteed that your objects will not be garbage-collected during a native method call. To ensure this, *local references* are created before, and destroyed right after, the native method call. Since their lifetime wraps the call, you know that the objects will be valid throughout the native method call.

Since these references are created and subsequently destroyed every time the function is called, you cannot make local copies in your native

---

methods, in **static** variables. If you want a reference that lasts across function invocations, you need a global reference. Global references are not created by the JVM, but the programmer can make a global reference out of a local one by calling specific JNI functions. When you create a global reference, you become responsible for the lifetime of the referenced object. The global reference (and the object it refers to) will be in memory until the programmer explicitly frees the reference with the appropriate JNI function. It's similar to **malloc( )** and **free( )** in C.

JNI and Java exceptions

With JNI, Java exceptions can be thrown, caught, printed, and rethrown just as they are inside a Java program. But it's up to the programmer to call dedicated JNI functions to deal with exceptions. Here are the JNI functions for exception handling:

♦ **Throw( )**
Throws an existing exception object. Used in native methods to rethrow an exception.

♦ **ThrowNew( )**
Generates a new exception object and throws it.

♦ **ExceptionOccurred( )**
Determines if an exception was thrown and not yet cleared.

♦ **ExceptionDescribe( )**
Prints an exception and the stack trace.

♦ **ExceptionClear( )**
Clears a pending exception.

♦ **FatalError( )**
Raises a fatal error. Does not return.

Among these, you can't ignore **ExceptionOccurred( )** and **ExceptionClear( )**. Most JNI functions can generate exceptions, and there is no language feature that you can use in place of a Java try block, so you must call **ExceptionOccurred( )** after each JNI function call to see if an exception was thrown. If you detect an exception, you may choose to handle it (and possibly rethrow it). You must make certain, however, that the exception is eventually cleared. This can be done in your function using **ExceptionClear( )** or in some other function if the exception is rethrown, but it must be done.

You must ensure that the exception is cleared, because otherwise the results will be unpredictable if you call a JNI function while an exception is pending. There are few JNI functions that are safe to call during an exception; among these, of course, are all the exception handling functions.

JNI and threading

Since Java is a multithreaded language, several threads can call a native method concurrently. (The native method might be suspended in the middle of its operation when a second thread calls it.) It's entirely up to the programmer to guarantee that the native call is thread-safe; i.e., it does not modify shared data in an unmonitored way. Basically, you have two options: declare the native method as **synchronized**, or implement some other strategy within the native method to ensure correct, concurrent data manipulation.

Also, you should never pass the **JNIEnv** pointer across threads, since the internal structure it points to is allocated on a per-thread basis and contains information that makes sense only in that particular thread.

Using a preexisting code base

The easiest way to implement JNI native methods is to start writing native method prototypes in a Java class, compile that class, and run the **.class** file through **javah**. But what if you have a large, preexisting code base that you want to call from Java? Renaming all the functions in your DLLs to match the JNI name mangling convention is not a viable solution. The best approach is to write a wrapper DLL "outside" your original code base. The Java code calls functions in this new DLL, which in turn calls your original DLL functions. This solution is not just a work-around; in most cases you must do this anyway because you must call JNI functions on the object references before you can use them.

Additional information

You can find further introductory material, including a C (rather than C++) example and discussion of Microsoft issues, in Appendix A of the first edition of this book, which can be found on the CD ROM bound in with this book, or in a free download from *www.BruceEckel.com*. More extensive information is available at *java.sun.com* (in the search engine, select "training & tutorials" for keywords "native methods"). Chapter 11 of *Core Java 2, Volume II*, by Horstmann & Cornell (Prentice-Hall, 2000) gives excellent coverage of native methods.

C: Java Programming Guidelines

This appendix contains suggestions to help guide you in performing low-level program design, and in writing code.

Naturally, these are guidelines and not rules. The idea is to use them as inspirations, and to remember that there are occasional situations where you need to bend or break a rule.

Design

1. **Elegance always pays off**. In the short term it might seem like it takes much longer to come up with a truly graceful solution to a problem, but when it works the first time and easily adapts to new situations instead of requiring hours, days, or months of struggle, you'll see the rewards (even if no one can measure them). Not only does it give you a program that's easier to build and debug, but it's also easier to understand and maintain, and that's where the financial value lies. This point can take some experience to understand, because it can appear that you're not being productive while you're making a piece of code elegant. Resist the urge to hurry; it will only slow you down.

2. **First make it work, then make it fast**. This is true even if you are certain that a piece of code is really important and that it will be a principal bottleneck in your system. Don't do it. Get the system going first with as simple a design as possible. Then if it isn't going fast enough, profile it. You'll almost always discover that "your"

bottleneck isn't the problem. Save your time for the really important stuff.

3. **Remember the "divide and conquer" principle**. If the problem you're looking at is too confusing, try to imagine what the basic operation of the program would be, given the existence of a magic "piece" that handles the hard parts. That "piece" is an object—write the code that uses the object, then look at the object and encapsulate *its* hard parts into other objects, etc.

4. **Separate the class creator from the class user (*client programmer*)**. The class user is the "customer" and doesn't need or want to know what's going on behind the scenes of the class. The class creator must be the expert in class design and write the class so that it can be used by the most novice programmer possible, yet still work robustly in the application. Library use will be easy only if it's transparent.

5. **When you create a class, attempt to make your names so clear that comments are unnecessary**. Your goal should be to make the client programmer's interface conceptually simple. To this end, use method overloading when appropriate to create an intuitive, easy-to-use interface.

6. **Your analysis and design must produce, at minimum, the classes in your system, their public interfaces, and their relationships to other classes, especially base classes**. If your design methodology produces more than that, ask yourself if all the pieces produced by that methodology have value over the lifetime of the program. If they do not, maintaining them will cost you. Members of development teams tend not to maintain anything that does not contribute to their productivity; this is a fact of life that many design methods don't account for.

7. **Automate everything**. Write the test code first (before you write the class), and keep it with the class. Automate the running of your tests through a makefile or similar tool. This way, any changes can be automatically verified by running the test code, and you'll immediately discover errors. Because you know that you have the safety net of your test framework, you will be bolder about making

sweeping changes when you discover the need. Remember that the greatest improvements in languages come from the built-in testing provided by type checking, exception handling, etc., but those features take you only so far. You must go the rest of the way in creating a robust system by filling in the tests that verify features that are specific to your class or program.

8. **Write the test code first (before you write the class) in order to verify that your class design is complete**. If you can't write test code, you don't know what your class looks like. In addition, the act of writing the test code will often flush out additional features or constraints that you need in the class—these features or constraints don't always appear during analysis and design. Tests also provide example code showing how your class can be used.

9. **All software design problems can be simplified by introducing an extra level of conceptual indirection**. This fundamental rule of software engineering[1] is the basis of abstraction, the primary feature of object-oriented programming.

10. **An indirection should have a meaning** (in concert with guideline 9). This meaning can be something as simple as "putting commonly used code in a single method." If you add levels of indirection (abstraction, encapsulation, etc.) that don't have meaning, it can be as bad as not having adequate indirection.

11. **Make classes as atomic as possible**. Give each class a single, clear purpose. If your classes or your system design grows too complicated, break complex classes into simpler ones. The most obvious indicator of this is sheer size: if a class is big, chances are it's doing too much and should be broken up.
    Clues to suggest redesign of a class are:
    1) A complicated switch statement: consider using polymorphism.
    2) A large number of methods that cover broadly different types of operations: consider using several classes.

---

[1] Explained to me by Andrew Koenig.

3) A large number of member variables that concern broadly different characteristics: consider using several classes.

12. **Watch for long argument lists**. Method calls then become difficult to write, read, and maintain. Instead, try to move the method to a class where it is (more) appropriate, and/or pass objects in as arguments.

13. **Don't repeat yourself**. If a piece of code is recurring in many methods in derived classes, put that code into a single method in the base class and call it from the derived-class methods. Not only do you save code space, you provide for easy propagation of changes. Sometimes the discovery of this common code will add valuable functionality to your interface.

14. **Watch for *switch* statements or chained *if-else* clauses**. This is typically an indicator of *type-check coding*, which means you are choosing what code to execute based on some kind of type information (the exact type may not be obvious at first). You can usually replace this kind of code with inheritance and polymorphism; a polymorphic method call will perform the type checking for you, and allow for more reliable and easier extensibility.

15. **From a design standpoint, look for and separate things that change from things that stay the same**. That is, search for the elements in a system that you might want to change without forcing a redesign, then encapsulate those elements in classes. You can learn significantly more about this concept in *Thinking in Patterns with Java*, downloadable at *www.BruceEckel.com*.

16. **Don't extend fundamental functionality by subclassing**. If an interface element is essential to a class it should be in the base class, not added during derivation. If you're adding methods by inheriting, perhaps you should rethink the design.

17. **Less is more**. Start with a minimal interface to a class, as small and simple as you need to solve the problem at hand, but don't try to anticipate all the ways that your class *might* be used. As the class is used, you'll discover ways you must expand the interface.

However, once a class is in use you cannot shrink the interface without disturbing client code. If you need to add more methods, that's fine; it won't disturb code, other than forcing recompiles. But even if new methods replace the functionality of old ones, leave the existing interface alone (you can combine the functionality in the underlying implementation if you want). If you need to expand the interface of an existing method by adding more arguments, create an overloaded method with the new arguments; this way you won't disturb any existing calls to the existing method.

18. **Read your classes aloud to make sure they're logical**. Refer to the relationship between a base class and derived class as "is-a" and member objects as "has-a."

19. **When deciding between inheritance and composition, ask if you need to upcast to the base type**. If not, prefer composition (member objects) to inheritance. This can eliminate the perceived need for multiple base types. If you inherit, users will think they are supposed to upcast.

20. **Use data members for variation in value and method overriding for variation in behavior**. That is, if you find a class that uses state variables along with methods that switch behavior based on those variables, you should probably redesign it to express the differences in behavior within subclasses and overridden methods.

21. **Watch for overloading**. A method should not conditionally execute code based on the value of an argument. In this case, you should create two or more overloaded methods instead.

22. **Use exception hierarchies**—preferably derived from specific appropriate classes in the standard Java exception hierarchy. The person catching the exceptions can then catch the specific types of exceptions, followed by the base type. If you add new derived exceptions, existing client code will still catch the exception through the base type.

23. **Sometimes simple aggregation does the job**. A "passenger comfort system" on an airline consists of disconnected elements:

seat, air conditioning, video, etc., and yet you need to create many of these in a plane. Do you make private members and build a whole new interface? No—in this case, the components are also part of the public interface, so you should create public member objects. Those objects have their own private implementations, which are still safe. Be aware that simple aggregation is not a solution to be used often, but it does happen.

24. **Consider the perspective of the client programmer and the person maintaining the code**. Design your class to be as obvious as possible to use. Anticipate the kind of changes that will be made, and design your class so that those changes will be easy.

25. **Watch out for "giant object syndrome."** This is often an affliction of procedural programmers who are new to OOP and who end up writing a procedural program and sticking it inside one or two giant objects. With the exception of application frameworks, objects represent concepts in your application, not the application.

26. **If you must do something ugly, at least localize the ugliness inside a class**.

27. **If you must do something nonportable, make an abstraction for that service and localize it within a class**. This extra level of indirection prevents the nonportability from being distributed throughout your program. (This idiom is embodied in the *Bridge* Pattern).

28. **Objects should not simply hold some data**. They should also have well-defined behaviors. (Occasionally, "data objects" are appropriate, but only when used expressly to package and transport a group of items when a generalized container is innappropriate.)

29. **Choose composition first when creating new classes from existing classes**. You should only used inheritance if it is required by your design. If you use inheritance where composition will work, your designs will become needlessly complicated.

30. **Use inheritance and method overriding to express differences in behavior, and fields to express variations in**

state. An extreme example of what not to do is inheriting different classes to represent colors instead of using a "color" field.

31. **Watch out for *variance***. Two semantically different objects may have identical actions, or responsibilities, and there is a natural temptation to try to make one a subclass of the other just to benefit from inheritance. This is called variance, but there's no real justification to force a superclass/subclass relationship where it doesn't exist. A better solution is to create a general base class that produces an interface for both as derived classes—it requires a bit more space, but you still benefit from inheritance, and will probably make an important discovery about the design.

32. **Watch out for *limitation* during inheritance**. The clearest designs add new capabilities to inherited ones. A suspicious design removes old capabilities during inheritance without adding new ones. But rules are made to be broken, and if you are working from an old class library, it may be more efficient to restrict an existing class in its subclass than it would be to restructure the hierarchy so your new class fits in where it should, above the old class.

33. **Use design patterns to eliminate "naked functionality."** That is, if only one object of your class should be created, don't bolt ahead to the application and write a comment "Make only one of these." Wrap it in a singleton. If you have a lot of messy code in your main program that creates your objects, look for a creational pattern like a factory method in which you can encapsulate that creation. Eliminating "naked functionality" will not only make your code much easier to understand and maintain, it will also make it more bulletproof against the well-intentioned maintainers that come after you.

34. **Watch out for "analysis paralysis."** Remember that you must usually move forward in a project before you know everything, and that often the best and fastest way to learn about some of your unknown factors is to go to the next step rather than trying to figure it out in your head. You can't know the solution until you *have* the solution. Java has built-in firewalls; let them work for

---

you. Your mistakes in a class or set of classes won't destroy the integrity of the whole system.

35. **When you think you've got a good analysis, design, or implementation, do a walkthrough**. Bring someone in from outside your group—this doesn't have to be a consultant, but can be someone from another group within your company. Reviewing your work with a fresh pair of eyes can reveal problems at a stage when it's much easier to fix them, and more than pays for the time and money "lost" to the walkthrough process.

Implementation

36. **In general, follow the Sun coding conventions**. These are available at *java.sun.com/docs/codeconv/index.html* (the code in this book follows these conventions as much as I was able). These are used for what constitutes arguably the largest body of code that the largest number of Java programmers will be exposed to. If you doggedly stick to the coding style you've always used, you will make it harder for your reader. Whatever coding conventions you decide on, ensure they are consistent throughout the project. There is a free tool to automatically reformat Java code at: *home.wtal.de/software-solutions/jindent*.

37. **Whatever coding style you use, it really does make a difference if your team (and even better, your company) standardizes on it**. This means to the point that everyone considers it fair game to fix someone else's coding style if it doesn't conform. The value of standardization is that it takes less brain cycles to parse the code, so that you can focus more on what the code means.

38. **Follow standard capitalization rules**. Capitalize the first letter of class names. The first letter of fields, methods, and objects (references) should be lowercase. All identifiers should run their words together, and capitalize the first letter of all intermediate words. For example:
ThisIsAClassName

thisIsAMethodOrFieldName
Capitalize *all* the letters of **static final** primitive identifiers that have constant initializers in their definitions. This indicates they are compile-time constants.
Packages are a special case—they are all lowercase letters, even for intermediate words. The domain extension (com, org, net, edu, etc.) should also be lowercase. (This was a change between Java 1.1 and Java 2.)

39. **Don't create your own "decorated" private data member names**. This is usually seen in the form of prepended underscores and characters. Hungarian notation is the worst example of this, where you attach extra characters that indicate data type, use, location, etc., as if you were writing assembly language and the compiler provided no extra assistance at all. These notations are confusing, difficult to read, and unpleasant to enforce and maintain. Let classes and packages do the name scoping for you.

40. **Follow a "canonical form"** when creating a class for general-purpose use. Include definitions for **equals( )**, **hashCode( )**, **toString( )**, **clone( )** (implement **Cloneable**), and implement **Comparable** and **Serializable**.

41. **Use the JavaBeans "get," "set," and "is" naming conventions** for methods that read and change **private** fields, even if you don't think you're making a JavaBean at the time. Not only does it make it easy to use your class as a Bean, but it's a standard way to name these kinds of methods and so will be more easily understood by the reader.

42. **For each class you create, consider including a *static public test( )* that contains code to test that class**. You don't need to remove the test code to use the class in a project, and if you make any changes you can easily rerun the tests. This code also provides examples of how to use your class.

43. **Sometimes you need to inherit in order to access *protected* members of the base class**. This can lead to a perceived need for multiple base types. If you don't need to upcast, first derive a new class to perform the protected access. Then make

that new class a member object inside any class that needs to use it, rather than inheriting.

44. **Avoid the use of *final* methods for efficiency purposes**. Use **final** only when the program is running, but not fast enough, and your profiler has shown you that a method invocation is the bottleneck.

45. **If two classes are associated with each other in some functional way (such as containers and iterators), try to make one an inner class of the other**. This not only emphasizes the association between the classes, but it allows the class name to be reused within a single package by nesting it within another class. The Java containers library does this by defining an inner **Iterator** class inside each container class, thereby providing the containers with a common interface. The other reason you'll want to use an inner class is as part of the **private** implementation. Here, the inner class beneficial for implementation hiding rather than the class association and prevention of namespace pollution noted above.

46. **Anytime you notice classes that appear to have high coupling with each other, consider the coding and maintenance improvements you might get by using inner classes**. The use of inner classes will not uncouple the classes, but rather make the coupling explicit and more convenient.

47. **Don't fall prey to premature optimization**. This way lies madness. In particular, don't worry about writing (or avoiding) native methods, making some methods **final**, or tweaking code to be efficient when you are first constructing the system. Your primary goal should be to prove the design, unless the design requires a certain efficiency.

48. **Keep scopes as small as possible so the visibility and lifetime of your objects are as small as possible**. This reduces the chance of using an object in the wrong context and hiding a difficult-to-find bug. For example, suppose you have a container and a piece of code that iterates through it. If you copy that code to use with a new container, you may accidentally end up

using the size of the old container as the upper bound of the new one. If, however, the old container is out of scope, the error will be caught at compile-time.

49. **Use the containers in the standard Java library**. Become proficient with their use and you'll greatly increase your productivity. Prefer **ArrayList** for sequences, **HashSet** for sets, **HashMap** for associative arrays, and **LinkedList** for stacks (rather than **Stack**) and queues.

50. **For a program to be robust, each component must be robust**. Use all the tools provided by Java: access control, exceptions, type checking, and so on, in each class you create. That way you can safely move to the next level of abstraction when building your system.

51. **Prefer compile-time errors to run-time errors**. Try to handle an error as close to the point of its occurrence as possible. Prefer dealing with the error at that point to throwing an exception. Catch any exceptions in the nearest handler that has enough information to deal with them. Do what you can with the exception at the current level; if that doesn't solve the problem, rethrow the exception.

52. **Watch for long method definitions**. Methods should be brief, functional units that describe and implement a discrete part of a class interface. A method that is long and complicated is difficult and expensive to maintain, and is probably trying to do too much all by itself. If you see such a method, it indicates that, at the least, it should be broken up into multiple methods. It may also suggest the creation of a new class. Small methods will also foster reuse within your class. (Sometimes methods must be large, but they should still do just one thing.)

53. **Keep things as "*private* as possible."** Once you publicize an aspect of your library (a method, a class, a field), you can never take it out. If you do, you'll wreck somebody's existing code, forcing them to rewrite and redesign. If you publicize only what you must, you can change everything else with impunity, and since designs tend to evolve this is an important freedom. In this way,

implementation changes will have minimal impact on derived classes. Privacy is especially important when dealing with multithreading—only **private** fields can be protected against un-**synchronized** use.

54. **Use comments liberally, and use the *javadoc* comment-documentation syntax to produce your program documentation**. However, the comments should add geniune meaning to the code; comments that only reiterate what the code is clearly expressing are annoying. Note that the typical verbose detail of Java class and method names reduce the need for as many comments.

55. **Avoid using "magic numbers"**—which are numbers hard-wired into code. These are a nightmare if you need to change them, since you never know if "100" means "the array size" or "something else entirely." Instead, create a constant with a descriptive name and use the constant identifier throughout your program. This makes the program easier to understand and much easier to maintain.

56. **When creating constructors, consider exceptions**. In the best case, the constructor won't do anything that throws an exception. In the next-best scenario, the class will be composed and inherited from robust classes only, so they will need no cleanup if an exception is thrown. Otherwise, you must clean up composed classes inside a **finally** clause. If a constructor must fail, the appropriate action is to throw an exception, so the caller doesn't continue blindly, thinking that the object was created correctly.

57. **If your class requires any cleanup when the client programmer is finished with the object, place the cleanup code in a single, well-defined method**—with a name like **cleanup( )** that clearly suggests its purpose. In addition, place a **boolean** flag in the class to indicate whether the object has been cleaned up so that **finalize( )** can check for "the death condition" (see Chapter 4).

58. **The responsibility of *finalize( )* can only be to verify "the death condition" of an object for debugging.** (See Chapter

4.) In special cases, it might be needed to release memory that would not otherwise be released by the garbage collector. Since the garbage collector might not get called for your object, you cannot use **finalize( )** to perform necessary cleanup. For that you must create your own "cleanup" method. In the **finalize( )** method for the class, check to make sure that the object has been cleaned up and throw a class derived from **RuntimeException** if it hasn't, to indicate a programming error. Before relying on such a scheme, ensure that **finalize( )** works on your system. (You might need to call **System.gc( )** to ensure this behavior.)

59.   **If an object must be cleaned up (other than by garbage collection) within a particular scope, use the following approach:** Initialize the object and, if successful, immediately enter a **try** block with a **finally** clause that performs the cleanup.

60.   **When overriding *finalize( )* during inheritance, remember to call *super.finalize( )*.** (This is not necessary if **Object** is your immediate superclass.) You should call **super.finalize( )** as the *final* act of your overridden **finalize( )** rather than the first, to ensure that base-class components are still valid if you need them.

61.   **When you are creating a fixed-size container of objects, transfer them to an array**—especially if you're returning this container from a method. This way you get the benefit of the array's compile-time type checking, and the recipient of the array might not need to cast the objects in the array in order to use them. Note that the base-class of the containers library, **java.util.Collection**, has two **toArray( )** methods to accomplish this.

62.   **Choose *interfaces* over *abstract* classes.** If you know something is going to be a base class, your first choice should be to make it an **interface**, and only if you're forced to have method definitions or member variables should you change it to an **abstract** class. An **interface** talks about what the client wants to do, while a class tends to focus on (or allow) implementation details.

63. **Inside constructors, do only what is necessary to set the object into the proper state**. Actively avoid calling other methods (except for **final** methods) since those methods can be overridden by someone else to produce unexpected results during construction. (See Chapter 7 for details.) Smaller, simpler constructors are less likely to throw exceptions or cause problems.

64. **To avoid a highly frustrating experience, make sure that there is only one unpackaged class of each name anywhere in your classpath**. Otherwise, the compiler can find the identically-named other class first, and report error messages that make no sense. If you suspect that you are having a classpath problem, try looking for **.class** files with the same names at each of the starting points in your classpath. Ideally, put all your classes within packages.

65. **Watch out for accidental overloading**. If you attempt to override a base-class method and you don't quite get the spelling right, you'll end up adding a new method rather than overriding an existing method. However, this is perfectly legal, so you won't get any error message from the compiler or run-time system—your code simply won't work correctly.

66. **Watch out for premature optimization**. First make it work, then make it fast—but only if you must, and only if it's proven that there is a performance bottleneck in a particular section of your code. Unless you have used a profiler to discover a bottleneck, you will probably be wasting your time. The hidden cost of performance tweaks is that your code becomes less understandable and maintainable.

67. **Remember that code is read much more than it is written**. Clean designs make for easy-to-understand programs, but comments, detailed explanations, and examples are invaluable. They will help both you and everyone who comes after you. If nothing else, the frustration of trying to ferret out useful information from the online Java documentation should convince you.

D: Resources

Software

The JDK from *java.sun.com*. Even if you choose to use a third-party development environment, it's always a good idea to have the JDK on hand in case you come up against what might be a compiler error. The JDK is the touchstone, and if there is a bug in it, chances are it will be well-known.

The HTML Java documentation from *java.sun.com*. I have never found a reference book on the standard Java libraries that wasn't out of date or missing information. Although the HTML documentation from Sun is shot-through with small bugs and is sometimes unusably terse, all the classes and methods are at least *there*. People are sometimes uncomfortable at first using an online resource rather than a printed book, but it's worth your while to get over this and open the HTML docs first, so you can at least get the big picture. If you can't figure it out at that point, then reach for the printed books.

Books

Thinking in Java, 1st Edition. Available as fully-indexed, color-syntax-highlighted HTML on the CD ROM bound in with this book, or as a free download from *www.BruceEckel.com*. Includes older material and material that was not considered interesting enough to carry through to the 2nd edition.

Core Java 2, by Horstmann & Cornell, Volume I—Fundamentals (Prentice-Hall, 1999). Volume II—Advanced Features, 2000. Huge, comprehensive, and the first place I go when I'm hunting for answers. The book I recommend when you've completed *Thinking in Java* and need to cast a bigger net.

Java in a Nutshell: A Desktop Quick Reference, 2nd Edition, by David Flanagan (O'Reilly, 1997). A compact summary of the online Java documentation. Personally, I prefer to browse the docs from *java.sun.com* online, especially since they change so often. However, many folks still like printed documentation and this fits the bill; it also provides more discussion than the online documents.

The Java Class Libraries: An Annotated Reference, by Patrick Chan and Rosanna Lee (Addison-Wesley, 1997). What the online reference *should* have been: enough description to make it usable. One of the technical reviewers for *Thinking in Java* said, "If I had only one Java book, this would be it (well, in addition to yours, of course)." I'm not as thrilled with it as he is. It's big, it's expensive, and the quality of the examples doesn't satisfy me. *But* it's a place to look when you're stuck and it seems to have more depth (and sheer size) than *Java in a Nutshell.*

Java Network Programming, by Elliotte Rusty Harold (O'Reilly, 1997). I didn't begin to understand Java networking until I found this book. I also find his Web site, Café au Lait, to be a stimulating, opinionated, and up-to-date perspective on Java developments, unencumbered by allegiances to any vendors. His regular updates keep up with fast-changing news about Java. See *metalab.unc.edu/javafaq/*.

JDBC Database Access with Java, by Hamilton, Cattell & Fisher (Addison-Wesley, 1997). If you know nothing about SQL and databases, this is a nice, gentle introduction. It also contains some of the details as well as an "annotated reference" to the API (again, what the online reference should have been). The drawback, as with all books in *The Java Series* ("The ONLY Books Authorized by JavaSoft") is that it's been whitewashed so that it says only wonderful things about Java—you won't find out about any dark corners in this series.

Java Programming with CORBA, by Andreas Vogel & Keith Duddy (John Wiley & Sons, 1997). A serious treatment of the subject with code examples for three Java ORBs (Visibroker, Orbix, Joe).

Design Patterns, by Gamma, Helm, Johnson & Vlissides (Addison-Wesley, 1995). The seminal book that started the patterns movement in programming.

Practical Algorithms for Programmers, by Binstock & Rex (Addison-Wesley, 1995). The algorithms are in C, so they're fairly easy to translate into Java. Each algorithm is thoroughly explained.

Analysis & design

Extreme Programming Explained, by Kent Beck (Addison-Wesley, 2000). I *love* this book. Yes, I tend to take a radical approach to things but I've always felt that there could be a much different, much better program development process, and I think XP comes pretty darn close. The only book that has had a similar impact on me was *PeopleWare* (described below), which talks primarily about the environment and dealing with corporate culture. *Extreme Programming Explained* talks about programming, and turns most things, even recent "findings," on their ear. They even go so far as to say that pictures are OK as long as you don't spend too much time on them and are willing to throw them away. (You'll notice that this book does *not* have the "UML stamp of approval" on its cover.) I could see deciding whether to work for a company based solely on whether they used XP. Small book, small chapters, effortless to read, exciting to think about. You start imagining yourself working in such an atmosphere and it brings visions of a whole new world.

UML Distilled, 2nd Edition, by Martin Fowler (Addison-Wesley, 2000). When you first encounter UML, it is daunting because there are so many diagrams and details. According to Fowler, most of this stuff is unnecessary so he cuts through to the essentials. For most projects, you only need to know a few diagramming tools, and Fowler's goal is to come up with a good design rather than worry about all the artifacts of getting there. A nice, thin, readable book; the first one you should get if you need to understand UML.

UML Toolkit, by Hans-Erik Eriksson & Magnus Penker, (John Wiley & Sons, 1997). Explains UML and how to use it, and has a case study in Java. An accompanying CD ROM contains the Java code and a cut-down version of Rational Rose. An excellent introduction to UML and how to use it to build a real system.

The Unified Software Development Process, by Ivar Jacobsen, Grady Booch, and James Rumbaugh (Addison-Wesley, 1999). I went in fully prepared to dislike this book. It seemed to have all the makings of a boring college text. I was pleasantly surprised—only pockets of the book contain explanations that seem as if those concepts aren't clear to the authors. The bulk of the book is not only clear, but enjoyable. And best of all, the process makes a lot of practical sense. It's not Extreme Programming (and does not have their clarity about testing) but it's also part of the UML juggernaut—even if you can't get XP adopted, most people have climbed aboard the "UML is good" bandwagon (regardless of their *actual* level of experience with it) and so you can probably get it adopted. I think this book should be the flagship of UML, and the one you can read after Fowler's *UML Distilled* when you want more detail.

Before you choose any method, it's helpful to gain perspective from those who are not trying to sell one. It's easy to adopt a method without really understanding what you want out of it or what it will do for you. Others are using it, which seems a compelling reason. However, humans have a strange little psychological quirk: If they want to believe something will solve their problems, they'll try it. (This is experimentation, which is good.) But if it doesn't solve their problems, they may redouble their efforts and begin to announce loudly what a great thing they've discovered. (This is denial, which is not good.) The assumption here may be that if you can get other people in the same boat, you won't be lonely, even if it's going nowhere (or sinking).

This is not to suggest that all methodologies go nowhere, but that you should be armed to the teeth with mental tools that help you stay in experimentation mode ("It's not working; let's try something else") and out of denial mode ("No, that's not really a problem. Everything's wonderful, we don't need to change"). I think the following books, read *before* you choose a method, will provide you with these tools.

Software Creativity, by Robert Glass (Prentice-Hall, 1995). This is the best book I've seen that discusses *perspective* on the whole methodology issue. It's a collection of short essays and papers that Glass has written and sometimes acquired (P.J. Plauger is one contributor), reflecting his many years of thinking and study on the subject. They're entertaining and only long enough to say what's necessary; he doesn't ramble and bore you. He's not just blowing smoke, either; there are hundreds of references to other papers and studies. All programmers and managers should read this book before wading into the methodology mire.

Software Runaways: Monumental Software Disasters, by Robert Glass (Prentice-Hall, 1997). The great thing about this book is that it brings to the forefront what we don't talk about: how many projects not only fail, but fail spectacularly. I find that most of us still think "That can't happen to me" (or "That can't happen *again*"), and I think this puts us at a disadvantage. By keeping in mind that things can always go wrong, you're in a much better position to make them go right.

Peopleware, 2nd Edition, by Tom Demarco and Timothy Lister (Dorset House, 1999). Although they have backgrounds in software development, this book is about projects and teams in general. But the focus is on the *people* and their needs, rather than the technology and its needs. They talk about creating an environment where people will be happy and productive, rather than deciding what rules those people should follow to be adequate components of a machine. This latter attitude, I think, is the biggest contributor to programmers smiling and nodding when XYZ method is adopted and then quietly doing whatever they've always done.

Complexity, by M. Mitchell Waldrop (Simon & Schuster, 1992). This chronicles the coming together of a group of scientists from different disciplines in Santa Fe, New Mexico, to discuss real problems that their individual disciplines couldn't solve (the stock market in economics, the initial formation of life in biology, why people do what they do in sociology, etc.). By crossing physics, economics, chemistry, math, computer science, sociology, and others, a multidisciplinary approach to these problems is developing. But more important, a different way of *thinking* about these ultra-complex problems is emerging: Away from mathematical determinism and the illusion that you can write an equation that predicts all behavior, and toward first *observing* and looking for a pattern and trying to emulate that pattern by any means possible. (The book chronicles, for example, the emergence of genetic algorithms.) This kind of thinking, I believe, is useful as we observe ways to manage more and more complex software projects.

Python

Learning Python, by Mark Lutz and David Ascher (O'Reilly, 1999). A nice programmer's introduction to what is rapidly becoming my favorite language, an excellent companion to Java. The book includes an introduction to JPython, which allows you to combine Java and Python in a single program (the JPython interpreter is compiled to pure Java bytecodes, so there is nothing special you need to add to accomplish this). This language union promises great possibilities.

My own list of books

Listed in order of publication. Not all of these are currently available.

Computer Interfacing with Pascal & C, (Self-published via the Eisys imprint, 1988. Only available via *www.BruceEckel.com*). An introduction to electronics from back when CP/M was still king and DOS was an upstart. I used high-level languages and often the parallel port of the computer to drive various electronic projects. Adapted from my columns in the first and best magazine I wrote for, *Micro Cornucopia*. (To paraphrase Larry O'Brien, long-time editor of *Software Development Magazine*: the best computer magazine ever published—they even had plans for building a robot in a flower pot!) Alas, Micro C became lost long before the Internet appeared. Creating this book was an extremely satisfying publishing experience.

Using C++, (Osborne/McGraw-Hill, 1989). One of the first books out on C++. This is out of print and replaced by its second edition, the renamed *C++ Inside & Out*.

C++ Inside & Out, (Osborne/McGraw-Hill, 1993). As noted, actually the 2nd edition of **Using C++**. The C++ in this book is reasonably accurate, but it's circa 1992 and *Thinking in C++* is intended to replace it. You can find out more about this book and download the source code at *www.BruceEckel.com*.

Thinking in C++, 1st Edition, (Prentice-Hall, 1995).

Thinking in C++, 2nd Edition, Volume 1, (Prentice-Hall, 2000). Downloadable from *www.BruceEckel.com*.

Black Belt C++, the Master's Collection, Bruce Eckel, editor (M&T Books, 1994). Out of print. A collection of chapters by various C++ luminaries based on their presentations in the C++ track at the Software Development Conference, which I chaired. The cover on this book stimulated me to gain control over all future cover designs.

Thinking in Java, 1ˢᵗ Edition, (Prentice-Hall, 1998). The first edition of this book won the *Software Development Magazine* Productivity Award, the *Java Developer's Journal* Editor's Choice Award, and the *JavaWorld Reader's Choice Award for best book*. Downloadable from *www.BruceEckel.com*.

Index

Please note that some names will be duplicated in capitalized form. Following Java style, the capitalized names refer to Java classes, while lowercase names refer to a general concept.

D

JProgressBar · 781
JRadioButton · 738, 750
JScrollPane · 712, 744, 755, 784
JSlider · 781
JSP · 960
JTabbedPane · 755
JTable · 784
JTextArea · 711, 790
JTextField · 708, 740
JTextPane · 747
JToggleButton · 736
JTree · 781
JVM (Java Virtual Machine) · 662

K

keyboard navigation, and Swing · 691
keyboard shortcuts · 765
keySet( ) · 511
keywords: class · 32, 38
Koenig, Andrew · 1079

L

label · 178
labeled break · 178
labeled continue · 178
late binding · 45, 311, 316
layout: controlling layout with layout
    managers · 712
lazy inizialization · 273
left-shift operator (<<) · 147
length, array member · 232
length, for arrays · 409
less than (<) · 141
less than or equal to (<=) · 141
lexicographic vs. alphabetic sorting · 436
library: creator, vs. client programmer ·
    243; design · 243; use · 244
LIFO · 471
lightweight: Swing components · 691
lightweight persistence · 613
LineNumberInputStream · 586
LineNumberReader · 591
linked list · 440
LinkedList · 467, 472, 505
list: drop-down list · 751
List · 408, 439, 440, 467, 753; sorting and
    searching · 511

list boxes · 753
listener adapters · 729
listener classes · 799
listener interfaces · 728
listeners and events · 723
Lister, Timothy · 1095
ListIterator · 467
literal: class literal · 664, 669; double · 156;
    float · 156; long · 156; values · 155
load factor, of a HashMap or HashSet · 491
loading: .class files · 247; initialization &
    class loading · 304; loding a class · 305
local loopback IP address · 907
localhost · 907; and RMI · 977
lock, for multithreading · 848
logarithms: natural logarithms · 156
logical: AND · 154; operator and short-
    circuiting · 144; operators · 143; OR ·
    154
long, literal value marker (L) · 156
Look & Feel: Pluggable · 787
lvalue · 134

M

main( ) · 277
maintenance, program · 85
management obstacles · 95
manifest file, for JAR files · 611, 816
map · 477
Map · 408, 439, 440, 476, 508
Map.Entry · 486
mark( ) · 593
Math.random( ) · 480; values produced by
    · 186
mathematical operators · 137
max( ) · 512
member: member function · 35; object · 37
member initializers · 332
memory exhaustion, solution via
    References · 495
mentoring: and training · 95, 96
menu: JPopupMenu · 766
menus: JDialog, JApplet, JFrame · 759
message box, in Swing · 756
message, sending · 33
meta-class · 662
method: adding more methods to a design
    · 268; aliasing during a method call ·
    1014; aliasing during method calls · 136;
    behavior of polymorphic methods inside

N

O

object · 31; aliasing · 136; arrays are first-class objects · 409; assigning objects by copying references · 134; assignment and reference copying · 134; business object/logic · 796; Class object · 633, 662, 848; creation · 192; equals( ) method · 142; equivalence · 141; equivalence vs reference equivalence · 142; final · 295; five stages of object design · 82; guidelines for object development · 83; immutable objects · 1047; interface to · 32; lock, for multithreading · 848; member · 37; object-oriented programming · 660; order of finalization of objects · 336; process of creation · 227; reference equivalence vs. object equivalence · 1025; serialization · 613; web of objects · 614, 1020

Object · 408; clone( ) · 1021, 1025; getClass( ) · 674; hashCode( ) · 477; standard root class, default inheritance from · 275; wait( ) and notify( ) methods · 866

object-oriented: analysis and design · 71; basic concepts of object-oriented programming (OOP) · 29

ObjectOutputStream · 614

obstacles, management · 95

Octal · 156

ODBC · 928

OMG · 981

ones complement operator · 146

OOP · 262; analysis and design · 71; basic characteristics · 31; basic concepts of object-oriented programming · 29; protocol · 350; Simula programming language · 32; substitutability · 31

operator · 133; + and += overloading for String · 277; +, for String · 1054; == and != · 1025; binary · 146; bitwise · 146; casting · 154; comma · 152; comma operator · 175; common pitfalls · 153; indexing operator [ ] · 231; logical · 143; logical operators and short-circuiting · 144; ones-complement · 146; operator overloading for String · 1054; overloading · 153; precedence · 134; precedence mnemonic · 158; relational · 141; shift · 147; ternary · 151; unary · 139, 146

optional methods, in the Java 2 containers · 516

OR · 154; (||) · 143

order: of constructor calls with inheritance · 330; of finalization of objects · 336; of initialization · 223, 304, 338

organization, code · 255

OutputStream · 581, 583, 913

OutputStreamWriter · 589, 590, 913

overflow: and primitive types · 169

overloading: and constructors · 194; distinguishing overloaded methods · 196; lack of name hiding during inheritance · 286; method overloading · 194; on return values · 202; operator + and += overloading for String · 277; operator overloading · 153; operator overloading for String · 1054; overloading vs. overriding · 286; vs. overriding · 324

overriding: and inner classes · 385; function · 42; overloading vs. overriding · 286; vs. overloading · 324

P

package · 244; access, and friendly · 255; and applets · 699; and directory structure · 254; creating unique package names · 247; default package · 257; names, capitalization · 116; visibility, friendly · 368

paintComponent( ) · 768, 776

Painting on a JPanel in Swing · 768

pair programming · 90

paralysis, analysis · 72

param, HTML keyword · 839

parameter, applet · 697

parameterized type · 455

parseInt( ) · 776

pass: pass by value · 1018; passing a reference into a method · 1014

Pattern: Command Pattern · 575

patterns, design · 86, 94

patterns, design patterns · 266

perfect hashing function · 488

performance: and final · 302

performance issues · 96

Perl programming language · 705

S

Tomcat, standard servlet container · 960
tool tips · 740
TooManyListenersException · 796, 814
toString( ) · 272, 452, 458, 500
training · 93; and mentoring · 95, 96
training seminars provided by Bruce Eckel
· 23
Transferable · 792
transient keyword · 624
translation unit · 245
Transmission Control Protocol (TCP) · 923
tree · 781
TreeMap · 476, 510, 642
TreeSet · 473, 506
true · 143
try · 286, 554; try block in exceptions · 535
two's complement, signed · 151
type: base · 39; data type equivalence to
class · 33; derived · 39; finding exact
type of a base reference · 662;
parameterized type · 455; primitive ·
105; primitive data types and use with
operators · 159; type checking and
arrays · 408; type safety in Java · 154;
type-safe downcast in run-time type
identification · 665; weak typing · 45
TYPE field, for primitive class literals · 665
type safe sets of constants · 361
type-conscious ArrayList · 454

U

UDP, User Datagram Protocol · 923
UML · 81; indicating composition · 37;
Unified Modeling Language · 35, 1093
unary: minus (-) · 139; operator · 146;
operators · 139; plus (+) · 139
unbind( ) · 978
unicast · 814; unicast events · 796
UnicastRemoteObject · 974
Unicode · 590
Unified Modeling Language (UML) · 35,
1093
unit testing · 277
unmodifiable, making a Collection or Map
unmodifiable · 513
unsupported methods, in the Java 2
containers · 516
UnsupportedOperationException · 516
upcasting · 47, 291, 312, 660; and interface
· 353; inner classes and upcasting · 368

updates of the book · 22
URL · 925
use case · 76; iteration · 84; scope · 84
User Datagram Protocol (UDP) · 923
user interface · 78; and threads, for
responsiveness · 831; responsive, with
threading · 826

V

value: preventing change at run-time · 294
value, HTML keyword · 839
variable: defining a variable · 174;
initialization of method variables · 220;
variable argument lists (unknown
quantity and type of arguments) · 235
vector: of change · 86
Vector · 505, 519, 521
vector of change · 397
versioning, serialization · 630
versions of Java · 22
visibility, package visibility, (friendly) ·
368
visual: programming · 800
Visual Basic, Microsoft · 800
visual programming environments · 690

W

wait( ) · 860, 866
Waldrop, M. Mitchell · 1095
weak: weakly typed language · 45
WeakHashMap · 498
WeakReference · 495
Web: displaying a Web page from within
an applet · 923; placing an applet inside
a Web page · 695; safety, and applet
restrictions · 692
web of objects · 614, 1020
West, BorderLayout · 713
while · 172
widening conversion · 155
wild-card · 73
WindowAdapter · 704
windowClosing( ) · 704, 771
windowed applications · 700
Windows Explorer, running Java
programs from · 705

X

Y

Z

Bruce Eckel's Hands-On Java Seminar
Multimedia CD
It's like coming to the seminar!
Available at *www.BruceEckel.com*

➢ The *Hands-On Java Seminar* captured on a Multimedia CD!

➢ Overhead slides and synchronized audio voice narration for all the lectures. Just play it to see and hear the lectures!

➢ Created and narrated by Bruce Eckel.

➢ Based on the material in this book.

➢ Demo lecture available at *www.BruceEckel.com*

End-User License Agreement for Microsoft Software

IMPORTANT-READ CAREFULLY: This Microsoft End-User License Agreement ("EULA") is a legal agreement between you (either an individual or a single entity) and Microsoft Corporation for the Microsoft software product included in this package, which includes computer software and may include associated media, printed materials, and "online" or electronic documentation ("SOFTWARE PRODUCT"). The SOFTWARE PRODUCT also includes any updates and supplements to the original SOFTWARE PRODUCT provided to you by Microsoft. By installing, copying, downloading, accessing or otherwise using the SOFTWARE PRODUCT, you agree to be bound by the terms of this EULA. If you do not agree to the terms of this EULA, do not install, copy, or otherwise use the SOFTWARE PRODUCT.

SOFTWARE PRODUCT LICENSE

The SOFTWARE PRODUCT is protected by copyright laws and international copyright treaties, as well as other intellectual property laws and treaties. The SOFTWARE PRODUCT is licensed, not sold.
1. GRANT OF LICENSE. This EULA grants you the following rights:
1.1 License Grant. Microsoft grants to you as an individual, a personal nonexclusive license to make and use copies of the SOFTWARE PRODUCT for the sole purposes of evaluating and learning how to use the SOFTWARE PRODUCT, as may be instructed in accompanying publications or documentation. You may install the software on an unlimited number of computers provided that you are the only individual using the SOFTWARE PRODUCT.
1.2 Academic Use. You must be a "Qualified Educational User" to use the SOFTWARE PRODUCT in the manner described in this section. To determine whether you are a Qualified Educational User, please contact the Microsoft Sales Information Center/One Microsoft Way/Redmond, WA 98052-6399 or the Microsoft subsidiary serving your country. If you are a Qualified Educational User, you may either:
(i) exercise the rights granted in Section 1.1, OR
(ii) if you intend to use the SOFTWARE PRODUCT solely for instructional purposes in connection with a class or other educational program, this EULA grants you the following alternative license models:
(A) Per Computer Model. For every valid license you have acquired for the SOFTWARE PRODUCT, you may install a single copy of the SOFTWARE PRODUCT on a single computer for access and use by an unlimited number of

student end users at your educational institution, provided that all such end users comply with all other terms of this EULA, OR
(B) Per License Model. If you have multiple licenses for the SOFTWARE PRODUCT, then at any time you may have as many copies of the SOFTWARE PRODUCT in use as you have licenses, provided that such use is limited to student or faculty end users at your educational institution and provided that all such end users comply with all other terms of this EULA. For purposes of this subsection, the SOFTWARE PRODUCT is "in use" on a computer when it is loaded into the temporary memory (i.e., RAM) or installed into the permanent memory (e.g., hard disk, CD ROM, or other storage device) of that computer, except that a copy installed on a network server for the sole purpose of distribution to other computers is not "in use". If the anticipated number of users of the SOFTWARE PRODUCT will exceed the number of applicable licenses, then you must have a reasonable mechanism or process in place to ensure that the number of persons using the SOFTWARE PRODUCT concurrently does not exceed the number of licenses.
2. DESCRIPTION OF OTHER RIGHTS AND LIMITATIONS.
• Limitations on Reverse Engineering, Decompilation, and Disassembly. You may not reverse engineer, decompile, or disassemble the SOFTWARE PRODUCT, except and only to the extent that such activity is expressly permitted by applicable law notwithstanding this limitation.
• Separation of Components. The SOFTWARE PRODUCT is licensed as a single product. Its component parts may not be separated for use on more than one computer.
• Rental. You may not rent, lease or lend the SOFTWARE PRODUCT.
• Trademarks. This EULA does not grant you any rights in connection with any trademarks or service marks of Microsoft.
• Software Transfer. The initial user of the SOFTWARE PRODUCT may make a one-time permanent transfer of this EULA and SOFTWARE PRODUCT only directly to an end user. This transfer must include all of the SOFTWARE PRODUCT (including all component parts, the media and printed materials, any upgrades, this EULA, and, if applicable, the Certificate of Authenticity). Such transfer may not be by way of consignment or any other indirect transfer. The transferee of such one-time transfer must agree to comply with the terms of this EULA, including the obligation not to further transfer this EULA and SOFTWARE PRODUCT.
• No Support. Microsoft shall have no obligation to provide any product support for the SOFTWARE PRODUCT.
• Termination. Without prejudice to any other rights, Microsoft may terminate this EULA if you fail to comply with the terms and conditions of this EULA. In

such event, you must destroy all copies of the SOFTWARE PRODUCT and all of its component parts.

3. COPYRIGHT. All title and intellectual property rights in and to the SOFTWARE PRODUCT (including but not limited to any images, photographs, animations, video, audio, music, text, and "applets" incorporated into the SOFTWARE PRODUCT), the accompanying printed materials, and any copies of the SOFTWARE PRODUCT are owned by Microsoft or its suppliers. All title and intellectual property rights in and to the content which may be accessed through use of the SOFTWARE PRODUCT is the property of the respective content owner and may be protected by applicable copyright or other intellectual property laws and treaties. This EULA grants you no rights to use such content. All rights not expressly granted are reserved by Microsoft.

4. BACKUP COPY. After installation of one copy of the SOFTWARE PRODUCT pursuant to this EULA, you may keep the original media on which the SOFTWARE PRODUCT was provided by Microsoft solely for backup or archival purposes. If the original media is required to use the SOFTWARE PRODUCT on the COMPUTER, you may make one copy of the SOFTWARE PRODUCT solely for backup or archival purposes. Except as expressly provided in this EULA, you may not otherwise make copies of the SOFTWARE PRODUCT or the printed materials accompanying the SOFTWARE PRODUCT.

5. U.S. GOVERNMENT RESTRICTED RIGHTS. The SOFTWARE PRODUCT and documentation are provided with RESTRICTED RIGHTS. Use, duplication, or disclosure by the Government is subject to restrictions as set forth in subparagraph (c)(1)(ii) of the Rights in Technical Data and Computer Software clause at DFARS 252.227-7013 or subparagraphs (c)(1) and (2) of the Commercial Computer Software-Restricted Rights at 48 CFR 52.227-19, as applicable. Manufacturer is Microsoft Corporation/One Microsoft Way/Redmond, WA 98052-6399.

6. EXPORT RESTRICTIONS. You agree that you will not export or re-export the SOFTWARE PRODUCT, any part thereof, or any process or service that is the direct product of the SOFTWARE PRODUCT (the foregoing collectively referred to as the "Restricted Components"), to any country, person, entity or end user subject to U.S. export restrictions. You specifically agree not to export or re-export any of the Restricted Components (i) to any country to which the U.S. has embargoed or restricted the export of goods or services, which currently include, but are not necessarily limited to Cuba, Iran, Iraq, Libya, North Korea, Sudan and Syria, or to any national of any such country, wherever located, who intends to transmit or transport the Restricted Components back to such country; (ii) to any end-user who you know or have reason to know will utilize the Restricted Components in the design, development or production of nuclear, chemical or biological weapons; or (iii) to any end-user who has been

prohibited from participating in U.S. export transactions by any federal agency of the U.S. government. You warrant and represent that neither the BXA nor any other U.S. federal agency has suspended, revoked, or denied your export privileges.

7. NOTE ON JAVA SUPPORT. THE SOFTWARE PRODUCT MAY CONTAIN SUPPORT FOR PROGRAMS WRITTEN IN JAVA. JAVA TECHNOLOGY IS NOT FAULT TOLERANT AND IS NOT DESIGNED, MANUFACTURED, OR INTENDED FOR USE OR RESALE AS ON-LINE CONTROL EQUIPMENT IN HAZARDOUS ENVIRONMENTS REQUIRING FAIL-SAFE PERFORMANCE, SUCH AS IN THE OPERATION OF NUCLEAR FACILITIES, AIRCRAFT NAVIGATION OR COMMUNICATION SYSTEMS, AIR TRAFFIC CONTROL, DIRECT LIFE SUPPORT MACHINES, OR WEAPONS SYSTEMS, IN WHICH THE FAILURE OF JAVA TECHNOLOGY COULD LEAD DIRECTLY TO DEATH, PERSONAL INJURY, OR SEVERE PHYSICAL OR ENVIRONMENTAL DAMAGE.

MISCELLANEOUS

If you acquired this product in the United States, this EULA is governed by the laws of the State of Washington.

If you acquired this product in Canada, this EULA is governed by the laws of the Province of Ontario, Canada. Each of the parties hereto irrevocably attorns to the jurisdiction of the courts of the Province of Ontario and further agrees to commence any litigation which may arise hereunder in the courts located in the Judicial District of York, Province of Ontario.

If this product was acquired outside the United States, then local law may apply.

Should you have any questions concerning this EULA, or if you desire to contact Microsoft for any reason, please contact Microsoft, or write: Microsoft Sales Information Center/One Microsoft Way/Redmond, WA 98052-6399.

LIMITED WARRANTY

LIMITED WARRANTY. Microsoft warrants that (a) the SOFTWARE PRODUCT will perform substantially in accordance with the accompanying written materials for a period of ninety (90) days from the date of receipt, and (b) any Support Services provided by Microsoft shall be substantially as described in applicable written materials provided to you by Microsoft, and Microsoft support engineers will make commercially reasonable efforts to solve any problem. To the extent allowed by applicable law, implied warranties on the SOFTWARE PRODUCT, if any, are limited to ninety (90) days. Some states/jurisdictions do not allow limitations on duration of an implied warranty, so the above limitation may not apply to you.

CUSTOMER REMEDIES. Microsoft's and its suppliers' entire liability and your exclusive remedy shall be, at Microsoft's option, either (a) return of the price paid, if any, or (b) repair or replacement of the SOFTWARE PRODUCT that does not meet Microsoft's Limited Warranty and that is returned to Microsoft with a copy of your receipt. This Limited Warranty is void if failure of the SOFTWARE PRODUCT has resulted from accident, abuse, or misapplication. Any replacement SOFTWARE PRODUCT will be warranted for the remainder of the original warranty period or thirty (30) days, whichever is longer. Outside the United States, neither these remedies nor any product support services offered by Microsoft are available without proof of purchase from an authorized international source.

NO OTHER WARRANTIES. TO THE MAXIMUM EXTENT PERMITTED BY APPLICABLE LAW, MICROSOFT AND ITS SUPPLIERS DISCLAIM ALL OTHER WARRANTIES AND CONDITIONS, EITHER EXPRESS OR IMPLIED, INCLUDING, BUT NOT LIMITED TO, IMPLIED WARRANTIES OR CONDITIONS OF MERCHANTABILITY, FITNESS FOR A PARTICULAR PURPOSE, TITLE AND NON-INFRINGEMENT, WITH REGARD TO THE SOFTWARE PRODUCT, AND THE PROVISION OF OR FAILURE TO PROVIDE SUPPORT SERVICES. THIS LIMITED WARRANTY GIVES YOU SPECIFIC LEGAL RIGHTS. YOU MAY HAVE OTHERS, WHICH VARY FROM STATE/JURISDICTION TO STATE/JURISDICTION.

LIMITATION OF LIABILITY. TO THE MAXIMUM EXTENT PERMITTED BY APPLICABLE LAW, IN NO EVENT SHALL MICROSOFT OR ITS SUPPLIERS BE LIABLE FOR ANY SPECIAL, INCIDENTAL, INDIRECT, OR CONSEQUENTIAL DAMAGES WHATSOEVER (INCLUDING, WITHOUT LIMITATION, DAMAGES FOR LOSS OF BUSINESS PROFITS, BUSINESS INTERRUPTION, LOSS OF BUSINESS INFORMATION, OR ANY OTHER PECUNIARY LOSS) ARISING OUT OF THE USE OF OR INABILITY TO USE THE SOFTWARE PRODUCT OR THE FAILURE TO PROVIDE SUPPORT SERVICES, EVEN IF MICROSOFT HAS BEEN ADVISED OF THE POSSIBILITY OF SUCH DAMAGES. IN ANY CASE, MICROSOFT'S ENTIRE LIABILITY UNDER ANY PROVISION OF THIS EULA SHALL BE LIMITED TO THE GREATER OF THE AMOUNT ACTUALLY PAID BY YOU FOR THE SOFTWARE PRODUCT OR U.S.$5.00; PROVIDED, HOWEVER, IF YOU HAVE ENTERED INTO A MICROSOFT SUPPORT SERVICES AGREEMENT, MICROSOFT'S ENTIRE LIABILITY REGARDING SUPPORT SERVICES SHALL BE GOVERNED BY THE TERMS OF THAT AGREEMENT. BECAUSE SOME STATES/JURISDICTIONS DO NOT ALLOW THE EXCLUSION OR LIMITATION OF LIABILITY, THE ABOVE LIMITATION MAY NOT APPLY TO YOU.

0495 Part No. 64358

LICENSE AGREEMENT FOR MindView, Inc.'s
Thinking in C: Foundations for Java & C++ CD ROM
by Chuck Allison
This CD is provided together with the book "Thinking in Java, 2nd edition."

READ THIS AGREEMENT BEFORE USING THIS "Thinking in C: Foundations for
C++ & Java" (Hereafter called "CD"). BY USING THE CD YOU AGREE TO BE
BOUND BY THE TERMS AND CONDITIONS OF THIS AGREEMENT. IF YOU DO
NOT AGREE TO THE TERMS AND CONDITIONS OF THIS AGREEMENT,
IMMEDIATELY RETURN THE UNUSED CD FOR A FULL REFUND OF MONIES
PAID, IF ANY.

SOFTWARE REQUIREMENTS
The purpose of this CD is to provide the Content, not the associated software
necessary to view the Content. The Content of this CD is in HTML for viewing
with Microsoft Internet Explorer 4 or newer, and uses Microsoft Sound Codecs
available in Microsoft's Windows Media Player for Windows. It is your
responsibility to correctly install the appropriate Microsoft software for your
system.

The text, images, and other media included on this CD ("Content") and their
compilation are licensed to you subject to the terms and conditions of this
Agreement by MindView, Inc., having a place of business at 5343 Valle Vista,
La Mesa, CA 91941. Your rights to use other programs and materials included
on the CD are also governed by separate agreements distributed with those
programs and materials on the CD (the "Other Agreements"). In the event of
any inconsistency between this Agreement and the Other Agreements, this
Agreement shall govern. By using this CD, you agree to be bound by the terms
and conditions of this Agreement. MindView, Inc. owns title to the Content and
to all intellectual property rights therein, except insofar as it contains materials
that are proprietary to third-party suppliers. All rights in the Content except
those expressly granted to you in this Agreement are reserved to MindView,
Inc. and such suppliers as their respective interests may appear.

1. LIMITED LICENSE
MindView, Inc. grants you a limited, nonexclusive, nontransferable license to
use the Content on a single dedicated computer (excluding network servers).
This Agreement and your rights hereunder shall automatically terminate if you
fail to comply with any provisions of this Agreement or any of the Other

Agreements. Upon such termination, you agree to destroy the CD and all copies of the CD, whether lawful or not, that are in your possession or under your control.

2. ADDITIONAL RESTRICTIONS

a. You shall not (and shall not permit other persons or entities to) directly or indirectly, by electronic or other means, reproduce (except for archival purposes as permitted by law), publish, distribute, rent, lease, sell, sublicense, assign, or otherwise transfer the Content or any part thereof.

b. You shall not (and shall not permit other persons or entities to) use the Content or any part thereof for any commercial purpose or merge, modify, create derivative works of, or translate the Content.

c. You shall not (and shall not permit other persons or entities to) obscure MindView's or its suppliers copyright, trademark, or other proprietary notices or legends from any portion of the Content or any related materials.

3. PERMISSIONS
a. Except as noted in the Contents of the CD, you must treat this software just like a book. However, you may copy it onto a computer to be used and you may make archival copies of the software for the sole purpose of backing up the software and protecting your investment from loss. By saying, "just like a book," MindView, Inc. means, for example, that this software may be used by any number of people and may be freely moved from one computer location to another, so long as there is no possibility of its being used at one location or on one computer while it is being used at another. Just as a book cannot be read by two different people in two different places at the same time, neither can the software be used by two different people in two different places at the same time.
b. You may show or demonstrate the un-modified Content in a live presentation, live seminar, or live performance as long as you attribute all material of the Content to MindView, Inc.
c. Other permissions and grants of rights for use of the CD must be obtained directly from MindView, Inc. at http://www.MindView.net. (Bulk copies of the CD may also be purchased at this site.)
DISCLAIMER OF WARRANTY

The Content and CD are provided "AS IS" without warranty of any kind, either express or implied, including, without limitation, any warranty of merchantability and fitness for a particular purpose. The entire risk as to the results and performance of the CD and Content is assumed by you. MindView, Inc. and its suppliers assume no responsibility for defects in the CD, the accuracy of the Content, or omissions in the CD or the Content. MindView, Inc. and its suppliers do not warrant, guarantee, or make any representations regarding the use, or the results of the use, of the product in terms of correctness, accuracy, reliability, currentness, or otherwise, or that the Content will meet your needs, or that operation of the CD will be uninterrupted or error-free, or that any defects in the CD or Content will be corrected. MindView, Inc. and its suppliers shall not be liable for any loss, damages, or costs arising from the use of the CD or the interpretation of the Content. Some states do not allow exclusion or limitation of implied warranties or limitation of liability for incidental or consequential damages, so all of the above limitations or exclusions may not apply to you.

In no event shall MindView, Inc. or its suppliers' total liability to you for all damages, losses, and causes of action (whether in contract, tort, or otherwise) exceed the amount paid by you for the CD.

MindView, Inc., and Prentice-Hall, Inc. specifically disclaim the implied warrantees of merchantability and fitness for a particular purpose. No oral or written information or advice given by MindView, Inc., Prentice-Hall, Inc., their dealers, distributors, agents or employees shall create a warrantee. You may have other rights, which vary from state to state.

Neither MindView, Inc., Bruce Eckel, Chuck Allison, Prentice-Hall, nor anyone else who has been involved in the creation, production or delivery of the product shall be liable for any direct, indirect, consequential, or incidental damages (including damages for loss of business profits, business interruption, loss of business information, and the like) arising out of the use of or inability to use the product even if MindView, Inc., has been advised of the possibility of such damages. Because some states do not allow the exclusion or limitation of liability for consequential or incidental damages, the above limitation may not apply to you.

This CD is provided as a supplement to the book "Thinking in Java 2nd edition." The sole responsibility of Prentice-Hall will be to provide a replacement CD in the event that the one that came with the book is defective. This replacement warrantee shall be in effect for a period of sixty days from the purchase date. MindView, Inc. does not bear any additional responsibility for the CD.

NO TECHNICAL SUPPORT IS PROVIDED WITH THIS CD ROM

The following are trademarks of their respective companies in the U.S. and may be protected as trademarks in other countries: Sun and the Sun Logo,

Thinking in C: Foundations for Java & C++

Multimedia Seminar-on-CD ROM

©2000 MindView, Inc. All rights reserved.

WARNING: BEFORE OPENING THE DISC PACKAGE, CAREFULLY READ THE TERMS AND CONDITIONS OF THE LICENSE AGREEMENT & WARANTEE LIMITATION ON THE PREVIOUS PAGES.

The CD ROM packaged with this book is a multimedia seminar consisting of synchronized slides and audio lectures. The goal of this seminar is to introduce you to the aspects of C that are necessary for you to move on to C++ or Java, leaving out the unpleasant parts that C programmers must deal with on a day-to-day basis but that the C++ and Java languages steer you away from. The CD also contains this book in HTML form along with the source code for the book.

This CD ROM will work with Windows (with a sound system). However, you must:

1. Install the most recent version of Microsoft's Internet Explorer. Because of the features provided on the CD, it will NOT work with Netscape Navigator. **The Internet Explorer software for Windows 9X/NT is included on the CD.**
2. Install Microsoft's *Windows Media Player*. **The Media Player software for Windows 9X/NT is included on the CD.** You can also go to **http://www.microsoft.com/windows/mediaplayer** and follow the instructions or links there to download and install the Media Player for your particular platform.
3. At this point you should be able to play the lectures on the CD. Using the Internet Explorer Web browser, open the file **Install.html** that you'll find on the CD. This will introduce you to the CD and provide further instructions about the use of the CD.